business 4e

O.C. Ferrell
University of New Mexico

Geoffrey A. Hirt
DePaul University

Linda Ferrell
University of New Mexico

business

SENIOR VICE PRESIDENT, PRODUCTS & MARKETS **KURT L. STRAND**

VICE PRESIDENT, CONTENT PRODUCTION & TECHNOLOGY SERVICES **KIMBERLY MERIWETHER DAVID**

MANAGING DIRECTOR **PAUL DUCHAM**

SENIOR BRAND MANAGER **ANKE BRAUN WEEKES**

EXECUTIVE DIRECTOR OF DEVELOPMENT **ANN TORBERT**

DEVELOPMENT EDITOR II **KELLY I. PEKELDER**

MARKETING MANAGER **MICHAEL GEDATUS**

MARKETING SPECIALIST **ELIZABETH STEINER**

DIRECTOR, CONTENT PRODUCTION **TERRI SCHIESL**

CONTENT PROJECT MANAGER **ANGELA NORRIS**

SENIOR BUYER **MICHAEL R. MCCORMICK**

DESIGN **DEBRA KUBIAK**

COVER IMAGE **BILL NOLL/GETTY IMAGES**

CONTENT LICENSING SPECIALIST **JOANNE MENNEMEIER**

TYPEFACE **10/12 TIMES LT STD ROMAN**

COMPOSITOR **LASERWORDS PRIVATE LIMITED**

PRINTER **R. R. DONNELLEY**

M: BUSINESS

This book is printed on acid-free paper.

2 3 4 5 6 7 8 9 0 DOW/DOW 1 0 9 8 7 6 5 4

ISBN 978-0-07-802315-6
MHID 0-07-802315-7

Library of Congress Control Number: 2013951450

www.mhhe.com

brief contents

contents

part four CREATING THE HUMAN RESOURCE ADVANTAGE 180

part five MARKETING: DEVELOPING RELATIONSHIPS 220

changes to the fourth edition

chapter one

- New features: "Demand Eclipses Supply: Bluefin Tuna" and "Gaining a Foot Ahead in the Athletic Industry"
- New entrepreneurship feature: "Mayorga Coffee Combines Business Skills with Social Responsibility"
- Updated figures: Figure 1.3 "Average Annual Unemployment Rate, Civilian Labor Force 16 Years and Over" and Figure 1.4 "Growth in U.S. Gross Domestic Product"
- Updated Table 1.2 "Comparative Analysis of Selected Countries"
- Expanded "Mixed Economies" section and coverage of state capitalism

chapter two

- New entrepreneurship feature: "Virtual Farm Bears Responsible Fruit"
- New features: "New Orleans Saints Faces Down Bounty Scandal," "Unilever Makes Palm Oil Sustainable," and "Web Marketers Experience Limitations on Online Tracking of Children"
- New figures: Figure 2.1 "Global Trust in Industry Sectors" and Figure 2.4 "Consumer Preferences for Doing Business with Sustainable and Socially Responsible Organizations"
- Updated tables: Table 2.2 "Percentage of U.S. Workforce Observing Specific Forms of Misconduct, 2009 and 2011," Table 2.4 "Ranking of Countries Based on Corruption of Public Sector," and Table 2.7 "A Selection of the World's Most Ethical Companies"
- New and updated examples of entities that bounced back from a misconduct disaster stronger than before; employee compensation from Goldman Sachs to JPMorgan; New Orleans mayor Ray Nagin; Lance Armstrong; and examples of misuse of company resources to take into account the growing misuse of social media sites at work
- New content on fairness and honesty; a section on the misuse of company time, ethical leadership, and insider trading; and a section on unemployment
- Expanded coverage on the Foreign Corrupt Practices Act and bribery

chapter three

- New features: "Viber Gives Skype a Run for Its Money" and "The Danger of Counterfeit Products in India"
- New entrepreneurship feature: "Uniqlo Brings Japanese Fashion to America"
- Examples on population, imports, and exports updated to be more current
- Updated Table 3.1 "U.S. Trade Deficit, 1990–2012," Table 3.2 "Top Ten Countries with Which United States Has Trade Deficits/Surpluses," Table 3.4 "U.S. Exporters and Value by Company Size," Table 3.5 "Top Global Franchises," and Table 3.6 "Well-Known Multinational Companies"
- Updated Figure 3.1 "Top Exporting Countries"
- New example of the trouble that foreign companies have had expanding into India; WTO's investigation that the United States unfairly levied anti-dumping measures against certain Chinese imports; and how some companies, including Caterpillar and General Electric, have begun moving their operations back to the United States due to the barriers and costs associated with outsourcing to faraway countries
- Expanded coverage of increasing business opportunity in Mexico, countries struggling economically in Europe (e.g., Greece), government ownership of Chinese companies and how it might increase risk, and Association of Southeast Asian Nations as a trading bloc

chapter four

- New entrepreneurship feature, "Vital Farms Knows the Value of Its Chickens"
- New features: "Vita Coco: Loved by Celebrities, Athletes, and Health-Conscious Consumers" and "SodaStream Challenges Top Dogs of the Soda Industry"
- New Table 4.4 "American Companies with More than Half of Their Revenues from Outside the United States"
- New examples: Stratus Building Solutions; conflict between Steve Wynn and long-time business partner Kazuo Okada; Facebook IPO; U.S. lawsuit filed against InBev to prevent a merger between the company and Grupo Modelo SAB

chapter five

- New entrepreneurship feature: "Kickstarter Allows Entrepreneurs to Introduce Products"
- New features: "The Environmentally Friendly Laundromat" and "Five Guys Builds Its Business on a Simpler Concept"
- New tables: Table 5.1 "Great Entrepreneurs of Innovative Companies," Table 5.3 "Number of Firms by Employment

Size," Table 5.5 "Challenges in Starting a New Business," Table 5.6 "Fastest Growing and Hottest New Franchises," and Table 5.7 "Most Business-Friendly Cities"

- New coverage of social entrepreneurship
- New examples: Oprah and her success, how Matt Chatham opened up a crepe business called SkyCrepers, and how Alexa Andrzejewski financed iPhone photo-sharing app Foodspotting

chapter six

- New entrepreneurship feature: "Shelli Gardner Leads Stampin' Up! through Human Resources Skills"
- New features: "Changing Management Styles: Looking through Apple-Colored Lenses" and "Successful Leaders Not Limited by Leadership Styles"
- Turned areas of management section into Table 6.3 "Areas of Management"
- New tables: Table 6.1 "CEO Compensation of Top Companies," Table 6.5 "Seven Tips for Successful Leadership"
- New examples: how FedEx set a goal of increasing its profit in a three-year period and how it plans to do this; the tactical plan Cisco set to slim down different areas of the company to increase competitiveness; and the preparedness of investment company Fred Alger Management Inc. after the terrorist attacks on September 11, 2001
- Tighter coverage of top management and elimination of "Where Do Managers Come From?" section
- Expanded leadership section, including explaining authentic leadership and adding subsection, "Employee Empowerment"

chapter seven

- New entrepreneurship feature: " Teamwork Key to Success of Silpada Designs"
- New features: "Peer Performance Reviews Encourage Teamwork and Communication" and "Boss-Less Organizations Have Their Benefits"
- New Table 7.1 "Employees Who View Their Corporate Cultures Positively vs. Negatively"
- New examples: Apple supplier Foxconn; how Susan Cain advises teams to work toward collaboration rather than collectivism; Cisco virtual teams; how Coca-Cola used a task force to examine pay and promotion practices after the company faced lawsuits alleging discrimination; and chemical manufacturing company AMVAC Chemical Corporation
- New concluding section: "Improving Communication Effectiveness"

chapter eight

- New entrepreneurship feature: "Aspire Group Helps Fill Seats at Stadium"
- New features: "Ford Examines Ways to Increase Sustainability of Cars" and "Panasonic Greens Its Supply Chain"
- New tables: Table 8.1 "The World's Top Five Outsourcing Providers" and Table 8.2 "2012 Airline Scorecard (best to worst)"
- New Figure 8.4 "J.D. Power and Associates Initial Automobile Quality Study"
- New examples: how Bare Escentuals Cosmetics uses social media to gather marketing research and interact with customers; how Johnson Controls is incorporating sustainability into many facets of its operations; and how Kia improved its quality control and changed consumer perceptions of its brand
- Updated coverage of the Malcolm Baldrige National Quality Award winners
- New concluding section, "Integrating Operations and Supply Chain Management"

chapter nine

- New features: "Companies Offer Green Incentives for Employees" and "The New Incentives of Generation Y"
- New entrepreneurship feature: "FullContact Wants Employees to Take Vacations"
- Updated tables: Table 9.1 "How to Retain Good Employees," Table 9.2 "How to Motivate Employees," and Table 9.5 "Companies with Excellent Motivational Strategies"
- Updated Figure 9.2 "Job Aspects Important to Employee Satisfaction"
- Coverage of variations on Theory Z section eliminated
- New trend in some businesses requiring their telecommuting workers to come back into the office (e.g., Yahoo!, Bank of America)
- Updated paragraph relating equity theory to CEO compensation

chapter ten

- New entrepreneurship feature: "Coffee & Power's Unique Compensation Plan for Employees"
- New features: "Hostess Brands Shutters Doors after Mediation Fails" and "Disabilities Create Diversity in the Workplace"
- Updated figures: Figure 10.2 "U.S. Population Employed by Age Group," Figure 10.3 "Performance Reviews: Those Who Believe Reviews Improve Employees' Performance," Figure 10.5 "Union Membership Rates by State," Figure 10.6 "Union Membership Rate for Private-Sector Workers"
- Updated tables: Table 10.7 "Costco versus Walmart" and Table 10.9 "The DiversityInc Top 50 Companies for Diversity"
- New current examples: Examples of firms requesting job applicants' Facebook passwords; how Yahoo! CEO Scott Thompson was fired after it was found that his résumé was inaccurate; and how many minorities are on the boards of Fortune 500 companies
- New concluding section, "Trends in Management of the Workforce"

chapter eleven

- New features: "Chinese Brands Struggle to Lift Quality Image" and "Are Your Clothes Green? Ask the Higg Index"

- New entrepreneurship feature: "Sport Clips: A New Kind of Salon"
- Updated Table 11.1 "U.S. Buying Power Statistics by Race" and new Table 11.2 "Companies with the Best Customer Service"
- New examples: Lego's targeting of its products to young girls; how beer companies Anheuser-Busch InBev and MillerCoors are trying to attract more of the Hispanic market; and Anheuser-Busch's niche marketing of Michelob Ultra Light Cider that is gluten free
- Expanded coverage of online surveys
- New concluding section: "Importance of Marketing to Business and Society"

chapter twelve

- New entrepreneurship feature: "Crocs: A 'Shoe In' for Success"
- New features: "Darden Restaurants Changes Tactics to Appeal to Consumers' Changing Tastes" and "Driving the Tiger: Demand for SUVs Grows in China"
- Updated Figure 12.3 "Colgate-Palmolive's Product Mix and Product Lines"
- New tables: Table 12.2 "The 10 Most Valuable Brands in the World" and Table 12.3 "Best-Selling Vehicle Brands"
- New examples: the Hewlett-Packard Touchpad failure versus the iPad's success; Amazon.com's evolving business model; text marketing; Cat® CT660 Vocational; Ford as an example of why firms must work to maintain their high quality
- New coverage of reference pricing.
- New concluding section, "Importance of Marketing Strategy"

chapter thirteen

- New features: "Flipping the Pages Is a Thing of the Past: The Rise of E-Textbooks" and "Marketers Find a New Communication Tool with Pinterest"
- New entrepreneurship feature: "Instagram Becomes an Instant Success in Digital Marketing"
- New figures: Figure 13.1 "Do You Use Social Networking Sites?" Figure 13.2 "Smart Phone Ownership by Age," and Figure 13.3 "Main Sources of Identity Theft"
- New examples, including Baidu as growing competitor to Google in China; Instagram and Pinterest as media-sharing sites; Facebook's Sponsored Stories; CafeMom, a niche social media site; and New Belgium's use of Facebook to connect with and analyze fans and customers.
- More emphasis on mobile marketing, new "Applications and Widgets" section

chapter fourteen

- New features: "Goodwill Contributes Significantly to Firm Value" and "Companies Investigate Ways to Integrate Financial Information and Sustainability Costs"
- New entrepreneurship feature: "Buffalo Wild Wings: From Accounting Mess to Success"
- Updated Table 14.1 "Prestige Ranking of Accounting Firms"
- New example: how Deloitte Touche Tohmatsu was charged by the Public Company Accounting Oversight Board for a violation of U.S. securities law
- Updated ratios and data from company financials: Table 14.4 "Starbucks Corporation Consolidated Statements of Earnings," Table 14.6 "Starbucks Corporation Consolidated Balance Sheets," Table 14.7 "Consolidated Statements of Cash Flows," Table 14.8 "Industry Analysis, Year Ending 2011"
- More information on Dodd-Frank Act, updated information about the financial difficulties of the PIGS nations (Portugal, Ireland, Greece, Spain)
- Concluding section: "Importance of Integrity in Accounting"

chapter fifteen

- New features: "Are Partnerships between Universities and Debit Card Companies Good for Students?" and "Banks Increase Investment in Sustainability"
- New entrepreneurship feature: "Time to Square Up without Cash or Credit Cards"
- Updated tables: Table 15.2 "Costs to Produce Pennies and Nickels" and Table 15.5 "Facts about ATM Use"; new Table 15.4 "Leading Diversified Financial Services Firms"
- New information regarding the status of credit card debt among lower- and middle-income households and college students; a comparison of the cost of E-Trade's, TDAmeritrade's, and Scottrade's trades compared to one by Morgan Stanley; information on deflation under "Store of Value" section; recent bank failures

chapter sixteen

- New features: "Finance Executives Recognize the Benefits of Method's Green Efficiencies" and "Social Media Companies Face Obstacles Going Public"
- New entrepreneurship feature: "Venture Firm Focuses on Smaller Clean-Tech Investments"
- Updated tables: Table 16.1 "Short-Term Investment Possibilities for Idle Cash," Table 16.3 "A Basic Stock Quote," and Table 16.4 "Estimated Common Stock Price/Earnings Ratios and Dividends for Selected Companies"
- Updated Figure 16.2 "Recent Performance of Stock Market and Dow Jones Industrial Average (^DJI)"
- Took out paragraph about electronic funds transfers and HSBC Finance Corporation
- Changed "Did You Know?" example of Microsoft to Coca-Cola
- Additional information about capital budgeting; competition between Apple and Android; information on the Dow Jones Industrial Average has been added, with an emphasis on the fact that young investors (such as those just graduating from college) should analyze the long-term trends of a stock when investing rather than just relying on short-term growth

business 4e

BROOKLYN
BATTERY
TUNNEL

chapter one

the dynamics of business + economics

We begin our study of business in this chapter by examining the fundamentals of business and economics. First, we introduce the nature of business, including its goals, activities, and participants. Next, we describe the basics of economics and apply them to the United States economy. Finally, we establish a framework for studying business in this text. ■

LEARNING OBJECTIVES

After reading this chapter, you will be able to:

- **LO 1-1** Define basic concepts such as business, product, and profit.
- **LO 1-2** Identify the main participants and activities of business and explain why studying business is important.
- **LO 1-3** Define economics and compare the four types of economic systems.
- **LO 1-4** Describe the role of supply, demand, and competition in a free-enterprise system.
- **LO 1-5** Specify why and how the health of the economy is measured.
- **LO 1-6** Trace the evolution of the American economy and discuss the role of the entrepreneur in the economy.

business individuals or organizations who try to earn a profit by providing products that satisfy people's needs

product a good or service with tangible and intangible characteristics that provide satisfaction and benefits

profit the difference between what it costs to make and sell a product and what a customer pays for it

nonprofit organizations organizations that may provide goods or services but do not have the fundamental purpose of earning profits

stakeholders groups that have a stake in the success and outcomes of a business

LO 1-1 Define basic concepts such as business, product, and profit.

THE NATURE OF BUSINESS

A **business** tries to earn a profit by providing products that satisfy people's needs. The outcome of its efforts is **products** that have both tangible and intangible characteristics that provide satisfaction and benefits. When you purchase a product, you are buying the benefits and satisfaction you think the product will provide. A Subway sandwich, for example, may be purchased to satisfy hunger, while a Ford Focus may be purchased to satisfy the need for transportation and the desire to present a certain image.

Seventh Generation is a leading brand of environmentally friendly household products. Its disinfectant cleaning products and wipes are marketed as having the ability to kill 99.99% of germs botanically.

Most people associate the word *product* with tangible goods—an automobile, computer, phone, coat, or some other tangible item. However, a product can also be a service, which occurs when people or machines provide or process something of value to customers. Dry cleaning, a checkup by a doctor, a performance by a basketball player—these are examples of services. Some services, such as Flickr, an online photo management and sharing application, do not charge a fee for use but obtain revenue from ads on their sites. A product can also be an idea. Accountants and attorneys, for example, generate ideas for solving problems.

The Goal of Business

The primary goal of all businesses is to earn a **profit**, the difference between what it costs to make and sell a product and what a customer pays for it. If a company spends $8.00 to manufacture, finance, promote, and distribute a product that it sells for $10.00, the business earns a profit of $2.00 on each product sold. Businesses have the right to keep and use their profits as they choose—within legal limits—because profit is the reward for the risks they take in providing products. Earning profits contributes to society by providing employment, which in turn provides money that is reinvested in the economy. In addition, profits must be earned in a responsible manner. Not all organizations are businesses, however. **Nonprofit organizations**, such as the Red Cross, Special Olympics, and other charities and social causes, do not have the fundamental purpose of earning profits, although they may provide goods or services and engage in fund raising.

To earn a profit, a person or organization needs management skills to plan, organize, and control the activities of the business and to find and develop employees so that it can make products consumers will buy. A business also needs marketing expertise to learn what products consumers need and want and to develop, manufacture, price, promote, and distribute those products. Additionally, a business needs financial resources and skills to fund, maintain, and expand its operations. Other challenges for businesspeople include abiding by laws and government regulations; acting in an ethical and socially responsible manner; and adapting to economic, technological, political, and social changes. Even nonprofit organizations engage in management, marketing, and finance activities to help reach their goals.

To achieve and maintain profitability, businesses have found that they must produce quality products, operate efficiently, and be socially responsible and ethical in dealing with customers, employees, investors, government regulators, and the community. Because these groups have a stake in the success and outcomes of a business, they are sometimes called **stakeholders**. Many businesses, for example, are concerned about how the production and distribution of their products affect the environment. Concerns about landfills becoming high-tech graveyards plague many electronics firms. Best Buy offers recycling of electronics at all of its stores. The stores take cell phones, wide-screen TVs, and most other electronic products in their green program, regardless of where they were purchased. Other businesses are concerned about the quality of life in the communities in which they operate. For example,

Charlotte Street Computers in Asheville, North Carolina, has created a refurbishing center for old computers. The center refurbishes the computers and then donates them to those in need.[1] Others are concerned with promoting business careers among African American, Hispanic, and Native American students. The Diversity Pipeline Alliance is a network of national organizations that work toward preparing students and professionals of color for leadership and management in the 21st-century workforce. The Pipeline assists individuals in getting into the appropriate college, pursuing a career in business, or earning an advanced degree in business.[2] Other companies, such as Home Depot, have a long history of supporting natural disaster victims, relief efforts, and recovery.

LO 1-2 Identify the main participants and activities of business and explain why studying business is important.

The People and Activities of Business

Figure 1.1 shows the people and activities involved in business. At the center of the figure are owners, employees, and customers; the outer circle includes the primary business activities—management, marketing, and finance. Owners have to put up resources—money or credit—to start a business. Employees are responsible for the work that goes on within a business. Owners can manage the business themselves or hire employees to accomplish this task. The chairman and CEO of Coca-Cola, Muhtar Kent, does not own Coca-Cola, but is an employee who is responsible for managing all the other employees in a way that earns a profit for investors, who are the real owners. Finally, and most importantly, a business's major role is to satisfy the customers who buy its goods or services. Note also that people and forces beyond an organization's control—such as legal and regulatory forces, the economy, competition, technology, the political environment, and ethical and social concerns—all have an impact on the daily operations of businesses. You will learn more about these participants in business activities throughout this book. Next, we will examine the major activities of business.

Management

Notice that in Figure 1.1 management and employees are in the same segment of the circle. This is because management involves coordinating employees' actions to achieve the firm's goals, organizing people to work efficiently, and motivating them to achieve the business's goals. Steve Ells, founder and co-CEO of Chipotle Grill, recognizes the importance of management to company success. Ells created a multibillion-dollar franchise that can partially be attributed to its highly efficient operations and an emphasis on social responsibility. Although employees at Chipotle Grill might start off at close to minimum wage, they can quickly advance to higher positions. The best store managers can continue to advance until they are making a salary of over $100,000 per year.[3] Management is also concerned with acquiring, developing, and using resources (including people) effectively and efficiently. Campbell's Soup enlists its workers to help squeeze more efficiency out of its plants. Operating efficiency comes from saving time, money, and effort.[4]

Production and manufacturing is another element of management. At Campbell's Soup, for example, a 20-person work team was created to determine how best to cut costs in some plants. In essence, managers plan, organize, staff, and control the tasks required to carry out the work of the company or nonprofit organization. We take a closer look at management activities in Parts 3 and 4 of this text.

Marketing

Marketing and consumers are in the same segment of Figure 1.1 because the focus of all marketing activities is satisfying customers. Marketing includes all the activities designed to provide goods and services that satisfy consumers' needs and wants. Marketers gather information and conduct research to determine what customers want. Using information gathered from marketing research, marketers plan and develop products and make decisions about how much to charge for their products and when and where to make them available. They also analyze the marketing environment to see whether products need to be modified. In response to First Lady Michelle Obama's campaign against childhood obesity, Walmart announced that

FIGURE 1.1
Overview of the Business World

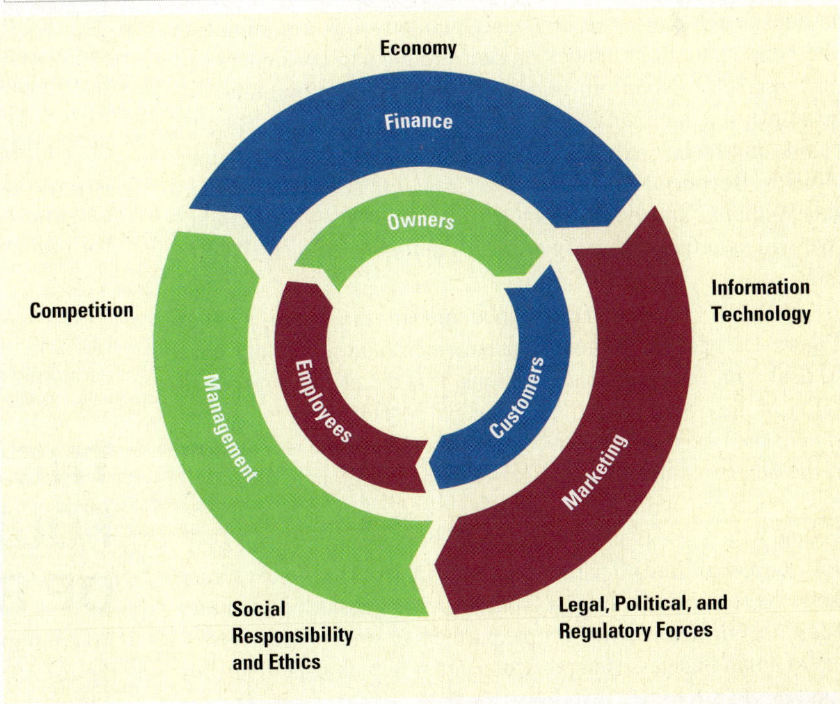

economics the study of how resources are distributed for the production of goods and services within a social system

it would lower the sugars, fats, and salts in its products over a five-year period. Such a response could be a smart move on Walmart's part because marketing research shows that consumers are becoming more health-conscious.[5] PepsiCo, for example, is expanding into healthier products such as Tropicana and oatmeal. CEO Indra Nooyi anticipates that healthy products will make up 30 percent of the company's product portfolio by the next decade.[6] Marketers use promotion—advertising, personal selling, sales promotion (coupons, games, sweepstakes, movie tie-ins), and publicity—to communicate the benefits and advantages of their products to consumers and increase sales. Nonprofit organizations also use promotion. For example, the National Fluid Milk Processor Promotion Board's "milk mustache" advertising campaign has featured Brooke Shields, Beyoncé Knowles, Sheryl Crow, Elizabeth Hurley, Serena Williams, and even animated "celebrities" such as Garfield.[7] We will examine marketing activities in Part 5 of this text.

Geico's rowing guinea pigs advertisement uses humor to demonstrate how much easier it is to save money using Geico insurance.

Finance Owners and finance are in the same part of Figure 1.1 because, although management and marketing have to deal with financial considerations, it is the primary responsibility of the owners to provide financial resources for the operation of the business. Moreover, the owners have the most to lose if the business fails to make a profit. Finance refers to all activities concerned with obtaining money and using it effectively. People who work as accountants, stockbrokers, investment advisors, or bankers are all part of the financial world. Owners sometimes have to borrow money from banks to get started or attract additional investors who become partners or stockholders. Owners of small businesses in particular often rely on bank loans for funding. Part 6 of this text discusses financial management.

Why Study Business?

Studying business can help you develop skills and acquire knowledge to prepare for your future career, regardless of whether you plan to work for a multinational *Fortune* 500 firm, start your own business, work for a government agency, or manage or volunteer at a nonprofit organization. The field of business offers a variety of interesting and challenging career opportunities throughout the world, such as marketing, human resources management, information technology, finance, production and operations, wholesaling and retailing, and many more.

Studying business can also help you better understand the many business activities that are necessary to provide satisfying goods and services—and that these activities carry a price tag. For example, if you buy a new compact disk, about half of the price goes toward activities related to distribution and the retailer's expenses and profit margins. The production (pressing) of the CD represents about $1, or a small percentage of its price. Most businesses charge a reasonable price for their products to ensure that they cover their production costs, pay their employees, provide their owners with a return on their investment, and perhaps give something back to their local communities. Bill Daniels founded Cablevision, building his first cable TV system in Casper, Wyoming, in 1953, and is now considered "the father of cable television." Prior to Daniels's passing in 2000, he had established a foundation that currently has funding of $1.1 billion and supports a diversity of causes from education to business ethics. During his life, he affected many individuals and organizations, and his business success has allowed his legacy to be one of giving and affecting communities throughout the United States.[8] Thus, learning about business can help you become a well-informed consumer and member of society.

Business activities help generate the profits that are essential not only to individual businesses and local economies but also to the health of the global economy. Without profits, businesses find it difficult, if not impossible, to buy more raw materials, hire more employees, attract more capital, and create additional products that in turn make more profits and fuel the world economy. Understanding how our free-enterprise economic system allocates resources and provides incentives for industry and the workplace is important to everyone.

LO 1-3 Define economics and compare the four types of economic systems.

THE ECONOMIC FOUNDATIONS OF BUSINESS

To continue our introduction to business, it is useful to explore the economic environment in which business is conducted. In this section, we examine economic systems, the free-enterprise

natural resources land, forests, minerals, water, and other things that are not made by people

human resources the physical and mental abilities that people use to produce goods and services; also called labor

financial resources the funds used to acquire the natural and human resources needed to provide products; also called capital

economic system a description of how a particular society distributes its resources to produce goods and services

communism first described by Karl Marx as a society in which the people, without regard to class, own all the nation's resources

The Young Americans Bank in Denver was created by cable magnate Bill Daniels. It is the only bank in the world that lends money to individuals under the age of 22.

system, the concepts of supply and demand, and the role of competition. These concepts play important roles in determining how businesses operate in a particular society.

Economics is the study of how resources are distributed for the production of goods and services within a social system. You are already familiar with the types of resources available. Land, forests, minerals, water, and other things that are not made by people are **natural resources**. **Human resources**, or labor, refers to the physical and mental abilities that people use to produce goods and services. **Financial resources**, or capital, are the funds used to acquire the natural and human resources needed to provide products. Because natural, human, and financial resources are used to produce goods and services, they are sometimes called *factors of production.* The firm can also have intangible resources such as a good reputation for quality products or being socially responsible. The goal is to turn the factors of production and intangible resources into a competitive advantage.

Economic Systems

An **economic system** describes how a particular society distributes its resources to produce goods and services. A central issue of economics is how to fulfill an unlimited demand for goods and services in a world with a limited supply of resources. Different economic systems attempt to resolve this central issue in numerous ways, as we shall see.

Although economic systems handle the distribution of resources in different ways, all economic systems must address three important issues:

1. What goods and services, and how much of each, will satisfy consumers' needs?
2. How will goods and services be produced, who will produce them, and with what resources will they be produced?
3. How are the goods and services to be distributed to consumers?

Communism, socialism, and capitalism, the basic economic systems found in the world today (Table 1.1), have fundamental differences in the way they address these issues. The factors of production in command economies are controlled by government planning. In many cases, the government owns or controls the production of goods and services. Communism and socialism are, therefore, considered command economies.

Communism Karl Marx (1818–1883) first described **communism** as a society in which the people, without regard to class, own all the nation's resources. In his ideal political-economic system, everyone contributes according to ability and receives benefits according to need. In a communist economy, the people (through the government) own and operate all businesses and factors of production. Central government planning determines what goods and services satisfy citizens' needs, how the goods and services are produced, and how they are distributed. However, no true communist economy exists today that satisfies Marx's ideal.

On paper, communism appears to be efficient and equitable, producing less of a gap between rich and poor. In practice, however, communist economies have been marked by low standards of living, critical shortages of consumer goods, high prices, corruption, and little freedom. Russia, Poland, Hungary, and other eastern European nations have turned away from communism and toward economic systems governed by supply and demand rather than by central planning. However, their experiments with alternative economic systems have been fraught with difficulty and hardship. Cuba continues to apply communist principles to its economy, but Cuba is also experiencing economic and political change. Countries such as Venezuela are trying to incorporate communist economic principles. However, communism is declining and its future as an economic system is uncertain. When Fidel Castro stepped down as president of Cuba, his younger brother Raul formally assumed the role and eliminated many of the bans, including allowing the purchase of electric appliances, microwaves, computers,

socialism an economic system in which the government owns and operates basic industries but individuals own most businesses

capitalism (free enterprise) an economic system in which individuals own and operate the majority of businesses that provide goods and services

free-market system pure capitalism, in which all economic decisions are made without government intervention

and cell phones. The communist country appears more open to free enterprise now.[9] Hundreds of thousands of Cuban workers are shifting from the public sector to the private sector. Similarly, China has become the first communist country to make strong economic gains by adopting capitalist approaches to business. The Chinese state is the largest shareholder among China's 150 largest companies and influences thousands of other businesses.[10] Economic prosperity has advanced in China with the government claiming to ensure market openness, equality, and fairness.[11]

Socialism **Socialism** is an economic system in which the government owns and operates basic industries—postal service, telephone, utilities, transportation, health care, banking, and some manufacturing—but individuals own most businesses. For example, in France the postal service industry La Posta is fully owned by the French government and makes a profit. Central planning determines what basic goods and services are produced, how they are produced, and how they are distributed. Individuals and small businesses provide other goods and services based on consumer demand and the availability of resources. Citizens are dependent on the government for many goods and services.

Most socialist nations, such as Sweden, India, and Israel, are democratic and recognize basic individual freedoms. Citizens can vote for political offices, but central government planners usually make decisions about what is best for the nation. People are free to go into the occupation of their choice, but they often work in government-operated organizations. Socialists believe their system permits a higher standard of living than other economic systems, but the difference often applies to the nation as a whole rather than to its individual citizens. Socialist economies profess egalitarianism—equal distribution of income and social services. They believe their economies are more stable than those of other nations. Although this may be true, taxes and unemployment are generally higher in socialist countries. Perhaps as a result, many socialist countries have also experienced economic difficulties.

Capitalism **Capitalism**, or **free enterprise**, is an economic system in which individuals own and operate the majority of businesses that provide goods and services. Competition, supply, and demand determine which goods and services are produced, how they are produced, and how they are distributed. The United States, Canada, Japan, and Australia are examples of economic systems based on capitalism.

There are two forms of capitalism: pure capitalism and modified capitalism. In pure capitalism, also called a **free-market system**, all economic decisions are made without government intervention. This economic system was first described by Adam Smith in *The Wealth of Nations* (1776). Smith, often called the father of capitalism, believed that the "invisible hand of competition" best regulates the economy. He argued that competition should determine what goods and services people need. Smith's system is also called *laissez-faire* ("let it be") *capitalism* because the government does not interfere in business.

Modified capitalism differs from pure capitalism in that the government intervenes and regulates business to some extent. One of the ways in which the United States and Canadian governments regulate business is through laws. Laws such as the Federal Trade Commission Act, which created the Federal Trade Commission to enforce antitrust laws, illustrate the importance

TABLE 1.1 Comparison of Communism, Socialism, and Capitalism

	Communism	Socialism	Capitalism
Business ownership	Most businesses are owned and operated by the government.	The government owns and operates major industries; individuals own small businesses.	Individuals own and operate all businesses.
Competition	None. The government owns and operates everything.	Restricted in major industries; encouraged in small business.	Encouraged by market forces and government regulations.
Profits	Excess income goes to the government.	Profits earned by small businesses may be reinvested in the business; profits from government-owned industries go to the government.	Individuals are free to keep profits and use them as they wish.
Product availability and price	Consumers have a limited choice of goods and services; prices are usually high.	Consumers have some choice of goods and services; prices are determined by supply and demand.	Consumers have a wide choice of goods and services; prices are determined by supply and demand.
Employment options	Little choice in choosing a career; most people work for government-owned industries or farms.	Some choice of careers; many people work in government jobs.	Unlimited choice of careers.

Source: "Gross Domestic Product or Expenditure, 1930–2002," *InfoPlease* (n.d.), www.infoplease.com/ipa/A0104575.html.

mixed economies economies that have elements from more than one economic system

The Federal Trade Commission enforces antitrust laws and monitors businesses to ensure fair competition.

of the government's role in the economy. In the most recent recession, the government provided loans and took ownership positions in banks such as Citigroup, AIG (an insurance company), and General Motors. These actions were thought necessary to keep these firms from going out of business and creating a financial disaster for the economy.

Mixed Economies No country practices a pure form of communism, socialism, or capitalism, although most tend to favor one system over the others. Most nations operate as **mixed economies**, which have elements from more than one economic system. In socialist Sweden, most businesses are owned and operated by private individuals. In capitalist United States, an independent federal agency operates the postal service and another independent agency operates the Tennessee Valley Authority, an electric utility. In Great Britain and Mexico, the governments are attempting to sell many state-run businesses to private individuals and companies. In Germany, the Deutsche Post is privatized and trades on the stock market. In once-communist Russia, Hungary, Poland, and other eastern European nations, capitalist ideas have been implemented, including private ownership of businesses.

Countries such as China and Russia have used state capitalism to advance the economy. State capitalism tries to integrate the powers of the state with the advantages of capitalism. It is led by the government but uses capitalistic tools such as listing state-owned companies on the stock market and embracing globalization.[12] State capitalism includes some of the world's largest companies such as Russia's Gazprom, which is the largest natural gas company. China's ability to make huge investments to the point of creating entirely new industries puts many private industries at a disadvantage.[13]

The Free-Enterprise System

Many economies—including those of the United States, Canada, and Japan—are based on free enterprise, and many communist and socialist countries, such as China and Russia, are applying more principles of free enterprise to their own economic systems. Free enterprise provides an opportunity for a business to succeed or fail on the basis of market demand. In a

DEMAND ECLIPSES SUPPLY: BLUEFIN TUNA

Bluefin tuna is immensely popular among sushi lovers, creating a high demand for the fish. Supply, on the other hand, is another matter. The bluefin population is being reduced through global overfishing and pollution. The Center for Biological Diversity requested endangered species status for bluefin, fearing current fishing practices might bring about extinction. The U.S. government declined the request. It argued that scientists need time to assess the current status of bluefin thanks, in part, to the impact on its spawning grounds from the BP *Deepwater Horizon* oil spill. It did, however, place the fish on its watch list.

Most scientists, environmentalists, and lawmakers agree the bluefin population has significantly declined, but many feel an international agreement on how best to preserve the population is preferable to a moratorium on fishing it. This assumes that fishermen will comply with regulations. Many fishermen currently fish more than the legal quota, with some fishing completely illegally. Reduced supply and steady demand are driving up the price of bluefin, making it a desirable catch. One fish brought in $736,000. Mitsubishi Corporation (the largest bluefin purchaser globally) has stored a large amount of frozen bluefin in defense of extinction. Unless there is an effective way to police fishing and preserve habitats, the bluefin may ultimately need official protection.[14]

Discussion Questions

1. Why is the price of bluefin tuna skyrocketing?
2. What are the ethical issues involved in selling bluefin tuna?
3. Why might the United States be reluctant to place the bluefin tuna on the endangered species list? What are some of the consequences of acting too slowly or too quickly in its assessment?

demand the number of goods and services that consumers are willing to buy at different prices at a specific time

supply the number of products—goods and services—that businesses are willing to sell at different prices at a specific time

free-enterprise system, companies that can efficiently manufacture and sell products that consumers desire will probably succeed. Inefficient businesses and those that sell products that do not offer needed benefits will likely fail as consumers take their business to firms that have more competitive products.

A number of basic individual and business rights must exist for free enterprise to work. These rights are the goals of many countries that have recently embraced free enterprise.

1. Individuals must have the right to own property and to pass this property on to their heirs. This right motivates people to work hard and save to buy property.

"Demand is the number of goods and services that consumers are willing to buy at different prices at a specific time."

2. Individuals and businesses must have the right to earn profits and to use the profits as they wish, within the constraints of their society's laws, principles, and values.
3. Individuals and businesses must have the right to make decisions that determine the way the business operates. Although there is government regulation, the philosophy in countries like the United States and Australia is to permit maximum freedom within a set of rules of fairness.
4. Individuals must have the right to choose what career to pursue, where to live, what goods and services to purchase, and more. Businesses must have the right to choose where to locate, what goods and services to produce, what resources to use in the production process, and so on.

Without these rights, businesses cannot function effectively because they are not motivated to succeed. Thus, these rights make possible the open exchange of goods and services. In the countries that favor free enterprise, such as the United States, citizens have the freedom to make many decisions about the employment they choose and create their own productivity systems. Many entrepreneurs are more productive in free-enterprise societies because personal and financial incentives are available that can aid in entrepreneurial success. For many entrepreneurs, their work becomes a part of their system of goals, values, and lifestyle. Consider the panelists ("sharks") on the ABC program *Shark Tank*. Panelists on *Shark Tank* give entrepreneurs a chance to receive funding to realize their dreams by deciding whether to invest in their projects. They include Barbara Corcoran, who built one of New York's largest real estate companies; Mark Cuban, founder of Broadcast.com and MicroSolutions; and Daymond John, founder of clothing company FUBU.[15]

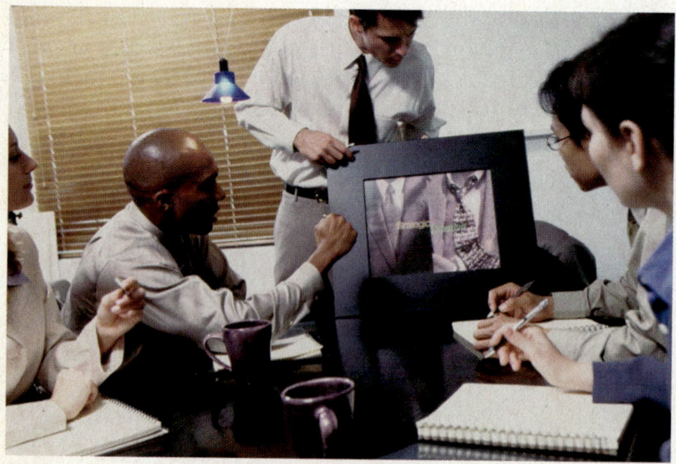

An entrepreneur presents his idea for a new product. Entrepreneurs are more productive in free-enterprise systems.

LO 1-4 Describe the role of supply, demand, and competition in a free-enterprise system.

The Forces of Supply and Demand

In the United States and in other free-enterprise systems, the distribution of resources and products is determined by supply and demand. **Demand** is the number of goods and services that consumers are willing to buy at different prices at a specific time. From your own experience, you probably recognize that consumers are usually willing to buy more of an item as its price falls because they want to save money. Consider handmade rugs, for example. Consumers may be willing to buy six rugs at $350 each, four at $500 each, but only two at $650 each. The relationship between the price and the number of rugs consumers are willing to buy can be shown graphically with a *demand curve* (see Figure 1.2).

Supply is the number of products that businesses are willing to sell at different prices at a specific time. In general, because the potential for profits is higher, businesses are willing to supply more of a good or service at higher prices. For example, a company that sells rugs may be willing to sell six at $650 each, four at $500 each, but just two at $350 each. The relationship

FIGURE 1.2
Equilibrium Price of Handmade Rugs

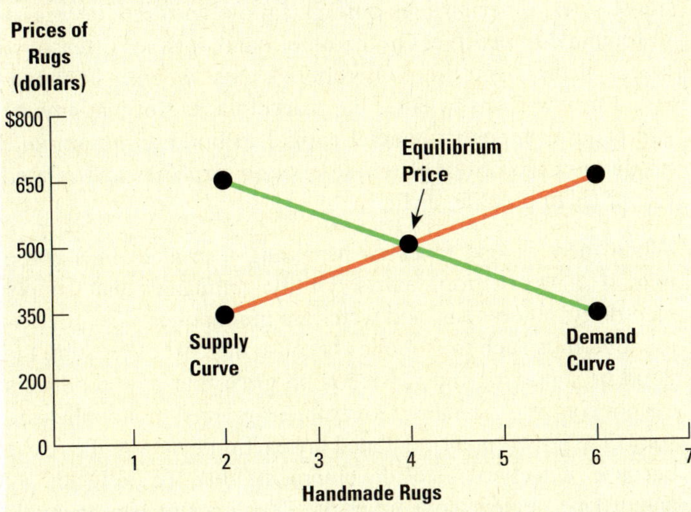

between the price of rugs and the quantity the company is willing to supply can be shown graphically with a *supply curve* (see Figure 1.2).

In Figure 1.2, the supply and demand curves intersect at the point where supply and demand are equal. The price at which the number of products that businesses are willing to supply equals the number of products that consumers are willing to buy at a specific point in time is the **equilibrium price**. In our rug example, the company is willing to supply four rugs at $500 each, and consumers are willing to buy four rugs at $500 each. Therefore, $500 is the equilibrium price for a rug at that point in time, and most rug companies will price their rugs at $500. As you might imagine, a business that charges more than $500 (or whatever the current equilibrium price is) for its rugs will not sell many and might not earn a profit. On the other hand, a business that charges less than $500 accepts a lower profit per rug than could be made at the equilibrium price.

If the cost of making rugs goes up, businesses will not offer as many at the old price. Changing the price alters the supply curve, and a new equilibrium price results. This is an ongoing process, with supply and demand constantly changing in response to changes in economic conditions, availability of resources, and degree of competition. For example, the price of oil can change rapidly and has been between $35 and $145 a barrel over the past five years. Prices for goods and services vary according to these changes in supply and demand. This concept is the force that drives the distribution of resources (goods and services, labor, and money) in a free-enterprise economy.

Critics of supply and demand say the system does not distribute resources equally. The forces of supply and demand prevent sellers who have to sell at higher prices (because their costs are high) and buyers who cannot afford to buy goods at the equilibrium price from participating in the market. According to critics, the wealthy can afford to buy more than they need, but the poor may be unable to buy enough of what they need to survive.

equilibrium price the price at which the number of products that businesses are willing to supply equals the number of products that consumers are willing to buy at a specific point in time

competition the rivalry among businesses for consumers' dollars

pure competition the market structure that exists when there are many small businesses selling one standardized product

The Nature of Competition

Competition, the rivalry among businesses for consumers' dollars, is another vital element in free enterprise. According to Adam Smith, competition fosters efficiency and low prices by forcing producers to offer the best products at the most reasonable price; those who fail to do so are not able to stay in business. Thus, competition should improve the quality of the goods and services available or reduce prices. For example, thanks to smart design and excellent timing, Apple dominates the market for downloadable music with its iTunes online service, iPod MP3 player, and iPhone. However, many companies have set their sights on capturing some of the firm's market share with new products of their own. Therefore, Apple must constantly seek to remain competitive by creating new innovations to maintain its market share—and sometimes capture market share from other companies. The new iPad device combines the features of the smart phone and the laptop into one product. The iPad also contains an interface that allows users to read books and take pictures, which will capture some of the e-reader market dominated by Amazon's Kindle Fire.[16]

> "Competition, the rivalry among businesses for consumers' dollars, is another vital element in free enterprise."

Within a free-enterprise system, there are four types of competitive environments: pure competition, monopolistic competition, oligopoly, and monopoly.

Pure competition exists when there are many small businesses selling one standardized product, such as agricultural commodities like wheat, corn, and cotton. No one business sells enough of the product to influence the product's price. And, because there is no difference in the products, prices are determined solely by the forces of supply and demand.

monopolistic competition the market structure that exists when there are fewer businesses than in a pure-competition environment and the differences among the goods they sell are small

oligopoly the market structure that exists when there are very few businesses selling a product

monopoly the market structure that exists when there is only one business providing a product in a given market

Monopolistic competition exists when there are fewer businesses than in a pure-competition environment and the differences among the goods they sell are small. Aspirin, soft drinks, and vacuum cleaners are examples of such goods. These products differ slightly in packaging, warranty, name, and other characteristics, but all satisfy the same consumer need. Businesses have some power over the price they charge in monopolistic competition because they can make consumers aware of product differences through advertising. Dyson, for example, attempts to differentiate its vacuum cleaners through product design, quality, and advertising. Consumers value some features more than others and are often willing to pay higher prices for a product with the features they want. For example, Advil, a nonprescription pain reliever, contains ibuprofen instead of aspirin. Consumers who cannot take aspirin or who believe ibuprofen is a more effective pain reliever may not mind paying a little extra for the ibuprofen in Advil.

An **oligopoly** exists when there are very few businesses selling a product. In an oligopoly, individual businesses have control over their products' price because each business supplies a large portion of the products sold in the marketplace. Nonetheless, the prices charged by different firms stay fairly close because a price cut or increase by one company will trigger a similar response from another company. In the airline industry, for example, when one airline cuts fares to boost sales, other airlines quickly follow with rate decreases to remain competitive. On the other hand, airlines often raise prices at the same time. Oligopolies exist when it is expensive for new firms to enter the marketplace. Not just anyone can acquire enough financial capital to build an automobile production facility or purchase enough airplanes and related resources to build an airline.

When there is one business providing a product in a given market, a **monopoly** exists. Utility companies that supply electricity, natural gas, and water are monopolies. The government permits such monopolies because the cost of creating the good or supplying the service is so great that new producers cannot compete for sales. Government-granted monopolies are subject to government-regulated prices. Some monopolies exist because of technological developments that are protected by patent laws. Patent laws grant the developer of new technology a period of time (usually 20 years) during which no other producer can use the same technology without the agreement of the original developer. The United States granted its first patent in 1790. Now its patent office receives hundreds of thousands of patent applications a year, although it is estimated that China will soon overtake the United States in patent filings.[17] This monopoly allows the developer to recover research, development, and production expenses and to earn a reasonable profit. An example of this type of monopoly is the dry-copier process developed by Xerox. Xerox's patents have expired, however, and many imitators have forced market prices to decline.

GAINING A FOOT AHEAD IN THE ATHLETIC INDUSTRY

Ken Hicks, president and CEO of Foot Locker, found a way to sustain the organization despite widespread economic contraction. During the most recent recession, many retailers, especially those located in shopping malls, had to shut down locations because shoppers were no longer spending their disposable income on nonessential items like branded footwear. This was a challenge for Foot Locker because it is known for selling branded items such as Nike. Yet under Hicks's leadership, Foot Locker has been successful in gaining sales by focusing more on corporate branding and emphasizing more profitable clothing items rather than shoes.

Foot Locker has different branches, such as Foot Locker, Lady Foot Locker, and Kids Foot Locker. Each branch was being branded together so that there was not a clear distinction between each store. Hicks realized that this was confusing to the customer. Foot Locker solved this problem by placing all these branches under separate marketing campaigns and reallocating the items in each store to differentiate them according to their target market. Foot Locker also changed the operational and pricing strategies to increase foot traffic and revenues.

During the economic contraction, many sellers turned to online retailing, but Foot Locker increased the number of employees and executives to emphasize customer-oriented service. As a result, profits have increased to $59 million from $37 million, and revenues increased 7.2 percent over the past year. By reorganizing the way it distributes products and focusing on customer service, Foot Locker was successful in maintaining an advantage over monopolistic competition.[18]

Discussion Questions

1. What are some ways that Foot Locker was able to weather the recession?
2. Why might it be problematic to have each brand branded together in a firm's marketing campaigns?
3. What might have been some of the advantages of increasing the number of employees rather than turning to more online retailing to cut costs?

economic expansion the situation that occurs when an economy is growing and people are spending more money; their purchases stimulate the production of goods and services, which in turn stimulates employment

inflation a condition characterized by a continuing rise in prices

economic contraction a slowdown of the economy characterized by a decline in spending and during which businesses cut back on production and lay off workers

recession a decline in production, employment, and income

unemployment the condition in which a percentage of the population wants to work but is unable to find jobs

Economic Cycles and Productivity

Expansion and Contraction Economies are not stagnant; they expand and contract. **Economic expansion** occurs when an economy is growing and people are spending more money. Their purchases stimulate the production of goods and services, which in turn stimulates employment. The standard of living rises because more people are employed and have money to spend. Rapid expansions of the economy, however, may result in **inflation**, a continuing rise in prices. Inflation can be harmful if individuals' incomes do not increase at the same pace as rising prices, reducing their buying power. Zimbabwe suffered from hyperinflation so severe that its inflation percentage rate rose into the hundreds of millions. With the elimination of the Zimbabwean dollar and certain price controls, the inflation rate began to decrease, but not before the country's economy was virtually decimated.[19]

Economic contraction occurs when spending declines. Businesses cut back on production and lay off workers, and the economy as a whole slows down. Contractions of the economy lead to **recession**—a decline in production, employment, and income. Recessions are often characterized by rising levels of **unemployment**, which is measured as the percentage of the population that wants to work but is unable to find jobs. Figure 1.3 shows the overall unemployment rate in the civilian labor force over the past 60 years. Rising unemployment levels tend to stifle demand for goods and services, which can have the effect of forcing prices downward, a condition known as *deflation*. The United States has experienced numerous recessions, the most recent ones occurring in 1990–1991, 2002–2003, and 2008–2011. The most recent recession (or economic slowdown) was caused by the collapse in housing prices and consumers' inability to stay current on their mortgage and credit card payments. This caused a crisis in the banking industry, with the government bailing out banks to keep them from failing. This in turn caused a slowdown in spending on consumer goods and an increase in employment. Unemployment reached 10 percent of the labor force. Don't forget that personal consumption makes up almost 70 percent of gross domestic product, so consumer behavior is extremely important for economic activity. A severe recession may turn into a **depression**, in which unemployment is very high, consumer spending is low, and business output is sharply reduced, such as what occurred in the United States in the early 1930s. The most recent recession is often called the Great Recession because it was the longest and most severe economic decline since the Great Depression.

Economies expand and contract in response to changes in consumer, business, and government spending. War also can affect an economy, sometimes stimulating it (as in the United States during World Wars I and II) and sometimes stifling it (as during the Vietnam, Persian Gulf, and Iraq Wars). Although fluctuations in the economy are inevitable and to a certain extent predictable, their effects—inflation and unemployment—disrupt lives and thus governments try to minimize them.

LO 1-5 Specify why and how the health of the economy is measured.

Measuring the Economy Countries measure the state of their economies to determine whether they are expanding or contracting and whether corrective action is necessary to

FIGURE 1.3
Average Annual Unemployment Rate, Civilian Labor Force 16 Years and Over

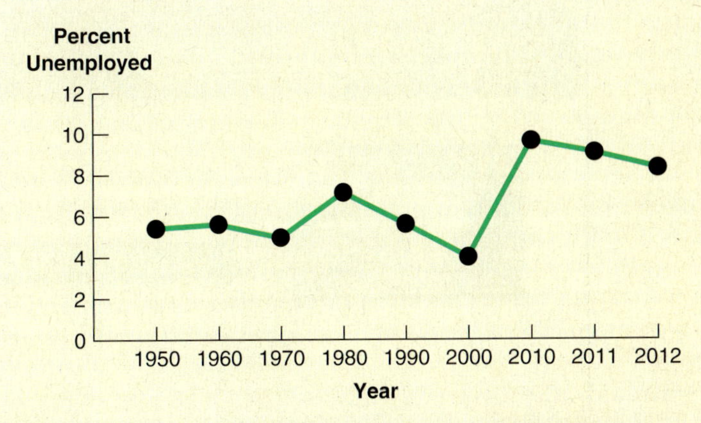

Source: "Employment Status of the Civilian Noninstitutional Population, 1940 to date," *Bureau of Labor Statistics*, www.bls.gov/cps/cpsaat01.pdf.

depression a condition of the economy in which unemployment is very high, consumer spending is low, and business output is sharply reduced

gross domestic product (GDP) the sum of all goods and services produced in a country during a year

budget deficit the condition in which a nation spends more than it takes in from taxes

minimize the fluctuations. One commonly used measure is **gross domestic product (GDP)**—the sum of all goods and services produced in a country during a year. GDP measures only those goods and services made within a country and therefore does not include profits from companies' overseas operations; it does include profits earned by foreign companies within the country being measured. However, it does not take into account the concept of GDP in relation to population (GDP per capita). Figure 1.4 shows the increase in GDP over the past 60 years, while Table 1.2 compares a number of economic statistics for a sampling of countries.

FIGURE 1.4
Growth in U.S. Gross Domestic Product

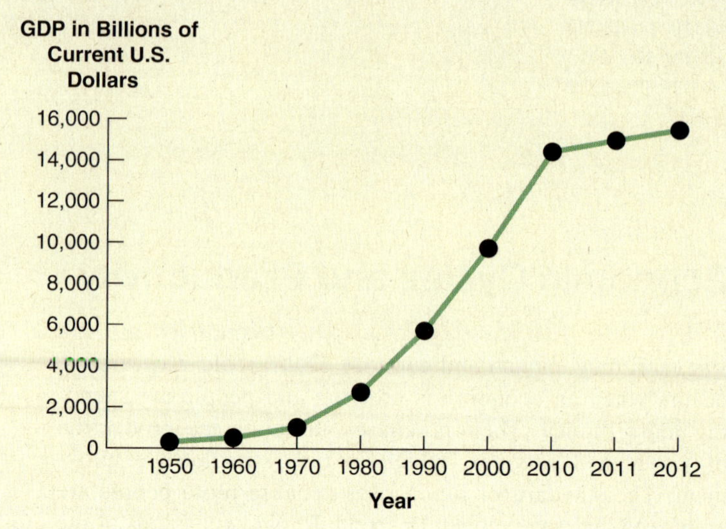

Source: U.S. Department of Commerce Bureau of Economic Analysis, www.bea.gov/national/index.htm#gdp.

Another important indicator of a nation's economic health is the relationship between its spending and income (from taxes). When a nation spends more than it takes in from taxes, it has a **budget deficit**. In the 1990s, the U.S. government eliminated its long-standing budget deficit by balancing the money spent for social, defense, and other programs with the amount of money taken in from taxes.

In recent years, however, the budget deficit has reemerged and grown to record levels, partly due to defense spending in the aftermath of the terrorist attacks of September 11, 2001. Massive government stimulus spending during the most recent recession also increased the national debt. Because many Americans do not want their taxes increased and Congress has difficulty agreeing on appropriate tax rates, it is difficult to increase taxes and reduce the deficit. Like consumers and businesses, when the government needs money, it borrows from the public, banks, and even foreign investors. The national debt (the amount of money the nation owes its lenders) exceeded $16 trillion in 2012, due largely to increased spending by the government and an economic stimulus package to help stave off the worst effects of the Great Recession.[20] This figure is especially worrisome because, to reduce the debt to a manageable level, the government has to either increase its revenues (raise taxes) or reduce spending on social, defense, and legal programs, neither of which is politically popular. The size of the national debt and little agreement on how to reduce the deficit caused the credit rating of the U.S. debt to go down in 2011. The national debt figure changes daily and can be seen at the Department of the Treasury, Bureau of the Public Debt, website. Table 1.3 describes some of the other ways we evaluate our nation's economy.

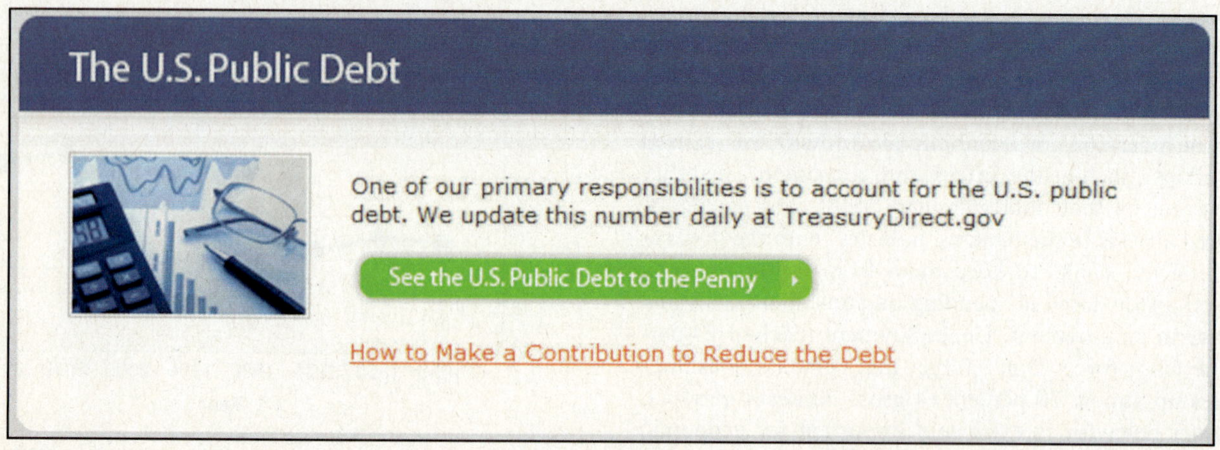

You can see what the U.S. government currently owes—down to the penny—by going to the website for the Bureau of the Public Debt, www.publicdebt.treas.gov/.

▼ TABLE 1.2 Comparative Analysis of Selected Countries

Country	GDP (U.S.$ in Billions)	GDP Per Capita	Unemployment Rate (%)	Inflation Rate (%)
Argentina	716.5	17,700	7.2	22.0
Australia	915.1	40,800	4.2	3.4
Brazil	2,294	11,800	6.0	6.6
Canada	1,389	40,500	7.5	2.9
China	11,300	8,400	6.5	5.5
France	2,214	35,100	9.2	2.3
Germany	3,114	38,100	6.0	2.5
India	4,421	3,700	9.8	8.9
Israel	237	31,500	5.6	3.5
Japan	4,444	34,700	4.6	−0.3
Mexico	1,667	14,700	5.2	3.4
Russia	2,383	16,700	6.6	8.4
South Africa	555	11,000	24.9	5.0
United Kingdom	2,288	36,500	8.1	4.5
U.S.	15,676	48,300	8.1	3.1

Sources: The CIA, *The World Fact Book,* www.cia.gov/library/publications/the-world-factbook/rankorder/rankorderguide.html; U.S. Department of Commerce Bureau of Economic Analysis, www.bea.gov/national/index.htm#gdp; Bureau of Labor Statistics, "Unemployment Unchanged at 7.8 Percent for December 2012," *National Conference of State Legislatures,* January 4, 2013, www.ncsl.org/issues-research/labor/national-employment-monthly-update.aspx.

LO 1-6 Trace the evolution of the American economy and discuss the role of the entrepreneur in the economy.

THE AMERICAN ECONOMY

As we said previously, the United States is a mixed economy with a foundation based on capitalism. The answers to the three basic economic issues are determined primarily by competition and the forces of supply and demand, although the federal government does intervene in economic decisions to a certain extent. To understand the current state of the American economy and its effect on business practices, it is helpful to examine its history and the roles of the entrepreneur and the government.

▼ TABLE 1.3 How Do We Evaluate Our Nation's Economy?

Unit of Measure	Description
Trade balance	The difference between our exports and our imports. If the balance is negative, as it has been since the mid-1980s, it is called a trade deficit and is generally viewed as unhealthy for our economy.
Consumer Price Index	Measures changes in prices of goods and services purchased for consumption by typical urban households.
Per capita income	Indicates the income level of "average" Americans. Useful in determining how much "average" consumers spend and how much money Americans are earning.
Unemployment rate	Indicates how many working-age Americans are not working who otherwise want to work.*
Inflation	Monitors price increases in consumer goods and services over specified periods of time. Used to determine if costs of goods and services are exceeding worker compensation over time.
Worker productivity	The amount of goods and services produced for each hour worked.

*Americans who do not work in a traditional sense, such as househusbands/housewives, are not counted as unemployed.

A Brief History of the American Economy

The Early Economy Before the colonization of North America, Native Americans lived as hunter/gatherers and farmers, with some trade among tribes. The colonists who came later operated primarily as an *agricultural economy.* People were self-sufficient and produced everything they needed at home, including food, clothing, and furniture. Abundant natural resources and a moderate climate nourished industries such as farming, fishing, shipping, and fur trading. A few manufactured goods, and money for the colonies' burgeoning industries came from England and other countries.

As the nation expanded slowly toward the West, people found natural resources such as coal, copper, and iron ore and used them to produce goods such as horseshoes, farm implements, and kitchen utensils. Farm

MAYORGA COFFEE COMBINES BUSINESS SKILLS WITH SOCIAL RESPONSIBILITY

Martin Mayorga, a Guatemalan native who grew up in the United States, founded Maryland-based Mayorga Coffee in 1997. Mayorga founded his enterprise with a commitment toward selling a high-quality product while promoting and improving the environmental and economic conditions of coffee farmers in Central and South America. As an entrepreneur entering an industry of monopolistic competition, Mayorga differentiates his business by incorporating social responsibility into his essential business practices. He promotes Organic and Rainforest Alliance certified coffees that are imported from their origin, which is an appealing option for the environmentally conscious consumer. Mayorga's success also comes from his ability to form long-term relationships with stakeholders, which has expanded his market presence. He has partnered with over 1,700 retail and food service organizations to sell his coffee products. Mayorga's entrepreneurial skills have paid off with $16 million in sales, ten retail locations, and a ranking among the Top 500 Hispanic-Owned Companies.[21]

families who produced surplus goods sold or traded them for things they could not produce themselves, such as fine furniture and window glass. Some families also spent time turning raw materials into clothes and household goods. Because these goods were produced at home, this system was called the domestic system.

The Industrial Revolution The 19th century and the Industrial Revolution brought the development of new technology and factories. The factory brought together all the resources needed to make a product—materials, machines, and workers. Work in factories became specialized as workers focused on one or two tasks. As work became more efficient, productivity increased, making more goods available at lower prices. Railroads brought major changes, allowing farmers to send their surplus crops and goods all over the nation for barter or for sale.

Factories began to spring up along the railways to manufacture farm equipment and a variety of other goods to be shipped by rail. Samuel Slater set up the first American textile factory after he memorized the plans for an English factory and emigrated to the United States. Eli Whitney revolutionized the cotton industry with his cotton gin. Francis Cabot Lowell's factory organized all the steps in manufacturing cotton cloth for maximum efficiency and productivity. John Deere's farm equipment increased farm production and reduced the number of farmers required to feed the young nation. Farmers began to move to cities to find jobs in factories and a higher standard of living. Henry Ford developed the assembly-line system to produce automobiles. Workers focused on one part of an automobile and then pushed it to the next stage until it rolled off the assembly line as a finished automobile. Ford's assembly line could manufacture many automobiles efficiently, and the price of his cars was $200, making them affordable to many Americans.

?

DID YOU KNOW?

Approximately 60 percent of adult women are engaged in the workforce.[22]

The Manufacturing and Marketing Economies Industrialization brought increased prosperity, and the United States gradually became a *manufacturing economy*—one devoted to manufacturing goods and providing services rather than producing agricultural products. The assembly line was applied to more industries, increasing the variety of goods available to the consumer. Businesses became more concerned with the needs of the consumer and entered the *marketing economy*. Expensive goods such as cars and appliances could be purchased on a time-payment plan. Companies conducted research to find out what products consumers needed and wanted. Advertising made consumers aware of products and important information about features, prices, and other competitive advantages.

Because these developments occurred in a free-enterprise system, consumers determined what goods and services were produced. They did this by purchasing the products they liked at prices they were willing to pay. The United States prospered, and American citizens had one of the highest standards of living in the world.

The Service and New Digital Economy After World War II, with the increased standard of living, Americans had more money and more time. They began to pay others to perform services that made their lives easier. Beginning in the 1960s, more and more women entered the workforce. The United States began experiencing major shifts in the population. The U.S. population grew 9.7 percent in the past decade to almost 314 million. This is the slowest pace of growth since the Great Depression, with the South leading the population gains. While the birth rate in the United States is declining, new immigrants help with population gains. The United States is growing at about the same rate as Mexico and Brazil.[23] The profile of the family is also changing: Today there are more

entrepreneur an individual who risks his or her wealth, time, and effort to develop for profit an innovative product or way of doing something

single-parent families and individuals living alone, and in two-parent families, both parents often work.

One result of this trend is that time-pressed Americans are increasingly paying others to do tasks they used to do at home, like cooking, laundry, landscaping, and child care. These trends have gradually changed the United States to a *service economy*—one devoted to the production of services that make life easier for busy consumers. Businesses increased their demand for services, especially in the areas of finance and information technology. Service industries such as restaurants, banking, health care, child care, auto repair, leisure-related industries, and even education are growing rapidly and may account for as much as 80 percent of the U.S. economy. These trends continue with advanced technology contributing to new service products based on technology and digital media that provide smart phones, social networking, and virtual worlds. More about the Internet, business, and new online social media can be found in Chapter 13.

The Role of the Entrepreneur

An **entrepreneur** is an individual who risks his or her wealth, time, and effort to develop for profit an innovative product or way of doing something. Wolfgang Puck, although an Austrian by birth, is a true American entrepreneur. He moved to Los Angeles to be a chef and opened Spago, an Italian-style trattoria that served good food that attracted movie stars. When people found his pizza so good that they took home extras to place in their freezers, he decided to build his frozen pizza into a multimillion-dollar business. Today, he has more than 20 restaurants and Wolfgang Express bistros in 80 locations.[24]

The free-enterprise system provides the conditions necessary for entrepreneurs to succeed. In the past, entrepreneurs were often inventors who brought all the factors of production together to produce a new product. Thomas Edison, whose inventions include the record player and light bulb, was an early American entrepreneur. Henry Ford was one of the first persons to develop mass assembly methods in the automobile industry. Other entrepreneurs, so-called captains of industry, invested in the country's growth. John D. Rockefeller built Standard Oil out of the fledgling oil industry, and Andrew Carnegie invested in railroads and founded the United States Steel Corporation. Andrew Mellon built the Aluminum Company of America and Gulf Oil. J. P. Morgan started financial institutions to fund the business activities of other entrepreneurs. Although these entrepreneurs were born in another century, their legacy to the American economy lives on in the companies they started, many of which still operate today. Milton Hershey began producing chocolate in 1894 in Lancaster, Pennsylvania. In 1900, the company was mass producing chocolate in many forms, lowering the cost of chocolate and making it more affordable to the masses, where it had once been a high-priced, luxury good. Early advertising touted chocolate as "a palatable confection and most nourishing food." Today, the Hershey Company employs more than 13,000 employees and sells almost $5 billion in chocolates and candies annually throughout the world.[25]

Entrepreneurs are constantly changing American business practices with new technology and innovative management techniques. Bill Gates, for example, built Microsoft, a software company whose products include Word and Windows, into a multibillion-dollar enterprise. Frederick Smith had an idea to deliver packages overnight, and now

Twitter founder Jack Dorsey launches the Square mobile credit card scanner in the hopes of revolutionizing the credit card industry.

his FedEx Company plays an important role in getting documents and packages delivered all over the world for businesses and individuals. Steve Jobs co-founded Apple and turned the company into a successful consumer electronics firm that revolutionized many industries, with products such as the iPod, iPhone, Mac computers, and iPad. The company went from near bankruptcy in the 1990s to become one of the most valuable brands in the entire world. Entrepreneurs have been associated with such uniquely American concepts as Dell Computers, Ben & Jerry's, Levi's, McDonald's, Dr Pepper, Apple, Google, Facebook, and Walmart. Walmart, founded by entrepreneur Sam Walton, was the first retailer to reach $100 billion in sales in one year and now routinely passes that mark, with more than $469 billion.[26] Sam Walton's heirs own about 47 percent of the company.[27] We will examine the importance of entrepreneurship further in Chapter 5.

> **"BUSINESS ETHICS GENERALLY REFERS TO THE STANDARDS AND PRINCIPLES USED BY SOCIETY TO DEFINE APPROPRIATE AND INAPPROPRIATE CONDUCT IN THE WORKPLACE."**

The Role of Government in the American Economy

The American economic system is best described as modified capitalism because the government regulates business to preserve competition and protect consumers and employees. Federal, state, and local governments intervene in the economy with laws and regulations designed to promote competition and to protect consumers, employees, and the environment. Many of these laws are discussed in the Appendix for Chapter 2.

Additionally, government agencies such as the U.S. Department of Commerce measure the health of the economy (GDP, productivity, and so on) and, when necessary, take steps to minimize the disruptive effects of economic fluctuations and reduce unemployment. When the economy is contracting and unemployment is rising, the federal government through the Federal Reserve Board (see Chapter 15) tries to spur growth so that consumers will spend more money and businesses will hire more employees. To accomplish this, it may reduce interest rates or increase its own spending for goods and services. When the economy expands so fast that inflation results, the government may intervene to reduce inflation by slowing down economic growth. This can be accomplished by raising interest rates to discourage spending by businesses and consumers. Techniques used to control the economy are discussed in Chapter 15.

Home Depot associates lay the foundation for a new house. Home Depot partners with Habitat for Humanity to build homes for disadvantaged families.

The Role of Ethics and Social Responsibility in Business

In the past few years, you may have read about a number of scandals at a number of well-known corporations, including Enron, Countrywide Financial, BP, and even leading banks such as Bank of America and Citigroup. In many cases, misconduct by individuals within these firms had an adverse effect on current and retired employees, investors, and others associated with these firms. In some cases, individuals went to jail for their actions. Top executives like Enron's Jeffrey Skilling and Tyco's Dennis Kozlowski received long prison sentences for their roles in corporate misconduct. These scandals undermined public confidence in corporate America and sparked a new debate about ethics in business. Business ethics generally refers to the standards and principles used by society to define appropriate and inappropriate conduct in the workplace. In many cases, these standards have been codified as laws prohibiting actions deemed unacceptable.

Society is increasingly demanding that businesspeople behave ethically and socially responsibly toward not only their customers but also employees, investors, government regulators, communities, and the natural environment. No area is more debated than online piracy. Software, music, and film executives want to defend their intellectual property. On the other hand, companies such as Google are concerned that strict laws would stifle innovation and enable censorship.[28] When actions are heavily criticized, a balance is usually required to support and protect various stakeholders.

While one view is that ethics and social responsibility are a good supplement to business activities, there is an alternative viewpoint. Research has shown that ethical behavior can not only enhance a company's reputation but can also drive profits.[29] The ethical and socially responsible conduct of companies such as Whole Foods, Starbucks, and the hotel chain Marriott provides evidence that good ethics is good business. There is growing recognition that the long-term value of conducting business in an ethical and socially responsible manner that considers the interests of all stakeholders creates superior financial performance.[30]

TEAM EXERCISE

Major economic systems, including capitalism, socialism, and communism, as well as mixed economies, were discussed in this chapter. Assuming that you want an economic system that is best for the majority, not just a few members of society, defend one of the economic systems as the best system. Form groups and try to reach agreement on one economic system. Defend why you support the system that you advance.

To promote socially responsible and ethical behavior while achieving organizational goals, businesses can monitor changes and trends in society's values. Businesses should determine what society wants and attempt to predict the long-term effects of their decisions. While it requires an effort to address the interests of all stakeholders, businesses can prioritize and attempt to balance conflicting demands. The goal is to develop a solid reputation of trust and avoid misconduct to develop effective workplace ethics.

CAN YOU LEARN BUSINESS IN A CLASSROOM?

Obviously, the answer is yes, or there would be no purpose for this textbook! To be successful in business, you need knowledge, skills, experience, and good judgment. The topics covered in this chapter and throughout this book provide some of the knowledge you need to understand the world of business. The examples and features within each chapter describe experiences to help you develop good business judgment. However, good judgment is based on knowledge and experience plus personal insight and understanding. Therefore, you need more courses in business, along with some practical experience in the business world, to help you develop the special insight necessary to put your personal stamp on knowledge as you apply it. The challenge in business is in the area of judgment, and judgment does not develop from memorizing an introductory business textbook. If you are observant in your daily experiences as an employee, as a student, and as a consumer, you will improve your ability to make good business judgments.

Figure 1.5 is an overview of how the chapters in this book are linked and how the chapters relate to the participants, the activities, and the environmental factors found in the business world. The topics presented in the chapters that follow will give you the best opportunity to begin the process of understanding the world of business.

FIGURE 1.5
The Organization of This Book

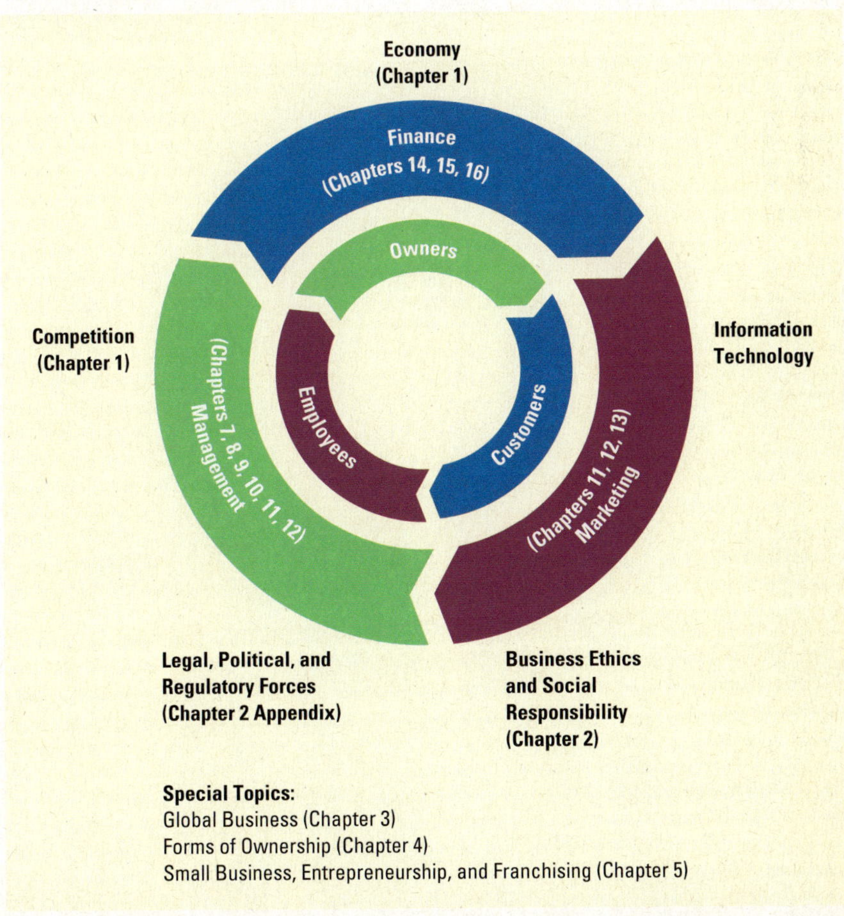

SO YOU WANT A JOB // in the Business World /

When most people think of a career in business, they see themselves entering the door to large companies and multinationals that they read about in the news and that are discussed in class. In a national survey, students indicated they would like to work for Google, Walt Disney, Apple, and Ernst & Young. In fact, most jobs are not with large corporations, but are in small companies, nonprofit organizations, government, and even self-employed individuals. There are 20 million individuals that the Small Business Administration says own their businesses and have no employees. In addition, there are nearly 5 million small businesses that employ 10 or fewer workers. With more than 75 percent of the economy based on services, there are jobs available in industries such as health care, finance, education, hospitality, entertainment, and transportation. The world is changing quickly and large corporations replace the equivalent of their entire workforce every four years.

The fast pace of technology today means that you have to be prepared to take advantage of emerging job opportunities and markets. You must also become adaptive and recognize that business is becoming more global, with job opportunities around the world. If you want to obtain such a job, you shouldn't miss a chance to spend some time overseas. To get you started on the path to thinking about job opportunities, consider all of the changes in business today that might affect your possible long-term track and that could bring you lots of success. You may want to stay completely out of large organizations and corporations and put yourself in a position for an entrepreneurial role as a self-employed contractor or small-business owner. However, there are many who feel that experience in larger businesses is helpful to your success later as an entrepreneur.

You're on the road to learning the key knowledge, skills, and trends that you can use to be a star in business. Business's impact on our society, especially in the area of sustainability and improvement of the environment, is a growing challenge and opportunity. Green businesses and green jobs in the business world are provided to give you a glimpse at the possibilities. Along the way, we will introduce you to some specific careers and offer advice on developing your own job opportunities. Research indicates that you won't be that happy with your job unless you enjoy your work and feel that it has a purpose. Since you spend most of your waking hours every day at work, you need to think seriously about what is important to you in a job.[31]

learn, practice, apply business and economic concepts!

M: Business was developed just for you—students on the go who need information packaged in a concise yet interesting format with multiple learning options. Check out the book's website to:

- Learn how the forces of supply and demand apply to business. (Solve the Dilemma)
- Know how to develop supply and demand curves. (Build Your Skills)
- Use supply and demand to determine an equilibrium price. (Build Your Skills)

While you are there, don't forget to enhance your skills. Practice and apply your knowledge, review the practice exercises, Student PPT® slides, and quizzes to review and apply chapter concepts. Additionally, *Connect® Business* is available for *M: Business*.

www.mhhe.com/ferrellm4e

Any organization, including nonprofits, has to manage the ethical behavior of employees and participants in the overall operations of the organization. The ethical conduct of employees creates a culture of trust and respect that makes a business productive. Although the mass media reports much misconduct in the business world, most businesses operate in an ethically and socially responsible manner. Any organizational decision may be judged as right or wrong, ethical or unethical, legal or illegal.

In this chapter, we take a look at the role of ethics and social responsibility in business decision making. First we define business ethics and examine why it is important to understand ethics' role in business. Next we explore a number

chapter two

business ethics + social responsibility

of business ethics issues to help you learn to recognize such issues when they arise. Finally, we consider steps businesses can take to improve ethical behavior in their organizations. The second half of the chapter focuses on social responsibility and unemployment. We survey some important issues and detail how companies have responded to them. ■

LEARNING OBJECTIVES

After reading this chapter, you will be able to:

LO 2-1 Define business ethics and social responsibility and examine their importance.

LO 2-2 Detect some of the ethical issues that may arise in business.

LO 2-3 Specify how businesses can promote ethical behavior.

LO 2-4 Explain the four dimensions of social responsibility.

LO 2-5 Debate an organization's social responsibilities to owners, employees, consumers, the environment, and the community.

business ethics principles and standards that determine acceptable conduct in business

social responsibility a business's obligation to maximize its positive impact and minimize its negative impact on society

LO 2-1 Define business ethics and social responsibility and examine their importance.

BUSINESS ETHICS AND SOCIAL RESPONSIBILITY

In this chapter, we define **business ethics** as the principles and standards that determine acceptable conduct in business organizations. Personal ethics, on the other hand, relates to an individual's values, principles, and standards of conduct. The acceptability of behavior in business is determined by not only the organization but also stakeholders such as customers, competitors, government regulators, interest groups, and the public as well as each individual's personal principles and values. The publicity and debate surrounding highly visible legal and ethical issues at a number of well-known firms, including Diamond Foods, Bank of America, and Citigroup, highlight the need for businesses to integrate ethics and responsibility into all business decisions. The most recent global financial crisis took a toll on consumer trust of financial services companies. Words used to describe these companies in a survey were "greedy," "impersonal," "opportunistic," and "distant." Most unethical activities within organizations are supported by an organizational culture that encourages employees to bend the rules. On the other hand, trust in business is the glue that holds relationships together. Texas Instruments, for example, has been recognized for its high integrity and strong ethical culture. In Figure 2.1, you can see that trust in banks is lower than in other industries.

Organizations that exhibit a high ethical culture encourage employees to act with integrity and adhere to business values.

SUSTAINABLE HARVEST™

RELATIONSHIP COFFEE

Sustainable Harvest imports specialty-grade coffee from 15 countries. The organization invests in training and development opportunities in the coffee communities from which it sources.

Many experts agree that ethical leadership, ethical values, and compliance are important in creating good business ethics. To truly create an ethical culture, however, managers must show a strong commitment to ethics and compliance. This "tone at the top" requires top managers to acknowledge their own role in supporting ethics and compliance, create strong relationships with the general counsel and the ethics and compliance department, clearly communicate company expectations for ethical behavior to all employees, educate all managers and supervisors in the business about the company's ethics policies, and train managers and employees on what to do if an ethics crisis occurs.[1]

Many consumers and social advocates believe that businesses should not only make a profit but also consider the social implications of their activities. Sustainable Harvest is an example of a leader in the social enterprise sector. We define **social responsibility** as a business's obligation to maximize its positive impact and minimize its negative impact on society. Although many people use the terms *social responsibility* and *ethics* interchangeably, they do not mean the same thing. Business ethics relates to an *individual's* or a *work group's* decisions that society evaluates as right or wrong, whereas social

"Many consumers and social advocates believe that businesses should not only make a profit but also consider the social implications of their activities."

VIRTUAL FARM BEARS RESPONSIBLE FRUIT

Zynga.org proves that companies can be both profitable and socially responsible. Zynga.org is the philanthropic arm of Zynga, a company known for its popular online video games such as FarmVille and Words With Friends. It is run by Laura Pincus Hartman, sister to Zynga founder Mark Pincus. Hartman's mission is to show that for-profit businesses can positively contribute to social change while maintaining their economic responsibilities. Zynga raises money by offering gamers a limited-edition virtual product, such as never-wilting sweet potatoes. The proceeds from these products are donated to organizations such as Habitat for Humanity to help alleviate poverty and improve infrastructure in developing countries. Although Zynga.org does not directly contribute to Zynga's bottom line, its philanthropic activities enhance the firm's reputation. By encouraging people to buy limited-edition virtual products for charity, Zynga.org also spreads awareness of the Zynga name and virtual products. Zynga has been able to link its philanthropic activities to its brand, demonstrating a prime example of how companies can integrate social responsibility into their business strategies.[2]

FIGURE 2.1
Global Trust in Industry Sectors

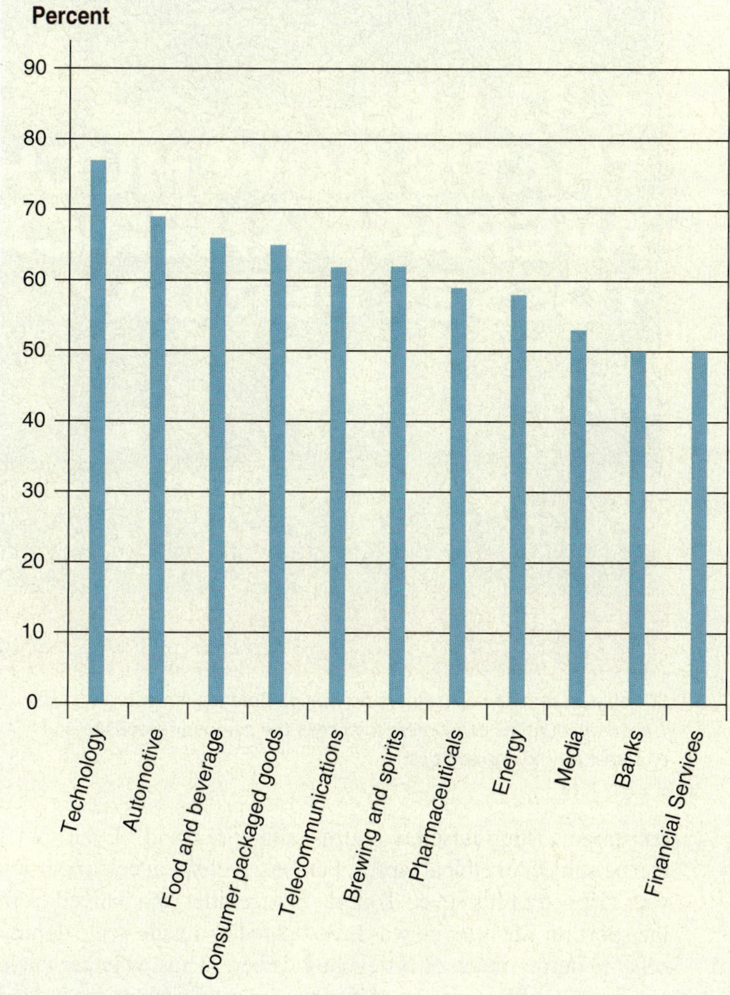

Source: Edelman, *Global Deck: 2013 Trust Barometer,* www.edelman.com/trust-downloads/global-results-2/.

responsibility is a broader concept that concerns the impact of the *entire business's* activities on society. From an ethical perspective, for example, we may be concerned about a health care organization overcharging the government for Medicare services. From a social responsibility perspective, we might be concerned about the impact that this overcharging will have on the ability of the health care system to provide adequate services for all citizens. It would appear that such concern is warranted. In one takedown, the Medicare Fraud Strike Task Force charged 107 individuals with fraud amounting to $452 million in false billing statements.[3]

On the other hand, misconduct does not necessarily have to spell doom for an organization. Hospital Corporation of America was one major health care organization accused of health care fraud more than a decade ago. However, the company worked hard to institute an ethics program that would completely change its ethical culture. The turnaround was so successful that it has been nominated as one of the world's most ethical companies. Hospital Corporation of America demonstrates how a company can learn from its mistakes and grow as an ethical firm.

The most basic ethical and social responsibility concerns have been codified by laws and regulations that encourage businesses to conform to society's standards, values, and attitudes. For example, after accounting scandals at a number of well-known firms in the early 2000s shook public confidence in the integrity of corporate America, the reputations of every U.S. company suffered regardless of their association with the scandals.[4] To help restore confidence in corporations and markets, Congress passed the Sarbanes-Oxley Act, which criminalized securities fraud and stiffened penalties for corporate fraud. After the financial crisis occurred in the most recent recession, the Dodd-Frank Act was passed to reform the financial industry and offer consumers protection against complex and/or deceptive financial products. At a minimum, managers are expected to obey all laws and regulations. Most legal issues arise as choices that society deems unethical, irresponsible, or otherwise unacceptable. However, all actions deemed unethical by society are not necessarily illegal, and both legal and ethical concerns change over time (see Table 2.1). Business law refers to the laws and regulations that govern the conduct of business. Many problems and conflicts in business can be avoided if owners, managers, and employees knew more about business law and the legal system. Business ethics, social responsibility, and laws together act as a compliance system, requiring that businesses and employees act responsibly in society. In this chapter, we explore ethics and social responsibility; the Appendix addresses business law, including the Sarbanes-Oxley Act and the Dodd-Frank Act.

TABLE 2.1 A Timeline of Ethical and Socially Responsible Activities

1960s	1970s	1980s	1990s	2000s
• Social issues • Consumer Bill of Rights • Disadvantaged consumer • Environmental issues • Product safety	• Business ethics • Social responsibility • Diversity • Bribery • Discrimination • Identifying ethical issues	• Standards for ethical conduct • Financial misconduct • Self-regulation • Codes of conduct • Ethics training	• Corporate ethics programs • Regulation to support business ethics • Health issues • Safe working conditions • Detecting misconduct	• Transparency in financial markets • Corporate misconduct • Intellectual property • Regulation of accounting and finance • Executive compensation

ethical issue an identifiable problem, situation, or opportunity that requires a person to choose from among several actions that may be evaluated as right or wrong, ethical or unethical

THE ROLE OF ETHICS IN BUSINESS

You have only to pick up *The Wall Street Journal* or *USA Today* to see examples of the growing concern about legal and ethical issues in business. For example, Wells Fargo & Company paid $85 million after it was accused of encouraging borrowers to take out subprime mortgage loans even when many were eligible for regular loans. Subprime mortgage borrowers are generally riskier and therefore pay higher interest rates. However, because subprime mortgages result in higher rates to the company, Wells Fargo allegedly gave individuals who qualified for lower rates subprime mortgages, a practice deemed to be highly unethical and deceptive.[5] Many of the largest banks have had to pay fines related to subprime loans and foreclosures. Regardless of what an individual believes about a particular action, if society judges it to be unethical or wrong, whether correctly or not, that judgment directly affects the organization's ability to achieve its business goals.[6]

green reflection | number 392

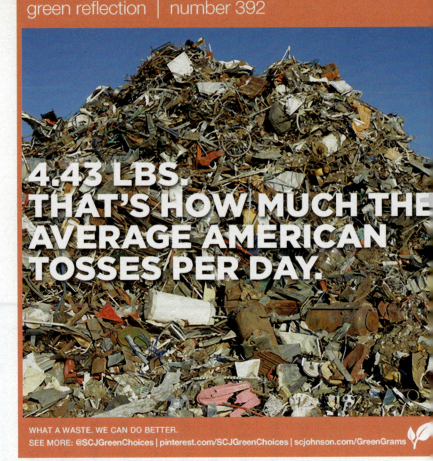

SC Johnson reminds consumers how much Americans waste every day. The ad encourages consumers to access the company's website and Pinterest for more green tips.

Well-publicized incidents of unethical and illegal activity—ranging from accounting fraud to using the Internet to steal another person's credit card number, from deceptive advertising of food and diet products to unfair competitive practices in the computer software industry—strengthen the public's perceptions that ethical standards and the level of trust in business need to be raised. Often, ethical conflicts evolve into legal disputes when cooperative conflict resolution cannot be accomplished. Headline-grabbing scandals like those associated with executive compensation and benefits packages create ethical concerns. Consumer outrage over executive compensation is prompting companies to begin reevaluating how they compensate their CEOs relative to corporate performance. JPMorgan cut CEO James Dimon's pay by 50 percent for 2012 after a high-risk trading scandal cost the firm more than $6.2 billion in trading losses.[7]

However, it is important to understand that business ethics goes beyond legal issues. Ethical conduct builds trust among individuals and in business relationships, which validates and promotes confidence in business relationships. Establishing trust and confidence is much more difficult in organizations that have reputations for acting unethically. If you were to discover, for example, that a manager had misled you about company benefits when you were hired, your trust and confidence in that company would probably diminish. And if you learned that a colleague had lied to you about something, you probably would not trust or rely on that person in the future.

Ethical issues are not limited to for-profit organizations either. Ethical issues include all areas of organizational activities, including government. In government, several politicians and some high-ranking officials have faced disciplinary actions over ethical indiscretions. Ex-New Orleans mayor Ray Nagin was indicted on charges that included money laundering, bribery, conspiracy, filing false tax returns, and wire fraud.[8] Even sports can be subject to ethical lapses. Famous cyclist Lance Armstrong was stripped of his seven Tour de France titles and banned from the sport for life after he was investigated in a wide-scale doping scheme during much of his cycling career.[9] Thus, whether made in science, politics, sports, or business, most decisions are judged as right or wrong, ethical or unethical. Negative judgments can affect an organization's ability to build relationships with customers and suppliers, attract investors, and retain employees.[10]

Although we will not tell you in this chapter what you ought to do, others—your superiors, co-workers, and family—will make judgments about the ethics of your actions and decisions. Learning how to recognize and resolve ethical issues is a key step in evaluating ethical decisions in business.

LO 2-2 Detect some of the ethical issues that may arise in business.

Recognizing Ethical Issues in Business

Recognizing ethical issues is the most important step in understanding business ethics. An **ethical issue** is an identifiable problem, situation, or opportunity that requires a person to choose from among several actions that may be evaluated as

bribes payments, gifts, or special favors intended to influence the outcome of a decision

Ralph Lauren reported that its subsidiary had bribed government officials in Argentina. Because it took quick action to address the misconduct, the company did not face charges.

Ethics is also related to the culture in which a business operates. In the United States, for example, it would be inappropriate for a businessperson to bring an elaborately wrapped gift to a prospective client on their first meeting—the gift could be viewed as a bribe. In Japan, however, it is considered impolite *not* to bring a gift. Experience with the culture in which a business operates is critical to understanding what is ethical or unethical.

To help you understand ethical issues that perplex businesspeople today, we will take a brief look at some of them in this section. Ethical issues can be more complex now than in the past. The vast number of news-format investigative programs has increased consumer and employee awareness of organizational misconduct. In addition, the multitude of cable channels and Internet resources has improved the awareness of ethical problems among the general public.

"Many business issues seem straightforward and easy to resolve on the surface but are in reality very complex."

right or wrong, ethical or unethical. In business, such a choice often involves weighing monetary profit against what a person considers appropriate conduct. The best way to judge the ethics of a decision is to look at a situation from a customer's or competitor's viewpoint: Should liquid-diet manufacturers make unsubstantiated claims about their products? Should an engineer agree to divulge her former employer's trade secrets to ensure that she gets a better job with a competitor? Should a salesperson omit facts about a product's poor safety record in his presentation to a customer? Such questions require the decision maker to evaluate the ethics of his or her choice.

Many business issues seem straightforward and easy to resolve on the surface but are in reality very complex. A person often needs several years of experience in business to understand what is acceptable or ethical. For example, it is considered improper to give or accept **bribes**, which are payments, gifts, or special favors intended to influence the outcome of a decision. A bribe benefits an individual or a company at the expense of other stakeholders. Companies that do business overseas should be aware that bribes are a significant ethical issue and are, in fact, illegal in many countries. In the United States, the Foreign Corrupt Practices Act imposes heavy penalties on companies found guilty of bribery. For instance, Paris-based telecommunications company Alcatel SA was fined more than $130 million after it was revealed that the company had paid "consultants" in Central America and Southeast Asia $8 million to try to get government contracts.[11]

The show Undercover Boss *gives managers and business owners the chance to understand how their subordinates feel as they take on the responsibilities of their employees. Many bosses develop a stronger appreciation for their employees' challenging jobs, as Kat Cole, president of Cinnabon Inc., did after spending time undercover in the company's retail locations.*

> ONE OF THE PRINCIPAL CAUSES OF UNETHICAL BEHAVIOR IN ORGANIZATIONS IS OVERLY AGGRESSIVE FINANCIAL OR BUSINESS OBJECTIVES.

One of the principal causes of unethical behavior in organizations is overly aggressive financial or business objectives. Many of these issues relate to decisions and concerns that managers have to deal with daily. It is not possible to discuss every issue, of course. However, a discussion of a few issues can help you begin to recognize the ethical problems with which businesspersons must deal. Many ethical issues in business can be categorized in the context of their relation with abusive and intimidating behavior, conflicts of interest, fairness and honesty, communications, misuse of company resources, and business associations. The National Business Ethics Survey found that workers witness many instances of ethical misconduct in their organizations (see Table 2.2).

Misuse of Company Time Theft of time is the number-one area of misconduct observed in the workplace.[12] One example of misusing time in the workplace is by engaging in activities that are not necessary for the job. For instance, many employees spend an average of one hour each day using social networking sites or watching YouTube. In this case, the employee is misusing not only time but also company resources by using the company's computer and Internet access for personal use.[13] Time theft costs can be difficult to measure but are estimated to cost companies hundreds of billions of dollars annually. It is widely believed that the average employee steals 4.5 hours a week with late arrivals, leaving early, long lunch breaks, inappropriate sick days, excessive socializing, and engaging in personal activities such as online shopping and watching sports while on the job. All of these activities add up to lost productivity and profits for the employer—and relate to ethical issues in the area of time theft.

TABLE 2.2 Percentage of U.S. Workforce Observing Specific Forms of Misconduct, 2009 and 2011

Behavior	2009 (%)	2011 (%)
Misuse of company time	n/a	33
Abusive behavior	22	21
Lying to employees	19	20
Company resource abuse	23	20
Violating company Internet-use policies	n/a	16
Discrimination	14	15
Conflicts of interest	16	15
Inappropriate social networking	n/a	14
Health or safety violations	11	13
Lying to outside stakeholders	12	12
Stealing	9	12
Falsifying time reports or hours worked	n/a	12

Source: Ethics Resource Center, *2011 National Business Ethics Survey®: Ethics in Transition* (Arlington, VA: Ethics Resource Center, 2012), pp. 39–40. Reprinted with permission.

Abusive and Intimidating Behavior Abusive or intimidating behavior is the second most common ethical problem for employees. These concepts can mean anything from physical threats, false accusations, profanity, insults, yelling, harshness, and unreasonableness to ignoring someone or simply being annoying; and the meaning of these words can differ by person—you probably have some ideas of your own. Abusive behavior can be placed on a continuum from a minor distraction to a disruption of the workplace. For example, what one person may define as yelling might be another's definition of normal speech. Civility in our society is a concern, and the workplace is no exception. The productivity level of many organizations has been diminished by the time spent unraveling abusive relationships.

Abusive behavior is difficult to assess and manage because of diversity in culture and lifestyle. What does it mean to speak profanely? Is profanity only related to specific words or other such terms that are common in today's business world? If you are using words that are normal in your language but that others consider to be profanity, have you just insulted, abused, or disrespected them?

Within the concept of abusive behavior, intent should be a consideration. If the employee was trying to convey a compliment but the comment was considered abusive, then it was probably a mistake. The way a word is said (voice inflection) can be important. Add to this the fact that we now live in a multicultural environment—doing business and working with many cultural groups—and the businessperson soon realizes the depth of the ethical and legal issues that may arise. There are problems of word meanings by age and within cultures. For example, an expression such as "Did you guys hook up last night?" can have various meanings, including some that could be considered offensive in a work environment.

Bullying is associated with a hostile workplace when a person or group is targeted and is threatened, harassed, belittled, verbally abused, or overly criticized. Bullying may create what some consider a hostile environment, a term generally associated with sexual harassment. Although sexual harassment has legal recourse, bullying has little legal recourse at this time. Bullying is a widespread problem in the United States and can cause psychological damage that can result in health-endangering consequences to the target. Surveys indicate that approximately one in three adults has experienced bullying in

TABLE 2.3 Actions Associated with Bullies

1. Spreading rumors to damage others
2. Blocking others' communication in the workplace
3. Flaunting status or authority to take advantage of others
4. Discrediting others' ideas and opinions
5. Use of e-mails to demean others
6. Failing to communicate or return communication
7. Insults, yelling, and shouting
8. Using terminology to discriminate by gender, race, or age
9. Using eye or body language to hurt others or their reputation
10. Taking credit for others' work or ideas

Source: © O.C. Ferrell, 2011.

the workplace, and one in seven workers witnesses bullying. Many victims and bystanders do not report bullying for fear of reprisals.[14] As Table 2.3 indicates, bullying can use a mix of verbal, nonverbal, and manipulative threatening expressions to damage workplace productivity. One may wonder why workers tolerate such activities. The problem is that 81 percent of workplace bullies are supervisors. A top officer at Boeing cited an employee survey indicating 26 percent had observed abusive or intimidating behavior by management.[15]

Misuse of Company Resources Misuse of company resources has been identified by the Ethics Resource Center as a leading issue in observed misconduct in organizations. Issues might include spending an excessive amount of time on personal e-mails, submitting personal expenses on company expense reports, or using the company copier for personal use. Although serious resource abuse can result in firing, some abuse can have legal repercussions. For example, one lawyer was found guilty of tax evasion after charging personal expenses through the law firm's bank account and manipulating the firm's ledgers to hide the misconduct.[16]

The most common way that employees abuse resources is by using company computers for personal use. Typical examples of using a computer for personal use include shopping on the Internet, downloading music, doing personal banking, surfing the Internet for entertainment purposes, or visiting Facebook. Some companies have chosen to block certain sites such as YouTube or Pandora from employees. However, other companies choose to take a more flexible approach. For example, many have instituted policies that allow for some personal computer use as long as the use does not detract significantly from the workday.

No matter what approach a business chooses to take, it must have policies in place to prevent company resource abuse. Because misuse of company resources is such a widespread problem, many companies, like Boeing, have implemented official policies delineating acceptable use of company resources. Boeing's policy states that use of company resources is acceptable when it does not result in "significant added costs, disruption of business processes, or any other disadvantage to the company." The policy further states that use of company resources for noncompany purposes is acceptable only when an employee receives explicit permission to do so. This kind of policy is in line with that of many companies, particularly large ones that can easily lose millions of dollars and thousands of hours of productivity to these activities.[17]

Conflict of Interest A conflict of interest, one of the most common ethical issues identified by employees, exists when a person must choose whether to advance his or her own personal interests or those of others. For example, a manager in a corporation is supposed to ensure that the company is profitable so that its stockholder-owners receive a return on their investment. In other words, the manager has a responsibility to investors. If she instead makes decisions that give her more power or money but do not help the company, then she has a conflict of interest—she is acting to benefit herself at the expense of her company and is not fulfilling her responsibilities as an employee. To avoid conflicts of interest, employees must be able to separate their personal financial interests from their business dealings. In the wake of the 2008 meltdown on Wall Street, stakeholders and legislators pushed for reform of the credit rating industry. Many cited rampant conflicts of interest between financial firms and the companies that rate them as part of the reason no one recognized the impending financial disaster. Conflict of interest has long been a serious problem in the financial industry because the financial companies pay the credit raters money to be rated. Because different rating companies exist, financial firms can also shop around for the best rating. There is no third-party mediator who oversees the financial industry and how firms are rated.[18]

Insider trading is an example of a conflict of interest. Insider trading is the buying or selling of stocks by insiders who possess material that is still not public. The Justice Department has taken an aggressive stance toward insider trading. For instance, Rajat Gupta, director of Goldman Sachs and Procter & Gamble, was arrested after being accused of passing insider information to his friend Raj Rajaratnam, former director of the hedge fund the Galleon Group. Rajaratnam himself was sentenced to 11 years in prison.[19] Bribery can also be a conflict of interest. Although bribery is an increasing issue in many countries, it is more prevalent in some countries than in others. Transparency International has developed a Corruption Perceptions Index (Table 2.4). Note that 18 countries are perceived as less corrupt than the United States.[20]

Fairness and Honesty

Fairness and honesty are at the heart of business ethics and relate to the general values of decision makers. Beyond obeying the law, businesspersons are expected not to harm customers, employees, clients, or competitors knowingly through deception, misrepresentation, coercion, or discrimination. Honesty and fairness can relate to how the employees use the resources of the organization. Fairness can be defined as being impartial and just, whereas honesty is defined as being truthful and trustworthy. In contrast, dishonesty is usually associated with a lack of

▼ **TABLE 2.4** Ranking of Countries Based on Corruption of Public Sector

Country Rank	CPI Score*	Least Corrupt	Country Rank	CPI Score*	Most Corrupt
1	90	Denmark	174	8	Somalia
1	90	Finland	174	8	North Korea
1	90	New Zealand	174	8	Afghanistan
4	88	Sweden	173	13	Sudan
5	87	Singapore	172	15	Myanmar
6	86	Switzerland	170	17	Uzbekistan
7	85	Australia	170	17	Turkmenistan
7	85	Norway	169	18	Iraq
9	84	Canada	165	19	Venezuela
9	84	Netherlands	165	19	Haiti
11	82	Iceland	165	19	Chad
12	80	Luxembourg	165	19	Burundi

* CPI 2012 score relates to perceptions of the degree of public sector corruption as seen by businesspeople and country analysts and ranges between 100 (highly clear) and 0 (highly corrupt). The United States is perceived as the 19th least-corrupt nation out of the 176 countries and territories surveyed.

Source: Extracted from the *Corruption Perceptions Index 2012.*

integrity, lack of disclosure, and lying. One common example of dishonesty is theft of office supplies. Approximately 35 percent of shrinkage—inventory losses due to shoplifting, employee theft, or errors—is a result of employee theft.[21] Although the majority of office supply thefts involve small things such as pencils or Post-it® Notes, some workers admit to stealing more expensive equipment such as laptops, PDAs, and cell phones. Employees should be aware of policies on taking items and recognize how these decisions relate to ethical behavior.

One aspect of fairness relates to competition. Although numerous laws have been passed to foster competition and make monopolistic practices illegal, companies sometimes gain control over markets by using questionable practices that harm competition. Bullying can also occur between companies that are intense competitors. For example, Pool Corporation, the largest U.S. distributor of pool products, was accused by the Federal Trade Commission of using anticompetitive tactics to bar new distributors from entering the market.[22] In many cases, the alleged misconduct not only can have monetary and legal implications but also can threaten reputation, investor confidence, and customer loyalty. In the case of Pool Corporation, the company had allegedly bullied pool manufacturers by threatening to refuse to distribute their products if they did business with other pool distributors. Such behavior is unacceptable. At the minimum, a business found guilty of anticompetitive practices will be forced to stop such conduct. However, many companies end up paying millions in penalties to settle allegations.[23]

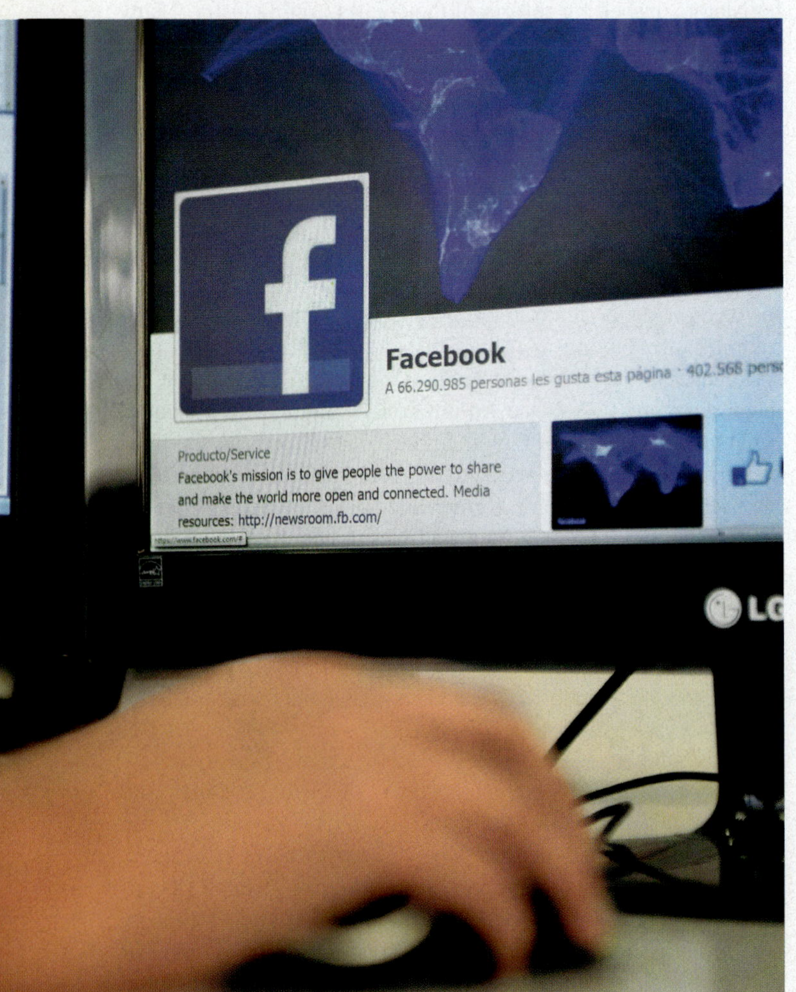

Misuse of company time through the use of personal social media is very costly to businesses.

Communications Communications is another area in which ethical concerns may arise. False and misleading advertising, as well as deceptive personal-selling tactics, anger consumers and can lead to the failure of a business. Truthfulness about product safety and quality are also important to consumers. Johnson & Johnson (J&J) faced a major crisis after undergoing 50 product recalls in a 15-month period. Many of the recalls related to product quality and safety issues, ranging from foul odors to the wrong amount of ingredients in medicines. Criticizing J&J for its product quality lapses and its handling of the crisis, the Food and Drug Administration placed three factories under its supervision for five years.[24]

Some companies fail to provide enough information for consumers about differences or similarities between products. For example, driven by high prices for medicines, many consumers

plagiarism the act of presenting someone else's work as your own without mentioning the source

are turning to Canadian, Mexican, and overseas Internet sources for drugs to treat a variety of illnesses and conditions. However, research suggests that a significant percentage of these imported pharmaceuticals may not actually contain the labeled drug, and the counterfeit drugs could even be harmful to those who take them.[25]

Another important aspect of communications that may raise ethical concerns relates to product labeling. This becomes an even greater concern with potentially harmful products such as cigarettes. In Europe, at least 30 percent of the front side of cigarette packaging and 40 percent of the back needs to be taken up by the warning. The Food and Drug Administration passed similar rules for the United States, but its ruling was blocked until the lawsuit between the FDA and cigarette companies is resolved.[26] However, labeling of other products raises ethical questions when it threatens basic rights, such as freedom of speech and expression. This is the heart of the controversy surrounding the movement to require warning labels on movies and videogames, rating their content, language, and appropriate audience age. Although people in the entertainment industry claim that such labeling violates their First Amendment right to freedom of expression, other consumers—particularly parents—believe that labeling is needed to protect children from harmful influences. Similarly, alcoholic beverage and cigarette manufacturers have argued that a total ban on cigarette and alcohol advertisements violates the First Amendment. Internet regulation, particularly that designed to protect children and the elderly, is on the forefront in consumer protection legislation. Because of the debate surrounding the acceptability of these business activities, they remain major ethical issues.

plagiarism.org

Business Relationships The behavior of businesspersons toward customers, suppliers, and others in their workplace may also generate ethical concerns. Ethical behavior within a business involves keeping company secrets, meeting obligations and responsibilities, and avoiding undue pressure that may force others to act unethically.

Managers in particular, because of the authority of their position, have the opportunity to influence employees' actions. For example, a manager might influence employees to use pirated computer software to save costs. The use of illegal software puts the employee and the company at legal risk, but employees may feel pressured to do so by their superior's authority. The National Business Ethics Survey found that employees who feel pressured to compromise ethical standards view top and middle managers as the greatest source of such pressure.[27]

It is the responsibility of managers to create a work environment that helps the organization achieve its objectives and fulfill its responsibilities. However, the methods that managers use to enforce these responsibilities should not compromise employee rights. Organizational pressures may encourage a person to engage in activities that he or she might otherwise view as unethical, such as invading others' privacy or stealing a competitor's secrets. The firm may provide only vague or lax supervision on ethical issues, creating the opportunity for misconduct. Managers who offer no ethical direction to employees create many opportunities for manipulation, dishonesty, and conflicts of interest.

Plagiarism—presenting someone else's work as your own without mentioning the source—is another ethical issue. As a student, you may be familiar with plagiarism in school, for example, copying someone else's term paper or quoting from a published work or Internet source without acknowledging it. In business, an ethical issue arises when an employee copies reports or presents the work or ideas of others as his or her own. A manager attempting to take credit for a subordinate's ideas is engaging in another type of plagiarism.

Making Decisions about Ethical Issues

Although we've presented a variety of ethical issues that may arise in business, it can be difficult to recognize specific ethical issues in practice. Whether a decision maker recognizes an issue as an ethical one often depends on the issue itself. Managers, for example, tend to be more concerned about issues that affect those close to them as well as issues that have immediate rather than long-term consequences. Thus, the perceived importance of an ethical issue substantially affects choices. However, only a few issues receive scrutiny, and most receive no attention at all.[28]

Table 2.5 lists some questions you may want to ask yourself and others when trying to determine whether an action is ethical. Open discussion of ethical issues does not eliminate ethical problems, but it does promote both trust and learning in an

TABLE 2.5 Questions to Consider in Determining Whether an Action Is Ethical

Are there any potential legal restrictions or violations that could result from the action?
Does your company have a specific code of ethics or policy on the action?
Is this activity customary in your industry? Are there any industry trade groups that provide guidelines or codes of conduct that address this issue?
Would this activity be accepted by your co-workers? Will your decision or action withstand open discussion with co-workers and managers and survive untarnished?
How does this activity fit with your own beliefs and values?

codes of ethics formalized rules and standards that describe what a company expects of its employees

organization.[29] When people feel that they cannot discuss what they are doing with their co-workers or superiors, there is a good chance that an ethical issue exists. Once a person has recognized an ethical issue and can openly discuss it with others, he or she has begun the process of resolving that issue.

LO 2-3 Specify how businesses can promote ethical behavior.

Improving Ethical Behavior in Business

Understanding how people make ethical choices and what prompts a person to act ethically or unethically may reverse the current trend toward unethical behavior in business. Ethical decisions in an organization are influenced by three key factors: individual moral standards, the influence of managers and co-workers, and the opportunity to engage in misconduct (Figure 2.2). Although you have great control over your personal ethics outside the workplace, your co-workers and superiors exert significant control over your choices at work through authority and example. In fact, the activities and examples set by co-workers, along with rules and policies established by the firm, are critical in gaining consistent ethical compliance in an organization. If the company fails to provide good examples and direction for appropriate conduct, confusion and conflict will develop and result in the opportunity for misconduct. If your boss or co-workers leave work early, you may be tempted to do so as well. If you see co-workers engaged in personal activities such as shopping online or watching YouTube, then you may be more likely to do so also. In addition, having sound personal values contributes to an ethical workplace.

> "Many employees use different ethical standards at work than they do at home."

Because ethical issues often emerge from conflict, it is useful to examine the causes of ethical conflict. Business managers and employees often experience some tension between their own ethical beliefs and their obligations to the organizations in which they work. Many employees use different ethical standards at work than they do at home. This conflict increases when employees feel that their company is encouraging unethical conduct or exerting pressure on them to engage in it.

It is difficult for employees to determine what conduct is acceptable within a company if the firm does not have established ethics policies and standards. And without such policies and standards, employees may base decisions on how their peers and superiors behave. Professional **codes of ethics** are formalized rules and standards that describe what the company expects of its employees. Codes of ethics do not have to be so detailed that they take into account every situation, but they should provide guidelines and principles that can help employees achieve organizational objectives and address risks in an acceptable and ethical way. Eaton's code of ethics, for instance, provides

NEW ORLEANS SAINTS FACES DOWN BOUNTY SCANDAL

Business ethics does not apply just to the corporate world. It applies to all organizations, including sports, politics, nonprofits, and more. The bounty scandal of the New Orleans Saints football organization is an example of ethical misconduct in leadership. The head coach, assistant coach, defensive coordinator, and general manager all received suspensions for offering a monetary award to the defensive line players who would "cart off" ($1,000) or "knock out" ($1,500) their opponents during games. These abusive and intimidating behaviors are not just a way to win games but are serious threats to the safety of the players.

According to most football players in the NFL, the bounty system is a common occurrence but is usually orchestrated on a small scale by the players without the knowledge of management. Under the leadership of the New Orleans Saints, the players succumbed to an ethical dilemma: Take out their opponents and receive the money to increase their chances of winning a game, or not get involved. The culture that the management of the Saints nurtured did not reflect the code of ethics the NFL promotes, which is player safety and competitive integrity. Some of the players were also suspended, but the suspensions were lifted after an appeals panel decided there was not enough evidence against them. This damaged reputation might take the team years to recover from. However, the New Orleans Saints team has learned the major lesson that ethical leadership is important to success.[30]

Discussion Questions

1. Describe the ethical issue the New Orleans Saints faced.
2. What does this situation say about the New Orleans Saints' organizational culture?
3. What are some ways the New Orleans Saints team might begin to rebuild its reputation?

FIGURE 2.2
Three Factors That Influence Business Ethics

Individual Standards and Values	+	Managers' and Co-workers' Influence	+	Opportunity: Codes and Compliance Requirements	=	Ethical/Unethical Choices in Business

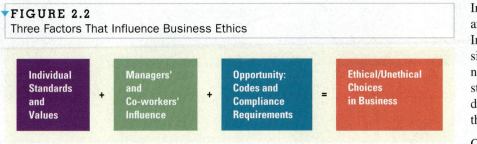

examples, questions, and other aids to help its employees across the globe understand the firm's ethical standards. The development of a code of ethics should include not only a firm's executives and board of directors, but also legal staff and employees from all areas of a firm.[31] Table 2.6 lists some key things to consider when developing a code of ethics.

Codes of ethics, policies on ethics, and ethics training programs advance ethical behavior because they prescribe which activities are acceptable and which are not, and they limit the opportunity for misconduct by providing punishments for violations of the rules and standards. Codes and policies on ethics encourage the creation of an ethical culture in the company. According to the National Business Ethics Survey (NBES), employees in organizations that have written codes of conduct and ethics training, ethics offices or hotlines, and systems for reporting are more likely to report misconduct when they observe it. The survey found that a company's ethical culture is the greatest determinant of future misconduct.[32]

The enforcement of ethical codes and policies through rewards and punishments increases the acceptance of ethical standards by employees. For example, employees at Granite Construction are highly encouraged to engage in ethical behavior. Granite Construction holds six mandatory training sessions to manage risks, offers computer-based training for employees, provides ethics training for board members, and uses Field Compliance Officers to monitor compliance throughout the company. Granite's strong ethics inspired the creation of the Construction Industry Ethics and Compliance Initiative, consisting of a network of construction firms dedicated to supporting ethics throughout the industry.[33]

whistleblowing the act of an employee exposing an employer's wrongdoing to outsiders, such as the media or government regulatory agencies

One of the most important components of an ethics program is a means through which employees can report observed misconduct anonymously. Although the risk of retaliation is still a major factor in whether an employee will report illegal conduct, the NBES found that whistleblowing has increased in the past few years. Approximately 65 percent of respondents said they reported misconduct when they observed it.[34] **Whistleblowing** occurs when an employee exposes an employer's wrongdoing to outsiders, such as the media or government regulatory agencies. However, more companies are establishing programs to encourage employees to report illegal or unethical practices internally so that they can take steps to remedy problems before they result in legal action or generate negative publicity. Unfortunately, whistleblowers are often treated negatively in organizations. The government seeks to discourage this practice by rewarding firms that encourage employees to report misconduct—with reduced fines and penalties when violations occur. Congress has also taken steps to close a legislative loophole in whistleblowing legislation that has led to the dismissal of many whistleblowers. In 2010, Congress passed the Dodd-Frank Act, which includes a "whistleblower bounty program." The Securities and Exchange Commission can now award whistleblowers between 10 and 30 percent of monetary sanctions over $1 million. The hope is that incentives will encourage more people to come forward with information regarding corporate misconduct. In fact, the National Business Ethics Survey estimates that 8 percent of employees who report misconduct could qualify for a bounty under the Dodd-Frank Act.[35]

TABLE 2.6 Key Things to Consider in Developing a Code of Ethics

- Create a team to assist with the process of developing the code (include management and nonmanagement employees from across departments and functions).
- Solicit input from employees from different departments, functions, and regions to compile a list of common questions and answers to include in the code document.
- Make certain that the headings of the code sections can be easily understood by all employees.
- Avoid referencing specific U.S. laws and regulations or those of specific countries, particularly for codes that will be distributed to employees in multiple regions.
- Hold employee group meetings on a complete draft version (including graphics and pictures) of the text, using language that everyone can understand.
- Inform employees that they will receive a copy of the code during an introduction session.
- Let all employees know that they will receive future ethics training that will, in part, cover the important information contained in the code document.

Source: Adapted from William Miller, "Implementing an Organizational Code of Ethics," *International Business Ethics Review* 7 (Winter 2004), pp. 1, 6–10.

Lance Armstrong confesses to Oprah Winfrey that he participated in a doping scheme throughout much of his cycling career. Armstrong was stripped of his Tour de France wins and banned from cycling for life.

> "The current trend is to move away from legally based ethical initiatives in organizations to cultural- or integrity-based initiatives that make ethics a part of core organizational values."

The current trend is to move away from legally based ethical initiatives in organizations to cultural- or integrity-based initiatives that make ethics a part of core organizational values. Organizations recognize that effective business ethics programs are good for business performance. Firms that develop higher levels of trust function more efficiently and effectively and avoid damaged company reputations and product images. Organizational ethics initiatives have been supportive of many positive and diverse organizational objectives, such as profitability, hiring, employee satisfaction, and customer loyalty.[36] Conversely, lack of organizational ethics initiatives and the absence of workplace values such as honesty, trust, and integrity can have a negative impact on organizational objectives and employee retention. According to one study, three of the most common factors that executives give for why turnover increases are employee loss of trust in the company, a lack of transparency among company leaders, and unfair employee treatment.[37] On the other hand, organizations that possess ethical leadership have been found to have higher employee morale, lower turnover, and a stronger ethical culture. Ethical leadership involves influencing others to achieve company goals while ensuring that these goals are achieved in an ethical manner. Ethical leadership is not limited solely to management but can be practiced and implemented by every employee at every level of the organization. Organizations with strong ethical leadership have mechanisms in place such as codes of conduct and anonymous reporting systems to develop a set of shared values for all employees. By embracing ethical leadership, companies can protect themselves from potential legal consequences while creating an ethical reputation that will help them succeed for many years. Starbucks's Howard Schultz and Berkshire Hathaway's Warren Buffett have often been identified as ethical leaders.

LO 2-4 Explain the four dimensions of social responsibility.

THE NATURE OF SOCIAL RESPONSIBILITY

There are four dimensions of social responsibility: economic, legal, ethical, and voluntary (including philanthropic) (Figure 2.3).[38] Earning profits is the economic foundation of the pyramid in Figure 2.3, and complying with the law is the next step. However, a business whose *sole* objective is to maximize profits is not likely to consider its social responsibility, although its activities will probably be legal. (We looked at ethical responsibilities in the first half of this chapter.) Finally, voluntary responsibilities are additional activities that may not be required but which promote human welfare or goodwill. Legal and economic concerns have long been acknowledged in business, but voluntary and ethical issues are more recent concerns.

Corporate citizenship is the extent to which businesses meet the legal, ethical, economic, and voluntary responsibilities placed on them by their various stakeholders. It involves the activities and organizational processes adopted by businesses to meet their social responsibilities. A commitment to corporate citizenship by a firm indicates a strategic focus on fulfilling the social responsibilities expected of it by its stakeholders. Corporate citizenship involves action and measurement of the extent to which a firm embraces the corporate citizenship philosophy and then follows through by implementing citizenship and social responsibility initiatives. One of the major corporate citizenship issues is the focus on preserving the environment. Consumers, governments, and special interest groups such as The Nature Conservancy are concerned about greenhouse gases and CO_2 carbon emissions that are contributing to global warming. The majority of people agree that climate change is a global emergency, but there is no agreement on how to solve the problem.[39] Another example of a corporate citizenship issue might be animal rights—an issue that is important to many stakeholders. As the organic and local foods movements grow and become more profitable, more and more stakeholders are calling for more humane practices in factory farms as well.[40] Large factory farms are where most Americans get their meat, but some businesses are looking at more animal-friendly options in response to public outcry.

corporate citizenship the extent to which businesses meet the legal, ethical, economic, and voluntary responsibilities placed on them by their stakeholders

FIGURE 2.3 The Pyramid of Social Responsibility

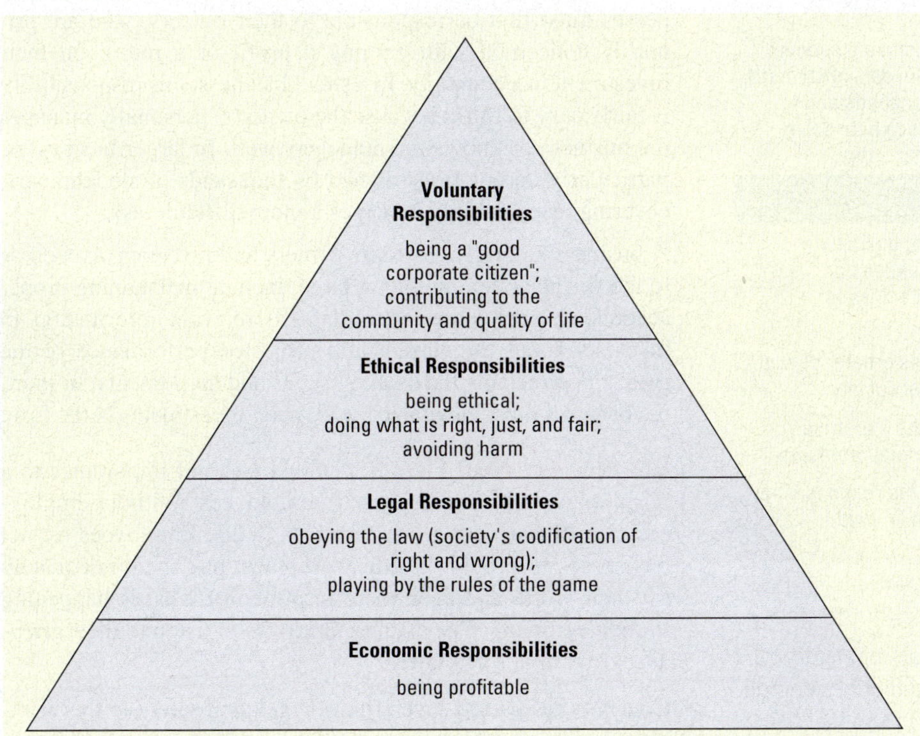

Source: From Archie B. Carroll, "The Pyramid of Corporate Social Responsibility: Toward the Moral Management of Organizational Stakeholders," *Business Horizons,* July/August 1991. Copyright © Elsevier. Reprinted with permission.

Part of the answer to the climate change crisis is alternative energy such as solar, wind, bio-fuels, and hydro applications. The drive for alternative fuels such as ethanol from corn has added new issues such as food price increases and food shortages. More than 2 billion consumers earn less than $2 a day in wages. Sharply increased food costs have led to riots and government policies to restrict trade in basic commodities such as rice, corn, and soybeans.[41]

To respond to these developments, most companies are introducing eco-friendly products and marketing efforts. Walmart is becoming very proactive in protecting the environment. The company is developing a new labeling system that shows consumers the carbon output of every product carried in Walmart's stores. Americans as consumers are generally concerned about the environment, but only 43 percent trust companies to tell them the truth in environmental marketing.[42] This is because most businesses are promoting themselves as green-conscious and concerned about the environment without actually making the necessary commitments to environmental health.

The Ethisphere Institute selects an annual list of the world's most ethical companies based on the following criteria: corporate citizenship and responsibility; corporate governance; innovation that contributes to the public well-being; industry leadership;

TABLE 2.7 A Selection of the World's Most Ethical Companies

Safeway, Inc.	Salesforce.com
ManpowerGroup	Cummins
Colgate-Palmolive Company	Xerox Corporation
PepsiCo	Eaton Corporation
Whole Foods Market, Inc.	Hospital Corporation of America
General Electric Company	eBay
T-Mobile USA	International Paper
The Sherwin-William Company	Adobe Systems Incorporated
Starbucks Coffee Company	UPS
Target	Accenture

Source: "2013 World's Most Ethical Companies," *Ethisphere*, http://m1.ethisphere.com/wme2013/index.html.

TABLE 2.8 The Arguments for and against Social Responsibility

For:

1. Business helped to create many of the social problems that exist today, so it should play a significant role in solving them, especially in the areas of pollution reduction and cleanup.
2. Businesses should be more responsible because they have the financial and technical resources to help solve social problems.
3. As members of society, businesses should do their fair share to help others.
4. Socially responsible decision making by businesses can prevent increased government regulation.
5. Social responsibility is necessary to ensure economic survival: If businesses want educated and healthy employees, customers with money to spend, and suppliers with quality goods and services in years to come, they must take steps to help solve the social and environmental problems that exist today.

Against:

1. It sidetracks managers from the primary goal of business—earning profits. Every dollar donated to social causes or otherwise spent on society's problems is a dollar less for owners and investors.
2. Participation in social programs gives businesses greater power, perhaps at the expense of particular segments of society.
3. Some people question whether business has the expertise needed to assess and make decisions about social problems.
4. Many people believe that social problems are the responsibility of government agencies and officials, who can be held accountable by voters.

executive leadership and tone from the top; legal, regulatory, and reputation track record; and internal systems and ethics/compliance program.[43] Table 2.7 shows 20 companies from that list.

Although the concept of social responsibility is receiving more and more attention, it is still not universally accepted. Table 2.8 lists some of the arguments for and against social responsibility.

LO 2-5 Debate an organization's social responsibilities to owners, employees, consumers, the environment, and the community.

Social Responsibility Issues

As with ethics, managers consider social responsibility on a daily basis. Among the many social issues that managers must consider are their firms' relations with owners and stockholders, employees, consumers, the environment, and the community. For example, Indra Nooyi, CEO of PepsiCo, believes that companies must embrace "purpose," not just for financial results, but also for the imprint they leave on society. She goes on to say that stakeholders, including employees, consumers, and regulators, "will leave no doubt that performance without purpose is not a long-term sustainable formula."[44]

Social responsibility is a dynamic area with issues changing constantly in response to society's demands. There is much evidence that social responsibility is associated with improved business performance. Consumers are refusing to buy from businesses that receive publicity about misconduct. A number of studies have found a direct relationship between social responsibility and profitability as well as a link that exists between employee commitment and customer loyalty—two major concerns of any firm trying to increase profits.[45] This section highlights a few of the many social responsibility issues that managers face; as managers become aware of and work toward the solution of current social problems, new ones will certainly emerge.

Relations with Owners and Stockholders Businesses must first be responsible to their owners, who are primarily concerned with earning a profit or a return on their investment in a company. In a small business, this responsibility is fairly easy to fulfill because the owner(s) personally manages the business or knows the managers well. In larger businesses, particularly corporations owned by thousands of stockholders, ensuring responsibility becomes a more difficult task.

A business's obligations to its owners and investors, as well as to the financial community at large, include maintaining proper accounting procedures, providing all relevant information to investors about the current and projected performance of the firm, and protecting the owners' rights and investments. In short, the business must maximize the owners' investments in the firm.

Employee Relations Another issue of importance to a business is its responsibilities to employees. Without employees, a business cannot carry out its goals. Employees expect businesses to provide a safe workplace, pay them adequately for their work, and keep them informed of what is happening in their company. They want employers to listen to their grievances and treat them fairly.

Congress has passed several laws regulating safety in the workplace, many of which are enforced by the Occupational Safety and Health Administration (OSHA). Labor unions have also made significant contributions to achieving safety in the workplace and improving wages and benefits. Most organizations now recognize

consumerism the activities that independent individuals, groups, and organizations undertake to protect their rights as consumers

sustainability conducting activities in a way that allows for the long-term well-being of the natural environment, including all biological entities

that the safety and satisfaction of their employees are critical ingredients in their success, and many strive to go beyond what is legally expected of them. Healthy, satisfied employees also supply more than just labor to their employers. Employers are beginning to realize the importance of obtaining input from even the lowest-level employees to help the company reach its objectives.

A major social responsibility for business is providing equal opportunities for all employees regardless of their sex, age, race, religion, or nationality. Women and minorities have been slighted in the past in terms of education, employment, and advancement opportunities; additionally, many of their needs have not been addressed by business. The Equal Employment Opportunity Commission (EEOC) found Bass Pro Shops guilty of racial discrimination in its hiring practices. According to the EEOC, managers at multiple Bass Pro Shops retailers would not hire nonwhite employees despite their qualifications.[46] Women, who continue to bear most child-rearing responsibilities, often experience conflict between those responsibilities and their duties as employees. Consequently, day care has become a major employment issue for women, and more companies are providing day care facilities as part of their effort to recruit and advance women in the workforce. In addition, companies are considering alternative scheduling such as flextime and job sharing to accommodate employee concerns. Telecommuting has grown significantly over the past 5 to 10 years as well. Many Americans today believe business has a social obligation to provide special opportunities for women and minorities to improve their standing in society.

Consumer Relations

A critical issue in business today is business's responsibility to customers, who look to business to provide them with satisfying, safe products and to respect their rights as consumers. The activities that independent individuals, groups, and organizations undertake to protect their rights as consumers are known as **consumerism**. To achieve their objectives, consumers and their advocates write letters to companies, lobby government agencies, make public service announcements, and boycott companies whose activities they deem irresponsible.

Many of the desires of those involved in the consumer movement have a foundation in John F. Kennedy's 1962 consumer bill of rights, which highlighted four rights. The *right to safety* means that a business must not knowingly sell anything that could result in personal injury or harm to consumers. Defective or dangerous products erode public confidence in the ability of business to serve society. They also result in expensive litigation that ultimately increases the cost of products for all consumers. The right to safety also means businesses must provide a safe place for consumers to shop.

The *right to be informed* gives consumers the freedom to review complete information about a product before they buy it. This means that detailed information about ingredients, risks, and instructions for use are to be printed on labels and packages. The *right to choose* ensures that consumers have access to a variety of products and services at competitive prices. The assurance of both satisfactory quality and service at a fair price is also a part of the consumer's right to choose. Some consumers are not being given this right. For instance, investigations by the Senate Commerce Committee found that phone-bill "cramming" has become a major issue. Cramming occurs when the phone company or a third party puts additional charges on the customer's bill. Officials believe that many of these charges are not authorized and that consumers remain unaware of them because they do not check their phone bills carefully enough.[47] The *right to be heard* assures consumers that their interests will receive full and sympathetic consideration when the government formulates policy. It also ensures the fair treatment of consumers who voice complaints about a purchased product.

The role of the Federal Trade Commission's Bureau of Consumer Protection exists to protect consumers against unfair, deceptive, or fraudulent practices. The bureau, which enforces a variety of consumer protection laws, is divided into five divisions. The Division of Enforcement monitors legal compliance and investigates violations of laws, including unfulfilled holiday delivery promises by online shopping sites, employment opportunities fraud, scholarship scams, misleading advertising for health care products, and more.

Sustainability Issues

Most people probably associate the term *environment* with nature, including wildlife, trees, oceans, and mountains. Until the 20th century, people generally thought of the environment solely in terms of how these resources could be harnessed to satisfy their needs for food, shelter, transportation, and recreation. As the earth's population swelled throughout the 20th century, however, humans began to use more and more of these resources and, with technological advancements, to do so with ever-greater efficiency. Although these conditions have resulted in a much-improved standard of living, they come with a cost. Plant and animal species, along with wildlife habitats, are disappearing at an accelerated rate, while pollution has rendered the atmosphere of some cities a gloomy haze. How to deal with these issues has become a major concern for business and society in the 21st century.

Although the scope of the word *sustainability* is broad, in this book we discuss the term from a strategic business perspective. Thus, we define **sustainability** as conducting activities in such a way as to provide for the long-term well-being of the natural environment, including all biological entities. Sustainability involves the interaction among nature and individuals, organizations, and business strategies and includes the assessment and improvement of business strategies, economic sectors, work practices, technologies, and lifestyles so that they maintain the health of the natural environment. In recent years, business has played a significant role in adapting, using, and maintaining the quality of sustainability.

Environmental protection emerged as a major issue in the 20th century in the face of increasing evidence that pollution, uncontrolled use of natural resources, and population growth were putting increasing pressure on the long-term sustainability of these resources. Governments around the globe responded with environmental protection laws during the 1970s. In recent years, companies have been increasingly incorporating these issues into their overall business strategies. Some nonprofit organizations have stepped forward to provide leadership in gaining the cooperation of diverse groups in responsible environmental activities. For example, the Coalition for Environmentally Responsible Economies (CERES)—a union of businesses, consumer groups, environmentalists, and other stakeholders—has established a set of goals for environmental performance.

In the following section, we examine some of the most significant sustainability and environmental health issues facing business and society today, including pollution and alternative energy.

Pollution. A major issue in the area of environmental responsibility is pollution. Water pollution results from dumping toxic chemicals and raw sewage into rivers and oceans, oil spills, and the burial of industrial waste in the ground where it may filter into underground water supplies. Fertilizers and insecticides used in farming and grounds maintenance also run off into water supplies with each rainfall. Water pollution problems are especially notable in heavily industrialized areas. Medical waste—such as used syringes, vials of blood, and HIV-contaminated materials—has turned up on beaches in New York, New Jersey, and Massachusetts as well as other places. Society is demanding that water supplies be clean and healthful to reduce the potential danger from these substances.

Air pollution is usually the result of smoke and other pollutants emitted by manufacturing facilities, as well as carbon monoxide and hydrocarbons emitted by motor vehicles. In addition to the health risks posed by air pollution, when some chemical compounds emitted by manufacturing facilities react with air and rain, acid rain results. Acid rain has contributed to the deaths of many forests and lakes in North America as well as in Europe. Air pollution may also contribute to global warming; as carbon dioxide collects in the earth's atmosphere, it traps the sun's heat and prevents the earth's surface from cooling. It is indisputable that the global surface temperature has been increasing over the past 35 years. Worldwide passenger vehicle ownership has been growing due to rapid industrialization and consumer purchasing power in China, India, and other developing countries with large populations. The most important way to contain climate change is to control carbon emissions. The move to green buildings, higher-mileage cars, and other emissions reductions resulting from better efficiency have the potential to generate up to 50 percent of the reductions needed to keep warming at no more than 28°C above present temperatures—considered the "safe" level.[48] The 2007 U.S. Federal Energy bill raised average fuel economy (CAFE) standards to 35 mpg for cars by 2020, while Europe has the goal of a 40 mpg standard by the same deadline. Because buildings create half of U.S. greenhouse emissions, there is tremendous opportunity to develop conservation measures. For example, some utilities charge more for electricity in peak demand periods, which encourages behavioral changes that reduce consumption. On the positive side, more than 100 million bicycles are produced annually worldwide, more than

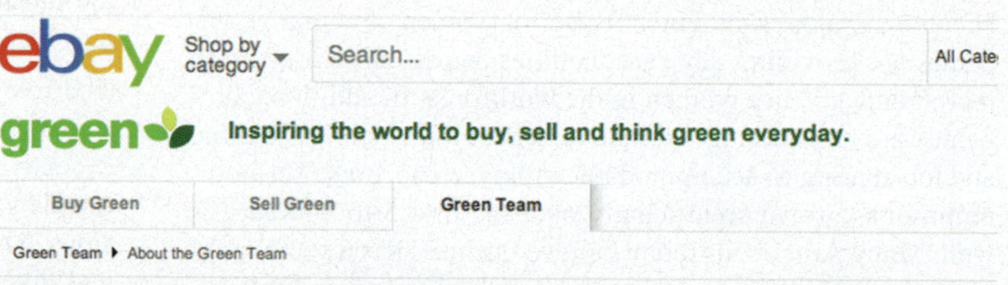

Inspiring the world to buy, sell and think green everyday.

Green Team ▸ About the Green Team
About the Green Team
We are a global team of 2,500+ eBay Inc. employees and more than 300,000 members of the eBay community. Together, we are committed to helping the world buy, sell and think green every day.
Green Team Talks

In 2007 the eBay Green Team started as a group of 40 passionate eBay employees who wanted to make our company a truly green place to work.

Not only does eBay encourage consumers to exchange and reuse goods, it also partnered with UPS to develop eco-friendly Priority Mail packaging.

FIGURE 2.4
Consumer Preferences for Doing Business with Sustainable and Socially Responsible Organizations

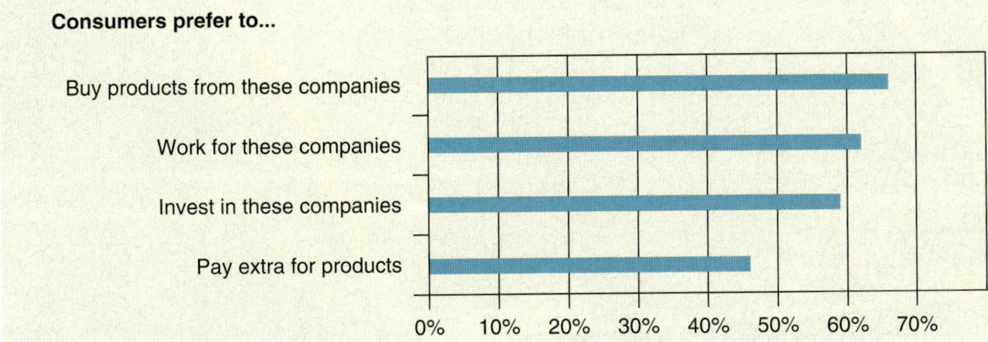

Source: Nielsen survey of 28,000 online respondents from 56 countries, Q3 2011.

double the passenger vehicles produced.[49] More and more consumers are recognizing the need to protect the planet. In fact, many consumers prefer to do business with companies that appear to invest in sustainability or other forms of corporate social responsibility, as Figure 2.4 demonstrates.

Land pollution is tied directly to water pollution because many of the chemicals and toxic wastes that are dumped on the land eventually work their way into the water supply. A study conducted by the Environmental Protection Agency found residues of prescription drugs, soaps, and other contaminants in virtually every waterway in the United States. Effects of these pollutants on humans and wildlife are uncertain, but there is some evidence to suggest that fish and other water-dwellers are starting to suffer serious effects.[50] Land pollution results from the dumping of residential and industrial waste, strip mining, forest fires, and poor forest conservation. In Brazil and other South American countries, rain forests are being destroyed—to make way for farms and ranches, at a cost of the extinction of the many animals and plants (some endangered species) that call the rain forest home. Large-scale deforestation also depletes the oxygen supply available to humans and other animals.

Related to the problem of land pollution is the larger issue of how to dispose of waste in an environmentally responsible manner. It takes 1,000 years for plastic bags to decompose. San Francisco has banned plastic bags; Ireland charges a nationwide tax of 15 cents on all supermarket shopping bags; and India will fine those caught handing out plastic bags.[51] Whole Foods, the nation's leading natural and organic supermarket, ended its use of plastic bags on Earth Day 2008.[52] Whole Foods estimates that this move will keep 150 million new plastic grocery bags out of the environment each year.

Alternative Energy. With ongoing plans to reduce global carbon emissions, countries and companies alike are looking toward alternative energy sources. Traditional fossil fuels are problematic because of their emissions but also because stores have been greatly depleted. Foreign fossil fuels are often imported from politically and economically unstable regions, often making it unsafe to conduct business there. The United States spends more than $1 billion a day on foreign oil.[53] With global warming concerns and rising gas prices, the U.S.

UNILEVER MAKES PALM OIL SUSTAINABLE

Unilever is working toward full sustainability when it comes to palm oil production. The process of extracting palm oil has gained global attention because of unsustainable practices such as deforestation, which has led to the destruction of native animal habitats. Because Unilever is a large company that works with an extensive supply chain, maintaining ethical sourcing practices can be a bit of a burden and are hard to track. Yet as the buyer, Unilever is responsible for any unethical sourcing practices in its supply chain.

Unilever is attempting to monitor its supply chain in two ways. First, it has invested $100 million to build a palm oil processing plant in Indonesia, the source of much of its palm oil, to ensure responsible practices. Second, Unilever is purchasing GreenPalm certificates from the Roundtable on Sustainable Palm Oil (RSPO) when it purchases palm oil from other processing companies. The RSPO monitors the practices of palm oil processing companies and issues them certificates when they meet sustainable, environmentally responsible standards. These certificates can then be purchased by companies such as Unilever in an attempt to ensure ethically sourced supply chains. This alleviates some of the skepticism about the origins of the palm oil. However, this method is not entirely dependable because the processing of all the palm oil is not completely traceable. Despite limitations, it is a step in the right direction for Unilever. The company hopes to have full sustainability in palm oil processing within the next 10 years.[54]

Discussion Questions

1. Why is it so difficult for large firms to monitor their supply chains?
2. What are some ways that Unilever is attempting to improve the sustainability of its supply chain?
3. What are some problems with relying on GreenPalm certificates? Do you think Unilever should do more to ensure the sustainability of its palm oil sourcing?

Solar power is growing in popularity as an alternative to traditional fuel sources, as this solar-powered race car demonstrates.

government has begun to recognize the need to look toward alternative forms of energy as a source of fuel and electricity. There have been many ideas as to which form of alternative energy would best suit the United States' energy needs. These sources include wind power, solar power, nuclear power, biofuels, electric cars, and hydro- and geothermal power. As of yet, no "best" form of alternative fuel has been selected to replace gasoline. Additionally, there are numerous challenges with the economic viability of alternative energy sources. For instance, wind and solar power cost significantly more than traditional energy; watts from wind power are estimated to be 290 percent higher than from natural gas, and the costs of solar photovoltaic is estimated to be 230 percent more expensive. Alternative energy will likely require government subsidies to make any significant strides. The bankruptcy scandal of the solar company Solyndra, which was granted a $527 million federally funded loan despite signs that the company was in trouble, has added fuel to the debate of whether alternative energy ventures should be subsidized.[55]

DID YOU KNOW?

In one year, Americans generated 230 million tons of trash and recycled 23.5 percent of it.[57]

Response to Environmental Issues. Partly in response to federal legislation such as the National Environmental Policy Act of 1969 and partly due to consumer concerns, businesses are responding to environmental issues. Many small and large companies, including Walt Disney Company, Chevron, and Scott Paper, have created an executive position—a vice president of environmental affairs—to help them achieve their business goals in an environmentally responsible manner. Some companies are finding that environmental consciousness can save them money. For instance, Walmart estimates that it has saved $1 million in electricity costs by installing solar panels on some of its stores.[56]

Many firms are trying to eliminate wasteful practices, the emission of pollutants, and/or the use of harmful chemicals from their manufacturing processes. Other companies are seeking ways to improve their products. Utility providers, for example, are increasingly supplementing their services with alternative energy sources, including solar, wind, and geothermal power. Environmentalists are concerned that some companies are merely

"Environmentalists are concerned that some companies are merely *greenwashing,* or 'creating a positive association with environmental issues for an unsuitable product, service, or practice.'"

greenwashing, or "creating a positive association with environmental issues for an unsuitable product, service, or practice."

In many places, local utility customers can even elect to purchase electricity from green sources—primarily wind power—for a few extra dollars a month. Austin Energy of Austin, Texas, has an award-winning GreenChoice program that includes many small and large businesses among its customers.[58] Indeed, a growing number of businesses and consumers are choosing green power sources where available. New Belgium Brewing Company, the third-largest craft brewer in the United States, is the first all-wind-powered brewery in the country. Many businesses have turned to *recycling,* the reprocessing of materials—aluminum, paper, glass, and some plastic—for reuse. Such efforts to make products, packaging, and processes more environmentally friendly have been labeled "green" business or marketing by the public and media. New Belgium, for instance, started selling aluminum cans of its beers because aluminum is easily recyclable and creates less waste. Lumber products at Home Depot may carry a seal from the Forest Stewardship Council to indicate that they were harvested from sustainable forests using environmentally friendly methods.[59]

It is important to recognize that, with current technology, environmental responsibility requires trade-offs. Society must weigh the huge costs of limiting or eliminating pollution against the health threat posed by the pollution. Environmental responsibility imposes costs on both business and the public. Although people certainly do not want oil fouling beautiful waterways and killing wildlife, they insist on low-cost, readily available gasoline and heating oil. People do not want to contribute to the growing garbage-disposal problem, but they often refuse to pay more for "green" products packaged in an environmentally friendly manner, to recycle as much of their own waste as possible, or to permit the building of additional waste-disposal facilities (the "not in my backyard," or NIMBY, syndrome). Managers must coordinate environmental goals with other social and economic ones.

Community Relations A final, yet very significant, issue for businesses concerns their responsibilities to the general welfare of the communities and societies in which they operate. Many businesses simply want to make their communities better places for everyone to live and work. The most common way that businesses exercise their community responsibility is through donations to local and national charitable organizations. For example, Safeway, the nation's fourth-largest grocer, has donated millions of dollars to organizations involved in medical research, such as Easter Seals and the Juvenile Diabetes Research Foundation International. The company's employees have also raised funds to support social causes of interest.[60] Even small companies participate in philanthropy through donations and volunteer support of local causes and national charities such as the Red Cross and the United Way.

UNEMPLOYMENT

After realizing that the current pool of prospective employees lacks many basic skills necessary to work, many companies have become concerned about the quality of education in the United States. Unemployment has become a significant problem over the past few years. In the years following 2008, unemployment reached as high as 10 percent in the United States. Although it is estimated to fall to between 7.4 percent and 7.9 percent of the population, many consumers remain unemployed.[61]

Although most would argue that unemployment is an economic issue, it also carries ethical implications. Consider the Occupy Wall Street protests. In the United States and other parts of the world, consumers got together to protest what they saw as the growing gap between the rich and the poor. One of the major issues was the fact that executives of Wall Street firms—some of them implicated in the misconduct leading up to the financial crisis—received high wages and bonuses while many employees were laid off or remained unemployed.[62] Although the protests eventually died down, this issue continues to be an ethical concern for many stakeholders.

Factory closures are another ethical issue because factories usually employ hundreds of workers. Sometimes it is necessary to close a plant due to economic reasons. However, when Caterpillar Inc. announced it was closing a Canadian factory, many questioned the ethics of the action. Workers of the factory had been locked out after they went on strike for higher wages. Critics believed the closure was retaliation for the problems caused by the strikes.[63]

Another criticism levied against companies involves hiring standards. Studies appear to show that although plenty of people are unemployed, approximately 35 percent of companies cite employees' lack of experience as why there are so many unfilled positions. Yet only about 28 percent are investing in more training and development for new hires. Although it is important for employees to have certain skills, many feel that businesses must be willing to train employees if they want to

Thousands of jobs were lost after the bookstore Borders closed down.

fill their vacancies and decrease the unemployment rate.[64]

On the other hand, several businesses are working to reduce unemployment. After realizing that the current pool of prospective employees lacks many basic skills necessary to work, Target made a commitment to donate $1 billion in its ongoing efforts to improve education. Through the retailer's Take Charge of Education program, customers using a Target REDcard can select a specific school to which Target will contribute 1 percent of their total purchase. The company also provides funds for building new school libraries.[65]

Additionally, businesses are beginning to take more responsibility for the hard-core unemployed. These are people who have never had a job or who have been unemployed for a long period of time. Some are mentally or physically handicapped; some are homeless. Organizations such as the National Alliance of Businessmen fund programs to train the hard-core unemployed so that they can find jobs and support themselves. Also, although numerous businesses laid off employees during the last recession, others were praised for their refusal to lay off workers. Boston Consulting Group (BCG), for instance, avoided laying off employees during the recession and even hired its largest number of recruits in 2010. As a result, employees at BCG are highly motivated and voted BCG as one of the best companies to work for.[66] Such commitment enhances self-esteem and helps people become productive members of society. ■

TEAM EXERCISE

Sam Walton, founder of Walmart, had an early strategy for growing his business related to pricing. The "Opening Price Point" strategy used by Walton involved offering the introductory product in a product line at the lowest point in the market. For example, a minimally equipped microwave oven would sell for less than anyone else in town could sell the same unit. The strategy was that if consumers saw a product, such as the microwave, and saw it as a good value, they would assume that all of the microwaves were good values. Walton also noted that most people don't buy the entry-level product; they want more features and capabilities and often trade up.

Form teams and assign the role of defending this strategy or casting this strategy as an unethical act. Present your thoughts on either side of the issue.

SO YOU WANT A JOB // in Business Ethics and Social Responsibility /

In the words of Kermit the Frog, "It's not easy being green." It may not be easy, but green business opportunities abound. A popular catchphrase, "Green is the new black," indicates how fashionable green business is becoming. Consumers are more in tune with and concerned about green products, policies, and behaviors by companies than ever before. Companies are looking for new hires to help them see their business creatively and bring insights to all aspects of business operations. The American Solar Energy Society estimates that the number of green jobs could rise to 40 million in the United States by 2030. Green business strategies not only give a firm a commercial advantage in the marketplace, but help lead the way toward a greener world. The fight to reduce our carbon footprint in an attempt against climate change has opened up opportunities for renewable energy, recycling, conservation, and increasing overall efficiency in the way resources are used. New businesses that focus on hydro, wind, and solar power are on the rise and will need talented businesspeople to lead them. Carbon emissions' trading is gaining popularity as large corporations and individuals alike seek to lower their footprints. A job in this growing field could be similar to that of a stock trader, or you could lead the search for carbon-efficient companies in which to invest.

In the ethics arena, current trends in business governance strongly support the development of ethics and compliance departments to help guide organizational integrity. This alone is a billion-dollar business, and there are jobs in developing organizational ethics programs, developing company policies, and training employees and management. An entry-level position might be as a communication specialist or trainer for programs in a business ethics department. Eventually, there's an opportunity to become an ethics officer that would have typical responsibilities of meeting with employees, the board of directors, and top management to discuss and provide advice about ethics issues in the industry, developing and distributing a code of ethics, creating and maintaining an anonymous, confidential service to answer questions about ethical issues, taking actions on possible ethics code violations, and reviewing and modifying the code of ethics of the organization.

There are also opportunities to help with initiatives to help companies relate social responsibility to stakeholder interests and needs. These jobs could involve coordinating and implementing philanthropic programs that give back to others important to the organization or developing a community volunteering program for employees. In addition to the human relations function, most companies develop programs to assist employees and their families to improve their quality of life. Companies have found that the healthier and happier employees are the more productive they will be in the workforce.

Social responsibility, ethics, and sustainable business practices are not a trend; they are good for business and the bottom line. New industries are being created and old ones are adapting to the new market demands, opening up varied job opportunities that will lead not only to a paycheck but also to the satisfaction of making the world a better place.[67]

chapter two appendix

the legal and regulatory environment

Business law refers to the rules and regulations that govern the conduct of business. Problems in this area come from the failure to keep promises, misunderstandings, disagreements about expectations, or, in some cases, attempts to take advantage of others. The regulatory environment offers a framework and enforcement system to provide a fair playing field for all businesses. The regulatory environment is created based on inputs from competitors, customers, employees, special interest groups, and the public's elected representatives. Lobbying by pressure groups who try to influence legislation often shapes the legal and regulatory environment.

SOURCES OF LAW

Laws are classified as either criminal or civil. *Criminal law* not only prohibits a specific kind of action, such as unfair competition or mail fraud, but also imposes a fine or imprisonment as punishment for violating the law. A violation of a criminal law is thus called a crime. *Civil law* defines all the laws not classified as criminal, and it specifies the rights and duties of individuals and organizations (including businesses). Violations of civil law may result in fines but not imprisonment. The primary difference between criminal and civil law is that criminal laws are enforced by the state or nation, whereas civil laws are enforced through the court system by individuals or organizations.

Criminal and civil laws are derived from four sources: the Constitution (constitutional law), precedents established by judges (common law), federal and state statutes (statutory law), and federal and state administrative agencies (administrative law). Federal administrative agencies established by Congress control and influence business by enforcing laws and regulations to encourage competition and protect consumers, workers, and the environment. The Supreme Court is the ultimate authority on legal and regulatory decisions for appropriate conduct in business.

COURTS AND THE RESOLUTION OF DISPUTES

The primary method of resolving conflicts and business disputes is through **lawsuits,** where one individual or organization takes another to court using civil laws. The legal system, therefore, provides a forum for businesspeople to resolve disputes based on our legal foundations. The courts may decide when harm or damage results from the actions of others.

["The primary method of resolving conflicts and business disputes is through lawsuits, where one individual or organization takes another to court using civil laws."]

Workers exit a Chrysler truck plant. Because it could not come to an agreement with its debt holders by a prescribed deadline, Chrysler was forced to file for bankruptcy during the most recent recession. Chrysler managed to survive bankruptcy, paid back its loans to the U.S. government, and became profitable once more.

Because lawsuits are so frequent in the world of business, it is important to understand more about the court system where such disputes are resolved. Both financial restitution and specific actions to undo wrongdoing can result from going before a court to resolve a conflict. All decisions made in the courts are based on criminal and civil laws derived from the legal and regulatory system.

A businessperson may win a lawsuit in court and receive a judgment, or court order, requiring the loser of the suit to pay monetary damages. However, this does not guarantee the victor will be able to collect those damages. If the loser of the suit lacks the financial resources to pay the judgment—for example, if the loser is a bankrupt business—the winner of the suit may not be able to collect the award. Most business lawsuits involve a request for a sum of money, but some lawsuits request that a court specifically order a person or organization to do or to refrain from doing a certain act, such as slamming telephone customers.

The Court System

Jurisdiction is the legal power of a court, through a judge, to interpret and apply the law and make a binding decision in a particular case. In some instances, other courts will not enforce the decision of a prior court because it lacked jurisdiction. Federal courts are granted jurisdiction by the Constitution or by Congress. State legislatures and constitutions determine which state courts hear certain types of cases. Courts of general jurisdiction hear all types of cases; those of limited jurisdiction hear only specific types of cases. The Federal Bankruptcy Court, for example, hears only cases involving bankruptcy. There is some combination of limited and general jurisdiction courts in every state.

In a **trial court** (whether in a court of general or limited jurisdiction and whether in the state or the federal system), two tasks must be completed. First, the court (acting through the judge or a jury) must determine the facts of the case. In other words, if there is conflicting evidence, the judge or jury must decide who to believe. Second, the judge must decide which law or set of laws is pertinent to the case and must then apply those laws to resolve the dispute.

An **appellate court,** on the other hand, deals solely with appeals relating to the interpretation of law. Thus, when you hear about a case being appealed, it is not retried but rather reevaluated. Appellate judges do not hear witnesses but instead base their decisions on a written transcript of the original trial. Moreover, appellate courts do not draw factual conclusions; the appellate judge is limited to deciding whether the trial judge made a mistake in interpreting the law that probably affected the outcome of the trial. If the trial judge made no mistake (or if mistakes would not have changed the result of the trial), the appellate court will let the trial court's decision stand. If the appellate court finds a mistake, it usually sends the case back to the trial court so that the mistake can be corrected. Correction may involve the granting of a new trial. On occasion, appellate courts modify the verdict of the trial court without sending the case back to the trial court.

Alternative Dispute Resolution Methods

Although the main remedy for business disputes is a lawsuit, other dispute resolution methods are becoming popular. The schedules of state and federal trial courts are often crowded; long delays between the filing of a case and the trial date are common. Further, complex cases can become quite expensive to pursue. As a result, many businesspeople are turning to alternative methods of resolving business arguments: mediation and arbitration, the mini-trial, and litigation in a private court.

Mediation is a form of negotiation to resolve a dispute by bringing in one or more third-party mediators, usually chosen by the disputing parties, to help reach a settlement. The mediator suggests different ways to resolve a dispute between the parties. The mediator's resolution is nonbinding—that is, the parties do not have to accept the mediator's suggestions; they are strictly voluntary.

Arbitration involves submission of a dispute to one or more third-party arbitrators, usually chosen by the disputing parties, whose decision usually is final. Arbitration differs from mediation in that an arbitrator's decision must be followed, whereas a mediator merely offers suggestions and facilitates negotiations. Cases may be submitted to arbitration because a contract—such as a labor contract—requires it or because the parties agree to do so. Some consumers are barred from taking claims to court by agreements drafted by banks, brokers, health plans, and others. Instead, they are required to take complaints to mandatory arbitration. Arbitration can be an attractive alternative to a lawsuit because it is often cheaper and quicker, and the parties frequently can choose arbitrators who are knowledgeable about the particular area of business at issue.

A method of dispute resolution that may become increasingly important in settling complex disputes is the **mini-trial,** in which both parties agree to present a summarized version of their case to an independent third party. That person then advises them of his or her impression of the probable outcome if the case were to be tried. Representatives of both sides then attempt to negotiate a settlement based on the advisor's recommendations. For example, employees in a large corporation who believe they have muscular or skeletal stress injuries caused by the strain of repetitive motion in using a computer could agree to a mini-trial to address a dispute related to damages. Although the mini-trial itself does not resolve the dispute, it can help the parties resolve the case before going to court. Because the mini-trial is not subject to formal court rules, it can save companies a great deal of money, allowing them to recognize the weaknesses in a particular case.

In some areas of the country, disputes can be submitted to a private nongovernmental court for resolution. In a sense, a **private court system** is similar to arbitration in that an independent third party resolves the case after hearing both sides of the story. Trials in private courts may be either informal or highly formal, depending on the people involved. Businesses typically agree to have their disputes decided in private courts to save time and money.

REGULATORY ADMINISTRATIVE AGENCIES

Federal and state administrative agencies (listed in Table A.1) also have some judicial powers. Many administrative agencies, such as the Federal Trade Commission, decide disputes that involve their regulations. In such disputes, the resolution process is usually called a hearing rather than a trial. In these cases, an administrative law judge decides all issues.

Federal regulatory agencies influence many business activities and cover product liability, safety, and the regulation or deregulation of public utilities. Usually, these bodies have the power to enforce specific laws, such as the Federal Trade Commission Act, and have some discretion in establishing operating rules and regulations to guide certain types of industry practices. Because of this discretion and overlapping areas of responsibility, confusion or conflict regarding which agencies have jurisdiction over which activities is common.

TABLE A.1 The Major Regulatory Agencies

Agency	Major Areas of Responsibility
Federal Trade Commission (FTC)	Enforces laws and guidelines regarding business practices; takes action to stop false and deceptive advertising and labeling.
Food and Drug Administration (FDA)	Enforces laws and regulations to prevent distribution of adulterated or misbranded foods, drugs, medical devices, cosmetics, veterinary products, and particularly hazardous consumer products.
Consumer Product Safety Commission (CPSC)	Ensures compliance with the Consumer Product Safety Act; protects the public from unreasonable risk of injury from any consumer product not covered by other regulatory agencies.
Interstate Commerce Commission (ICC)	Regulates franchises, rates, and finances of interstate rail, bus, truck, and water carriers.
Federal Communications Commission (FCC)	Regulates communication by wire, radio, and television in interstate and foreign commerce.
Environmental Protection Agency (EPA)	Develops and enforces environmental protection standards and conducts research into the adverse effects of pollution.
Federal Energy Regulatory Commission (FERC)	Regulates rates and sales of natural gas products, thereby affecting the supply and price of gas available to consumers; also regulates wholesale rates for electricity and gas, pipeline construction, and U.S. imports and exports of natural gas and electricity.
Equal Employment Opportunity Commission (EEOC)	Investigates and resolves discrimination in employment practices.
Federal Aviation Administration (FAA)	Oversees the policies and regulations of the airline industry.
Federal Highway Administration (FHA)	Regulates vehicle safety requirements.
Occupational Safety and Health Administration (OSHA)	Develops policy to promote worker safety and health and investigates infractions.
Securities and Exchange Commission (SEC)	Regulates corporate securities trading and develops protection from fraud and other abuses; provides an accounting oversight board.

> OF ALL THE FEDERAL REGULATORY UNITS, THE FEDERAL TRADE COMMISSION (FTC) MOST INFLUENCES BUSINESS ACTIVITIES RELATED TO QUESTIONABLE PRACTICES THAT CREATE DISPUTES BETWEEN BUSINESSES AND THEIR CUSTOMERS.

Of all the federal regulatory units, the **Federal Trade Commission (FTC)** most influences business activities related to questionable practices that create disputes between businesses and their customers. Although the FTC regulates a variety of business practices, it allocates a large portion of resources to curbing false advertising, misleading pricing, and deceptive packaging and labeling. When it receives a complaint or otherwise has reason to believe that a firm is violating a law, the FTC issues a complaint stating that the business is in violation.

If a company continues the questionable practice, the FTC can issue a cease-and-desist order, which is an order for the business to stop doing whatever has caused the complaint. In such cases, the charged firm can appeal to the federal courts to have the order rescinded. However, the FTC can seek civil penalties in court—up to a maximum penalty of $10,000 a day for each infraction—if a cease-and-desist order is violated. In its battle against unfair pricing, the FTC has issued consent decrees alleging that corporate attempts to engage in price fixing or invitations to competitors to collude are violations even when the competitors in question refuse the invitations. The commission can also require companies to run corrective advertising in response to previous ads considered misleading.

The FTC also assists businesses in complying with laws. New marketing methods are evaluated every year. When general sets of guidelines are needed to improve business practices in a particular industry, the FTC sometimes encourages firms within that industry to establish a set of trade practices voluntarily. The FTC may even sponsor a conference bringing together industry leaders and consumers for the purpose of establishing acceptable trade practices.

Unlike the FTC, other regulatory units are limited to dealing with specific products, services, or business activities. The Food and Drug Administration (FDA) enforces regulations prohibiting the sale and distribution of adulterated, misbranded, or hazardous food and drug products. For example, the FDA outlawed the sale and distribution of most over-the-counter hair-loss remedies after research indicated that few of the products were effective in restoring hair growth.

The Environmental Protection Agency (EPA) develops and enforces environmental protection standards and conducts research into the adverse effects of pollution. The Consumer Product Safety Commission recalls about 300 products a year, ranging from small, inexpensive toys to major appliances. The Consumer Product Safety Commission's website provides details regarding current recalls.

The Consumer Product Safety commission has fallen under increasing scrutiny in the wake of a number of product safety scandals involving children's toys. The most notable of these issues was lead paint discovered in toys produced in China. Other problems have included the manufacture of toys that include small magnets that pose a choking hazard and lead-tainted costume jewelry.[68]

IMPORTANT ELEMENTS OF BUSINESS LAW

To avoid violating criminal and civil laws, as well as discouraging lawsuits from consumers, employees, suppliers, and others, businesspeople need to be familiar with laws that address business practices.

The Uniform Commercial Code

At one time, states had their own specific laws governing various business practices, and transacting business across state lines was difficult because of the variation in the laws from state to state. To simplify commerce, every state—except Louisiana—has enacted the Uniform Commercial Code (Louisiana has enacted portions of the code). The **Uniform Commercial Code (UCC)** is a set of statutory laws covering several business law topics. Article II of the Uniform Commercial Code, which is discussed in the following paragraphs, has a significant impact on business.

Sales Agreements Article II of the Uniform Commercial Code covers sales agreements for goods and services such as installation but does not cover the sale of stocks and bonds, personal services, or real estate. Among its many provisions, Article II stipulates that a sales agreement can be enforced even though it does not specify the selling price or the time or place of delivery. It also requires that a buyer pay a reasonable price for goods at the time of delivery if the buyer and seller have not reached an agreement on price. Specifically, Article II addresses the rights of buyers and sellers, transfers of ownership, warranties, and the legal placement of risk during manufacture and delivery.

Article II also deals with express and implied warranties. An **express warranty** stipulates the specific terms the seller will honor. Many automobile manufacturers, for example, provide three-year or 36,000-mile warranties on their vehicles, during which period they will fix any and all defects specified in the warranty. An **implied warranty** is imposed on the producer or seller by law, although it may not be a written document provided at the time of sale. Under Article II, a consumer may assume that the product for sale has a clear title (in other words, that it is not stolen) and that the product will serve the purpose for which it was made and sold as well as function as advertised.

The Law of Torts and Fraud

A **tort** is a private or civil wrong other than breach of contract. For example, a tort can result if the driver of a Domino's Pizza delivery car loses control of the vehicle and damages property or injures a person. In the case of the delivery car accident, the injured persons might sue the driver and the owner of the company—Domino's in this case—for damages resulting from the accident.

Fraud is a purposefully unlawful act to deceive or manipulate to damage others. Thus, in some cases, a tort may also represent a violation of criminal law. Health care fraud has become a major issue in the courts.

An important aspect of tort law involves **product liability**—businesses' legal responsibility for any negligence in the design, production, sale, and consumption of products. Product liability laws have evolved from both common and statutory law. Some states have expanded the concept of product liability to include injuries by products whether or not the producer is proven negligent. Under this strict product liability, a consumer who files suit because of an injury has to prove only that the product was defective, that the defect caused the injury, and that the defect made the product unreasonably dangerous. For example, a carving knife is expected to be sharp and is not considered defective if you cut your finger using it. But an electric knife could be considered defective and unreasonably dangerous if it continued to operate after being switched off.

Reforming tort law, particularly in regard to product liability, has become a hot political issue as businesses look for relief from huge judgments in lawsuits. Although many lawsuits are warranted—few would disagree that a wrong has occurred when a patient dies because of negligence during a medical procedure or when a child is seriously injured by a defective toy, and that the families deserve some compensation—many suits are not. Because of multimillion-dollar judgments, companies are trying to minimize their liability, and sometimes they pass on the costs of the damage awards to their customers in the form of higher prices. Some states have passed laws limiting damage awards and some tort reform is occurring at the federal level. Table A.2 lists the state courts systems the U.S. Chamber of Commerce's Institute for Legal Reform has identified as being "friendliest" and "least friendly" to business in terms of juries' fairness, judges' competence and impartiality, and other factors.

TABLE A.2 State Court Systems' Reputations for Supporting Business

Most Friendly to Business	Least Friendly to Business
Delaware	Mississippi
Nebraska	West Virginia
Virginia	Alabama
Iowa	Louisiana
Idaho	California
Utah	Texas
New Hampshire	Illinois
Minnesota	Montana
Kansas	Arkansas
Wisconsin	Missouri

Source: U.S. Chamber of Commerce Institute for Legal Reform, in Martin Kasindorf, "Robin Hood Is Alive in Court, Say Those Seeking Lawsuit Limits," *USA Today,* March 8, 2004, p. 4A.

The Law of Contracts

Virtually every business transaction is carried out by means of a **contract,** a mutual agreement between two or more parties that can be enforced in a court if one party chooses not to comply with the terms of the contract. If you rent an apartment or house, for example, your lease is a contract. If you have borrowed money under a student loan program, you have a contractual agreement to repay the money. Many aspects of contract law are covered under the Uniform Commercial Code.

A "handshake deal" is in most cases as fully and completely binding as a written, signed contract agreement. Indeed, many oil-drilling and construction contractors have for years agreed to take on projects on the basis of such handshake deals. However, individual states require that some contracts be in writing to be enforceable. Most states require that at least some of the following contracts be in writing:

- Contracts involving the sale of land or an interest in land
- Contracts to pay somebody else's debt
- Contracts that cannot be fulfilled within one year
- Contracts for the sale of goods that cost more than $500 (required by the Uniform Commercial Code)

Only those contracts that meet certain requirements—called *elements*—are enforceable by the courts. A person or business seeking to enforce a contract must show that it contains the following elements: voluntary agreement, consideration, contractual capacity of the parties, and legality.

For any agreement to be considered a legal contract, all persons involved must agree to be bound by the terms of the contract.

Voluntary agreement typically comes about when one party makes an offer and the other accepts. If both the offer and the acceptance are freely, voluntarily, and knowingly made, the acceptance forms the basis for the contract. If, however, either the offer or the acceptance is the result of fraud or force, the individual or organization subject to the fraud or force can void, or invalidate, the resulting agreement or receive compensation for damages.

The second requirement for enforcement of a contract is that it must be supported by *consideration*—that is, money or something of value must be given in return for fulfilling a contract. As a general rule, a person cannot be forced to abide by the terms of a promise unless that person receives a consideration. The something of value could be money, goods, services, or even a promise to do or not to do something.

Contractual capacity is the legal ability to enter into a contract. As a general rule, a court cannot enforce a contract if either party to the agreement lacks contractual capacity. A person's contractual capacity may be limited or nonexistent if he or she is a minor (under the age of 18), mentally unstable, retarded, insane, or intoxicated.

Legality is the state or condition of being lawful. For an otherwise binding contract to be enforceable, both the purpose of and the consideration for the contract must be legal. A contract in which a bank loans money at a rate of interest prohibited by law, a practice known as usury, would be an illegal contract, for example. The fact that one of the parties may commit an illegal act while performing a contract does not render the contract itself illegal, however.

Breach of contract is the failure or refusal of a party to a contract to live up to his or her promises. In the case of an apartment lease, failure to pay rent would be considered breach of contract. The breaching party—the one who fails to comply—may be liable for monetary damages that he or she causes the other person.

The Law of Agency

An **agency** is a common business relationship created when one person acts on behalf of another and under that person's control. Two parties are involved in an agency relationship: The **principal** is the one who wishes to have a specific task accomplished; the **agent** is the one who acts on behalf of the principal to accomplish the task. Authors, movie stars, and athletes often employ agents to help them obtain the best contract terms.

An agency relationship is created by the mutual agreement of the principal and the agent. It is usually not necessary that such an agreement be in writing, although putting it in writing is certainly advisable. An agency relationship continues as long as both the principal and the agent so desire. It can be terminated by mutual agreement, by fulfillment of the purpose of the agency, by the refusal of either party to continue in the relationship, or by the death of either the principal or the agent. In most cases, a principal grants authority to the agent through a formal *power of attorney,* which is a legal document authorizing a person to act as someone else's agent. The power of attorney can be used for any agency relationship, and its use is not limited to lawyers. For instance, in real estate transactions, often a lawyer or real estate agent is given power of attorney with the authority to purchase real estate for the buyer. Accounting firms often give employees agency relationships in making financial transactions.

> "An agency is a common business relationship created when one person acts on behalf of another and under that person's control."

Both officers and directors of corporations are fiduciaries, or people of trust, who use due care and loyalty as an agent in making decisions on behalf of the organization. This relationship creates a duty of care, also called duty of diligence, to make informed decisions. These agents of the corporation are not held responsible for negative outcomes if they are informed and diligent in their decisions. The duty of loyalty means that all decisions should be in the interests of the corporation and its stakeholders. Many people believe that executives at financial firms such as Countrywide Financial, Lehman Brothers, and Merrill Lynch failed to carry out their fiduciary duties. Lawsuits from shareholders called for the officers and directors to pay large sums of money from their own pockets.

The Law of Property

Property law is extremely broad in scope because it covers the ownership and transfer of all kinds of real, personal, and intellectual property. **Real property** consists of real estate and everything permanently attached to it; **personal property** basically is everything else. Personal property can be further subdivided into tangible and intangible property. *Tangible property* refers to items that have a physical existence, such as automobiles, business inventory, and clothing. *Intangible property* consists of rights and duties; its existence may be represented by a document or by some other tangible item. For example, accounts receivable, stock in a corporation, goodwill, and trademarks are all examples of intangible personal property. **Intellectual property** refers to property, such as musical works, artwork, books, and computer software, that is generated by a person's creative activities.

Copyrights, patents, and trademarks provide protection to the owners of property by giving them the exclusive right to use it. *Copyrights* protect the ownership rights on material (often intellectual property) such as books, music, videos, photos, and computer software. The creators of such works, or their heirs, generally have exclusive rights to the published or unpublished works for the creator's lifetime plus 70 years. *Patents* give inventors exclusive rights to their invention for 20 years. The most intense competition for patents is in the pharmaceutical industry. Most patents take a minimum of 18 months to secure.

A *trademark* is a brand (name, mark, or symbol) that is registered with the U.S. Patent and Trademark Office and is thus legally protected from use by any other firm. Among the symbols that have been so protected are McDonald's golden arches and Coca-Cola's distinctive bottle shape. It is estimated that large multinational firms may have as many as 15,000 conflicts related to trademarks. Companies are diligent about protecting their trademarks both to avoid confusion in consumers' minds and because a term that becomes part of everyday language can no longer be trademarked. The names *aspirin* and *nylon*, for example, were once the exclusive property of their creators but became so widely used as product names (rather than brand names) that now anyone can use them.

As the trend toward globalization of trade continues, and more and more businesses trade across national boundaries, protecting property rights, particularly intellectual property such as computer software, has become an increasing challenge. Although a company may be able to register as a trademark a brand name or symbol in its home country, it may not be able to secure that protection abroad. Some countries have copyright and patent laws that are less strict than those of the United States; some countries will not enforce U.S. laws. China, for example, has often been criticized for permitting U.S. goods to be counterfeited there. Such counterfeiting harms not only the sales of U.S. companies but also their reputations if the knockoffs are of poor quality. Thus, businesses engaging in foreign trade may have to take extra steps to protect their property because local laws may be insufficient to protect them.

The Law of Bankruptcy

Although few businesses and individuals intentionally fail to repay (or default on) their debts, sometimes they cannot fulfill their financial obligations. Individuals may charge goods and services beyond their ability to pay for them. Businesses may take on too much debt to finance growth, or business events such as an increase in the cost of commodities can bankrupt a company. An option of last resort in these cases is bankruptcy, or legal insolvency. Some well-known companies that have declared bankruptcy include Hostess, American Airlines, and Eastman Kodak. Individuals or companies may ask a bankruptcy court to declare them unable to pay their debts and thus release them from the obligation of repaying those debts. The debtor's assets may then be sold to pay off as much of the debt as possible. In the case of a personal bankruptcy, although the individual is released from repaying debts and can start over with a clean slate, obtaining credit after bankruptcy proceedings is very difficult. About 2 million households in the United States filed for bankruptcy in 2005, the most ever. However, a new, more restrictive law went into effect in late 2005, allowing fewer consumers to use bankruptcy to eliminate their debts. The law makes it harder for consumers to prove that they should be allowed to clear their debts for what is called a "fresh start" or Chapter 7 bankruptcy. Although the person or company in debt usually initiates bankruptcy proceedings, creditors may also initiate them. The subprime mortgage crisis of early 2008 caused a string of bankruptcies among individuals and Chapter 7 and 11 bankruptcies among banks and other businesses as well. Tougher bankruptcy laws and a slowing economy converged on the subprime crisis to create a situation in which bankruptcy filings skyrocketed. Table A.3 describes the various levels of bankruptcy protection a business or individual may seek.

LAWS AFFECTING BUSINESS PRACTICES

One of the government's many roles is to act as a watchdog to ensure that businesses behave in accordance with the wishes of society. Congress has enacted a number of laws that affect business practices; some of the most important of these are summarized in Table A.4. Many state legislatures have enacted similar laws governing business within specific states.

The **Sherman Antitrust Act,** passed in 1890 to prevent businesses from restraining trade and monopolizing markets, condemns "every contract, combination, or conspiracy in restraint of trade." For example, a request that a competitor agree to fix prices or divide markets would, if accepted, result in a violation of the Sherman Act. AT&T faced serious resistance from the U.S. Justice Department after it announced its bid to acquire T-Mobile. Because there are only a few dominant cell phone carriers in the market, the Justice Department believed that the merger would make AT&T too powerful. Critics feared that

TABLE A.3 Types of Bankruptcy

Chapter 7	Requires that the business be dissolved and its assets liquidated, or sold, to pay off the debts. Individuals declaring Chapter 7 retain a limited amount of exempt assets, the amount of which may be determined by state or federal law, at the debtor's option. Although the type and value of exempt assets varies from state to state, most states' laws allow a bankrupt individual to keep an automobile, some household goods, clothing, furnishings, and at least some of the value of the debtor's residence. All nonexempt assets must be sold to pay debts.
Chapter 11	Temporarily frees a business from its financial obligations while it reorganizes and works out a payment plan with its creditors. The indebted company continues to operate its business during bankruptcy proceedings. Often, the business sells off assets and less-profitable subsidiaries to raise cash to pay off its immediate obligations.
Chapter 13	Similar to Chapter 11 but limited to individuals. This proceeding allows an individual to establish a three- to five-year plan for repaying his or her debt. Under this plan, an individual ultimately may repay as little as 10 percent of his or her debt.

TABLE A.4 Major Federal Laws Affecting Business Practices

Act (Date Enacted)	Purpose
Sherman Antitrust Act (1890)	Prohibits contracts, combinations, or conspiracies to restrain trade; establishes as a misdemeanor monopolizing or attempting to monopolize.
Clayton Act (1914)	Prohibits specific practices such as price discrimination, exclusive dealer arrangements, and stock acquisitions in which the effect may notably lessen competition or tend to create a monopoly.
Federal Trade Commission Act (1914)	Created the Federal Trade Commission; also gives the FTC investigatory powers to be used in preventing unfair methods of competition.
Robinson-Patman Act (1936)	Prohibits price discrimination that lessens competition among wholesalers or retailers; prohibits producers from giving disproportionate services of facilities to large buyers.
Wheeler-Lea Act (1938)	Prohibits unfair and deceptive acts and practices regardless of whether competition is injured; places advertising of foods and drugs under the jurisdiction of the FTC.
Lanham Act (1946)	Provides protections and regulation of brand names, brand marks, trade names, and trademarks.
Celler-Kefauver Act (1950)	Prohibits any corporation engaged in commerce from acquiring the whole or any part of the stock or other share of the capital assets of another corporation when the effect substantially lessens competition or tends to create a monopoly.
Fair Packaging and Labeling Act (1966)	Makes illegal the unfair or deceptive packaging or labeling of consumer products.
Magnuson-Moss Warranty (FTC) Act (1975)	Provides for minimum disclosure standards for written consumer product warranties; defines minimum consent standards for written warranties; allows the FTC to prescribe interpretive rules in policy statements regarding unfair or deceptive practices.
Consumer Goods Pricing Act (1975)	Prohibits the use of price maintenance agreements among manufacturers and resellers in interstate commerce.
Antitrust Improvements Act (1976)	Requires large corporations to inform federal regulators of prospective mergers or acquisitions so that they can be studied for any possible violations of the law.
Trademark Counterfeiting Act (1980)	Provides civil and criminal penalties against those who deal in counterfeit consumer goods or any counterfeit goods that can threaten health or safety.
Trademark Law Revision Act (1988)	Amends the Lanham Act to allow brands not yet introduced to be protected through registration with the Patent and Trademark Office.
Nutrition Labeling and Education Act (1990)	Prohibits exaggerated health claims and requires all processed foods to contain labels with nutritional information.
Telephone Consumer Protection Act (1991)	Establishes procedures to avoid unwanted telephone solicitations; prohibits marketers from using automated telephone dialing system or an artificial or prerecorded voice to certain telephone lines.
Federal Trademark Dilution Act (1995)	Provides trademark owners the right to protect trademarks and requires relinquishment of names that match or parallel existing trademarks.
Digital Millennium Copyright Act (1998)	Refined copyright laws to protect digital versions of copyrighted materials, including music and movies.
Children's Online Privacy Protection Act (2000)	Regulates the collection of personally identifiable information (name, address, e-mail address, hobbies, interests, or information collected through cookies) online from children under age 13.
Sarbanes-Oxley Act (2002)	Made securities fraud a criminal offense; stiffened penalties for corporate fraud; created an accounting oversight board; and instituted numerous other provisions designed to increase corporate transparency and compliance.
Do Not Call Implementation Act (2003)	Directs FCC and FTC to coordinate so their rules are consistent regarding telemarketing call practices, including the Do Not Call Registry.
Dodd-Frank Wall Street Reform and Consumer Protection Act (2010)	Increases accountability and transparency in the financial industry, protects consumers from deceptive financial practices, and establishes the Bureau of Consumer Financial Protection.

the merger would lead to higher prices for consumers. Due to increased pressure from the Justice Department, AT&T dropped its bid to acquire T-Mobile—a move that cost it a $4 billion charge.[69] The Sherman Antitrust Act, still highly relevant 100 years after its passage, is being copied throughout the world as the basis for regulating fair competition.

Because the provisions of the Sherman Antitrust Act are rather vague, courts have not always interpreted it as its creators

> OUR USE AND DEPENDENCE ON THE INTERNET IS INCREASINGLY CREATING A POTENTIAL LEGAL PROBLEM FOR BUSINESSES.

intended. The Clayton Act was passed in 1914 to limit specific activities that can reduce competition. The **Clayton Act** prohibits price discrimination, tying and exclusive agreements, and the acquisition of stock in another corporation when the effect may be to substantially lessen competition or tend to create a monopoly. In addition, the Clayton Act prohibits members of one company's board of directors from holding seats on the boards of competing corporations. The act also exempts farm cooperatives and labor organizations from antitrust laws.

In spite of these laws regulating business practices, there are still many questions about the regulation of business. For instance, it is difficult to determine what constitutes an acceptable degree of competition and whether a monopoly is harmful to a particular market. Many mergers were permitted that resulted in less competition in the banking, publishing, and automobile industries. In some industries, such as utilities, it is not cost effective to have too many competitors. For this reason, the government permits utility monopolies, although recently, the telephone, electricity, and communications industries have been deregulated. Furthermore, the antitrust laws are often rather vague and require interpretation, which may vary from judge to judge and court to court. Thus, what one judge defines as a monopoly or trust today may be permitted by another judge a few years from now. Businesspeople need to understand what the law says on these issues and try to conduct their affairs within the bounds of these laws.

THE INTERNET: LEGAL AND REGULATORY ISSUES

Our use and dependence on the Internet is increasingly creating a potential legal problem for businesses. With this growing use come questions of maintaining an acceptable level of privacy for consumers and proper competitive use of the medium. Some might consider that tracking individuals who visit or hit their website by attaching a cookie (identifying you as a website visitor for potential recontact and tracking your movement throughout the site) is an improper use of the Internet for business purposes. Others may find such practices acceptable and similar to the practices of non-Internet retailers who copy information from checks or ask customers for their name, address, or phone number before they will process a transaction. There are few specific laws that regulate business on the Internet, but the standards for acceptable behavior that are reflected in the basic laws and

Whether you like it or not, Google, like Yahoo! and AOL, tracks people's web browsing patterns. By tracking the sites you visit, the companies' advertisers can aim ads targeted closer to your interests.

regulations designed for traditional businesses can be applied to business on the Internet as well. One law aimed specifically at advertising on the Internet is the CAN-SPAM Act of 2004. The law restricts unsolicited e-mail advertisements by requiring the consent of the recipient. Furthermore, the CAN-SPAM Act follows the opt-out model wherein recipients can elect to not receive further e-mails from a sender simply by clicking a link.[70]

The central focus for future legislation of business conducted on the Internet is the protection of personal privacy. The present basis of personal privacy protection is the U.S. Constitution, various Supreme Court rulings, and laws such as the 1971 Fair Credit Reporting Act, the 1978 Right to Financial Privacy Act, and the 1974 Privacy Act, which deals with the release of government records. With few regulations on the use of information by businesses, companies legally buy and sell information on customers to gain competitive advantage. Sometimes existing laws are not enough to protect people, and the ease with which information on customers can be obtained becomes a problem. For example, identity theft has increased due to the proliferation of the use of the Internet. A disturbing trend is how many children have had their identities stolen. One study of 40,000 children revealed that more than 10 percent have had their Social Security numbers stolen. The rates of child identity theft have risen since the advent of the Internet.[71] It has been suggested that the treatment of personal data as property will ensure privacy rights by recognizing that customers have a right to control the use of their personal data.

WEB MARKETERS EXPERIENCE LIMITATIONS ON ONLINE TRACKING OF CHILDREN

Web marketers may soon see restrictions placed on their ability to collect information about children. COPPA, the Children's Online Privacy Protection Act, is looking to pursue stricter privacy measures on online tracking that has been leaving room for children to be tracked through games, apps, social networks, and websites. The privacy measures are aimed directly at users under the age of 13. Although COPPA prohibits websites from collecting certain types of information on children under 13 without parental consent, the growing use of smart phones and other devices has provided online marketers with an opportunity to bypass these rules.

The proposed changes are expected to close loopholes that allow companies to access children specifically with third-party advertising through Facebook and iPhone games without parental consent. These changes would also include blocking cookies and/or disabling geolocation systems, which can be used to target children with advertising, specifically on smart phones. For websites to gain consent, parents would have to provide their e-mail addresses or names.

Updating COPPA could help protect child safety and enable parents to feel more secure when their children download apps or games on mobile devices. On the other hand, many companies are against the rules, saying they already take measures to protect children's anonymity. They also claim that additional regulations could hinder online advertising, which is necessary to finance the free online content they offer to children.[72]

Discussion Questions

1. Why do regulators think it necessary to update COPPA?
2. What are some of the proposed changes that regulators are recommending?
3. What are some of the arguments that companies have against new regulations?

Internet use is different from traditional interaction with businesses in that it is readily accessible, and most online businesses can develop databases of information on customers. Congress has restricted the development of databases on children using the Internet. The Children's Online Privacy Protection Act of 2000 prohibits website and Internet providers from seeking personal information from children under age 13 without parental consent. Companies are still running afoul of COPPA. Playdom, a Disney-owned online game company, was forced to pay $3 million to settle allegations that it had collected and disclosed the personal information of children under 13 years of age.[73]

The Internet has also created a copyright dilemma for some organizations that have found that the web addresses of other online firms either match or are very similar to their company trademark. "Cybersquatters" attempt to sell back the registration of these matching sites to the trademark owner. Companies such as Taco Bell, MTC, and KFC have paid thousands of dollars to gain control of domain names that match or parallel company trademarks. The Federal Trademark Dilution Act of 1995 helps companies address this conflict. The act provides trademark owners the right to protect trademarks, prevents the use of trademark-protected entities, and requires the relinquishment of names that match or closely parallel company trademarks. The reduction of geographic barriers, speed of response, and memory capability of the Internet will continue to create new challenges for the legal and regulatory environment in the future.

LEGAL PRESSURE FOR RESPONSIBLE BUSINESS CONDUCT

To ensure greater compliance with society's desires, both federal and state governments are moving toward increased organizational accountability for misconduct. Before 1991, laws mainly punished those employees directly responsible for an offense. Under new guidelines established by the Federal Sentencing Guidelines for Organizations (FSGO), however, both the responsible employees and the firms that employ them are held accountable for violations of federal law. Thus, the government now places responsibility for controlling and preventing misconduct squarely on the shoulders of top management. The main objectives of the federal guidelines are to train employees, self-monitor and supervise employee conduct, deter unethical acts, and punish those organizational members who engage in illegal acts.

"To ensure greater compliance with society's desires, both federal and state governments are moving toward increased organizational accountability for misconduct."

A 2004 amendment to the FSGO requires that a business's governing authority be well informed about its ethics program with respect to content, implementation, and effectiveness. This places the responsibility squarely on the shoulders of the firm's leadership, usually the board of directors. The board must ensure that a high-ranking manager is accountable for the day-to-day operational oversight of the ethics program. The board must provide for adequate authority, resources, and access to the board or an appropriate subcommittee of the board. The board must ensure that confidential mechanisms are available so that the organization's employees and agents may report or seek guidance about potential or actual misconduct without fear of retaliation. Finally, the board is required to oversee the discovery of risks and to design, implement, and modify approaches to deal with those risks.

If an organization's culture and policies reward or provide opportunities to engage in misconduct through lack of managerial concern or failure to comply with the seven minimum requirements of the FSGO (provided in Table A.5), then the organization may incur not only penalties but also the loss of customer trust, public confidence, and other intangible assets. For this reason, organizations cannot succeed solely through a legalistic approach to compliance with the sentencing guidelines; top management must cultivate high ethical standards that will serve as barriers to illegal conduct. The organization must want to be a good citizen and recognize the importance of compliance to successful workplace activities and relationships.

The federal guidelines also require businesses to develop programs that can detect—and that will deter employees from engaging in—misconduct. To be considered effective, such compliance programs must include disclosure of any wrongdoing, cooperation with the government, and acceptance of responsibility for the misconduct. Codes of ethics, employee ethics training, hotlines (direct 800 phone numbers), compliance directors, newsletters, brochures, and other communication methods are typical components of a compliance program. The ethics component, discussed in Chapter 2, acts as a buffer, keeping firms away from the thin line that separates unethical and illegal conduct.

Despite the existing legislation, a number of ethics scandals in the early 2000s led Congress to pass—almost unanimously—the **Sarbanes-Oxley Act,** which criminalized securities fraud and strengthened penalties for corporate fraud. It also created an accounting oversight board that requires corporations to establish codes of ethics for financial reporting and to develop greater transparency in financial reports to investors and other interested parties. Additionally, the law requires top corporate executives to sign off on their firms' financial reports, and they risk fines and jail sentences if they misrepresent their companies' financial position. Table A.6 summarizes the major provisions of the Sarbanes-Oxley Act.

The Sarbanes-Oxley Act has created a number of concerns and is considered burdensome and expensive to corporations. Large corporations report spending more than $4 million each year to comply with the Act according to Financial Executives International. The Act has caused more than 500 public companies a year to report problems in their accounting systems. Additionally, Sarbanes-Oxley failed to prevent and detect the widespread misconduct of financial institutions that led to the financial crisis.

On the other hand, there are many benefits, including greater accountability of top managers and boards of directors, that improve investor confidence and protect employees, especially their retirement plans. It is believed that the law has more benefits than drawbacks—with the greatest benefit being that boards of directors and top managers are better informed. Some companies such as Cisco and Pitney Bowes report improved efficiency and cost savings from better financial information.

In spite of the benefits Sarbanes-Oxley offers, it did not prevent widespread corporate corruption from leading to the most recent recession. The resulting financial crisis prompted

"In spite of the benefits Sarbanes-Oxley offers, it did not prevent widespread corporate corruption from leading to the most recent recession."

TABLE A.5 Seven Steps to Compliance

1. Develop standards and procedures to reduce the propensity for criminal conduct.
2. Designate a high-level compliance manager or ethics officer to oversee the compliance program.
3. Avoid delegating authority to people known to have a propensity to engage in misconduct.
4. Communicate standards and procedures to employees, other agents, and independent contractors through training programs and publications.
5. Establish systems to monitor and audit misconduct and to allow employees and agents to report criminal activity.
6. Enforce standards and punishments consistently across all employees in the organization.
7. Respond immediately to misconduct and take reasonable steps to prevent further criminal conduct.

Source: United States Sentencing Commission, *Federal Sentencing Guidelines for Organizations,* 1991.

the Obama administration to create new regulation to reform Wall Street and the financial industry. In 2010, the Dodd-Frank Wall Street Reform and Consumer Protection Act was passed. In addition to new regulations for financial institutions, the legislation created a Consumer Financial Protection Bureau (CFPB) to protect consumers from complex or deceptive financial products. Table A.7 highlights some of the major provisions of the Dodd-Frank Act.

TABLE A.6 Major Provisions of the Sarbanes-Oxley Act

1. Requires the establishment of a Public Company Accounting Oversight Board in charge of regulations administered by the Securities and Exchange Commission.
2. Requires CEOs and CFOs to certify that their companies' financial statements are true and without misleading statements.
3. Requires that corporate boards of directors' audit committees consist of independent members who have no material interests in the company.
4. Prohibits corporations from making or offering loans to officers and board members.
5. Requires codes of ethics for senior financial officers; code must be registered with the SEC.
6. Prohibits accounting firms from providing both auditing and consulting services to the same client without the approval of the client firm's audit committee.
7. Requires company attorneys to report wrongdoing to top managers and, if necessary, to the board of directors; if managers and directors fail to respond to reports of wrongdoing, the attorney should stop representing the company.
8. Mandates whistleblower protection for persons who disclose wrongdoing to authorities.
9. Requires financial securities analysts to certify that their recommendations are based on objective reports.
10. Requires mutual fund managers to disclose how they vote shareholder proxies, giving investors information about how their shares influence decisions.
11. Establishes a 10-year penalty for mail/wire fraud.
12. Prohibits the two senior auditors from working on a corporation's account for more than five years; other auditors are prohibited from working on an account for more than seven years. In other words, accounting firms must rotate individual auditors from one account to another from time to time.

Source: From O.C. Ferrell, John Fraedrich, and Linda Ferrell, *Business Ethics*, 8e, pp. 108–109.

TABLE A.7 Major Provisions of the Dodd-Frank Wall Street Reform and Consumer Protection Act

1. Enhances stability of the finance industry through the creation of two new financial agencies, the Financial Oversight Stability Council and the Office of Financial Research.
2. Institutes an orderly liquidation procedure for the Federal Deposit Insurance Corporation to liquidate failing companies.
3. Eliminates the Office of Thrift Supervision and transfers its powers to the Comptroller of the Currency.
4. Creates stronger regulation and greater oversight of hedge funds.
5. Establishes the Federal Insurance Agency to gather information and oversee the insurance industry for risks.
6. Requires regulators to have regulations in place for banks. Also prohibits and/or limits proprietary trading, hedge fund sponsorship and private equity funds, and relationships with hedge funds and private equity funds.
7. Regulates derivatives and complex financial instruments by limiting where they can be traded and ensuring that traders have the financial resources to meet their responsibilities.
8. Provides a framework for creating risk-management standards for financial market utilities and the payment, clearing, and settlement activities performed by institutions.
9. Improves investor protection through acts such as creating a whistleblower bounty program and increasing consumer access to their credit scores.
10. Institutes the Bureau of Consumer Financial Protection to educate consumers and protect them from deceptive financial products.
11. Attempts to reform the Federal Reserve in ways that include limiting the Federal Reserve's lending authority, reevaluating methods for Federal Reserve regulations and the appointment of Federal Reserve Bank directors, and instituting additional disclosure requirements.
12. Reforms mortgage activities with new provisions that include increasing the lender's responsibility to ensure the borrower can pay back the loan, prohibiting unfair lending practices, requiring additional disclosure in the mortgage loan process, and imposing penalties against those found guilty of noncompliance with the new standards.

Source: *Brief Summary of the Dodd-Frank Wall Street Reform and Consumer Protection Act,* http://banking.senate.gov/public/_files/070110_Dodd_Frank_Wall_Street_Reform_comprehensive_summary_Final.pdf.

learn, practice, apply business ethics!

M: Business **was developed just for you—students on the go who need information packaged in a concise yet interesting format with multiple learning options.**

Check out the book's website to:

- **Solve a consumer privacy issue. (Solve the Dilemma)**
- **Learn about important issues in business ethics. (Build Your Skills)**
- **Determine how you would react to observed misconduct. (Build Your Skills)**

While you are there, don't forget to enhance your skills. Practice and apply your knowledge, review the practice exercises, Student PPT® slides, and quizzes to review and apply chapter concepts. Additionally, *Connect® Business* is available for *M: Business*.

www.mhhe.com/ferrellm4e

The Dodd-Frank Act contains 16 titles meant to increase consumer protection, enhance transparency and accountability in the financial sector, and create new financial agencies. In some ways, Dodd-Frank is attempting to improve upon provisions laid out in the Sarbanes-Oxley Act. For instance, Dodd-Frank takes whistleblower protection a step further by offering additional incentives to whistleblowers for reporting misconduct. If whistleblowers report misconduct that results in penalties of more than $1 million, the whistleblower will be entitled to a percentage of the settlement.[74] Additionally, complex financial instruments must now be made more transparent so that consumers will have a better understanding of what these instruments involve.

The act also created three new agencies: the Consumer Financial Protection Bureau (CFPB), the Office of Financial Research, and the Financial Stability Oversight Council. Although the CFPB was created to protect consumers, the other two agencies work to maintain stability in the financial industry so such a crisis will not recur in the future.[75] Although it is too early to tell whether these regulations will serve to create widescale positive financial reform, the Dodd-Frank Act is certainly leading to major changes on Wall Street and in the financial sector.

chapter three

business in a borderless world

Consumers around the world can drink Coca-Cola and Pepsi; eat at McDonald's and Pizza Hut; see movies from Mexico, England, France, Australia, and China; and watch CNN and MTV on Samsung and Panasonic televisions. It may surprise you that the Japanese firm Komatsu sells earth-moving equipment to China that is manufactured in Peoria, Illinois.[1] The products you consume today are just as likely to have been made in China, Korea, or Germany as in the United States. Likewise, consumers in other countries buy Western electrical equipment, clothing, rock music, cosmetics, and toiletries as well as computers, robots, and earth-moving equipment.

Many U.S. firms are finding that international markets provide tremendous opportunities for growth. Accessing these markets can promote innovation while intensifying global competition spurs companies to market better and less expensive products. Today, the more than 7 billion people who inhabit the earth comprise one tremendous marketplace.

In this chapter, we explore business in this exciting global marketplace. First, we look at the nature of international business, including barriers and promoters of trade across international boundaries. Next, we consider the levels of organizational involvement in international business. Finally, we briefly discuss strategies for trading across national borders. ■

LEARNING OBJECTIVES

After reading this chapter, you will be able to:

- **LO 3-1** Explore some of the factors within the international trade environment that influence business.
- **LO 3-2** Investigate some of the economic, legal-political, social, cultural, and technological barriers to international business.
- **LO 3-3** Specify some of the agreements, alliances, and organizations that may encourage trade across international boundaries.
- **LO 3-4** Summarize the different levels of organizational involvement in international trade.
- **LO 3-5** Contrast two basic strategies used in international business.

international business the buying, selling, and trading of goods and services across national boundaries

absolute advantage a monopoly that exists when a country is the only source of an item, the only producer of an item, or the most efficient producer of an item

comparative advantage the basis of most international trade, when a country specializes in products that it can supply more efficiently or at a lower cost than it can produce other items

LO 3-1 Explore some of the factors within the international trade environment that influence business.

THE ROLE OF INTERNATIONAL BUSINESS

International business refers to the buying, selling, and trading of goods and services across national boundaries. Falling political barriers and new technology are making it possible for more and more companies to sell their products overseas as well as at home. And, as differences among nations continue to narrow, the trend toward the globalization of business is becoming increasingly important. Starbucks serves millions of global customers at more than 5,500 shops in more than 50 countries.[3] The Internet provides many companies easier entry to access global markets than opening brick-and-mortar stores.[4] Amazon.com, an online retailer, has distribution centers from Nevada to Germany that fill millions of orders a day and ship them to customers in every corner of the world. Unilever gets half of its sales from emerging markets.[5] Indeed, most of the world's population and two-thirds of its total purchasing power are outside the United States.

When McDonald's sells a Big Mac in Moscow, Sony sells a stereo in Detroit, or a small Swiss medical supply company sells a shipment of orthopedic devices to a hospital in Monterrey, Mexico, the sale affects the economies of the countries involved. The U.S. market, with nearly 314 million consumers, makes up only a small part of the more than 7 billion people elsewhere in the world to whom global companies must consider marketing. Global marketing requires balancing your global brand with the needs of local consumers.[6] To begin our study of international business, we must first consider some economic issues: why nations trade, exporting and importing, and the balance of trade.

?

DID YOU KNOW?

Subway has surpassed McDonald's as the largest global restaurant chain with over 39,000 locations.[2]

Why Nations Trade

Nations and businesses engage in international trade to obtain raw materials and goods that are otherwise unavailable to them or are available elsewhere at a lower price than that at which they themselves can produce. A nation, or individuals and organizations from a nation, sell surplus materials and goods to acquire funds to buy the goods, services, and ideas its people need. Poland and Hungary, for example, want to trade with Western nations so that they can acquire new technology and techniques to revitalize their formerly communist economies. Which goods and services a nation sells depends on what resources it has available.

Some nations have a monopoly on the production of a particular resource or product. Such a monopoly, or **absolute advantage**, exists when a country is the only source of an item, the only producer of an item, or the most efficient producer of an item. Because South Africa has the largest deposits of diamonds in the world, one company, De Beers Consolidated Mines Ltd., controls a major portion of the world's diamond trade and uses its control to maintain high prices for gem-quality diamonds. The United States, until recently, held an absolute advantage in oil-drilling equipment. But an absolute advantage not based on the availability of natural resources rarely lasts, and Japan and Russia are now challenging the United States in the production of oil-drilling equipment.

Most international trade is based on **comparative advantage**, which occurs when a country specializes in products that it can supply more efficiently or at a lower cost than it can produce other items. The United States has a comparative advantage in producing agricultural commodities such as corn and wheat. The United States at one time had a comparative advantage in manufacturing automobiles, heavy machinery, airplanes, and weapons; other countries now hold the comparative advantage for many of these products.

> "Falling political barriers and new technology are making it possible for more and more companies to sell their products overseas as well as at home."

outsourcing the transferring of manufacturing or other tasks—such as data processing—to countries where labor and supplies are less expensive

> **OUTSOURCING HAS BECOME A CONTROVERSIAL PRACTICE IN THE UNITED STATES BECAUSE MANY JOBS HAVE MOVED OVERSEAS WHERE THOSE TASKS CAN BE ACCOMPLISHED FOR LOWER COSTS.**

Other countries, particularly India and Ireland, are also gaining a comparative advantage over the United States in the provision of some services, such as call-center operations, engineering, and software programming. As a result, U.S. companies are increasingly **outsourcing**, or transferring manufacturing and other tasks to countries where labor and supplies are less expensive. Outsourcing has become a controversial practice in the United States because many jobs have moved overseas where those tasks can be accomplished for lower costs. For example, the Philippines has surpassed India as the popular choice for call-center jobs. Call-center jobs are appealing to many Filipinos because the pay is almost as much as the average family income within the country. English is also one of the country's official languages, which makes it easier to communicate with English-speaking customers.[7]

American companies such as KFC have become widely popular in China. Some have more sales in China than they have in the United States.

exporting the sale of goods and services to foreign markets

importing the purchase of goods and services from foreign sources

balance of trade the difference in value between a nation's exports and its imports

trade deficit a nation's negative balance of trade, which exists when that country imports more products than it exports

balance of payments the difference between the flow of money into and out of a country

Nike outsources its manufacturing to Asian countries such as Vietnam, where labor costs are less expensive.

Trade between Countries

To obtain needed goods and services and the funds to pay for them, nations trade by exporting and importing. **Exporting** is the sale of goods and services to foreign markets. The United States exported more than $2.1 trillion in goods and services in 2012.[8] In China, General Motors is targeting wealthier customers with the Cadillac, middle management with the Buick Excelle, office workers with the Chevrolet Spark, and rural consumers with the Wuling minivan.[9] U.S. companies that view China as both a growth market for exports and a market for lower-cost labor for imports and can strategically integrate these into their operations enjoy significantly higher profits than companies who focus only on one of these opportunities.[10] U.S. businesses export many goods and services, particularly agricultural, entertainment (movies, television shows, and so on), and technological products. **Importing** is the purchase of goods and services from foreign sources. Many of the goods you buy in the United States are likely to be imports or to have some imported components. Sometimes, you may not even realize they are imports. The United States imported more than $2.7 trillion in goods and services in 2012.[11]

Balance of Trade

You have probably read or heard about the fact that the United States has a trade deficit, but what is a trade deficit? A nation's **balance of trade** is the difference in value between its exports and imports. Because the United States (and some other nations as well) imports more products than it exports, it has a negative balance of trade, or **trade deficit**. Table 3.1 shows the trade deficit for the United States. In 2012, the United States had a trade deficit of $539.5 billion.[12] The trade deficit fluctuates according to such factors as the health of the United States and other economies, productivity, perceived quality, and exchange rates. Trade deficits are harmful because they can mean the failure of businesses, the loss of jobs, and a lowered standard of living.

Of course, when a nation exports more goods than it imports, it has a favorable balance of trade, or trade surplus. Until about 1970, the United States had a trade surplus due to an abundance of natural resources and the relative efficiency of its manufacturing systems. Table 3.2 shows the top 10 countries with which the United States has a trade deficit and a trade surplus.

The difference between the flow of money into and out of a country is called its **balance of payments**. A country's balance of trade, foreign investments, foreign aid, loans, military expenditures, and money spent by tourists comprise its balance of payments. As you might expect, a country with a trade surplus generally has a favorable balance of payments

TABLE 3.1 U.S. Trade Deficit, 1990–2012 (in billions of dollars)

	1990	2000	2005	2006	2007	2008	2009	2010	2011	2012
Exports	$535.2	$1,072.8	$1,287.4	$1,459.8	$1,654.6	$1,842.7	$1,575.0	$2,837.6	$2,103.1	$2,194.5
Imports	616.1	1,449.5	1,996.1	2,213.1	2,351.3	2,541.0	1,956.3	2,337.6	2,661.1	2,734.0
Trade surplus/ deficit	−80.9	−376.7	−708.6	−753.3	−696.7	−698.3	−381.3	−500.0	−558.0	−539.5

Sources: U.S. Bureau of the Census, Foreign Trade Division, *U.S. Trade in Goods and Services—Balance of Payments (BOP) Basis,* February 10, 2012, www.census.gov/foreign-trade/statistics/historical/gands.pdf. "U.S. International Transactions: Fourth Quarter and Year 2012," U.S. Department of Commerce Bureau of Labor Economic Analysis, www.bea.gov/newsreleases/international/transactions/transnewsrelease.htm.

Bumrungrad Hospital in Thailand offers world-class and destination health-care services. Notice the presence of Starbucks on the first floor of the hospital.

TABLE 3.2 Top Ten Countries with Which United States Has Trade Deficits/Surpluses

Trade Deficit	Trade Surplus
1. China	Hong Kong
2. Germany	United Arab Emirates
3. Japan	Australia
4. Mexico	Brazil
5. Canada	Netherlands
6. Saudi Arabia	Singapore
7. Ireland	Belgium
8. Italy	Panama
9. Venezuela	Chile
10. South Korea	Qatar

Sources: U.S. Bureau of the Census, "Top Ten Countries with Which the U.S. Has a Trade Deficit," November 2012, www.census.gov/foreign-trade/top/dst/current/deficit.html; "Top Ten Countries with Which the U.S. Has a Trade Surplus," November 2012, www.census.gov/foreign-trade/top/dst/current/surplus.html.

because it is receiving more money from trade with foreign countries than it is paying out. When a country has a trade deficit, more money flows out of the country than into it. If more money flows out of the country than into it from tourism and other sources, the country may experience declining production and higher unemployment because less money is available for spending.

INTERNATIONAL TRADE BARRIERS

Completely free trade seldom exists. When a company decides to do business outside its own country, it will encounter a number of barriers to international trade. Any firm considering international business must research the other country's economic, legal, political, social, cultural, and technological background. Such research will help the company choose an appropriate level of involvement and operating strategies, as we will see later in this chapter.

LO 3-2 Investigate some of the economic, legal-political, social, cultural, and technological barriers to international business.

Economic Barriers

When looking at doing business in another country, managers must consider a number of basic economic factors, such as economic development, infrastructure, and exchange rates.

infrastructure the physical facilities that support a country's economic activities, such as railroads, highways, ports, airfields, utilities and power plants, schools, hospitals, communication systems, and commercial distribution systems

exchange rate the ratio at which one nation's currency can be exchanged for another nation's currency

Economic Development

When considering doing business abroad, U.S. businesspeople need to recognize that they cannot take for granted that other countries offer the same things as are found in *industrialized nations*—economically advanced countries such as the United States, Japan, Great Britain, and Canada. Many countries in Africa, Asia, and South America, for example, are in general poorer and less economically advanced than those in North America and Europe; they are often called *less-developed countries* (LDCs). LDCs are characterized by low per-capita income (income generated by the nation's production of goods and services divided by the population), which means that consumers are less likely to purchase nonessential products. Nonetheless, LDCs represent a potentially huge and profitable market for many businesses because they may be buying technology to improve their infrastructures, and much of the population may desire consumer products. For example, automobile manufacturers are looking toward LDCs as a way to expand their customer base. The rising middle class has caused many consumers in India and China to desire their own vehicles. Companies such as General Motors are partnering with domestic manufacturers to create electric vehicles for the Chinese market.[13]

A country's level of development is determined in part by its **infrastructure**, the physical facilities that support its economic activities, such as railroads, highways, ports, airfields, utilities and power plants, schools, hospitals, communication systems, and commercial distribution systems. When doing business in LDCs, for example, a business may need to compensate for rudimentary distribution and communication systems or even a lack of technology.

Exchange Rates The ratio at which one nation's currency can be exchanged for another nation's currency is the **exchange rate**. Exchange rates vary daily and can be found in newspapers and through many sites on the Internet. Familiarity with exchange rates is important because they affect the cost of imports and exports. When the value of the U.S. dollar declines relative to other currencies, such as the euro, the price of imports becomes relatively expensive for U.S. consumers. On the other hand, U.S. exports become relatively cheap for international markets—in this example, the European Union.

Occasionally, a government may intentionally alter the value of its currency through fiscal policy. Devaluation decreases the value of currency in relation to other currencies. If the U.S.

"Devaluation decreases the value of currency in relation to other currencies."

VIBER GIVES SKYPE A RUN FOR ITS MONEY

One of the biggest competitors to Skype hires about 40 percent of its workforce from the eastern European country of Belarus. Belarus is a mixed-market economy with Soviet-era policies. In Belarus, censorship is common and freedoms are limited. Yet through a combination of ingenuity, technological knowledge, and the ability to span global barriers, the Israeli app development company Viber is becoming a formidable competitor to Skype.

Viber was started by two Israeli friends who realized that although Skype was an effective technology for desktops, it was not very effective on smart phones. They developed the Viber app to enable users to make phone calls and share text messages and photo messages from across the world for free, using their iPhones, Androids, or Blackberrys. No user registration is required to use Viber, another difference from Skype. Viber went from 18 users on its first day to more than 100 million users today.

Viber hires a significant portion of its workforce from Belarus at a fraction of what it would cost in Israel or the United States. Companies that have operations in Belarus pay no corporate income taxes, and a developer's salary from Israel equals the salaries of several Belarusian developers. Despite the lower costs and state ownership of the economy, Belarus's capital is becoming an information technology hub, and many students are graduating from Belarusian universities with degrees in information technology, mathematics, and sciences. One major barrier to investing in Belarus is political. If the authoritarian government decides to limit the operations of foreign companies, this could profoundly affect Viber.[14]

Discussion Questions

1. What is unique about Belarus that makes it an unusual choice for a small business?
2. What are some advantages of hiring software developers from Belarus?
3. What are some potential barriers Viber might encounter in Belarus?

government were to devalue the dollar, it would lower the cost of American goods abroad and make trips to the United States less expensive for foreign tourists. Thus, devaluation encourages the sale of domestic goods and tourism. Mexico has repeatedly devalued the peso for this reason. Revaluation, which increases the value of a currency in relation to other currencies, occurs rarely.

Ethical, Legal, and Political Barriers

A company that decides to enter the international marketplace must contend with potentially complex relationships among the different laws of its own nation, international laws, and the laws of the nation with which it will be trading; various trade restrictions imposed on international trade; changing political climates; and different ethical values. Legal and ethical requirements for successful business are increasing globally. For instance, India has strict limitations on foreign retailers that want to operate within the country. Until recently, foreign retailers were required to partner with a domestic firm if they wanted to do business within India. Walmart partnered with Bharti Enterprises to gain entry into the country. India has now reduced the restrictions slightly. Single-brand retailers such as Nike can now own their own stores in India without a partner, but multibrand retailers such as Walmart are still limited by the former restrictions.[15]

Counterfeit products such as these fake luxury handbags are major challenges for international firms.

Laws and Regulations The United States has a number of laws and regulations that govern the activities of U.S. firms engaged in international trade. For example, the Webb-Pomerene Export Trade Act of 1918 exempts American firms from antitrust laws if those firms are acting together to enter international trade. This law allows selected U.S. firms to form monopolies to compete with foreign monopolistic organizations, although they are not allowed to limit free trade and competition within the United States or to use unfair methods of competition in international trade. The United States also has a variety of friendship, commerce, and navigation treaties with other nations. These treaties allow business to be transacted between citizens of the specified countries. For example, Belgium is a gateway to European markets and has lowered its taxes to give U.S. companies greater reason to locate their European operations there. Belgium has the lowest patent income tax and has 0 percent withholding tax on corporate dividends and interest from a U.S. company. This prevents a company from paying both U.S. and Belgian tax, or double taxation.[16]

Once outside U.S. borders, businesspeople are likely to find that the laws of other nations differ from those of the United States. Many of the legal rights that Americans take for granted do not exist in other countries, and a firm doing business abroad must understand and obey the laws of the host country. Some countries have strict laws limiting the amount of local currency that can be taken out of the country and the amount of currency that can be brought in; others limit how foreign companies can operate within the country.

As mentioned earlier, for many years Indian law restricted companies such as Walmart from opening stores in the country unless they created a joint venture with a domestic firm. The Indian government began to relax these restrictions, allowing some companies the opportunity to develop their own subsidiaries in India. However, proposed legislation is creating a turbulent environment for foreign businesses because the Indian government has contemplated regulations that could increase their tax liability or even require them to open technology production facilities within the country. Proposals such as these could limit the imports of certain products.[17]

Some countries have copyright and patent laws that are less strict than those of the United States, and some countries fail to honor U.S. laws. Because copying is a tradition in China and Vietnam and laws protecting copyrights and intellectual property are weak and minimally enforced, those countries are flooded with counterfeit videos, movies, CDs, computer software, furniture, and clothing. Companies are angry because the counterfeits harm not only their sales, but also their reputations if the knockoffs are of poor quality. Such counterfeiting is not limited to China or Vietnam. It is estimated that nearly half of all software installed on personal computers worldwide is illegally pirated or copied, amounting to more than $58 billion in global

import tariff a tax levied by a nation on goods imported into the country

exchange controls regulations that restrict the amount of currency that can be bought or sold

quota a restriction on the number of units of a particular product that can be imported into a country

embargo a prohibition on trade in a particular product

revenue losses annually.[18] In countries where these activities occur, laws against them may not be sufficiently enforced if counterfeiting is deemed illegal. Thus, businesses engaging in foreign trade may have to take extra steps to protect their products because local laws may be insufficient to do so.

Tariffs and Trade Restrictions Tariffs and other trade restrictions are part of a country's legal structure but may be established or removed for political reasons. An **import tariff** is a tax levied by a nation on goods imported into the country. A *fixed tariff* is a specific amount of money levied on each unit of a product brought into the country, while an *ad valorem tariff* is based on the value of the item. Most countries allow citizens traveling abroad to bring home a certain amount of merchandise without paying an import tariff. A U.S. citizen may bring $200 worth of merchandise into the United States duty free. After that, U.S. citizens must pay an ad valorem tariff based on the cost of the item and the country of origin. Thus, identical items purchased in different countries might have different tariffs.

Countries sometimes levy tariffs for political reasons, as when they impose sanctions against other countries to protest their actions. However, import tariffs are more commonly imposed to protect domestic products by raising the price of imported ones. Such protective tariffs have become controversial as Americans become increasingly concerned over the U.S. trade deficit. Protective tariffs allow more expensive domestic goods to compete with foreign ones. For example, the United States has lost a significant number of steelworks over the past few decades to foreign competition in places such as China. Other markets can produce steel more cheaply than the United States. Many people and special interest groups in the United States, such as unions, would like to see tariffs placed on Chinese steel, which is significantly less expensive, to protect remaining U.S. steel production. The United States has also imposed tariffs on imported sugar for almost two centuries. The European Union levies tariffs on many products, including some seafood imports.

Critics of protective tariffs argue that their use inhibits free trade and competition. Supporters of protective tariffs say they insulate domestic industries, particularly new ones, against well-established foreign competitors. Once an industry matures, however, its advocates may be reluctant to let go of the tariff that protected it. Tariffs also help when, because of low labor costs and other advantages, foreign competitors can afford to sell their products at prices lower than those charged by domestic companies. Some Americans argue that tariffs should be used to keep domestic wages high and unemployment low.

Exchange controls restrict the amount of currency that can be bought or sold. Some countries control their foreign trade by forcing businesspeople to buy and sell foreign products through a central bank. If John Deere, for example, receives payments for its tractors in a foreign currency, it may be required to sell the currency to that nation's central bank. When foreign currency is in short supply, as it is in many less-developed countries, the government uses foreign currency to purchase necessities and capital goods and produces other products locally, thus limiting its need for foreign imports.

A **quota** limits the number of units of a particular product that can be imported into a country. A quota may be established by voluntary agreement or by government decree. The United States imposes quotas on certain goods, such as garments produced in Vietnam and China. Quotas are designed to protect the industries and jobs of the country imposing the quota.

An **embargo** prohibits trade in a particular product. Embargoes are generally directed at specific goods or countries and may be established for political, economic, health, or religious reasons. While the United States maintains a trade embargo

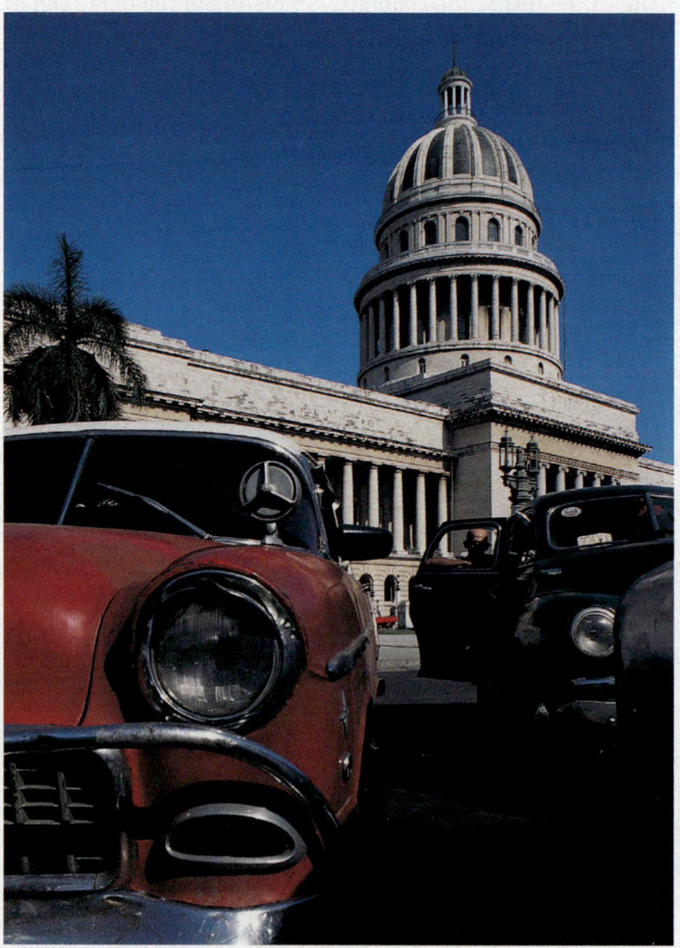

Due to the U.S. embargo against Cuba, many Cubans drive older automobiles.

dumping the act of a country or business selling products at less than what it costs to produce them

cartel a group of firms or nations that agrees to act as a monopoly and not compete with each other, in order to generate a competitive advantage in world markets

with Cuba, European hotel chains are engaged in a building boom on the Caribbean island, where tourism is the number-one industry. U.S. hotel chains are eager to build in Cuba but have no opportunity until the embargo is lifted. Until recently, U.S. tourists were forbidden by the U.S. government to vacation in Cuba because of the embargo. However, the government has begun to allow more Americans to visit Cuba with certain restrictions.[19] It may be surprising to know that U.S. farmers export hundreds of millions of dollars worth of commodities to Cuba each year, based on a 2000 law that provided permission for some trade to the embargoed country.[20] Health embargoes prevent the importing of various pharmaceuticals, animals, plants, and agricultural products. Muslim nations forbid the importation of alcoholic beverages on religious grounds.

One common reason for setting quotas or tariffs is to prohibit **dumping**, which occurs when a country or business sells products at less than what it costs to produce them. For instance, the United States set a tariff on Chinese solar panels after an investigation alleged that Chinese companies had been dumping solar panels by charging extremely low prices.[21] A company may dump its products for several reasons. Dumping permits quick entry into a market. Sometimes dumping occurs when the domestic market for a firm's product is too small to support an efficient level of production. In other cases, technologically obsolete products that are no longer salable in the country of origin are dumped overseas. Dumping is relatively difficult to prove, but even the suspicion of dumping can lead to the imposition of quotas or tariffs.

Political Barriers Unlike legal issues, political considerations are seldom written down and often change rapidly. Nations that have been subject to economic sanctions for political reasons in recent years include Cuba, Iran, Syria, and North Korea. Although these were dramatic events, political considerations affect international business daily as governments enact tariffs, embargoes, or other types of trade restrictions in response to political events.

Businesses engaged in international trade must consider the relative instability of countries such as Iraq, Haiti, and Venezuela. Political unrest in countries such as Pakistan, Somalia, and the Democratic Republic of the Congo may create a hostile or even dangerous environment for foreign businesses. Natural disasters can make the region even more unstable. Even a developed country such as Japan had its social, economic, and political institutions stressed by the 2011 earthquake and tsunamis. Finally, a sudden change in power can result in a regime that is hostile to foreign investment. Some businesses have been forced out of a country altogether, as when Hugo Chávez conducted a socialist revolution in Venezuela to force out or take over American oil companies. Whether they like it or not, companies are often involved directly or indirectly in international politics.

Political concerns may lead a group of nations to form a **cartel**, a group of firms or nations that agrees to act as a monopoly and not compete with each other, to generate a competitive advantage in world markets. Probably the most famous cartel is OPEC, the Organization of Petroleum Exporting Countries, founded in the 1960s to increase the price of petroleum throughout the world and to maintain high prices. By working to ensure stable oil prices, OPEC hopes to enhance the economies of its member nations.

Dumping can spark trade wars. After the Obama administration imposed stiff tariffs on Chinese-made tires it alleged were being dumped on the U.S. market, China retaliated by slapping tariffs on U.S. chicken products exported to China.

THE DANGER OF COUNTERFEIT PRODUCTS IN INDIA

Counterfeiting is a serious crime, but it has become one of India's most lucrative business trades. Illiteracy rates in India contribute to this issue, creating a major sociocultural barrier. The packaging, font, and colors of the counterfeit products are identical to those of the brand name, but the counterfeit products add or omit a letter in the actual spelling of the brand name. This makes it impossible for those who cannot read to tell the difference. For example, consumers in India often mistake the counterfeit Voroline for Unilever's Vaseline. These counterfeits are being sold at the same price as the brand names, but they are less expensive to make so manufacturers are making significant profits. Retailers are also investing in the counterfeit products because they are offered a higher margin percentage. Products that are counterfeited range from beauty products to automobile parts to pharmaceuticals.

This is where counterfeiting becomes dangerous. Thousands of deaths have been associated with motor vehicle accidents whose vehicles had counterfeit parts in them. The same is true for medications. Often drugs will not contain the active ingredients needed to cure an ailment, or they may contain toxins that are fatal to those who ingest them. Many companies are recognizing the danger that counterfeiting imposes on people and are finding ways to defend their products as well as protect their consumers. Hewlett-Packard, for example, has come up with a barcode system for pharmaceuticals by which consumers can use their smart phones to scan the barcode and authenticate the brand. Other companies have developed similar systems involving text messaging and scanning of products for the same purpose.[22]

Discussion Questions

1. Why is counterfeiting so popular in places such as India?
2. Why is it hard for Indian consumers to detect counterfeit products?
3. How are companies fighting against counterfeit products?

Social and Cultural Barriers

Most businesspeople engaged in international trade underestimate the importance of social and cultural differences, but these differences can derail an important transaction. For example, when Big Boy opened a restaurant in Bangkok, it quickly became popular with European and American tourists, but the local Thais refused to eat there. Instead, they placed gifts of rice and incense at the feet of the Big Boy statue (a chubby boy holding a hamburger) because it reminded them of Buddha. In Japan, customers tiptoed around a logo painted on the floor at the entrance to an Athlete's Foot store because in Japan it is considered taboo to step on a crest.[23] And in Russia, consumers found the American-style energetic happiness of McDonald's employees insincere and offensive when the company opened its first stores there.[24] Unfortunately, cultural norms are rarely written down, and what is written down may well be inaccurate.

Cultural differences include differences in spoken and written language. Although it is certainly possible to translate words from one language to another, the true meaning is sometimes misinterpreted or lost. Consider some translations that went awry in foreign markets:

- Scandinavian vacuum manufacturer Electrolux used the following in an American campaign: "Nothing sucks like an Electrolux."
- The Coca-Cola name in China was first read as "Ke-kou-ke-la," meaning "bite the wax tadpole."
- In Italy, a campaign for Schweppes Tonic Water translated the name into Schweppes Toilet Water.[25]

Translators cannot just translate slogans, advertising campaigns, and website language; they must know the cultural differences that could affect a company's success.

Differences in body language and personal space also affect international trade. Body language is nonverbal, usually unconscious communication through gestures, posture, and facial expression. Personal space is the distance at which one person feels comfortable talking to another. Americans tend to stand a moderate distance away from the person with whom they are speaking. Arab businessmen tend to stand face-to-face with the object of their conversation. Additionally, gestures vary from culture to culture, and gestures considered acceptable in American society—pointing, for example—may be considered rude in others. Table 3.3 shows some of the behaviors considered rude or unacceptable in other countries. Such cultural differences may generate uncomfortable feelings or misunderstandings when businesspeople of different countries negotiate with each other.

Family roles also influence marketing activities. Many countries do not allow children to be used in advertising, for example. Advertising that features people in nontraditional social roles may or may not be successful either. One airline featured advertisements with beautiful hostesses serving champagne on a flight. The ad does not seem unusual in Western markets, but there was a major backlash in the Middle East. Saudi Arabia even considered restricting the airline from flights in that country. Not only is alcohol usage forbidden among Muslims, unveiled women are not allowed to interact with men—especially without their husbands around. Some in Saudi Arabia saw the airline as being insensitive to their religious beliefs and customs.[26]

▼ **TABLE 3.3** Cultural Behavioral Differences

Region	Gestures Viewed as Rude or Unacceptable
Japan, Hong Kong, Middle East	Summoning with the index finger
Middle and Far East	Pointing with index finger
Thailand, Japan, France	Sitting with soles of shoes showing
Brazil, Germany	Forming a circle with fingers (the "O.K." sign in the United States)
Japan	Winking means "I love you"
Buddhist countries	Patting someone on the head

Source: Adapted from Judie Haynes, "Communicating with Gestures," *EverythingESL* (n.d.), www.everythingesl.net/inservices/body_language.php.

The people of other nations quite often have a different perception of time as well. Americans value promptness; a business meeting scheduled for a specific time seldom starts more than a few minutes late. In Mexico and Spain, however, it is not unusual for a meeting to be delayed half an hour or more. Such a late start might produce resentment in an American negotiating in Spain for the first time.

Companies engaged in foreign trade must observe the national and religious holidays and local customs of the host country. In many Islamic countries, for example, workers expect to take a break at certain times of the day to observe religious rites. Companies also must monitor their advertising to guard against offending customers. In Thailand and many other countries, public displays of affection between the sexes are unacceptable in advertising messages; in many Middle Eastern nations, it is unacceptable to show the soles of one's feet.[27] In Russia, smiling is considered appropriate only in private settings, not in business.

With the exception of the United States, most nations use the metric system. This lack of uniformity creates problems for both buyers and sellers in the international marketplace. American sellers, for instance, must package goods destined for foreign markets in liters or meters, and Japanese sellers must convert to the English system if they plan to sell a product in the United States. Tools also must be calibrated in the correct system if they are to function correctly. Hyundai and Honda service technicians need metric tools to make repairs on those cars.

The literature dealing with international business is filled with accounts of sometimes humorous but often costly mistakes that occurred because of a lack of understanding of the social and cultural differences between buyers and sellers. Such problems cannot always be avoided, but they can be minimized through research on the cultural and social differences of the host country.

Technological Barriers

Many countries lack the technological infrastructure found in the United States, and some marketers are viewing such barriers as opportunities. For instance, marketers are targeting many countries such as India and China and some African countries where there are few private phone lines. Citizens of these countries are turning instead to wireless communication through cell phones. Technological advances are creating additional global marketing opportunities. Along with opportunities, changing technologies also create new challenges and competition. The U.S. market share of the personal computer market is dropping as new competitors emerge that are challenging U.S. PC makers. In fact, of the top five PC companies—Lenovo, Hewlett-Packard, Dell, Acer, and Asus—three are from Asian countries. Recently, Lenovo surpassed Hewlett-Packard as the world's largest PC company.[28] On the other hand, Apple Inc.'s iPad and other tablet computer makers have already begun eroding the market share of traditional personal computers, leading many to believe that personal computers have hit the maturity stage of the product life cycle.

LO 3-3 Specify some of the agreements, alliances, and organizations that may encourage trade across international boundaries.

TRADE AGREEMENTS, ALLIANCES, AND ORGANIZATIONS

Although these economic, political, legal, and sociocultural issues may seem like daunting barriers to international trade, there are also organizations and agreements—such as the General Agreement on Tariffs and Trade, the World Bank, and the International Monetary Fund—that foster international

Cell phone services are taking off in Africa. They offer a viable alternative to landlines, which require infrastructure not always available in rural areas.

General Agreement on Tariffs and Trade (GATT) a trade agreement, originally signed by 23 nations in 1947, that provided a forum for tariff negotiations and a place where international trade problems could be discussed and resolved

World Trade Organization (WTO) international organization dealing with the rules of trade between nations

North American Free Trade Agreement (NAFTA) agreement that eliminates most tariffs and trade restrictions on agricultural and manufactured products to encourage trade among Canada, the United States, and Mexico

trade and can help companies get involved in and succeed in global markets. Various regional trade agreements, such as the North American Free Trade Agreement and the European Union, also promote trade among member nations by eliminating tariffs and trade restrictions. In this section, we'll look briefly at these agreements and organizations.

General Agreement on Tariffs and Trade

During the Great Depression of the 1930s, nations established so many protective tariffs covering so many products that international trade became virtually impossible. By the end of World War II, there was considerable international momentum to liberalize trade and minimize the effects of tariffs. The **General Agreement on Tariffs and Trade (GATT)**, originally signed by 23 nations in 1947, provided a forum for tariff negotiations and a place where international trade problems could be discussed and resolved. More than 100 nations abided by its rules. GATT sponsored rounds of negotiations aimed at reducing trade restrictions. The most recent round, the Uruguay Round (1988–1994), further reduced trade barriers for most products and provided new rules to prevent dumping.

The **World Trade Organization (WTO)**, an international organization dealing with the rules of trade between nations, was created in 1995 by the Uruguay Round. Key to the World Trade Organization are the WTO agreements, which are the legal ground rules for international commerce. The agreements were negotiated and signed by most of the world's trading nations and ratified by their parliaments. The goal is to help producers of goods and services and exporters and importers conduct their business. In addition to administering the WTO trade agreements, the WTO presents a forum for trade negotiations, monitors national trade policies, provides technical assistance and training for developing countries, and cooperates with other international organizations. Based in Geneva, Switzerland, the WTO has also adopted a leadership role in negotiating trade disputes among nations.[29] For example, the WTO investigated China's allegations that the United States unfairly applied antidumping measures on Chinese imports of kitchen appliances, paper, and other products. The United States filed a case with the WTO claiming that China was unfairly subsidizing cars and automobile parts. China and the United States have undergone many such trade conflicts over the years.[30]

The North American Free Trade Agreement

The **North American Free Trade Agreement (NAFTA)**, which went into effect on January 1, 1994, effectively merged Canada, the United States, and Mexico into one market of nearly 440 million consumers. NAFTA virtually eliminated all tariffs on goods produced and traded among Canada, Mexico, and the United States to create a free trade area. NAFTA makes it easier for U.S. businesses to invest in Mexico and Canada; provides protection for intellectual property (of special interest to high-technology and entertainment industries); expands trade by requiring equal treatment of U.S. firms in both countries; and simplifies country-of-origin rules, hindering Japan's use of Mexico as a staging ground for further penetration into U.S. markets.

Canada's more than 34 million consumers are relatively affluent, with a per capita GDP of $40,500.[31] Trade between the United States and Canada totals approximately $430 billion. About 80 percent of Canada's exports go to the United States, including gold, oil, and uranium.[32] In fact, Canada is the single largest trading partner of the United States.[33]

With a per capita GDP of $14,700, Mexico's 115 million consumers are less affluent than Canadian consumers.[34] However, trade with the United States and Mexico has tripled since NAFTA was initiated. Annual trade between the United States and Mexico totals more than $450 billion.[35] Millions of Americans cite their heritage as Mexican, making them the most populous Hispanic group in the country. These individuals often have close ties to relatives in Mexico and assist in Mexican–U.S. economic development and trade. Mexico is on a course of a market economy, rule of law, respect for human rights, and responsible public policies. There is also a commitment to the environment and sustainable human development. Many U.S. companies have taken advantage of Mexico's low labor costs and proximity to the United States to set up production

> "NAFTA makes it easier for U.S. businesses to invest in Mexico and Canada."

European Union (EU) a union of European nations established in 1958 to promote trade among its members; one of the largest single markets today

NAFTA, which went into effect on January 1, 1994, has increased trade among Mexico, the United States, and Canada.

facilities, sometimes called *maquiladoras.* Mexico is also attracting major technological industries, including electronics, software, and aerospace. Business opportunities for Mexico have been increasing in other ways as well. For instance, Mexico now has higher growth than Brazil and may become one of the world's top 10 largest economies. Oil production is proving very profitable for Mexico, contributing to the country's quickly growing economy. Business loans in Mexico have also been increasing. In addition, as labor costs continue to rise in China, many U.S. businesses are increasingly considering outsourcing to Mexico to save costs.[36]

However, there is great disparity within Mexico. The country's southern states cannot seem to catch up with the more affluent northern states on almost any socioeconomic indicator. For example, 47 percent of rural Mexicans in the south are considered extremely poor, compared with just 12 percent in the north. The disparities are growing, as can be seen comparing the south to the northern industrial capital of Monterrey, which is beginning to seem like south Texas.[37] However, drug gang wars threaten the economic stability of Mexico, especially in the northern states close to the U.S. border. On the other hand, this situation is improving as the economy is growing and violence is decreasing.

Despite its benefits, NAFTA has been controversial, and disputes continue to arise over the implementation of the trade agreement. For example, a trucking dispute between the United States and Mexico resulted in a ban on Mexican trucks operating within the U.S. border. In retaliation, Mexico instituted a punitive tariff on U.S. imports, claiming that the ban violated NAFTA. Americans in support of the ban felt it was necessary to protect the jobs of U.S. truck and warehouse workers. The dispute was eventually resolved, with President Obama agreeing to lift the ban in exchange for tougher standards for Mexican trucks crossing the border.[38] Although many Americans feared the agreement would erase jobs in the United States, Mexicans have been disappointed that the agreement failed to create more jobs. Moreover, Mexico's rising standard of living has increased the cost of doing business there; many hundreds of *maquiladoras* have closed their doors and transferred work to China and other nations where labor costs are cheaper. Indeed, China has become the United States' second-largest importer.[39] On the other hand, high transportation costs, intellectual property theft, higher labor costs, and the difficulty management often incurs in controlling a business so far away and under a communist regime are now causing some manufacturers to reconsider opting for Mexican factories over China, as mentioned earlier.

Although NAFTA has been controversial, it has become a positive factor for U.S. firms wishing to engage in international marketing. Because licensing requirements have been relaxed under the pact, smaller businesses that previously could not afford to invest in Mexico and Canada will be able to do business in those markets without having to locate there. NAFTA's long phase-in period provided time for adjustment by those firms affected by reduced tariffs on imports. Furthermore, increased competition should lead to a more efficient market, and the long-term prospects of including most countries in the Western Hemisphere in the alliance promise additional opportunities for U.S. marketers.

The European Union

The **European Union (EU)**, also called the *European Community* or *Common Market,* was established in 1958 to promote trade among its members, which initially included Belgium, France, Italy, West Germany, Luxembourg, and the Netherlands. East and West Germany united in 1991, and by 1995 the United Kingdom, Spain, Denmark, Greece, Portugal, Ireland, Austria, Finland, and Sweden had joined as well. The Czech Republic, Estonia, Hungary, Latvia, Lithuania, Poland, Slovakia, and Slovenia joined in 2004. In 2007, Bulgaria and Romania also became members, Cyprus and Malta joined in 2008, and Croatia joined in 2013, which brought total membership to 28. Macedonia, Iceland, and Turkey are candidate countries that hope to join the European Union in the near future.[40] Until 1993, each nation functioned as a separate market, but at that time members officially unified into one of the largest single world markets, which today has nearly half a billion consumers with a GDP of more than $15.5 trillion.[41]

To facilitate free trade among members, the EU is working toward standardization of business regulations and requirements, import duties, and value-added taxes; the elimination of customs checks; and the creation of a standardized currency

Asia-Pacific Economic Cooperation (APEC) an international trade alliance that promotes open trade and economic and technical cooperation among member nations

for use by all members. Many European nations (Austria, Belgium, Finland, France, Germany, Greece, Ireland, Italy, Luxembourg, the Netherlands, Portugal, Spain, and Slovenia) link their exchange rates to a common currency, the *euro;* however, several EU members have rejected use of the euro in their countries. Although the common currency requires many marketers to modify their pricing strategies and will subject them to increased competition, the use of a single currency frees companies that sell goods among European countries from the nuisance of dealing with complex exchange rates.[42] The long-term goals are to eliminate all trade barriers within the EU, improve the economic efficiency of the EU nations, and stimulate economic growth, thus making the union's economy more competitive in global markets, particularly against Japan and other Pacific Rim nations, and North America. However, several disputes and debates still divide the member nations, and many barriers to completely free trade remain. Consequently, it may take many years before the EU is truly one deregulated market.

The EU has also enacted some of the world's strictest laws concerning antitrust issues, which have had unexpected consequences for some non-European firms. For example, European antitrust regulators resisted the New York Stock Exchange's proposed merger with German marketplace organizer Deutsche Börse. They believed the merger would give the combined companies too much market power, thus decreasing competition.[43]

The prosperity of the EU has suffered in recent years. EU members experienced a severe economic crisis in 2010 that required steep bailouts from the International Monetary Fund (IMF). The first country to come to the forefront was Greece, which had so much debt that it risked default. With an increase in Greek bond yields and credit risks—along with a severe deficit and other negative economic factors—the country's economy plummeted. Because Greece uses the euro as its currency, the massive downturn decreased the euro's value. This had a profound effect on other countries in the Euro zone. (The Euro zone refers collectively to European member countries that have adopted the euro as their form of currency.) Ireland and Portugal were particularly vulnerable because they had some of the region's largest deficits.[44] Ireland began experiencing problems similar to Greece, including a debt crisis, failing economic health, and rising bond yields.[45] Both Ireland and Portugal required bailout packages. In 2012, Spain and Cyprus also requested bailouts.

Greece continued to struggle even after the initial bailout because it did not have enough funds to repay its bondholders. Greece was forced to default. Other countries in the EU are also struggling. The European Commission has expressed concerns at economic imbalances in Italy, Spain, France, and Slovenia. Countries deemed to have excessive imbalances could face fines if they do not improve. With their economies interconnected, most of the countries in the European Union have been affected by the debt crisis. One exception, however, appears to be Germany.[46] Germany has largely avoided the economic woes plaguing other countries. It has many exporting companies and has a smaller budget deficit and smaller household debt, which has enabled it to weather the crisis better.[47]

Most of these European countries are a part of the European Union. Iceland is a candidate country that hopes to join the EU in the near future.

Asia-Pacific Economic Cooperation

The **Asia-Pacific Economic Cooperation (APEC)**, established in 1989, promotes open trade and economic and technical cooperation among member nations, which initially included Australia, Brunei Darussalam, Canada, Indonesia, Japan, Korea, Malaysia, New Zealand, the Philippines, Singapore, Thailand, and the United States. Since then, the alliance has grown to include China, Hong Kong, Chinese Taipei, Mexico, Papua New Guinea, Chile, Peru, Russia, and Vietnam. The 21-member alliance represents approximately 41 percent of the world's population, 44 percent of world trade, and 54 percent of world GDP. APEC differs from other international trade alliances in its commitment to facilitating business and its practice of allowing the business/private sector to participate in a wide range of APEC activities.[48]

Association of Southeast Asian Nations (ASEAN) a trade alliance that promotes trade and economic integration among member nations in Southeast Asia

World Bank an organization established by the industrialized nations in 1946 to loan money to underdeveloped and developing countries; formally known as the International Bank for Reconstruction and Development

Companies of the APEC have become increasingly competitive and sophisticated in global business in the past three decades. The Japanese and South Koreans in particular have made tremendous inroads on world markets for automobiles, cameras, and audio and video equipment. Products from Samsung, Sony, Sanyo, Toyota, Daewoo, Mitsubishi, Suzuki, and Toshiba are sold all over the world and have set standards of quality by which other products are often judged. The People's Republic of China, a country of 1.3 billion people, has launched a program of economic reform to stimulate its economy by privatizing many industries, restructuring its banking system, and increasing public spending on infrastructure (including railways and telecommunications). As a result, China has become a manufacturing powerhouse, with an estimated economic growth rate of 8 percent a year.[49] China's export market has consistently outpaced its import growth in recent years and its GDP is the world's second-largest economy, behind the United States.

Increased industrialization has also caused China to become the world's largest emitter of greenhouse gases. China mainly uses coal-fired power plants; in fact, it builds a new one every 10 days, so it has become the world's largest emitter of carbon dioxide. As companies transfer their manufacturing to China, they increase their CO_2 emissions because China emits 22 percent more than the global average of carbon per kilowatt-hour.[50] On the other hand, China has also begun a quest to become a world leader in green initiatives and renewable energy. This is an increasingly important quest as the country becomes more polluted.

Another risk area for China is the fact that the government owns or has stakes in so many enterprises. On the one hand, China's system of state-directed capitalism has benefited the country because reforms and decisions can be made more quickly. On the other hand, state-backed companies lack many of the competitors that private industries have. Remember that competition often spurs innovation and lowers costs. If China's firms lack sufficient competition, their costs may very likely increase. China's growing debt liabilities have also caused concern among foreign investors. Although exports and manufacturing have improved, China's corporate debt has risen. Because many large companies in China are state-owned, the country's economy may be affected if these corporations cannot manage their debt.[51]

Less-visible Pacific Rim regions, such as Thailand, Singapore, Taiwan, Vietnam, and Hong Kong, have also become major manufacturing and financial centers. Vietnam, with one of the world's most open economies, has bypassed its communist government with private firms moving ahead despite bureaucracy, corruption, and poor infrastructure. In a country of 88 million, Vietnamese firms now compete internationally with an agricultural miracle, making the country one of the world's main providers of farm produce. Coach Inc. wants to increase its presence in Vietnam, while Guess Inc. is considering an expansion of its production facilities in Vietnam along with Cambodia and Indonesia.[52]

APEC
Asia-Pacific
Economic Cooperation

Association of Southeast Asian Nations

The **Association of Southeast Asian Nations (ASEAN)**, established in 1967, promotes trade and economic integration among member nations in Southeast Asia, including Malaysia, the Philippines, Singapore, Thailand, Brunei Darussalam, Vietnam, Laos, Myanmar, Indonesia, and Cambodia.[53] The 10-member alliance represents 600 million people with a GDP of $2 trillion.[54] ASEAN's goals include the promotion of free trade, peace, and collaboration between its members.[55] In 1993, ASEAN began to reduce or phase out tariffs among countries and eliminate nontariff trade barriers.[56] This elimination of tariffs will encourage additional trade among countries and could be beneficial to businesses that want to export to other countries in the trading bloc.

However, ASEAN is facing challenges in becoming a unified trade bloc. Unlike members of the European Union, the economic systems of ASEAN members are quite different, with political systems including dictatorships (Myanmar), democracies (Philippines and Malaysia), constitutional monarchies (Thailand and Cambodia), and communism (Vietnam).[57] Major conflicts have also occurred between member nations.

Despite these challenges, ASEAN plans to increase economic integration by 2015, but unlike the European Union, it will not have a common currency or fully free labor flows between member-nations. In this way, ASEAN plans to avoid some of the pitfalls that occurred among nations in the EU during the latest worldwide recession.[58]

World Bank

The **World Bank**, more formally known as the International Bank for Reconstruction and Development, was established by the industrialized nations, including the United States, in 1946 to loan money to underdeveloped and developing countries.

It loans its own funds or borrows funds from member countries to finance projects ranging from road and factory construction to the building

International Monetary Fund (IMF) organization established in 1947 to promote trade among member nations by eliminating trade barriers and fostering financial cooperation

of medical and educational facilities. The World Bank and other multilateral development banks (banks with international support that provide loans to developing countries) are the largest source of advice and assistance for developing nations. The International Development Association and the International Finance Corporation are associated with the World Bank and provide loans to private businesses and member countries.

International Monetary Fund

The **International Monetary Fund (IMF)** was established in 1947 to promote trade among member nations by eliminating trade barriers and fostering financial cooperation. It also makes short-term loans to member countries that have balance-of-payment deficits and provides foreign currencies to member nations. The International Monetary Fund tries to avoid financial crises and panics by alerting the international community about countries that will not be able to repay their debts. The IMF's Internet site provides additional information about the organization, including news releases, frequently asked questions, and members.

> "The IMF is the closest thing the world has to an international central bank."

The IMF is the closest thing the world has to an international central bank. If countries get into financial trouble, they can borrow from the World Bank. However, the global economic crisis created many challenges for the IMF because it was forced to increase its loans significantly to both emerging economies and more-developed nations. The usefulness of the IMF for developed countries is limited because these countries use private markets as a major source of capital.[59] Yet the European debt crisis changed this somewhat. Portugal, Ireland, Greece, and Spain (often referred to with the acronym PIGS) required billions of dollars in bailouts from the IMF to keep their economies afloat.

LO 3-4 Summarize the different levels of organizational involvement in international trade.

GETTING INVOLVED IN INTERNATIONAL BUSINESS

Businesses may get involved in international trade at many levels—from a small Kenyan firm that occasionally exports African crafts to a huge multinational corporation such as Shell Oil that sells products around the globe. The degree of commitment of resources and effort required increases according to the level at which a business involves itself in international trade. This section examines exporting and importing, trading companies, licensing and franchising, contract manufacturing, outsourcing, joint ventures, direct investment, and multinational corporations.

Exporting and Importing

Many companies first get involved in international trade when they import goods from other countries for resale in their own businesses. For example, a grocery store chain may import bananas from Honduras and coffee from Colombia. A business may get involved in exporting when it is called upon to supply a foreign company with a particular product. Such exporting enables enterprises of all sizes to participate in international business. Exporting to other countries becomes a necessity for established countries that seek to

UNIQLO BRINGS JAPANESE FASHION TO AMERICA

Founded in 1984 in Hiroshima, Japan, Uniqlo is a sportswear retail operation that takes its inspiration from retailers such as H&M and the Gap with their stylish looks at affordable prices. Uniqlo is known for its innovative products, including a synthetic material called HeatTech that stays dry even if the person wearing it is sweating. Uniqlo has become globally successful with 1,100 stores.

However, Uniqlo has encountered challenges when expanding in the United States. Although Americans seemed to like Uniqlo products, the company had difficulties opening successful retail operations. Uniqlo opened stores in New Jersey, only to shut them down quickly thereafter because Americans were not familiar with the brand. Uniqlo launched a marketing campaign featuring everyday people in New York City wearing the Uniqlo brand. Uniqlo has been attracting the American consumer ever since. Location was also a factor. The first store it opened was in a regular-sized unit in a mall. Now it is opening its stores in buildings that are tall and can be seen from the highway.[60]

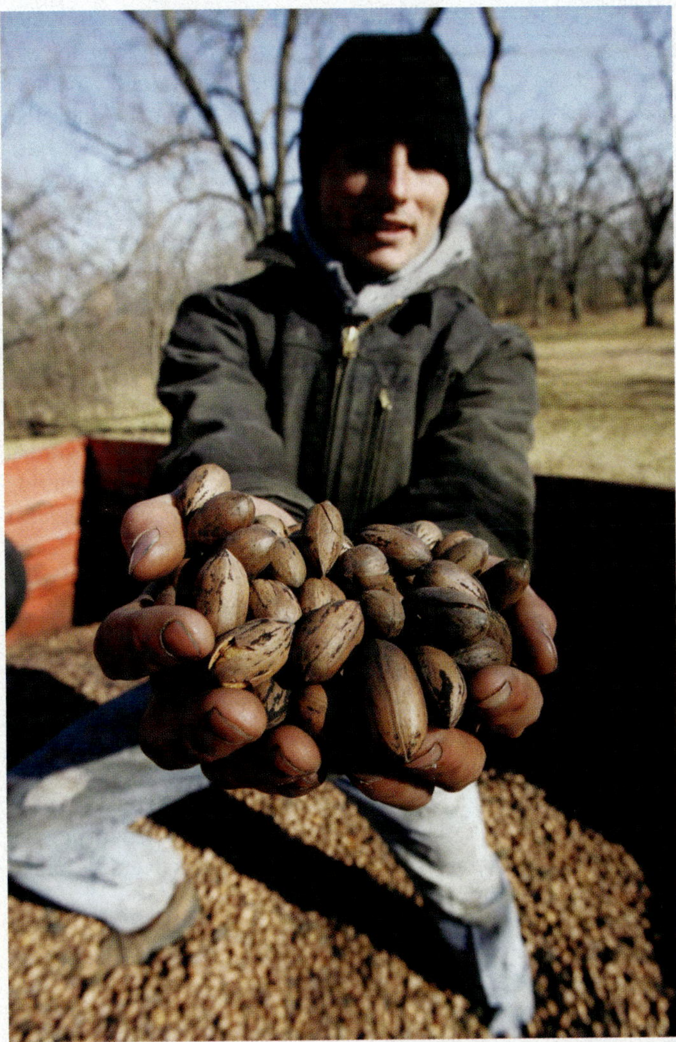

The United States is exporting a record number of pecans.

grow continually. Products often have higher sales growth potential in foreign countries than they have in the parent country. For instance, General Motors and YUM! Brands sell more of their products in China than in the United States. Walmart experienced sales growth in international markets. Table 3.4 shows the number of U.S. exporters and the export value by company size, and Figure 3.1 shows some of the world's largest exporting countries.

Exporting sometimes takes place through **countertrade agreements**, which involve bartering products for other products instead of for currency. Such arrangements are fairly common in international trade, especially between Western companies and eastern European nations. An estimated 40 percent or more of all international trade agreements contain countertrade provisions.

countertrade agreements foreign trade agreements that involve bartering products for other products instead of for currency

trading company a firm that buys goods in one country and sells them to buyers in another country

Although a company may export its wares overseas directly or import goods directly from their manufacturer, many choose to deal with an intermediary, commonly called an *export agent.* Export agents seldom produce goods themselves; instead, they usually handle international transactions for other firms. Export agents either purchase products outright or take them on consignment. If they purchase them outright, they generally mark up the price they have paid and attempt to sell the product in the international marketplace. They are also responsible for storage and transportation.

An advantage of trading through an agent instead of directly is that the company does not have to deal with foreign currencies or the red tape (paying tariffs and handling paperwork) of international business. A major disadvantage is that, because the export agent must make a profit, either the price of the product must be increased or the domestic company must provide a larger discount than it would in a domestic transaction.

Trading Companies

A **trading company** buys goods in one country and sells them to buyers in another country. Trading companies handle all activities required to move products from one country to another, including consulting, marketing research, advertising, insurance, product research and design, warehousing, and foreign exchange services to companies interested in selling their products in foreign markets. Trading companies are similar to export agents, but their role in international trade is larger. By linking sellers and buyers of goods in different countries, trading companies promote international trade. The best-known U.S. trading company is Sears World Trade, which specializes in consumer goods, light industrial items, and processed foods.

Licensing and Franchising

Licensing is a trade arrangement in which one company—the *licensor*—allows another company—the *licensee*—to use

TABLE 3.4 U.S. Exporters and Value by Company Size

	Number of Exporters	Percentage	Value (millions of dollars)	Percentage
Unknown	112,166	38.3	$106,751	9.4
Small (<100 employees)	158,607	54.2	171,286	15.1
Medium (100–499 employees)	15,888	5.4	105,376	9.3
Large (>500 employees)	6,470	2.2	754,222	66.3

Source: U.S. Bureau of the Census, "Exhibit 1a: 2010 Exports by Company Type and Employment Size," www.census.gov/foreign-trade/Press-Release/edb/2010/exh1a.pdf.

licensing a trade agreement in which one company—the licensor—allows another company—the licensee—to use its company name, products, patents, brands, trademarks, raw materials, and/or production processes in exchange for a fee or royalty

franchising a form of licensing in which a company—the franchiser—agrees to provide a franchisee a name, logo, methods of operation, advertising, products, and other elements associated with a franchiser's business in return for a financial commitment and the agreement to conduct business in accordance with the franchiser's standard of operations

contract manufacturing the hiring of a foreign company to produce a specified volume of the initiating company's product to specification; the final product carries the domestic firm's name

FIGURE 3.1
Top Exporting Countries

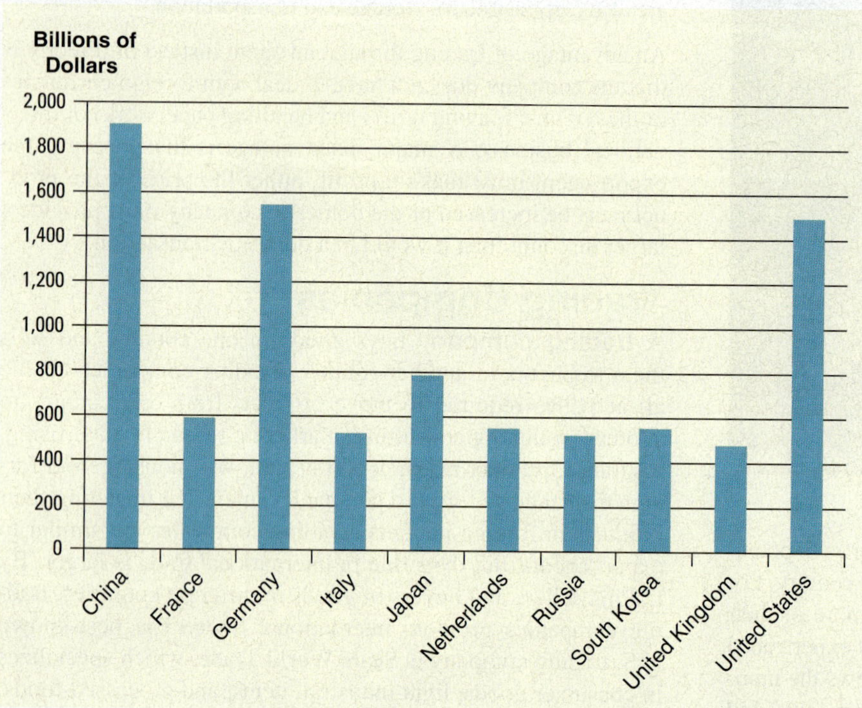

Source: "Country Comparison: Exports," *The World Factbook,* https://www.cia.gov/library/publications/the-world-factbook/rankorder/2078rank.html.

its company name, products, patents, brands, trademarks, raw materials, and/or production processes in exchange for a fee or royalty. The Coca-Cola Company and PepsiCo frequently use licensing as a means to market their soft drinks, apparel, and other merchandise in other countries. Licensing is an attractive alternative to direct investment when the political stability of a foreign country is in doubt or when resources are unavailable for direct investment. Licensing is especially advantageous for small manufacturers wanting to launch a well-known brand internationally. Yoplait is a French yogurt that is licensed for production in the United States.

Franchising is a form of licensing in which a company—the *franchiser*—agrees to provide a *franchisee* the name, logo, methods of operation, advertising, products, and other elements associated with the franchiser's business in return for a financial commitment and the agreement to conduct business in accordance with the franchiser's standard of operations. Wendy's, McDonald's, Pizza Hut, and Holiday Inn are well-known franchisers with international visibility. Table 3.5 lists some of the top global franchises.

Licensing and franchising enable a company to enter the international marketplace without spending large sums of money abroad or hiring or transferring personnel to handle overseas affairs. They also minimize problems associated with shipping costs, tariffs, and trade restrictions, and they allow the firm to establish goodwill for its products in a foreign market, which will help the company if it decides to produce or market its products directly in the foreign country at some future date. However, if the licensee (or franchisee) does not maintain high standards of quality, the product's image may be hurt; therefore, it is important for the licensor to monitor its products overseas and to enforce its quality standards.

Contract Manufacturing

Contract manufacturing occurs when a company hires a foreign company to produce a specified volume of the firm's product to specification; the final product carries the domestic firm's name. Spalding, for example, relies on contract manufacturing for its sports equipment; Reebok uses Korean contract manufacturers to manufacture many of its athletic shoes.

Outsourcing

Earlier, we defined outsourcing as transferring manufacturing or other tasks (such as information technology operations) to companies in countries where labor and supplies are less expensive. Many U.S. firms have outsourced tasks to India, Ireland, Mexico, and the Philippines, where there are many well-educated workers and significantly lower labor costs. Services, such as taxes or customer service, can also be outsourced.

Although outsourcing has become politically controversial in recent years amid concerns over jobs lost to overseas workers, foreign companies transfer tasks and jobs to U.S. companies—sometimes called *insourcing*—far more often than U.S. companies outsource tasks and jobs abroad.[61] However, some firms are bringing their outsourced jobs back after concerns that

TABLE 3.5 Top Global Franchises

Franchise	Country	Ranking
Subway	United States	1
McDonald's	United States	2
InterContinental Hotels Group	United Kingdom	13
Kumon North America, Inc.	Japan	18
Tim Hortons	Canada	20
DIA-FRANCHISE	Spain	25
Europcar	France	28
Yogun Fruz	Canada	38
Cartridge World	Australia	46
Ben & Jerry's	United States	56

Source: "Top 100 Global Franchises Rankings," *Franchise Direct*, www.franchisedirect.com/top100globalfranchises/rankings/.

foreign workers were not adding enough value. Companies such as General Electric and Caterpillar are returning to the United States due to increasing labor costs in places such as China, the expense of shipping products across the ocean, and fears of fraud or intellectual property theft. Companies from other countries have also been moving some of their production to the United States; Chinese computer-maker Lenovo is opening a production facility in the United States. Apple also announced it would start building a line of Mac computers in America.[62]

Offshoring

Offshoring is the relocation of a business process by a company, or a subsidiary, to another country. Offshoring is different than outsourcing; the company retains control of the process because it is not subcontracting to a different company. Companies may choose to offshore for a number of reasons, ranging from lower wages for skilled labor to taking advantage of time zone differences to offer services around the clock. Some banks have chosen not to outsource because of concerns about data security in other countries. These institutions may instead engage in offshoring, which allows a company more control over international operations because the offshore office is an extension of the company. Barclays Bank, for instance, has an international offshore banking unit called Barclays Wealth International. This branch helps the company better serve wealthy clients with international banking needs.[63]

offshoring The relocation of business processes by a company or subsidiary to another country. Offshoring is different than outsourcing because the company retains control of the offshored processes.

joint venture the sharing of the costs and operation of a business between a foreign company and a local partner

strategic alliance a partnership formed to create competitive advantage on a worldwide basis

This Subway restaurant is part of the huge Souq Sharq shopping center in Kuwait City, Kuwait.

Joint Ventures and Alliances

Many countries, particularly LDCs, do not permit direct investment by foreign companies or individuals. A company may also lack sufficient resources or expertise to operate in another country. In such cases, a company that wants to do business in another country may set up a **joint venture** by finding a local partner (occasionally, the host nation itself) to share the costs and operation of the business. For example, Brazilian conglomerate Odebrecht created a joint venture with state-owned oil company Petróleos de Venezuela. Odebrecht paid $50 million, or a 40 percent stake, to search for oil in the Venezuelan state of Zulia. Because the oil industry is nationalized in Venezuela, foreign oil companies must enter into joint ventures if they want to explore for and drill oil in the country.[64]

In some industries, such as automobiles and computers, strategic alliances are becoming the predominant means of competing. A **strategic alliance** is a partnership formed to create competitive advantage on a worldwide basis. In such industries, international competition is so fierce and the costs of competing on a global basis are so high that few firms have the resources to go it alone, so they collaborate with other companies. An example of a strategic alliance is the partnership between Australian airlines Virgin Blue and SkyWest. By forming an alliance, the two airlines hope to tap into the increased demand from the mining industry for flights to distant mining sites. As part of the agreement, SkyWest can use as many as 18 Virgin Blue turbo-prop aircraft for 10 years. In addition to penetrating a lucrative market, Virgin Blue hopes the alliance will help it to extend its influence into regional markets and steal market share from its competitor, QantasLink.[65]

Direct Investment

Companies that want more control and are willing to invest considerable resources in international business may consider

direct investment the ownership of overseas facilities

multinational corporation (MNC) a corporation that operates on a worldwide scale, without significant ties to any one nation or region

direct investment, the ownership of overseas facilities. Direct investment may involve the development and operation of new facilities—such as when Starbucks opens a new coffee shop in Japan—or the purchase of all or part of an existing operation in a foreign country. India's Tata Motors purchased Jaguar and Land Rover from Ford Motor Company. Tata, a maker of cars and trucks, is attempting to broaden its global presence, including manufacturing these vehicles in the United Kingdom.[66]

The highest level of international business involvement is the **multinational corporation (MNC)**, a corporation, such as IBM or ExxonMobil, that operates on a worldwide scale, without significant ties to any one nation or region. Table 3.6 lists some well-known multinationals from different countries. MNCs are more than simple corporations. They often have greater assets than some of the countries in which they do business. Nestlé, with headquarters in Switzerland, operates more than 400 factories around the world and receives revenues from Europe; North, Central, and South America; Africa; and Asia.[67] The Royal Dutch/Shell Group, one of the world's major oil producers, is another MNC. Its main offices are located in The Hague and London. Other MNCs include BASF, British Petroleum, Matsushita, Mitsubishi, Siemens, Texaco, Toyota, and Unilever. Many MNCs have been targeted by antiglobalization activists at global business forums, and some protests have turned violent. The activists contend that MNCs increase the gap between rich and poor nations, misuse and misallocate scarce resources, exploit the labor markets in LDCs, and harm their natural environments.[68]

INTERNATIONAL BUSINESS STRATEGIES

Planning in a global economy requires businesspeople to understand the economic, legal, political, and sociocultural realities of the countries in which they will operate. These factors will affect the strategy a business chooses to use outside its own borders.

Walmart has chosen to invest directly in China. However, it must still make adjustments to fit with the local culture. For instance, Walmart, which is normally against trade unions, was pressured to allow its Chinese employees to unionize.

TABLE 3.6 Well-Known Multinational Companies

Company	Country	Description
Royal Dutch Shell	Netherlands	Oil and gas
Toyota	Japan	Automobiles
Walmart	United States	Retail
Siemens	Germany	Engineering and electronics
Nestlé	Switzerland	Nutritional, snack-food, and health-related consumer goods
Samsung	South Korea	Subsidiaries specializing in electronics, electronic components, telecommunications equipment, medical equipment, and more
Unilever	United Kingdom	Consumer goods including cleaning and personal care, foods, beverages
Boeing	United States	Aerospace and defense
Lenovo	China	Computer technology
Subway	United States	Largest fast-food chain

LO 3-5 Contrast two basic strategies used in international business.

Developing Strategies

Companies doing business internationally have traditionally used a **multinational strategy**, customizing their products, promotion, and distribution according to cultural, technological, regional, and national differences. To succeed in India, for example, McDonald's had to adapt its products to respect religious customs. McDonald's India does not serve beef or pork products and has vegetarian dishes for its largely vegetarian consumer base. Many soap and detergent manufacturers have adapted their products to local water conditions, washing equipment, and washing habits. For customers in some less-developed countries, Colgate-Palmolive Co. has developed an inexpensive, plastic, hand-powered washing machine for use in households that have no electricity. Even when products are standardized, advertising often has to be modified to adapt to language and cultural differences. Also, celebrities used in advertising in the United States may be unfamiliar to foreign consumers and thus would not be effective in advertising products in other countries.

TEAM EXERCISE

Visit Transparency International's Country Corruption Index website at **http://cpi.transparency.org/cpi2011/results/**. Form groups and select two countries. Research some of the economic, ethical, legal, regulatory, and political barriers that would have an impact on international trade. Be sure to pair a fairly ethical country with a fairly unethical country (Sweden with Myanmar, Australia with Haiti). Report your findings.

More and more companies are moving from this customization strategy to a **global strategy (globalization)**, which involves standardizing products (and, as much as possible, their promotion and distribution) for the whole world as if it were a single entity. Examples of globalized products are American clothing, movies, music, and cosmetics. As it has become a global brand, Starbucks has standardized its products and stores. Starbucks was ranked as the world's most engaged brand in terms of online activities, even surpassing Coca-Cola, which is another global brand.

Before moving outside their own borders, companies must conduct environmental analyses to evaluate the potential of and problems associated with various markets and to determine what strategy is best for doing business in those markets. Failure to do so may result in losses and even negative publicity. Some companies rely on local managers to gain greater insights and faster response to changes within a country. Astute businesspeople today "think globally, act locally." That is, while constantly being aware of the total picture, they adjust their firms' strategies to conform to local needs and tastes.

multinational strategy a plan, used by international companies, that involves customizing products, promotion, and distribution according to cultural, technological, regional, and national differences

global strategy (globalization) a strategy that involves standardizing products (and, as much as possible, their promotion and distribution) for the whole world as if it were a single entity

Managing the Challenges of Global Business

As we've pointed out in this chapter, many past political barriers to trade have fallen or been minimized, expanding and opening new market opportunities. Managers who can meet the challenges of creating and implementing effective and sensitive business strategies for the global marketplace can help lead their companies to success. Knowing how to deal with global competition and reach markets in other countries is important. The Commercial Service is the global business solutions unit of the U.S. Department of Commerce that offers U.S. firms wide and deep practical knowledge of international markets and industries, a unique global network, inventive use of information technology, and a focus on small and mid-sized businesses. Another example is the benchmarking of best international practices that benefits U.S. firms, which is conducted by the network of CIBERs (Centers for International Business Education and Research) at leading business schools in the

SO YOU WANT A JOB // in Global Business /

Have you always dreamt of traveling the world? Whether backpacking your way through Central America or sipping espressos at five-star European restaurants is your style, the increasing globalization of business might just give you your chance to see what the world has to offer. Most new jobs will have at least some global component, even if located within the United States, so being globally aware and keeping an open mind to different cultures is vital in today's business world. Think about the 1.3 billion consumers in China that have already purchased 500 million mobile phones. In the future, some of the largest markets will be in Asia.

Many jobs discussed in chapters throughout this book tend to have strong international components. For example, product management and distribution management are discussed as marketing careers in Chapter 12. As more and more companies sell products around the globe, their function, design, packaging, and promotions need to be culturally relevant to many people in many places. Products very often cross multiple borders before reaching the final consumer, both in their distribution and through the supply chain to produce the products.

Jobs exist in export and import management, product and pricing management, distribution and transportation, and advertising. Many "born global" companies such as Google operate virtually and consider all countries their market. Many companies sell their products through eBay and other Internet sites and never leave the United States. Today communication and transportation facilitates selling and buying products worldwide with delivery in a few days. You may have sold or purchased a product on eBay outside the United States without thinking about how easy and accessible international markets are to business. If you have, welcome to the world of global business.

To be successful, you must have an idea not only of differing regulations from country to country but also of different language, ethics, and communication styles and varying needs and wants of international markets. From a regulatory side, you may need to be aware of laws related to intellectual property, copyrights, antitrust, advertising, and pricing in every country. Translating is never only about translating the language. Perhaps even more important is ensuring that your message gets through. Whether on a product label or in advertising or promotional materials, the use of images and words varies widely across the globe.

United States. These CIBERs are funded by the U.S. government to help U.S. firms become more competitive globally. A major element of the assistance that these governmental organizations can provide firms (especially for small and medium-sized firms) is knowledge of the internationalization process.[69] Small businesses, too, can succeed in foreign markets when their managers have carefully studied those markets and prepared and implemented appropriate strategies. Being globally aware is therefore an important quality for today's managers and will become a critical attribute for managers in the 21st century. ■

learn, practice, apply global business concepts!

M: Business was developed just for you—students on the go who need information packaged in a concise yet interesting format with multiple learning options. Check out the book's website to:

- Identify cultural norms of different countries. (Build Your Skills)
- Understand major challenges to global expansion. (Solve the Dilemma)
- Consider the different ways to expand a business globally. (Solve the Dilemma)

While you are there, don't forget to enhance your skills. Practice and apply your knowledge, review the practice exercises, Student PPT® slides, and quizzes to review and apply chapter concepts. Additionally, *Connect® Business* is available for *M: Business.*

www.mhhe.com/ferrellm4e

FedEx
FedEx
Express

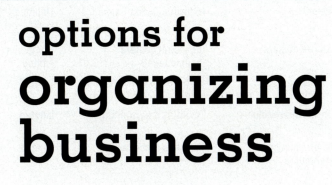

options for organizing business

The legal form of ownership taken by a business is seldom of great concern to you as a customer. When you eat at a restaurant, you probably don't care whether the restaurant is owned by one person (a sole proprietorship), has two or more owners who share the business (a partnership), or is an entity owned by many stockholders (a corporation); all you want is good food. If you buy a foreign car, you probably don't care whether the company that made it has laws governing its form of organization that are different from those for businesses in the United States. You are buying the car because it is well made, fits your price range, or appeals to your sense of style. Nonetheless, a business's legal form of ownership affects how it operates, how much taxes it pays, and how much control its owners have.

This chapter examines three primary forms of business ownership—sole proprietorship, partnership, and corporation—and weighs the advantages and disadvantages of each. These forms are the most often used whether the business is a traditional brick-and-mortar company, an online-only one, or a combination of both. We also take a look at S corporations, limited liability companies, and cooperatives and discuss some trends in business ownership. You may wish to refer to Table 4.1 to compare the various forms of business ownership mentioned in the chapter. ■

LEARNING OBJECTIVES

After reading this chapter, you will be able to:

LO 4-1 Define and examine the advantages and disadvantages of the sole proprietorship form of organization.

LO 4-2 Identify two types of partnership and evaluate the advantages and disadvantages of the partnership form of organization.

LO 4-3 Describe the corporate form of organization and cite the advantages and disadvantages of corporations.

LO 4-4 Define and debate the advantages and disadvantages of mergers, acquisitions, and leveraged buyouts.

▼ **TABLE 4.1** Various Forms of Business Ownership

Structure	Ownership	Taxation	Liability	Use
Sole Proprietorship	1 owner	Individual income taxed	Unlimited	Owned by a single individual and is the easiest way to conduct business
Partnership	2 or more owners	Individual owners' income taxed	Somewhat limited	Easy way for two individuals to conduct business
Corporation	Any number of shareholders	Corporate and shareholder taxed	Limited	A legal entity with shareholders or stockholders
S Corporation	Up to 100 shareholders	Taxed as a partnership	Limited	A legal entity with tax advantages for restricted number of shareholders
Limited Liability Company	Unlimited number of shareholders	Taxed as a partnership	Limited	Avoids personal lawsuits

LO 4-1 Define and examine the advantages and disadvantages of the sole proprietorship form of organization.

SOLE PROPRIETORSHIPS

Sole proprietorships, businesses owned and operated by one individual, are the most common form of business organization in the United States. Common examples include many restaurants, hair salons, flower shops, dog kennels, and independent grocery stores. Many sole proprietors focus on services—small retail stores, financial counseling, appliance repair, child care, and the like—rather than on the manufacture of goods, which often requires large sums of money not available to most small businesses. As you can see in Figure 4.1, proprietorships far outnumber corporations, but they net far fewer sales and less income.

"Sole proprietorships constitute approximately three-fourths of all businesses in the United States."

▼**FIGURE 4.1**
Comparison of Sole Proprietorships, Partnerships, and Corporations

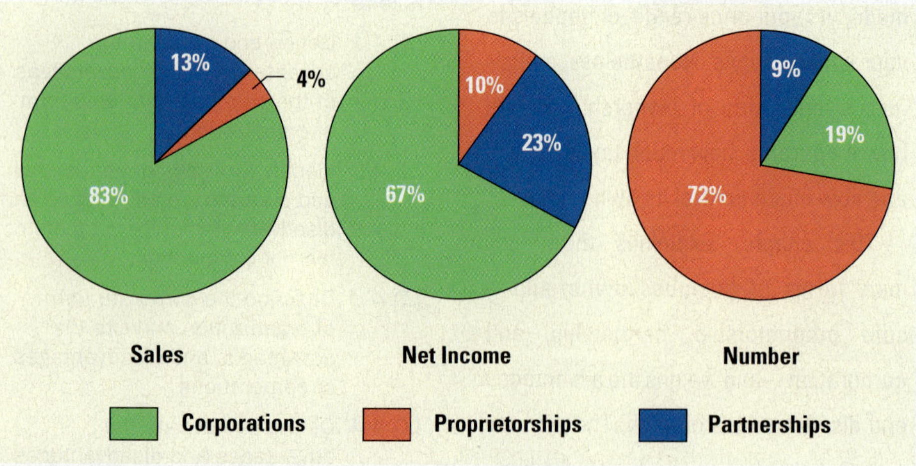

	Corporations	Proprietorships	Partnerships
Sales	83%	4%	13%
Net Income	67%	10%	23%
Number	19%	72%	9%

Source: U.S. Bureau of the Census, *Statistical Abstract of the United States,* www.census.gov/prod/2009pubs/10statab/business.pdf.

Sole proprietorships are typically small businesses employing fewer than 50 people. (We'll look at small businesses in greater detail in Chapter 5.) Sole proprietorships constitute approximately three-fourths of all businesses in the United States. In many areas, small businesses make up the vast majority of the economy.

Advantages of Sole Proprietorships

Sole proprietorships are generally managed by their owners. Because of this simple management structure, the owner/manager can make decisions quickly. This is just one of many advantages of the sole proprietorship form of business.

Ease and Cost of Formation

Forming a sole proprietorship is relatively easy and inexpensive. In some states, creating a sole proprietorship involves merely announcing the new business in the local newspaper. Other proprietorships, such as barber shops and restaurants, may require state and local licenses and permits because of the nature of the business. The cost of these permits may run from $25 to $100. No lawyer is needed to create such enterprises, and the owner can usually take care of the required paperwork without outside assistance.

Of course, an entrepreneur starting a new sole proprietorship must find a suitable site from which to operate the business. Some sole proprietors look no farther than their garage or a spare bedroom when seeking a workshop or office. Among the more famous businesses that sprang to life in their founders' homes are Google, Walt Disney, Dell, eBay, Hewlett-Packard, Apple, and Mattel.[1] Computers, personal

sole proprietorships businesses owned and operated by one individual; the most common form of business organization in the United States

Many local restaurants are sole proprietorships.

Distribution and Use of Profits All profits from a sole proprietorship belong exclusively to the owner. He or she does not have to share them with any partners or stockholders. The owner decides how to use the funds—for expansion of the business, or salary increases, for travel to purchase additional inventory, or to find new customers.

Flexibility and Control of the Business The sole proprietor has complete control over the business and can make decisions on the spot without anyone else's approval. This control allows the owner to respond quickly to competitive business conditions or to changes in the economy. The ability to quickly change prices or products can provide a competitive advantage for the business.

Government Regulation Sole proprietorships have the most freedom from government regulation. Many government regulations—federal, state, and local—apply only to businesses that have a certain number of employees, and securities laws apply only to corporations that issue stock. Nonetheless, sole proprietors must ensure that they follow all laws that do apply to their business. For example, sole proprietorships must be careful to obey employee and consumer protection regulation.

"Sole proprietorships have the most freedom from government regulation."

copiers, scanners, and other high-tech gadgets have been a boon for home-based businesses, permitting them to interact quickly with customers, suppliers, and others. Many independent salespersons and contractors can perform their work using a smart phone or tablet computer as they travel. E-mail and social networks have made it possible for many proprietorships to develop in the services area. Internet connections also allow small businesses to establish websites to promote their products and even to make low-cost long-distance phone calls with voice over Internet protocol (VOIP) technology. One of the most famous services using VOIP is Skype, which allows people to make free calls over the Internet.

Secrecy Sole proprietorships make possible the greatest degree of secrecy. The proprietor, unlike the owners of a partnership or corporation, does not have to discuss publicly his or her operating plans, minimizing the possibility that competitors can obtain trade secrets. Financial reports need not be disclosed, as do the financial reports of publicly owned corporations.

Taxation Profits from sole proprietorships are considered personal income and are taxed at individual tax rates. The owner, therefore, pays one income tax that includes the business and individual income. Another tax benefit is that a sole proprietor is allowed to establish a tax-exempt retirement account or a tax-exempt profit-sharing account. Such accounts are exempt from current income tax, but payments taken after retirement are taxed when they are received.

Closing the Business A sole proprietorship can be dissolved easily. No approval of co-owners or partners is necessary. The only legal condition is that all financial obligations must be paid or resolved.

Disadvantages of Sole Proprietorships

What may be seen as an advantage by one person may turn out to be a disadvantage to another. For profitable businesses managed by capable owners, many of the following factors do

> IT IS USUALLY DIFFICULT FOR A SMALL SOLE PROPRIETORSHIP TO MATCH THE WAGES AND BENEFITS OFFERED BY A LARGE COMPETING CORPORATION BECAUSE THE PROPRIETORSHIP'S PROFITS MAY NOT BE AS HIGH.

not cause problems. On the other hand, proprietors starting out with little management experience and little money are likely to encounter many of the disadvantages.

Unlimited Liability The sole proprietor has unlimited liability in meeting the debts of the business. In other words, if the business cannot pay its creditors, the owner may be forced to use personal, nonbusiness holdings such as a car or a home to pay off the debts. There are only a few states in which houses and homesteads cannot be taken by creditors, even if the proprietor declares bankruptcy. The more wealth an individual has, the greater is the disadvantage of unlimited liability.

Limited Sources of Funds Among the relatively few sources of money available to the sole proprietorship are banks, friends, family, the Small Business Administration, or his or her own funds. The owner's personal financial condition determines his or her credit standing. Additionally, sole proprietorships may have to pay higher interest rates on funds borrowed from banks than do large corporations because they are considered greater risks. Often, the only way a sole proprietor can borrow for business purposes is to pledge a car, a house, other real estate, or other personal assets to guarantee the loan. If the business fails, the owner may lose the personal assets as well as the business. Publicly owned corporations, in contrast, can not only obtain funds from commercial banks but can also sell stocks and bonds to the public to raise money. If a public company goes out of business, the owners do not lose personal assets.

Limited Skills The sole proprietor must be able to perform many functions and possess skills in diverse fields such as management, marketing, finance, accounting, bookkeeping, and personnel management. Business owners can rely on specialized professionals, such as accountants or attorneys, for help or advice. Companies can even hire companies that specialize in janitorial services. For instance, Stratus Building Solutions offers janitorial and cleaning services to businesses. The international franchise offers sustainable cleaning services approved by the Environmental Protection Agency. Many organizations find it more cost-effective to hire companies like Stratus Building Solutions than spend money to hire their own personnel to do the job.[2] In the end, however, it is up to the business owner to make the final decision in all areas of the business.

Lack of Continuity The life expectancy of a sole proprietorship is directly linked to that of the owner and his or her ability to work. The serious illness of the owner could result in failure of the business if competent help cannot be found.

It is difficult to arrange for the sale of a proprietorship and at the same time assure customers that the business will continue to meet their needs. For instance, how does one sell a veterinary practice? A veterinarian's major asset is patients. If the vet dies suddenly, the equipment can be sold, but the patients will not necessarily remain loyal to the office. On the other hand, a veterinarian who wants to retire could take in a younger partner and sell the practice to the partner over time. One advantage to the partnership is that some of the customers are likely to stay with the business, even if ownership changes.

Lack of Qualified Employees It is usually difficult for a small sole proprietorship to match the wages and

VITAL FARMS KNOWS THE VALUE OF ITS CHICKENS

Over the past several decades, there has been a shift from small-scale, independently owned farms to large-scale, corporately owned agricultural farms. However, Vital Farms has been able to maintain a small-scale operation successfully. This S corporation, based out of Austin, Texas, was established to produce humane eggs and poultry as opposed to cage-raised chickens. All of Vital Farm's eggs and poultry are purchased from local family farms, or sole proprietors, whose hens are pastured and given the ability to forage. The company's birds are 100 percent certified organic; their feed is pesticide-free. Vital Farms is also concerned about its more direct impact on the environment. The birds are regularly rotated to different pastures, which helps prevent overgrazing and ensures that the hens are receiving the best possible vegetation. In addition, the company uses 100 percent recycled pulp cartons. Vital Farms supplies hundreds of stores nationwide, including most Whole Foods stores. The business's annual revenues are $4.9 million, proving that it pays to be small-scale and sustainably minded.[3]

partnership a form of business organization defined by the Uniform Partnership Act as "an association of two or more persons who carry on as co-owners of a business for profit"

general partnership a partnership that involves a complete sharing in both the management and the liability of the business

Sole proprietorships have greater difficulty attracting talented employees because larger corporations such as JPMorgan Chase Bank often have higher profits and can pay better wages.

benefits offered by a large competing corporation because the proprietorship's profits may not be as high. In addition, there is little room for advancement within a sole proprietorship, so the owner may have difficulty attracting and retaining qualified employees. On the other hand, the trend of large corporations downsizing and outsourcing tasks has created renewed opportunities for small businesses to acquire well-trained employees.

Taxation Although we listed taxation as an advantage for sole proprietorships, it can also be a disadvantage, depending on the proprietor's income. Under current tax rates, sole proprietors pay a higher marginal tax rate than do small corporations on income of less than $75,000. However, sole proprietorships avoid the double taxation that occurs with corporations. The tax effect often determines whether a sole proprietor chooses to incorporate his or her business.

LO 4-2 Identify two types of partnership and evaluate the advantages and disadvantages of the partnership form of organization.

PARTNERSHIPS

One way to minimize the disadvantages of a sole proprietorship and maximize its advantages is to have more than one owner. Most states have a model law governing partnerships based on the Uniform Partnership Act. This law defines a **partnership** as "an association of two or more persons who carry on as co-owners of a business for profit." Partnerships are the least used form of business (see Figure 4.1). They are typically larger than sole proprietorships but smaller than corporations.

Partnerships can be a fruitful form of business, as long as you follow some basic keys to success, which are outlined in Table 4.2.

Types of Partnership

There are two basic types of partnership: general partnership and limited partnership. A **general partnership** involves a complete sharing in the management of a business. In a general partnership, each partner has unlimited liability for the debts of the business. For example, Cirque du Soleil grew from a group of Quebec street performers, who acted as partners, into a half-billion-dollar global company. Cirque du Soleil, however, ended its 16-year run as a partnership in the year 2000. Guy Laliberté bought out the other principal partner, Daniel Gauthier. Laliberté maintains a controlling share of the company, and Dubai's state-run private equity firm, Istithmar World, along

TABLE 4.2 Keys to Success in Business Partnerships

1. Keep profit sharing and ownership at 50/50, or you have an employer/employee relationship.
2. Partners should have different skill sets to complement one another.
3. Honesty is critical.
4. Must maintain face-to-face communication in addition to phone and e-mail.
5. Maintain transparency, sharing more information over time.
6. Be aware of funding constraints, and do not put yourself in a situation in which neither you nor your partner can secure additional financial support.
7. To be successful, you need experience.
8. Whereas family should be a priority, be careful to minimize the number of associated problems.
9. Do not become too infatuated with "the idea" as opposed to implementation.
10. Couple optimism with realism in sales and growth expectations and planning.

Source: Abstracted from J. Watananbe, "14 Reasons Why 80% of New Business Partnerships Would Fail Within Their First 5 Years of Existence," http://ezinearticles.com/?14-Reasons-Why-80-Percent-Of-New-Business-Partnerships-Would-Fail-Within-Their-First-5-Years-Of-Exis&id=472498.

limited partnership a business organization that has at least one general partner, who assumes unlimited liability, and at least one limited partner, whose liability is limited to his or her investment in the business

articles of partnership legal documents that set forth the basic agreement between partners

with real estate developer Nakheel picked up a 20 percent stake in Cirque du Soleil for more global expansion of permanent show venues.[4] Professionals such as lawyers, accountants, and architects often join together in general partnerships.

A **limited partnership** has at least one general partner, who assumes unlimited liability, and at least one limited partner, whose liability is limited to his or her investment in the business. Limited partnerships exist for risky investment projects in which the chance of loss is great. The general partners accept the risk of loss; the limited partners' losses are limited to their initial investment. Limited partners do not participate in the management of the business but share in the profits in accordance with the terms of a partnership agreement. Usually, the general partner receives a larger share of the profits after the limited partners have received their initial investment back. Popular examples are oil-drilling partnerships and real estate partnerships.

Articles of Partnership

Articles of partnership are legal documents that set forth the basic agreement between partners. Most states require articles of partnership, but even if they are not required, it makes good sense for partners to draw them up. Articles of partnership usually list the money or assets that each partner has contributed (called *partnership capital*), state each partner's individual management role or duty, specify how the profits and losses of the partnership will be divided among the partners, and describe how a partner may leave the partnership as well as any other restrictions that might apply to the agreement. Table 4.3 lists some of the issues and provisions that should be included in articles of partnership.

Advantages of Partnerships

Law firms, accounting firms, and investment firms with several hundred partners have partnership agreements that are quite complicated in comparison with the partnership agreement among two or three people owning a computer repair shop. The advantages must be compared with those offered by other forms of business organization, and not all apply to every partnership.

Ease of Organization Starting a partnership requires little more than drawing up articles of partnership. No legal charters have to be granted, but the name of the business should be registered with the state.

Availability of Capital and Credit When a business has several partners, it has the benefit of a combination of talents and skills and pooled financial resources. Partnerships tend to be larger than sole proprietorships and therefore have greater earning power and better credit ratings. Because

"WHEN A BUSINESS HAS SEVERAL PARTNERS, IT HAS THE BENEFIT OF A COMBINATION OF TALENTS."

TABLE 4.3 Issues and Provisions in Articles of Partnership

1. Name, purpose, location
2. Duration of the agreement
3. Authority and responsibility of each partner
4. Character of partners (general or limited, active or silent)
5. Amount of contribution from each partner
6. Division of profits or losses
7. Salaries of each partner
8. How much each partner is allowed to withdraw
9. Death of partner
10. Sale of partnership interest
11. Arbitration of disputes
12. Required and prohibited actions
13. Absence and disability
14. Restrictive covenants
15. Buying and selling agreements

In 1996, Stanford students Sergey Brin and Larry Page partnered to form the search engine Google as part of a research project. The company was incorporated in 1998 and is now the world's top search engine.

many limited partnerships have been formed for tax purposes rather than for economic profits, the combined income of all U.S. partnerships is quite low, as shown in Figure 4.1. Nevertheless, the professional partnerships of many lawyers, accountants, and banking firms make quite large profits. For instance, the partners in the international law firm Davis Polk & Wardwell LLP take home an average of more than $2 million a year.[5]

Combined Knowledge and Skills Partners in the most successful partnerships acknowledge each other's talents and avoid confusion and conflict by specializing in a particular area of expertise such as marketing, production, accounting, or service. The diversity of skills in a partnership makes it possible for the business to be run by a management team of specialists instead of by a generalist sole proprietor. Co-founders Barry Nalebuff and Seth Goldman credit this diversity as being a key component in the success of their company, Honest Tea. In less than a decade, Honest Tea went from $250,000 to $13.5 million in annual sales and attracted the attention of Coca-Cola. Coca-Cola bought a 40 percent stake in the company.[6] Service-oriented partnerships in fields such as law, financial planning, and accounting may attract customers because clients may think that the service offered by a diverse team is of higher quality than that provided by one person. Larger law firms, for example, often have individual partners who specialize in certain areas of the law—such as family, bankruptcy, corporate, entertainment, and criminal law.

Decision Making Small partnerships can react more quickly to changes in the business environment than can large partnerships and corporations. Such fast reactions are possible because the partners are involved in day-to-day operations and can make decisions quickly after consultation. Large partnerships with hundreds of partners in many states are not common. In those that do exist, decision making is likely to be slow. However, some partnerships have been successful despite their large size. The accounting firm of Baird, Kurtz & Dodson is the 10th largest accounting and advisory firm in the United States, with approximately 250 partners and principals and 1,200 personnel. Some have attributed BKD's success to its strong diversification techniques and ability to operate in different market niches.[7]

Regulatory Controls Like a sole proprietorship, a partnership has fewer regulatory controls affecting its activities than does a corporation. A partnership does not have to file public financial statements with government agencies or send out quarterly financial statements to several thousand owners, as do corporations such as Apple and Ford Motor Co. A partnership does, however, have to abide by all laws relevant to the industry or profession in which it operates as well as state and federal laws relating to hiring and firing, food handling, and so on, just as the sole proprietorship does.

Disadvantages of Partnerships

Partnerships have many advantages compared to sole proprietorships and corporations, but they also have some disadvantages. Limited partners have no voice in the management of the partnership, and they may bear most of the risk of the business while the general partner reaps a larger share of the benefits. There may be a change in the goals and objectives of one partner but not the other, particularly when the partners are multinational organizations. This can cause friction, giving rise to an enterprise that fails to satisfy both parties or even forcing an end to the partnership. Many partnership disputes wind up in court or require outside mediation. A partnership can be jeopardized when two business partners cannot resolve disputes. For instance, Steve Wynn, CEO of Wynn Resorts, had a lawsuit filed against his company by long-time business partner Kazuo Okada. Okada claims that Wynn blocked him from viewing financial records of a $135 million donation that the company gave to the University of Macau. Okada believed the donation might not have constituted an appropriate use of the company's funds.[8] In some cases, the ultimate solution may be dissolving the partnership. Major disadvantages of partnerships include the following.

Unlimited Liability In general partnerships, the general partners have unlimited liability for the debts incurred by the business, just as the sole proprietor has unlimited liability for his or her business. Such unlimited liability can be a distinct disadvantage to one partner if his or her personal financial resources are greater than those of the others. A potential partner should check to make sure that all partners have comparable resources to help the business in time of trouble. This disadvantage is eliminated for limited partners, who can lose only their initial investment.

["All partners are responsible for the business actions of all others."]

Business Responsibility All partners are responsible for the business actions of all others. Partners may have the ability to commit the partnership to a contract without approval of the other partners. A bad decision by one partner may put the

corporation a legal entity, created by the state, whose assets and liabilities are separate from its owners'

stock shares of a corporation that may be bought or sold

dividends profits of a corporation that are distributed in the form of cash payments to stockholders

other partners' personal resources in jeopardy. Personal problems such as a divorce can eliminate a significant portion of one partner's financial resources and weaken the financial structure of the whole partnership.

Life of the Partnership A partnership is terminated when a partner dies or withdraws. In a two-person partnership, if one partner withdraws, the firm's liabilities would be paid off and the assets divided between the partners. Obviously, the partner who wishes to continue in the business would be at a serious disadvantage. The business could be disrupted, financing would be reduced, and the management skills of the departing partner would be lost. The remaining partner would have to find another or reorganize the business as a sole proprietorship. In very large partnerships such as those found in law firms and investment banks, the continuation of the partnership may be provided for in the articles of partnership. The provision may simply state the terms for a new partnership agreement among the remaining partners. In such cases, the disadvantage to the other partners is minimal.

Selling a partnership interest has the same effect as the death or withdrawal of a partner. It is difficult to place a value on a partner's share of the partnership. No public value is placed on the partnership, as there is on publicly owned corporations. What is a law firm worth? What is the local hardware store worth? Coming up with a fair value that all partners can agree to is not easy. Selling a partnership interest is easier if the articles of partnership specify a method of valuation. Even if there is not a procedure for selling one partner's interest, the old partnership must still be dissolved and a new one created. In contrast, in the corporate form of business, the departure of owners has little effect on the financial resources of the business, and the loss of managers does not cause long-term changes in the structure of the organization.

Distribution of Profits Profits earned by the partnership are distributed to the partners in the proportions specified in the articles of partnership. This may be a disadvantage if the division of the profits does not reflect the work each partner puts into the business. You may have encountered this disadvantage while working on a student group project: You may have felt that you did most of the work and that the other students in the group received grades based on your efforts. Even the perception of an unfair profit-sharing agreement may cause tension between the partners, and unhappy partners can have a negative effect on the profitability of the business.

Limited Sources of Funds As with a sole proprietorship, the sources of funds available to a partnership are limited. Because no public value is placed on the business (such as the current trading price of a corporation's stock), potential partners do not know what one partnership share is worth. Moreover, because partnership shares cannot be bought and sold easily in public markets, potential owners may not want to tie up their money in assets that cannot be readily sold on short notice. Accumulating enough funds to operate a national business, especially a business requiring intensive investments in facilities and equipment, can be difficult. Partnerships also may have to pay higher interest rates on funds borrowed from banks than do large corporations because partnerships may be considered greater risks.

Taxation of Partnerships

Partnerships are quasi-taxable organizations. This means that partnerships do not pay taxes when submitting the partnership tax return to the Internal Revenue Service. The tax return simply provides information about the profitability of the organization and the distribution of profits among the partners. Partners must report their share of profits on their individual tax returns and pay taxes at the income tax rate for individuals.

LO 4-3 Describe the corporate form of organization and cite the advantages and disadvantages of corporations.

CORPORATIONS

When you think of a business, you probably think of a huge corporation such as General Electric, Procter & Gamble, or Sony because a large portion of your consumer dollars go to such corporations. A **corporation** is a legal entity, created by the state, whose assets and liabilities are separate from its owners'. As a legal entity, a corporation has many of the rights, duties, and powers of a person, such as the right to receive, own, and transfer property. Corporations can enter into contracts with individuals or with other legal entities, and they can sue and be sued in court.

Corporations account for the majority of all U.S. sales and income. Thus, most of the dollars you spend as a consumer probably go to incorporated businesses (see Figure 4.1). Most corporations are not mega-companies like General Mills or Ford Motor Co.; even small businesses can incorporate. As we shall see later in the chapter, many smaller firms elect to incorporate as S corporations, which operate under slightly different rules and have greater flexibility than do traditional C corporations like General Mills.

Corporations are typically owned by many individuals and organizations who own shares of the business, called **stock** (thus, corporate owners are often called *shareholders* or *stockholders*). Stockholders can buy, sell, give or receive as gifts, or inherit their shares of stock. As owners, the stockholders are entitled to all profits that are left after all the corporation's other obligations have been paid. These profits may be distributed in the form of cash payments called **dividends**. For example, if a corporation earns $100 million after expenses and taxes and decides to pay the owners $40 million in dividends, the stockholders receive 40 percent of the profits in cash dividends. However, not all after-tax profits are paid to stockholders in

corporate charter a legal document that the state issues to a company based on information the company provides in the articles of incorporation

dividends. Some corporations may retain profits to expand the business. For example, Berkshire Hathaway has always retained its earnings and reinvested them for the shareholders. This has resulted in an average 20 percent increase in per share investment over a 40-year period.[9]

Creating a Corporation

A corporation is created, or incorporated, under the laws of the state in which it incorporates. The individuals creating the corporation are known as *incorporators.* Each state has a specific procedure, sometimes called *chartering the corporation,* for incorporating a business. Most states require a minimum of three incorporators; thus, many small businesses can be and are incorporated. Another requirement is that the new corporation's name cannot be similar to that of another business. In most states, a corporation's name must end in "company," "corporation," "incorporated," or "limited" to show that the owners have limited liability. (In this text, however, the word *company* means any organization engaged in a commercial enterprise and can refer to a sole proprietorship, a partnership, or a corporation.)

The incorporators must file legal documents generally referred to as *articles of incorporation* with the appropriate state office (often the secretary of state). The articles of incorporation contain basic information about the business. The following 10 items are found in the Model Business Corporation Act, issued by the American Bar Association, which is followed by most states:

1. Name and address of the corporation.
2. Objectives of the corporation.
3. Classes of stock (common, preferred, voting, nonvoting) and the number of shares for each class of stock to be issued.
4. Expected life of the corporation. (Corporations are usually created to last forever.)
5. Financial capital required at the time of incorporation.
6. Provisions for transferring shares of stock between owners.
7. Provisions for the regulation of internal corporate affairs.
8. Address of the business office registered with the state of incorporation.
9. Names and addresses of the initial board of directors.
10. Names and addresses of the incorporators.

Based on the information in the articles of incorporation, the state issues a **corporate charter** to the company. After securing this charter, the owners hold an organizational meeting at which they establish the corporation's bylaws and elect a board of directors. The bylaws might set up committees of the board of directors and describe the rules and procedures for their operation.

Types of Corporations

If the corporation does business in the state in which it is chartered, it is known as a *domestic corporation.* In other states where the corporation does business, it is known as a *foreign corporation.* If a corporation does business outside the nation in which it is incorporated, it is called an *alien corporation.* A corporation may be privately or publicly owned.

"A corporation may be privately or publicly owned."

VITA COCO: LOVED BY CELEBRITIES, ATHLETES, AND HEALTH-CONSCIOUS CONSUMERS

Vita Coco made its debut in the beverage market during the summer of 2004. Michael Kirban and Ira Liran first learned about coconut water from a couple of Brazilian girls they met at a bar in Manhattan. Liran then went to Brazil, did some research, visited coconut plantations, and decided that it was possible to sell this beverage in America. Not only was it possible; it became a highly sought-after beverage. With celebrity investors knocking on its doors with a desire to purchase shares, Vita Coco grew quickly as a privately held company to become the top coconut-water brand. Although 80 percent of shares are owned by the co-founders and a Belgian investment firm, the other 20 percent are owned by the firm's employees and several celebrity investors. Madonna is one of the firm's most well-known celebrity investors.

Vita Coco's product opened up an alternative to several segments in the beverage industry. Health-conscious consumers like it because it is all natural and provides nutrients inherent in the coconut. Others choose it as an alternative to water for its sweet taste. Athletes are also drinking Vita Coco instead of traditional sports drinks because it offers hydration without making the stomach feel full or upset and because it contains potassium, which prevents muscle cramping. Vita Coca seems well poised to challenge top players in the sports and health beverage industries.[10]

Discussion Questions

1. Why do you think Vita Coco has become so popular?
2. Why might celebrity investors want to purchase shares in Vita Coco?
3. Do you believe Vita Coco will succeed in challenging top players in the sports and health beverage industries?

private corporation a corporation owned by just one or a few people who are closely involved in managing the business

public corporation a corporation whose stock anyone may buy, sell, or trade

A **private corporation** is owned by just one or a few people who are closely involved in managing the business. These people, often a family, own all the corporation's stock, and no stock is sold to the public. Many corporations are quite large, yet remain private, including Cargill, a farm products business. It is the nation's largest private corporation with annual revenues of well over $100 billion.

The snack and food company Mars is privately owned by the Mars family. The company became one of the world's largest candy makers when Mars purchased chewing-gum company Wm. Wrigley Jr. Company in 2008.

Founded at the end of the Civil War, descendents of the original founder have owned equity in the company for more than 140 years.[11] The third-largest privately held company in the United States is Mars, Incorporated. In 1911, Frank C. Mars made the first Mars candies in his Tacoma, Washington kitchen and established Mars' first roots as a confectionery company. In the 1920s, Forrest E. Mars, Sr. joined his father in business and together they launched the MILKY WAY® bar. In 1932, Forrest, Sr. moved to the United Kingdom with a dream of building a business based on the objective of creating a "mutuality of benefits for all stakeholders"—this objective serves as the foundation of Mars, Incorporated today. Based in McLean, Virginia, with operations across 74 countries, Mars has annual net sales of more than $33 billion, six business segments including Petcare, Chocolate, Wrigley, Food, Drinks, Symbioscience, and more than 72,000 Associates worldwide. Mars is now one of the world's leading petcare, chocolate, gum, food and drinks company with 11 billion dollar brands including PEDIGREE®, WHISKAS®, ORBIT®, EXTRA®, UNCLE BENS®, M&M'S®, and SNICKERS®.[12] As a private, family owned business, Mars remains successful to this day, largely because of success of its established iconic brands.[13] Other well-known privately held companies include Chrysler, Publix Supermarkets, Dollar General, and MGM Entertainment. Privately owned corporations are not required to disclose financial information publicly, but they must, of course, pay taxes.

A **public corporation** is one whose stock anyone may buy, sell, or trade. Many of the largest U.S. public corporations have

TABLE 4.4 American Companies with More than Half of Their Revenues from Outside the United States

Company	Description
Caterpillar, Inc.	Designs, manufactures, markets, and sells machinery, engines, and financial products
Dow Chemical	Manufactures chemicals, with products including plastics, oil, and crop technology
General Electric	Operates in the technology infrastructure, energy, capital finance, and consumer and industrial fields, with products including appliances, locomotives, weapons, lighting, and gas
General Motors	Sells automobiles with brands including Chevrolet, Buick, Cadillac, and Isuzu
IBM	Conducts technological research, develops intellectual technology including software and hardware, and offers consulting services
Intel	Manufactures and develops semiconductor chips and microprocessors
McDonald's	Operates second-largest chain of fast-food restaurants worldwide after Subway
Nike	Designs, develops, markets, and sells athletic shoes and clothing
Procter & Gamble	Sells consumer goods with brands including Tide, Bounty, Crest, and Iams
Yum! Brands	Operates and licenses restaurants including Taco Bell, Kentucky Fried Chicken, and Pizza Hut

initial public offering (IPO) selling a corporation's stock on public markets for the first time

quasi-public corporations corporations owned and operated by the federal, state, or local government

nonprofit corporations corporations that focus on providing a service rather than earning a profit but are not owned by a government entity

board of directors a group of individuals, elected by the stockholders to oversee the general operation of the corporation, who set the corporation's long-range objectives

become multinational companies with much of their sales coming from overseas markets. Table 4.4 lists 10 U.S. corporations with more than half of their revenue coming from outside of the United States. Thousands of smaller public corporations in the United States have annual sales under $10 million. In large public corporations such as AT&T, the stockholders are often far removed from the management of the company. In other public corporations, the managers are often the founders and the major shareholders. NASCAR, for example, was founded by William France in 1948, and ever since then his descendents have manned the helm as CEO. Grandson Brian France currently fills the post.[14] *Forbes* Global 2000 companies generate around $36 trillion in revenues, $2.64 trillion in profits, and $149 trillion in assets. They are worth $37 trillion in market value. The United States still has the majority of the Global 2000 companies, but other nations are catching up. The rankings of the Global 2000 span across 62 countries.[15] Publicly owned corporations must disclose financial information to the public under specific laws that regulate the trade of stocks and other securities.

A private corporation that needs more money to expand or to take advantage of opportunities may have to obtain financing by going public through an **initial public offering (IPO)**, that is, becoming a public corporation by selling stock so that it can be traded in public markets. Among much hype, Facebook released its IPO at $38 a share, with a total valuation of $104 billion for the digital media giant. However, afterward, share values fell steeply, leading to losses and allegations that Morgan Stanley and other Wall Street companies had overvalued the firm even though they had cut Facebook's earnings forecasts before the IPO was launched. This led to lawsuits against the underwriters and against the NASDAQ stock market for trading missteps.[16]

Also, privately owned firms are occasionally forced to go public with stock offerings when a major owner dies and the heirs have large estate taxes to pay. The tax payment may be possible only with the proceeds of the sale of stock. This happened to the brewer Adolph Coors Inc. After Adolph Coors died, the business went public, and his family sold shares of stock to the public to pay the estate taxes.

On the other hand, public corporations can be taken private when one or a few individuals (perhaps the management of the firm) purchase all the firm's stock so that it can no longer be sold publicly. Taking a corporation private may be desirable when new owners want to exert more control over the firm or they want to avoid the necessity of public disclosure of future activities for competitive reasons. For example, RCN Corporation, a broadband provider, was purchased by a private equity group, Abry Partners LLC, for about $535 million in cash. Abry's goal with the purchase is to expand its companies, offering broadband and cable service in New York, Boston, and Philadelphia.[17] Taking a corporation private is also one technique for avoiding a takeover by another corporation.

"Taking a corporation private is also one technique for avoiding a takeover by another corporation."

Quasi-public corporations and nonprofits are two types of public corporations. **Quasi-public corporations** are owned and operated by the federal, state, or local government. The focus of these entities is to provide a service to citizens, such as mail delivery, rather than earning a profit. Indeed, many quasi-public corporations operate at a loss. Examples of quasi-public corporations include the National Aeronautics and Space Administration (NASA) and the U.S. Postal Service.

Like quasi-public corporations, **nonprofit corporations** focus on providing a service rather than earning a profit, but they are not owned by a government entity. Organizations such as the Sesame Workshop, the Elks Clubs, the American Lung Association, the American Red Cross, museums, and private schools provide services without a profit motive. To fund their operations and services, nonprofit organizations solicit donations from individuals and companies and grants from the government and other charitable foundations.

Elements of a Corporation

The Board of Directors A **board of directors**, elected by the stockholders to oversee the general operation of the corporation, sets the long-range objectives of the corporation. It is the board's responsibility to ensure that the objectives are achieved on schedule. Board members are legally liable for the mismanagement of the firm or for any misuse of funds. An important duty of the board of directors is to hire corporate officers, such as the president and the chief executive officer (CEO), who are responsible to the directors for the management and daily operations of the firm. The role and expectations of the board of directors took on greater significance after the accounting scandals of the early 2000s and the passage of

Berkshire Hathaway's board includes many well-known businesspeople, including Microsoft founder Bill Gates, former president of Yahoo! Susan Decker, and CEO of NBCUniversal Stephen B. Burke.

the Sarbanes-Oxley Act.[18] As a result, most corporations have restructured how they compensate board directors for their time and expertise.

However, some experts now speculate that Sarbanes-Oxley did little to motivate directors to increase company oversight. One notable case of alleged director misconduct involves a lawsuit filed by the SEC against three directors of DHB Industries. The SEC accused these directors of purposefully ignoring red flags that indicated company misconduct. However, such lawsuits are the exception to the norm. If it cannot be proven that directors did not act in good faith, it is hard for the SEC to develop a case against them.[19] At the same time, the pay rate of directors is rising, and median pay is more than $200,000 a year for directors at the 500 largest companies. Although such pay is meant to attract top-quality directors, concerns exist over whether excessive pay will have unintended consequences. Some believe that pay greater than $200,000 will cause directors to be more complacent and overlook potential misconduct in order to keep their positions.[20]

Directors can be employees of the company *(inside directors)* or people unaffiliated with the company *(outside directors).* Inside directors are usually the officers responsible for running the company. Outside directors are often top executives from other companies, lawyers, bankers, even professors. Directors today are increasingly chosen for their expertise, competence, and ability to bring diverse perspectives to strategic discussions. Outside directors are also thought to bring more independence to the monitoring function because they are not bound by past allegiances, friendships, a current role in the company, or some other issue that may create a conflict of interest. Many of the corporate scandals uncovered in recent years might have been prevented if each of the companies' boards of directors had been better qualified, more knowledgeable, and more independent.

There is a growing shortage of available and qualified board members. Boards are increasingly telling their own CEOs that they should be focused on serving their company, not serving on outside boards. Because of this, the average CEO sits on fewer than one outside board. This represents a decline from a decade ago when the average was two. Because many CEOs are

SODASTREAM CHALLENGES TOP DOGS OF THE SODA INDUSTRY

Daniel Birnbaum, CEO of SodaStream, sees plastic bottles as a thing of the past. SodaStream manufactures home carbonation systems that allow consumers to make their own sodas. The home carbonation systems include a reusable bottle, which cuts back on the plastic ending up in landfills. Although SodaStream controls less than 1 percent of the global soda market, Birnbaum hopes that one day SodaStream will be its leader. The company sells its products in retailers ranging from Sears and Walmart to Bloomingdale's and Williams-Sonoma.

SodaStream became a public corporation in 2010 with an initial public offering of $109 million in the United States. Its share price has been as high as $79.92 but has fluctuated greatly as the firm continues to be the underdog in a fierce competition between the two heavyweight corporations—PepsiCo and Coca-Cola. PepsiCo and Coca-Cola are becoming increasingly green, posing challenges for SodaStream and its green message. However, SodaStream continues to be visibly critical of the amount of waste created by beverage companies and was even given a cease-and-desist letter from Coca-Cola regarding one of its marketing campaigns. The campaign featured a cage full of discarded plastic and canned sodas collected from dumpsites—which included Coca-Cola products. Birnbaum's response was to point to the massive amounts of litter Coca-Cola has produced worldwide. He also implied that if Coke wants to claim any of its discarded trademark waste, it should be forced to claim all of it. Although SodaStream has a long way to go, it is clear the corporation is prepared to take on the U.S. soda titans.[21]

Discussion Questions

1. Why do you think SodaStream's stock has fluctuated greatly?
2. How has Daniel Birnbaum differentiated SodaStream from its competitors?
3. Who do you think is SodaStream's target market?

turning down outside positions, many companies have taken steps to ensure that boards have experienced directors. They have increased the mandatory retirement age to 72 or older, and some have raised it to 75 or even older. Minimizing the amount of overlap between directors sitting on different boards helps to limit conflicts of interest and provides for independence in decision making.

Stock Ownership Corporations issue two types of stock: preferred and common. Owners of **preferred stock** are a special class of owners because, although they generally do not have any say in running the company, they have a claim to profits before any other stockholders do. Other stockholders do not receive any dividends unless the preferred stockholders have already been paid. Dividend payments on preferred stock are usually a fixed percentage of the initial issuing price (set by the board of directors). For example, if a share of preferred stock originally cost $100 and the dividend rate was stated at 7.5 percent, the dividend payment will be $7.50 per share per year. Dividends are usually paid quarterly. Most preferred stock carries a cumulative claim to dividends. This means that if the company does not pay preferred-stock dividends in one year because of losses, the dividends accumulate to the next year. Such dividends unpaid from previous years must also be paid to preferred stockholders before other stockholders can receive any dividends.

Owners of preferred stock have first claim to company profits.

Although owners of **common stock** do not get such preferential treatment with regard to dividends, they do get some say in the operation of the corporation. Their ownership gives them the right to vote for members of the board of directors and on other important issues. Common stock dividends may vary according to the profitability of the business, and some corporations do not issue dividends at all, but instead plow their profits back into the company to fund expansion.

preferred stock
a special type of stock whose owners, though not generally having a say in running the company, have a claim to profits before other stockholders do

common stock
stock whose owners have voting rights in the corporation, yet do not receive preferential treatment regarding dividends

Common stockholders are the voting owners of a corporation. They are usually entitled to one vote per share of common stock. During an annual stockholders' meeting, common stockholders elect a board of directors. Some boards find it easier than others to attract high-profile individuals. For example, the board of Procter & Gamble consists of Ernesto Zedillo, former president of Mexico; Kenneth I. Chenault, CEO of the American Express Company; Scott Cook, founder of Intuit Inc.; as well as the CEO of Archer Daniels Midland, the CEO of Boeing, and the CEO of Hewlett-Packard.[22] Because they can choose the board of directors, common stockholders have some say in how the company will operate. Common stockholders may vote by *proxy,* which is a written authorization by which stockholders assign their voting privilege to someone else, who then votes for his or her choice at the stockholders' meeting. It is a normal practice for management to request proxy statements from shareholders who are not planning to attend the annual meeting. Most owners do not attend annual meetings of the very large companies, such as Westinghouse or Boeing, unless they live in the city where the meeting is held.

> "Common stockholders are the voting owners of a corporation."

Common stockholders have another advantage over preferred shareholders. In most states, when the corporation decides to sell new shares of common stock in the marketplace, common stockholders have the first right, called a *preemptive right,* to purchase new shares of the stock from the corporation. A preemptive right is often included in the articles of incorporation. This right is important because it allows stockholders to purchase new shares to maintain their original positions. For example, if a stockholder owns 10 percent of a corporation that decides to issue new shares, that stockholder has the right to buy enough of the new shares to retain the 10 percent ownership.

> "OF ALL THE FORMS OF BUSINESS ORGANIZATION, THE PUBLIC CORPORATION FINDS IT EASIEST TO RAISE MONEY."

Advantages of Corporations

Because a corporation is a separate legal entity, it has some very specific advantages over other forms of ownership. The biggest advantage may be the limited liability of the owners.

Limited Liability Because the corporation's assets (money and resources) and liabilities (debts and other obligations) are separate from its owners', in most cases the stockholders are not held responsible for the firm's debts if it fails. Their liability or potential loss is limited to the amount of their original investment. Although a creditor can sue a corporation for not paying its debts, even forcing the corporation into bankruptcy, it cannot make the stockholders pay the corporation's debts out of their personal assets. Occasionally, the owners of a private corporation may pledge personal assets to secure a loan for the corporation; this would be most unusual for a public corporation.

Ease of Transfer of Ownership Stockholders can sell or trade shares of stock to other people without causing the termination of the corporation, and they can do this without the prior approval of other shareholders. The transfer of ownership (unless it is a majority position) does not affect the daily or long-term operations of the corporation.

Perpetual Life A corporation usually is chartered to last forever unless its articles of incorporation stipulate otherwise. The existence of the corporation is unaffected by the death or withdrawal of any of its stockholders. It survives until the owners sell it or liquidate its assets. However, in some cases, bankruptcy ends a corporation's life. Bankruptcies occur when companies are unable to compete and earn profits. Eventually, uncompetitive businesses must close or seek protection from creditors in bankruptcy court while the business tries to reorganize.

BP is the sixth-largest corporation in the world.

External Sources of Funds Of all the forms of business organization, the public corporation finds it easiest to raise money. When a corporation needs to raise more money, it can sell more stock shares or issue bonds (corporate "IOUs," which pledge to repay debt), attracting funds from anywhere in the United States and even overseas. The larger a corporation becomes, the more sources of financing are available to it. We take a closer look at some of these in Chapter 15.

Expansion Potential Because large public corporations can find long-term financing readily, they can easily expand into national and international markets. And, as a legal entity, a corporation can enter into contracts without as much difficulty as a partnership.

Disadvantages of Corporations

Corporations have some distinct disadvantages resulting from tax laws and government regulation.

Double Taxation As a legal entity, the corporation must pay taxes on its income just like you do. When after-tax corporate profits are paid out as dividends to the stockholders, the dividends are taxed a second time as part of the individual owner's income. This process creates double taxation for the stockholders of dividend-paying corporations. Double taxation does not occur with the other forms of business organization.

Forming a Corporation The formation of a corporation can be costly. A charter must be obtained, and this usually requires the services of an attorney and payment of legal fees. Filing fees ranging from $25 to $150 must be paid to the state that awards the corporate charter, and certain states require that an annual fee be paid to maintain the charter. Today, a number of Internet services such as LegalZoom.com and Business.com make it easier, quicker, and less costly to form a corporation. However, in making it easier for people to form businesses without expert consultation, these services have increased the risk that people will not choose the kind of organizational form that is right for them. Sometimes, one form works better than another. The business's founders may fail to take into account disadvantages, such as double taxation with corporations.

joint venture a partnership established for a specific project or for a limited time

S corporation corporation taxed as though it were a partnership with restrictions on shareholders

limited liability company (LLC) form of ownership that provides limited liability and taxation like a partnership but places fewer restrictions on members

cooperative (co-op) an organization composed of individuals or small businesses that have banded together to reap the benefits of belonging to a larger organization

Disclosure of Information Corporations must make information available to their owners, usually through an annual report to shareholders. The annual report contains financial information about the firm's profits, sales, facilities and equipment, and debts, as well as descriptions of the company's operations, products, and plans for the future. Public corporations must also file reports with the Securities and Exchange Commission (SEC), the government regulatory agency that regulates securities such as stocks and bonds. The larger the firm, the more data the SEC requires. Because all reports filed with the SEC are available to the public, competitors can access them. Additionally, complying with securities laws takes time.

Employee–Owner Separation Many employees are not stockholders of the company for which they work. This separation of owners and employees may cause employees to feel that their work benefits only the owners. Employees without an ownership stake do not always see how they fit into the corporate picture and may not understand the importance of profits to the health of the organization. If managers are part owners but other employees are not, management–labor relations take on a different, sometimes difficult, aspect from those in partnerships and sole proprietorships. However, this situation is changing as more corporations establish employee stock ownership plans (ESOPs), which give shares of the company's stock to its employees. Such plans build a partnership between employee and employer and can boost productivity because they motivate employees to work harder so that they can earn dividends from their hard work as well as from their regular wages.

DID YOU KNOW?

The first corporation with a net income of more than $1 billion in one year was General Motors, with a net income in 1955 of $1,189,477,082.[23]

OTHER TYPES OF OWNERSHIP

In this section, we take a brief look at joint ventures, S corporations, limited liability companies, and cooperatives—businesses formed for special purposes.

Joint Ventures

A **joint venture** is a partnership established for a specific project or for a limited time. The partners in a joint venture may be individuals or organizations, as in the case of the international joint ventures discussed in Chapter 3. Control of a joint venture may be shared equally, or one partner may control decision making. Joint ventures are especially popular in situations that call for large investments, such as extraction of natural resources and the development of new products. For example, TEMCO LLC is a joint venture between Cargill and wholesale agricultural products company CHS Inc. The two companies are using the joint venture to capitalize on global opportunities for grain exporting. The joint venture was later expanded to export food grains to markets in Asia and other Pacific countries.[24]

S Corporations

An **S corporation** is a form of business ownership that is taxed as though it were a partnership. Net profits or losses of the corporation pass to the owners, thus eliminating double taxation. The benefit of limited liability is retained. Formally known as Subchapter S Corporations, they have become a popular form of business ownership for entrepreneurs and represent almost half of all corporate filings.[25] Vista Bank Texas is an S Corporation, and the owners get the benefits of tax advantages and limited liability. Advantages of S corporations include the simple method of taxation, the limited liability of shareholders, perpetual life, and the ability to shift income and appreciation to others. Disadvantages include restrictions on the number (100) and types (individuals, estates, and certain trusts) of shareholders and the difficulty of formation and operation.

Limited Liability Companies

A **limited liability company (LLC)** is a form of business ownership that provides limited liability, as in a corporation, but is taxed like a partnership. Although relatively new in the United States, LLCs have existed for many years abroad. Professionals such as lawyers, doctors, and engineers often use the LLC form of ownership. Many consider the LLC a blend of the best characteristics of corporations, partnerships, and sole proprietorships. One of the major reasons for the LLC form of ownership is to protect the members' personal assets in case of lawsuits. LLCs are flexible, simple to run, and do not require the members to hold meetings, keep minutes, or make resolutions, all of which are necessary in corporations. For example, Segway, which markets the Segway Human Transporter, is a limited liability company.

Cooperatives

Another form of organization in business is the **cooperative** or **co-op**, an organization composed of individuals or small

> "COMPANIES LARGE AND SMALL ACHIEVE GROWTH AND IMPROVE PROFITABILITY BY EXPANDING THEIR OPERATIONS, OFTEN BY DEVELOPING AND SELLING NEW PRODUCTS OR SELLING CURRENT PRODUCTS TO NEW GROUPS OF CUSTOMERS IN DIFFERENT GEOGRAPHIC AREAS."

REI is organized as a consumer cooperative.

businesses that have banded together to reap the benefits of belonging to a larger organization. Oglethorpe Power Corp., for example, is a power cooperative based in the suburbs of Atlanta;[26] Ocean Spray is a cooperative of cranberry farmers. REI operates a bit differently because it is owned by consumers rather than farmers or small businesses. A co-op is set up not to make money as an entity but so that its members can become more profitable or save money. Co-ops are generally expected to operate without profit or to create only enough profit to maintain the co-op organization.

Many cooperatives exist in small farming communities. The co-op stores and markets grain; orders large quantities of fertilizer, seed, and other supplies at discounted prices; and reduces costs and increases efficiency with good management. A co-op can purchase supplies in large quantities and pass the savings on to its members. It also can help distribute the products of its members more efficiently than each could on an individual basis. A cooperative can advertise its members' products and thus generate demand. Ace Hardware, a cooperative of independent hardware store owners, allows its members to share in the savings that result from buying supplies in large quantities; it also provides advertising, which individual members might not be able to afford on their own.

LO 4-4 Define and debate the advantages and disadvantages of mergers, acquisitions, and leveraged buyouts.

TRENDS IN BUSINESS OWNERSHIP: MERGERS AND ACQUISITIONS

Companies large and small achieve growth and improve profitability by expanding their operations, often by developing and selling new products or selling current products to new groups of customers in different geographic areas. Such growth, when carefully planned and controlled, is usually beneficial to the firm and ultimately helps it reach its goal of enhanced profitability. But companies also grow by merging with or purchasing other companies.

A **merger** occurs when two companies (usually corporations) combine to form a new company. An **acquisition** occurs when one company purchases another, generally by buying most of its stock. The acquired company may become a subsidiary of the buyer, or its operations and assets may be merged with those of the buyer. The government sometimes scrutinizes mergers and acquisitions in an attempt to protect customers from monopolistic practices. For example, the decision to authorize Whole Foods' acquisition of Wild Oats was carefully analyzed, as was the merger of Sirius and XM Satellite Radio. The United States filed a lawsuit to block the merger of Anheuser-Busch InBev IV, makers of the popular Bud Light beer, with Grupo Modelo SAB, which owns the Corona brand. The U.S. government feared the merger would give the larger company too much power over pricing.[27] Acquisitions sometimes involve the purchase of a division or some other part of a company rather than the entire company. The late 1990s saw a merger and acquisition frenzy, which is slowing in the 21st century (see Table 4.5).

merger the combination of two companies (usually corporations) to form a new company

acquisition the purchase of one company by another, usually by buying its stock

US Airways and American Airlines announced a merger to form a more competitive global airline. The merger would cost $11 billion.

When firms that make and sell similar products to the same customers merge, it is known as a *horizontal merger,* as when Martin Marietta and Lockheed, both defense contractors, merged to form Lockheed Martin. Horizontal mergers, however, reduce the number of corporations competing within an industry, and for this reason they are usually reviewed carefully by federal regulators before the merger is allowed to proceed.

When companies operating at different but related levels of an industry merge, it is known as a *vertical merger.* In many instances, a vertical merger results when one corporation merges with one of its customers or suppliers. For example, if Burger King were to purchase a large Idaho potato farm—to ensure a ready supply of potatoes for its french fries—a vertical merger would result.

A *conglomerate merger* results when two firms in unrelated industries merge. For example, the purchase of Sterling Drug, a pharmaceutical firm, by Eastman Kodak, best-known for its films and cameras, represents a conglomerate merger because the two companies are of different industries. (Kodak later sold Sterling Drug to a pharmaceutical company.)

When a company (or an individual), sometimes called a *corporate raider,* wants to acquire or take over another company, it first offers to buy some or all of the other company's stock at a premium over its current price in a *tender offer.* Most such offers are friendly, with both groups agreeing to the proposed deal, but some are hostile, when the second company does not want to be taken over. Openwave Systems Inc. adopted a poison pill plan to discourage hostile takeovers. (A poison pill is an attempt to make a takeover less attractive to a potential acquirer.) Openwave's plan is set to go off if an outside company acquires 4.99 percent of Openwave's stock. In that case, shareholders would be given the ability to gain more shares, which in turn would dilute the stock ownership of the acquiring company.[28]

To head off a hostile takeover attempt, a threatened company's managers may use one or more of several techniques. They may ask stockholders not to sell to the raider; file a lawsuit in an effort to abort the takeover; institute a *poison pill* (in which the firm allows stockholders to buy more shares of stock at

TABLE 4.5 Major Mergers and Acquisitions Worldwide, 2000–2011

Rank	Year	Acquirer	Target	Transaction Value (in millions of U.S. dollars)
1	2000	America Online Inc. (AOL) (*Merger*)	Time Warner	$164,747
2	2000	Glaxo Wellcome Plc.	SmithKline Beecham Plc.	75,961
3	2004	Royal Dutch Petroleum Co.	Shell Transport & Trading Co.	74,559
4	2006	AT&T Inc.	BellSouth Corporation	72,671
5	2001	Comcast Corporation	AT&T Broadband & Internet Svcs.	72,041
6	2004	JPMorgan Chase & Co.	Bank One Corporation	58,761
7	2010	Kraft	Cadbury	19,500
8	2008	Bank of America	Countrywide	4,000
9	2008	JPMorgan Chase & Co.	Bear Stearns Companies Inc.	1,100
10	2011	Southwest Airlines	AirTran Holdings	1,000

Unless noted, deal was an acquisition.

Sources: Institute of Mergers, Acquisitions and Alliances Research, *Thomson Financial,* www.imaa-institute.org/en/publications+mergers+acquisitions+m&a.php#Reports; "JPMorgan Chase Completes Bear Stearns Acquisition," JPMorganChase News Release, May 31, 2008, www.bearstearns.com/includes/pdfs/PressRelease_BSC_31May08.pdf; David Mildenberg and Guy Beaudin, "Kraft Acquires Cadbury," *Bloomberg Businessweek,* January 3, 2010, www.businessweek.com/managing/content/feb2010/ca2010028_928488.htm; "Southwest Completes Purchase of Orlando-Based AirTran," *Orlando Sentinel,* May 2, 2011, http://articles.orlandosentinel.com/2011-05-02/business/os-southwest-airtran-reuters-update2-20110502_1_southwest-executive-vice-president-southwest-brand-airtran-holdings.

leveraged buyout (LBO) a purchase in which a group of investors borrows money from banks and other institutions to acquire a company (or a division of one), using the assets of the purchased company to guarantee repayment of the loan

prices lower than the current market value) or *shark repellant* (in which management requires a large majority of stockholders to approve the takeover); or seek a *white knight* (a more acceptable firm that is willing to acquire the threatened company). In some cases, management may take the company private or even take on more debt so that the heavy debt obligation will scare off the raider.

In a **leveraged buyout (LBO)**, a group of investors borrows money from banks and other institutions to acquire a company (or a division of one), using the assets of the purchased company to guarantee repayment of the loan. In some LBOs, as much as 95 percent of the buyout price is paid with borrowed money, which eventually must be repaid.

Because of the explosion of mergers, acquisitions, and leveraged buyouts in the 1980s and 1990s, financial journalists coined the term *merger mania.* Many companies joined the merger mania simply to enhance their own operations by consolidating them with the operations of other firms. Mergers and acquisitions enabled these companies to gain a larger market share in their industries, acquire valuable assets such as new products or plants and equipment, and lower their costs. Mergers also represent a means of making profits quickly, as was the case during the 1980s when many companies' stock was undervalued. Quite simply, such companies represent a bargain to other companies that can afford to buy them. Additionally, deregulation of some industries has permitted consolidation of firms within those industries for the first time, as is the case in the banking and airline industries.

Some people view mergers and acquisitions favorably, pointing out that they boost corporations' stock prices and market

SO YOU'D LIKE // to Start a Business /

If you have a good idea and want to turn it into a business, you are not alone. Small businesses are popping up all over the United States, and the concept of entrepreneurship is hot. Entrepreneurs seek opportunities and creative ways to make profits. Business emerges in a number of organizational forms, each with its own advantages and disadvantages. Sole proprietorships are the most common form of business organization in the U.S. They tend to be small businesses and can take pretty much any form—anything from a hair salon to a scuba shop, from an organic produce provider to a financial advisor. Proprietorships are everywhere serving consumers' wants and needs. Proprietorships have a big advantage in that they tend to be simple to manage—decisions get made quickly when the owner and the manager are the same person, and they are fairly simple and inexpensive to set up. Rules vary by state, but at most all you will need is a license from the state.

Many people have been part of a partnership at some point in their life. Group work in school is an example of a partnership. If you ever worked as a DJ on the weekend with your friend and split the profits, then you have experienced a partnership. Partnerships can be either general or limited. General partners have unlimited liability and share completely in the management, debts, and profits of the business. Limited partners, on the other hand, consist of at least one general partner and one or more limited partners who do not participate in the management of the company but share in the profits. This form of partnership is used more often in risky investments in which the limited partner stands only to lose his or her initial investment. Real estate limited partnerships are an example of how investors can minimize their financial exposure, given the poor performance of the real estate market in recent years. Although it has its advantages, partnership is the least used form of business. Part of the reason is that all partners are responsible for the actions and decisions of all other partners, whether or not all of the partners were involved. Usually, partners will have to write up an articles of partnership that outlines respective responsibilities in the business. Even in states where it is not required, it is a good idea to draw up this document as a way to cement each partner's role and hopefully minimize conflict. Unlike a corporation, proprietorships and partnerships both expire upon the death of one or more of those involved.

Corporations tend to be larger businesses but do not need to be. A corporation can consist of nothing more than a small group of family members. To become a corporation, you will have to file in the state under which you wish to incorporate. Each state has its own procedure for incorporation, meaning there are no general guidelines to follow. You can make your corporation private or public, meaning the company issues stocks, and shareholders are the owners. Although incorporating is a popular form of organization because it gives the company an unlimited lifespan and limited liability (meaning that if your business fails, you cannot lose personal funds to make up for losses), there is a downside: You will be taxed as a corporation and as an individual, resulting in double taxation. No matter what form of organization suits your business idea best, there is a world of options out there for you if you want to be or experiment with being an entrepreneur.

learn, practice, apply knowledge for starting a business!

M: Business **was developed just for you—students on the go who need information packaged in a concise yet interesting format with multiple learning options.**

Check out the book's website to:

- **Consider the advantages and disadvantages of partnerships. (Solve the Dilemma)**
- **Consider the advantages and disadvantages of corporations. (Build Your Skills)**
- **Consider the advantages and disadvantages of sole proprietorships. (Build Your Skills)**
- **Determine which business organization to choose for different situations. (Build Your Skills)**

While you are there, don't forget to enhance your skills. Practice and apply your knowledge, review the practice exercises, Student PPT® slides, and quizzes to review and apply chapter concepts. Additionally, *Connect® Business* is available for *M: Business*.

www.mhhe.com/ferrellm4e

value, to the benefit of their stockholders. In many instances, mergers enhance a company's ability to meet foreign competition in an increasingly global marketplace. Additionally, companies that are victims of hostile takeovers generally streamline their operations, reduce unnecessary staff, cut costs, and otherwise become more efficient with their operations, which benefits their stockholders whether or not the takeover succeeds.

Critics, however, argue that mergers hurt companies because they force managers to focus their efforts on avoiding takeovers rather than managing effectively and profitably. Some companies have taken on a heavy debt burden to stave off a takeover, later to be forced into bankruptcy when economic downturns left them unable to handle the debt. Mergers and acquisitions also can damage employee morale and productivity as well as the quality of the companies' products.

Many mergers have been beneficial for all involved; others have had damaging effects for the companies, their employees, and customers. No one can say whether mergers will continue to slow, but many experts say the utilities, telecommunications, financial services, natural resources, computer hardware and software, gaming, managed health care, and technology industries are likely targets. ■

TEAM EXERCISE

Form groups and find examples of mergers and acquisitions. Mergers can be broken down into traditional mergers, horizontal mergers, vertical mergers, and conglomerate mergers. When companies are found, note how long the merger or acquisition took, if there were any requirements by the government before approval of the merger or acquisition, and if any failed mergers or acquisitions were found that did not achieve government approval. Report your findings to the class and explain what the companies hoped to gain from the merger or acquisition.

chapter five

small business, entrepreneurship, + franchising

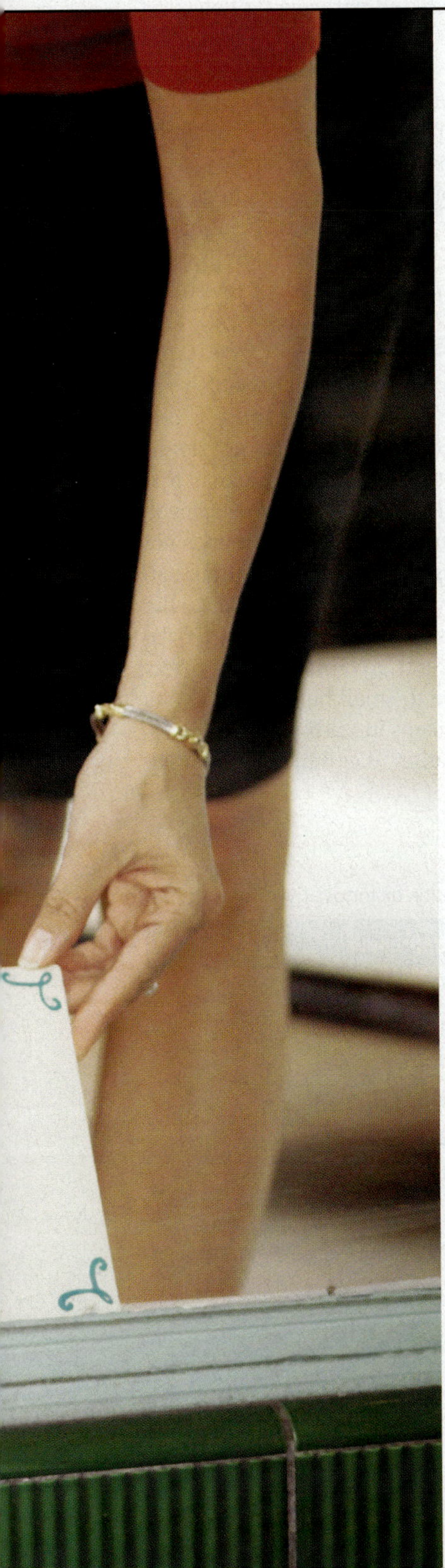

Although many business students go to work for large corporations upon graduation, others may choose to start their own business or to find employment opportunities in small organizations with 500 or fewer employees. Small businesses employ more than half of all private-sector employees.[1] Each small business represents the vision of its owners to succeed through providing new or better products. Small businesses are the heart of the U.S. economic and social system because they offer opportunities and demonstrate the freedom of people to make their own destinies. Today, the entrepreneurial spirit is growing around the world, from Russia and China to India, Germany, Brazil, and Mexico. For instance, even though China remains a communist country, private companies employ more than 90 percent of the country's workers. However, the state owns shares in many of these businesses.[2]

This chapter surveys the world of entrepreneurship and small business. First we define entrepreneurship and small business and examine the role of small business in the American economy. Then we explore the advantages and disadvantages of small-business ownership and analyze why small businesses succeed or fail. Next, we discuss how an entrepreneur goes about starting a business and the challenges facing small businesses today. Finally, we look at entrepreneurship in larger organizations. ■

LEARNING OBJECTIVES

After reading this chapter, you will be able to:

- **LO 5-1** Define entrepreneurship and small business.
- **LO 5-2** Investigate the importance of small business in the U.S. economy and why certain fields attract small business.
- **LO 5-3** Specify the advantages of small-business ownership.
- **LO 5-4** Summarize the disadvantages of small-business ownership and analyze why many small businesses fail.
- **LO 5-5** Describe how you go about starting a small business and what resources are needed.
- **LO 5-6** Evaluate the demographic, technological, and economic trends that are affecting the future of small business.
- **LO 5-7** Explain why many large businesses are trying to "think small."

enterpreneurship the process of creating and managing a business to achieve desired objectives

small business any independently owned and operated business that is not dominant in its competitive area and does not employ more than 500 people

Small Business Administration (SBA) an independent agency of the federal government that offers managerial and financial assistance to small businesses

LO 5-1 Define entrepreneurship and small business.

THE NATURE OF ENTREPRENEURSHIP AND SMALL BUSINESS

In Chapter 1, we defined an entrepreneur as a person who risks his or her wealth, time, and effort to develop for profit an innovative product or way of doing something. **Entrepreneurship** is the process of creating and managing a business to achieve desired objectives. Many large businesses you may recognize (Levi Strauss and Co., Procter & Gamble, McDonald's, Dell Computers, Microsoft, and Google) all began as small businesses based on the visions of their founders. Some entrepreneurs who start small businesses have the ability to see emerging trends; in response, they create a company to provide a product that serves customer needs. For example, rather than inventing a major new technology, an innovative company may take advantage of technology to create new markets, such as Amazon.com. Or it may offer a familiar product that has been improved or placed in a unique retail environment, such as Starbucks and its coffee shops. A company may innovate by focusing on a particular market segment and delivering a combination of features that consumers in that segment could not find anywhere else. For instance, Patagonia creates apparel using organic cotton and other sustainable materials, which appeals to consumers who care about the environment.

Of course, smaller businesses do not have to evolve into such highly visible companies to be successful, but those entrepreneurial efforts that result in rapidly growing businesses gain visibility along with success. Entrepreneurs who have achieved success, like Michael Dell (Dell Computers), Bill Gates (Microsoft), Larry Page and Sergey Brin (Google), and the late Steve Jobs (Apple) are some of the most well known. Table 5.1 lists some of the greatest entrepreneurs of the past few decades.

The entrepreneurship movement is accelerating, and many new, smaller businesses are emerging. Technology once available only to the largest firms can now be obtained by a small business. Websites, podcasts, online videos, social media, cell phones, and even expedited delivery services enable small businesses to be more competitive with today's giant corporations. Small businesses can also form alliances with other companies to produce and sell products in domestic and global markets.

Another growing trend among small businesses is social entrepreneurship. *Social entrepreneurs* are individuals who use entrepreneurship to address social problems. Social entrepreneurs have the same skill sets and operate by the same principles as other entrepreneurs but view their organizations as vehicles to create social change. Although these entrepreneurs often start their own nonprofit organizations, they can also operate for-profit organizations committed to solving social issues. CEO of TOMS Shoes Blake Mycoskie is an example of a social entrepreneur who founded the firm with the purpose to donate one pair of shoes to a child in need for every pair of shoes sold to consumers. Muhammad Yunus, founder of micro-lending organization Grameen Bank, is another example of a social entrepreneur. Yunus seeks to combat poverty by providing small loans to low-income individuals to start their own businesses.

What Is a Small Business?

This question is difficult to answer because smallness is relative. In this book, we will define a **small business** as any independently owned and operated business that is not dominant in its competitive area and does not employ more than 500 people. A local Mexican restaurant may be the most patronized Mexican restaurant in your community, but because it does not dominate the restaurant industry as a whole, the restaurant can be considered a small business. This definition is similar to the one used by the **Small Business Administration (SBA)**, an independent agency of the federal government that offers managerial and financial assistance to small businesses. On its website, the SBA outlines the first steps in starting a small business and offers a wealth of information to current and potential small-business owners.

TABLE 5.1 Great Entrepreneurs of Innovative Companies

Company	Entrepreneur
Hewlett-Packard	Bill Hewlett, David Packard
Walt Disney Productions	Walt Disney
Starbucks	Howard Schultz
Amazon.com	Jeff Bezos
Dell	Michael Dell
Microsoft	Bill Gates
Apple	Steve Jobs
Walmart	Sam Walton
Google	Larry Page, Sergey Brin
Ben & Jerry's	Ben Cohen, Jerry Greenfield
Ford	Henry Ford
General Electric	Thomas Edison

The Role of Small Business in the American Economy

No matter how you define a small business, one fact is clear: They are vital to the American economy. As you can see in Table 5.2, more than 99 percent of all U.S. firms are classified as small businesses, and they employ 50 percent of private workers. Small firms are also important as exporters, representing 97.5 percent of U.S. exporters of goods and contributing 31 percent of the value of exported goods.[3] In addition, small businesses are largely responsible for fueling job creation and innovation. Small businesses also provide opportunities for minorities and women to succeed in business. Women-owned businesses are responsible for more than 23 million American jobs and contribute almost $3 trillion to the national economy. Women own more than 8 million businesses nationwide, with great success in the professional services, retail, communication, and administrative industries.[4] Minority-owned businesses have been growing faster than other classifiable firms as well, representing 21.3 percent of all small businesses. The number of minority-owned businesses is increasing at a rate of 30 percent, even higher than for women-owned firms. For example, Sacred Power is a Native American–owned power and telecommunications company that generates solar, thermal, and wind energy. As a small business, Sacred Power produces and sells alternative energy to larger power companies for distribution to consumers around the Southwest.

Job Creation The energy, creativity, and innovative abilities of small-business owners have resulted in jobs for many people. In fact, in the past 17 years, 65 percent of net new jobs annually were created by small businesses.[5] Table 5.3 indicates that 99.7 percent of all businesses employ fewer than 500 people. Businesses employing 19 or fewer people account for 90 percent of all businesses.[6]

Many small businesses today are being started because of encouragement from larger ones. Many new jobs are also created by big-company/small-company alliances. Whether through formal joint ventures, supplier relationships, or product or marketing cooperative projects, the rewards of collaborative relationships are creating many jobs for small-business owners and their employees. In India, many small information technology (IT) firms provide IT services to global markets. Because of lower costs, international companies often can find Indian businesses to provide their information-processing solutions.[7]

TABLE 5.2 Importance of Small Businesses to Our Economy

Small firms represent 99.7 percent of all employer firms.
Small firms have generated 65 percent of net new jobs over the past 17 years.
Small firms hire approximately 43 percent of high-tech workers (such as scientists, engineers, computer programmers, and others).
Small firms produce 13 times more patents per employee than large patenting firms.
Small firms employ half of all private-sector employees.
Small firms pay 44 percent of the total U.S. private payroll.

Source: "FAQs," U.S. Small Business Administration, http://web.sba.gov/faqs/faqIndexAll.cfm?areaid=24.

TABLE 5.3 Number of Firms by Employment Size

Firm Size	Number of Firms	Percentage of All Firms
0–19 employees	5,160,404	90
20–99 employees	475,125	8.3
100–499 employees	81,773	1.4
500+ employees	17,236	0.3

Source: "Statistics of U.S. Businesses (SUSB)," *Statistics of U.S. Businesses,* http://www.census.gov/econ/susb/index.html.

Innovation Perhaps one of the most significant strengths of small businesses is their ability to innovate and to bring significant benefits to customers. Small firms produce more than half of all innovations. Among the important 20th-century innovations by U.S. small firms are the airplane, the audio tape recorder, fiber-optic examining equipment, the heart valve, the optical scanner, the pacemaker, the personal computer, soft contact lenses, the Internet, and the zipper. Not all innovations are based on new technology. Consider Oprah Winfrey's success. She developed her own brand image and media production company. She went from having nothing to amassing a fortune of $2.3 billion as one of the most recognizable figures in global media. After 26 years on her CBS talk show, she created the Oprah Winfrey Network.[8]

The innovation of successful firms takes many forms. For instance, small firms make up approximately 52 percent of home-based businesses and 2 percent of franchises. Many of today's largest businesses started off as small firms that used innovation to achieve success.[9] Small businessman Ray Kroc found a new way to sell hamburgers and turned his ideas into one of the most successful fast-food franchises in the world—McDonald's. Small businesses have become an integral part of our lives. James Dyson's name is synonymous with high-quality vacuum cleaners. Today, his more than $1 billion company produces a bagless vacuum cleaner that commands 25 percent of the U.S. market. However, it took a lot of work to achieve such success. Dyson developed 5,127 prototypes before he got the design and function right. Similarly, Bikram Choudhury's name is associated with yoga. Bikram Yoga uses a sequence of 26 signature poses, and the business has expanded to training courses, books, CDs, clothing, and numerous franchises. Choudhury is credited with popularizing yoga in the United States and with turning "his particular brand of yoga into the McDonald's of a $3 billion industry."[10] Entrepreneurs provide fresh ideas and usually have greater flexibility to change than do large companies.

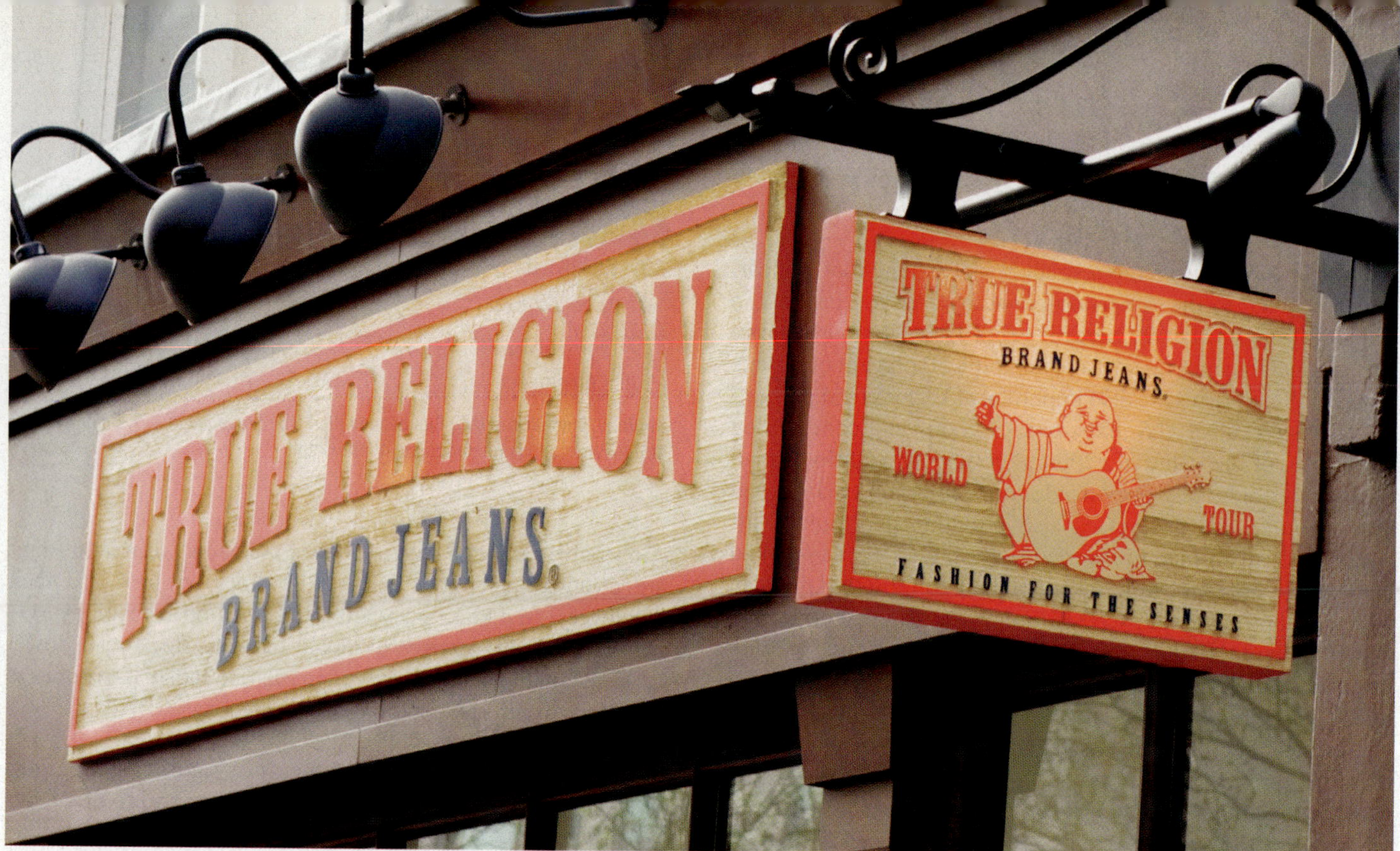

Jeffrey Lubell founded premium apparel company True Religion in 2002. It has gone on to be listed among Forbes' best publicly traded small companies in America.

LO 5-2 Investigate the importance of small business in the U.S. economy and why certain fields attract small business.

Industries That Attract Small Business

Small businesses are found in nearly every industry, but retailing and wholesaling, services, manufacturing, and high technology are especially attractive to entrepreneurs. These fields are relatively easy to enter and require low initial financing. Small-business owners in these industries also find it easier to focus on specific groups of consumers; new firms in these industries initially suffer less from heavy competition than do established firms.

Retailing and Wholesaling Retailers acquire goods from producers or wholesalers and sell them to consumers. Main streets and shopping centers and malls are generally lined with independent music stores, sporting-goods stores, dry cleaners, boutiques, drugstores, restaurants, caterers, service stations, and hardware stores that sell directly to consumers. Retailing attracts entrepreneurs because gaining experience and exposure in retailing is relatively easy. Additionally, an entrepreneur opening a new retail store does not have to spend the large sums of money for the equipment and distribution systems that a manufacturing business requires. All that a new retailer needs is a lease on store space, merchandise, money to sustain the business, knowledge about prospective customers' needs and desires, and basic management and marketing skills. However, it is important for entrepreneurs to anticipate the costs of opening a retail or wholesale business beforehand. When Sharon Munroe wanted to open up a retail consignment store in Austin, Texas, she knew she would not be able to get a loan from the bank. She therefore estimated her cash flow projections beforehand. Monroe spent more than $30,000 to open her store Little Green Beans, which covered rent/operating costs, public relations, marketing, IT, and miscellaneous expenses. She was able to avoid inventory costs by agreeing to split the profits of the sales with her consigners.[11]

Wholesalers supply products to industrial, retail, and institutional users for resale or for use in making other products. Wholesaling activities range from planning and negotiating for supplies, promoting, and distributing (warehousing and transporting) to providing management and merchandising assistance to clients. Wholesalers are extremely important for many products, especially consumer goods, because of the marketing activities they perform. Although it is true that wholesalers themselves can be eliminated, their functions must be passed on to some other organization such as the producer, or another intermediary, often a small business. Frequently, small businesses are closer to the final customers and know what it takes to keep them satisfied. Some smaller businesses start out manufacturing but find their real niche as a supplier or distributor of larger firms' products.

> "The service sector includes businesses that do not actually produce tangible goods."

Services The service sector includes businesses that do not actually produce tangible goods. The service sector accounts for

The retailing industry is particularly attractive to entrepreneurs. Fresh & Easy is a chain of retail grocery stores owned by U.K. grocery and general merchandise retailer Tesco.

80 percent of U.S. jobs, excluding farmworkers. Real estate, insurance and personnel agencies, barbershops, banks, television and computer repair shops, copy centers, dry cleaners, and accounting firms are all service businesses. Services also attract individuals—such as beauticians, morticians, jewelers, doctors, and veterinarians—whose skills are not usually required by large firms. Many of these service providers are retailers who provide their services to ultimate consumers.

Manufacturing Manufacturing goods can provide unique opportunities for small businesses. Started in 1988, the Malcolm Baldrige Award recognizes achievements in quality and performance in businesses of all sizes. It is designed to spur competitive business practices in American industry. MidwayUSA, a shooting and gun supply business in Missouri and a previous winner of the award, takes the Malcolm Baldrige criteria seriously. CEO Larry Potterfield has incorporated Baldrige principles into Midway's operations, planning, and strategic decision making. His goal is to use these best practices to make MidwayUSA into "the best-run business in America."[12] Small businesses sometimes have an advantage over large firms because they can customize products to meet specific customer needs and wants. Such products include custom artwork, jewelry, clothing, and furniture.

DID YOU KNOW?

Small businesses hire 43 percent of high-tech workers in the United States.[14]

High Technology *High technology* is a broad term used to describe businesses that depend heavily on advanced scientific and engineering knowledge. People who were able to innovate or identify new markets in the fields of computers, biotechnology, genetic engineering, robotics, and other markets have become today's high-tech giants. Mark Zuckerberg, the CEO of Facebook (a social networking website), for instance, has created a company that is one of the fastest growing dot-coms in history. Facebook has more than 1 billion monthly active users, and more than half of all active users log on to the site on any given day. Facebook has also contributed to the global economy through employment opportunities and support for businesses. A Deloitte study estimates that Facebook added approximately $20 billion in value to the European economy alone.[13] In general, high-technology businesses require greater capital and have higher initial startup costs than do other small businesses. Many of the biggest, nonetheless, started out in garages, basements, kitchens, and dorm rooms.

LO 5-3 Specify the advantages of small-business ownership.

ADVANTAGES OF SMALL-BUSINESS OWNERSHIP

There are many advantages to establishing and running a small business. These can be categorized into personal advantages and business advantages. Table 5.4 lists some of the traits that can help entrepreneurs succeed.

Independence

Independence is probably one of the leading reasons that entrepreneurs choose to go into business for themselves. Being a small-business owner means being your own boss. Many people start their own businesses because they believe they will do better for themselves than they could do by remaining with their current employer or by changing jobs. They may feel stuck on the corporate ladder and that no business would take them seriously enough to fund their ideas.

KICKSTARTER ALLOWS ENTREPRENEURS TO INTRODUCE PRODUCTS

Got a project idea but you can't find funding? Kickstarter might be the answer. In 2009, Perry Chen, Yancey Strickler, and Charles Adler established Kickstarter in Manhattan as a web platform that engages in "crowd-sourced financing." Entrepreneurs post their ideas on the site, and funders can choose whether to finance them. In return, funders get a free item, a finished product at a steep discount, or stock in the small business. Since its launch, the site has featured more than 26,000 creative projects in fields such as technology, design, music, art, and more. Kickstarter takes an all-or-nothing approach, so entrepreneurs must reach a certain financing goal on the website to receive any funding.

In an uncertain economic climate in which funding is scarce, Kickstarter enables funders to find and choose projects and share in the financial risks. Entrepreneurs benefit not only from funding but also from feedback provided by consumers and investors. This feedback enables entrepreneurs to understand market needs and tailor their products accordingly, a significant component to product success. Since its launch, Kickstarter has raised over $75 million for creative projects and has a 44 percent success rate. Thanks to Kickstarter, many of the products featured on its site have the chance to move quickly from introduction to growth.[15]

TABLE 5.4 10 Successful Traits of Young Entrepreneurs

Intuitive	Persistent
Creative	Innovative
Productive	Frugal
Patient	Friendly
Charismatic	Fearless

Source: Yan Susanto, "10 Successful Traits of Young Entrepreneurs," *Retire @21,* April 10, 2009, www.retireat21.com/blog/10-successful-traits-of-young-entrepreneurs.

Sometimes people who venture forth to start their own small business are those who simply cannot work for someone else. Such people may say that they just do not fit the corporate mold.

More often, small-business owners just want the freedom to choose whom they work with, the flexibility to pick where and when to work, and the option of working in a family setting. The availability of the computer, copy machine, fax, and Internet has permitted many people to work at home. In the past, most of them would have needed the support that an office provides.

Costs

As already mentioned, small businesses often require less money to start and maintain than do large ones. Obviously, a firm with just 25 people in a small factory spends less money on wages and salaries, rent, utilities, and other expenses than does a firm employing tens of thousands of people in several large facilities. Rather than maintain the expense of keeping separate departments for accounting, advertising, and legal counseling, small businesses often hire other firms (sometimes small businesses themselves) to supply these services as they are needed. Additionally, small-business owners can sometimes rely on friends and family members to help them save money by volunteering to work on a difficult project.

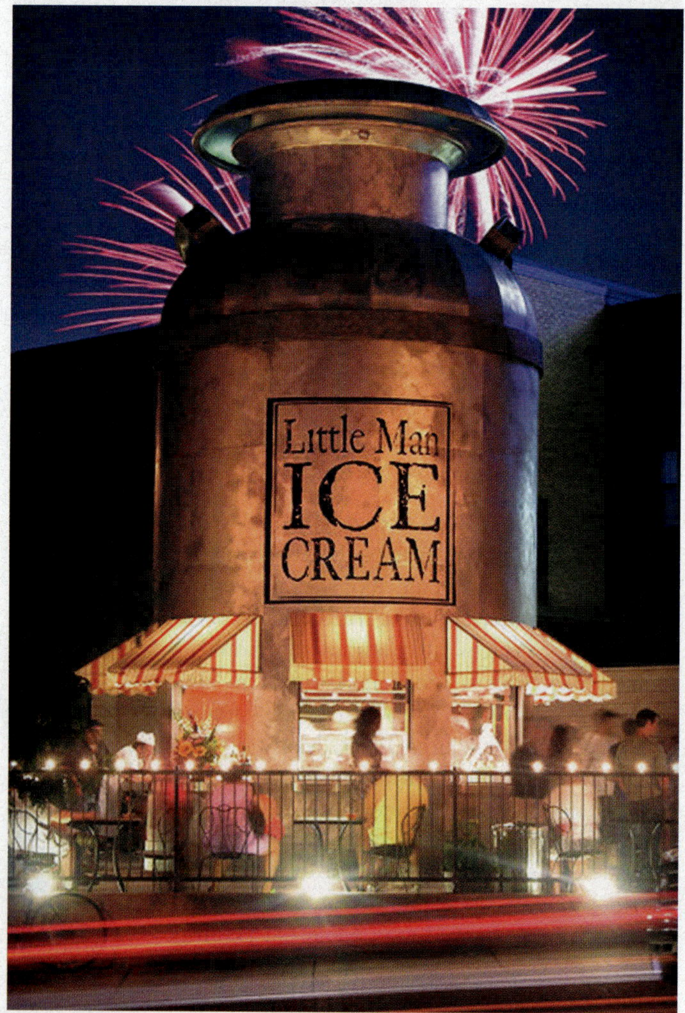

Independently owned ice cream business Little Man Ice Cream can charge premium prices because of the quality of the product and the unique atmosphere.

Entrepreneurs experience a great deal of independence but also a great deal of stress. Many fail.

Flexibility

With small size comes the flexibility to adapt to changing market demands. Small businesses usually have only one layer of management—the owners. Decisions therefore can be made and executed quickly. In larger firms, decisions about even routine matters can take weeks because they must pass through multiple levels of management before action is authorized. When Taco Bell introduces a new product, for example, it must first research what consumers want, then develop the product and test it before introducing it nationwide—a process that sometimes takes years. An independent snack shop, however, can develop and introduce a new product (perhaps to meet a customer's request) in a much shorter time.

Focus

Small firms can focus their efforts on a precisely defined market niche—that is, a specific group of customers. Many large corporations must compete in the mass market or for large market segments. Smaller firms can develop products for particular groups of customers or to satisfy a need that other companies have not addressed. For example, Fatheadz, based in Indianapolis, Indiana, focuses on producing sunglasses for people with big heads. To be an official "fathead," you need a ball cap size of at least 7⅝ and a head circumference above the ear of at least 23.5 inches. The idea arose when Rico Elmore was walking down the Las Vegas strip with his brother and realized that he had lost his sunglasses. He went to a nearby sunglass shop, and out of 300 pairs of glasses, he could not find one that fit. He decided to start a company addressing this need, and Fatheadz now distributes its designs in Walmart optical stores throughout the country.[16] By targeting small niches or product needs, small businesses can sometimes avoid competition from larger firms, helping them to grow into stronger companies.

Reputation

Small firms, because of their capacity to focus on narrow niches, can develop enviable reputations for quality and service. A good example of a small business with a formidable reputation is W. Atlee Burpee and Co., which has the country's premier bulb and seed catalog. Burpee has an unqualified returns policy (complete satisfaction or your money back) that demonstrates a strong commitment to customer satisfaction.

LO 5-4 Summarize the disadvantages of small-business ownership and analyze why many small businesses fail.

DISADVANTAGES OF SMALL-BUSINESS OWNERSHIP

The rewards associated with running a small business are so enticing that it's no wonder many people dream of it. However, as with any undertaking, small-business ownership has its disadvantages.

undercapitalization
the lack of funds to operate a business normally

High Stress Level

A small business is likely to provide a living for its owner, but not much more (although there are exceptions as some examples in this chapter have shown). There are ongoing worries about competition, employee problems, new equipment, expanding inventory, rent increases, or changing market demand. In addition to other stresses, small-business owners tend to be victims of physical and psychological stress. The small-business person is often the owner, manager, sales force, shipping and receiving clerk, bookkeeper, and custodian. Having to multitask can result in long hours for most small-business owners. Many creative persons fail, not because of their business concepts, but rather because of difficulties in managing their business.

High Failure Rate

Despite the importance of small businesses to our economy, there is no guarantee of success. Half of all new employer firms fail within the first five years.[17] Restaurants are a case in point. Look around your own neighborhood, and you can probably spot the locations of several restaurants that are no longer in business.

Small businesses fail for many reasons (see Table 5.5). A poor business concept—such as insecticides for garbage cans (research found that consumers are not concerned with insects in their garbage)—will produce disaster nearly every time. Expanding a hobby into a business may work if a genuine market niche exists, but all too often people start such a business without identifying a real need for the goods or services. Other notable causes of small-business failure include the burdens imposed by government regulation, insufficient funds to withstand slow sales, and vulnerability to competition from larger companies. However, three major causes of small-business failure deserve a close look: undercapitalization, managerial inexperience or incompetence, and inability to cope with growth.

Undercapitalization The shortest path to failure in business is **undercapitalization**, the lack of funds to operate a business normally. Too many entrepreneurs think that all they need is enough money to get started, that the business can survive on cash generated from sales soon thereafter. But almost all businesses suffer from seasonal variations in sales, which make cash tight, and few businesses make money from

TABLE 5.5 Challenges in Starting a New Business

1. Underfunded (not providing adequate startup capital)
2. Not understanding your competitive niche
3. Lack of effective utilization of websites and social media
4. Lack of a marketing and business plan
5. If operating a retail store, poor site selection
6. Pricing mistakes—too high or too low
7. Underestimating the time commitment for success
8. Not finding complementary partners to bring in additional expertise
9. Not hiring the right employees and/or not training them properly
10. Not understanding legal and ethical responsibilities

THE ENVIRONMENTALLY FRIENDLY LAUNDROMAT

Concern for customer service and a clean environment are the ideas that sparked the Eco Laundry Company. Frustrated with missing items and bad customer service, founder Phillipe Christodoulou decided to redefine the Laundromat experience by opening a Laundromat that incorporated sustainable practices and a high level of customer service. For instance, the machines at Eco Laundry are more water and energy efficient than machines you would find in most Laundromats, with recycled steel built into their surfaces. The Laundromats themselves are painted with oil-free paint, their lights are energy efficient, and their floors are made from organic materials. Additionally, Eco Laundry uses biodegradable soaps and detergents.

Recognizing that his Laundromats still use large amounts of water, Christodoulou gives back to the environment by planting trees. So far he has planted more than 300 trees. Eco Laundry engages in more sustainable pickup and delivery services, which are done by bike or on foot so as not to contribute to pollution. Employees hand-fold the laundered clothes and put them in a reusable laundry bag made from recycled cotton. Eco Laundry also offers a dry-cleaning service that does not use chemicals at all.

The business appears to be doing well. It began in Buenos Aires and has opened up a franchise location in Chelsea, New York. The company also has several requests from six countries for franchise locations, presenting opportunities for additional growth.[18]

Discussion Questions

1. What are some of the issues that caused Phillipe Christodoulou to create Eco Laundry?
2. How does Eco Laundry differentiate itself from other Laundromats?
3. How might Eco Laundry benefit by adopting a franchise model?

the start. Many small rural operations cannot obtain financing within their own communities because small rural banks often lack the necessary financing expertise or assets sizable enough to counter the risks involved with small-business loans. Without sufficient funds, the best small-business idea in the world will fail.

Managerial Inexperience or Incompetence

Poor management is the cause of many business failures. Just because an entrepreneur has a brilliant vision for a small business does not mean he or she has the knowledge or experience to manage a growing business effectively. A person who is good at creating great product ideas and marketing them may lack the skills and experience to make good management decisions in hiring, negotiating, finance, and control. Moreover, entrepreneurs may neglect those areas of management they know little about or find tedious, at the expense of the business's success.

Inability to Cope with Growth Sometimes, the very factors that are advantages for a small business turn into serious disadvantages when the time comes to grow. Growth often requires the owner to give up a certain amount of direct authority, and it is frequently hard for someone who has called all the shots to give up control. It has often been said that the greatest impediment to the success of a business is the entrepreneur. Similarly, growth requires specialized management skills in areas such as credit analysis and promotion—skills that the founder may lack or not have time to apply. The founders of many small businesses, including Dell Computers, found that they needed to bring in more experienced managers to help manage their companies through growing pains.

Poorly managed growth probably affects a company's reputation more than anything else, at least initially. And products that do not arrive on time or goods that are poorly made can quickly reverse a success. The principal immediate threats to small and midsized businesses include rising inflation, energy and other supply shortages or cost escalations, and excessive household and/or corporate debt.

LO 5-5 Describe how you go about starting a small business and what resources are needed.

STARTING A SMALL BUSINESS

We've told you how important small businesses are, and why they succeed and fail, but *how do you go about* starting your own business in the first place? To start any business, large or small, you must have some kind of general idea. Sam Walton, founder of Walmart stores, had a vision of a discount retailing enterprise that spawned the world's largest retailing empire and changed the way companies look at business. Next, you need to devise a strategy to guide planning and development in the business. Finally, you must make decisions about form of ownership, the financial resources needed, and whether to acquire an existing business, start a new one, or buy a franchise.

business plan
a precise statement of the rationale for a business and a step-by-step explanation of how it will achieve its goals

The Business Plan

A key element of business success is a **business plan**—a precise statement of the rationale for the business and a step-by-step explanation of how it will achieve its goals. The business plan should include an explanation of the business, an analysis of the competition, estimates of income and expenses, and other information. It should also establish a strategy for acquiring sufficient funds to keep the business going. Many financial institutions decide whether to loan a small business money based on its business plan. A good business plan should act as a guide and reference document—not a shackle that limits the business's flexibility and decision-making ability. The business plan must be revised periodically to ensure that the firm's goals and strategies adapt to changes in the environment. Business plans allow companies to assess market potential, determine price and manufacturing requirements, identify optimal distribution channels, and refine product selection. Former Patriots football linebacker Matt Chatham developed an innovative idea for a crepe franchise operation. Chatham wanted to create a franchise that would sell bigger, bolder, more Americanized crepes. These franchises would be located in mall food courts and other high-traffic areas. Chatham's idea won him first place at a business-plan competition at Babson College. He received $60,000 to launch his business concept. His first SkyCrepers shop opened in August 2011.[19] The Small Business Administration website provides an overview of a plan for small businesses to use to gain financing.

Forms of Business Ownership

After developing a business plan, the entrepreneur has to decide on an appropriate legal form of business ownership—whether it is best to operate as a sole proprietorship, partnership, or corporation—and to examine the many factors that affect that decision, which we explored in Chapter 4.

Financial Resources

The expression "it takes money to make money" holds especially true in developing a business enterprise. To make money from a small business, the owner must first provide or obtain money (capital) to get started and to keep it running smoothly. Even a small retail store will probably need at least $50,000 in initial financing to rent space, purchase or lease necessary equipment and furnishings, buy the initial inventory, and provide working capital. Often, the small-business owner has to put up a significant percentage of the necessary capital. Few new business owners have a large amount of their own capital and must look to other sources for additional financing.

venture capitalists persons or organizations that agree to provide some funds for a new business in exchange for an ownership interest or stock

Equity Financing The most important source of funds for any new business is the owner. Many owners include among their personal resources ownership of a home, the accumulated value in a life-insurance policy, or a savings account. A new business owner may sell or borrow against the value of such assets to obtain funds to operate a business. Additionally, the owner may bring useful personal assets—such as a computer, desks and other furniture, a car or truck—as part of his or her ownership interest in the firm. Such financing is referred to as *equity financing* because the owner uses real personal assets rather than borrowing funds from outside sources to get started in a new business. The owner can also provide working capital by reinvesting profits into the business or simply by not drawing a full salary.

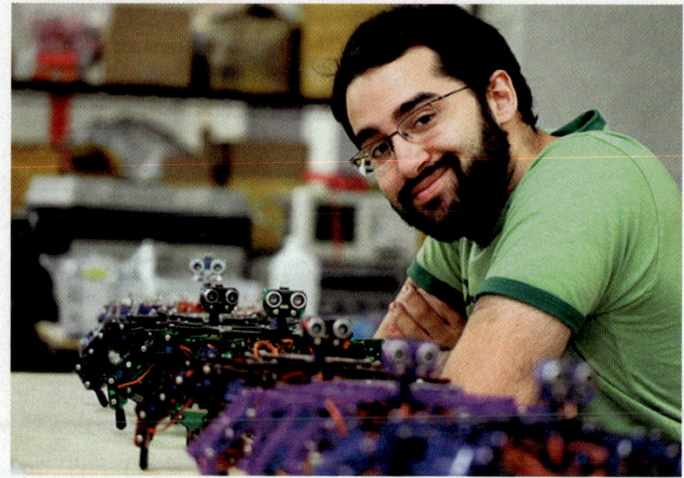

Some of the advantages of small businesses include flexibility, lower startup costs, and perhaps most desirable, the ability to be your own boss.

Small businesses can also obtain equity financing by finding investors for their operations. They may sell stock in the business to family members, friends, employees, or other investors. For example, Alexa Andrzejewski created photo-sharing site Foodspotting after realizing that although there are many reviews online about specific restaurants, there were none about favorite meals or dishes. In 2010, the Foodspotting iPhone app was released that allows food lovers to recommend or bookmark their favorite foods and look up these "best options" at restaurants. The company initially raised $750,000 in seed funding and raised $3 million more from investors interested in the concept.[20] **Venture capitalists** are persons or organizations that agree to provide some funds for a new business in exchange for an ownership interest or stock. Venture capitalists hope to purchase the stock of a small business at a low price and then sell the stock for a profit after the business has grown successful. Although these forms of equity financing have helped many small businesses, they require the small-business owner to share the profits of the business—and sometimes control as well—with the investors.

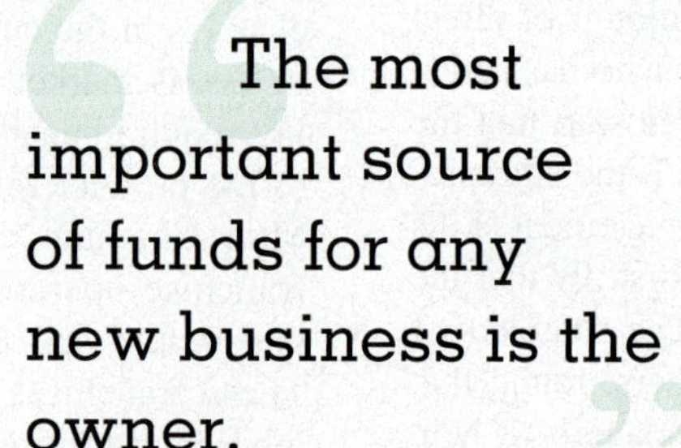
"The most important source of funds for any new business is the owner."

Debt Financing New businesses sometimes borrow more than half of their financial resources. Banks are the main suppliers of external financing to small businesses. On the federal level, the Small Business Administration offers financial assistance to qualifying businesses. They can also look to family and friends as sources for long-term loans or other assets, such as computers or an automobile, that are exchanged for an ownership interest in a business. In such cases, the business owner can usually structure a favorable repayment schedule and sometimes negotiate an interest rate below current bank rates. If the business goes bad, however, the emotional losses for all concerned may greatly exceed the money involved. Anyone lending a friend or family member money for a venture should state the agreement clearly in writing before any money changes hands.

SOUL
CAFE

Small-business owners often use debt financing from banks or the Small Business Administration to start their own organization.

The amount a bank or other institution is willing to loan depends on its assessment of the venture's likelihood of success and of the entrepreneur's ability to repay the loan. The bank will often require the entrepreneur to put up *collateral,* a financial interest in the property or fixtures of the business, to guarantee payment of the debt. Additionally, the small-business owner may have to provide personal property as collateral, such as his or her home, in which case the loan is called a *mortgage.* If the small business fails to repay the loan, the lending institution may eventually claim and sell the collateral or mortgage to recover its loss.

Banks and other financial institutions can also grant a small business a *line of credit*—an agreement by which a financial

franchise a license to sell another's products or to use another's name in business, or both

franchiser the company that sells a franchise

franchisee the purchaser of a franchise

institution promises to lend a business a predetermined sum on demand. A line of credit permits an entrepreneur to take quick advantage of opportunities that require external funding. Small businesses may obtain funding from their suppliers in the form of a *trade credit*—that is, suppliers allow the business to take possession of the needed goods and services and pay for them at a later date or in installments. Occasionally, small businesses engage in *bartering*—trading their own products for the goods and services offered by other businesses. For example, an accountant may offer accounting services to an office supply firm in exchange for office supplies and equipment.

Additionally, some community groups sponsor loan funds to encourage the development of particular types of businesses. State and local agencies may guarantee loans, especially to minority business people or for development in certain areas.

> "Many small-business owners find entry into the business world through franchising."

Approaches to Starting a Small Business

Starting from Scratch versus Buying an Existing Business Although entrepreneurs often start new small businesses from scratch much the way we have discussed in this section, they may elect instead to buy an existing business. This has the advantage of providing a built-in network of customers, suppliers, and distributors and reducing some of the guesswork inherent in starting a new business from the ground up. However, an entrepreneur who buys an existing business also takes on any problems the business already has.

Franchising Many small-business owners find entry into the business world through franchising. A license to sell another's products or to use another's name in business, or both, is a **franchise**. The company that sells a franchise is the **franchiser**. Dunkin' Donuts, Subway, and Jiffy Lube are well-known franchisers with national visibility. The purchaser of a franchise is called a **franchisee**.

The franchisee acquires the rights to a name, logo, methods of operation, national advertising, products, and other elements associated with the franchiser's business in return for a financial commitment and the agreement to conduct business in accordance with the franchiser's standard of operations. The initial fee to join a franchise varies greatly. In addition, franchisees buy equipment, pay for training, and obtain a mortgage or lease. The franchisee also pays the franchiser a monthly or annual fee based on a percentage of sales or profits. In return, the franchisee often receives building specifications and designs, site recommendations, management and accounting support, and perhaps most importantly, immediate name recognition. Visit the website of the International Franchise Association to learn more on this topic.

The practice of franchising first began in the United States in the 19th century when Singer used it to sell sewing machines. The method of goods distribution soon became commonplace in the automobile, gasoline, soft drink, and hotel industries. The concept of franchising grew especially rapidly during the 1960s, when it expanded to diverse industries. Table 5.6 shows the 10 fastest growing franchises and the top 10 hottest new franchises.

TABLE 5.6 Fastest Growing and Hottest New Franchises

Top 10 Fastest Growing Franchises	Top 10 Hottest New Franchises
Stratus Building Solutions	No Mas Vello
Subway	Complete Nutrition
CleanNet USA Inc.	Yogurtland Franchising Inc.
Vanguard Cleaning Systems	ShelfGenie Franchise Systems LLC
H&R Block	The Senior's Choice Inc.
Dunkin' Donuts	CPR-Cell Phone Repair
Chester's	Get in Shape for Women
Liberty Tax Service	Signal 88 Security
7-Eleven Inc.	Menchie's
Anytime Fitness	Smashburger Franchising LLC

Source: "2012 Fastest-Growing Franchise Rankings," *Entrepreneur,* http://www.entrepreneur.com/franchises/rankings/fastestgrowing-115162/2012,-1.html; http://www.entrepreneur.com/franchises/rankings/topnew-115520/2012,-1.html.

The entrepreneur will find that franchising has both advantages and disadvantages. Franchising allows a franchisee the opportunity to set up a small business relatively quickly, and because of its association with an established brand, a franchise outlet often reaches the break-even point faster than an independent business would. Franchisees commonly report the following advantages:

- Management training and support
- Brand-name appeal
- Standardized quality of goods and services
- National and local advertising programs
- Financial assistance
- Proven products and business formats
- Centralized buying power
- Site selection and territorial protection
- Greater chance for success[21]

However, the franchisee must sacrifice some freedom to the franchiser. Some shortcomings experienced by franchisees include:

- Franchise fees and profit sharing with the franchiser
- Strict adherence to standardized operations
- Restrictions on purchasing
- Limited product line
- Possible market saturation
- Less freedom in business decisions[22]

Strict uniformity is the rule rather than the exception. Entrepreneurs who want to be their own bosses are often frustrated with the restrictions of a franchise.

Help for Small-Business Managers

Because of the crucial role that small business and entrepreneurs play in the U.S. economy, a number of organizations offer programs to improve the small-business owner's ability to compete. These include entrepreneurial training programs and programs sponsored by the Small Business Administration. Such programs provide small-business owners with invaluable assistance in managing their businesses, often at little or no cost to the owner.

Entrepreneurs can learn critical marketing, management, and finance skills in seminars and college courses. In addition, knowledge, experience, and judgment are necessary for success in a new business. Although knowledge can be communicated and some experiences can be simulated in the classroom, good judgment must be developed by the entrepreneur. Local chambers of commerce and the U.S. Department of Commerce offer information and assistance helpful in operating a small business. National publications such as *Inc.* and *Entrepreneur* share statistics, advice, tips, and success/failure stories. Additionally, most urban areas have weekly business journal/newspapers that provide stories on local businesses as well as on business techniques that a manager or small business can use.

The Small Business Administration offers many types of management assistance to small businesses, including counseling for firms in difficulty, consulting on improving operations, and training for owner/managers and their employees. Among its many programs, the SBA funds Small Business Development Centers (SBDCs). These are business clinics, usually located on college campuses, that provide counseling at no charge and training at only a nominal charge. SBDCs are often the SBA's principal means of providing direct management assistance.

The Service Corps of Retired Executives (SCORE) and the Active Corps of Executives (ACE) are volunteer agencies funded by the SBA to provide advice for owners of small firms. Both are staffed by experienced managers whose talents and experience the small firms could not ordinarily afford.[23] The SBA also has organized Small Business Institutes (SBIs) on almost 500 university and college campuses in the United States. Seniors, graduate students, and faculty at each SBI provide onsite management counseling.

Finally, the small-business owner can obtain advice from other small-business owners, suppliers, and even customers. A customer may approach a small business it frequents with a request for a new product, for example, or a supplier may offer suggestions for improving a manufacturing process. Networking—building relationships and sharing information with colleagues—is vital for any businessperson, whether you

FIVE GUYS BUILDS ITS BUSINESS ON A SIMPLER CONCEPT

Jerry Murrell, owner of the Five Guys burger restaurant, was nervous about franchising. He understood that expansion could jeopardize the company culture that he and his sons had created. In 2002, Murrell took the chance. Today, Five Guys is the fastest growing restaurant chain with more than 1,000 stores nationwide.

In 1986, Murrell used his sons' tuition money to start the restaurant after two of his sons decided not to attend college. The original "five guys" were Murrell and his four sons (he later had another son). All sons now have significant positions within the company.

Five Guys embraces a simple concept: sell high-quality food. The restaurant uses fresh meat in its burgers and fries its food in peanut oil (to eliminate trans fats). Five Guys does not serve milk shakes because the company refuses to use frozen products. The company even taste-tested 16 mayonnaise options to find the best one.

Five Guys' food has simple directions for preparation, and the kitchens don't have timers. To keep the preparation process simple, the company does not offer menu options such as chicken sandwiches. Five Guys also has no drive-thru service and refuses to deliver—even to the Pentagon.

Rather than dissuading customers, Five Guys' simplicity has made it successful. Five Guys relies on word-of-mouth communication rather than advertising, and customers give the restaurant rave reviews. The company continues to grow and is considering expanding into Europe. Five Guys is carving out its own niche among burger chains.[24]

Discussion Questions

1. What are some of the risks involved with turning Five Guys into a franchise?
2. What differentiates Five Guys' products from those of other fast-food burger franchises?
3. Describe some of the ways in which Murrell and his family retain control over the Five Guys franchise.

The Latino population is the biggest and fastest growing minority segment in the United States—and a lucrative market for businesses looking for ways to meet the segment's many needs.

work for a huge corporation or run your own small business. Communicating with other business owners is a great way to find ideas for dealing with employees and government regulation, improving processes, or solving problems. New technology is making it easier to network. For example, some states are establishing social networking sites for the use of their businesses to network and share ideas.

LO 5-6 Evaluate the demographic, technological, and economic trends that are affecting the future of small business.

THE FUTURE FOR SMALL BUSINESS[25]

Although small businesses are crucial to the economy, their size and limited resources can make them more vulnerable to turbulence and change in the marketplace than large businesses. Next, we take a brief look at the demographic, technological, and economic trends that will have the most impact on small business in the future.

Demographic Trends

America's baby boom started in 1946 and ended in 1964. Many boomers are over 50, and in the next few years, millions more will pass that mark. The baby boomer generation represents 27 percent of Americans.[26] This segment of the population is wealthy, but many small businesses do not actively pursue it. Some exceptions, however, include Gold Violin, which sells designer canes and other products online and through a catalog, and LifeSpring, which delivers nutritional meals and snacks directly to the customer. Industries such as travel, financial planning, and health care will continue to grow as boomers age. Many experts believe that the boomer demographic is the market of the future.

Another market with huge potential for small business is the echo boomers, also called millennials or Generation Y.

"COMMUNICATING WITH OTHER BUSINESS OWNERS IS A GREAT WAY TO FIND IDEAS FOR DEALING WITH EMPLOYEES AND GOVERNMENT REGULATION, IMPROVING PROCESSES, OR SOLVING PROBLEMS."

Millennials number around 75 million and possess a number of unique characteristics. Born between 1977 and 1994, this cohort is not solely concerned about money. Those who fall into this group are also concerned with advancement, recognition, and improved capabilities. They need direct, timely feedback and frequent encouragement and recognition. Millennials do well when training sessions combine entertainment with learning. Working remotely is more acceptable to this group than previous generations, and virtual communication may become as important as face-to-face meetings.[27]

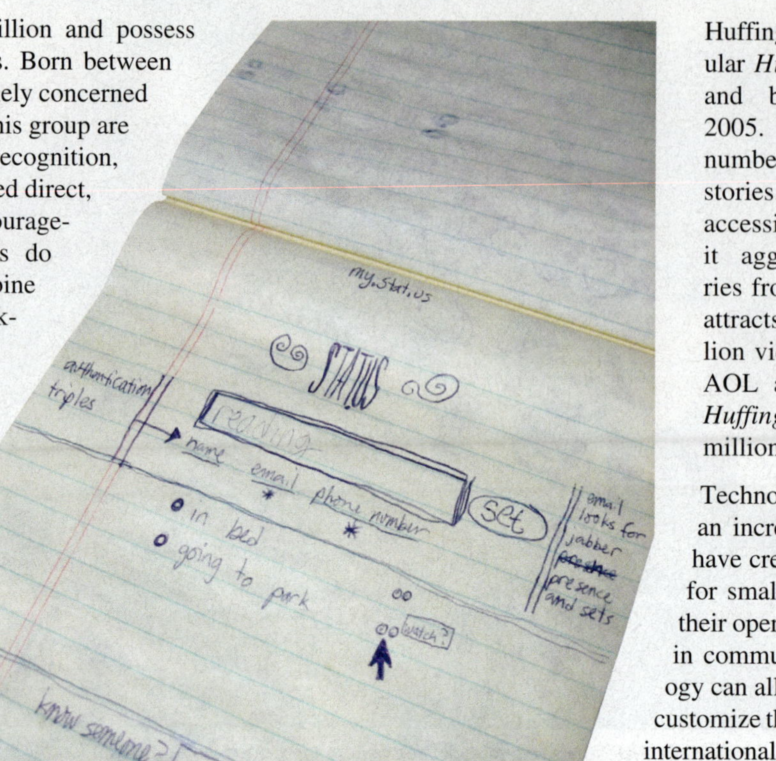

Yet another trend is the growing number of immigrants living in the United States, who now represent about 16 percent of the population. If this trend continues, by 2050 nearly one in five Americans will be classified as immigrants. The Latino population, the nation's largest minority group, is expected to triple in size by 2050.[28]

This vast group provides still another greatly untapped market for small businesses. Retailers who specialize in ethnic products, and service providers who offer bi- or multilingual employees, will find a large amount of business potential in this market. Table 5.7 ranks top cities in the United States for small businesses and startups.

Technological and Economic Trends

Advances in technology have opened up many new markets to small businesses. Undoubtedly, the Internet will continue to provide new opportunities for small businesses. Arianna Huffington launched the popular *Huffington Post,* a news and blogging website, in 2005. The site has broken a number of important news stories. Partly because of its accessible format and the way it agglomerates news stories from many sites, HuffPo attracts approximately 25 million views a month. In 2011, AOL agreed to acquire the *Huffington Post* for $315 million.[29]

TABLE 5.7 Most Business-Friendly Cities

1. Oklahoma City, Oklahoma
2. Dallas–Fort Worth, Texas
3. San Antonio, Texas
4. Austin, Texas
5. Atlanta, Georgia
6. Colorado Springs, Colorado
7. Omaha, Nebraska

Source: Thumbtack.com Small Business Survey, done in partnership with Kauffman Foundation, "7 Most Business-Friendly Cities," *CNN*, June 11, 2012, http://money.cnn.com/galleries/2012/smallbusiness/1206/gallery.best-places-launch-cities/index.html.

Technological advances and an increase in service exports have created new opportunities for small companies to expand their operations abroad. Changes in communications and technology can allow small companies to customize their services quickly for international customers. Also, free trade agreements and trade alliances are helping to create an environment in which small businesses have fewer regulatory and legal barriers.

In recent years, economic turbulence has provided both opportunities and threats for small businesses. As large information technology companies such as Cisco, Oracle, and Sun Microsystems had to recover from an economic slowdown and an oversupply of Internet infrastructure products, some smaller firms found new niche markets. Smaller companies can react quickly to change and can stay close to their customers. While well-funded dot-coms were failing, many small businesses were learning how to use the Internet to promote themselves and sell products online. For example, arts and crafts dealers and makers of specialty products found they could sell their wares on existing websites such as eBay. Service providers related to tourism, real estate, and construction also found they could reach customers through their own or existing websites.

Deregulation of the energy market and interest in alternative fuels and in fuel conservation have spawned many small businesses. Southwest Windpower Inc. manufactures and markets small wind turbines for producing electric power for homes, sailboats, and telecommunications. Solar Attic Inc. has developed a process to recover heat from home attics to use in heating water or swimming pools. As entrepreneurs begin to realize that worldwide energy markets are valued in the hundreds of billions of dollars, the number of innovative companies entering this market will increase. In addition, many small businesses have the desire and employee commitment to purchase such environmentally friendly products. New Belgium

intrapreneurs individuals in large firms who take responsibility for the development of innovations within the organizations

Brewing Company received the U.S. Environmental Protection Agency and Department of Energy Award for leadership in conservation for making a 10-year commitment to purchase wind energy. The company's employees unanimously agreed to cover the increased costs of wind-generated electricity from the employee profit-sharing program.

The future for small business remains promising. The opportunities to apply creativity and entrepreneurship to serve customers are unlimited. Whereas large organizations such as Walmart typically must adapt to change slowly, a small business can adapt immediately to customer and community needs and changing trends. This flexibility provides small businesses with a definite advantage over large companies.

LO 5-7 Explain why many large businesses are trying to "think small."

MAKING BIG BUSINESSES ACT "SMALL"

The continuing success and competitiveness of small businesses through rapidly changing conditions in the business world have led many large corporations to take a closer look at what makes their smaller rivals tick. More and more firms are emulating small businesses in an effort to improve their own bottom line. Beginning in the 1980s and continuing through the present, the buzzword in business has been to *downsize* or *right-size* to reduce management layers, corporate staff, and work tasks to make the firm more flexible, resourceful, and innovative. Many well-known U.S. companies, including IBM, Ford, Apple Inc., General Electric, Xerox, and 3M, have downsized to improve their competitiveness, as have German, British, and Japanese firms. Other firms have sought to make their businesses "smaller" by making their operating units function more like independent small businesses, each responsible for its profits, losses, and resources. Of course, some large corporations, such as Southwest Airlines, have acted like small businesses from their inception, with great success.

While trying to capitalize on small-business success in introducing innovative new products, more and more companies are attempting to instill a spirit of entrepreneurship into even the largest firms. In major corporations, **intrapreneurs**, like entrepreneurs, take responsibility for, or "champion," the development of innovations of any kind *within* the larger organization.[30] Often, they use company resources and time to develop a new product for the company. ■

TEAM EXERCISE

Explore successful global franchises. Go to the companies' websites and find the requirements for applying for three franchises. The chapter provides examples of successful franchises. What do the companies provide, and what is expected to be provided by the franchiser? Compare and contrast each group's findings for the franchises researched. For example, at Subway, the franchisee is responsible for the initial franchise fee, finding locations, leasehold improvements and equipment, hiring employees and operating restaurants, and paying an 8 percent royalty to the company and a fee into the advertising fund. The company provides access to formulas and operational systems, store design and equipment ordering guidance, a training program, an operations manual, a representative on-site during opening, periodic evaluations and ongoing support, and informative publications.

SO YOU WANT TO BE // an Entrepreneur or Small-Business Owner /

In times when jobs are scarce, many people turn to entrepreneurship as a way to find employment. As long as there are unfulfilled needs from consumers, there will be a demand for entrepreneurs and small businesses. Entrepreneurs and small-business owners have been, and will continue to be, a vital part of the U.S. economy, whether in retailing, wholesaling, manufacturing, technology, or services. Creating a business around your idea has a lot of advantages. For many people, independence is the biggest advantage of forming their own small business, especially for those who do not work well in a corporate setting and like to call their own shots. Smaller businesses are also cheaper to start up than large ones in terms of salaries, infrastructure, and equipment. Smallness also provides a lot of flexibility to change with the times. If consumers suddenly start demanding new and different products or services, a small business is more likely to deliver quickly.

Starting your own business is not easy, especially in slow economic times. Even in a good economy, turning an idea into a business has a very high failure rate. The possibility of failure can increase even more when money is tight. Reduced revenues and expensive materials can hurt a small business more than a large one because small businesses have fewer resources. When people are feeling the pinch from rising food and fuel prices, they tend to cut back on other expenditures—which could potentially harm your small business. The increased cost of materials will also affect your bottom line. However, several techniques can help your company survive:

- Set clear payment schedules for all clients. Small businesses tend to be worse about collecting payments than large ones, especially if the clients are acquaintances. However, you need to keep cash flowing into the company to keep the business going.
- Take the time to learn about tax breaks. A lot of people do not realize all the deductions they can claim on items such as equipment and health insurance.
- Focus on your current customers, and don't spend a lot of time looking for new ones. It is far less expensive for a company to keep its existing customers happy.
- Although entrepreneurs and small-business owners are more likely to be friends with their customers, do not let this be a temptation to give things away for free. Make it clear to your customers what the basic price is for what you are selling and charge for extra features, extra services, and so on.
- Make sure the office has the conveniences employees need—like a good coffee maker and other drinks and snacks. This will not only make your employees happy, but it will also help maintain productivity by keeping employees closer to their desks.
- Use your actions to set an example. If money is tight, show your commitment to cutting costs and making the business work by doing simple things like taking the bus to work or bringing a sack lunch every day.
- Don't forget to increase productivity in addition to cutting costs. Try not to focus so much attention on cost cutting that you don't try to increase sales.

In unsure economic times, these measures should help new entrepreneurs and small-business owners sustain their businesses. Learning how to run a business on a shoestring is a great opportunity to cut the fat and to establish lean, efficient operations.[31]

learn, practice, apply entrepreneurial skills!

M: Business was developed just for you—students on the go who need information packaged in a concise yet interesting format with multiple learning options. Check out the book's website to:

- Learn about the advantages and disadvantages of small businesses. (Solve the Dilemma)
- Evaluate a proposed business startup. (Solve the Dilemma)
- Determine your creativity. (Build Your Skills)

While you are there, don't forget to enhance your skills. Practice and apply your knowledge, review the practice exercises, Student PPT® slides, and quizzes to review and apply chapter concepts. Additionally, *Connect® Business* is available for *M: Business*.

www.mhhe.com/ferrellm4e

chapter six

the nature of management

For any organization—small or large, for profit or nonprofit—to achieve its objectives, it must have equipment and raw materials to turn into products to market, employees to make and sell the products, and financial resources to purchase additional goods and services, pay employees, and generally operate the business. To accomplish this, it must also have one or more managers to plan, organize, staff, direct, and control the work that goes on.

This chapter introduces the field of management. It examines and surveys the various functions, levels, and areas of management in business. The skills that managers need for success and the steps that lead to effective decision making are also discussed. ■

LEARNING OBJECTIVES

After reading this chapter, you will be able to:

LO 6-1 Define management and explain its role in the achievement of organizational objectives.

LO 6-2 Describe the major functions of management.

LO 6-3 Distinguish among three levels of management and the concerns of managers at each level.

LO 6-4 Specify the skills managers must have to be successful.

LO 6-5 Describe the different types of leaders and how leadership can be used to empower employees.

LO 6-6 Summarize the systematic approach to decision making used by many business managers.

management a process designed to achieve an organization's objectives by using its resources effectively and efficiently in a changing environment

managers those individuals in organizations who make decisions about the use of resources and who are concerned with planning, organizing, staffing, directing, and controlling the organization's activities to reach its objectives

LO 6-1 Define management and explain its role in the achievement of organizational objectives.

THE IMPORTANCE OF MANAGEMENT

Management is a process designed to achieve an organization's objectives by using its resources effectively and efficiently in a changing environment. *Effectively* means having the intended result; *efficiently* means accomplishing the objectives with a minimum of resources. **Managers** make decisions about the use of the organization's resources and are concerned with planning, organizing, staffing, directing, and controlling the organization's activities to reach its objectives. The decision to introduce new products to reach objectives is often a key management duty. After several years of decline in the automobile industry, Ford management introduced the Ford Fiesta from Europe into the United States. The car provides good driving dynamics, European styling, a starting price of $16,000, and up to 40 mpg. The car fits well with Ford's existing product mix in the United States.[1] Management is universal. It takes place not only in business, but also in government, the military, labor unions, hospitals, schools, and religious groups—any organization requiring the coordination of resources.

Sergio Marchionne, the CEO of Fiat, saved the company from near bankruptcy and put it on the road to multimillion dollar profits and the purchase of Chrysler. Since then, Chrylser has returned to profitability.

Every organization must acquire resources (people, raw materials and equipment, money, and information) to effectively pursue its objectives and coordinate their use to turn out a final good or service. Employees are one of the most important resources in helping a business attain its objectives. Successful companies recruit, train, compensate, and provide benefits (such as shares of stock and health insurance) to foster employee loyalty. Acquiring suppliers is another important part of managing resources and in ensuring that products are made available to customers. As firms reach global markets, companies such as Walmart, Corning, and Charles Schwab enlist hundreds of diverse suppliers that provide goods and services to support operations. A good supplier maximizes efficiencies and provides creative solutions to help the company reduce expenses and reach its objectives. Finally, the manager needs adequate financial resources to pay for essential activities. Primary funding comes from owners and shareholders as well as banks and other financial institutions. All these resources and activities must be coordinated and controlled if the company is to earn a profit. Organizations must also have adequate supplies of resources of all types, and managers must carefully coordinate their use if they are to achieve the organization's objectives.

LO 6-2 Describe the major functions of management.

MANAGEMENT FUNCTIONS

To harmonize the use of resources so that the business can develop, produce, and sell products, managers engage in a series of activities: planning, organizing, staffing, directing, and controlling (Figure 6.1). Although this book discusses each of the five functions separately, they are interrelated; managers may perform two or more of them at the same time.

Planning

Planning, the process of determining the organization's objectives and deciding how to accomplish them, is the first function of management. Planning is a crucial activity, for it designs the map that lays the groundwork for the other functions. It involves forecasting events and determining the best course of action from a set of options or choices. The plan itself specifies what should be done, by whom, where, when, and how. For example, General Electric implemented a plan to improve its reputation for sustainability and to reduce costs resulting from inefficiencies. Its planning resulted in a program called "Ecomagination," which addresses sustainability through calling attention to GE's solar energy programs, hybrid locomotives, fuel cell development, lower-emissions aircraft, and development of lighter and stronger materials, among many other projects. Ecomagination is part of GE's specific plans to produce products with an emphasis on clean technology and renewable energy.[2] The program has a presence on Facebook, Twitter, and other websites to create conversations to assist in planning. All businesses—from the smallest restaurant to the largest multinational corporation—need to develop plans for achieving success. But before an organization can plan a course of action, it must first determine what it wants to achieve.

planning the process of determining the organization's objectives and deciding how to accomplish them; the first function of management

mission the statement of an organization's fundamental purpose and basic philosophy

FIGURE 6.1
The Functions of Management

Managers				
Planning activities to achieve the organization's objectives	**Organizing** resources and activities to achieve the organization's objectives	**Staffing** the organization with qualified people	**Directing** employees' activities toward achievement of objectives	**Controlling** the organization's activities to keep it on course

Mission

A **mission**, or mission statement, is a declaration of an organization's fundamental purpose and basic philosophy. It seeks to answer the question "What business are we in?" Good mission statements are clear and concise statements that explain the organization's reason for existence. A well-developed mission statement, no matter what the industry or size of business, will answer five basic questions:

1. Who are we?
2. Who are our customers?
3. What is our operating philosophy (basic beliefs, values, ethics, and so on)?
4. What are our core competencies and competitive advantages?
5. What are our responsibilities with respect to being a good steward of environmental, financial, and human resources?

A mission statement that delivers a clear answer to these questions provides the foundation for the development of a strong organizational culture, a good marketing plan, and a coherent business strategy. Sustainable cleaning products company Seventh Generation states that its mission is to "inspire a revolution that nurtures the health of the next seven generations."[3]

Goals

A goal is the result that a firm wishes to achieve. A company almost always has multiple goals, which illustrates the complex nature of business. A goal has three key components: an attribute sought, such as profits, customer satisfaction, or product quality; a target to be achieved, such as the volume of sales or extent of management

SHELLI GARDNER LEADS STAMPIN' UP! THROUGH HUMAN RESOURCES SKILLS

Stampin' Up! is a rubber-stamp company co-founded by CEO Shelli Gardner. It sells rubber stamps, ink, scrapbooking materials, and other items for those with a creative flair. Gardner's goal in life was to be a great mom, and she holds her relationships with friends and family as one of her highest values. People who know her say that her human relations skills have contributed to her success. Gardner and her sister shared an interest in stamping and established the direct selling firm in Utah with her family savings. She has since built a manufacturing factory in Utah so that her employees would not be faced with the decision of leaving their home town. The company has been growing over the past 12 years with more than $100 million in sales and plans to expand internationally. Because of Gardner's concern for others, she has set up the Sterling and Shelli Gardner Foundation, which works to fulfill philanthropic needs in her community. In 1999, she was awarded Entrepreneur of the Year by Ernst and Young.[4]

strategic plans those plans that establish the long-range objectives and overall strategy or course of action by which a firm fulfills its mission

tactical plans short-range plans designed to implement the activities and objectives specified in the strategic plan

training to be achieved; and a time frame, which is the time period in which the goal is to be achieved. FedEx, for example, set a goal of increasing its profit by $1.7 billion in a three-year period. FedEx plans to get much of this additional profit from its Express unit. To be successful, goals should be specific. One way FedEx plans to increase its profit is by purchasing more efficient aircraft to save on fuel costs. In fiscal year 2012, the firm replaced 21 Boeing 727s with more fuel-efficient Boeing 767s and Boeing 757s.[5] To be successful at achieving goals, it is necessary to know what is to be achieved, how much, when, and how succeeding at a goal is to be determined.

Objectives Objectives, the ends or results desired by an organization, derive from the organization's mission. A business's objectives may be elaborate or simple. Common objectives relate to profit, competitive advantage, efficiency, and growth. The principal difference between goals and objectives is that objectives are generally stated in such a way that they are measurable. Organizations with profit as an objective want to have money and assets left over after paying off business expenses. Objectives regarding competitive advantage are generally stated in terms of percentage of sales increase and market share, with the goal of increasing those figures. Efficiency objectives involve making the best use of the organization's resources. Dalhousie University has developed energy calculators for small and medium-sized businesses to help them become more aware of their energy usage and reduce their energy expenditure. Growth objectives relate to an organization's ability to adapt and get new products to the marketplace in a timely fashion. One of the most important objectives for businesses is sales. For example, when the Fiat 500 was introduced in the United States, the first year's sales objectives were 50,000 units. Sales slightly below 20,000 units prompted Fiat to replace its U.S. sales chief and hire Jennifer Lopez to be spokeswoman in its new advertisements.[6] Objectives provide direction for all managerial decisions; additionally, they establish criteria by which performance can be evaluated.

Plans There are three general types of plans for meeting objectives—strategic, tactical, and operational. A firm's highest managers develop its **strategic plans**, which establish the long-range objectives and overall strategy or course of action by which the firm fulfills its mission. Strategic plans generally cover periods ranging from one year or longer. They include plans to add products, purchase companies, sell unprofitable segments of the business, issue stock, and move into international markets. For example, Ford sold its Volvo division to China's Geely automotive group to acquire new resources and increase profits. Faced with stiff competition, rising costs, and slowing sales, some companies are closing U.S. plants and moving production to factories abroad. For example, Converse Inc. (tennis shoes), Lionel LLC (model trains), and Zebco (fishing reels) all stopped U.S. production in favor of Asian factories. Strategic plans must take into account the organization's capabilities and resources, the changing business environment, and organizational objectives. Plans should be market-driven, matching customers' desire for value with operational capabilities, processes, and human resources.[7]

Private-equity firms Apollo Global Management and Metropoulos made the strategic plan to purchase the Hostess snack business after the firm declared bankruptcy.

> "Strategic plans generally cover periods ranging from one year or longer."

Tactical plans are short range and designed to implement the activities and objectives specified in the strategic plan. These plans, which usually cover a period of one year or less, help keep the organization on the course established in the strategic plan. Because tactical plans allow the organization to react to changes in the environment while continuing to focus on the company's overall strategy, management must periodically review and update them. Declining performance or failure to meet objectives set out in tactical plans may be one reason for revising them. As part of changes to its tactical planning, Cisco made the decision to slim

operational plans very short-term plans that specify what actions individuals, work groups, or departments need to accomplish to achieve the tactical plan and ultimately the strategic plan

crisis management (contingency planning) an element in planning that deals with potential disasters such as product tampering, oil spills, fire, earthquake, computer virus, or reputation crisis

According to the firm, Nokia has a contingency plan in case its Windows Phone is unsuccessful. Microsoft later announced it was acquiring Nokia.

down different areas of the company. This included reducing its number of councils (internal committees) to three main ones whose focus will be setting direction for projects rather than engaging in tactical planning. Tactical planning will be more decentralized.[8] The differences between the two types of planning result in different activities in the short-term versus the long-term. For instance, a strategic plan might include the use of social media to reach consumers. A tactical plan could involve finding ways to increase traffic to the site or promoting premium content to those who visit the site. A fast-paced and ever-changing market requires companies to develop short-run or tactical plans to deal with the changing environment.

A retailing organization with a five-year strategic plan to invest $5 billion in 500 new retail stores may develop five tactical plans (each covering one year) specifying how much to spend to set up each new store, where to locate, and when to open each new store. Tactical plans are designed to execute the overall strategic plan. Because of their short-term nature, they are easier to adjust or abandon if changes in the environment or the company's performance so warrant.

Operational plans are very short term and specify what actions specific individuals, work groups, or departments need to accomplish to achieve the tactical plan and ultimately the strategic plan. They apply to details in executing activities in one month, week, or even day. For example, a work group may be assigned a weekly production quota to ensure that sufficient products are available to elevate market share (tactical goal) and ultimately help the firm be number one in its product category (strategic goal). Returning to our retail store example, operational plans may specify the schedule for opening one new store, hiring and training new employees, obtaining merchandise, and opening for actual business.

Another element of planning is **crisis management** or **contingency planning**, which deals with potential disasters such as product tampering, oil spills, fire, earthquake, computer viruses, or even a reputation crisis due to unethical or illegal conduct by one or more employees. Unfortunately, many businesses do not have updated contingency plans to handle the types of crises that their companies might encounter. A recent study reveals that more than 85 percent of small or midsized businesses have ineffective or outdated emergency recovery plans.[9] Businesses that have correct and well-thought-out contingency plans tend to respond more effectively when problems occur than do businesses who lack such planning.

Many companies, including Ashland Oil, H. J. Heinz, and Johnson & Johnson, have crisis management teams to deal specifically with problems, permitting other managers to continue to focus on their regular duties. Some companies even hold periodic disaster drills to ensure that their employees know how to respond when a crisis does occur. After the horrific earthquake in Japan, many companies in U.S. earthquake zones reevaluated their crisis management plans. Crisis management plans generally cover maintaining business operations throughout a crisis and communicating with the public, employees, and officials about the nature of and the company's response to the problem. Communication is especially important to minimize panic and damaging rumors; it also demonstrates that the company is aware of the problem and plans to respond.

Sometimes disasters occur that no one can anticipate, but companies can still plan for how to react to the disaster. The investment company Fred Alger Management Inc. was one company that displayed exemplary disaster recovery planning. When the company's core investment team—including its president—was killed during the September 11 attacks (the office was located in the World Trade Center), the firm relied upon its employee assistance programs and a recovery office located in New Jersey to help weather the emergency. Ten years later, the successful company continues to maintain disaster recovery plans, such as an unoccupied office for emergencies and the use of vendors to back up essential data in case the company's own data are destroyed.[10] Incidents such as this highlight the importance of planning for crises and the need to respond publicly and quickly when a disaster occurs.

organizing the structuring of resources and activities to accomplish objectives in an efficient and effective manner

staffing the hiring of people to carry out the work of the organization

downsizing the elimination of a significant number of employees from an organization

Organizing

Rarely are individuals in an organization able to achieve common goals without some form of structure. **Organizing** is the structuring of resources and activities to accomplish objectives in an efficient and effective manner. Managers organize by reviewing plans and determining what activities are necessary to implement them; then, they divide the work into small units and assign it to specific individuals, groups, or departments. As companies reorganize for greater efficiency, more often than not, they are organizing work into teams to handle core processes such as new product development instead of organizing around traditional departments such as marketing and production. Organizing occurs continuously because change is inevitable.

Organizing is important for several reasons. It helps create synergy, whereby the effect of a whole system equals more than that of its parts. It also establishes lines of authority, improves communication, helps avoid duplication of resources, and can improve competitiveness by speeding up decision making. When Japanese consumer electronics firm Panasonic decided to reorganize its business, it reduced its workforce, formed overseas alliances to expand into new product areas such as industrial-use solar systems, and stopped investing in less profitable areas. Although eliminating jobs was a difficult move, Panasonic believed that it must reduce redundancies and streamline operations to create a more efficient business.[11] Because organizing is so important, we'll take a closer look at it in Chapter 7.

Staffing

Once managers have determined what work is to be done and how it is to be organized, they must ensure that the organization has enough employees with appropriate skills to do the work. Hiring people to carry out the work of the organization is known as **staffing**. Beyond recruiting people for positions within the firm, managers must determine what skills are needed for specific jobs, how to motivate and train employees, how much to pay, what benefits to provide, and how to prepare employees for higher-level jobs in the firm at a later date. These elements of staffing will be explored in detail in Chapters 9 and 10.

Another aspect of staffing is **downsizing**, the elimination of significant numbers of employees from an organization, which has been a pervasive and much-talked-about trend. Staffing can be outsourced to companies that focus on hiring and managing employees. For instance, the Bartech Group provides search and staffing services, workforce solutions, business processes outsourcing, and consulting services. The Bartech Group bills and manages $1 billion for customers such as General Motors and Eaton.[12] Many firms downsize by outsourcing production, sales, and technical positions to companies in other countries with lower labor costs. Downsizing has helped numerous firms reduce costs quickly and become more profitable (or become profitable after lengthy losses) in a short period of time. Whether it is called downsizing, rightsizing, trimming the fat, or the new reality in business, the implications of downsizing have been dramatic. During the recent economic recession, many companies laid off workers to cut costs. The nationwide unemployment rate climbed above 10 percent, but after the recovery, unemployment dropped significantly.[13]

Downsizing and outsourcing, however, have painful consequences. Obviously, the biggest casualty is those who lose their jobs, along with their incomes, insurance, and pensions. Some find new jobs quickly; others do not. Another victim is the morale of the remaining employees at downsized firms. Those left behind often feel insecure, angry, and sad, and their productivity may decline as a result, the opposite of the effect sought. Studies have found that firms that lay off more than 10 percent of their surviving workforce can expect to see turnover increase to 15.5 percent versus 10.4 percent at firms that do not have layoffs.[14]

After a downsizing situation, an effective manager will promote optimism and positive thinking and minimize criticism and fault-finding. Management should also build teamwork and encourage positive group discussions. Honest communication is important during a time of change and will lead to

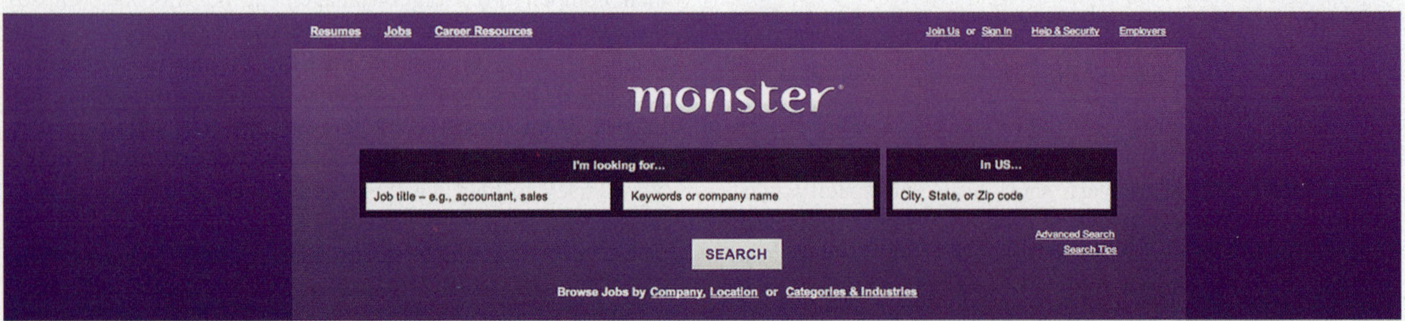

Some companies choose to recruit people to hire through online job websites such as Monster.com. Monster.com is one of the world's largest employment websites. Using websites like Monster.com falls under the staffing function of management.

directing motivating and leading employees to achieve organizational objectives

controlling the process of evaluating and correcting activities to keep the organization on course

trust. In reality, when departments are downsized, the remaining employees end up working harder to fill the gaps left by layoffs. Truthfulness about what has happened and about future expectations is essential.

Directing

Once the organization has been staffed, management must direct the employees. **Directing** is motivating and leading employees to achieve organizational objectives. Good directing involves telling employees what to do and when to do it through the implementation of deadlines and then encouraging them to do their work. For example, as a sales manager, you would need to learn how to motivate salespersons; provide leadership; teach sales teams to be responsive to customer needs; and manage organizational issues as well as evaluate sales results. Finally, directing also involves determining and administering appropriate rewards and recognition. All managers are involved in directing, but it is especially important for lower-level managers who interact daily with the employees operating the organization. For example, an assembly-line supervisor for Frito-Lay must ensure that her workers know how to use their equipment properly and have the resources needed to carry out their jobs safely and efficiently, and she must motivate her workers to achieve their expected output of packaged snacks.

> ["Participation makes workers feel important, and the company benefits."]

Managers may motivate employees by providing incentives—such as the promise of a raise or promotion—for them to do a good job. But most workers want more than money from their jobs: They need to know that their employer values their ideas and input. Managers should give younger employees some decision-making authority as soon as possible. Smart managers, therefore, ask workers to contribute ideas for reducing costs, making equipment more efficient, improving customer service, or even developing new products. For example, Travelocity has made employee engagement a top priority to bring customer service to the highest level. This participation makes workers feel important, and the company benefits. Recognition and appreciation are often the best motivators. Employees who understand more about their effect on the financial success of the company may be induced to work harder for that success, and managers who understand the needs and desires of workers can encourage their employees to work harder and more productively. The motivation of employees is discussed in detail in Chapter 9.

Controlling

Planning, organizing, staffing, and directing are all important to the success of an organization, whether its objective is earning a profit or something else. But what happens when a firm fails to reach its goals despite a strong planning effort? **Controlling** is the process of evaluating and correcting activities to keep the organization on course. Control involves five activities: (1) measuring performance, (2) comparing present performance with standards or objectives, (3) identifying deviations from the standards, (4) investigating the causes of deviations, and (5) taking corrective action when necessary.

Controlling and planning are closely linked. Planning establishes goals and standards. By monitoring performance and comparing it with standards, managers can determine whether performance is on target. When performance is substandard, management must determine why and take appropriate actions to get the firm back on course. In short, the control function helps managers assess the success of their plans. You might relate this to your performance in this class. If you did not perform as well on early projects or exams, you must take corrective action such as increasing studying or using website resources to achieve your overall objective of getting an A or B in the course. When the outcomes of plans do not meet expectations, the control process facilitates revision of the plans. Control can take many forms such as visual inspections, testing, and statistical modeling processes. The basic idea is to ensure that operations meet requirements and are satisfactory to reach objectives.

The control process also helps managers deal with problems arising outside the firm. For example, if a firm is the subject of negative publicity, management should use the control process to determine why and to guide the firm's response.

LO 6-3 Distinguish among three levels of management and the concerns of managers at each level.

TYPES OF MANAGEMENT

All managers—whether the sole proprietor of a jewelry store or the hundreds of managers of a large company such as Paramount Pictures—perform the five functions just discussed. In the case of the jewelry store, the owner handles all the functions, but in a large company with more than one manager, responsibilities must be divided and delegated. This division of responsibility

top managers the president and other top executives of a business, such as the chief executive officer (CEO), chief financial officer (CFO), and chief operations officer (COO), who have overall responsibility for the organization

middle managers those members of an organization responsible for the tactical planning that implements the general guidelines established by top management

is generally achieved by establishing levels of management and areas of specialization—finance, marketing, and so on.

Levels of Management

As we have hinted, many organizations have multiple levels of management—top management, middle management, and first-line, or supervisory, management. These levels form a pyramid, as shown in Figure 6.2. As the pyramid shape implies, there are generally more middle managers than top managers, and still more first-line managers. Very small organizations may have only one manager (typically, the owner), who assumes the responsibilities of all three levels. Large businesses have many managers at each level to coordinate the use of the organization's resources. Managers at all three levels perform all five management functions, but the amount of time they spend on each function varies, as we shall see (Figure 6.3).

?

DID YOU KNOW?

Only 4 percent of *Fortune* 500 CEOs are women.[15]

Top Management

In businesses, **top managers** include the president and other top executives, such as the chief executive officer (CEO), chief financial officer (CFO), and chief operations officer (COO), who have overall responsibility for the organization. For example, Mark Zuckerberg, CEO and founder of Facebook, manages the overall strategic direction of the company and plays a key role in representing the company to stakeholders. Sheryl Sandberg, Facebook's chief operating officer, is responsible for the daily operation of the company. The COO reports to the CEO and is often considered to be number two in command. In public corporations, even chief executive officers have a boss—the firm's board of directors.

FIGURE 6.2
Levels of Management

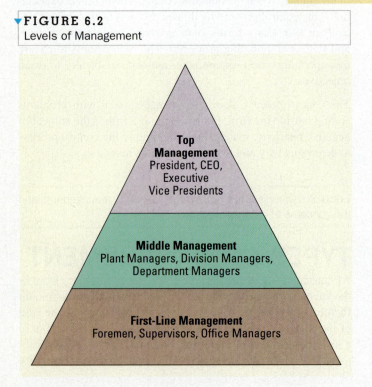

Level	Positions
Top Management	President, CEO, Executive Vice Presidents
Middle Management	Plant Managers, Division Managers, Department Managers
First-Line Management	Foremen, Supervisors, Office Managers

Interestingly, Mark Zuckerberg is an example of a CEO who does not receive high annual compensation. In 2012, it was announced that Zuckerberg would go from a base salary of $600,000 to an annual pay of just $1 per year.

Top-level managers spend most of their time planning. They make the organization's strategic decisions, decisions that focus on an overall scheme or key idea for using resources to take advantage of opportunities. They decide whether to add products, acquire companies, sell unprofitable business segments, and move into foreign markets. Top managers also represent their company to the public and to government regulators.

Given the importance and range of top managements' decisions, top managers generally have many years of varied experience and command top salaries. In addition to salaries, top managers' compensation packages typically include bonuses, long-term incentive awards, stock, and stock options. Table 6.1 lists the compensation packages of different CEOs. Top managers are also concerned with issues such as diversity. Bringing together diverse groups of people with different perspectives can greatly enhance a firm's creativity and productivity. Managers from companies devoted to workforce diversity devised five rules that make diversity recruiting work (see Table 6.2 on page 128).

Middle Management

Rather than making strategic decisions about the whole organization, **middle managers** are responsible for tactical planning that will implement the general guidelines established by top management. Thus, their responsibility is more narrowly focused than that of top

first-line managers those who supervise both workers and the daily operations of an organization

▼ **FIGURE 6.3**
Importance of Management Functions to Managers in Each Level

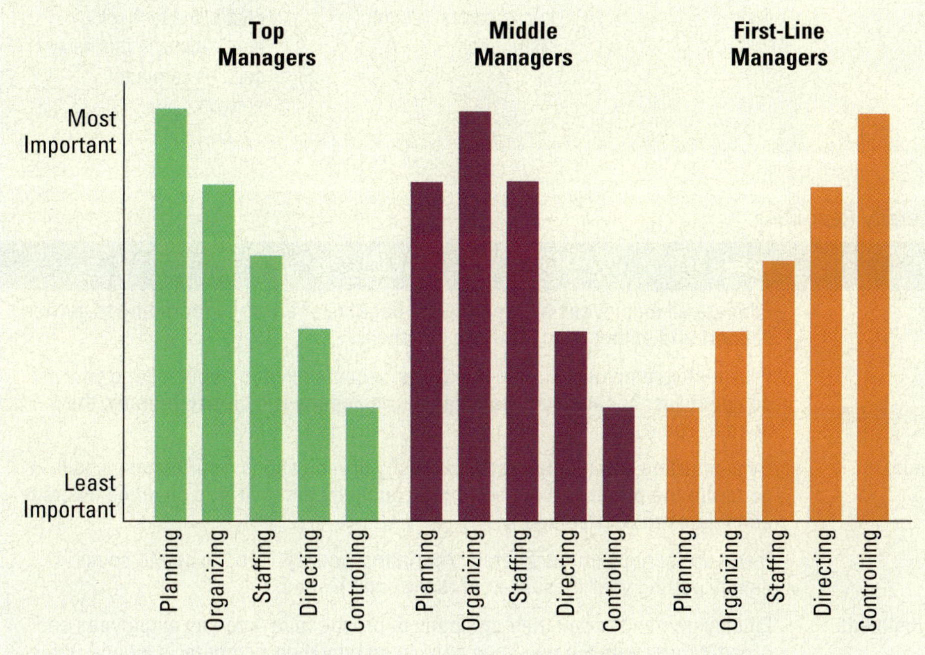

managers. Middle managers are involved in the specific operations of the organization and spend more time organizing than other managers. In business, plant managers, division managers, and department managers make up middle management. The product manager for laundry detergent at a consumer products manufacturer, the department chairperson in a university, and the head of a state public health department are all middle managers. The ranks of middle managers have been shrinking as more and more companies downsize to be more productive.

First-Line Management Most people get their first managerial experience as **first-line managers**, those who supervise workers and the daily operations of the organization. They are responsible for implementing the plans established by middle management and directing workers' daily performance on the job. They spend most of their time directing and controlling. Common titles for first-line managers are foreman, supervisor, and office service manager.

Areas of Management

At each level, there are managers who specialize in the basic functional areas of business: finance, production and operations, human resources (personnel), marketing, and administration. Each of these management areas is important to a business's success. For instance, a firm cannot survive without someone obtaining needed financial resources (financial managers) or staff (human resources managers). Although larger firms will most likely have all these managers and even more, depending on that particular firm's needs, in smaller firms these important tasks may fall to the owner or a few employees. Yet whether or not companies have managers for specific areas, every company must have someone responsible for obtaining financial resources, transforming resources into finished products for the marketplace, hiring and/or dealing with staff, marketing products, handling the firm's information technology resources, and managing a business segment or the overall business. These different types of managers are discussed in more detail in Table 6.3.

"Most people get their first managerial experience as first-line managers."

▼ **TABLE 6.1** CEO Compensation of Top Companies

CEO	Company	Compensation (millions)
Larry Ellison	Oracle	$96,160,696
Robert Iger	Walt Disney Productions	37,103,208
Mark G. Parker	Nike	35,212,678
Kenneth I. Chenault	American Express	28,590,114
Muhtar Kent	Coca-Cola	21,608,751
James P. Gorman	Morgan Stanley	10,379,760
Tim Cook	Apple	4,174,992
Mark Zuckerberg	Facebook	1,990,714
Warren Buffett	Berkshire Hathaway	423,923
John Mackey	Whole Foods	69,019

*2012 compensation results compiled from publicly available data.

financial managers those who focus on obtaining needed funds for the successful operation of an organization and using those funds to further organizational goals

production and operations managers those who develop and administer the activities involved in transforming resources into goods, services, and ideas ready for the marketplace

human resources managers those who handle the staffing function and deal with employees in a formalized manner

marketing managers those who are responsible for planning, pricing, and promoting products and making them available to customers through distribution

information technology (IT) managers those who are responsible for implementing, maintaining, and controlling technology applications in business, such as computer networks

TABLE 6.2 Five Rules of Successful Diversity Recruiting

Rule	Action
1. Get everyone involved.	Educate all employees on the tangible benefits of diversity recruiting to garner support and enthusiasm for those initiatives.
2. Showcase your diversity.	Prospective employees are not likely to become excited about joining your company just because you say that your company is diversity-friendly; they need to see it.
3. Work with diversity groups within your community.	By supporting community-based diversity organizations, your company will generate the priceless word-of-mouth publicity that will lead qualified diversity candidates to your company.
4. Spend money.	If you are serious about diversity recruiting, you will need to spend some money getting your message out to the right places.
5. Sell, sell, sell—and measure your return on investment.	Employers need to sell their company to prospective diversity employees and present them with a convincing case as to why their company is a good fit for the diversity candidate.

Source: Adapted from Juan Rodriguez, "The Five Rules of Successful Diversity Recruiting," *Diversityjobs.com,* www.diversityjobs.com/Rules-of-Successful-Diversity-Recruiting.

TABLE 6.3 Areas of Management

Manager	Function
Financial Manager	Focuses on obtaining the money needed for the successful operation of the organization and using that money to further with organizational goals
Production and Operations Manager	Develops and administers the activities involved in transforming resources into goods, services, and ideas ready for the marketplace
Human Resources Manager	Handles the staffing function and deals with employees in a formalized manner
Marketing Manager	Responsible for planning, pricing, and promoting products and making them available to customers through distribution
Information Technology (IT) Manager	Responsible for implementing, maintaining, and controlling technology applications in business, such as computer networks
Administrative Manager	Manages an entire business or a major segment of a business; does not specialize in a particular function but coordinate the activities of specialized managers

LO 6-4 Specify the skills managers must have to be successful.

SKILLS NEEDED BY MANAGERS

Managers are typically evaluated using the metrics of how effective and efficient they are. Managing effectively and efficiently requires certain skills—technical expertise, conceptual skills, analytical skills, and human relations skills. Table 6.4 (on page 130) describes some of the roles managers may fulfill.

Technical Expertise

Managers need **technical expertise**, the specialized knowledge and training required to perform jobs related to their area of management. Accounting managers need to be able to perform accounting jobs, and production managers need to be able to perform production jobs. Although a production manager may not actually perform a job, he or she needs technical expertise to train employees, answer questions, provide guidance, and solve problems. Technical skills are most needed by first-line managers and are least critical to top-level managers.

administrative managers those who manage an entire business or a major segment of a business; they are not specialists but coordinate the activities of specialized managers

technical expertise the specialized knowledge and training needed to perform jobs that are related to particular areas of management

conceptual skills the ability to think in abstract terms and to see how parts fit together to form the whole

analytical skills the ability to identify relevant issues, recognize their importance, understand the relationships between them, and perceive the underlying causes of a situation

CHANGING MANAGEMENT STYLES: LOOKING THROUGH APPLE-COLORED LENSES

With the passing of Apple founder and CEO Steve Jobs, eyes are now turned to new CEO Tim Cook. Tim Cook was Apple's corporate operations officer for many years before becoming CEO, so his focus has been on operational and financial strategies. Unlike Jobs, Cook has taken a more traditional approach in his management style by prioritizing project and supply chain management over creative engineering, attending investor meetings, being accessible to the media, and paying out dividends to stockholders, among other activities. He still maintains the secretive nature of the company but also has the human relations skills that Jobs seemed to lack.

Yet although Cook seems to possess the technical expertise and analytical skills necessary for the CEO position, some fear that he lacks the conceptual skills that made Jobs such a visionary. Conceptual skills provide the ability to think in abstract terms and see how parts fit together into a whole. Jobs was considered a creative builder adept at recognizing consumer needs and developing revolutionary products that changed the marketplace. A major concern is that Cook might emphasize the business side of Apple over creatively designed products, leading to fears that Cook's leadership might change Apple's culture for the worse. On the other hand, others feel that Cook might bring Apple into a new era of competitiveness. The change in tone of the company is the big difference between the leadership styles of Cook and Jobs. Time will tell whether this change of tone will be a benefit for Apple in the long run.[16]

Discussion Questions

1. How does Tim Cook's management style differ from Steve Jobs's?
2. What skills does Tim Cook possess that give him an advantage as a manager?
3. Do you think Tim Cook will be as effective at running Apple as Steve Jobs?

Conceptual Skills

Conceptual skills, the ability to think in abstract terms, and to see how parts fit together to form the whole, are needed by all managers, but particularly top-level managers. Top management must be able to evaluate continually where the company will be in the future. Conceptual skills also involve the ability to think creatively. Recent scientific research has revealed that creative thinking, which is behind the development of many innovative products, including fiber optics and compact disks, can be learned. As a result, IBM, AT&T, GE, Hewlett-Packard, Intel, and other top U.S. firms hire creative consultants to teach their managers how to think creatively.

Flight attendant David Holmes became a YouTube sensation by rapping passenger instructions on Southwest Airlines flights. Southwest Airlines' managers and employees are well-known for their excellent human relations skills and making the workplace fun.

Analytical Skills

Analytical skills refer to the ability to identify relevant issues and recognize their importance, understand the relationships between them, and perceive the underlying causes of a situation. When managers have identified critical factors and causes, they can take appropriate action. All managers need to think logically, but this skill is probably most important to the success of top-level managers. To be

TABLE 6.4 Managerial Roles

Type of Role	Specific Role	Examples of Role Activities
Decisional	Entrepreneur	Commit organizational resources to develop innovative goods and services; decide to expand internationally to obtain new customers for the organization's products.
	Disturbance handler	Move quickly to take corrective action to deal with unexpected problems facing the organization from the external environment, such as a crisis like an oil spill, or from the internal environment, such as producing faulty goods or services.
	Resource allocator	Allocate organizational resources among different functions and departments of the organization; set budgets and salaries of middle and first-level managers.
	Negotiator	Work with suppliers, distributors, and labor unions to reach agreements about the quality and price of input, technical, and human resources; work with other organizations to establish agreements to pool resources to work on joint projects.
Informational	Monitor	Evaluate the performance of managers in different functions and take corrective action to improve their performance; watch for changes occurring in the external and internal environment that may affect the organization in the future.
	Disseminator	Inform employees about changes taking place in the external and internal environment that will affect them and the organization; communicate to employees the organization's vision and purpose.
	Spokesperson	Launch a national advertising campaign to promote new goods and services; give a speech to inform the local community about the organization's future intentions.
Interpersonal	Figurehead	Outline future organizational goals to employees at company meetings; open a new corporate headquarters building; state the organization's ethical guidelines and the principles of behavior employees are to follow in their dealings with customers and suppliers.
	Leader	Provide an example for employees to follow; give direct commands and orders to subordinates; make decisions concerning the use of human and technical resources; mobilize employee support for specific organizational goals.
	Liaison	Coordinate the work of managers in different departments; establish alliances between different organizations to share resources to produce new goods and services.

Source: Gareth R. Jones and Jennifer M. George, *Essentials of Contemporary Management* (Burr Ridge, IL: McGraw-Hill/Irwin, 2007, 3rd edition), p. 14.

analytical, it is necessary to think about a broad range of issues and to weigh different options before taking action. Because analytical skills are so important, questions that require analytical skills are often a part of job interviews. Questions such as "Tell me how you would resolve a problem at work if you had access to a large amount of data?" may be part of the interview process. The answer would require the interviewee to explain how to sort data to find relevant facts that could resolve the issue. Analytical thinking is required in complex or difficult situations when the solution is often not clear. Resolving ethical issues often requires analytical skills.

Human Relations Skills

People skills, or **human relations skills**, are the ability to deal with people, both inside and outside the organization. Those who can relate to others, communicate well with others, understand the needs of others, and show a true appreciation for others are generally more successful than managers who lack such skills. People skills are especially important in hospitals, airline companies, banks, and other organizations that provide services. For example, at Southwest Airlines, every new employee attends "You, Southwest and Success," a day-long class designed to teach employees about the airline and its reputation for impeccable customer service. All employees in management positions at Southwest take mandatory leadership classes that address skills related to listening, staying in touch with employees, and handling change without compromising values.

LO 6-5 Describe the different types of leaders and how leadership can be used to empower employees.

LEADERSHIP

Leadership is the ability to influence employees to work toward organizational goals. Strong leaders manage and pay attention to the culture of their organizations and the needs of their customers. Table 6.5 offers some tips for successful leadership.

Managers often can be classified into three types based on their leadership style. *Autocratic leaders* make all the decisions and then tell employees what must be done and how to do it. They generally use their authority and economic rewards to get employees to comply with their directions. Martha Stewart is an example of an autocratic leader. She built up her media empire

human relations skills the ability to deal with people, both inside and outside the organization

leadership the ability to influence employees to work toward organizational goals

TABLE 6.5 Tips for Successful Leadership

1. Act as a role model for employees
2. Clearly communicate company expectations and mission
3. Encourage employee participation and creativity
4. Communicate core values
5. Listen as much as you speak and encourage feedback
6. Empower employees to make decisions
7. Identify and guard against ethical risks
8. Build sincere relationships
9. Evaluate employee success and failures
10. Engage the workforce in continuous improvement

"Strong leaders also realize the value that employees can provide by participating in the firm's corporate culture."

by paying close attention to every detail.[17] *Democratic leaders* involve their employees in decisions. The manager presents a situation and encourages his or her subordinates to express opinions and contribute ideas. The manager then considers the employees' points of view and makes the decision. Herb Kelleher, co-founder of Southwest Airlines, had a democratic leadership style. Under his leadership, employees were encouraged to discuss concerns and provide input.[18] *Free-rein leaders* let their employees work without much interference. The manager sets performance standards and allows employees to find their own ways to meet them. For this style to be effective, employees must know what the standards are, and they must be motivated to attain them. The free-rein style of leadership can be a powerful motivator because it demonstrates a great deal of trust and confidence in the employee. Warren Buffett, CEO of Berkshire Hathaway, exhibits free-rein leadership among the managers who run the company's various businesses.

The effectiveness of the autocratic, democratic, and free-rein styles depends on several factors. One consideration is the type of employees. An autocratic style of leadership is generally best for stimulating unskilled, unmotivated employees; highly skilled, trained, and motivated employees may respond better to democratic or free-rein leadership styles. Employees who have been involved in decision making generally require less supervision than those not similarly involved. Other considerations are the manager's abilities and the situation itself. When a situation requires quick decisions, an autocratic style of leadership may be best because the manager does not have to consider input from a lot of people. If a special task force must be set up to solve a quality-control problem, a normally democratic manager may give free rein to the task force. Many managers, however, are unable to use more than one style of leadership. Some are incapable of allowing their subordinates to participate in decision making, let alone make any decisions. Thus, which leadership style is best depends on specific circumstances, and effective managers will strive to adapt their leadership style as circumstances warrant. Many organizations offer programs to develop leadership skills. When plans fail, very often leaders are held responsible for what goes wrong. For example, Hewlett-Packard's CEO Leo Apotheker was let go after HP's stock dropped 45 percent under his leadership. Potential contributors to the drop in stock included HP's failed computer tablet and its announcement that it might sell its PC business.[19]

Another type of leadership style that has been gaining in popularity is authentic leadership. Authentic leadership is a bit different from the other three leadership styles because it is not exclusive. Both democratic and free-rein leaders could qualify as authentic leaders, depending on how they conduct themselves among stakeholders. Authentic leaders are passionate about the goals and mission of the company, display corporate values in the workplace, and form long-term relationships with stakeholders.[20] Kim Jordan of New Belgium Brewing Company is an authentic leader. As co-founder of the company, she helped develop the firm's core values and has ensured that everything New Belgium does aligns with these values.

Although leaders might incorporate different leadership styles, depending on the business and the situation, all leaders must be able to align employees behind a common vision to be effective.[21] Strong leaders also realize the value that employees can provide by participating in the firm's corporate culture. It is important for companies to develop leadership training programs for employees. Because managers cannot oversee everything that goes on in the company, empowering employees to take more responsibility for their decisions can aid in organizational growth and productivity. Leadership training also enables a smooth transition when an executive or manager leaves the organization. For instance, when CEO Jim Skinner of McDonald's retired in 2012, he made sure the current chief operating officer had enough leadership experience to take over the position of CEO. Although it is common for stock prices to drop whenever an effective leader leaves the organization, in this case, investors seemed so reassured that the new

SUCCESSFUL LEADERS NOT LIMITED BY LEADERSHIP STYLES

Leadership is a dynamic and complex skill that can be separated into three categories: autocratic, democratic, and free-rein. However, within these categories are a number of leadership styles and characteristics. For instance, Microsoft founder Bill Gates was an autocratic leader who, according to psychoanalyst Michael Maccoby, had a narcissistic leadership style. Although this leadership style does not allow for dissent, these leaders tend to have large groups that follow them if their vision is powerful enough. Autocratic leader Frederick Smith is characterized as having a no-excuse personality type. He views leadership as taking control and making the hard decisions, suitable for creating the highly efficient FedEx.

Herb Kelleher of Southwest Airlines and Carlos Ghosn of Nissan are in the democratic leadership category. Kelleher has a mindful leadership style because he is good at understanding the environment of his company by listening to others. Ghosn is more of a charismatic or transformational leader because he can inspire his employees and align them under a common vision. Free-rein or laissez-faire leadership is rarer, but one good example is Google's CEO Larry Page. Google's idea of leadership is allowing every employee to be a leader within the company.

So what do all these very different leaders have in common that make them successful? More than half of the most successful CEOs are considered to be creative builders or visionaries who can inspire others.[22]

Discussion Questions

1. Why might an autocratic style be suitable for certain organizations?
2. Why do you think Google has a free-rein style of leadership?
3. What are the similarities that many successful leaders share despite differences in leadership style?

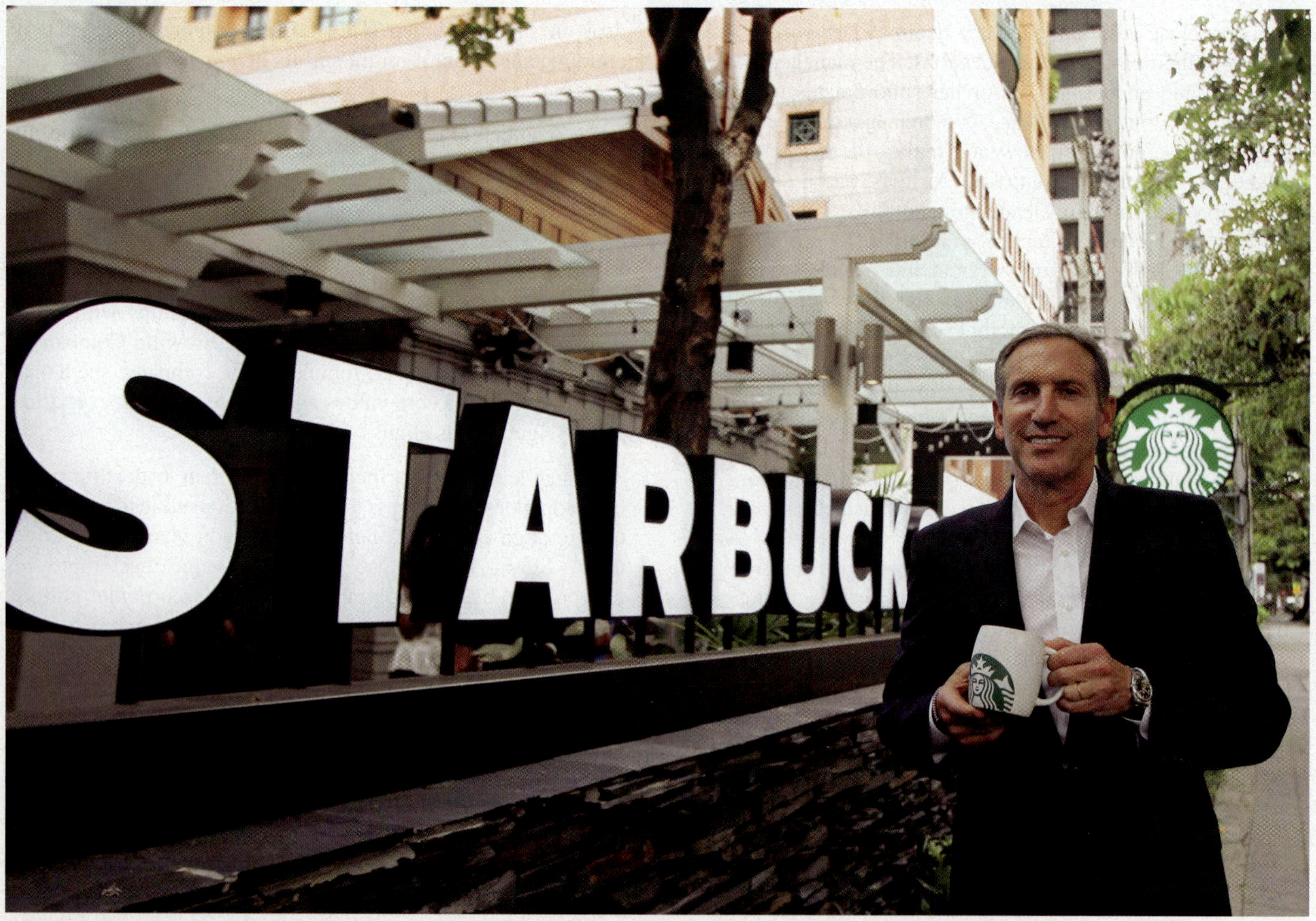

Howard Schultz, founder and CEO of Starbucks, has great human relations skills, as demonstrated by his ability to relate to others. Under his leadership, Starbucks decided to offer health insurance to its part-time workers.

leader was up to the task that stock prices hardly dropped when Skinner's resignation was announced.[23]

Employee Empowerment

Businesses are increasingly realizing the benefits of participative corporate cultures characterized by employee empowerment. **Employee empowerment** occurs when employees are provided with the ability to take on responsibilities and make decisions about their jobs. Employee empowerment does not mean that managers are not needed. Managers are important for guiding employees, setting goals, making major decisions, and performing according to other responsibilities emphasized throughout this chapter. However, companies that have a participative corporate culture can be beneficial because employees feel that they are taking an active role in the firm's success.

Leaders who wish to empower employees must adopt systems that support an employee's ability to provide input and feedback on company decisions. Employees must be encouraged to participate actively in decision making. Although this might be simpler for some employees, other employees might find it difficult if they come from more of an autocratic or authoritarian background where lower-level employees were discouraged from speaking up. Managers also might find it difficult to support a participative culture if they come from similar backgrounds. One of the best ways to overcome these challenges is through employee and managerial training. As mentioned earlier, employees should be trained in leadership skills, including teamwork, conflict resolution, and decision making. Managers should also be trained in ways to empower employees to make decisions while also guiding employees in challenging situations in which the right decision might not be so clear.[24]

A section on leadership would not be complete without a discussion of leadership in teams. In today's business world, decisions made by teams are becoming the norm. Employees at Zappos, for instance, often work in teams and are encouraged to make decisions they believe will reinforce the company's mission and values. Teamwork has often been an effective way to encourage employee empowerment. Although decision making in teams is collective, the most effective teams are those in which all employees are encouraged to contribute their ideas and recommendations. Because each employee can bring in his or her own unique insights, teams often result in innovative ideas or decisions that would not have been reached by only one or two people. However, truly empowering employees in team decision making can be difficult. It is quite common for more outspoken employees to dominate the team and/or for the team to engage in groupthink, in which team members go with the majority rather than what they think is the right decision. Training employees on how to listen to one another and provide relevant feedback can help prevent these common challenges. Another way is to rotate the team leader so that no one person can assume dominance.[25]

employee empowerment when employees are provided with the ability to take on responsibilities and make decisions about their jobs

LO 6-6 Summarize the systematic approach to decision making used by many business managers.

DECISION MAKING

Managers make many kinds of decisions, such as the hours in a workday, which employees to hire, what products to introduce, and what price to charge for a product. Decision making is important in all management functions and at all levels, whether the decisions are on a strategic, tactical, or operational level. A systematic approach using the following six steps usually leads to more-effective decision making: (1) recognizing and defining the decision situation, (2) developing options to resolve the situation, (3) analyzing the options, (4) selecting the best option, (5) implementing the decision, and (6) monitoring the consequences of the decision (Figure 6.4).

Recognizing and Defining the Decision Situation

The first step in decision making is recognizing and defining the situation. The situation may be negative—for example, huge losses on a particular product—or positive—for example, an opportunity to increase sales.

Situations calling for small-scale decisions often occur without warning. Situations requiring large-scale decisions, however, generally occur after some warning signs. Effective managers pay attention to such signals. Declining profits, small-scale losses in previous years, inventory buildup, and retailers' unwillingness to stock a product are signals that may foreshadow huge losses to come. If managers pay attention to such signals, problems can be contained.

Once a situation has been recognized, management must define it. Losses reveal a problem—for example, a failing product. One manager may define the situation as a product-quality problem; another may define it as a change in consumer preference. These two viewpoints may lead to vastly different solutions. The first manager, for example, may seek new sources of raw materials of better quality. The second manager may believe that the product has reached the end of its lifespan and decide to discontinue it. This example emphasizes the importance of carefully defining the problem rather than jumping to conclusions.

Developing Options

Once the decision situation has been recognized and defined, the next step is to develop a list of possible courses of action. The best lists include both standard and creative plans. As a general rule, more time and expertise are devoted to the development stage of decision making when the decision is of major importance. When the decision is of less importance, less time and

> AFTER DEVELOPING A LIST OF POSSIBLE COURSES OF ACTION, MANAGEMENT SHOULD ANALYZE THE PRACTICALITY AND APPROPRIATENESS OF EACH OPTION.

FIGURE 6.4
Steps in the Decision-Making Process

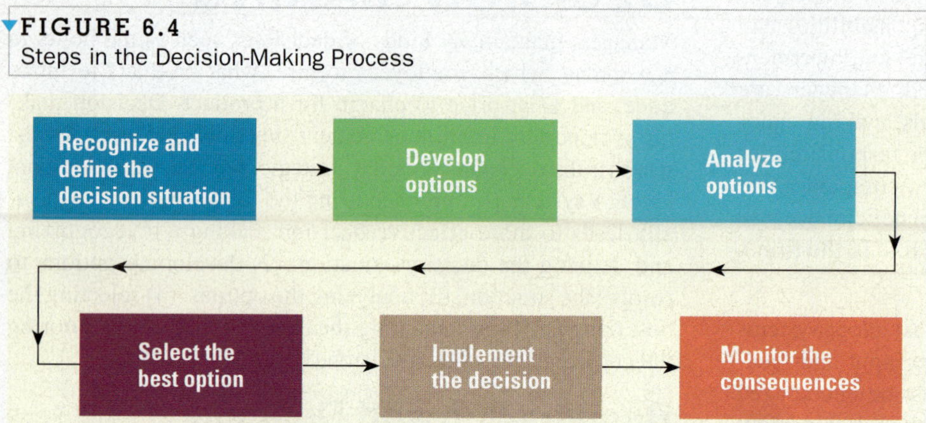

expertise will be spent on this stage. Options may be developed individually, by teams, or through analysis of similar situations in comparable organizations. Creativity is a very important part of selecting the most viable option. Creativity depends on new and useful ideas, regardless of where they originate or the method used to create them. The best option can range from a required solution to an identified problem or a volunteered solution to an observed problem by an outside work group member.[26]

Technology can help managers maintain an agenda, analyze options, and make decisions.

Analyzing Options

After developing a list of possible courses of action, management should analyze the practicality and appropriateness of each option. An option may be deemed impractical because of a lack of financial resources, legal restrictions, ethical and social responsibility considerations, authority constraints, technological constraints, economic limitations, or simply a lack of information and expertise. For example, a small computer manufacturer may recognize an opportunity to introduce a new type of computer but lack the financial resources to do so. Other options may be more practical for the computer company: It may consider selling its technology to another computer company that has adequate resources, or it may allow itself to be purchased by a larger company that can introduce the new technology.

When assessing appropriateness, the decision maker should consider whether the proposed option adequately addresses the situation. When analyzing the consequences of an option, managers should consider its impact on the situation and on the organization as a whole. For example, when considering a price cut to boost sales, management must think about the consequences of the action on the organization's cash flow and consumers' reaction to the price change.

Selecting the Best Option

When all courses of action have been analyzed, management must select the best one. Selection is often a subjective procedure because many situations do not lend themselves to quantitative analysis. Of course, it is not always necessary to select only one option and reject all others; it may be possible to select and use a combination of several options. William Wrigley Jr. made a decision to sell his firm to Mars for $23 billion. The firm was founded by his great-grandfather in 1891, but hard times forced Wrigley to take what was considered to be the best option. This option was to create the Mars-Wrigley firm, currently the world's largest confectionary company with a distribution network in 180 countries.[27] A different set of choices would have been available to the company had it been able to purchase Hershey for $12 billion a few years earlier.

Implementing the Decision

To deal with the situation at hand, the selected option or options must be put into action. Implementation can be fairly simple or very complex, depending on the nature of the decision. Effective implementation of a decision to abandon a product, close a plant, purchase a new business, or something similar requires planning. For example, when a product is dropped, managers must decide how to handle distributors and customers and what to do with the idle production facility. Additionally, they should anticipate resistance from people within the organization. (People tend to resist change because they fear the unknown.) Finally, management should be ready to deal with the unexpected consequences. No matter how well planned implementation is, unforseen problems will arise. Management must be ready to address these situations when they occur.

Monitoring the Consequences

After managers have implemented the decision, they must determine whether it has accomplished the desired result.

Without proper monitoring, the consequences of decisions may not be known quickly enough to make efficient changes. If the desired result is achieved, management can reasonably conclude that it made a good choice. If the desired result is not achieved, further analysis is warranted. Was the decision simply wrong, or did the situation change? Should some other option have been implemented?

If the desired result is not achieved, management may discover that the situation was incorrectly defined from the beginning. That may require starting the decision-making process all over again. Finally, management may determine that the decision was good even though the desired results have not yet shown up, or it may determine a flaw in the decision's implementation. In the latter case, management would not change the decision but would change the way in which it is implemented.

MANAGEMENT IN PRACTICE

Management is not a cut-and-dried process. There is no mathematical formula for managing an organization and achieving organizational goals, although many managers passionately wish for one! Managers plan, organize, staff, direct, and control, but management expert John P. Kotter says even these functions can be boiled down to two basic activities:

1. Figuring out what to do despite uncertainty, great diversity, and an enormous amount of potentially relevant information, and
2. Getting things done through a large and diverse set of people despite having little direct control over most of them.[28]

Managers spend as much as 75 percent of their time working with others—not only with subordinates but with bosses, people outside their hierarchy at work, and people outside the organization itself. In these interactions, they discuss anything and everything remotely connected with their business.

Managers spend a lot of time establishing and updating an agenda of goals and plans for carrying out their responsibilities. An **agenda** contains both specific and vague items, covering short-term goals and long-term objectives. Like a calendar, an agenda helps the manager figure out what must be done and how to get it done to meet the objectives set by the organization.

agenda a calender, containing both specific and vague items, that covers short-term goals and long-term objectives

networking the building of relationships and sharing of information with colleagues who can help managers achieve the items on their agendas

"Managers spend a lot of time establishing and updating an agenda of goals and plans for carrying out their responsibilities."

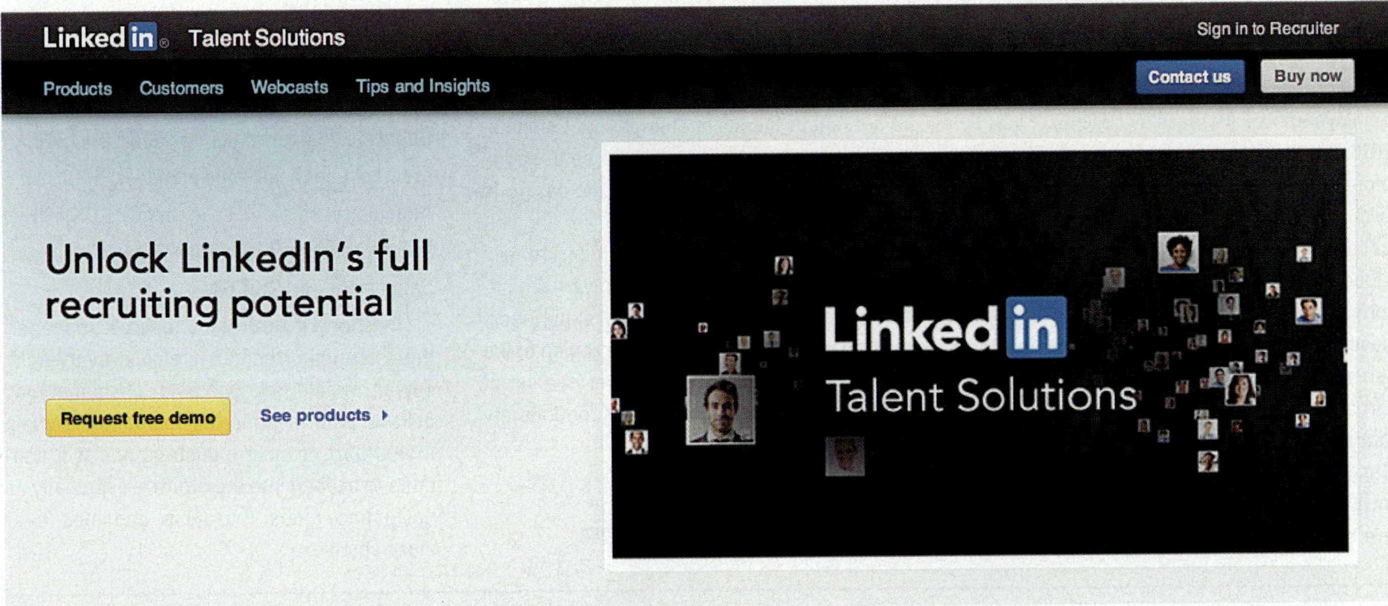

Websites like LinkedIn are helping managers and employees network with one another to achieve their professional goals.

Technology tools such as smart phones can help managers manage their agendas, contacts, communications, and time.

Managers also spend a lot of time **networking**—building relationships and sharing information with colleagues who can help them achieve the items on their agendas. Managers spend much of their time communicating with a variety of people and participating in activities that on the surface do not seem to have much to do with the goals of their organization. Nevertheless, these activities are crucial to getting the job done. Networks are not limited to immediate subordinates and bosses; they include other people in the company as well as customers, suppliers, and friends. These contacts provide managers with information and advice on diverse topics. Managers ask, persuade, and even intimidate members of their network to get information and to get things done. Networking helps managers carry out their responsibilities. Social media sites have increased the ability of both managers and subordinates to network. Internal social networks such as Yammer allow employees to connect with one another, and social networks such as Facebook or Twitter enable managers to connect with customers. Sales managers are even using social networks to communicate with their distributors. LinkedIn has been used for job networking and is gaining in popularity among the younger generation as an alternative to traditional job hunting. Some speculate that social networks might eventually replace traditional résumés and job boards.[29]

Finally, managers spend a great deal of time confronting the complex and difficult challenges of the business world today. Some of these challenges relate to rapidly changing technology (especially in production and information processing), increased scrutiny of individual and corporate ethics and social responsibility, the impact of social media, the changing nature of the workforce, new laws and regulations, increased global competition and more challenging foreign markets, declining educational standards (which may limit the skills and knowledge of the future labor and customer pool), and time itself—that is, making the best use of it. But such diverse issues cannot simply be plugged into a computer program that supplies correct, easy-to-apply solutions. It is only through creativity and imagination that managers can make effective decisions that benefit their organizations. ■

TEAM EXERCISE

Form groups and assign the responsibility of locating examples of crisis management implementation for companies dealing with natural disasters (explosions, fires, earthquakes, and so on), technology disasters (viruses, plane crashes, compromised customer data, and so on), or ethical or legal disasters. How did these companies communicate with key stakeholders? What measures did the company take to provide support to those involved in the crisis? Report your findings to the class.

SO YOU WANT TO BE A MANAGER // What Kind of Manager Do You Want to Be? /

Managers are needed in a wide variety of organizations. Experts suggest that employment will increase by millions of jobs by 2016. But the requirements for the jobs become more demanding with every passing year—with the speed of technology and communication increasing by the day, and the stress of global commerce increasing pressures to perform. However, if you like a challenge and if you have the right kind of personality, management remains a viable field. Even as companies are forced to restructure, management remains a vital role in business. In fact, the Bureau of Labor Statistics predicts that management positions in public relations, marketing, and advertising are set to increase around 12 percent overall between 2006 and 2016. Financial managers will be in even more demand, with jobs increasing 13 percent in the same time period. Computer and IT managers will continue to be in strong demand, with the number of jobs increasing 16 percent between 2006 and 2016.[30]

Salaries for managerial positions remain strong overall. Although pay can vary significantly, depending on your level of experience, the firm where you work, and the region of the country where you live, following is a list of the nationwide average incomes for a variety of managers:

Chief executive officer: $210,120
Computer and IT manager: $131,940
Marketing manager: $134,680
Financial manager: $139,690
General and operations manager: $141,170
Medical/health services manager: $110,390
Administrative services manager: $100,480
Human resources manager: $124,180
Sales manager: $127,630[31]

In short, if you want to be a manager, there are opportunities in almost every field. Fewer middle management positions may be available in firms, but managers remain a vital part of most industries and will continue to be long into the future—especially as navigating global business becomes ever more complex.

learn, practice, apply managerial skills!

M: Business was developed just for you—students on the go who need information packaged in a concise yet interesting format with multiple learning options. Check out the book's website to:

- Learn how to determine business strengths and weaknesses. (Solve the Dilemma)
- Understand the different functions of management. (Build Your Skills)
- Learn how to identify opportunities and business strategies. (Solve the Dilemma)
- Engage in the planning process. (Solve the Dilemma)

While you are there, don't forget to enhance your skills. Practice and apply your knowledge, review the practice exercises, Student PPT® slides, and quizzes to review and apply chapter concepts. Additionally, *Connect® Business* is available for *M: Business.*

www.mhhe.com/ferrellm4e

chapter seven

organization, teamwork, + communication

An organization's structure determines how well it makes decisions and responds to problems, and it influences employees' attitudes toward their work. A suitable structure can minimize a business's costs and maximize its efficiency. Even companies that operate within the same industry may use different organizational structures. For example, in the medical device industry, 3M is organized by line of business (health care products, office products, security tools), whereas Medtronic has similar business groups, but it also has top-level, functional units that focus on legal issues, strategy, and human resources operating above each of the lines of business.[1]

Because a business's structure can so profoundly affect its success, this chapter will examine organizational structure in detail. First, we discuss how an organization's culture affects its operations. Then we consider the development of structure, including how tasks and responsibilities are organized through specialization and departmentalization. Next, we explore some of the forms organizational structure may take. Finally, we consider communications within business. ■

LEARNING OBJECTIVES

After reading this chapter, you will be able to:

- **LO 7-1** Define organizational structure and relate how organizational structures develop.
- **LO 7-2** Describe how specialization and departmentalization help an organization achieve its goals.
- **LO 7-3** Determine how organizations assign responsibility for tasks and delegate authority.
- **LO 7-4** Compare and contrast some common forms of organizational structure.
- **LO 7-5** Distinguish between groups and teams and identify the types of groups that exist in organizations.
- **LO 7-6** Describe how communication occurs in organizations.

organizational culture a firm's shared values, beliefs, traditions, philosophies, rules, and role models for behavior

structure the arrangement or relationship of positions within an organization

ORGANIZATIONAL CULTURE

One of the most important aspects of organizing a business is determining its **organizational culture**, a firm's shared values, beliefs, traditions, philosophies, rules, and role models for behavior. Also called corporate culture, an organizational culture exists in every organization, regardless of size, organizational type, product, or profit objective. Sometimes behaviors, programs, and policies enhance and support the organizational culture. For example, because The Container Store views employees as its most important stakeholders, it holds a "We Love Our Employees" Day on Valentine's Day to honor its employees. Events such as these make employees feel appreciated, which contributes to the organization's low turnover rate.[2] A firm's culture may be expressed formally through its mission statement, codes of ethics, memos, manuals, and ceremonies, but it is more commonly expressed informally. Examples of informal expressions of culture include dress codes (or the lack thereof), work habits, extracurricular activities, and stories. Employees often learn the accepted standards through discussions with co-workers.

TOMS Shoes' organizational culture is determined by the founder's desire to provide as many shoes as possible to children in developing countries (where shoeless children walk for miles to get water, food, and medical care). Blake Mycoskie gives hundreds of thousands of shoes to children around the world each year, creating a strong organizational culture of giving back and corporate social responsibility. His company operates with a program that for every pair of shoes purchased, a pair will be donated to children in need.[3] Disneyland/DisneyWorld and McDonald's have organizational cultures focused on cleanliness, value, and service. The Zappos.com company created a culture of "fun and a little weirdness." The company has a flexible work environment with very few rules, and employees are encouraged to socialize and engage in unique activities (such as ringing cowbells when visitors arrive). Zappos' goal is to make both employees and customers feel good. Customer service is such a must at Zappos that new hires must work for one month at a call center, even if the new employees are not going to be interacting with customers normally.[4] When such values and philosophies are shared by all members of an organization, they will be expressed in its relationships with stakeholders. However, organizational cultures that lack such positive values may result in employees who are unproductive and indifferent and have poor attitudes, which will be reflected externally to customers. The corporate culture may have contributed to the misconduct at a number of well-known companies. A survey found that executives in financial and technology companies are mostly cutthroat in collecting intelligence about competition, creating a corporate culture in which unethical acts might be tolerated if it means beating the competition.[5]

Organizational culture helps ensure that all members of a company share values and suggests rules for how to behave and deal with problems within the organization. Table 7.1 confirms that executives in this study believe that corporate culture has

PEER PERFORMANCE REVIEWS ENCOURAGE TEAMWORK AND COMMUNICATION

Would you rather have your boss or your peers evaluate your performance? Some companies have begun to use peer performance reviews as a way to flatten the organization, enhance communication, and encourage teamwork among work colleagues. LivingSocial, for instance, uses an employee-recognition software that allows its 5,000 employees to provide feedback on their peers. This feedback is then used to determine bonuses.

The reasoning behind peer-reviewed performance evaluations is clear: Colleagues often have a better idea of your true work performance than managers. Using more people can also eliminate biases and distribute rewards more equally. By placing more power in the hands of employees, organizations can encourage employees to communicate with one another about their progress. Perhaps most important, peer reviews remind employees from different departments that they are on the same team working to advance company goals.

However, the peer performance review is not without obstacles. Individuals tend to choose more positive or negative extremes in their ratings. In addition, employees may not be familiar with all the responsibilities of their peers. The LRN company addresses some of these issues by allowing employees to choose 20 people to evaluate their progress. Afterward, the employees read their peers' evaluations and rate themselves. These ratings determine the amount of bonus they receive. Despite the potential downsides of peer evaluations, peer performance reviews often add a greater sense of perceived legitimacy and employee empowerment.[6]

Discussion Questions

1. How do peer performance reviews enhance communication?
2. Why might peer performance reviews be more reliable than traditional ones?
3. How has LRN gotten past obstacles in peer performance reviews?

TABLE 7.1 Employees Who View Their Corporate Cultures Positively vs. Negatively

	Employees who view their culture negatively	Employees who view their culture positively
Committed toward the organization	17%	86%
Satisfied with the organization	13%	87%
Likely to recommend their organization to others	13%	88%
Intend to leave the organization	63%	10%
Alignment with leadership	8%	59%

n = 236 management and human resources professionals from U.S. companies with more than 100 employees.

Source: Survey conducted by Critical Metrics, LLC, *CRO Magazine* 3, no. 3, June 2012, www.thecro.com/content/quantifying-corporate-culture.

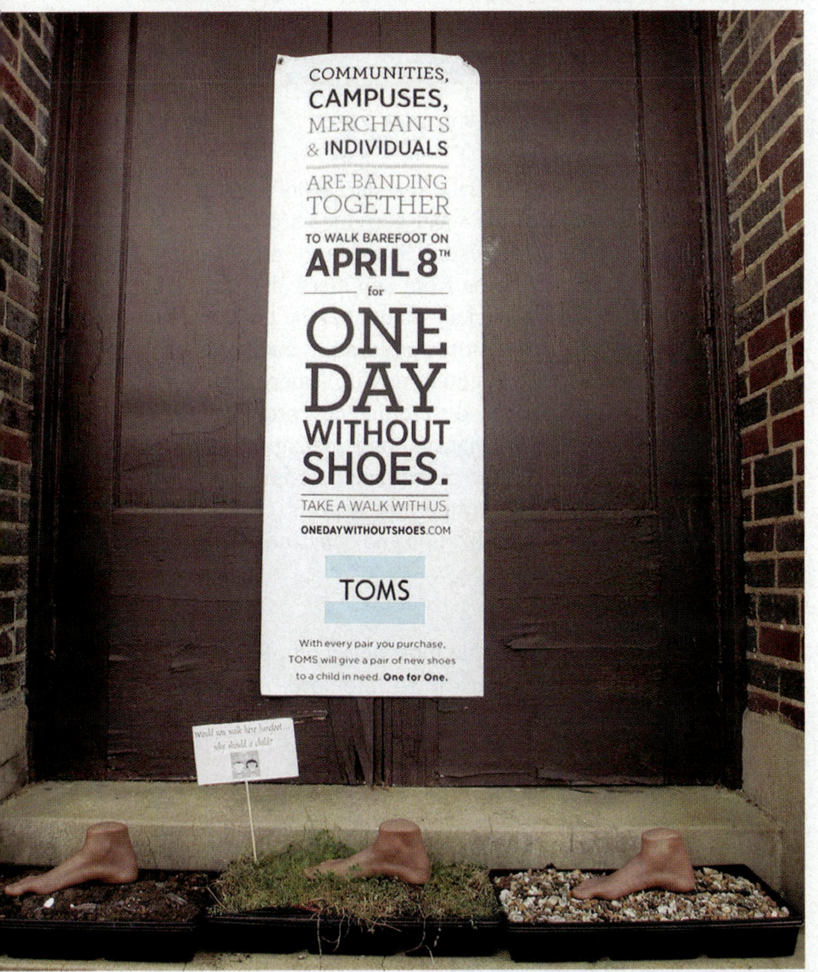

The organizational structure at TOMS Shoes consists of two parts. The for-profit component of the company manages overall operations. Its nonprofit component, Friends of TOMS, is responsible for volunteer activities and shoe donations.

a significant impact on organizational performance and the ability to retain good employees. The key to success in any organization is satisfying stakeholders, especially customers. Establishing a positive organizational culture sets the tone for all other decisions, including building an efficient organizational structure.

LO 7-1 Define organizational structure and relate how organizational structures develop.

DEVELOPING ORGANIZATIONAL STRUCTURE

Structure is the arrangement or relationship of positions within an organization. Rarely is an organization, or any group of individuals working together, able to achieve common objectives without some form of structure, whether that structure is explicitly defined or only implied. A professional baseball team such as the Colorado Rockies is a business organization with an explicit formal structure that guides the team's activities so that it can increase game attendance, win games, and sell souvenirs such as T-shirts. But even an informal group playing softball for fun has an organization that specifies who will pitch, catch, bat, coach, and so on. Governments and nonprofit organizations also have formal organizational structures to facilitate the achievement of their objectives. Getting people to work together efficiently and coordinating the skills of diverse individuals require careful planning. Developing appropriate organizational structures is therefore a major challenge for managers in both large and small organizations.

An organization's structure develops when managers assign work tasks and activities to specific individuals or work groups and coordinate the diverse activities required to reach the firm's objectives. When Macy's, for example, has a sale, the store manager must work with the advertising department to make the public aware of the sale, with department managers to ensure that extra salespeople are scheduled to handle the increased customer traffic, and with merchandise buyers to ensure that enough sale merchandise is available to meet expected consumer demand. All the people occupying these positions must work together to achieve the store's objectives.

The best way to begin to understand how organizational structure develops is to consider the evolution of a new business such as a clothing store. At first, the business is a sole proprietorship

> GROWTH REQUIRES ORGANIZING—THE STRUCTURING OF HUMAN, PHYSICAL, AND FINANCIAL RESOURCES TO ACHIEVE OBJECTIVES IN AN EFFECTIVE AND EFFICIENT MANNER.

in which the owner does everything—buys, prices, and displays the merchandise; does the accounting and tax records; and assists customers. As the business grows, the owner hires a salesperson and perhaps a merchandise buyer to help run the store. As the business continues to grow, the owner hires more salespeople. The growth and success of the business now require the owner to be away from the store frequently, meeting with suppliers, engaging in public relations, and attending trade shows. Thus, the owner must designate someone to manage the salespeople and maintain the accounting, payroll, and tax functions. If the owner decides to expand by opening more stores, still more managers will be needed. Figure 7.1 shows these stages of growth with three **organizational charts** (visual displays of organizational structure, chain of command, and other relationships).

Growth requires organizing—the structuring of human, physical, and financial resources to achieve objectives in an effective and efficient manner. Growth necessitates hiring people who have specialized skills. With more people and greater specialization, the organization needs to develop a formal structure to function efficiently. Imagine the organizational changes that Nathan's Famous hot dogs underwent from 1916, when it operated a single Coney Island hot dog shop, to a company that now operates an international chain of fast-food restaurants as well as selling food products through supermarkets. The company sells more than 425 million hot dogs a year and generates more than $66 million in revenue.[7] As we shall see, structuring an organization requires management to assign work tasks to specific individuals and departments and assign responsibility for the achievement of specific organizational objectives.

LO 7-2 Describe how specialization and departmentalization help an organization achieve its goals.

ASSIGNING TASKS

For a business to earn profits from the sale of its products, its managers must first determine what activities are required to achieve its objectives. At Celestial Seasonings, for example, employees must purchase herbs from suppliers, dry the herbs and place them in tea bags, package and label the tea, and then ship the packages to grocery stores around the country. Other necessary activities include negotiating with supermarkets and other retailers for display space, developing new products, planning advertising, managing finances, and managing employees. All these activities must be coordinated, assigned to work groups, and controlled. Two important aspects of assigning these work activities are specialization and departmentalization.

Specialization

After identifying all activities that must be accomplished, managers then break these activities down into specific tasks that

FIGURE 7.1
The Evolution of a Clothing Store, Phases 1, 2, and 3

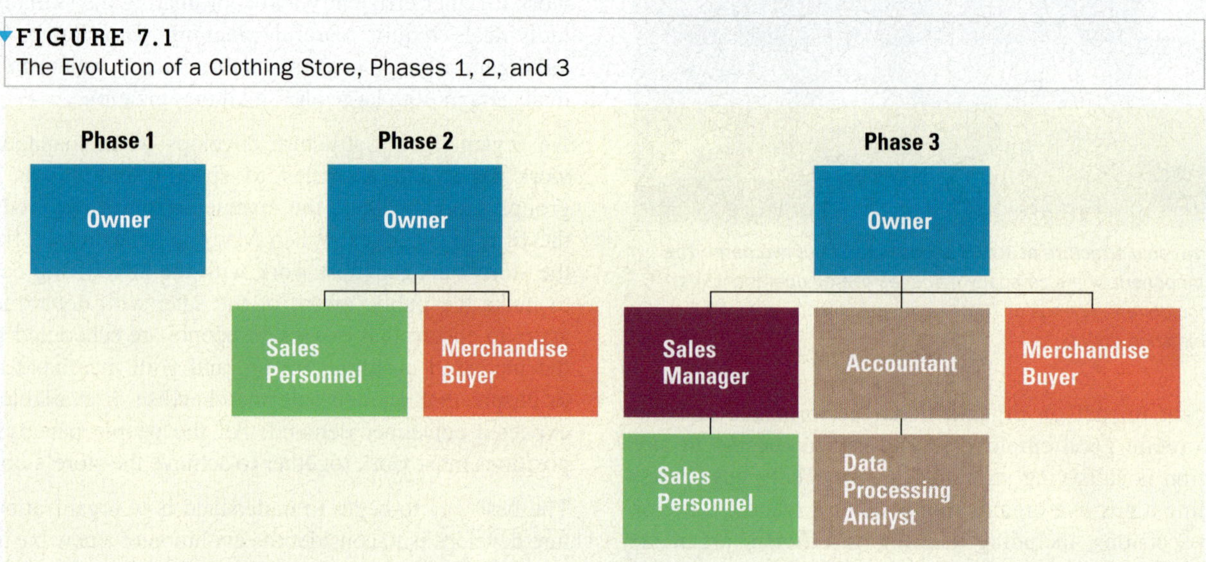

organizational chart a visual display of the organizational structure, lines of authority (chain of command), staff relationships, permanent committee arrangements, and lines of communication

specialization the division of labor into small, specific tasks and the assignment of employees to do a single task

departmentalization the grouping of jobs into working units usually called departments, units, groups, or divisions

can be handled by individual employees. This division of labor into small, specific tasks and the assignment of employees to do a single task is called **specialization**.

The rationale for specialization is efficiency. People can perform more efficiently if they master just one task rather than all tasks. In *The Wealth of Nations,* 18th-century economist Adam Smith discussed specialization, using the manufacture of straight pins as an example. Individually, workers could produce 20 pins a day when each employee produced complete pins. Thus, 10 employees working independently of each other could produce 200 pins a day. However, when one worker drew the wire, another straightened it, a third cut it, and a fourth ground the point, 10 workers could produce 48,000 pins per day.[8] To save money and achieve the benefits of specialization, some companies outsource and hire temporary workers to provide key skills. Many highly skilled, diverse, experienced workers are available through temp agencies.

Specialization means workers do not waste time shifting from one job to another, and training is easier. However, efficiency is not the only motivation for specialization. Specialization also occurs when the activities that must be performed within an organization are too numerous for one person to handle. Recall the example of the clothing store. When the business was young and small, the owner could do everything; but when the business grew, the owner needed help waiting on customers, keeping the books, and managing other business activities.

Overspecialization can have negative consequences. Employees may become bored and dissatisfied with their jobs, and the result of their unhappiness is likely to be poor-quality work, more injuries, and high employee turnover. In extreme cases, employees in crowded specialized electronic plants are unable to form working relationships with one another. At Foxconn, a multinational electronics manufacturing firm and one of the suppliers of Apple iPhones and iPods, lack of working relationships, long work hours, low pay, and other conditions have resulted in employee dissatisfaction and, tragically, depression and even suicide.[9] This is why some manufacturing firms allow job rotation so that employees do not become dissatisfied and leave. Although some degree of specialization is necessary for efficiency, because of differences in skills, abilities, and interests, all people are not equally suited for all jobs. We examine some strategies to overcome these issues in Chapter 9.

"Specialization means workers do not waste time shifting from one job to another, and training is easier."

Job specialization is common in automobile manufacturing. By dividing work into smaller specialized tasks, employees can perform their work more quickly and efficiently.

Departmentalization

After assigning specialized tasks to individuals, managers next organize workers doing similar jobs into groups to make them easier to manage. **Departmentalization** is the grouping of jobs into working units usually called departments, units, groups, or divisions. As we shall see, departments are commonly organized by function, product, geographic region, or customer (Figure 7.2). Most companies use more than one departmentalization plan to enhance productivity. For instance, many consumer goods manufacturers have departments for specific product lines (beverages, frozen dinners, canned goods, and so on) as well as departments dealing with legal, purchasing, finance, human resources, and other business functions. For smaller companies, accounting can be set up online, almost as an automated department. Accounting software can handle electronic transfers so you never have to worry about a late bill. Many city governments also have departments for specific services (for instance, police, fire, waste disposal) as well as departments for legal, human resources, and other business functions. Figure 7.3 (on page 145) depicts the organizational chart for the city of Corpus Christi, Texas, showing these departments.

functional departmentalization the grouping of jobs that perform similar functional activities, such as finance, manufacturing, marketing, and human resources

Functional Departmentalization

Functional departmentalization groups jobs that perform similar functional activities, such as finance, manufacturing, marketing, and human resources. Each of these functions is managed by an expert in the work done by the department—an engineer supervises the production department; a financial executive supervises the finance department. This approach is common in small organizations. Green Mountain Coffee is departmentalized into six functions: sales and marketing, operations, human resources, finance, information systems, and social responsibility. A weakness of functional departmentalization is that, because it tends to emphasize departmental units rather than the organization as a whole, decision making that involves more than one department may be slow, and it requires greater coordination. Thus, as businesses grow, they tend to adopt other approaches to organizing jobs.

Product Departmentalization

Product departmentalization, as you might guess, organizes jobs around the products of the firm. Procter & Gamble has global units, such as laundry and cleaning products, paper products, and health care products. Each division develops and implements its own product plans, monitors the results, and takes corrective action as necessary. Functional activities—production, finance, marketing, and others—are located within each product division.

FIGURE 7.2
Departmentalization

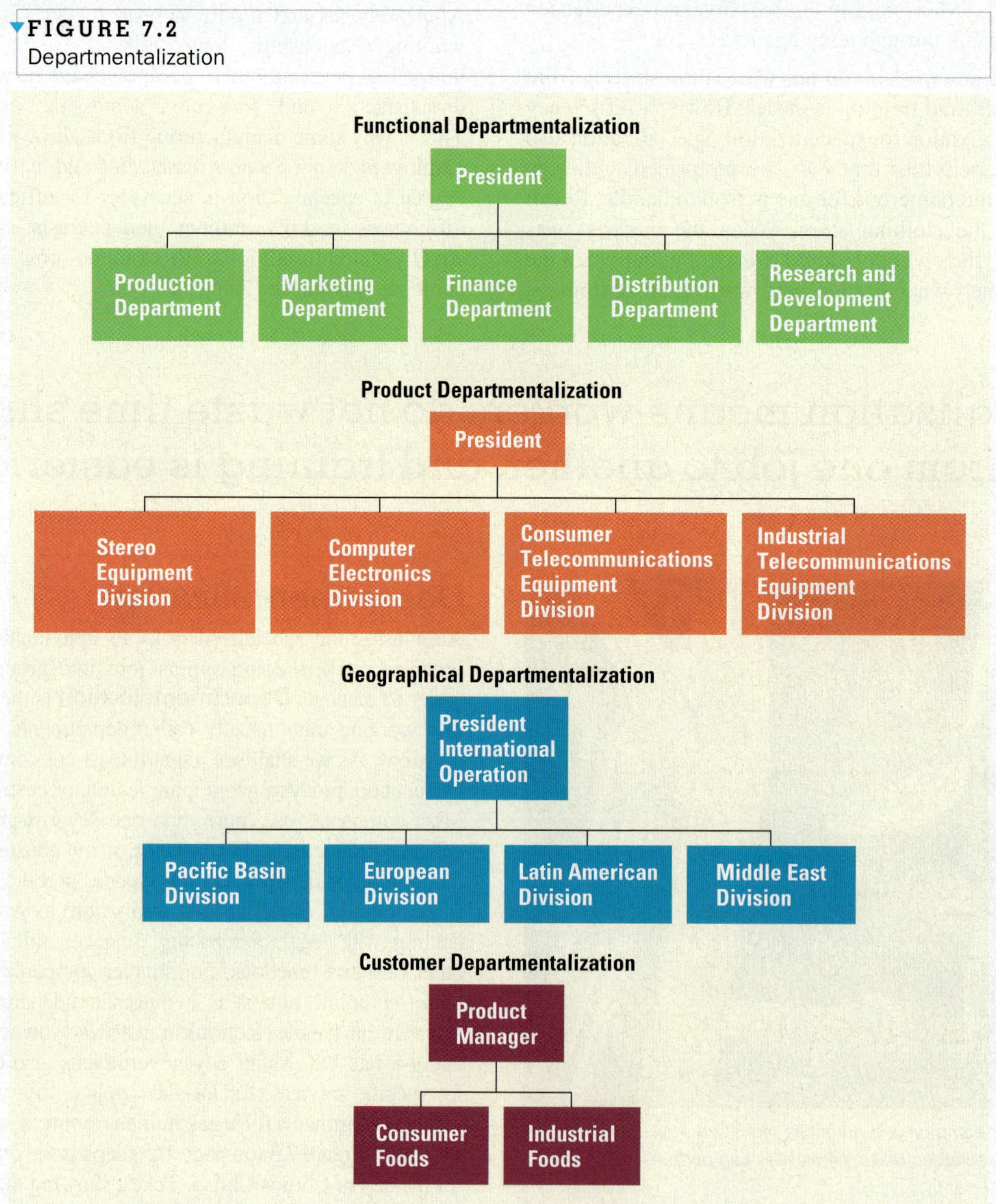

product departmentalization the organization of jobs in relation to the products of the firm

geographical departmentalization the grouping of jobs according to geographic location, such as state, region, country, or continent

Consequently, organizing by products duplicates functions and resources and emphasizes the product rather than achievement of the organization's overall objectives. However, it simplifies decision making and helps coordinate all activities related to a product or product group. The Campbell Soup Company is organized into four segments: (1) U.S. Soup, Sauces and Beverages, which includes Campbell's soups, Swanson broth, Prego pasta sauce, V8 juice and juice drinks, Campbell's tomato juice, and related products; (2) Baking and Snacking, which includes Pepperidge Farm cookies, crackers, bakery, and frozen products and Arnott's biscuits and salty snacks; (3) International Soup, Sauces and Beverages, which includes soup, sauces, and beverages sold outside the United States; and (4) North America Foodservice, which includes prepared food operations. Campbell's has actually adopted a combination of two types of departmentalization. Although it clearly separates baking and snacking products from soups and beverages, the company also chooses to divide its segments into geographic regions—a type of geographic departmentalization.[10]

Geographical Departmentalization **Geographical departmentalization** groups jobs according to geographic location, such as a state, region, country, or continent. Frito-Lay, for example, is organized into four regional divisions, allowing the company to get closer to its customers and respond more quickly and efficiently to regional competitors. Multinational corporations often use a geographical approach because of vast differences between different regions. Coca-Cola, General Motors, and Caterpillar are organized by region.

FIGURE 7.3
An Organizational Chart for the City of Corpus Christi, Texas

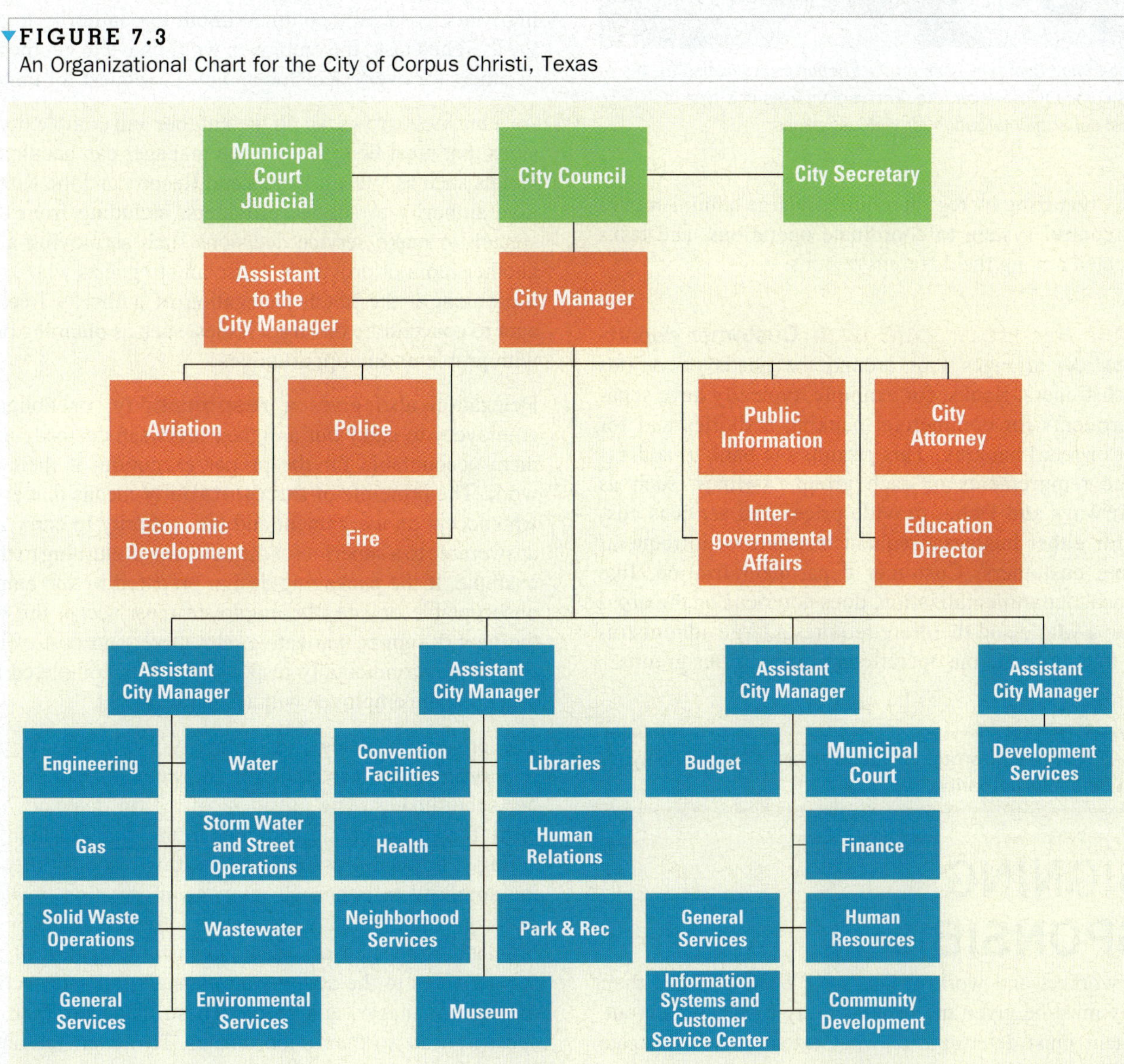

Source: "City of Corpus Christi Organizational Chart," City of Corpus Christi, www.cctexas.com/files/g5/cityorgchart.pdf.

customer departmentalization the arrangement of jobs around the needs of various types of customers

delegation of authority giving employees not only tasks but also the power to make commitments, use resources, and take whatever actions are necessary to carry out those tasks

responsibility the obligation, placed on employees through delegation, to perform assigned tasks satisfactorily and be held accountable for the proper execution of work

accountability the principle that employees who accept an assignment and the authority to carry it out are answerable to a superior for the outcome

The Campbell Soup Company uses product departmentalization to organize its company. However, the firm also engages in a type of geographical departmentalization for various regions.

However, organizing by region requires a large administrative staff and control system to coordinate operations, and tasks are duplicated among the different regions.

Customer Departmentalization

Customer departmentalization arranges jobs around the needs of various types of customers. Banks, for example, typically have separate departments for commercial banking activities and for consumer or retail banking. This permits the bank to address the unique requirements of each group. Airlines, such as British Airways and Delta, provide prices and services customized for either business/frequent travelers or infrequent/vacationing customers. Customer departmentalization, like geographical departmentalization, does not focus on the organization as a whole and therefore requires a large administrative staff to coordinate the operations of the various groups.

LO 7-3 Determine how organizations assign responsibility for tasks and delegate authority.

ASSIGNING RESPONSIBILITY

After all workers and work groups have been assigned their tasks, they must be given the responsibility to carry them out. Management must determine to what extent it will delegate responsibility throughout the organization and how many employees will report to each manager.

Delegation of Authority

Delegation of authority means not only giving tasks to employees but also empowering them to make commitments, use resources, and take whatever actions are necessary to carry out those tasks. Let's say a marketing manager at Nestlé has assigned an employee to design a new package that is less wasteful (more environmentally responsible) than the current package for one of the company's frozen-dinner lines. To carry out the assignment, the employee needs access to information and the authority to make certain decisions on packaging materials, costs, and so on. Without the authority to carry out the assigned task, the employee would have to get the approval of others for every decision and every request for materials.

As a business grows, so do the number and complexity of decisions that must be made; no one manager can handle them all. Hotels such as Westin Hotels and Resorts and the Ritz-Carlton give authority to service providers, including front desk personnel, to make service decisions such as moving a guest to another room or providing a discount to guests who experience a problem at the hotel. Delegation of authority frees a manager to concentrate on larger issues, such as planning or dealing with problems and opportunities.

Delegation also gives a **responsibility**, or obligation, to employees to carry out assigned tasks satisfactorily and holds them accountable for the proper execution of their assigned work. The principle of **accountability** means that employees who accept an assignment and the authority to carry it out are answerable to a superior for the outcome. Returning to the Nestlé example, if the packaging design prepared by the employee is unacceptable or late, the employee must accept the blame. If the new design is innovative, attractive, and cost-efficient, as well as environmentally responsible, or is completed ahead of schedule, the employee will accept the credit.

The process of delegating authority establishes a pattern of relationships and accountability between a superior and his or her subordinates. The president of a firm delegates responsibility for all marketing activities to the vice president of marketing. The vice president accepts this responsibility and has the authority to obtain all relevant information, make certain decisions, and delegate any or all activities to his or her subordinates. The vice president, in turn, delegates all advertising activities to the advertising manager, all sales activities to the sales manager, and so on. These managers then delegate specific tasks to their subordinates. However, the act of delegating authority to a subordinate does not relieve the superior of accountability for the delegated job. Even though the vice president of marketing delegates work to subordinates, he or she is still ultimately accountable to the president for all marketing activities.

Degree of Centralization

The extent to which authority is delegated throughout an organization determines its degree of centralization.

Centralized Organizations In a **centralized organization**, authority is concentrated at the top, and very little decision-making authority is delegated to lower levels. Although decision-making authority in centralized organizations rests with top levels of management, a vast amount of responsibility for carrying out daily and routine procedures is delegated to even the lowest levels of the organization. Many government organizations, including the U.S. Army, the Postal Service, and the IRS, are centralized.

Businesses tend to be more centralized when the decisions to be made are risky and when low-level managers are not highly skilled in decision making. In the banking industry, for example, authority to make routine car loans is given to all loan managers, whereas the authority to make high-risk loans, such as for a large residential development, may be restricted to upper-level loan officers.

Overcentralization can cause serious problems for a company, in part because it may take longer for the organization as a whole to implement decisions and to respond to changes and problems on a regional scale. McDonald's, for example, was one of the last chains to introduce a chicken sandwich because of the amount of research, development, test marketing, and layers of approval the product had to go through.

Decentralized Organizations A **decentralized organization** is one in which decision-making authority is delegated as far down the chain of command as possible. Decentralization is characteristic of organizations that operate in complex, unpredictable environments. Businesses that face intense competition often decentralize to improve responsiveness and enhance creativity. Lower-level managers who interact with the external environment often develop a good understanding of it and thus are able to react quickly to changes. Green Mountain Coffee has a very decentralized, flat organizational structure.

centralized organization a structure in which authority is concentrated at the top, and very little decision-making authority is delegated to lower levels

decentralized organization an organization in which decision-making authority is delegated as far down the chain of command as possible

Delegating authority to lower levels of managers may increase the organization's productivity. Decentralization requires that lower-level managers have strong decision-making skills. In recent years, the trend has been toward more decentralized organizations, and some of the largest and most successful companies, including GE, IBM, Google, and Nike, have decentralized decision-making authority. McDonald's, realizing most of its growth outside the United States, is becoming increasingly decentralized and "glo-cal," varying products in specific markets to meet consumer demands better. This change in organizational structure for McDonald's is fostering greater innovation and local market success. McDonald's, which was long known for the homogeneity of its products, has embraced local cuisine on a limited scale. For instance, because cows are sacred in India, McDonald's has introduced the McVeggie and the Veg McMuffin. It also sells the Spicy Paneer Wrap, made with

BOSS-LESS ORGANIZATIONS HAVE THEIR BENEFITS

Can you imagine working in an organization where there is no boss? Some businesses are eliminating the management position in the ultimate flat organizational structure. Flat organizations occur when there is no traditional hierarchical management system and decisions are made democratically. Valve Corp, a videogame development company, is an example of a business that has instituted this type of management style. Each employee gives input as to salary determinations, who they will work with, what their assignments will be, and who they will hire and fire.

Boss-less organizations can work only in firms that are relatively small with employees who are self-motivated and independent. Because of the democratic quality of this style, decisions can sometimes take a long time to make, and it can be difficult to find inefficiencies immediately in employees or processes. However, the potential for creativity and innovation is high in companies that adopt this practice. In some cases, the employees exhibit higher performance than in traditional management structures. Employees generally form work teams and have high levels of responsibility and accountability. Communication within the company is usually of higher quality and happens more quickly.

Although this kind of management system is hard to implement, after it takes hold, it can be very effective. Yet there can be a significant downside: Employees who are ambitious might not like this kind of environment because there are no titles or heads of departments, which limits promotion opportunities.[11]

Discussion Questions

1. What are some benefits in organizations where there is no boss?
2. What are some disadvantages in organizations where there is no boss?
3. Why would big companies have trouble implementing this management structure?

span of management the number of subordinates who report to a particular manager

organizational layers the levels of management in an organization

chicken, paneer cheese, and spicy batter, to appeal to Indians' preferences for spicy food.[12] Diversity and decentralization seem to be McDonald's keys to being better, not just bigger. Nonprofit organizations benefit from decentralization as well.

Span of Management

How many subordinates should a manager manage? There is no simple answer. Experts generally agree, however, that top managers should not directly supervise more than four to eight people, whereas lower-level managers who supervise routine tasks are capable of managing a much larger number of subordinates. For example, the manager of the finance department may supervise 25 employees, whereas the vice president of finance may supervise only five managers. **Span of management** refers to the number of subordinates who report to a particular manager. A *wide span of management* exists when a manager directly supervises a very large number of employees. A *narrow span of management* exists when a manager directly supervises only a few subordinates (Figure 7.4). At Whole Foods, the best employees are recruited and placed in small teams. Employees are empowered to discount, give away, and sample products as well as to assist in creating a respectful workplace where goals are achieved, individual employees succeed, and customers are core in business decisions. Whole Foods teams get to vote on new employee hires as well. This approach allows Whole Foods to offer unique and "local market" experiences in each of its stores. This level of customization is in contrast to more centralized national supermarket chains such as Kroger, Safeway, and Publix.[13]

FIGURE 7.4
Span of Management: Wide Span and Narrow Span

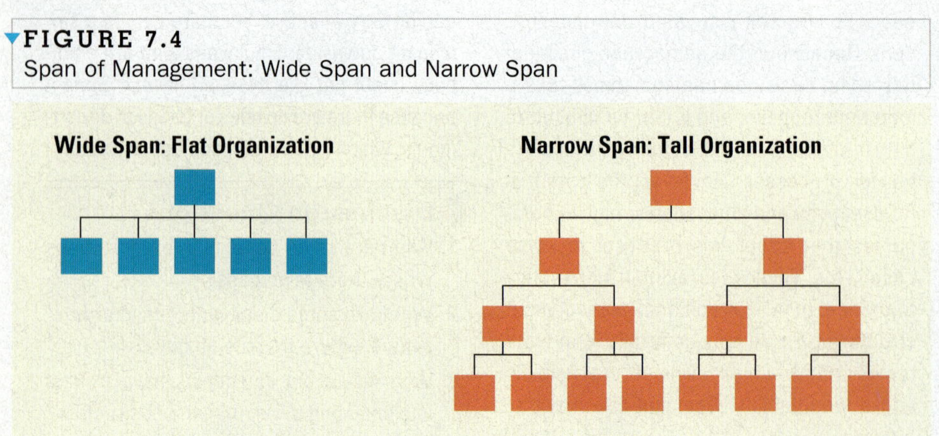

Should the span of management be wide or narrow? To answer this question, several factors need to be considered. A narrow span of management is appropriate when superiors and subordinates are not in close proximity, the manager has many responsibilities in addition to the supervision, the interaction between superiors and subordinates is frequent, and problems are common. However, when superiors and subordinates are located close to one another, the manager has few responsibilities other than supervision, the level of interaction between superiors and subordinates is low, few problems arise, subordinates are highly competent, and a set of specific operating procedures governs the activities of managers and their subordinates, a wide span of management will be more appropriate. Narrow spans of management are typical in centralized organizations; wide spans of management are more common in decentralized firms.

Organizational Layers

Complementing the concept of span of management is **organizational layers**, the levels of management in an organization. A company with many layers of managers is considered tall; in a tall organization, the span of management is narrow (see Figure 7.4). Because each manager supervises only a few subordinates, many layers of management are necessary to carry out the operations of the business. McDonald's, for example, has a tall organization with many layers, including store managers, district managers, regional managers, and functional managers (finance, marketing, and so on), as well as a chief executive officer and many vice presidents. Because there are more managers in tall organizations than in flat organizations, administrative costs are usually higher. Communication is slower because information must pass through many layers.

> "A company with many layers of managers is considered tall."

Organizations with few layers are flat and have wide spans of management. When managers supervise a large number of employees, fewer management layers are needed to conduct the organization's activities. Managers in flat organizations typically perform more administrative duties than managers in tall organizations because there are fewer of them. They also spend more time supervising and working with subordinates.

Many of the companies that have decentralized also flattened their structures and widened their spans of management, often by eliminating layers of middle management. As mentioned earlier in this chapter, Green Mountain Coffee has both a decentralized and flat organizational structure. Other corporations, including Avon, AT&T, and Ford Motor Company, embraced a more decentralized structure to reduce costs, speed up decision making, and boost overall productivity.

line structure the simplest organizational structure, in which direct lines of authority extend from the top manager to the lowest level of the organization

line-and-staff structure a structure having a traditional line relationship between superiors and subordinates and also specialized managers—called staff managers—who are available to assist line managers

multidivisional structure a structure that organizes departments into larger groups called divisions

LO 7-4 Compare and contrast some common forms of organizational structure.

FORMS OF ORGANIZATIONAL STRUCTURE

Along with assigning tasks and the responsibility for carrying them out, managers must consider how to structure their authority relationships—that is, what structure the organization itself will have and how it will appear on the organizational chart. Common forms of organization include line structure, line-and-staff structure, multidivisional structure, and matrix structure.

Line Structure

The simplest organizational structure, **line structure**, has direct lines of authority that extend from the top manager to employees at the lowest level of the organization. For example, a convenience store employee at 7-Eleven may report to an assistant manager, who reports to the store manager, who reports to a regional manager, or, in an independent store, directly to the owner (Figure 7.5). This structure has a clear chain of command, which enables managers to make decisions quickly. A mid-level manager facing a decision must consult only one person, his or her immediate supervisor. However, this structure requires managers to possess a wide range of knowledge and skills. They are responsible for a variety of activities and must be knowledgeable about them all. Line structures are most common in small businesses.

Line-and-Staff Structure

The **line-and-staff structure** has a traditional line relationship between superiors and subordinates, and specialized managers—called staff managers—are available to assist line managers (Figure 7.6). Line managers can focus on their area of expertise in the operation of the business, whereas staff managers provide advice and support to line departments on specialized matters such as finance, engineering, human resources, and the law. In the city of Corpus Christi (refer to Figure 7.3), for example, assistant city managers are line managers who oversee groups of related departments. However, the city attorney, police chief, and fire chief are effectively staff managers who report directly to the city manager (the city equivalent of a business chief executive officer). Staff managers do not have direct authority over line managers or over the line manager's subordinates, but they do have direct authority over subordinates in their own departments. However, line-and-staff organizations may experience problems with overstaffing and ambiguous lines of communication. In addition, employees may become frustrated because they lack the authority to carry out certain decisions.

Multidivisional Structure

As companies grow and diversify, traditional line structures become difficult to coordinate, making communication difficult and decision making slow. When the weaknesses of the structure—the "turf wars," miscommunication, and working at cross-purposes—exceed the benefits, growing firms tend to restructure, often into the divisionalized form. A **multidivisional structure** organizes departments into larger groups called divisions. Just as departments might be formed on the basis of geography, customer, product, or a combination of these, so too divisions can be formed based on any of these methods of organizing. Within each of these divisions, departments may be organized by product, geographic region, function, or some combination of all three. Indra Nooyi, CEO of PepsiCo, rearranged the company's organizational structure. Prior to her tenure, PepsiCo was organized geographically. She created new units—PepsiCo Americas Foods (PAF), PepsiCo Americas Beverages (PAB), PepsiCo Europe, and PepsiCo Asia, Middle

FIGURE 7.5
Line Structure

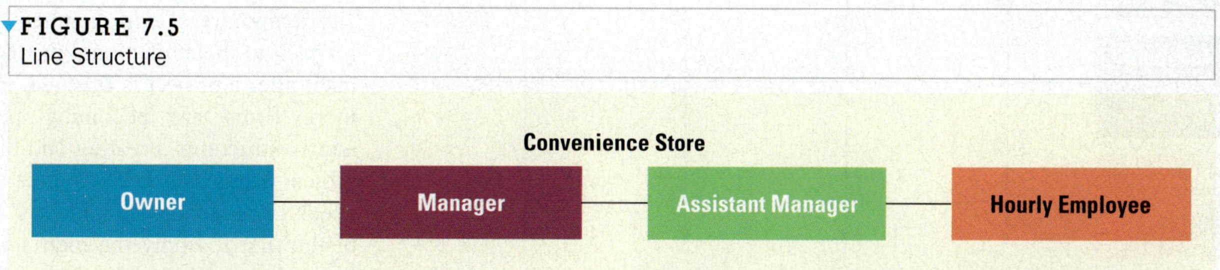

FIGURE 7.6
Line-and-Staff Structure

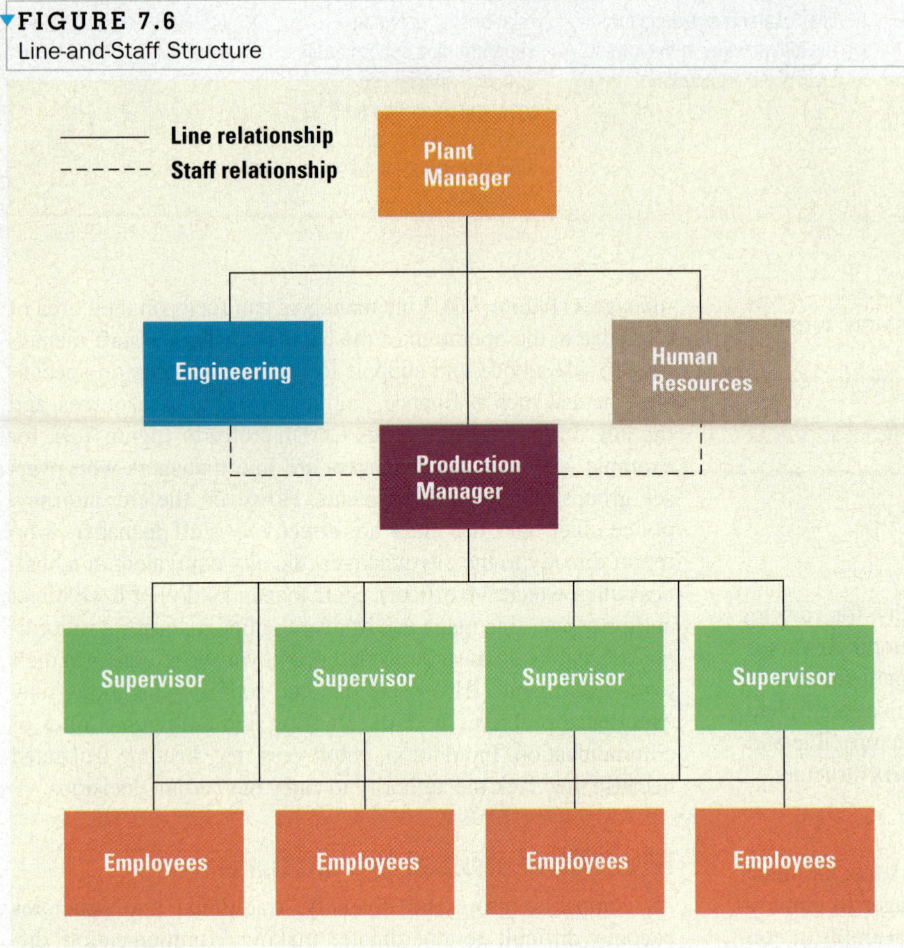

FIGURE 7.7
Matrix Structure

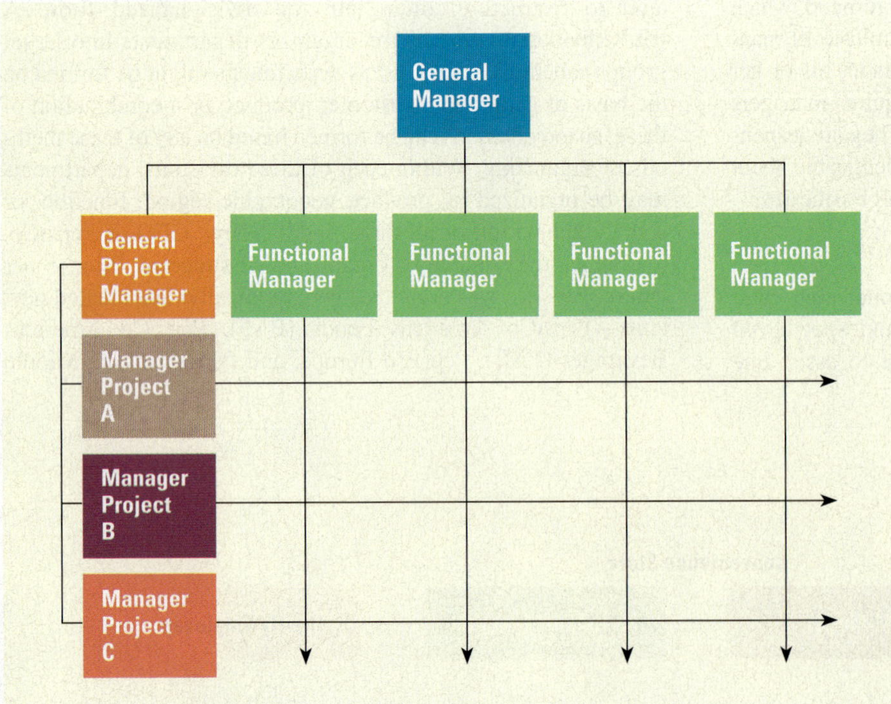

East & Africa—that span international boundaries and make it easier for employees in different geographic regions to share business practices.[14]

Multidivisional structures permit delegation of decision-making authority, allowing divisional and department managers to specialize. They allow those closest to the action to make the decisions that will affect them. Delegation of authority and divisionalized work also mean that better decisions are made faster, and they tend to be more innovative. Most important, by focusing each division on a common region, product, or customer, each is more likely to provide products that meet the needs of its particular customers. However, the divisional structure inevitably creates work duplication, which makes it more difficult to realize the economies of scale that result from grouping functions.

Matrix Structure

Another structure that attempts to address issues that arise with growth, diversification, productivity, and competitiveness is the matrix. A **matrix structure**, also called a project-management structure, sets up teams from different departments, thereby creating two or more intersecting lines of authority (Figure 7.7). One of the first organizations to design and implement a matrix structure was the National Aeronautics and Space Administration (NASA) for the space program because it needed to coordinate different projects at the same time. The matrix structure superimposes project-based departments on the more traditional, function-based departments. Project teams bring together specialists from a variety of areas to work together on a single project, such as developing a new fighter jet. In this arrangement, employees are responsible to two managers—functional managers and project managers. Matrix structures are usually temporary: Team members typically go back to their functional or line department after a project is finished. However, more firms are becoming permanent matrix structures, creating and dissolving project teams as needed to meet customer needs. The aerospace industry was one of the first to apply the matrix structure, but today it is used by universities and

matrix structure a structure that sets up teams from different departments, thereby creating two or more intersecting lines of authority; also called a project-management structure

group two or more individuals who communicate with one another, share a common identity, and have a common goal

team a small group whose members have complementary skills; have a common purpose, goals, and approach; and hold themselves mutually accountable

schools, accounting firms, banks, and organizations in other industries.

Matrix structures provide flexibility, enhanced cooperation, and creativity, and they enable the company to respond quickly to changes in the environment by giving special attention to specific projects or problems. However, they are generally expensive and quite complex, and employees may be confused as to whose authority has priority—the project manager's or the immediate supervisor's.

LO 7-5 Distinguish between groups and teams and identify the types of groups that exist in organizations.

THE ROLE OF GROUPS AND TEAMS IN ORGANIZATIONS

Regardless of how they are organized, most of the essential work of business occurs in individual work groups and teams, so we'll take a closer look at them now. Although some experts do not make a distinction between groups and teams, in recent years there has been a gradual shift toward an emphasis on teams and managing them to enhance individual and organizational success. Some experts now believe that highest productivity results only when groups become teams.[15]

Traditionally, a **group** has been defined as two or more individuals who communicate with one another, share a common identity, and have a common goal. A **team** is a small group whose members have complementary skills; have a common purpose, goals, and approach; and hold themselves mutually accountable.[16] All teams are groups, but not all groups are teams. Table 7.2 points out some important differences between them. Work groups emphasize individual work products, individual accountability, and even individual leadership. Salespeople working independently for the same company could be a work group. In contrast, work teams share leadership roles, have both individual and mutual accountability, and create collective work products. In other words, a work group's performance depends on what its members do as individuals, whereas a team's performance is based on creating a knowledge center and a competency to work together to accomplish a goal. On the other hand, it is also important for team members to retain their individuality and avoid becoming just another face in the crowd. According to former corporate lawyer and negotiations consultant Susan Cain, the purpose of teams should be toward collaboration versus collectivism. Although the team is working toward a common goal, it is important for all team members to contribute their ideas actively and work together to achieve this common goal.[17]

The type of groups an organization establishes depends on the tasks it needs to accomplish and the situation it faces. Some specific kinds of groups and teams include committees, task forces, project teams, product-development teams, quality-assurance teams, and self-directed work teams. All of these can be *virtual teams*—employees in different locations who rely on e-mail, audio conferencing, fax, Internet, videoconferencing, or other technological tools to accomplish their goals. With more than 84 percent of American employees working in a different location than their supervisors, virtual teams are becoming a part of everyday business.[18] Virtual teams have also opened up opportunities for different companies. Not only does Cisco Systems Inc. work in virtual teams, but the company makes networking technology to support videoconferencing. At Cisco Europe, 10,000 employees across 21 countries developed a set of team operating principles to aid team collaboration.[19]

TABLE 7.2 Differences between Groups and Teams

Working Group	Team
Has strong, clearly focused leader	Has shared leadership roles
Has individual accountability	Has individual and group accountability
Has the same purpose as the broader organizational mission	Has a specific purpose that the team itself delivers
Creates individual work products	Creates collective work products
Runs efficient meetings	Encourages open-ended discussion and active problem-solving meetings
Measures its effectiveness indirectly by its effects on others (for instance, financial performance of the business)	Measures performance directly by assessing collective work products
Discusses, decides, and delegates	Discusses, decides, and does real work together

Source: Robert Gatewood, Robert Taylor, and O.C. Ferrell, *Management: Comprehension Analysis and Application,* 1995, p. 427. Copyright © 1995 Richard D. Irwin, a Times Mirror Higher Education Group, Inc., company. Reproduced with permission of the McGraw-Hill Companies.

committee a permanent, formal group that performs a specific task

task force a temporary group of employees responsible for bringing about a particular change

project teams groups similar to task forces that normally run their operation and have total control of a specific work project

product-development teams a specific type of project team formed to devise, design, and implement a new product

quality-assurance teams (or quality circles) small groups of workers brought together from throughout the organization to solve specific quality, productivity, or service problems

Committees

A **committee** is usually a permanent, formal group that performs some specific task. For example, many firms have a compensation or finance committee to examine the effectiveness of these areas of operation as well as the need for possible changes. Ethics committees are formed to develop and revise codes of ethics, suggest methods for implementing ethical standards, and review specific issues and concerns.

Task Forces

A **task force** is a temporary group of employees responsible for bringing about a particular change. They typically come from across all departments and levels of an organization. Task force membership is usually based on expertise rather than organizational position. Occasionally, a task force may be formed from individuals outside a company. Coca-Cola has often used task forces to address problems and provide recommendations for improving company practices or products. Although some task forces might last a few months, others last for years. When Coca-Cola faced lawsuits alleging discrimination practices in hiring and promotion, it developed a five-year task force to examine pay and promotion practices among minority employees. Its experiences helped Coca-Cola realize the advantages of having a cross-functional task force made up of employees from different departments, and it continued to use task forces to tackle major company issues. Other companies that have recognized the benefits of task forces include IBM, Prudential, and General Electric.[20]

Teams

Teams are becoming far more common in the U.S. workplace as businesses strive to enhance productivity and global competitiveness. In general, teams have the benefit of being able to pool members' knowledge and skills and make greater use of them than can individuals working alone. Team building is becoming increasingly popular in organizations, with around half of executives indicating their companies had team-building training. Teams require harmony, cooperation, synchronized effort, and flexibility to maximize their contribution.[21] Teams can also create more solutions to problems than can individuals. Furthermore, team participation enhances employee acceptance of, understanding of, and commitment to team goals. Teams motivate workers by providing internal rewards in the form of an enhanced sense of accomplishment for employees as they achieve more, and external rewards in the form of praise and certain perks. Consequently, they can help get workers more involved. They can help companies be more innovative, and they can boost productivity and cut costs.

According to psychologist Ivan Steiner, team productivity peaks at about five team members. People become less motivated and group coordination becomes more difficult after this size. Jeff Bezos, Amazon.com CEO, says that he has a "two-pizza rule": If a team cannot be fed by two pizzas, it is too large. Keep teams small enough that everyone gets a piece of the action.[22]

Project Teams

Project teams are similar to task forces, but normally they run their operation and have total control of a specific work project. Like task forces, their membership is likely to cut across the firm's hierarchy and be composed of people from different functional areas. They are almost always temporary, although a large project, such as designing and building a new airplane at Boeing Corporation, may last for years.

Product-development teams are a special type of project team formed to devise, design, and implement a new product. Sometimes product-development teams exist within a functional area—research and development—but now they more frequently include people from numerous functional areas and may even include customers to help ensure that the end product meets the customers' needs. At specialty chemical manufacturing company AMVAC Chemical Corporation, its product-development team works on developing new agricultural chemical products such as herbicides, fungicides, and insecticides. The firm's team works to create solutions for diseases, weeds, and other issues that hinder plant growth. The team consists of scientists and agronomists to collaborate on new and improved products that meet the needs of the end users best.[23]

> "Teams are becoming far more common in the U.S. workplace as businesses strive to enhance productivity and global competitiveness."

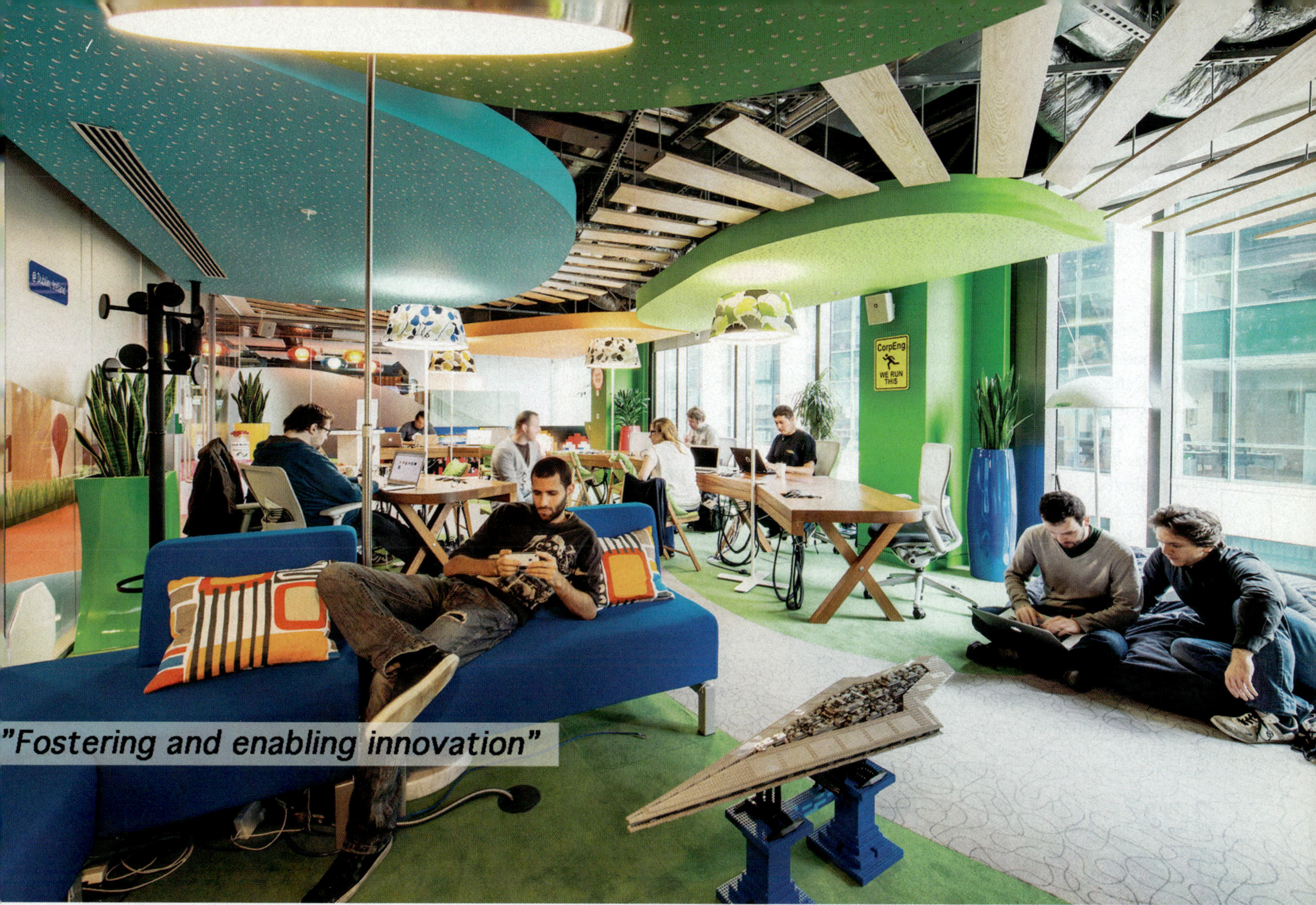

At Google, small teams work on research and engineering projects that often last 6–12 months.

Quality-Assurance Teams **Quality-assurance teams**, sometimes called **quality circles**, are fairly small groups of workers brought together from throughout the organization to solve specific quality, productivity, or service problems. Although the *quality circle* term is not as popular as it once was, the concern about quality is stronger than ever. Companies such as IBM and Xerox as well as companies in the automobile industry have used quality circles to shift the organization to a more participative culture. The use of teams to address quality issues will no doubt continue to increase throughout the business world.

TEAMWORK KEY TO SUCCESS OF SILPADA DESIGNS

When Bonnie Kelly and Teresa Walsh signed on as room mothers at a local school, they could not imagine that they would one day start a company. In 1997, the two women teamed up to develop Silpada Designs, a direct-selling jewelry company, as a way of manifesting their interests in fashion and empowering women. They began by showing women how to make different outfits from what they currently had and selling jewelry from a local manufacturer. As the business grew, customers opened up their homes for parties, and Kelly and Walsh began to hire independent sales representatives. This required the women to encourage teamwork among corporate headquarters, distributors, and sales representatives. Indeed, the ability that the two women have to work as a team has greatly contributed to the company's success. Silpada was acquired by Avon in 2010 but still operates as an independent company. Today, the firm has $280 million in annual sales, 33,000 independent representatives, and average party sales of $1,000.[24]

self-directed work team (SDWT) a group of employees responsible for an entire work process or segment that delivers a product to an internal or external customer

Self-directed Work Teams

A **self-directed work team (SDWT)** is a group of employees responsible for an entire work process or segment that delivers a product to an internal or external customer.[25] SDWTs permit the flexibility to change rapidly to meet the competition or respond to customer needs. The defining characteristic of an SDWT is the extent to which it is empowered or given authority to make and implement work decisions. Thus, SDWTs are designed to give employees a feeling of ownership of a whole job. Employees at 3M as well as an increasing number of companies encourage employees to be active to perform a function or operational task. With shared team responsibility for work outcomes, team members often have broader job assignments and cross-train to master other jobs, thus permitting greater team flexibility.

DID YOU KNOW?

A survey of managers and executives found that they feel 28 percent of meetings are a waste of time and that information could be communicated more effectively using other methods.[26]

LO 7-6 Describe how communication occurs in organizations.

COMMUNICATING IN ORGANIZATIONS

Communication within an organization can flow in a variety of directions and from a number of sources, each using both oral and written forms of communication. The success of communication systems within the organization has a tremendous effect on the overall success of the firm. Communication mistakes can lower productivity and morale.

Alternatives to face-to-face communications—such as meetings—are growing, thanks to technology such as voice-mail, e-mail, social media, wikis, and online newsletters. Many companies use internal networks called intranets to share information with employees. Intranets increase communication across different departments and levels of management and help with the flow of everyday business activities. Another innovative approach is cloud computing. Rather than using physical products, companies using cloud computing technology can access computing resources and information over a network. Cloud computing allows companies to have more control over computing resources and can be less expensive than hardware or software. Salesforce.com uses cloud computing in its customer relationship management solutions.[27] Companies can integrate aspects of social media such as wikis into their intranets, allowing employees to post comments and pictures, participate in polls, and create group calendars. However, increased access to the Internet at work has also created many problems, including employee abuse of company mail and Internet access.[28]

Formal Communication

Formal channels of communication are intentionally defined and designed by the organization. They represent the flow of communication within the formal organizational structure, as shown on organizational charts. Traditionally, formal communication patterns were classified as vertical and horizontal, but with the increased use of teams and matrix structures, formal communication may occur in a number of patterns (Figure 7.8).

Upward communication flows from lower to higher levels of the organization and includes information such as progress reports, suggestions for improvement, inquiries, and grievances. *Downward communication* refers to the traditional flow of information from upper organizational levels to lower levels. This type of communication typically involves directions, the assignment of tasks and responsibilities, performance feedback, and certain details about the organization's strategies and goals. Speeches, policy and procedures manuals, employee handbooks, company leaflets, telecommunications, and job descriptions are examples of downward communication.

Horizontal communication involves the exchange of information among colleagues and peers on the same organizational level, such as across or within departments. Horizontal information informs, supports, and coordinates activities both within the department and with other departments. At times, the business will formally require horizontal communication among particular organizational members, as is the case with task forces or project teams.

With more and more companies downsizing and increasing the use of self-managed work teams, many workers are being required to communicate with others in different departments and on different levels to solve problems and coordinate work. When these individuals from different units and organizational levels communicate, it is *diagonal communication.* One benefit of companies doing more with fewer employees is that productivity (output per work hour) increased by 9.5 percent in one year. Increased productivity allows companies to increase wages and leads to increased standards of living.[29]

Informal Communication Channels

Along with the formal channels of communication shown on an organizational chart, all firms communicate informally as well. Communication between friends, for instance, cuts across department, division, and even management–subordinate boundaries. Such friendships and other nonwork social relationships comprise the *informal organization* of a firm, and their impact can be great.

The most significant informal communication occurs through the **grapevine**, an informal channel of communication, separate from management's formal, official communication channels. Grapevines exist in all organizations. Information passed along the grapevine may relate to the job or organization, or it may be gossip and rumors unrelated to either. The accuracy of grapevine information has been of great concern to managers.

grapevine an informal channel of communication, separate from management's formal, official communication channels

In addition, managers can turn the grapevine to their advantage. Using it as a sounding device for possible new policies is one example. Managers can obtain valuable information from the grapevine that could improve decision making. Some organizations use the grapevine to their advantage by floating ideas, soliciting feedback, and reacting accordingly. People love to gossip, and managers need to be aware that grapevines exist in every organization. Managers who understand how the grapevine works also can use it to their advantage by feeding it facts to squelch rumors and incorrect information.

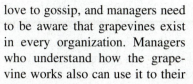

FIGURE 7.8
The Flow of Communication in an Organizational Hierarchy

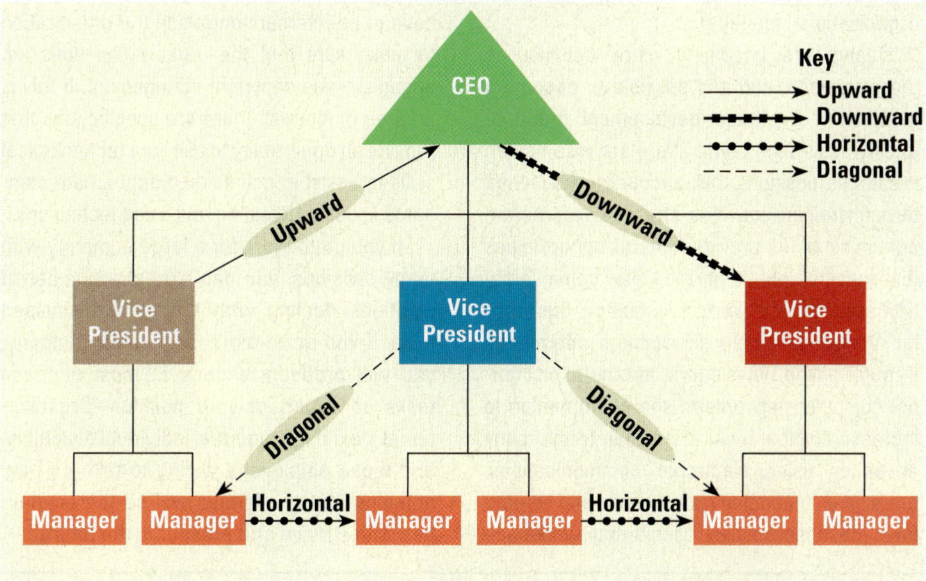

Monitoring Communications

Technological advances and the increased use of electronic communication in the workplace have made monitoring its use necessary for most companies. Failing to monitor employees' use of e-mail, social media, and the Internet can be costly. Many companies require employees to sign and follow a policy on appropriate Internet use. These agreements often require employees to use corporate computers only for work-related activities. In addition, several companies use software programs to monitor employee computer usage.[30] Instituting practices that show respect for employee privacy but do not abdicate employer responsibility are increasingly necessary in today's workplace. Several websites provide model policies and detailed guidelines for conducting electronic monitoring, including the Model Electronic Privacy Act on the American Civil Liberties Union site.

Improving Communication Effectiveness

Without effective communication, the activities and overall productivity of projects, groups, teams, and individuals will be diminished. Communication is an important area for a firm to address at all levels of management. Apple supplier Foxconn is one example of how essential communication is to a firm. Despite criticisms of unfair labor conditions, the Fair Labor Association determined that Foxconn had formal procedures in place at its factories to prevent many major accidents. However, it concluded that the firm had a communication problem. These procedures were not being communicated to the factory workers, contributing to unsafe practices and two tragic explosions.[31]

One of the major issues of effective communication is in obtaining feedback. If feedback is not provided, then communication will be ineffective and can drag down overall performance. Managers should always encourage feedback, including concerns and challenges about issues. Listening is a skill that involves hearing, and most employees listen much more than they actively communicate to others. Therefore, managers should encourage employees to provide feedback—even if it is negative. This will allow the organization to identify strengths and weaknesses and make adjustments when needed. At the same time, strong feedback mechanisms help empower employees because they feel that their voices are being heard.

Interruptions can be a serious threat to effective communication. Various activities can interrupt the message. For example, interjecting a remark can create discontinuance in the communication process or disrupt the uniformity of the message. Even small interruptions can be a problem if the messenger cannot adequately understand or interpret the communicator's message. One suggestion is to give the communicator space or time to make another statement rather than quickly responding or making your own comment.

Strong and effective communication channels are a requirement for companies to distribute information to different levels of the company. Businesses have several channels for communication, including face-to-face, e-mail, phone, and written communication (for example, memos). Each channel has advantages and disadvantages, and some are more appropriate to use than others. For instance, a small task requiring little instruction might be communicated through a short memo or e-mail. An in-depth task would most likely require a phone conversation or face-to-face contact. E-mail has become especially helpful for businesses, and both employees and managers are increasingly using e-mail rather than memos or phone conversations. However, it is important for employees to use e-mail correctly. It is quite easy to send the wrong e-mail to the wrong person, and messages sent over e-mail can be misinterpreted. Inappropriate e-mails can be forwarded without a second thought, and employees have gotten in trouble for sending personal e-mails in the workplace. It is therefore important for companies to communicate their e-mail policies throughout the organization. Communicators using e-mail, whether managers or employees, must exert caution before pushing that Send button.

Communication is necessary in helping every organizational member understand what is expected of him or her. Many business problems can be avoided if clear communication exists within the company. Even the best business strategies are of little use if those who will oversee them cannot understand what is intended. Communication might not seem to be as big of a concern to management as finances, human resources, and marketing, but in reality it can make the difference between successful implementation of business activities and failure. ■

TEAM EXERCISE

Assign the responsibility of providing the organizational structure for a company one of your team members has worked for. Was your organization centralized or decentralized in terms of decision making? Would you consider the span of control to be wide or narrow? Were any types of teams, committees, or task forces used in the organization? Report your work to the class.

SO YOU WANT A JOB // in Managing Organizational Culture, Teamwork, and Communication /

Jobs dealing with organizational culture and structure are usually at the top of the organization. If you want to be a CEO or high-level manager, you will help shape these areas of business. On the other hand, if you are an entrepreneur or small-business person, you will need to make decisions about assigning tasks, departmentalization, and assigning responsibility. Even managers in small organizations have to make decisions about decentralization, span of management, and forms of organizational structure. Although these decisions may be part of your job, there are usually no job titles dealing with these specific areas. Specific jobs that attempt to improve organizational culture could include ethics and compliance positions as well as those that are in charge of communicating memos, manuals, and policies that help establish the culture. These positions will be in communications, human resources, and positions that assist top organizational managers.

Teams are becoming more common in the workplace, and it is possible to become a member of a product-development group or quality-assurance team. There are also human resources positions that encourage teamwork through training activities. The area of corporate communications provides lots of opportunities for specific jobs that facilitate communication systems. Thanks to technology, there are job positions to help disseminate information through online newsletters, intranets, or internal computer networks to share information to increase collaboration. In addition to the many advances using electronic communications, there are technology concerns that create new job opportunities. Monitoring workplace communications such as the use of e-mail and the Internet have created new industries. There have to be internal controls in the organization to make sure that the organization does not engage in any copyright infringement. If this is an area of interest, there are specific jobs that provide an opportunity to use your technological skills to assist in maintaining appropriate standards in communicating and using technology.

If you go to work for a large company with many divisions, you can expect a number of positions dealing with the tasks discussed here. If you go to work for a small company, you will probably engage in most of these tasks as a part of your position. Organizational flexibility requires individual flexibility, and those employees willing to take on new domains and challenges will be the employees who survive and prosper in the future.

learn, practice, apply organization, teamwork, and communication skills to improve your business!

M: Business was developed just for you—students on the go who need information packaged in a concise yet interesting format with multiple learning options.

Check out the book's website to:

- Understand how to display leadership in a group setting. (Solve the Dilemma)
- Evaluate the advantages and disadvantages of teams. (Solve the Dilemma)
- Determine the characteristics of a good team. (Build Your Skills)

While you are there, don't forget to enhance your skills. Practice and apply your knowledge, review the practice exercises, Student PPT® slides, and quizzes to review and apply chapter concepts. Additionally, *Connect® Business* is available for *M: Business.*

www.mhhe.com/ferrellm4e

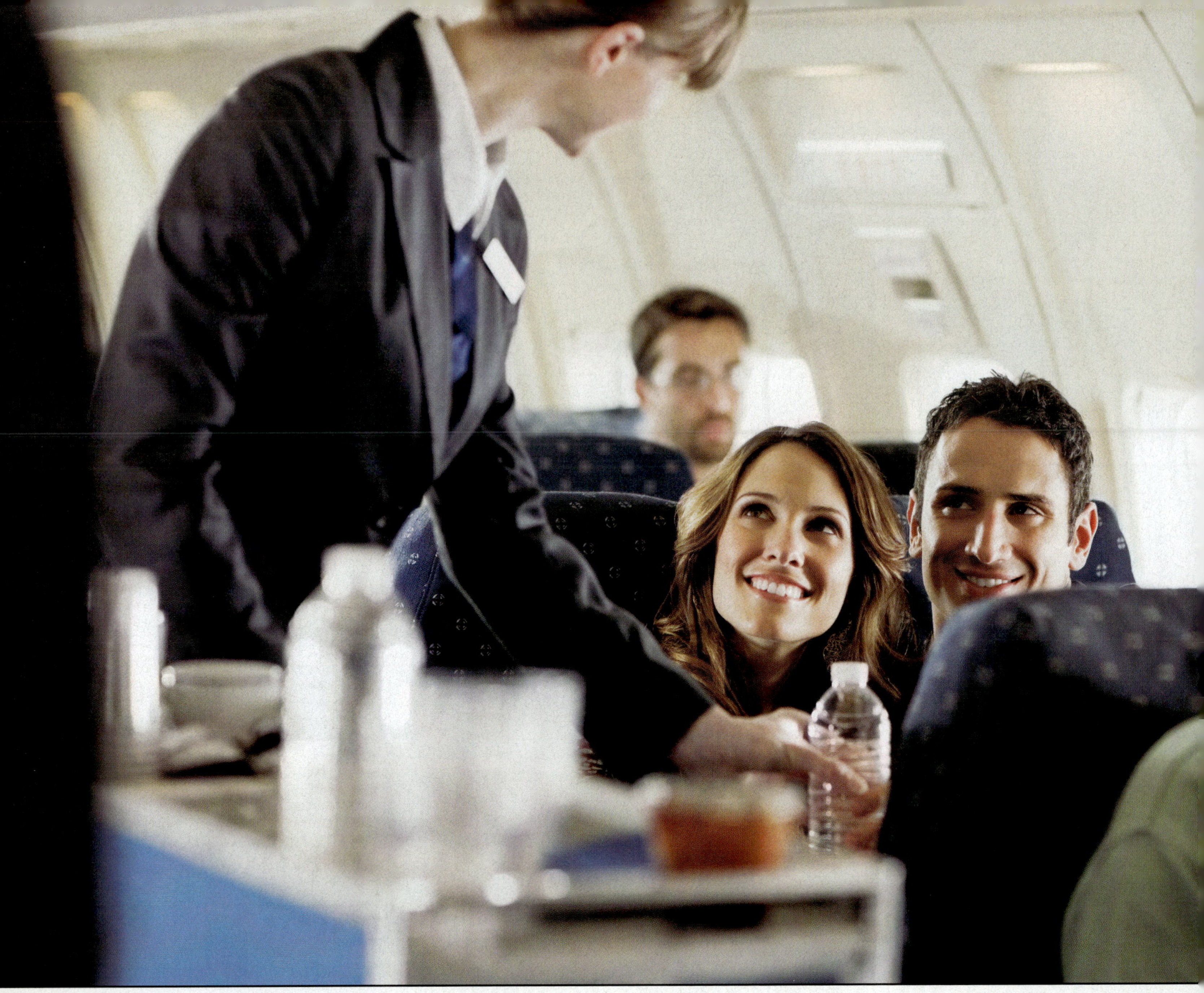

All organizations create products—goods, services, or ideas—for customers. Thus, organizations as diverse as Toyota, Campbell Soup, UPS, and a public hospital share a number of similarities relating to how they transform resources into the products we consume. Most hospitals use similar admission procedures, whereas online social media companies, like Facebook and Twitter, use their technology and operating systems to create social networking opportunities and sell advertising. Such similarities are to be expected. But even organizations in unrelated industries take similar steps in creating goods or services. The check-in procedures of hotels and commercial airlines are comparable, for example. The way Subway assembles a sandwich and the way GMC assembles a truck are similar (both use automation and an assembly line). These similarities are the result of operations management, the focus of this chapter.

Here, we discuss the role of production or operations management in acquiring and managing the resources necessary to create goods and services. Production and operations management involves planning and designing

chapter eight

managing service + manufacturing operations

the processes that will transform those resources into finished products, managing the movement of those resources through the transformation process, and ensuring that the products are of the quality expected by customers. ■

LEARNING OBJECTIVES

After reading this chapter, you will be able to:

- **LO 8-1** Define operations management and differentiate between operations and manufacturing.
- **LO 8-2** Explain how operations management differs in manufacturing and service firms.
- **LO 8-3** Describe the elements involved in planning and designing an operations system.
- **LO 8-4** Specify some techniques managers may use to manage the logistics of transforming inputs into finished products.
- **LO 8-5** Assess the importance of quality in operations management.

operations management (OM) the development and administration of the activities involved in transforming resources into goods and services

manufacturing the activities and processes used in making tangible products; also called production

production the activities and processes used in making tangible products; also called manufacturing

operations the activities and processes used in making both tangible and intangible products

inputs the resources—such as labor, money, materials, and energy—that are converted into outputs

outputs the goods, services, and ideas that result from the conversion of inputs

LO 8-1 Define operations management and differentiate between operations and manufacturing.

THE NATURE OF OPERATIONS MANAGEMENT

Operations management (OM), the development and administration of the activities involved in transforming resources into goods and services, is of critical importance. Operations managers oversee the transformation process and the planning and designing of operations systems, managing logistics, quality, and productivity. Quality and productivity have become fundamental aspects of operations management because a company that cannot make products of the quality desired by consumers, using resources efficiently and effectively, will not be able to remain in business. OM is the core of most organizations because it is responsible for the creation of the organization's goods and services. Some organizations like General Motors produce tangible products, but service is an important part of the total product for the customer.

Historically, operations management has been called "production" or "manufacturing" primarily because of the view that it was limited to the manufacture of physical goods. Its focus was on methods and techniques required to operate a factory efficiently. The change from "production" to "operations" recognizes the increasing importance of organizations that provide services and ideas. In addition, the term *operations* represents an interest in viewing the operations function as a whole rather than simply as an analysis of inputs and outputs.

Today, OM includes a wide range of organizational activities and situations outside of manufacturing, such as health care, food service, banking, entertainment, education, transportation, and charity. Thus, we use the terms **manufacturing** and **production** interchangeably to represent the activities and processes used in making *tangible* products, whereas we use the broader term **operations** to describe those processes used in the making of *both tangible and intangible products.* Manufacturing provides tangible products such as Hewlett-Packard's latest printer, and operations provides intangibles such as a stay at Wyndham Hotels and Resorts.

The Transformation Process

At the heart of operations management is the transformation process through which **inputs** (resources such as labor, money, materials, and energy) are converted into **outputs** (goods, services, and ideas). The transformation process combines inputs in predetermined ways using different equipment, administrative procedures, and technology to create a product (Figure 8.1). To ensure that this process generates quality products efficiently, operations managers control the process by taking measurements (feedback) at various points in the transformation process and comparing them to previously established standards. If there is any deviation between the actual and desired outputs, the manager may take some sort of corrective action. All adjustments made to create a satisfying product are a part of the transformation process.

FIGURE 8.1
The Transformation Process of Operations Management

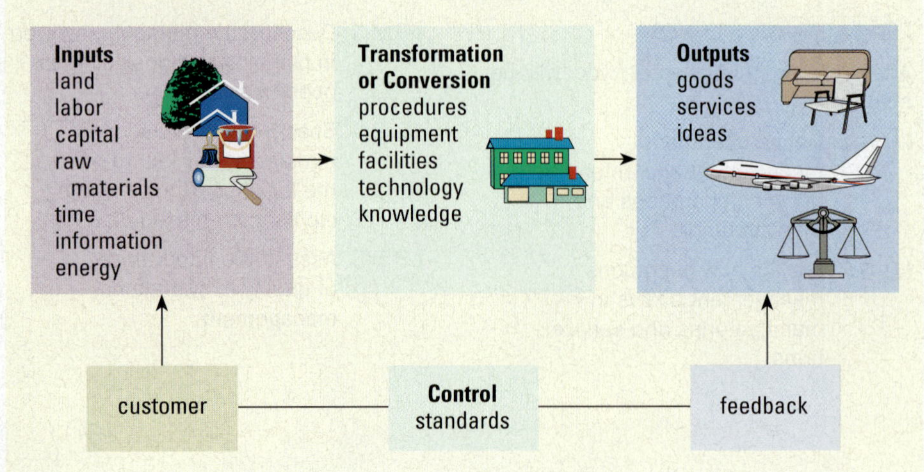

Transformation may take place through one or more processes. In a business that manufactures oak furniture, for example, inputs pass through several processes before being turned into the final outputs—furniture that has been designed to meet the desires of customers (Figure 8.2). The furniture maker must first strip the oak trees of their bark and saw them into appropriate sizes—one step in the transformation process. Next, the firm dries the strips of oak lumber, a second form of transformation. Third, the dried wood is routed into its appropriate shape and made smooth. Fourth, workers assemble

ASPIRE GROUP HELPS FILL SEATS AT STADIUMS

Addressing supply and demand for services can be a daunting task, especially for sporting events. Having spent 30 years working for various athletic teams, Bernie Mullin saw an opportunity to assist universities and professional organizations in filling empty stadium seats. Because services are susceptible to perishability and cannot be stored for later use, colleges are in danger of a significant loss of money not only from lack of ticket sales but also from a lack of sports donations. Aspire Group was founded in 2008 to rejuvenate team appreciation with alumni and former ticket holders. Aspire Group's salespeople use the Sport Market Research database to personalize the way they sell to the customer and use this information to re-inspire team loyalty. Georgia Tech and the Los Angeles Dodgers are among Aspire Group's clients; Aspire helped them make over $4 million in ticket sales over two years and increased ticket sales revenue by 280 percent. Despite the fact that the company is only four years old, Aspire Group is estimated to gross $500,000 off ticket sales of $5 million.[1]

FIGURE 8.2
Inputs, Outputs, and Transformation Processes in the Manufacture of Oak Furniture

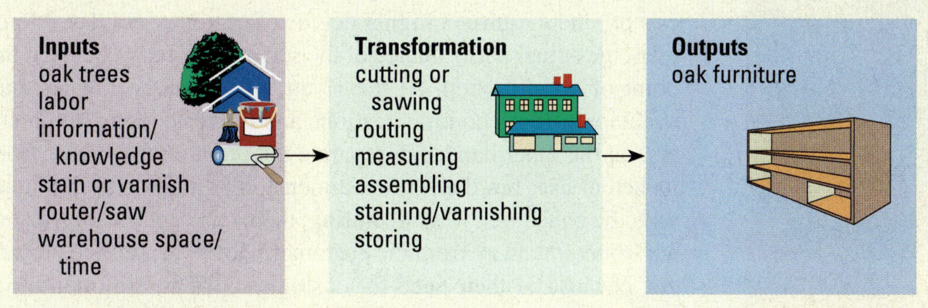

and treat the wood pieces, then stain or varnish the piece of assembled furniture. Finally, the completed piece of furniture is stored until it can be shipped to customers at the appropriate time. Of course, many businesses choose to eliminate some of these stages by purchasing already processed materials—lumber, for example—or outsourcing some tasks to third-party firms with greater expertise.

LO 8-2 Explain how operations management differs in manufacturing and service firms.

Operations Management in Service Businesses

Different types of transformation processes take place in organizations that provide services, such as airlines, colleges, and most nonprofit organizations. An airline transforms inputs such as employees, time, money, and equipment through processes such as booking flights, flying airplanes, maintaining equipment, and training crews. The output of these processes is flying passengers and/or packages to their destinations. In a nonprofit organization like Habitat for Humanity, inputs such as money, materials, information, and volunteer time and labor are used to transform raw materials into homes for needy families. In this setting, transformation processes include fundraising and promoting the cause to gain new volunteers and donations of supplies, as well as pouring concrete, raising walls, and setting roofs. Transformation processes occur in all organizations, regardless of what they produce or their objectives. For most organizations, the ultimate objective is for the produced outputs to be worth more than the combined costs of the inputs.

Unlike tangible goods, services are effectively actions or performances that must be directed toward the consumers who use them. Thus, there is a significant customer-contact component to most services. Examples of high-contact services include health care, real estate, tax preparation, and food service. At the Inn at Little Washington in Washington, Virginia, for example, food servers are critical to delivering the perfect dining experience expected by the most discriminating diners. Wait staff are expected not only to be courteous but also to demonstrate a detailed knowledge of the restaurant's offerings and even to assess the mood of guests to respond to diners appropriately.[2] Low-contact services, such as online auction services like eBay, often have a strong high-tech component.

Regardless of the level of customer contact, service businesses strive to provide a standardized process, and technology offers an interface that creates an automatic and structured response. The ideal service provider will be high-tech and high-touch. Southwest, for example, strives to maintain an excellent website; friendly, helpful customer contact; and satellite TV service at every seat on each plane. Thus, service organizations must build their operations around good execution, which comes from hiring and training excellent employees, developing flexible systems, customizing services, and maintaining adjustable capacity to deal with fluctuating demand.[3]

Another challenge related to service operations is that the output is generally intangible and even perishable. Few services can be saved, stored, resold, or returned.[4] A seat on an airline or a table

THE ACTUAL PERFORMANCE OF THE SERVICE TYPICALLY OCCURS AT THE POINT OF CONSUMPTION.

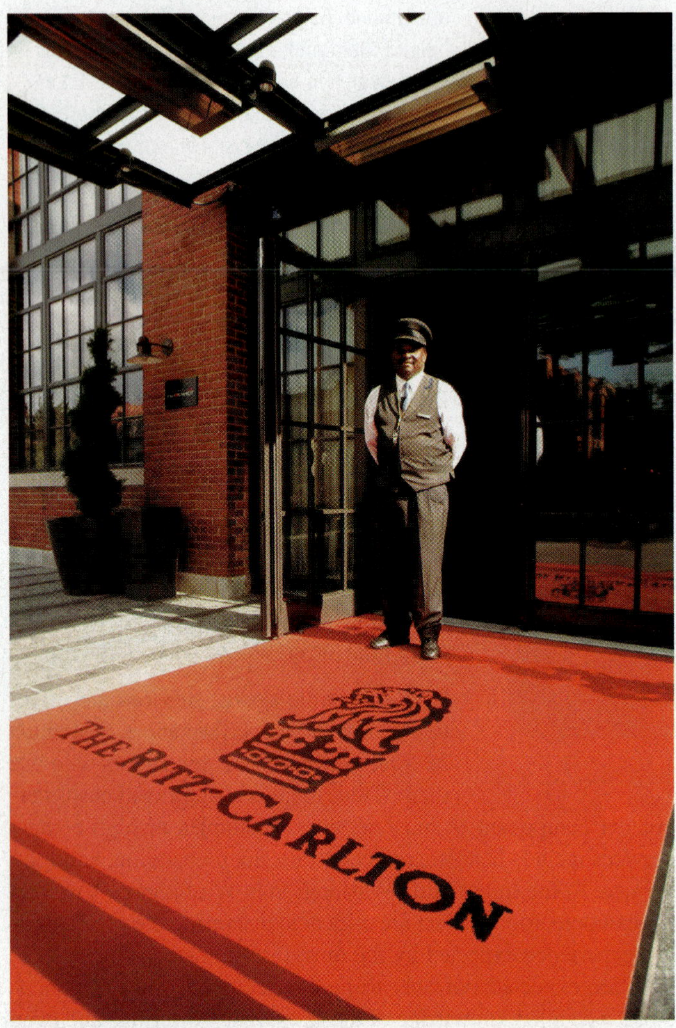

Although service organizations tend to vary depending on the service provider, businesses strive to standardize operations to ensure a high level of quality. The Ritz-Carlton has become famous for its high level of customer service.

in a restaurant, for example, cannot be sold or used at a later date. Because of the perishability of services, it can be extremely difficult for service providers to estimate the demand accurately to match the right supply of a service. If an airline overestimates demand, for example, it will still have to fly each plane even with empty seats. The flight costs the same regardless of whether it is 50 percent full or 100 percent full, but the former will result in much higher costs per passenger. If the airline underestimates demand, the result can be long lines of annoyed customers or even the necessity of bumping some customers off of an overbooked flight.

Businesses that manufacture tangible goods and those that provide services or ideas are similar yet different. For example, both types of organizations must make design and operating decisions. Most goods are manufactured prior to purchase, but most services are performed after purchase. Flight attendants at Southwest Airlines, hotel service personnel, and even the New York Giants football team engage in performances that are a part of the total product. Though manufacturers and service providers often perform similar activities, they also differ in several respects. We can classify these differences in five basic ways.

Nature and Consumption of Output First, manufacturers and service providers differ in the nature and consumption of their output. For example, the term *manufacturer* implies a firm that makes tangible products. A service provider, on the other hand, produces more intangible outputs such as U.S. Postal Service delivery of priority mail or a business stay in a Hyatt hotel. As mentioned earlier, the very nature of the service provider's product requires a higher degree of customer contact. Moreover, the actual performance of the service typically occurs at the point of consumption. At the Hyatt, the business traveler may evaluate in-room communications and the restaurant. Automakers, on the other hand, can separate the production of a car from its actual use, but the service dimension requires closer contact with the consumer. Manufacturing, then, can occur in an isolated environment, away from the customer. However, service providers, because of their need for customer contact, are often more limited than manufacturers in selecting work methods, assigning jobs, scheduling work, and exercising control over operations. At FedEx, the Quality Improvement Process (QIP) includes sayings such as "Do it right the first time," and "Make the first time you do it the only time anyone has to do it." The quality of the service experience is often controlled by a service contact employee. However, some hospitals are studying the manufacturing processes and quality-control mechanisms applied in the automotive industry in an effort to improve their service quality. By analyzing work processes to find unnecessary steps to eliminate and using teams to identify and address problems as soon as they occur, these hospitals are slashing patient waiting times, decreasing inventories of wheelchairs, readying operating rooms sooner, and generally moving patients through their hospital visit more quickly, with fewer errors and at a lower cost.[5]

Uniformity of Inputs A second way to classify differences between manufacturers and service providers has to do with the uniformity of inputs. Manufacturers typically have more control over the amount of variability of the resources they use than do service providers. For example, each customer calling Fidelity Investments is likely to require different services due to differing needs, whereas many of the tasks required to manufacture a Ford Focus are the same across each unit of output. Consequently, the products of service organizations tend to be more customized than those of their manufacturing counterparts. Consider, for example, a haircut versus a bottle of

Subway's inputs are sandwich components such as bread, tomatoes, and lettuce, while its outputs are customized sandwiches.

shampoo. The haircut is much more likely to incorporate your specific desires (customization) than is the bottle of shampoo.

Uniformity of Output Manufacturers and service providers also differ in the uniformity of their output, the final product. Because of the human element inherent in providing services, each service tends to be performed differently. Not all grocery checkers, for example, wait on customers in the same way. If a barber or stylist performs 15 haircuts in a day, it is unlikely that any two of them will be exactly the same. Consequently, human and technological elements associated with a service can result in a different day-to-day or even hour-to-hour performance of that service. The service experience can even vary at McDonald's or Burger King despite the fact that the two chains employ very similar procedures and processes. Moreover, no two customers are exactly alike in their perception of the service experience. Health care offers another excellent example of this challenge. Every diagnosis, treatment, and surgery varies because every individual is different. In manufacturing, the high degree of automation available allows manufacturers to generate uniform outputs and, thus, the operations are more effective and efficient. For example, we would expect every TAG Heuer or Rolex watch to maintain very high standards of quality and performance.

Labor Required A fourth point of difference is the amount of labor required to produce an output. Service providers are generally more labor-intensive (require more labor) because of the high level of customer contact, perishability of the output (must be consumed immediately), and high degree of variation of inputs and outputs (customization). For example, Adecco provides temporary support personnel. Each temporary worker's performance determines Adecco's product quality. A manufacturer, on the other hand, is likely to be more capital-intensive because of the machinery and technology used in the mass production of highly similar goods. For instance, it would take a considerable investment for Ford to make an electric car that has batteries with a longer life.

Measurement of Productivity The final distinction between service providers and manufacturers involves the measurement of productivity for each output produced. For manufacturers, measuring productivity is fairly straightforward because of the tangibility of the output and its high degree of uniformity. For the service provider, variations in demand (for example, higher demand for air travel in some seasons than in others), variations in service requirements from job to job, and the intangibility of the product make productivity measurement more difficult. Consider, for example, how much easier it is to measure the productivity of employees involved in the production of Intel computer processors as opposed to serving the needs of Prudential Securities' clients.

It is convenient and simple to think of organizations as being either manufacturers or service providers as in the preceding discussion. In reality, however, most organizations are a combination of the two, with both tangible and intangible qualities embodied in what they produce. For example, Porsche provides customer services such as toll-free hotlines and warranty protection, whereas banks may sell checks and other tangible products that complement their primarily intangible product offering. Thus, we consider "products" to include both tangible physical goods and intangible service offerings. It is the level of tangibility of its principal product that tends to classify a company as either a manufacturer or a service provider. From an OM standpoint, this level of tangibility greatly influences the nature of the company's operational processes and procedures.

LO 8-3 Describe the elements involved in planning and designing an operations system.

PLANNING AND DESIGNING OPERATIONS SYSTEMS

Before a company can produce any product, it must first decide what it will produce and for what group of customers. It must then determine what processes it will use to make these products as well as the facilities it needs to produce them. These decisions comprise operations planning. Although planning was once the sole realm of the production and operations department, today's successful companies involve all departments within an organization, particularly marketing and research and development, in these decisions.

Planning the Product

Before making any product, a company first must determine what consumers want and then design a product to satisfy that

FORD EXAMINES WAYS TO INCREASE SUSTAINABILITY OF CARS

How do you take 800 pounds off a 5,500-pound pickup? Ford Motor is attempting to do exactly that in an effort to improve its vehicles' fuel efficiency. The White House is in the process of implementing new gas fuel requirements for passenger cars and trucks to nearly double their mileage standards—to 54.5 mpg by the year 2025. Many auto companies are therefore taking the initiative to begin manufacturing products with improved fuel efficiency now, years before compliance is required. Ford and other companies are looking for innovative ways to increase the miles per gallon efficiency of their automobiles, including introducing different materials into their supply chains. As a result, Ford is investigating increasing the usage of aluminum in its vehicles instead of steel to reduce weight. Last year, the company also introduced a more fuel-efficient V-6 engine into production with their F-150s as an alternative to the V-8 engine.

Although many critics of the impending fuel efficiency standards point to increased costs and reduced safety as a result of using aluminum, U.S. automakers appear to be embracing this opportunity to improve the quality of their vehicles and develop their brands as fuel-efficient. Further, introducing more rigorous fuel standards is expected to spur job growth in addition to increasing sales. Consumers still list fuel efficiency as a main concern when purchasing a vehicle, and American companies do not want to be left behind as foreign vehicles become largely more fuel efficient.[6]

Discussion Questions

1. Why is Ford trying to increase the sustainability of its cars?
2. Why is Ford looking toward aluminum as an alternative material for its vehicles?
3. What are some of the disadvantages of using aluminum materials in cars?

want. Most companies use marketing research (discussed in Chapter 11) to determine the kinds of goods and services to provide and the features they must possess. Twitter and Facebook provide new opportunities for businesses to discover what consumers want, then design the product accordingly. For instance, mineral-based makeup company Bare Escentuals Cosmetics uses Facebook to interact with its customers and generate feedback. From Facebook, Bare Escentuals learned that customers preferred makeup packaging that was more portable so it would be easier to take the makeup with them. This feedback led the company to redesign its packaging by adopting the more portable "Click, Lock, Go" container. By listening to its customers, Bare Escentuals was able to meet their needs more effectively, leading to greater customer satisfaction.[7] Marketing research can also help gauge the demand for a product and how much consumers are willing to pay for it. But when a market's environment changes, firms have to be flexible.

Developing a product can be a lengthy, expensive process. For example, in the automobile industry, developing the new technology for night vision, parking assist systems, and a satellite service that locates and analyzes car problems has been a lengthy, expensive process. Most companies work to reduce development time and costs. For example, through Web collaboration, faucet manufacturer Moen reduced the time required to take an idea to a finished product in stores to just 16 months, a drop of 33 percent.[8] Once management has developed an idea for a product that customers will buy, it must then plan how to produce the product.

Within a company, the engineering or research and development department is charged with turning a product idea into a workable design that can be produced economically. In smaller companies, a single individual (perhaps the owner) may be solely responsible for this crucial activity. Regardless of who is responsible for product design, planning does not stop with a blueprint for a product or a description of a service; it must also work out efficient production of the product to ensure that enough is available to satisfy consumer demand. How does a lawn mower company transform steel, aluminum, and other materials into a mower design that satisfies consumer and environmental requirements? Operations managers must plan for the types and quantities of materials needed to produce the product, the skills and quantity of people needed to make the product, and the actual processes through which the inputs must pass in their transformation to outputs.

Designing the Operations Processes

Before a firm can begin production, it must first determine the appropriate method of transforming resources into the desired product. Often, consumers' specific needs and desires dictate a process. Customer needs, for example, require all 3/4-inch bolts to have the same basic thread size, function, and quality; if they did not, engineers and builders could not rely on 3/4-inch bolts in their construction projects. A bolt manufacturer, then, will likely use a standardized process so that every 3/4-inch bolt produced is like every other one. On the other hand, a bridge often must be customized so that it is appropriate for the site and expected load; furthermore, the bridge must be constructed on site rather than in a factory. Typically, products are designed to be manufactured by one of three processes: standardization, modular design, or customization.

Standardization Most firms that manufacture products in large quantities for many customers have found that they can make them cheaper and faster by standardizing designs.

standardization the making of identical interchangeable components or products

modular design the building of an item in self-contained units, or modules, that can be combined or interchanged to create different products

customization the making of products to meet a particular customer's needs or wants

capacity the maximum load that an organizational unit can carry or operate

Standardization is the making of identical, interchangeable components or even complete products. With standardization, a customer may not get exactly what he or she wants, but the product generally costs less than a custom-designed product. Television sets, ballpoint pens, and tortilla chips are standardized products; most are manufactured on an assembly line. Standardization speeds up production and quality control and reduces production costs. And, as in the example of the 3/4-inch bolts, standardization provides consistency so that customers who need certain products to function uniformly all the time will get a product that meets their expectations. Standardization becomes more complex on a global scale because different countries have different standards for quality. To help solve this problem, the International Organization for Standardization (ISO) has developed a list of global standards that companies can adopt to assure stakeholders that they are complying with the highest quality, environmental, and managerial guidelines.

Modular Design

Modular design involves building an item in self-contained units, or modules, that can be combined or interchanged to create different products. Dell laptops, for example, are composed of a number of components—LCD screen, AC adapter, keyboard, motherboard, and so on—that can be installed in different configurations to meet customers' needs.[9] Because many modular components are produced as integrated units, the failure of any portion of a modular component usually means replacing the entire component. Modular design allows products to be repaired quickly, thus reducing the cost of labor, but the component itself is expensive, raising the cost of repair materials. Many automobile manufacturers use modular design in the production process. Manufactured homes are built on a modular design and often cost about one-fourth as much as a conventionally built house.

Customization

Customization is the making of products to meet a particular customer's needs or wants. Products produced in this way are generally unique. Such products include repair services, photocopy services, custom artwork, jewelry, and furniture as well as large-scale products such as bridges, ships, and computer software. Custom designs are used in communications and service products. A web-based design service, myemma.com, creates a custom template using a company's logo and colors to create a unique page for a website. It also provides tools for interacting with customers and tracking deliveries.[10] Ship design is another industry that uses customization. Builders generally design and build each ship to meet the needs of the customer who will use it. Delta Marine Industries, for example, custom-builds each luxury yacht to the customer's exact specifications and preferences for things like helicopter garages, golf courses, and swimming pools. Mass customization relates to making products that meet the needs or wants of a large number of individual customers. The customer can select the model, size, color, style, or design of the product. Dell can customize a computer with the exact configuration that fits a customer's needs. Services such as fitness programs and travel packages can also be custom designed for a large number of individual customers. For both goods and services, customers get to make choices and have options to determine the final product.

Planning Capacity

Planning the operational processes for the organization involves two important areas: capacity planning and facilities planning. The term **capacity** basically refers to the maximum load that an organizational unit can carry or operate. The unit of measurement may be a worker or machine, a department, a branch, or even an entire plant. Maximum capacity can be stated in terms of the inputs or outputs provided. For example, an electric plant might state plant capacity in terms of the maximum number of kilowatt-hours that can be produced without causing a power outage, whereas a restaurant might state capacity in terms of the maximum number of customers who can be effectively—comfortably and courteously—served at any one particular time.

DID YOU KNOW?

Hershey has the production capacity to make more than 80 million chocolate kisses per day.[11]

Efficiently planning the organization's capacity needs is an important process for the operations manager. Capacity levels that fall short can result in unmet demand and, consequently, lost customers. On the other hand, when there is more capacity available than needed, operating costs are driven up needlessly due to unused and often expensive resources. To avoid such situations, organizations must accurately forecast demand and then plan capacity based on these forecasts. Another reason for the importance of efficient capacity planning has to do with long-term commitment of resources. Often, once a capacity decision—such as factory size—has been implemented, it is very difficult to change the decision without incurring substantial costs. Large companies have come to realize that although change can be expensive, not adjusting to future demand and stakeholder desires will be more expensive

Apple stores are designed to make the most efficient use of space. The layout of the stores allows customers to test its products before purchasing.

in the long run. For this reason, Honda has begun to adopt ISO 14001 guidelines for environmental management systems in its factories. These systems help firms monitor their impact on the environment. Many of Honda's North American factories have received certification.[12]

Planning Facilities

Once a company knows what process it will use to create its products, it then can design and build an appropriate facility in which to make them. Many products are manufactured in factories, but others are produced in stores, at home, or where the product ultimately will be used. Companies must decide where to locate their operations facilities, what layout is best for producing their particular product, and even what technology to apply to the transformation process.

Many firms are developing both a traditional organization for customer contact and a virtual organization. Charles Schwab Corporation, a securities brokerage and investment company, maintains traditional offices and has developed complete telephone and Internet services for customers. Through its website, investors can obtain personal investment information and trade securities over the Internet without leaving their home or office.

Facility Location Where to locate a firm's facilities is a significant question because, once the decision has been made and implemented, the firm must live with it due to the high costs involved. When a company decides to relocate or open a facility at a new location, it must pay careful attention to factors such as proximity to market, availability of raw materials, availability of transportation, availability of power, climatic influences, availability of labor, community characteristics (quality of life), and taxes and inducements. Inducements and tax reductions have become an increasingly important criterion in recent years. To increase production and to provide incentives for small startups, many states are offering tax inducements for solar companies. State governments are willing to forgo some tax revenue in exchange for job growth, getting in on a burgeoning industry as well as the good publicity generated by the company. In a very solar-friendly state like Colorado, companies may get tax reductions for starting production, and consumers receive additional rebates for installing solar systems in their homes and businesses.[13] Apple has followed the lead of other major companies by locating its manufacturing facilities in China to take advantage of lower labor and production costs. The facility-location decision is complex because it involves the evaluation of many factors, some of which cannot

fixed-position layout a layout that brings all resources required to create the product to a central location

project organization a company that uses a fixed-position layout because it is typically involved in large, complex projects such as construction or exploration

process layout a layout that organizes the transformation process into departments that group related processes

intermittent organizations organizations that deal with products of less magnitude than do project organizations; their products are not necessarily unique but possess a significant number of differences

product layout a layout requiring production to be broken down into relatively simple tasks assigned to workers, who are usually positioned along an assembly line

be measured with precision. Because of the long-term impact of the decision, however, it is one that cannot be taken lightly.

Facility Layout Arranging the physical layout of a facility is a complex, highly technical task. Some industrial architects specialize in the design and layout of certain types of businesses. There are three basic layouts: fixed-position, process, and product.

A company using a **fixed-position layout** brings all resources required to create the product to a central location. The product—perhaps an office building, house, hydroelectric plant, or bridge—does not move. A company using a fixed-position layout may be called a **project organization** because it is typically involved in large, complex projects such as construction or exploration. Project organizations generally make a unique product, rely on highly skilled labor, produce very few units, and have high production costs per unit.

Firms that use a **process layout** organize the transformation process into departments that group related processes. A metal fabrication plant, for example, may have a cutting department, a drilling department, and a polishing department. A hospital may have an X-ray unit, an obstetrics unit, and so on. These types of organizations are sometimes called **intermittent organizations**, which deal with products of less magnitude than do project organizations, and their products are not necessarily unique but possess a significant number of differences. Doctors, makers of custom-made cabinets, commercial printers, and advertising agencies are intermittent organizations because they tend to create products to customers' specifications and produce relatively few units of each product. Because of the low level of output, the cost per unit of product is generally high.

The **product layout** requires production to be broken down into relatively simple tasks assigned to workers, who are usually positioned along an assembly line. Workers remain in one location, and the product moves from one worker to another. Each person in turn performs his or her required tasks or activities. Companies that use assembly lines are usually known as **continuous manufacturing organizations**, so named because once they are set up, they run continuously, creating products with many similar characteristics. Examples of products produced on assembly lines are automobiles, television sets, vacuum cleaners, toothpaste, and meals from a cafeteria. Continuous manufacturing organizations using a product layout are characterized by the standardized product they produce, the large number of units produced, and the relatively low unit cost of production.

Many companies actually use a combination of layout designs. For example, an automobile manufacturer may rely on an assembly line (product layout) but may also use a process layout to manufacture parts.

Technology Every industry has a basic, underlying technology that dictates the nature of its transformation process. The steel industry continually tries to improve steelmaking techniques. The health care industry performs research into medical technologies and pharmaceuticals to improve the quality of health care service. Two developments that have strongly influenced the operations of many businesses are computers and robotics.

> "Every industry has a basic, underlying technology that dictates the nature of its transformation process."

Computers have been used for decades and on a relatively large scale since IBM introduced its 650 series in the late 1950s. The operations function makes great use of computers in all phases of the transformation process. **Computer-assisted design (CAD)**, for example, helps engineers design components, products, and processes on the computer instead of on paper. **Computer-assisted manufacturing (CAM)** goes a step further, employing specialized computer systems to actually guide and control the transformation processes. Such systems can monitor the transformation process, gathering information about the equipment used to produce the products and about the product itself as it goes from one stage of the transformation process to the next. The computer provides information to an

continuous manufacturing organizations companies that use continuously running assembly lines, creating products with many similar characteristics

computer-assisted design (CAD) the design of components, products, and processes on computers instead of on paper

computer-assisted manufacturing (CAM) manufacturing that employs specialized computer systems to actually guide and control the transformation processes

flexible manufacturing the direction of machinery by computers to adapt to different versions of similar operations

computer-integrated manufacturing (CIM) a complete system that designs products, manages machines and materials, and controls the operations function

operator who may, if necessary, take corrective action. In some highly automated systems, the computer itself can take corrective action. At Dell's OptiPlex Plant, electronic instructions are sent to double-decker conveyor belts that speed computer components to assembly stations. Two-member teams are told by computers which PC or server to build, with initial assembly taking only three to four minutes. Then more electronic commands move the products (more than 20,000 machines on a typical day) to a finishing area to be customized, boxed, and sent to waiting delivery trucks.

Using **flexible manufacturing**, computers can direct machinery to adapt to different versions of similar operations. For example, with instructions from a computer, one machine can be programmed to carry out its function for several versions of an engine without shutting down the production line for refitting.

Robots are also becoming increasingly useful in the transformation process. These "steel-collar" workers have become particularly important in industries such as nuclear power, hazardous-waste disposal, ocean research, and space construction and maintenance, in which human lives would otherwise be at risk. Robots are used in numerous applications by companies around the world. Many assembly operations—cars, television sets, telephones, stereo equipment, and numerous other products—depend on industrial robots. The Robotic Industries Association estimates that about 225,000 robots are now at work in U.S. factories, making the United States one of the two largest users of robotics, second only to Japan.[14] Researchers continue to make more sophisticated robots, and some speculate that in the future, robots will not be limited to space programs and production and operations, but will also be able to engage in farming, laboratory research, and even household activities. Moreover, robotics are increasingly being used in the medical field. More than 1 million robots are being used in manufacturing around the world, most of them in high-tech industries.

When all these technologies—CAD/CAM, flexible manufacturing, robotics, computer systems, and more—are integrated, the result is **computer-integrated manufacturing (CIM)**, a complete system that designs products, manages machines and materials, and controls the operations function. Companies adopt CIM to boost productivity and quality and reduce costs. Such technology, and computers in particular, will continue to make strong inroads into operations on two fronts—one dealing with the technology involved in manufacturing and one dealing with the administrative functions and processes used by operations managers. The operations manager must be willing

PANASONIC GREENS ITS SUPPLY CHAIN

Many companies have begun to incorporate sustainability into their business models. However, one area that is particularly difficult for companies to tackle is greening their supply chains. This is in part due to the long value chain that most products travel through before reaching their final destination. This makes it difficult for businesses to track how their products are created, assembled, produced, and transported—and even harder to ensure that the entire process is sustainable.

However, one company that has seen success in this area is Japanese company Panasonic. Panasonic has launched its Green Plan 2018 with the goal to become the world's top green electronics business, tackling both its operations and the daily lives of its customers. Panasonic has implemented a recycling-based manufacturing process by which products are manufactured in a way that minimizes waste, reduces resource consumption, and maximizes materials to be reused. This approach allows materials from previously used electronics to be reused to create new products. Panasonic has also set up a special recycling facility to help in the implementation of its recycling-based manufacturing process—allowing the company to have more control over its supply chain. In addition, engineers at this facility have designed new methods of creating products that are easier to disassemble, ultimately saving time, money, and energy.

Although there is a long road ahead in greening the world's supply chains, Panasonic has made progress. Panasonic has demonstrated innovative ways to redesign and create a supply chain that reduces resource consumption, increases recycled materials, and reduces waste.[15]

Discussion Questions

1. Why is it difficult to monitor the sustainability of an organization's supply chain?
2. What are some of the ways Panasonic has been able to "green" its supply chain?
3. Why do you think companies are trying to increase the sustainability of their operations and supply chains?

to work with computers and other forms of technology and to develop a high degree of computer literacy.

Sustainability and Manufacturing

Manufacturing and operations systems are moving quickly to establish environmental sustainability and minimize negative impact on the natural environment. Sustainability deals with conducting activities in such a way as to provide for the long-term well-being of the natural environment, including all biological entities. Sustainability issues are becoming increasingly important to stakeholders and consumers because they pertain to the future health of the planet. Some sustainability issues include pollution of the land, air, and water, climate change, waste management, deforestation, urban sprawl, protection of biodiversity, and genetically modified foods.

For example, Johnson Controls has incorporated sustainability into many facets of its operations. The company purchases green energy, works with suppliers to "green" its supply chain, and designs more eco-friendly products. Overseeing these activities is Johnson Controls' Global Environmental Sustainability Council, which measures the company's progress toward its sustainability goals. Johnson Controls also opened up a battery recycling facility to encourage stakeholders to recycle their lead-acid batteries rather than disposing of them improperly.[16]

New Belgium Brewing is another company that illustrates green initiatives in operations and manufacturing. New Belgium was the first brewery to adopt 100 percent wind-powered electricity, reducing carbon emissions by 1,800 metric tons a year. It uses a steam condenser to capture hot water to be reused for boiling the next batch of barley and hops. Then the steam is redirected to heat the floor tiles and de-ice the loading docks in cold Colorado weather. Used barley and hops are given to local farmers to feed cattle. The company is moving to aluminum cans because they can be recycled an infinite number of times, and recycling one can save enough electricity to run a television for three hours or save a half gallon of gasoline.

supply chain management connecting and integrating all parties or members of the distribution system to satisfy customers

Johnson Controls and New Belgium Brewing demonstrate that reducing waste, recycling, conserving, and using renewable energy not only protect the environment but also can gain the support of stakeholders. Green operations and manufacturing can improve a firm's reputation along with customer and employee loyalty, leading to improved profits.

Much of the movement to green manufacturing and operations is the belief that global warming and climate change must decline. The McKinsey Global Institute (MGI) says that just by investing in existing technologies, the world's energy use could be reduced by 50 percent by the year 2020. Creating green buildings and higher-mileage cars could yield $900 billion in savings per year by 2020.[17] Companies like General Motors and Ford are adapting to stakeholder demands for greater sustainability by producing smaller and more fuel-efficient cars. For example, the Chevy Volt can run for up to 35 miles on one overnight charge before switching to a gas-powered generator. The Volt is also a FlexFuel vehicle, which means that it can use either traditional gasoline or E85 ethanol, which some people believe is better for the environment.[18] Green products produced through green operations and manufacturing are our future. A report authored by the Center for American Progress cites ways that cities and local governments can play a role. For example, Los Angeles plans to save the city utility costs by retrofitting hundreds of city buildings while creating a green careers training program for low-income residents. Newark, New Jersey, and Richmond, California, also have green jobs training programs. Albuquerque, New Mexico, was the first city to sign on to a pledge to build a green economy as part of its efforts to create green jobs to stimulate the city's economy.[19] Government initiatives provide space for businesses to innovate their green operations and manufacturing.

The outdoor clothing company Patagonia is always looking for a greener way to design, produce, and recycle its products. The company's mission statement: Build the best product, cause no unnecessary harm, and use business to inspire and implement solutions to the environmental crisis.

LO 8-4 Specify some techniques managers may use to manage the logistics of transforming inputs into finished products.

MANAGING THE SUPPLY CHAIN

A major function of operations is **supply chain management**, which refers to connecting and integrating all parties or members of the distribution system to satisfy customers.[20] Also called

purchasing the buying of all the materials needed by the organization; also called procurement

inventory all raw materials, components, completed or partially completed products, and pieces of equipment a firm uses

inventory control the process of determining how many supplies and goods are needed and keeping track of quantities on hand, where each item is, and who is responsible for it

economic order quantity (EOQ) model a model that identifies the optimum number of items to order to minimize the costs of managing (ordering, storing, and using) them

just-in-time (JIT) inventory management a technique using smaller quantities of materials that arrive "just in time" for use in the transformation process and therefore require less storage space and other inventory management expense

logistics, supply chain management includes all the activities involved in obtaining and managing raw materials and component parts, managing finished products, packaging them, and getting them to customers. Sunny Delight had to re-create its supply chain quickly after spinning off from Procter & Gamble. This means it had to develop ordering, shipping, and billing, as well as warehouse management systems and transportation, so it could focus on growing and managing the Sunny Delight brand.[21] The supply chain integrates firms such as raw material suppliers, manufacturers, retailers, and ultimate consumers into a seamless flow of information and products.[22] Some aspects of logistics (warehousing, packaging, distributing) are so closely linked with marketing that we will discuss them in Chapter 12. In this section, we look at purchasing, managing inventory, outsourcing, and scheduling, which are vital tasks in the transformation of raw materials into finished goods. To illustrate logistics, consider a hypothetical small business—we'll call it Rushing Water Canoes Inc.—that manufactures aluminum canoes, which it sells primarily to sporting goods stores and river-rafting expeditions. Our company also makes paddles and helmets, but the focus of the following discussion is the manufacture of the company's quality canoes as they proceed through the logistics process.

Purchasing

Purchasing, also known as procurement, is the buying of all the materials needed by the organization. The purchasing department aims to obtain items of the desired quality in the right quantities at the lowest possible cost. Rushing Water Canoes, for example, must procure not only aluminum and other raw materials, and various canoe parts and components, but also machines and equipment, manufacturing supplies (oil, electricity, and so on), and office supplies to make its canoes. People in the purchasing department locate and evaluate suppliers of these items. They must constantly be on the lookout for new materials or parts that will do a better job or cost less than those currently being used. The purchasing function can be quite complex and is one area made much easier and more efficient by technological advances.

Not all companies purchase all the materials needed to create their products. Oftentimes, they can make some components more economically and efficiently than can an outside supplier. Coors, for example, manufactures its own cans at a subsidiary plant. On the other hand, firms sometimes find that it is uneconomical to make or purchase an item and, instead, arrange to lease it from another organization. Some airlines, for example, lease airplanes rather than buy them. Whether to purchase, make, or lease a needed item generally depends on cost as well as on product availability and supplier reliability.

Managing Inventory

Once the items needed to create a product have been procured, some provision has to be made for storing them until they are needed. Every raw material, component, completed or partially completed product, and piece of equipment a firm uses—its **inventory**—must be accounted for, or controlled. There are three basic types of inventory. *Finished-goods inventory* includes those products that are ready for sale, such as a fully assembled automobile ready to ship to a dealer. *Work-in-process inventory* consists of those products that are partly completed or are in some stage of the transformation process. At McDonald's, a cooking hamburger represents work-in-process inventory because it must go through several more stages before it can be sold to a customer. *Raw materials inventory* includes all the materials that have been purchased to be used as inputs for making other products. Nuts and bolts are raw materials for an automobile manufacturer, whereas hamburger patties, vegetables, and buns are raw materials for the fast-food restaurant. Our fictional Rushing Water Canoes has an inventory of materials for making canoes, paddles, and helmets as well as its inventory of finished products for sale to consumers. **Inventory control** is the process of determining how many supplies and goods are needed and keeping track of quantities on hand, where each item is, and who is responsible for it.

Coca-Cola distribution centers work with wholesalers and retailers to ensure there is enough inventory to handle customer demand.

DHL helps manage the supply and transportation of products, whether it be via truck, rail, air, or ocean transport.

Operations management must be closely coordinated with inventory control. The production of televisions, for example, cannot be planned without some knowledge of the availability of all the necessary materials—the chassis, picture tubes, color guns, and so forth. Also, each item held in inventory—any type of inventory—carries with it a cost. For example, storing fully assembled televisions in a warehouse to sell to a dealer at a future date requires not only the use of space but also the purchase of insurance to cover any losses that might occur due to fire or other unforeseen events.

Inventory managers spend a great deal of time trying to determine the proper inventory level for each item. The answer to the question of how many units to hold in inventory depends on variables such as the usage rate of the item, the cost of maintaining the item in inventory, future costs of inventory and other procedures associated with ordering or making the item, and the cost of the item itself. For example, the price of copper has fluctuated between $1.50 and $4 a pound over the past five years. Firms using copper wiring for construction, copper pipes for plumbing, and other industries requiring copper have to analyze the trade-offs between inventory costs and expected changes in the price of copper. Several approaches may be used to determine how many units of a given item should be procured at one time and when that procurement should take place.

“Operations management must be closely coordinated with inventory control.”

The Economic Order Quantity Model To control the number of items maintained in inventory, managers need to determine how much of any given item they should order. One popular approach is the **economic order quantity (EOQ) model**, which identifies the optimum number of items to order to minimize the costs of managing (ordering, storing, and using) them.

Just-in-Time Inventory Management An increasingly popular technique is **just-in-time (JIT) inventory management**, which eliminates waste by using smaller quantities of materials that arrive “just in time” for use in the transformation process and therefore require less storage space and other inventory management expense. JIT minimizes inventory by providing an almost continuous flow of items from suppliers to the production facility. Many U.S. companies, including Hewlett-Packard, IBM, and Harley Davidson, have adopted JIT to reduce costs and boost efficiency.

Let’s say that Rushing Water Canoes uses 20 units of aluminum from a supplier per day. Traditionally, its inventory manager

material-requirements planning (MRP) a planning system that schedules the precise quantity of materials needed to make the product

might order enough for one month at a time: 440 units per order (20 units per day times 22 workdays per month). The expense of such a large inventory could be considerable because of the cost of insurance coverage, recordkeeping, rented storage space, and so on. The just-in-time approach would reduce these costs because aluminum would be purchased in smaller quantities, perhaps in lot sizes of 20, which the supplier would deliver once a day. Of course, for such an approach to be effective, the supplier must be extremely reliable and relatively close to the production facility.

On the other hand, there are some downsides to just-in-time inventory management that marketers must take into account. When the earthquake and tsunami hit Japan, resulting in a nuclear reactor crisis, several Japanese companies halted their operations. Some multinationals relied so much upon their Japanese suppliers that their supply chains were also affected. In the case of natural disasters, having only enough inventory to meet current needs could create delays in production and hurt the company's bottom line. For this reason, many economists suggest that businesses store components that are essential for production and diversify their supply chains. That way, if a natural disaster knocks out a major supplier, the company can continue to operate.[23]

Material-Requirements Planning Another inventory management technique is **material-requirements planning (MRP)**, a planning system that schedules the precise quantity of materials needed to make the product. The basic components of MRP are a master production schedule, a bill of materials, and an inventory status file. At Rushing Water Canoes, for example, the inventory-control manager will look at the production schedule to determine how many canoes the company plans to make. He or she will then prepare a bill of materials—a list of all the materials needed to make that quantity of canoes. Next, the manager will determine the quantity of these items that RWC already holds in inventory (to avoid ordering excess materials) and then develop a schedule for ordering and accepting delivery of the right quantity of materials to satisfy the firm's needs. Because of the large number of parts and materials that go into a typical production process, MRP must be done on a computer. It can be, and often is, used in conjunction with just-in-time inventory management.

Outsourcing

Increasingly, outsourcing has become a component of supply chain management in operations. As we mentioned in Chapter 3, outsourcing refers to the contracting of manufacturing or other tasks to independent companies, often overseas. Many companies elect to outsource some aspects of their operations to companies that can provide these products more efficiently, at a lower cost, and with greater customer satisfaction. Globalization has put pressure on supply chain managers to improve speed and balance resources against competitive pressures. Companies outsourcing to China, in particular, face heavy regulation, high transportation costs, inadequate facilities, and unpredictable supply chain execution. Therefore, suppliers need to provide useful, timely, and accurate information about every aspect of the quality requirements, schedules, and solutions to dealing with problems. Companies that hire suppliers must also make certain that their suppliers are following company standards; failure to do so could lead to criticism of the parent company. For example, Hershey was criticized for sourcing from suppliers that used child labor on chocolate plantations. Although suppliers are responsible for hiring underage workers, it is ultimately the responsibility

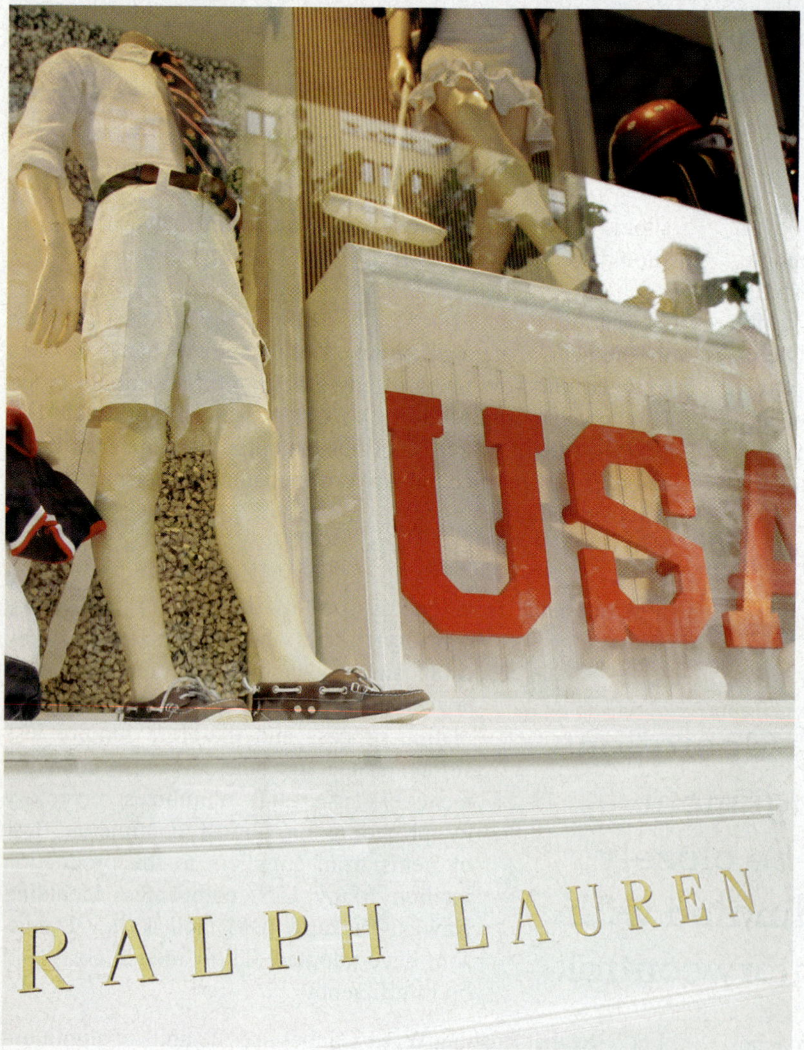

Ralph Lauren came under fire for outsourcing U.S. Olympic uniforms to China.

routing the sequence of operations through which the product must pass

scheduling the assignment of required tasks to departments or even specific machines, workers, or teams

of Hershey to ensure the compliance of suppliers in its supply chain.[24]

Many high-tech firms have outsourced the production of chips, computers, and telecom equipment to Asian companies. The hourly labor costs in countries such as China, India, and Vietnam are far less than in the United States, Europe, or even Mexico. These developing countries have improved their manufacturing capabilities, infrastructure, and technical and business skills, making them more attractive regions for global sourcing. For instance, Nike outsources almost all of its production to Asian countries such as China and Vietnam. On the other hand, the cost of outsourcing halfway around the world must be considered in decisions. Although information technology is often outsourced today, transportation, human resources, services, and even marketing functions can be outsourced. Our hypothetical Rushing Water Canoes might contract with a local janitorial service to clean its offices and with a local accountant to handle routine bookkeeping and tax-preparation functions.

Outsourcing, once used primarily as a cost-cutting tactic, has increasingly been linked with the development of competitive advantage through improved product quality, speeding up the time it takes products to get to the customer, and overall supply-chain efficiencies. Table 8.1 provides the world's top five outsourcing providers that assist mainly in information technology. Outsourcing allows companies to free up time and resources to focus on what they do best and to create better opportunities to focus on customer satisfaction. Many executives view outsourcing as an innovative way to boost productivity and remain competitive against low-wage offshore factories. However, outsourcing may create conflict with labor and negative public opinion when it results in U.S. workers being replaced by lower-cost workers in other countries.

> "Many executives view outsourcing as an innovative way to boost productivity and remain competitive against low-wage offshore factories."

TABLE 8.1 The World's Top Five Outsourcing Providers

Company	Services
Accenture	Management consulting, technology, and outsourcing
Infosys	Business consulting, IT services, product engineering
HCL Technologies	Offshore and IT software development
CBRE	Commercial real estate services
ISS	Facility services

Source: "The 2012 Global Outsourcing 100," International Association of Outsourcing Professionals, www.iaop.org/content/19/165/3437.

Routing and Scheduling

After all materials have been procured and their use determined, managers must then consider the **routing**, or sequence of operations through which the product must pass. For example, before employees at Rushing Water Canoes can form aluminum sheets into a canoe, the aluminum must be cut to size. Likewise, the canoe's flotation material must be installed before workers can secure the wood seats. The sequence depends on the product specifications developed by the engineering department of the company.

Once management knows the routing, the actual work can be scheduled. **Scheduling** assigns the tasks to be done to departments or even specific machines, workers, or teams. At Rushing Water, cutting aluminum for the company's canoes might be scheduled to be done by the "cutting and finishing" department on machines designed especially for that purpose.

Many approaches to scheduling have been developed, ranging from simple trial and error to highly sophisticated computer programs. One popular method is the *Program Evaluation and Review Technique (PERT),* which identifies all the major activities or events required to complete a project, arranges them in a sequence or path, determines the critical path, and estimates the time required for each event. Producing a McDonald's Big Mac, for example, involves removing meat, cheese, sauce, and vegetables from the refrigerator; grilling the hamburger patties; assembling the ingredients; placing the completed Big Mac in its package; and serving it to the customer (Figure 8.3). The cheese, pickles, onions, and sauce cannot be put on before the hamburger patty is completely grilled and placed on the bun. The path that requires the longest time from start to finish is called the *critical path* because it determines the minimum amount of time in which the process can be completed. If any of the activities on the critical path for production of the Big Mac fall behind schedule, the sandwich will not be completed on time, causing customers to wait longer than they usually would.

FIGURE 8.3
A Hypothetical PERT Diagram for a McDonald's Big Mac

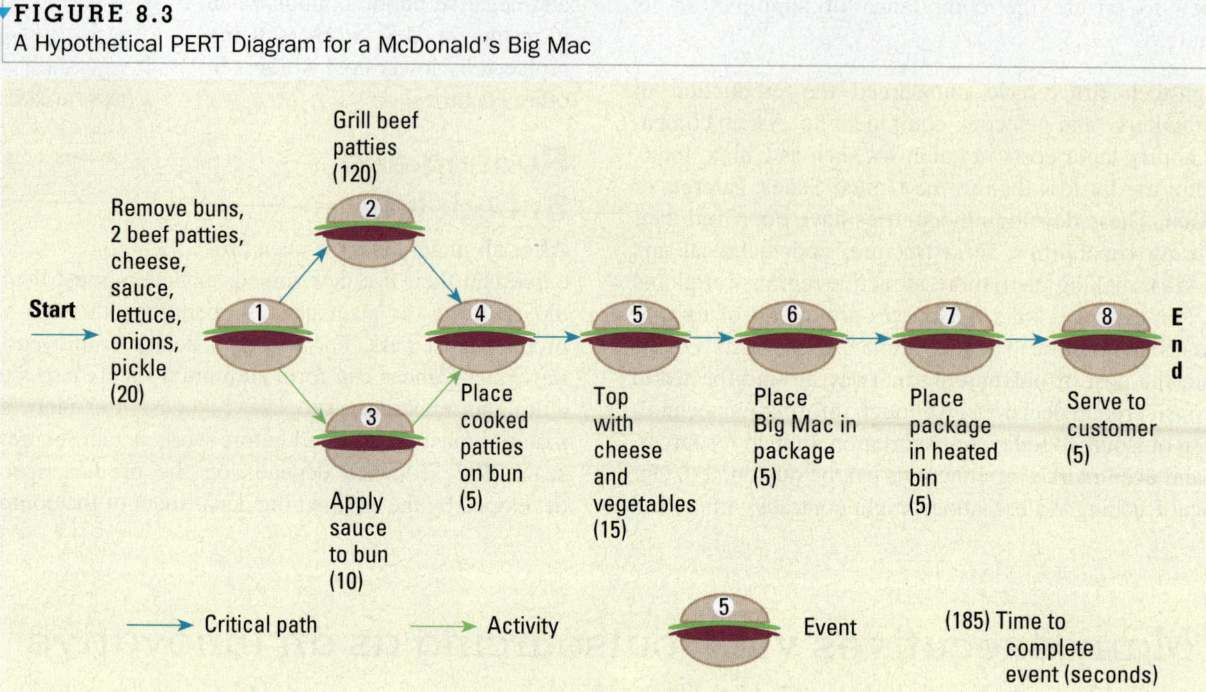

LO 8-5 Assess the importance of quality in operations management.

MANAGING QUALITY

Quality, like cost and efficiency, is a critical element of operations management, for defective products can quickly ruin a firm. Quality reflects the degree to which a good or service meets the demands and requirements of customers. Customers are increasingly dissatisfied with the quality of service provided by many airlines. Table 8.2 gives the rankings of U.S. airlines in certain operational areas. Determining quality can be difficult because it depends on customers' perceptions of how well the product meets or exceeds their expectations. For example, customer satisfaction on airlines can vary wildly depending on individual customers' perspectives. However, the airline industry is notorious for its dissatisfied customers. Flight delays are a common complaint from airline passengers; 20 percent of all flights arrive more than 15 minutes late. However, most passengers do not select an airline based on how often flights arrive on time.[25]

The fuel economy of an automobile or its reliability (defined in terms of frequency of repairs) can be measured with some degree of precision. Although automakers rely on their own measures of vehicle quality, they also look to independent sources such as the J.D. Power and Associates annual initial quality survey for confirmation of their quality assessment as well as consumer perceptions of quality for the industry, as indicated in Figure 8.4.

It is especially difficult to measure quality characteristics when the product is a service. A company has to decide exactly

TABLE 8.2 2012 Airline Scorecard (best to worst)

Rank	Overall Rank	Late Flights	Canceled Flights	Extreme Delays	Bumped Passengers	Lost Bags	Complaints
1	Delta	Alaska	Delta	US Airways	jetBlue	jetBlue	Southwest
2	Alaska	Delta	Southwest	Alaska	Delta	Delta	Alaska
3	US Airways	US Airways	US Airways	Delta	Alaska	US Airways	Delta
4	Southwest	jetBlue	Alaska	Southwest	US Airways	Southwest	jetBlue
5	jetBlue	Southwest	jetBlue	United	American	American	American
6	American	United	United	American	Southwest	Alaska	US Airways
7	United	American	American	jetBlue	United	United	United

Source: FlightStats.com; Department of Transportation.

quality control the processes an organization uses to maintain its established quality standards

total quality management (TQM) a philosophy whereby uniform commitment to quality in all areas of an organization will promote a culture that meets customers' perceptions of quality

which quality characteristics it considers important and then define those characteristics in terms that can be measured. The inseparability of production and consumption and the level of customer contact influence the selection of characteristics of the service that are most important. Employees in high-contact services such as hairstyling, education, legal services, and even the barista at Starbucks are an important part of the product.

The Malcolm Baldrige National Quality Award is given each year to companies that meet rigorous standards of quality. The Baldrige criteria are (1) leadership, (2) information and analysis, (3) strategic planning, (4) human resource development and management, (5) process management, (6) business results, and (7) customer focus and satisfaction. The criteria have become a worldwide framework for driving business improvement. Four companies won the award in 2012, representing four categories: Lockheed Martin Missiles and Fire Control (manufacturing); MESA Products, Inc. (small business); North Mississippi Health Services (health care); and the City of Irving (nonprofit).[26]

Quality is so important that we need to examine it in the context of operations management. **Quality control** refers to the processes an organization uses to maintain its established quality standards. Kia recognized the importance of quality control when it sought to revamp its image. For years, Kia vehicles were seen as low quality. To change consumer perceptions of the Kia brand, the company had its quality-control managers instead of sales executives provide final approval for its products, implemented benchmarks for improving product quality, developed strong marketing campaigns promoting the brand, and cut dealers that it did not feel were supporting the Kia franchise. Kia's quality efforts were largely successful; its overall sales grew 27 percent in a one-year period.[27] Quality has become a major concern in many organizations, particularly in light of intense foreign competition and increasingly demanding customers. To regain a competitive edge, a number of firms have adopted a total quality management approach. **Total quality management (TQM)** is a philosophy whereby uniform commitment to quality in all areas of the organization will promote a culture that meets customers' perceptions of quality. It involves coordinating efforts to improve customer satisfaction, increasing employee participation, forming and strengthening supplier partnerships, and facilitating an organizational culture of continuous quality improvement. TQM requires constant improvements in all areas of the company as well as employee empowerment.

Continuous improvement of an organization's goods and services is built around the notion that quality is free; by contrast, *not* having high-quality goods and services can be very expensive, especially in terms of dissatisfied customers.[28] A primary tool of the continuous improvement process is *benchmarking,* the measuring and evaluating of the quality of the organization's goods, services, or processes as compared with the quality produced by the best-performing companies in the industry.[29] Benchmarking lets the organization know where it stands competitively in its industry, thus giving it a goal to aim for over time. Now that online digital media are becoming more important in businesses, companies such as Compuware Gomez offer benchmarking tools so companies can monitor and compare the success of their websites. Such tools allow companies to track traffic to the site versus competitors' sites. Studies have shown a direct link between website performance and online sales, meaning this type of benchmarking is important.[30]

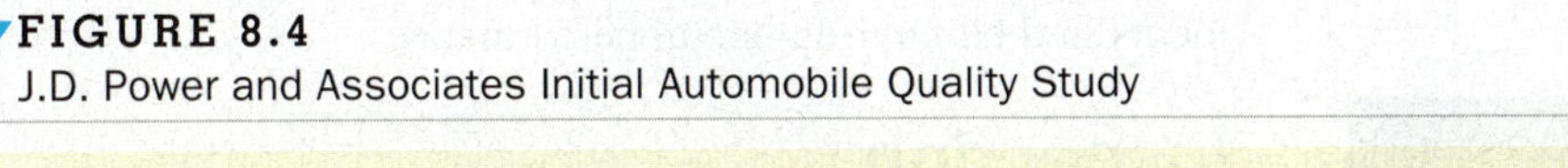

FIGURE 8.4
J.D. Power and Associates Initial Automobile Quality Study

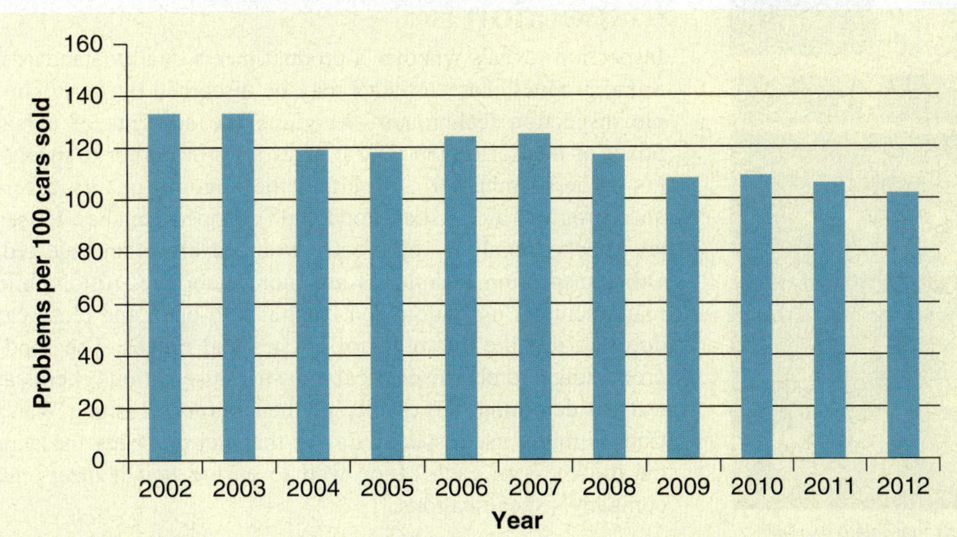

Source: J.D. Power and Associates, "2012 U.S. Initial Quality Study," June 20, 2012, http://autos.jdpower.com/content/press-release/ws4mUEA/2012-u-s-initial-quality-study.htm.

Companies employing total quality management (TQM) programs know that quality control should be incorporated throughout the transformation process, from the initial plans to the development of a specific product through the product and production-facility design processes to the actual manufacture of the product. In other words, they view quality control as an element of the product itself rather than as simply a function of the operations process. When a company makes the product correctly from

statistical process control a system in which management collects and analyzes information about the production process to pinpoint quality problems in the production system

ISO 9000 a series of quality assurance standards designed by the International Organization for Standardization (ISO) to ensure consistent product quality under many conditions

ISO 14000 a comprehensive set of environmental standards that encourages companies to conduct business in a cleaner, safer, and less wasteful way. ISO 14000 provides a uniform set of standards globally.

the outset, it eliminates the need to rework defective products, expedites the transformation process itself, and allows employees to make better use of their time and materials. One method through which many companies have tried to improve quality is **statistical process control**, a system in which management collects and analyzes information about the production process to pinpoint quality problems in the production system.

International Organization for Standardization (ISO)

Regardless of whether a company has a TQM program for quality control, it must first determine what standard of quality it desires and then assess whether its products meet that standard. Product specifications and quality standards must be set so the company can create a product that will compete in the marketplace. Rushing Water Canoes, for example, may specify that each of its canoes has aluminum walls of a specified uniform thickness, that the front and back be reinforced with a specified level of steel, and that each contain a specified amount of flotation material for safety. Production facilities must be designed that can produce products with the desired specifications.

Quality standards can be incorporated into service businesses as well. A hamburger chain, for example, may establish standards relating to how long it takes to cook an order and serve it to customers, how many fries are in each order, how thick the burgers are, or how many customer complaints might be acceptable. Once the desired quality characteristics, specifications, and standards have been stated in measurable terms, the next step is inspection.

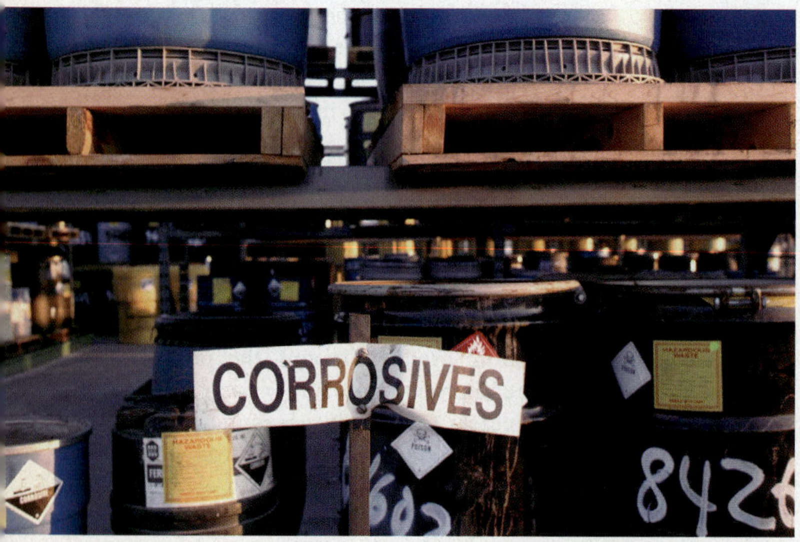

The ISO 9000 standards are international standards that relate to quality management. ISO 14000 standards relate to environmental management—managing businesses to minimize harmful effects to the environment.

The International Organization for Standardization (ISO) has created a series of quality management standards—**ISO 9000**—designed to ensure the customer's quality standards are met. The standards provide a framework for documenting how a certified business keeps records, trains employees, tests products, and fixes defects. To obtain ISO 9000 certification, an independent auditor must verify that a business's factory, laboratory, or office meets the quality standards spelled out by the International Organization for Standardization. The certification process can require significant investment, but for many companies, the process is essential to being able to compete. Thousands of companies have been certified, including General Electric Analytical Instruments, which has applied ISO standards to everything from the design to the manufacturing practices of its global facilities.[31] Certification has become a virtual necessity for doing business in Europe in some high-technology businesses. ISO 9002 certification was established for service providers. **ISO 14000** is a comprehensive set of environmental standards that encourages a cleaner and safer world. ISO 14000 is a valuable standard because, currently, considerable variation exists between the regulations in different nations and even regions within a nation. These variations make it difficult for organizations committed to sustainability to find acceptable global solutions to problems. The goal of the ISO 14000 standards is to promote a more uniform approach to environmental management and to help companies attain and measure improvements in their environmental performance.

Inspection

Inspection reveals whether a product meets quality standards. Some product characteristics may be discerned by fairly simple inspection techniques—weighing the contents of cereal boxes or measuring the time it takes for a customer to receive his or her hamburger. As part of the ongoing quality assurance program at Hershey Foods, all wrapped Hershey Kisses are checked, and all imperfectly wrapped kisses are rejected. Other inspection techniques are more elaborate. Automobile manufacturers use automated machines to open and close car doors to test the durability of latches and hinges. The food-processing and pharmaceutical industries use various chemical tests to determine the quality of their output. Rushing Water Canoes might use a special device that can precisely measure the thickness of each canoe wall to ensure that it meets the company's specifications.

Organizations normally inspect purchased items, work-in-process, and finished items. The inspection of purchased items and finished items takes place after the fact; the inspection of work-in-process is preventive. In other words, the purpose of inspection of purchased items and finished items is to determine what the quality level is. For items that are being worked on—an automobile moving down the assembly line or a canoe being assembled—the purpose of the inspection is to find defects before the product is completed so that necessary corrections can be made.

Sampling

An important question relating to inspection is how many items should be inspected. Should all canoes produced by Rushing Water be inspected or just some of them? Whether to inspect 100 percent of the output or only part of it is related to the cost of the inspection process, the destructiveness of the inspection process (some tests last until the product fails), and the potential cost of product flaws in terms of human lives and safety.

Some inspection procedures are quite expensive, use elaborate testing equipment, destroy products, and/or require a significant number of hours to complete. In such cases, it is usually desirable to test only a sample of the output. If the sample passes inspection, the inspector may assume that all the items in the lot from which the sample was drawn would also pass inspection. By using principles of statistical inference, management can employ sampling techniques that ensure a relatively high probability of reaching the right conclusion—that is, rejecting a lot that does not meet standards and accepting a lot that does. Nevertheless, there will always be a risk of making an incorrect conclusion—accepting a population that *does not* meet standards (because the sample was satisfactory) or rejecting a population that *does* meet standards (because the sample contained too many defective items).

Sampling is likely to be used when inspection tests are destructive. Determining the life expectancy of light bulbs by turning them on and recording how long they last would be foolish: There is no market for burned-out light bulbs. Instead, a generalization based on the quality of a sample would be applied to the entire population of light bulbs from which the sample was drawn. However, human life and safety often depend on the proper functioning of specific items, such as the navigational systems installed in commercial airliners. For such items, even though the inspection process is costly, the potential cost of flawed systems—in human lives and safety—is too great not to inspect 100 percent of the output.

TEAM EXERCISE

Form groups and assign the responsibility of finding companies that outsource their production to other countries. What are the key advantages of this outsourcing decision? Do you see any drawbacks or weaknesses in this approach? Why would a company not outsource when such a tactic can be undertaken to cut manufacturing costs? Report your findings to the class.

INTEGRATING OPERATIONS AND SUPPLY CHAIN MANAGEMENT

Managing operations and supply chains can be complex and challenging due to the number of independent organizations that must perform their responsibilities in creating product quality. Managing supply chains requires constant vigilance and the ability to make quick tactical changes. For example, an Australian firm experienced severe supply chain problems when it sent 50 goldfish to media companies as part of a public relations campaign. The fish died in transit, requiring the company to issue an apology and donate money to animal protection organizations.[32] Even Apple Inc., the most admired company in the world, has had supply chain problems. Reports of forced overtime, underage workers, and dangerous conditions at its Chinese supplier factories have resulted in negative publicity for the company.[33] Therefore, managing the various partners involved in supply chains and operations is important because many stakeholders hold the firm responsible for appropriate conduct related to product quality. This requires the company to exercise oversight over all suppliers involved in producing a product. Encouraging suppliers to report problems, issues, or concerns requires excellent communication systems to obtain feedback. Ideally, suppliers will report potential problems before they reach the next level of the supply chain, which reduces damage.

Despite the challenges of monitoring global operations and supply chains, there are steps businesses can take to manage these risks. All companies that work with global suppliers should adopt a Global Supplier Code of Conduct and ensure that it is effectively communicated. Additionally, companies should encourage compliance and procurement employees to work together to find ethical suppliers at reasonable costs. Those in procurement are concerned with the costs of obtaining materials for the company. As a result, supply chain and procurement managers must work together to make operational decisions to ensure the selection of the best suppliers from an ethical and cost-effective standpoint. Businesses must also work to make certain that their supply chains are diverse. Having only a few suppliers in one area can disrupt operations if a disaster strikes. Finally, companies must perform regular audits on its suppliers and take action against those found to be in violation of company standards.[34] ■

SO YOU WANT A JOB // in Operations Management /

Although you might not have been familiar with terms such as *supply chain* or *logistics* or *total quality management* before taking this course, careers abound in the operations management field. You will find these careers in a wide variety of organizations—manufacturers, retailers, transportation companies, third-party logistics firms, government agencies, and service firms. Approximately $1.3 trillion is spent on transportation, inventory, and related logistics activities, and logistics alone accounts for more than 9.5 percent of U.S. gross domestic product.[35] Closely managing how a company's inputs and outputs flow from raw materials to the end consumer is vital to a firm's success. Successful companies also need to ensure that quality is measured and actively managed at each step.

Supply chain managers have a tremendous impact on the success of an organization. These managers are engaged in every facet of the business process, including planning, purchasing, production, transportation, storage and distribution, customer service, and more. Their performance helps organizations control expenses, boost sales, and maximize profits.

Warehouse managers are a vital part of manufacturing operations. A typical warehouse manager's duties include overseeing and recording deliveries and pickups, maintaining inventory records and the product tracking system, and adjusting inventory levels to reflect receipts and disbursements. Warehouse managers also have to keep in mind customer service and employee issues. Warehouse managers can earn up to $60,000 in some cases.

Operations management is also required in service businesses. With more than 80 percent of the U.S. economy in services, jobs exist for services operations. Many service contact operations require standardized processes that often use technology to provide an interface that provides an automatic quality performance. Consider jobs in health care, the travel industry, fast food, and entertainment. Think of any job or task that is a part of the final product in these industries. Even an online retailer such as Amazon.com has a transformation process that includes information technology and human activities that facilitate a transaction. These services have a standardized process and can be evaluated based on their level of achieved service quality.

Total quality management is becoming a key attribute for companies to ensure that quality pervades all aspects of the organization. Quality assurance managers may make salaries in the $55,000 to $65,000 range. These managers monitor and advise on how a company's quality management system is performing and publish data and reports regarding company performance in both manufacturing and service industries.

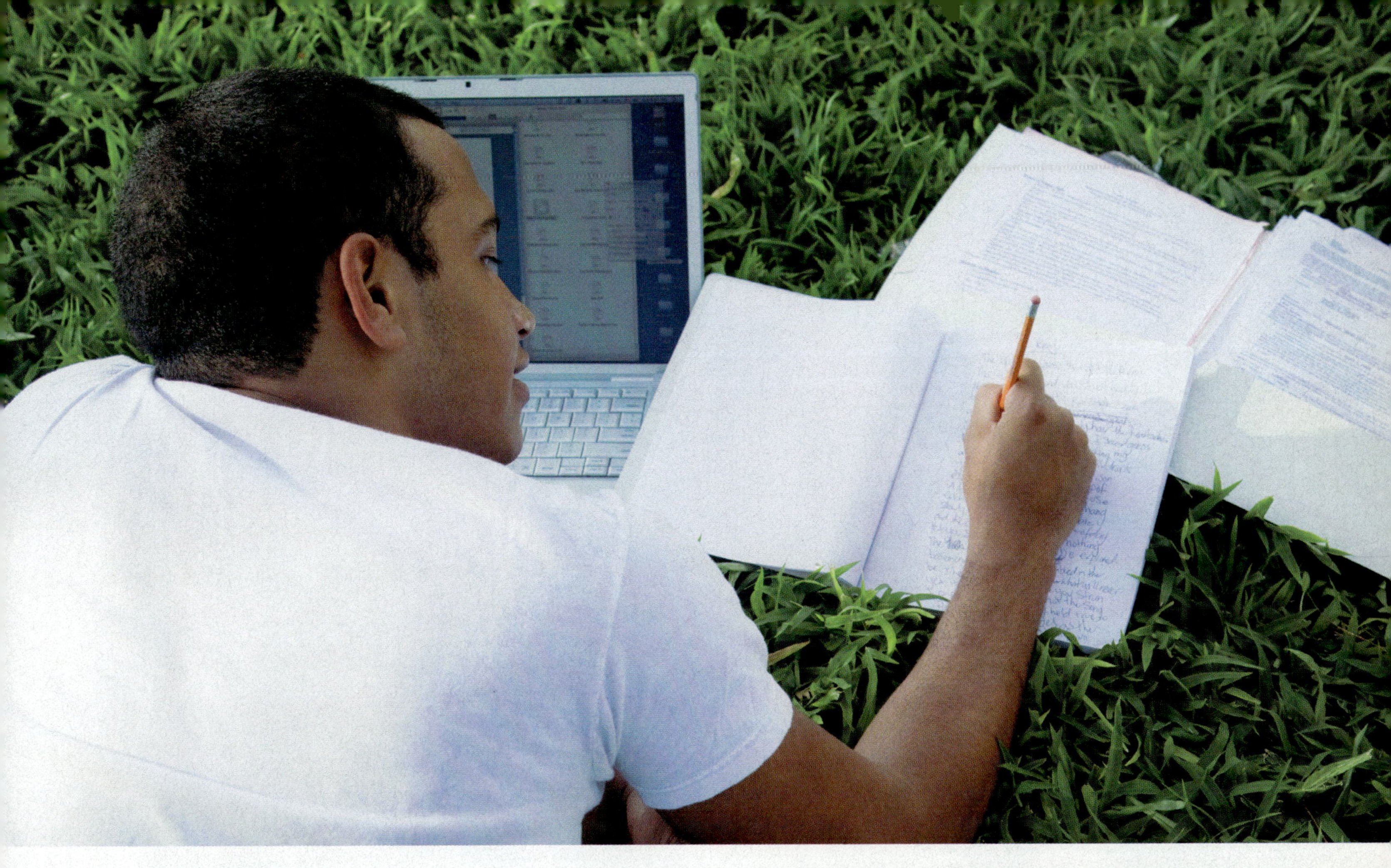

learn, practice, apply operations management!

M: Business was developed just for you—students on the go who need information packaged in a concise yet interesting format with multiple learning options.

Check out the book's website to:

- Understand the importance of identifying operations problems before product introductions. (Solve the Dilemma)
- Consider solutions to resolve operational difficulties for successful product introduction. (Solve the Dilemma)
- Learn how to analyze the cycle time of a business. (Build Your Skills)

While you are there, don't forget to enhance your skills. Practice and apply your knowledge, review the practice exercises, Student PPT® slides, and quizzes to review and apply chapter concepts. Additionally, *Connect® Business* is available for *M: Business.*

www.mhhe.com/ferrellm4e

chapter nine

motivating the workforce

Because employees do the actual work of the business and influence whether the firm achieves its objectives, most top managers agree that employees are an organization's most valuable resource. To achieve organizational objectives, employees must have the motivation, ability (appropriate knowledge and skills), and tools (proper training and equipment) to perform their jobs. Chapter 10 covers topics related to managing human resources, such as those listed earlier. This chapter focuses on how to motivate employees.

We examine employees' needs and motivation, managers' views of workers, and several strategies for motivating employees. Managers who understand the needs of their employees can help them reach higher levels of productivity and thus contribute to the achievement of organizational goals. ■

LEARNING OBJECTIVES

After reading this chapter, you will be able to:

LO 9-1 Define human relations and determine why its study is important.

LO 9-2 Summarize early studies that laid the groundwork for understanding employee motivation.

LO 9-3 Compare and contrast the human-relations theories of Abraham Maslow and Frederick Herzberg.

LO 9-4 Investigate various theories of motivation, including Theories X, Y, and Z; equity theory; and expectancy theory.

LO 9-5 Describe some of the strategies that managers use to motivate employees.

human relations the study of the behavior of individuals and groups in organizational settings

motivation an inner drive that directs a person's behavior toward goals

morale an employee's attitude toward his or her job, employer, and colleagues

intrinsic reward the personal satisfaction and enjoyment felt after attaining a goal

extrinsic rewards benefits and/or recognition received from someone else

LO 9-1 Define human relations and determine why its study is important.

NATURE OF HUMAN RELATIONS

What motivates employees to perform on the job is the focus of **human relations**, the study of the behavior of individuals and groups in organizational settings. In business, human relations involves motivating employees to achieve organizational objectives efficiently and effectively. The field of human relations has become increasingly important over the years as businesses strive to understand how to boost workplace morale, maximize employees' productivity and creativity, and motivate their ever more diverse employees to be more effective.

Motivation is an inner drive that directs a person's behavior toward goals. A goal is the satisfaction of some need, and a need is the difference between a desired state and an actual state. Both needs and goals can be motivating. Motivation explains why people behave as they do; similarly, a lack of motivation explains, at times, why people avoid doing what they should do. Motivating employees to do the wrong things or for the wrong reasons can be problematic, however. Encouraging employees to take excessive risks through high compensation, for example, led to the downfall of AIG and most major U.S. banks in the most recent recession. Also, encouraging employees to lie to customers or to create false documentation is unethical and could even have legal ramifications. A person who recognizes or feels a need is motivated to take action to satisfy the need and achieve a goal (Figure 9.1). Consider a person who takes a job as a salesperson. If his or her performance is far below other salespeople's, he or she will likely recognize a need to increase sales. To satisfy that need and achieve success, the person may try to acquire new insights from successful salespeople or obtain additional training to improve sales skills. In addition, a sales manager might try different means to motivate the salesperson to work harder and to improve his or her skills. Human relations is concerned with the needs of employees, their goals and how they try to achieve them, and the impact of those needs and goals on job performance.

Many companies offer onsite day care as a benefit for employees who have children. Company benefits such as these tend to increase employee satisfaction and motivation.

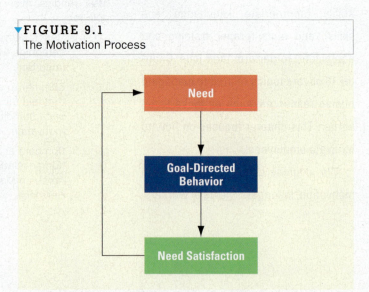

Effectively motivating employees helps keep them engaged in their work. Engagement involves emotional involvement and commitment. Being engaged results in carrying out the expectations and obligations of employment. Many employees are actively engaged in their jobs, whereas others are not. Some employees do the minimum amount of work required to get by, and some employees are completely disengaged. Motivating employees to stay engaged is a key responsibility of management. For example, to test whether his onsite production managers were fully engaged in their jobs, former Van Halen frontman David Lee Roth placed a line in the band's rider asking for a bowl of M&Ms with the brown ones removed. It was a means for the band to test local stage production crews' attention to detail. Because their shows were highly technical, David Lee Roth would demand a complete recheck of everything if he found brown M&Ms in the bowl.[1]

FIGURE 9.1
The Motivation Process

Need → Goal-Directed Behavior → Need Satisfaction → (back to Need)

▼ **TABLE 9.1** How to Retain Good Employees

1.	Challenge your employees.
2.	Provide adequate incentives.
3.	Don't micromanage.
4.	Create a work-friendly environment.
5.	Provide opportunities for employee growth.

Source: Adapted from Geoff Williams, "Retaining Employees: 5 Things You Need to Know," *The Huffington Post,* February 2, 2012, www.huffingtonpost.com/2012/02/01/retaining-employees-5-things-you-need-to-know_n_976767.html.

▼ **TABLE 9.2** How to Motivate Employees

1.	Interact with employees in a friendly and open manner.
2.	Equitably dispense rewards and other incentives.
3.	Create a culture of collaboration.
4.	Provide both positive feedback and constructive criticism.
5.	Make employees feel as if they are partners rather than workers.
6.	Handle conflicts in an open and professional manner.
7.	Provide continuous opportunities for improvement and employee growth.
8.	Encourage creativity in problem solving.
9.	Recognize employees for jobs well done.
10.	Allow employees to make mistakes, as these become learning opportunities.

One prominent aspect of human relations is **morale**—an employee's attitude toward his or her job, employer, and colleagues. High morale contributes to high levels of productivity, high returns to stakeholders, and employee loyalty. Conversely, low morale may cause high rates of absenteeism and turnover (when employees quit or are fired and must be replaced by new employees). Google recognizes the value of happy, committed employees and strives to engage in practices that will minimize turnover. Employees have the opportunity to have a massage every other week; onsite laundry service; free all-you-can-eat gourmet meals and snacks; and the "20% a week" rule, which allows engineers to work on whatever project they want for one day each week.[2]

Employees are motivated by their perceptions of extrinsic and intrinsic rewards. An **intrinsic reward** is the personal satisfaction and enjoyment that you feel from attaining a goal. For example, in this class you may feel personal enjoyment in learning how business works and aspire to have a career in business or to operate your own business one day. **Extrinsic rewards** are benefits and/or recognition that you receive from someone else. In this class, your grade is extrinsic recognition of your efforts and success in the class. In business, praise and recognition, pay increases, and bonuses are extrinsic rewards. If you believe that your job provides an opportunity to contribute to society or the environment, then that aspect would represent an intrinsic reward. Both intrinsic and extrinsic rewards contribute to motivation that stimulates employees to do their best in contributing to business goals.

Respect, involvement, appreciation, adequate compensation, promotions, a pleasant work environment, and a positive organizational culture are all morale boosters. Table 9.1 lists some ways to retain good employees. Facebook offers a comprehensive benefits package including 100 percent coverage of medical, dental, and vision insurance; four weeks of vacation; stock options; and free food at its two eateries. Many companies offer a diverse array of benefits designed to improve the quality of employees' lives and increase their morale and satisfaction. Some of the "best companies to work for" offer onsite day care, concierge services (for instance, dry cleaning, shoe repair, prescription renewal), domestic partner benefits to same-sex couples, and fully paid sabbaticals.[3] Table 9.2 offers suggestions for how leaders can motivate employees on a daily basis.

DID YOU KNOW?

Absenteeism can cost a company as much as 36 percent of payroll.[4]

LO 9-2 Summarize early studies that laid the groundwork for understanding employee motivation.

HISTORICAL PERSPECTIVES ON EMPLOYEE MOTIVATION

Throughout the 20th century, researchers have conducted numerous studies to identify ways to motivate workers and increase productivity. From these studies have come theories that have been applied to workers with varying degrees of success. A brief discussion of two of these theories—the classical theory of motivation and the Hawthorne studies—provides a background for understanding the present state of human relations.

> More and more corporations are tying pay to performance to motivate [employees].

Classical Theory of Motivation

The birth of the study of human relations can be traced to time and motion studies conducted at the turn of the century by Frederick W. Taylor and Frank and Lillian Gilbreth. Their studies analyzed how workers perform specific work tasks in an effort to improve the employees' productivity. These efforts led to the application of scientific principles to management.

According to the **classical theory of motivation**, money is the sole motivator for workers. Taylor suggested that workers who were paid more would produce more, an idea that would benefit both companies and workers. To improve productivity, Taylor thought that managers should break down each job into its component tasks (specialization), determine the best way to perform each task, and specify the output to be achieved by a worker performing the task. Taylor also believed that incentives would motivate employees to be more productive. Thus, he suggested that managers link workers' pay directly to their output. He developed the piece-rate system, under which employees were paid a certain amount for each unit they produced; those who exceeded their quota were paid a higher rate per unit for all the units they produced.

We can still see Taylor's ideas in practice today in the use of financial incentives for productivity. Moreover, companies are increasingly striving to relate pay to performance at both the hourly and managerial level. Incentive planners choose an individual incentive to motivate and reward their employees. In contrast, team incentives are used to generate partnership and collaboration to accomplish organizational goals. Boeing develops sales teams for most of its products, including commercial airplanes. The team dedicated to each product shares in the sales incentive program.

More and more corporations are tying pay to performance to motivate—even up to the CEO level. The topic of executive pay has become controversial in recent years, and many corporate boards of directors have taken steps to link executive compensation more closely to corporate performance. Despite these changes, many top executives still receive large compensation packages. John Hammergren, CEO of McKesson, is the highest paid executive, with $131 million in annual compensation.[5] However, later studies showed that other factors are also important in motivating workers.

COMPANIES OFFER GREEN INCENTIVES FOR EMPLOYEES

Some large businesses are providing incentives for employees to adopt green practices both at work and at home. For instance, Sony Pictures' Living La Vida Verde provides cash rebates on qualifying purchases of hybrid cars and residential solar power installations. Its Giving Green for Green allows employees to nominate environmental organizations in their communities for grants and encourages employees to submit ideas on how to green the workplace. Its Volunteerism program encourages employees to volunteer their time on environmental projects.

Lockheed Martin has also been recognized for its green incentives, particularly regarding transportation. The company offers Grab-and-Go bicycles for campus use, carpool planning, and annual eco-passes for the local light rail system. Its Go Green program has instituted Green Zones in the workplace where employees in these areas are responsible for turning off computers and lights when they leave work for the day. It also features a National Environmental Education Week that encourages employees to recognize their habits and their impact on the environment.

Google is another company that has become well-known for its green incentives. The company offers discounts on residential solar power installations, carpooling, and alternative transportation methods for employees. In addition, Google has instituted Google Bike to Work Day to discourage the use of vehicles. With companies like Sony, Lockheed Martin, and Google encouraging green behaviors among employees, perhaps it is businesses that will make the greatest contribution toward sustainable environmental practices.[6]

Discussion Questions

1. Why do you think businesses are providing employees with incentives to go green?
2. Describe some of the incentives that Sony Pictures, Lockheed Martin, and Google offer employees to engage in more sustainable practices.
3. Do you think these incentives are genuine efforts to encourage sustainability? Or are they more of a marketing initiative to make the businesses look good?

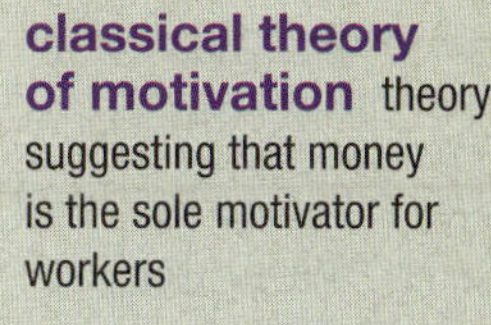

classical theory of motivation theory suggesting that money is the sole motivator for workers

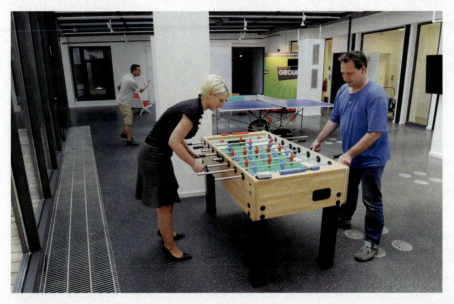

Providing nontraditional benefits such as foosball lets employees have fun and creates a happier work environment.

The Hawthorne Studies

Elton Mayo and a team of researchers from Harvard University wanted to determine what physical conditions in the workplace—such as light and noise levels—would stimulate employees to be most productive. From 1924 to 1932, they studied a group of workers at the Hawthorne Works Plant of the Western Electric Company and measured their productivity under various physical conditions.

What the researchers discovered was quite unexpected and very puzzling: Productivity increased regardless of the physical conditions. This phenomenon has been labeled the Hawthorne effect. When questioned about their behavior, the employees expressed satisfaction because their co-workers in the experiments were friendly and, more important, because their supervisors had asked for their help and cooperation in the study. In other words, they were responding to the attention they received, not the changing physical work conditions. The researchers concluded that social and psychological factors could significantly affect productivity and morale. Medtronic, often called the "Microsoft of the medical-device industry," has a built-in psychological factor that influences employee morale. The company makes life-saving medical devices, such as pacemakers, neurostimulators, and stents. New hires at Medtronic receive medallions inscribed with a portion of the firm's mission statement, "alleviate pain, restore health, and extend life." There is an annual party where people whose bodies function thanks to Medtronic devices give testimonials. Obviously, Medtronic employees feel a sense of satisfaction in their jobs. Figure 9.2 indicates how employees value a healthy work/life balance.

FIGURE 9.2

Job Aspects Important to Employee Satisfaction

Aside from salary, which one of the following aspects of your job is most tied to your satisfaction?

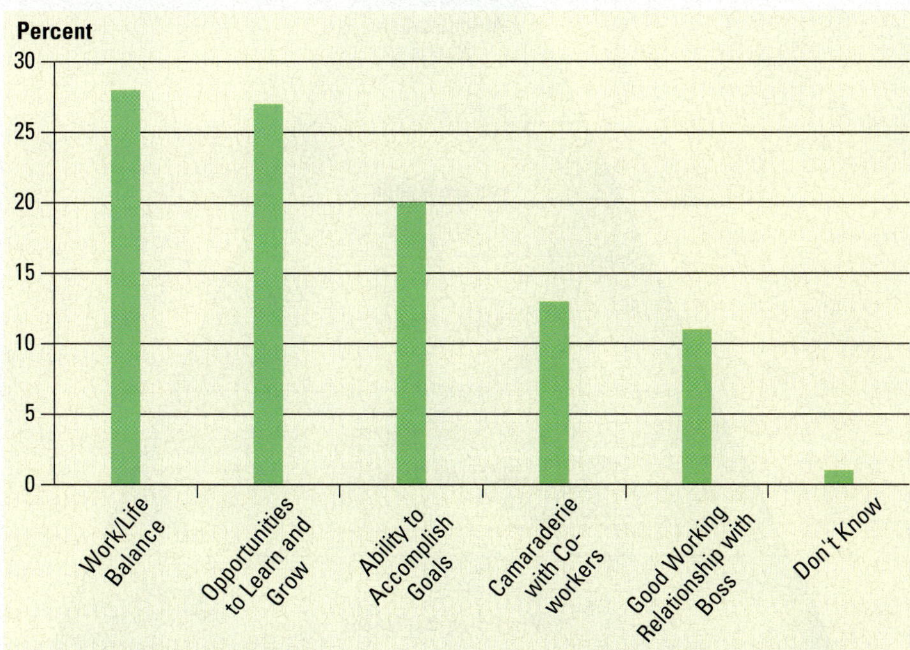

Source: "OfficeTeam Survey: Work/Life Balance, Learning Opportunities Have Greatest Impact on Job Satisfaction," *PR Newswire,* January 26, 2012, www.prnewswire.com/news-releases/officeteam-survey-worklife-balance-learning-opportunities-have-greatest-impact-on-job-satisfaction-138116108.html.

The Hawthorne experiments marked the beginning of a concern for human relations in the workplace. They revealed that human factors do influence workers' behavior and that managers who understand the needs, beliefs, and expectations of people have the greatest success in motivating their workers.

THEORIES OF EMPLOYEE MOTIVATION

The research of Taylor, Mayo, and many others has led to the development of a number of theories that attempt to describe what motivates employees to perform. In this section, we discuss some of the most

Maslow's hierarchy a theory that arranges the five basic needs of people—physiological, security, social, esteem, and self-actualization—into the order in which people strive to satisfy them

physiological needs the most basic human needs to be satisfied—water, food, shelter, and clothing

security needs the need to protect oneself from physical and economic harm

social needs the need for love, companionship, and friendship—the desire for acceptance by others

esteem needs the need for respect—both self-respect and respect from others

important of these theories. The successful implementation of ideas based on these theories will vary, of course, depending on the company, its management, and its employees. It should be noted, too, that what worked in the past may no longer work today. Good managers must have the ability to adapt their ideas to an ever-changing, diverse group of employees.

LO 9-3 Compare and contrast the human-relations theories of Abraham Maslow and Frederick Herzberg.

Maslow's Hierarchy of Needs

Psychologist Abraham Maslow theorized that people have five basic needs: physiological, security, social, esteem, and self-actualization. **Maslow's hierarchy** arranges these needs in the order in which people strive to satisfy them (Figure 9.3).

Physiological needs, the most basic and first needs to be satisfied, are the essentials for living—water, food, shelter, and clothing. According to Maslow, humans devote all their efforts to satisfying physiological needs until they are met. Only when these needs are met can people focus their attention on satisfying the next level of needs—security.

Security needs relate to protecting yourself from physical and economic harm. Actions that may be taken to achieve security include reporting a dangerous workplace condition to management, maintaining safety equipment, and purchasing insurance with income protection in the event you become unable to work. Once security needs have been satisfied, people may strive for social goals.

Social needs are the need for love, companionship, and friendship—the desire for acceptance by others. To fulfill social needs, a person may try many things: making friends with a co-worker, joining a group, volunteering at a hospital, throwing a party. Once their social needs have been satisfied, people attempt to satisfy their need for esteem.

Esteem needs relate to respect—both self-respect and respect from others. One aspect of esteem needs is competition—the need to feel that you can do something better than anyone else. Competition often motivates people to increase their productivity. Esteem needs are not as easily satisfied as the needs at lower levels in Maslow's hierarchy because they do not always provide tangible evidence of success. However, these needs can be realized through rewards and increased involvement in organizational activities. Until esteem needs are met, people focus their attention on achieving respect. When they feel they have achieved some measure of respect, self-actualization becomes the major goal of life.

Self-actualization needs, at the top of Maslow's hierarchy, mean being the best you can be. Self-actualization involves maximizing your potential. A self-actualized person feels that she or he is living life to its fullest in every way. For Stephen King, self-actualization might mean being praised as the best

FIGURE 9.3
Maslow's Hierarchy of Needs

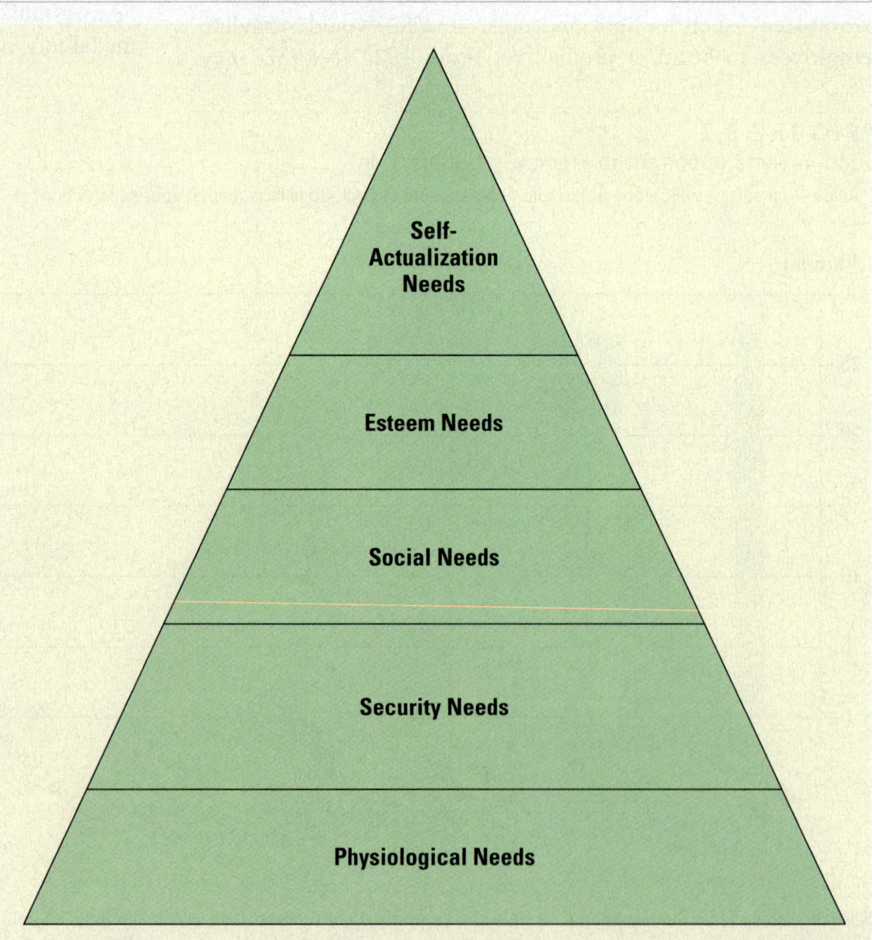

Source: Adapted from Abraham H. Maslow, "A Theory of Human Motivation," *Psychology Review* 50 (1943), pp. 370–396. American Psychology Association.

fiction writer in the world; for actress Halle Berry, it might mean winning an Oscar.

Maslow's theory maintains that the more basic needs at the bottom of the hierarchy must be satisfied before higher-level goals can be pursued. Thus, people who are hungry and homeless are not concerned with obtaining respect from their colleagues. Only when physiological, security, and social needs have been more or less satisfied do people seek esteem. Maslow's theory also suggests that if a low-level need is suddenly reactivated, the individual will try to satisfy that need rather than higher-level needs. Many laid-off workers probably shift their focus from high-level esteem needs to the need for security. Managers should learn from Maslow's hierarchy that employees will be motivated to contribute to organizational goals only if they are able first to satisfy their physiological, security, and social needs through their work.

self-actualization needs the need to be the best one can be; at the top of Maslow's hierarchy

hygiene factors aspects of Herzberg's theory of motivation that focus on the work setting and not the content of the work; these aspects include adequate wages, comfortable and safe working conditions, fair company policies, and job security

motivational factors aspects of Herzberg's theory of motivation that focus on the content of the work itself; these aspects include achievement, recognition, involvement, responsibility, and advancement

> Maslow's theory maintains that the more basic needs at the bottom of the hierarchy must be satisfied before higher-level goals can be pursued.

Herzberg's Two-Factor Theory

In the 1950s, psychologist Frederick Herzberg proposed a theory of motivation that focuses on the job and on the environment where work is done. Herzberg studied various factors relating to the job and their relation to employee motivation and concluded that they can be divided into hygiene factors and motivational factors (Table 9.3).

Hygiene factors, which relate to the work setting and not to the content of the work, include adequate wages, comfortable and safe working conditions, fair company policies, and job security. These factors do not necessarily motivate employees to excel, but their absence may be a potential source of dissatisfaction and high turnover. Employee safety and comfort are clearly hygiene factors.

TABLE 9.3 Herzberg's Hygiene and Motivational Factors

Hygiene Factors	Motivational Factors
Company policies	Achievement
Supervision	Recognition
Working conditions	Work itself
Relationships with peers, supervisors, and subordinates	Responsibility
Salary	Advancement
Security	Personal growth

Many people feel that a good salary is one of the most important job factors, even more important than job security and the chance to use one's mind and abilities. Salary and security, two of the hygiene factors identified by Herzberg, make it possible for employees to satisfy the physiological and security needs identified by Maslow. However, the presence of hygiene factors is unlikely to motivate employees to work harder. For example, many people do not feel motivated to pursue a career as a gastroenterologist (doctors who specialize in the digestive system). Although the job is important and pays more than $250,000 on average, the tasks are routine and most patients are not looking forward to their appointments.[7]

Motivational factors, which relate to the content of the work itself, include achievement, recognition, involvement, responsibility, and advancement. The absence of motivational

Best Buy empowers its employees to answer customer questions, resolve issues, and provide quality service.

Theory X McGregor's traditional view of management whereby it is assumed that workers generally dislike work and must be forced to do their jobs

Theory Y McGregor's humanistic view of management whereby it is assumed that workers like to work and that under proper conditions employees will seek out responsibility in an attempt to satisfy their social, esteem, and self-actualization needs

factors may not result in dissatisfaction, but their presence is likely to motivate employees to excel. Many companies are beginning to employ methods to give employees more responsibility and control and to involve them more in their work, which serves to motivate them to higher levels of productivity and quality. L.L. Bean employees have tremendous latitude to satisfy customers' needs. One employee drove 500 miles from Maine to New York to deliver a canoe to a customer who was leaving on a trip. L.L. Bean also ranks high in employee satisfaction. When the company decided to close down a call center, L.L. Bean allowed the call-center employees to act as home-based agents rather than laying them off and outsourcing the work. Besides empowering employees, the company has strict service training, answering every call within 20 seconds.[8]

Herzberg's motivational factors and Maslow's esteem and self-actualization needs are similar. Workers' low-level needs (physiological and security) have largely been satisfied by minimum-wage laws and occupational-safety standards set by various government agencies and are therefore not motivators. Consequently, to improve productivity, management should focus on satisfying workers' higher-level needs (motivational factors) by providing opportunities for achievement, involvement, and advancement and by recognizing good performance.

LO 9-4 Investigate various theories of motivation, including Theories X, Y, and Z; equity theory; and expectancy theory.

McGregor's Theory X and Theory Y

In *The Human Side of Enterprise,* Douglas McGregor related Maslow's ideas about personal needs to management. McGregor contrasted two views of management—the traditional view, which he called Theory X, and a humanistic view, which he called Theory Y.

According to McGregor, managers adopting **Theory X** assume that workers generally dislike work and must be forced to do their jobs. They believe that the following statements are true of workers:

1. The average person naturally dislikes work and will avoid it when possible.
2. Most workers must be coerced, controlled, directed, or threatened with punishment to get them to work toward the achievement of organizational objectives.
3. The average worker prefers to be directed and to avoid responsibility, has relatively little ambition, and wants security.[9]

Managers who subscribe to the Theory X view maintain tight control over workers, provide almost constant supervision, try to motivate through fear, and make decisions in an autocratic fashion, eliciting little or no input from their subordinates. The Theory X style of management focuses on physiological and security needs and virtually ignores the higher needs discussed by Maslow. Foxconn, a manufacturing company that creates components for tech products such as the Apple iPad, is a company that had adopted the Theory X perspective. In China, Foxconn workers live in crowded dorms and often work more than 60 hours per week.

THE NEW INCENTIVES OF GENERATION Y

The workforce is facing a huge generational shift. As the population ages, the new generation, Generation Y (also known as millennials), are moving into the workforce. Four generations might be working together on a daily basis. However, such a wide range of ages creates the potential for conflict.

Older workers often view millennials as entitled, impatient, and overly casual. However, millennials also tend to be more tech-savvy, collaborative, desirous of responsibility, and innovative. Many companies are already starting to offer different incentives targeted directly to Gen Y priorities, including faster promotions and greater work flexibility. These motivational factors differ from previous generations—for example, millennials tend to prioritize lifestyle over salary. Millennials also view several career changes as a likely reality in their work lives.

Along with altering incentives, workspaces are also changing. Although millennials view an engaging workplace as most important and meeting-room quality as least important, baby boomers rank these items in reverse. Millennials prefer casual and fast interactions. This is aided by their use of technology, which requires less time and decorum. In response, many companies are creating shared working environments with less formality and structure. However, with all the changes occurring in the workplace, companies must be careful not to alienate the members of the older generation. The challenge is to think about the best way to motivate all individuals working for them and tailor incentives to different styles and preferences. With four generations now employed in the workplace, companies must be sensitive to what drives each age group and reward them accordingly.[10]

Discussion Questions

1. Why are businesses having to adapt their incentives for workers?
2. Why is there potential conflict between older workers and younger workers?
3. How is the workplace changing as Generation Y moves into the workforce?

Theory Z a management philosophy that stresses employee participation in all aspects of company decision making

equity theory an assumption that how much people are willing to contribute to an organization depends on their assessment of the fairness, or equity, of the rewards they will receive in exchange

The Theory X view of management does not take into account people's needs for companionship, esteem, and personal growth, whereas Theory Y, the contrasting view of management, does. Managers subscribing to the **Theory Y** view assume that workers like to work and that under proper conditions employees will seek out responsibility in an attempt to satisfy their social, esteem, and self-actualization needs. McGregor describes the assumptions behind Theory Y in the following way:

1. The expenditure of physical and mental effort in work is as natural as play or rest.
2. People will exercise self-direction and self-control to achieve objectives to which they are committed.
3. People will commit to objectives when they realize that the achievement of those goals will bring them personal reward.
4. The average person will accept and seek responsibility.
5. Imagination, ingenuity, and creativity can help solve organizational problems, but most organizations do not make adequate use of these characteristics in their employees.
6. Organizations today do not make full use of workers' intellectual potential.[11]

Obviously, managers subscribing to the Theory Y philosophy have a management style very different from managers subscribing to the Theory X philosophy. Theory Y managers maintain less control and supervision, do not use fear as the primary motivator, and are more democratic in decision making, allowing subordinates to participate in the process. Theory Y managers address the high-level needs in Maslow's hierarchy as well as physiological and security needs. For instance, Google is one well-known example of a company that has adopted the Theory Y philosophy. From its famous employee perks to the 20 percent time it gives its employees to pursue company projects they find interesting, Google believes that its employees are motivated and creative enough to profit the company significantly.[12] Today, Theory Y enjoys widespread support and may have displaced Theory X.

> Theory Y managers maintain less control and supervision, do not use fear as the primary motivator, and are more democratic in decision making.

Theory Z

Theory Z is a management philosophy that stresses employee participation in all aspects of company decision making. It was first described by William Ouchi in his book *Theory Z—How American Business Can Meet the Japanese Challenge.* Theory Z incorporates many elements associated with the Japanese approach to management, such as trust and intimacy, but Japanese ideas have been adapted for use in the United States. In a Theory Z organization, managers and workers share responsibilities; the management style is participative; and employment is long term and often lifelong. Japan has faced a significant period of slowing economic progress and competition from China and other Asian nations. This has led to experts questioning Theory Z, particularly at firms such as Sony and Toyota. Theory Z results in employees feeling organizational ownership. Research has found that such feelings of ownership may produce positive attitudinal and behavioral effects for employees.[13] In a Theory Y organization, managers focus on assumptions about the nature of the worker. The two theories can be seen as complementary. Table 9.4 compares the traditional American management style, the Japanese management style, and Theory Z (the modified Japanese management style).

Equity Theory

According to **equity theory**, how much people are willing to contribute to an organization depends on their assessment of the fairness, or equity, of the rewards they will receive in exchange. In a fair situation, a person receives rewards proportional to the contribution he or she makes to the organization. However, in practice, equity is a subjective notion. Each worker regularly develops a personal input-output ratio by taking stock of his or her contribution (inputs) to the organization in time, effort, skills, and experience and assessing the rewards (outputs) offered by the organization in pay, benefits, recognition, and promotions. The worker compares his or her ratio to the input-output ratio of some other person—a "comparison other," who may be a co-worker, a friend working in another organization, or an "average" of several people working in the organization. If the two ratios are close, the individual will feel that he or she is being treated equitably.

Let's say you have a high-school education and earn $25,000 a year. When you compare your input-output ratio with that of a co-worker who has a college degree and makes $35,000 a year,

TABLE 9.4 Comparison of American, Japanese, and Theory Z Management Styles

	American	Japanese	Theory Z
Duration of employment	Relatively short term; workers subject to layoffs when business slows	Lifelong; no layoffs	Long term; layoffs rare
Rate of promotion	Rapid	Slow	Slow
Amount of specialization	Considerable; worker develops expertise in one area only	Minimal; worker develops expertise in all aspects of the organization	Moderate; worker learns all aspects of the organization
Decision making	Individual	Consensual; input from all concerned parties is considered	Consensual; emphasis on quality
Responsibility	Assigned to the individual	Shared by the group	Assigned to the individual
Control	Explicit and formal	Less explicit and less formal	Informal but with explicit performance measures
Concern for workers	Focus is on work only	Focus extends to worker's whole life	Focus includes worker's life and family

Source: Adapted from William Ouchi, *Theory Z—How American Business Can Meet the Japanese Challenge,* p. 58. © 1981. Reproduced with permission of Westview Press via Copyright Clearance Center.

you will probably feel that you are being paid fairly. However, if you perceive that your personal input-output ratio is lower than that of your college-educated co-worker, you may feel that you are being treated unfairly and be motivated to seek change. Or if you learn that your co-worker who makes $35,000 has only a high-school diploma, you may feel cheated by your employer. To achieve equity, you could try to increase your outputs by asking for a raise or promotion. You could also try to have your co-worker's inputs increased or his or her outputs decreased. Failing to achieve equity, you may be motivated to look for a job at a different company.

Equity theory might explain why many consumers are upset about CEO compensation. Although the job of the CEO can be incredibly stressful, the fact that he or she takes home millions in compensation, bonuses, and stock options has been questioned. The high unemployment rate coupled with the misconduct that occurred at some large corporations prior to the recession contributed largely to the Occupy Wall Street protests. To counter this perception of pay inequality, several corporations have now begun to tie CEO compensation with company performance. If the company performs poorly for the year, then firms such as Goldman Sachs will cut bonuses and other compensation.[14] Although lower compensation rates might appease the general public, some companies are worried that lower pay might deter talented individuals from wanting to assume the position of CEO at their firms.

Because almost all the issues involved in equity theory are subjective, they can be problematic. Author David Callahan has argued that feelings of inequity may underlie some unethical or illegal behavior in business. For example, due to employee theft and shoplifting, Walmart experiences billions in inventory losses every year. Some employees may take company resources to restore what they perceive to be equity. Theft of company resources is a major ethical issue, based on a survey by the Ethics Resource Center.[15] Callahan believes that employees who do not feel they are being treated equitably may be motivated to equalize the situation by lying, cheating, or otherwise "improving" their pay, perhaps by stealing.[16] Managers should try to avoid equity problems by ensuring that rewards are distributed on the basis of performance and that all employees clearly understand the basis for their pay and benefits.

Expectancy Theory

Psychologist Victor Vroom described **expectancy theory**, which states that motivation depends not only on how much a person wants something but also on the person's perception of how likely he or she is to get it. A person who wants something and has reason to be optimistic will be strongly motivated. For example, say you really want a promotion. And let's say because you have taken some night classes to improve your skills, and moreover, have just made a large, significant sale, you feel confident that you are qualified and able to handle the new position. Therefore, you are motivated to try to get the

Your motivation depends not only on how much you want something, but also on how likely you believe you are to get it.

expectancy theory the assumption that motivation depends not only on how much a person wants something but also on how likely he or she is to get it

behavior modification changing behavior and encouraging appropriate actions by relating the consequences of behavior to the behavior itself

job rotation movement of employees from one job to another in an effort to relieve the boredom often associated with job specialization

job enlargement the addition of more tasks to a job instead of treating each task as separate

job enrichment the incorporation of motivational factors, such as opportunity for achievement, recognition, responsibility, and advancement, into a job

promotion. In contrast, if you do not believe you are likely to get what you want, you may not be motivated to try to get it, even though you really want it.

STRATEGIES FOR MOTIVATING EMPLOYEES

Based on the various theories that attempt to explain what motivates employees, businesses have developed several strategies for motivating their employees and boosting morale and productivity. Some of these techniques include behavior modification and job design as well as the already described employee involvement programs and work teams.

LO 9-5 Describe some of the strategies that managers use to motivate employees.

Behavior Modification

Behavior modification involves changing behavior and encouraging appropriate actions by relating the consequences of behavior to the behavior itself. The concept of behavior modification was developed by psychologist B.F. Skinner, who showed that there are two types of consequences that can modify behavior—reward and punishment. Skinner found that behavior that is rewarded will tend to be repeated, whereas behavior that is punished will tend to be eliminated. For example, employees who know that they will receive a bonus such as an expensive restaurant meal for making a sale over $2,000 may be more motivated to make sales. Workers who know they will be punished for being tardy are likely to make a greater effort to get to work on time.

However, the two strategies may not be equally effective. Punishing unacceptable behavior may provide quick results but lead to undesirable long-term side effects, such as employee dissatisfaction and increased turnover. In general, rewarding appropriate behavior is a more effective way to modify behavior.

Job Design

Herzberg identified the job itself as a motivational factor. Managers have several strategies that they can use to design jobs to help improve employee motivation. These include job rotation, job enlargement, job enrichment, and flexible scheduling strategies.

Job Rotation

Job rotation allows employees to move from one job to another in an effort to relieve the boredom that is often associated with job specialization. Businesses often turn to specialization in hopes of increasing productivity, but there is a negative side effect to this type of job design: Employees become bored and dissatisfied, and productivity declines. Job rotation reduces this boredom by allowing workers to undertake a greater variety of tasks and by giving them the opportunity to learn new skills. With job rotation, an employee spends a specified amount of time performing one job and then moves on to another, different job. The worker eventually returns to the initial job and begins the cycle again.

Job rotation is a good idea, but it has one major drawback. Because employees may eventually become bored with all the jobs in the cycle, job rotation does not totally eliminate the problem of boredom. Job rotation is extremely useful, however, when a person is being trained for a position that requires an understanding of various units in an organization. Eli Lilly is a strong believer in the benefits of job rotation. The company leaves employees in their current jobs and asks them to take on short-term assignments outside their field of expertise or interest. The results of the process have been positive, and Nokia is trying the same process with similar outcomes.[17] Many executive training programs require trainees to spend time learning a variety of specialized jobs. Job rotation is also used to cross-train today's self-directed work teams.

Job Enlargement

Job enlargement adds more tasks to a job instead of treating each task as separate. Like job rotation, job enlargement was developed to overcome the boredom associated with specialization. The rationale behind this strategy is that jobs are more satisfying as the number of tasks performed by an individual increases. Employees sometimes enlarge, or craft, their jobs by noticing what needs to be done and then changing tasks and relationship boundaries to adjust. Individual orientation and motivation shape opportunities to craft new jobs and job relationships. Job enlargement strategies have been more successful in increasing job satisfaction than have job rotation strategies. IBM, AT&T, and Maytag are among the many companies that have used job enlargement to motivate employees.

Job Enrichment

Job enrichment incorporates motivational factors such as opportunity for achievement, recognition, responsibility, and advancement into a job. It gives workers not only more tasks within the job, but more control and authority over the job. Job enrichment programs enhance a worker's feeling of responsibility and provide opportunities for growth and advancement when the worker is able to take on the more challenging tasks. Hyatt Hotels Corporation and General Foods

flextime a program that allows employees to choose their starting and ending times, provided that they are at work during a specified core period

compressed workweek a four-day (or shorter) period during which an employee works 40 hours

job sharing performance of one full-time job by two people on part-time hours

use job enrichment to improve the quality of work life for their employees. The potential benefits of job enrichment are great, but it requires careful planning and execution.

Flexible Scheduling Strategies

Many U.S. workers work a traditional 40-hour workweek consisting of five 8-hour days with fixed starting and ending times. Facing problems of poor morale and high absenteeism as well as a diverse workforce with changing needs, many managers have turned to flexible scheduling strategies such as flextime, compressed workweeks, job sharing, part-time work, and telecommuting. A survey by CareerBuilder.com showed that 40 percent of working fathers were offered flexible work schedules versus 53 percent of working mothers.[18]

Flextime is a program that allows employees to choose their starting and ending times, as long as they are at work during a specified core period (Figure 9.4). It does not reduce the total number of hours that employees work; instead, it gives employees more flexibility in choosing which hours they work. A firm may specify that employees must be present from 10:00 a.m. to 3:00 p.m. One employee may choose to come in at 7:00 a.m. and leave at the end of the core time, perhaps to attend classes at a nearby college after work. Another employee, a mother who lives in the suburbs, may come in at 9:00 a.m. to have time to drop off her children at a day-care center and commute by public transportation to her job. Flextime provides many benefits, including improved ability to recruit and retain workers who wish to balance work and home life. Customers can be better served by allowing more coverage of customers over longer hours, workstations and facilities can be used better by staggering employee use, and rush hour traffic may be reduced. In addition, flexible schedules have been associated with an increase in healthy behaviors on the part of employees. More-flexible schedules are associated with healthier lifestyle choices such as increased physical activity and healthier sleep habits.[19]

> "Flextime provides many benefits, including improved ability to recruit and retain workers who wish to balance work and home life."

Related to flextime are the scheduling strategies of the compressed workweek and job sharing. The **compressed workweek** is a four-day (or shorter) period in which an employee works 40 hours. Under such a plan, employees typically work 10 hours per day for four days and have a three-day weekend. The compressed workweek reduces the company's operating expenses because its actual hours of operation are reduced. It is also sometimes used by parents who want to have more days off to spend with their families. The U.S. Bureau of Labor Statistics notes that the following career options provide greater flexibility in scheduling: medical transcriptionist, financial manager, nurse, database administrator, accountant, software developer, physical therapist assistant, paralegal, graphic designer, and private investigator.[20]

Job sharing occurs when two people do one job. One person may work from 8:00 a.m. to 12:30 p.m.; the second person comes in at 12:30 p.m. and works until 5:00 p.m. Job sharing gives both people the opportunity to work as well as time to fulfill other obligations,

FIGURE 9.4
Flextime, Showing Core and Flexible Hours

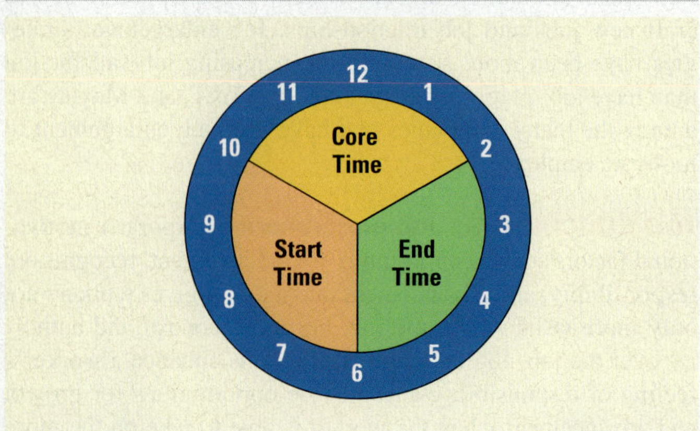

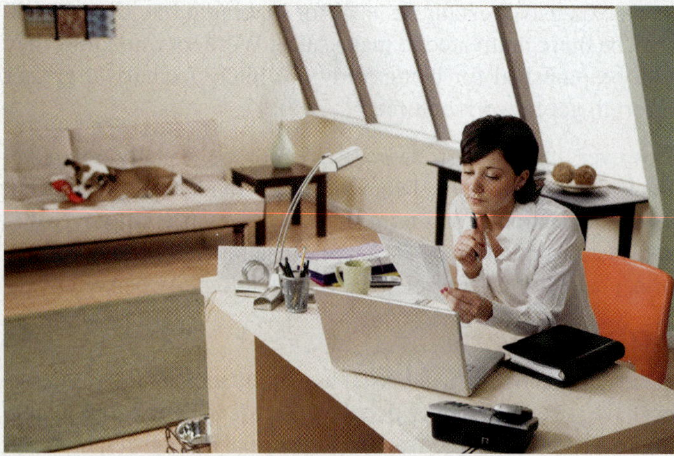

Working away from your desk is becoming increasingly common. Telecommuting, job sharing, and flextime can be beneficial for employees who cannot work normal work hours.

FULLCONTACT WANTS EMPLOYEES TO TAKE VACATIONS

At FullContact, employees can get paid to take a vacation. FullContact is a digital contact management company that consolidates contacts for individuals or businesses in one place. Bart Lorang founded the company in 2010 because he recognized that people have their contact information in various places. Because the information is spread out, it is usually not updated or complete. FullContact uses an algorithm that pulls all contact information together and ensures that it is complete and accurate.

Yet despite the uniqueness of his company, Lorang is becoming just as well-known for the way he motivates his employees. He calls FullContact's vacation policy "paid, paid vacation" because it offers employees a minimum of 15 days of paid vacation with a possible added bonus of $7,500. To qualify for the extra money, the employees must disconnect from work completely while they are on vacation—no e-mail or voice-mail. Lorang's incentives seem to be a step in the right direction; studies show that employee benefits have a direct positive impact on organizational success.[21]

such as parenting or school. With job sharing, the company has the benefit of the skills of two people for one job, often at a lower total cost for salaries and benefits than one person working eight hours a day would be paid.

Two other flexible scheduling strategies attaining wider use include allowing full-time workers to work part time for a certain period and allowing workers to work at home either full or part time. Employees at some firms may be permitted to work part time for several months to care for a new baby or an elderly parent or just to slow down for a little while to "recharge their batteries." When the employees return to full-time work, they are usually given a position comparable to their original full-time position. Other firms are allowing employees to telecommute or telework (work at home a few days of the week), staying connected via computers, modems, and telephones. Most telecommuters tend to combine going into the office with working from home. Only about 2.8 million employees (not including entrepreneurs) cite the home as their primary workplace.[22]

Although many employees ask for the option of working at home to ease the responsibilities of caring for family members, some have discovered that they are more productive at home without the distractions of the workplace. An assessment of 12 company telecommuting programs, including Apple, AT&T, and the state of California, found that positive productivity changes occurred. Perhaps due to the positive morale that telecommuting can create, 82 percent of *Fortune*'s "100 Best Companies to Work For" allow their employees to telecommute at least part of the time.[23] Other employees, however, have discovered that they are not suited for working at home. For telecommuting to work, it must be a feasible alternative and must not create significant costs for the company.[24] Bank of America, Yahoo!, and Best Buy are all eliminating their work-at-home programs because they feel that being present in the workplace increases collaboration and productivity. Still, work-at-home programs can help reduce overhead costs for businesses. For example, some companies used to maintain a surplus of office space but have reduced the surplus through employee telecommuting, "hoteling" (being assigned to a desk through a reservation system), and "hot-desking" (several people using the same desk but at different times).

Companies are turning to flexible work schedules to provide more options to employees who are trying to juggle their work duties with other responsibilities and needs. Preliminary results indicate that flexible scheduling plans increase job satisfaction, which, in turn, leads to increases in productivity. Some recent research, however, has indicated there are potential problems with telecommuting. Some managers are reluctant to adopt the practice because the pace of change in today's workplace is faster than ever, and telecommuters may be left behind or actually cause managers more work in helping them stay abreast of changes. Some employers also worry that telecommuting workers create a security risk by creating more opportunities for computer hackers or equipment thieves. Some employees have found that working outside the office may hurt career advancement opportunities, and some report that instead of helping them balance work and family responsibilities, telecommuting increases the strain by blurring the barriers between the office and home. Co-workers call at all hours, and telecommuters are apt to continue to work when

Businesses have come up with different ways to motivate employees, including rewards such as trophies and plaques to show the company's appreciation.

SO YOU THINK // You May Be Good at Motivating a Workforce /

If you are good at mediation and smoothing conflict, and have a good understanding of motivation and human relations theories, then you might be a good leader, human resources manager, or training expert. Most organizations, especially as they grow, will need to implement human relations programs. These are necessary to teach employees about sensitivity to other cultures, religions, and beliefs as well as for teaching the workforce about the organization so that members understand how they fit in the larger picture. Employees need to appreciate the benefits of working together to make the firm run smoothly, and they need to understand how their contributions help the firm. To stay motivated, most employees need to feel like what they do each day contributes something of value to the firm. Disclosing information and including employees in decision-making processes will also help employees feel valuable and wanted within the firm.

There are many ways employers can reward and encourage employees. However, employers must be careful when considering what kinds of incentives to use. Different cultures value different kinds of incentives more highly than others. For example, a Japanese worker would probably not like it if she were singled out from the group and given a large cash bonus as reward for her work. Japanese workers tend to be more group oriented, and therefore anything that singles out individuals would not be an effective way of rewarding and motivating. American workers, on the other hand, are very individualistic, and a raise and public praise might be more effective. However, what might motivate a younger employee (bonuses, raises, and perks) may not be the same as what motivates a more seasoned, experienced, and financially successful employee (recognition, opportunity for greater influence, and increased training). Motivation is not an easy thing to understand, especially as firms become more global and more diverse.

Another important part of motivation is enjoying where you work and your career opportunities. Here is a list of the best places to do business and start careers in the United States, according to *Forbes* magazine. Chances are, workers who live in these places have encountered fewer frustrations than those places at the bottom of the list and, therefore, would probably be more content with where they work.[25]

Best Places for Business and Careers[26]

Rank	Metro Area	Job Growth Projected Rank	Metro Area Population (In Thousands)
1.	Raleigh, NC	11	1,140
2.	Des Moines, IA	23	572
3.	Provo, UT	16	531
4.	Lexington, KY	96	474
5.	Fort Collins, CO	31	301
6.	Nashville, TN	54	1,597
7.	Austin, TX	3	1,738
8.	San Antonio, TX	8	2,151
9.	Denver, CO	50	2,562
10.	Dallas, TX	19	4,264

TABLE 9.5 Companies with Excellent Motivational Strategies

Company	Motivational Strategies
3M	Gives employees 15–20 percent of their time to pursue own projects
Google	Perks include a massage every other week, free gourmet lunches, tuition reimbursement, a volleyball court, and time to work on own projects
Whole Foods	Employees receive 20 percent discounts on company products, the opportunity to gain stock options, and the ability to make major decisions in small teams
Patagonia	Provides areas for yoga and aerobics, in-house childcare services, organic food in its café, and opportunities to go surfing during the day
The Container Store	Provides more than 260 hours of employee training and hosts "We Love Our Employees" Day
Southwest Airlines	Gives employees permission to interact with passengers as they see fit, provides free or discounted flights, and hosts the "Adopt-a-Pilot" program to connect pilots with students across the nation
Nike	Offers tuition assistance, product discounts, onsite fitness centers, and the ability for employees to give insights on how to improve the firm
Apple	Creates a fast-paced, innovative work environment where employees are encouraged to debate ideas
Marriott	Offers discounts at hotels across the world as well as free hotel stays and travel opportunities for employees with exceptional service
Zappos	Creates a fun, zany work environment for employees and empowers them to take as much time as needed to answer customer concerns

they are not supposed to (after regular business hours or during vacation time).

Importance of Motivational Strategies

Motivation is more than a tool that managers can use to foster employee loyalty and boost productivity. It is a process that affects all the relationships within an organization and influences many areas such as pay, promotion, job design, training opportunities, and reporting relationships. Employees are motivated by the nature of the relationships they have with their supervisors, by the nature of their jobs, and by characteristics of the organization. Table 9.5 shows companies with excellent motivational strategies, along with the types of strategies they use to motivate employees. Even the economic environment can change an employee's motivation. In a slow growth or recession economy, sales can flatten or decrease, and morale can drop because of the need to cut jobs. In the most recent recession, many workers feared losing their jobs and increased the amount they were saving. The firm may have to work harder to keep good employees and motivate all employees to work to overcome obstacles. In good economic times, employees may be more demanding and be on the lookout for better opportunities. New rewards or incentives may help motivate workers in such economies. Motivation tools, then, must be varied as well. Managers can further nurture motivation by being honest, supportive, empathic, accessible, fair, and open. Motivating employees to increase satisfaction and productivity is an important concern for organizations seeking to remain competitive in the global marketplace. ■

TEAM EXERCISE

Form groups and outline a compensation package that you would consider ideal in motivating an employee, recognizing performance, and assisting the company in attaining its cost-to-performance objectives. Think about the impact of intrinsic and extrinsic motivation and recognition. How can flexible scheduling strategies be used effectively to motivate employees? Report your compensation package to the class.

learn, practice, apply motivational tools for employees!

M: Business was developed just for you—students on the go who need information packaged in a concise yet interesting format with multiple learning options.

Check out the book's website to:

- Learn about methods of employee motivation. (Solve the Dilemma)
- Consider how to make work more like play. (Build Your Skills)
- Learn the value of motivating employees to compete against a goal. (Build Your Skills)

While you are there, don't forget to enhance your skills. Practice and apply your knowledge, review the practice exercises, Student PPT® slides, and quizzes to review and apply chapter concepts. Additionally, *Connect® Business* is available for *M: Business.*

www.mhhe.com/ferrellm4e

Employee Bene

managing human resources

If a business is to achieve success, it must have sufficient numbers of employees who are qualified and motivated to perform the required duties. Thus, managing the quantity (from hiring to firing) and quality (through training, compensating, and so on) of employees is an important business function. Meeting the challenge of managing increasingly diverse human resources effectively can give a company a competitive edge in a global marketplace.

This chapter focuses on the quantity and quality of human resources. First we look at how human resources managers plan for, recruit, and select qualified employees. Next we look at training, appraising, and compensating employees, aspects of human resources management designed to retain valued employees. Along the way, we'll also consider the challenges of managing unionized employees and workplace diversity. ■

LEARNING OBJECTIVES

After reading this chapter, you will be able to:

- **LO 10-1** Define human resources management and explain its significance.
- **LO 10-2** Summarize the processes of recruiting and selecting human resources for a company.
- **LO 10-3** Discuss how workers are trained and their performance appraised.
- **LO 10-4** Identify the types of turnover companies may experience and explain why turnover is an important issue.
- **LO 10-5** Specify the various ways a worker may be compensated.
- **LO 10-6** Discuss some of the issues associated with unionized employees, including collective bargaining and dispute resolution.
- **LO 10-7** Describe the importance of diversity in the workforce.

human resources management (HRM) all the activities involved in determining an organization's human resources needs as well as acquiring, training, and compensating people to fill those needs

job analysis the determination, through observation and study, of pertinent information about a job—including specific tasks and necessary abilities, knowledge, and skills

job description a formal, written explanation of a specific job, usually including job title, tasks, relationship with other jobs, physical and mental skills required, duties, responsibilities, and working conditions

job specification a description of the qualifications necessary for a specific job in terms of education, experience, and personal and physical characteristics

LO 10-1 Define human resources management and explain its significance.

THE NATURE OF HUMAN RESOURCES MANAGEMENT

Chapter 1 defined human resources as labor, the physical and mental abilities that people use to produce goods and services. **Human resources management (HRM)** refers to all the activities involved in determining an organization's human resources needs as well as acquiring, training, and compensating people to fill those needs. Human resources managers are concerned with maximizing the satisfaction of employees and motivating them to meet organizational objectives productively. In some companies, this function is called personnel management.

Today's organizations are more diverse, with a greater range of women, minorities, and older workers.

HRM has increased in importance over the past few decades, in part because managers have developed a better understanding of human relations through the work of Maslow, Herzberg, and others. Moreover, the human resources themselves are changing. Employees today are concerned not only about how much a job pays; they are concerned also with job satisfaction, personal performance, recreation, benefits, the work environment, and their opportunities for advancement. Once dominated by white men, today's workforce includes significantly more women, African Americans, Hispanics, and other minorities as well as disabled and older workers. Human resources managers must be aware of these changes and leverage them to increase the productivity of their employees. Every manager practices some of the functions of human resources management at all times.

PLANNING FOR HUMAN RESOURCES NEEDS

When planning and developing strategies for reaching the organization's overall objectives, a company must consider whether it will have the human resources necessary to carry out its plans. After determining how many employees and what skills are needed to satisfy the overall plans, the human resources department (which may range from the owner in a small business to hundreds of people in a large corporation) ascertains how many employees the company currently has and how many will be retiring or otherwise leaving the organization during the planning period. With this information, the human resources manager can then forecast how many more employees the company will need to hire and what qualifications they must have or determine whether layoffs are required to meet demand more efficiently. HRM planning also requires forecasting the availability of people in the workforce who will have the necessary qualifications to meet the organization's future needs. The human resources manager then develops a strategy for satisfying the organization's human resources needs. As organizations strive to increase efficiency through outsourcing, automation, or learning to use temporary workers effectively, hiring needs can change dramatically.

recruiting forming a pool of qualified applicants from which management can select employees

Next, managers analyze the jobs within the organization so that they can match the human resources to the available assignments. **Job analysis** determines, through observation and study, pertinent information about a job—the specific tasks that comprise it; the knowledge, skills, and abilities necessary to perform it; and the environment in which it will be performed. Managers use the information obtained through a job analysis to develop job descriptions and job specifications.

A **job description** is a formal, written explanation of a specific job that usually includes job title, tasks to be performed (for instance, waiting on customers), relationship with other jobs, physical and mental skills required (such as lifting heavy boxes or calculating data), duties, responsibilities, and working conditions. Job seekers might turn to online websites or databases to help find job descriptions for specific occupations. For instance, the Occupational Information Network has an online database with hundreds of occupational descriptors. These descriptors describe the skills, knowledge, and education needed to fulfill a particular occupation (for instance, human resources).[1] A **job specification** describes the qualifications necessary for a specific job in terms of education (some jobs require a college degree), experience, personal characteristics (ads frequently request outgoing, hardworking persons), and physical characteristics. Both the job description and job specification are used to develop recruiting materials such as newspapers, trade publications, and online advertisements.

LO 10-2 Summarize the processes of recruiting and selecting human resources for a company.

RECRUITING AND SELECTING NEW EMPLOYEES

After forecasting the firm's human resources needs and comparing them to existing human resources, the human resources manager should have a general idea of how many new employees the firm needs to hire. With the aid of job analyses, management can then recruit and select employees who are qualified to fill specific job openings.

Recruiting

Recruiting means forming a pool of qualified applicants from which management can select employees. There are two sources from which to develop this pool of applicants—internal and external.

Internal sources of applicants include the organization's current employees. Many firms have a policy of giving first consideration to their own employees—or promoting from within. The cost of hiring current employees to fill job openings is inexpensive when compared with the cost of hiring from external sources, and it is good for employee morale. However, hiring from within creates another job vacancy to be filled.

External sources of applicants consist of advertisements in newspapers and professional journals, employment agencies, colleges, vocational schools, recommendations from current employees, competing firms, unsolicited applications, online websites, and social networking sites such as LinkedIn. Internships are also a good way to solicit for potential employees. Many companies hire college students or recent graduates to low-paying internships that give them the opportunity to get hands-on experience on the job. If the intern proves to be a good fit, an organization may then hire the intern as a full-time worker. There are also hundreds of websites where employers can post job openings and job seekers can post their résumés, including Monster.com, USAJobs, Simply Hired, SnagaJob, and CareerBuilder.com. TheLadders.com is a website that focuses on career-driven professionals who make salaries of $40,000 or more. Employers looking for employees for specialized jobs can use more focused sites such as computerwork.com. Increasingly, companies can turn to their own websites for potential candidates: Nearly all of the *Fortune* 500 firms provide career websites where they recruit, provide employment

TheLadders.com is a website that targets career-driven professionals.

selection the process of collecting information about applicants and using that information to make hiring decisions

information, and take applications. Using these sources of applicants is generally more expensive than hiring from within, but it may be necessary if there are no current employees who meet the job specifications or there are better-qualified people outside of the organization. Recruiting for entry-level managerial and professional positions is often carried out on college and university campuses. For managerial or professional positions above the entry level, companies sometimes depend on employment agencies or executive search firms, sometimes called *headhunters,* which specialize in luring qualified people away from other companies. Employers are also increasingly using professional social networking sites such as LinkedIn and Viadeo as recruitment tools.

Selection

Selection is the process of collecting information about applicants and using that information to decide which ones to hire. It includes the application itself as well as interviewing, testing, and reference checking. This process can be quite lengthy and expensive. Procter & Gamble, for example, offers online applications for jobs in 80 countries. The first round of evaluation involves assessment, and if this stage goes well, the candidate interviews in the region or country to which the applicant applied.[2] Such rigorous scrutiny is necessary to find those applicants who can do the work expected and fit into the firm's structure and culture. If an organization finds the "right" employees through its recruiting and selection process, it will not have to spend as much money later in recruiting, selecting, and training replacement employees.

The Application In the first stage of the selection process, the individual fills out an application form and perhaps has a brief interview. The application form asks for the applicant's name, address, telephone number, education, and previous work experience. The goal of this stage of the selection process is to get acquainted with the applicants and to weed out those who are obviously not qualified for the job. Figure 10.1 indicates how much time human resources managers spend reviewing applications. For employees with work experience, most companies ask for the following information before contacting a potential candidate: current salary, reason for seeking a new job, years of experience, availability, and level of interest in the position. In addition to identifying obvious qualifications, the application can provide subtle clues about whether a person is appropriate for a particular job. For instance, an applicant who gives unusually creative answers may be perfect for a position at an advertising agency; a person who turns in a sloppy, hurriedly scrawled application probably would not be appropriate for a technical job requiring precise adjustments. Many companies now accept online applications. The online application for Target is designed not only to collect biographical data on the applicant but also to create a picture of the applicant and how that person might contribute to the company. The completion of the survey takes about 15–45 minutes, depending on the position. To get a better view of the fit between the applicant and the company, the online application contains a questionnaire that asks applicants more specific questions, from how they might react in a certain situation to personality attributes like self-esteem or ability to interact with people.

FIGURE 10.1
How Much Time Do Human Resources Managers Spend Reviewing Applications?

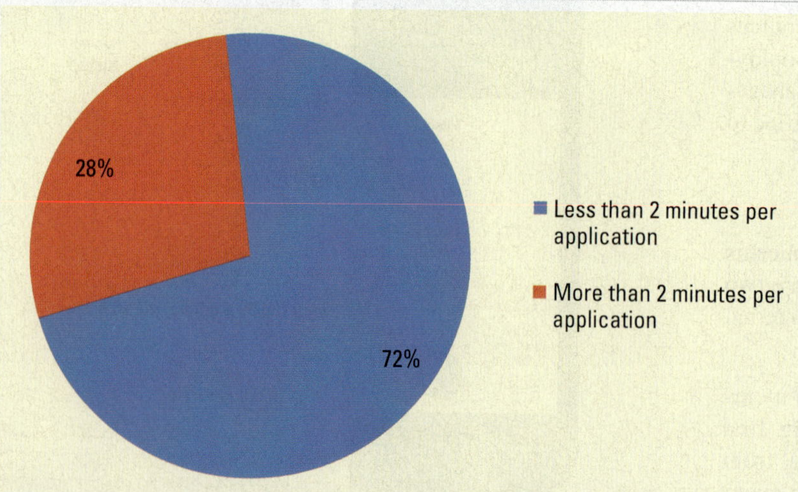

Source: CareerBuilder survey of 2,662 hiring managers.

The Interview The next phase of the selection process involves interviewing applicants. Table 10.1 provides some insights on finding the right work environment. Interviews allow management to obtain detailed information about the applicant's experience and skills, reasons for changing jobs, attitudes toward the job, and an idea of whether the person would fit in with the company. Table 10.2 lists some of the most common questions asked by interviewers; Table 10.3 reveals some common mistakes candidates make in interviewing. Furthermore, the interviewer can answer the applicant's questions about the requirements for the job, compensation, working conditions, company policies, organizational culture, and so on. A potential employee's questions may be just as revealing as his or her answers. Today's students might be surprised to have an interviewer ask them, "What's on your Facebook account?" or have them show the interviewer their Facebook accounts. Currently, these are legal questions for an interviewer to ask.

Testing Another step in the selection process is testing. Ability and performance tests are used to determine whether an applicant has the skills necessary for the job. Aptitude, IQ, or personality tests may be used to assess an applicant's potential for a certain kind of work and his or her ability to fit into

> BACKGROUND CHECKING IS IMPORTANT BECAUSE APPLICANTS MAY MISREPRESENT THEMSELVES ON THEIR APPLICATIONS OR RÉSUMÉS.

Personality tests such as Myers-Briggs are used to assess an applicant's potential for a certain kind of job. For instance, extroversion and a love of people would be good qualities for a sales or retail job.

the organization's culture. One of the most commonly used tests is the Myers-Briggs Type Indicator. The Myers-Briggs Type Indicator Test is used worldwide by millions of people each year. Although polygraph (lie detector) tests were once a common technique for evaluating the honesty of applicants, in 1988 their use was restricted to specific government jobs and those involving security or access to drugs. Applicants may also undergo physical examinations to determine their suitability for some jobs, and many companies require applicants to be screened for illegal drug use. Illegal drug use and alcoholism can be particularly damaging to businesses. It has been estimated that 8.4 percent of full-time employees engage in illicit drug use, 29.7 percent engage in binge drinking, and 8.5 percent are considered to be heavy drinkers.[3] Small businesses may have a higher percentage of these employees because they do not engage in systematic drug testing. If you employ a drug or alcohol abuser, you can expect a 33 percent loss in productivity from this employee. Loss in productivity from alcohol abuse alone costs companies $134 billion each year. Health care costs are also more expensive for those who abuse alcohol—twice more than those for employees who do not abuse alcohol.[4]

Because computer knowledge is a requirement for many jobs today, certain companies also require an applicant to take a typing test or tests to determine their knowledge of MS Word, Excel, PowerPoint, and/or other necessary programs. Like the application form and the interview, testing serves to eliminate those who do not meet the job specifications.

TABLE 10.1 Interviewing Tips

1. Evaluate the work environment. Do employees seem to get along and work well in teams?
2. Evaluate the attitude of employees. Are employees happy, tense, or overworked?
3. Are employees enthusiastic and excited about their work?
4. What is the organizational culture, and would you feel comfortable working there?

Source: Adapted from "What to Look for During Office Visits," http://careercenter.tamu.edu/guides/interviews/lookforinoffice.cfm?sn=parents.

TABLE 10.2 Most Common Questions Asked during the Interview

1. Tell me about yourself.
2. Why should I hire you?
3. Please tell me about your future objectives.
4. Has your education prepared you for your career?
5. Have you been a team player?
6. Did you encounter any conflict with your previous professors or employer? What are the steps that you have taken to resolve this issue?
7. What is your biggest weakness?
8. How would your professors describe you?
9. What are the qualities that a manager should possess?
10. If you could turn back time, what would you change?

Source: "Job Interview Skills Training: Top Ten Interview Questions for College Graduates," February 17, 2010, www.articlesbase.com/business-articles/job-interview-skills-training-top-ten-interview-questions-for-college-graduates-1871741.html.

Reference Checking Before making a job offer, the company should always check an applicant's references. Reference checking usually involves verifying educational background and previous work experience. An Internet search is often done to determine social media activities or other public activities. Until recently, the city of Bozeman, Montana, asked potential applicants for their passwords to their e-mail addresses and social networking sites. Although public Internet searches are usually deemed acceptable, asking for private information—although legal—is deemed to be intrusive by many job seekers.[5] Public companies are likely to do more extensive background searches to make sure applicants are not misrepresenting themselves.

Background checking is important because applicants may misrepresent themselves on their applications or résumés. The Yahoo! board of directors faced an embarrassment

GoodHire specializes in background checks. Background checks are important for detecting past misconduct or criminal activities committed by job applicants.

TABLE 10.3 Mistakes Made in Interviewing

1. Not taking the interview seriously.
2. Not dressing appropriately (dressing down).
3. Not appropriately discussing experience, abilities, and education.
4. Being too modest about your accomplishments.
5. Talking too much.
6. Too much concern about compensation.
7. Speaking negatively of a former employer.
8. Not asking enough or appropriate questions.
9. Not showing the proper enthusiasm level.
10. Not engaging in appropriate follow-up to the interview.

Source: "Avoid the Top 10 Job Interview Mistakes," All Business, www.allbusiness.com/human-resources/careers-job-interview/1611-1.html.

TABLE 10.4 Top 10 Résumé Lies

1. Stretching dates of employment
2. Inflating past accomplishments and skills
3. Enhancing job titles and responsibilities
4. Education exaggeration and fabricating degrees
5. Unexplained gaps and periods of "self employment"
6. Omitting past employment
7. Faking credentials
8. Fabricating reasons for leaving previous job
9. Providing fraudulent references
10. Misrepresenting military record

Source: Christopher T. Marquet and Lisa J. B. Peterson, "Résumé Fraud: The Top 10 Lies," www.marquetinternational.com/pdf/Resume%20Fraud-Top%20Ten%20Lies.pdf. Reprinted with permission of Christopher T. Marquet.

after a hedge fund manager announced that Yahoo! CEO Scott Thompson did not have one of the degrees stated on his résumé. The CEO resigned after this inaccuracy was revealed.[6] As Table 10.4 illustrates, some of the most common types of résumé lies include the faking of credentials, overstatements of skills or accomplishments, lies concerning education or degrees, omissions of past employment, and the falsification of references.[7]

Reference checking is a vital, albeit often overlooked, stage in the selection process. Managers charged with hiring should be aware, however, that many organizations will confirm only that an applicant is a former employee, perhaps with beginning and ending work dates, and will not release details about the quality of the employee's work.

Legal Issues in Recruiting and Selecting

Legal constraints and regulations are present in almost every phase of the recruitment and selection process, and a violation of these regulations can result in lawsuits and fines. Therefore,

Title VII of the Civil Rights Act prohibits discrimination in employment and created the Equal Employment Opportunity Commission

managers should be aware of these restrictions to avoid legal problems. Some of the laws affecting human resources management are discussed here.

Because one law pervades all areas of human resources management, we'll take a quick look at it now. **Title VII of the Civil Rights Act** of 1964 prohibits discrimination in employment. It also created the Equal Employment Opportunity Commission (EEOC), a federal agency dedicated to increasing job opportunities for women and minorities and eliminating job discrimination based on race, religion, color, sex, national origin, or handicap. As a result of Title VII, employers must not impose sex distinctions in job specifications, job descriptions, or newspaper advertisements. In 2012, workplace discrimination charges filed with the Equal Employment Opportunity Commission numbered 99,412. The EEOC received more than 30,000 complaints for sexual discrimination, which includes sexual harassment and denial of employment or loss of a job because of pregnancy.[8] Sexual harassment often makes up the largest number of claims the EEOC encounters each day. The Civil Rights Act of 1964 also outlaws the use of discriminatory tests for applicants. Aptitude tests and other indirect tests must be validated; in other words, employers must be able to demonstrate that scores on such tests are related to job performance, so that no one race has an advantage in taking the tests or is alternatively discriminated against. Although many hope for improvements in organizational diversity, only 3.8 percent of *Fortune* 500 companies are run by people of color. Despite the low number, this is an improvement from the mid-1990s when no *Fortune* 500 company had a person of color as CEO. Additionally, 9.8 percent of board seats are now held by racial minorities.[9]

Other laws affecting HRM include the Americans with Disabilities Act (ADA), which prevents discrimination against disabled persons. It also classifies people with AIDS as handicapped and, consequently, prohibits using a positive AIDS test as reason to deny an applicant employment. The Age Discrimination in Employment Act specifically outlaws discrimination based on age. Its focus is banning hiring practices that discriminate against people aged 40 years and older. Generally, when companies need employees, recruiters head to college campuses, and when downsizing is necessary, many older workers are offered early retirement. Forced retirement based on age, however, is generally considered to be illegal in the United States, although claims of forced retirement still abound. Until recently, employees in the United Kingdom could be forced to retire at age 65. However, a new law abolished the default retirement age.[10] Indeed there are many benefits that companies are realizing in hiring older workers. Some of these benefits include the fact that they are more dedicated, punctual, honest, and detail-oriented; are good listeners; take pride in their work; exhibit good organizational skills; are efficient and confident; are mature; can be seen as role models; have good communication skills; and offer an opportunity for a reduced labor cost because of already having insurance plans.[11] Figure 10.2 shows that although the hiring of older workers has increased in the past few years, the hiring of younger workers has increased at a slower rate.

The Equal Pay Act mandates that men and women who do equal work must receive the same wage. Wage differences are acceptable only if they are attributed to seniority, performance, or qualifications. In the United States, the typical full-time female employee earns 19 percent less than the average full-time male employee. In a study by PayScale, some of the biggest gender pay gaps can be found in positions such as chief executive (women earn 71 percent of what men earn), hospital administrator (women earn 77 percent of what men earn), and chief operating officer (women earn 80 percent of what men earn). Performance quality in these jobs is relatively subjective. Jobs such as engineers, actuaries, or electricians, where the performance evaluation is more objective, result in greater salary parity between men and women.[12] However, despite the wage inequalities that still exist, women in the workplace are becoming increasingly accepted among both genders. The working mother is no longer a novelty; in fact, many working mothers seek the same amount of achievement as working men and women who are not mothers.

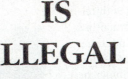

Federal law prohibits discrimination because of RACE, COLOR, RELIGION, NATIONAL ORIGIN, SEX, AGE (40 YEARS AND OVER), AND/OR PHYSICAL OR MENTAL HANDICAP AND RETALIATION FOR PARTICIPATING IN ACTIVITIES PROTECTED BY THE CIVIL RIGHTS STATUTES.
Employees or applicants for employment with NOAA who believe that they have been discriminated or retaliated against may contact an EEO Counselor. The Counselor will attempt to resolve the matter and furnish information about filing a complaint of discrimination.
To preserve your rights under the law, you must contact an EEO Counselor within 45 CALENDAR DAYS of the date of alleged discrimination.
TO INITIATE EEO COUNSELING OR FOR MORE INFORMATION, CONTACT:
Civil Rights Office, NOAA
VOICE (301) 713-0500
TDD (301) 713-0982
1-800-452-6728

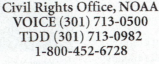

FIGURE 10.2
U.S. Population Employed by Age Group (in thousands)

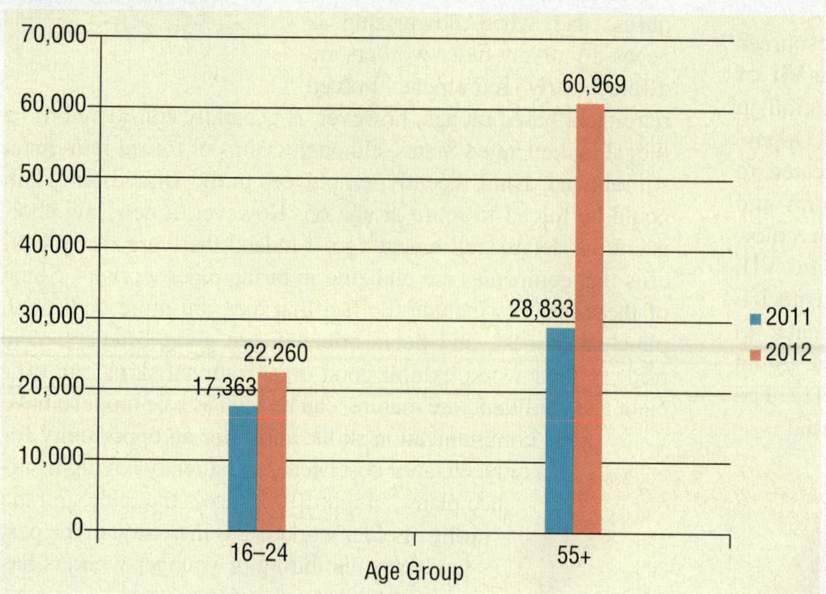

Source: U.S. Department of Labor, Bureau of Labor Statistics, labor force statistics from the *Current Population Survey*, www.bls.gov/cps/demographics.htm#age.

DEVELOPING THE WORKFORCE

Once the most qualified applicants have been selected, have been offered positions, and have accepted their offers, they must be formally introduced to the organization and trained so they can begin to be productive members of the workforce. **Orientation** familiarizes the newly hired employees with fellow workers, company procedures, and the physical properties of the company. It generally includes a tour of the building; introductions to supervisors, co-workers, and subordinates; and the distribution of organizational manuals describing the organization's policy on vacations, absenteeism, lunch breaks, company benefits, and so on. Orientation also involves socializing the new employee into the ethics and culture of the new company. Many larger companies now show videotapes of procedures, facilities, and key personnel in the organization to help speed the adjustment process.

LO 10-3 Discuss how workers are trained and their performance appraised.

Training and Development

Although recruiting and selection are designed to find employees who have the knowledge, skills, and abilities the company needs, new employees still must undergo **training** to learn how to do their specific job tasks. *On-the-job training* allows workers to learn by actually performing the tasks of the job, whereas *classroom training* teaches employees with lectures, conferences, videotapes, case studies, and web-based training. For instance, McDonald's trains those interested in company operations and leadership development at the Fred L. Turner Training Center, otherwise known as Hamburger University. Hamburger University employs full-time professors to train students in a variety of topics, including crew development, restaurant management, middle management, and executive development. Training includes classroom instruction, hands-on instruction, and computer e-learning.[13] **Development** is training that augments the skills and knowledge of managers and professionals. Training and development are also used to improve the skills of employees in their present positions and to prepare them for increased responsibility and job promotions. Training is therefore a vital function of human resources management. At the Container Store, for example, first-year sales personnel receive 263 hours of training about the company's products.[14] Companies are engaging in more experiential and involvement-oriented training exercises for employees. Use of role-plays, simulations, and online training methods are becoming increasingly popular in employee training.

Assessing Performance

Assessing an employee's performance—his or her strengths and weaknesses on the job—is one of the most difficult tasks for managers. However, performance appraisal is crucial because

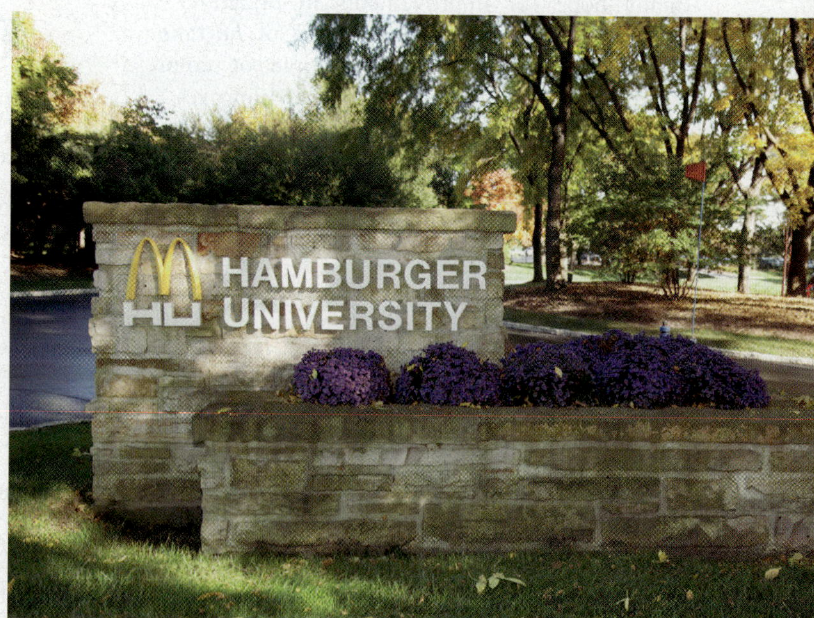

McDonald's has expanded its famous Hamburger University into China. This branch of Hamburger University will train a new generation of Chinese students in such areas as restaurant management, leadership development, and other skills.

orientation familiarizing newly hired employees with fellow workers, company procedures, and the physical properties of the company

training teaching employees to do specific job tasks through either classroom development or on-the-job experience

development training that augments the skills and knowledge of managers and professionals

it gives employees feedback on how they are doing and what they need to do to improve. It also provides a basis for determining how to compensate and reward employees, and it generates information about the quality of the firm's selection, training, and development activities. Table 10.5 identifies 16 characteristics that may be assessed in a performance review.

Performance appraisals may be objective or subjective. An objective assessment is quantifiable. For example, a Westinghouse employee might be judged by how many circuit boards he typically produces in one day or by how many of his boards have defects. A Century 21 real estate agent might be judged by the number of houses she has shown or the number of sales she has closed. A company can also use tests as an objective method of assessment. Whatever method they use, managers must take into account the work environment when they appraise performance objectively.

When jobs do not lend themselves to objective appraisal, the manager must relate the employee's performance to some other standard. One popular tool used in subjective assessment is the ranking system, which lists various performance factors on which the manager ranks employees against each other. Although used by many large companies, ranking systems are unpopular with many employees. Qualitative criteria, such as teamwork and communication skills, used to evaluate employees are generally hard to gauge. Such grading systems have triggered employee lawsuits that allege discrimination in grade/ranking assignments. For example, one manager may grade a company's employees one way, whereas another manager grades a group more harshly depending on the manager's grading style. If layoffs occur, then employees graded by the second manager may be more likely to lose their jobs. Other criticisms of grading systems include unclear wording or inappropriate words that a manager may unintentionally write in a performance evaluation, like *young* or *pretty* to describe an employee's appearance. These liabilities can all be fodder for lawsuits if employees allege that they were treated unfairly. It is therefore crucial for managers to use clear language in performance evaluations and be consistent with all employees. Several employee grading computer packages have been developed to make performance evaluations easier for managers and clearer for employees.[15] Figure 10.3 demonstrates that employers are more likely to believe that performance reviews improve employee performance than employees do.

Another performance appraisal method used by many companies is the 360-degree feedback system, which provides feedback from a panel that typically includes superiors, peers, and subordinates. Because of the tensions it may cause, peer appraisal appears to be difficult for many. However, companies that have success with 360-degree feedback tend to be open to learning and willing to experiment and are led by executives who are direct about the expected benefits as well as the

TABLE 10.5 Performance Characteristics

- **Productivity**—rate at which work is regularly produced
- **Quality**—accuracy, professionalism, and deliverability of produced work
- **Job knowledge**—understanding of the objectives, practices, and standards of work
- **Problem solving**—ability to identify and correct problems effectively
- **Communication**—effectiveness in written and verbal exchanges
- **Initiative**—willingness to identify and address opportunities for improvement
- **Adaptability**—ability to become comfortable with change
- **Planning and organization skills**—reflected through the ability to schedule projects, set goals, and maintain organizational systems
- **Teamwork and cooperation**—effectiveness of collaborations with co-workers
- **Judgment**—ability to determine appropriate actions in a timely manner
- **Dependability**—responsiveness, reliability, and conscientiousness demonstrated on the job
- **Creativity**—extent to which resourceful ideas, solutions, and methods for task completion are proposed
- **Sales**—demonstrated through success in selling products, services, yourself, and your company
- **Customer service**—ability to communicate effectively with customers, address problems, and offer solutions that meet or exceed their expectations
- **Leadership**—tendency and ability to serve as a doer, guide, decision maker, and role model
- **Financial management**—appropriateness of cost controls and financial planning within the scope defined by the position

Source: "Performance Characteristics," Performance Review from www.salary.com/Careerresources/docs/related_performance_review_part2_popup.html. Used with permission.

Amazon.com holds a job fair in the virtual world Second Life. Companies have started using digital media for posting job applications, holding job fairs, and even training employees.

challenges.[16] Managers and leaders with a high emotional intelligence (sensitivity to their own as well as others' emotions) assess and reflect upon their interactions with colleagues on a daily basis. In addition, they conduct follow-up analysis on their projects, asking the right questions and listening carefully to responses without getting defensive of their actions.[17]

Whether the assessment is objective or subjective, it is vital for the manager to discuss the results with the employee, so that the employee knows how well he or she is doing the job. The results of a performance appraisal become useful only when they are communicated, tactfully, to the employee and presented as a tool to allow the employee to grow and improve in his or her position and beyond. Performance appraisals are also used to determine whether an employee should be promoted, transferred, or terminated from the organization.

LO 10-4 Identify the types of turnover companies may experience and explain why turnover is an important issue.

Turnover

Turnover, which occurs when employees quit or are fired and must be replaced by new employees, results in lost productivity from the vacancy, costs to recruit replacement employees, management time devoted to interviewing, training, and socialization expenses for new employees. However, some companies have created innovative solutions for reducing turnover. Accenture, a global management consulting firm, has 275,000 employees around the world who travel frequently. Because of the hectic pace of the job and constant traveling, the company has instituted a unique wellness program offered to its on-the-go employees to encourage them to take care of their health while getting their jobs done. This program is personalized to the lifestyles of the employees and offers health tips and exercises that are effective but not time consuming. Accenture employees have rated this program as fun and relevant to their lives, resulting in higher job satisfaction. Job satisfaction is one of the best ways of reducing turnover.[18] Part of the reason for turnover may be overworked employees as a result of downsizing and a lack of training and advancement opportunities.[19] Figure 10.4 provides some of the top reasons employees give for leaving the company. Of course, turnover is not always an unhappy occasion when it takes the form of a promotion or transfer.

A **promotion** is an advancement to a higher-level job with increased authority, responsibility, and pay. In some companies and most labor unions, seniority—the length of time a person

"The results of a performance appraisal become useful only when they are communicated, tactfully, to the employee and presented as a tool to allow the employee to grow and improve in his or her position and beyond."

FIGURE 10.3
Performance Reviews: Those Who Believe Reviews Improve Employees' Performance

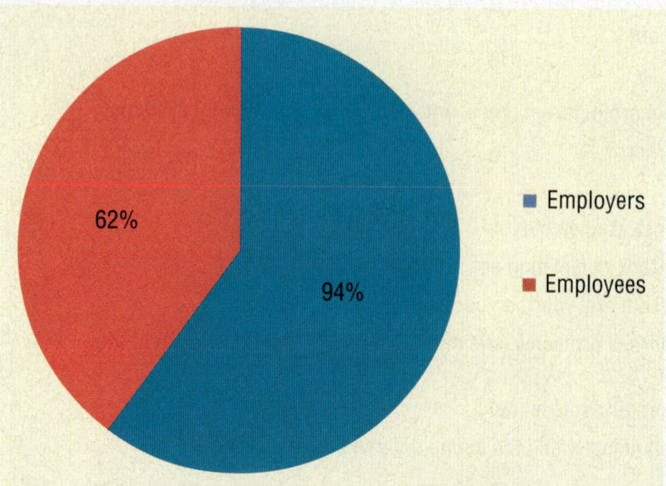

Source: Robert Half survey of 1,400 chief financial officers and 422 workers.

turnover occurs when employees quit or are fired and must be replaced by new employees

promotion an advancement to a higher-level job with increased authority, responsibility, and pay

transfer a move to another job within the company at essentially the same level and wage

separations employment changes involving resignation, retirement, termination, or layoff

has been with the company or at a particular job classification—is the key issue in determining who should be promoted. Most managers base promotions on seniority only when they have candidates with equal qualifications: Managers prefer to base promotions on merit.

Many companies in recent years are choosing to downsize by eliminating jobs. Reasons for downsizing might be due to financial constraints or the need to become more productive and competitive.

FIGURE 10.4
Reasons Employees Do Not Work Out in a Position (aside from poor performance)

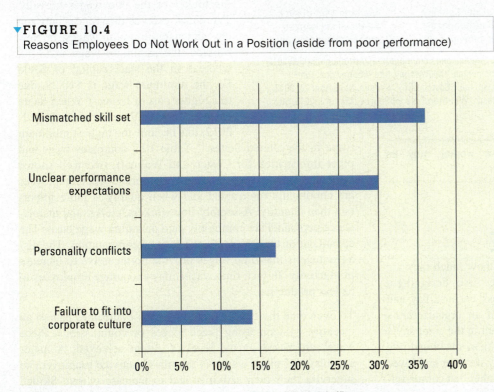

Source: Robert Half Finance & Accounting survey of 1,400 chief financial officers.

A **transfer** is a move to another job within the company at essentially the same level and wage. Transfers allow workers to obtain new skills or to find a new position within an organization when their old position has been eliminated because of automation or downsizing.

Separations occur when employees resign, retire, are terminated, or are laid off. Employees may be terminated, or fired, for poor performance, violation of work rules, absenteeism, and so on. Businesses have traditionally been able to fire employees *at will,* that is, for any reason other than for race, religion, sex, or age, or because an employee is a union organizer. However, recent legislation and court decisions now require companies to fire employees fairly, for just cause only. Managers must take care, then, to warn employees when their performance is unacceptable and may lead to dismissal, elevating the importance of performance evaluations. They should also document all problems and warnings in employees' work records. To avoid the possibility of lawsuits from individuals who may feel they have been fired unfairly, employers should provide clear, business-related reasons for any firing, supported by written documentation if possible. Employee disciplinary procedures should be carefully explained to all employees and should be set forth in employee handbooks. Table 10.6 illustrates what *not* to do when you are terminated.

Many companies have downsized in recent years, laying off tens of thousands of employees in their effort to become more productive and competitive. For example, Gap had to lay off workers after it decided to close 200 stores in the United States. Declining sales convinced Gap to adapt its marketing strategy and focus more on the overseas market.[20] Layoffs are sometimes temporary; employees may be brought back when business conditions improve. When layoffs are to be permanent, employers often help employees find other jobs and may extend benefits while the employees search for new employment. Such actions help lessen the trauma of the layoffs. Fortunately, there are several business areas that are choosing not to downsize.

A well-organized human resources department strives to minimize losses due to separations and transfers because recruiting and training new employees is very expensive. Note that a high turnover

wage/salary survey a study that tells a company how much compensation comparable firms are paying for specific jobs that the firms have in common

wages financial rewards based on the number of hours the employee works or the level of output achieved

rate in a company may signal problems with the selection and training process, the compensation program, or even the type of company. To help reduce turnover, companies have tried a number of strategies, including giving employees more interesting job responsibilities (job enrichment), allowing for increased job flexibility, and providing more employee benefits.

Designing a fair compensation plan is a difficult task because it involves evaluating the relative worth of all jobs within the business while allowing for individual efforts. Compensation for a specific job is typically determined through a **wage/salary survey**, which tells the company how much compensation comparable firms are paying for specific jobs that the firms have in common. Compensation for individuals within a specific job category depends on both the compensation for that job and the individual's productivity. Therefore, two employees with identical jobs may not receive exactly the same pay because of individual differences in performance.

TABLE 10.6 What You Should Not Do When You Are Terminated

1. Do not tell off your boss and co-workers, even if you think they deserve it.
2. Do not damage company property or steal something.
3. Do not forget to ask for a reference.
4. Do not badmouth your employer or any of your co-workers to your replacement.
5. Do not badmouth your employer to a prospective employer when you go on a job interview.

Source: Dawn Rosenberg McKay, "Five Things Not to Do When You Leave Your Job," http://careerplanning.about.com/od/jobseparation/a/leave_mistakes.htm.

TABLE 10.7 Costco versus Walmart

	Costco	Walmart
Number of employees	160,000+	2,200,000
Revenues	$97 billion	$446 billion
Average pay per hour	$17	$12.67
World's most admired ranking	23	27
Strengths	Management quality; financial soundness; people management	Management quality; financial soundness; global competitiveness

Sources: CNN, "Fortune Global 500," *CNNMoney,* http://money.cnn.com/magazines/fortune/global500/2012/snapshots/2255.html; CNN, "World's Most Admired Companies," *CNNMoney,* http://money.cnn.com/magazines/fortune/most-admired/2013/list/?iid=wma_sp_full; "Costco CEO," *Snopes,* November 28, 2012, http://www.snopes.com/politics/business/costcoceo.asp; "Wal-Mart," NYJobSource, March 3, 2013, http://nyjobsource.com/walmart.html.

LO 10-5 Specify the various ways a worker may be compensated.

COMPENSATING THE WORKFORCE

People generally don't work for free, and how much they are paid for their work is a complicated issue. Also, designing a fair compensation plan is an important task because pay and benefits represent a substantial portion of an organization's expenses. Wages that are too high may result in the company's products being priced too high, making them uncompetitive in the market. Wages that are too low may damage employee morale and result in costly turnover. Remember that compensation is one of the hygiene factors identified by Herzberg.

Financial Compensation

Financial compensation falls into two general categories—wages and salaries. **Wages** are financial rewards based on the number of hours the employee works or the level of output achieved. Wages based on the number of hours worked are called time wages. The federal minimum wage increased to $7.25 per hour in 2009 for covered nonexempt workers.[21] Tipped wages must be $2.13 per hour as long as tips plus the wage of $2.13 per hour equal the minimum wage of $7.25 per hour.[22] Many states also mandate minimum wages; when the two wages are in conflict, the higher of the two wages prevails. There may even be differences between city and state minimum wages. In New Mexico, the minimum wage is $7.50, whereas in the state capital of Santa Fe, the minimum wage is $10.29, due to a higher cost of living.[23] When Santa Fe went to $10.29 per hour on May 1, 2012, this became the highest minimum wage in the United States.[24] Table 10.7 compares wage and other information for Costco and Walmart, two well-known discount chains. Time wages are appropriate when employees are continually interrupted and when quality is more important than quantity. Assembly-line workers, clerks, and maintenance personnel are commonly paid on a time-wage basis. The advantage of time wages is the ease of computation. The disadvantage is that time wages provide no incentive to increase productivity. In fact, time wages may encourage employees to be less productive.

To overcome these disadvantages, many companies pay on an incentive system, using piece wages or commissions. Piece wages are based on the level of output achieved. A major advantage of piece wages is that they motivate employees to supervise their own activities and to increase output. Skilled craftworkers are often paid on a piece-wage basis.

commission an incentive system that pays a fixed amount or a percentage of the employee's sales

salary a financial reward calculated on a weekly, monthly, or annual basis

bonuses monetary rewards offered by companies for exceptional performance as incentives to increase productivity further

profit sharing a form of compensation whereby a percentage of company profits is distributed to the employees whose work helped to generate them

benefits nonfinancial forms of compensation provided to employees, such as pension plans, health insurance, paid vacation and holidays, and the like

COFFEE & POWER'S UNIQUE COMPENSATION PLAN FOR EMPLOYEES

Coffee & Power is a job-selling startup that was founded by Philip Rosedale. The site allows people to post jobs they need done or jobs or services they can perform. In other words, the website acts as a hub to connect service providers with customers. These services range from software to physical labor.

Not only is the business unique, but so is the way it compensates employees. Rosedale gives his 15 full- and part-time employees 1,200 stock options with instructions to award them to their peers who are deserving of a bonus. This approach is effective because employees know who has contributed to projects in a more significant way than management does. The advantages to this method are employee accountability and openness to feedback. It also allows for quiet employees to be recognized by management. Disadvantages include the possibility of this method turning into a popularity contest and leading to hard feelings among those who are not recognized.[25]

The other incentive system, **commission**, pays a fixed amount or a percentage of the employee's sales. Kele & Co Jewelers in Plainfield, Illinois, makes sterling silver jewelry and offers semi-precious and gemstones at affordable prices. Its handcrafted jewelry is sold through the Internet (www.keleonline.com) and through independent sales representatives (ISRs) all over the country. The unique aspect of Kele's sales process is its innovative sales and commission structure. ISRs have no minimum sales quotas, sales are shared among team members during training and after being promoted, and there is no requirement to purchase inventory because jewelry is shipped from Kele headquarters. ISRs receive a 30 to 50 percent commission on sales. The goal is to increase the profit margin and earning potential of the salespeople. The company's goal is to become the largest direct sales company in the industry.[26] This method motivates employees to sell as much as they can. Some companies also combine payment based on commission with time wages or salaries.

A **salary** is a financial reward calculated on a weekly, monthly, or annual basis. Salaries are associated with white-collar workers such as office personnel, executives, and professional employees. Although a salary provides a stable stream of income, salaried workers may be required to work beyond usual hours without additional financial compensation.

In addition to the basic wages or salaries paid to employees, a company may offer **bonuses** for exceptional performance as an incentive to increase productivity further. Many workers receive a bonus as a thank you for good work and an incentive to continue working hard. Many owners and managers are recognizing that simple bonuses and perks foster happier employees and reduce turnover. In 2012, the CEO of Lenovo, Yang Yuanqing, received a bonus that was $3 million larger than the year before. He then did something unexpected—he divided it up among the company's 100,000 lower-level employees. His actions demonstrated an appreciation for the hard work and commitment of the company's employees.[27]

Another form of compensation is **profit sharing**, which distributes a percentage of company profits to the employees whose work helped to generate those profits. Some profit-sharing plans involve distributing shares of company stock to employees. Usually referred to as *ESOPs*—employee stock ownership plans—they have been gaining popularity in recent years. One reason for the popularity of ESOPs is the sense of partnership that they create between the organization and employees. Profit sharing can also motivate employees to work hard because increased productivity and sales mean that the profits or the stock dividends will increase. Many organizations offer employees a stake in the company through stock purchase plans, ESOPs, or stock investments through 401(k) plans. Employees below senior management levels rarely received stock options until recently. Companies are adopting broad-based stock option plans to build a stronger link between employees' interests and the organization's interests. ESOPs have met with enormous success over the years, and employee-owned stock has even outperformed the stock market during certain periods. Many businesses have found employee stock options a great way to boost productivity and increase morale. There are an estimated 13,000 ESOPs in the United States.[28]

Benefits

Benefits are nonfinancial forms of compensation provided to employees, such as pension plans for retirement; health, disability, and life insurance; holidays and paid days off for vacation or illness; credit union membership; health programs; child care; elder care; assistance with adoption; and more. According to the Bureau of Labor Statistics, employer costs for employee compensation for private industry workers in the United States

> The most common counseling services offered include drug- and alcohol-abuse treatment programs, fitness programs, smoking cessation clinics, stress-management clinics, financial counseling, family counseling, and career counseling.

average $28.89 per hour worked. Wages and salaries account for approximately 70.3 percent of those costs, while benefits account for 29.7 percent of the cost. Legally required benefits (Social Security, Medicare, federal and state employment insurance, and workers' compensation) account for 8.2 percent of total compensation.[29] Such benefits increase employee security and, to a certain extent, their morale and motivation.

Table 10.8 lists some of the benefits Internet search engine Google offers its employees. Although health insurance is a common benefit for full-time employees, rising health care costs

TABLE 10.8 Google's Employee Benefits

- Health insurance:
  - Employee medical insurance
  - Dental insurance
  - Vision insurance
- Vacation (15 days per year for one–three years' employment; 20 days off for four–five years' employment; 25 days for more than six years' employment)
- Twelve paid holidays/year
- Savings plans
  - 401(k) retirement plan, matched by Google
  - Flexible spending accounts
- Disability and life insurance
- Employee Assistance Program
- Free lunches and snacks
- Massages, gym membership, hair stylist, fitness class, and bike repair
- Weekly activities
- Maternity leave
- Adoption assistance
- Tuition reimbursement
- Employee referral plan
- Onsite doctor
- Backup child care
- Holiday parties, health fair, credit union, roller hockey, outdoor volleyball court, discounts for local attractions

Source: Google, "Google Benefits," www.google.com/about/jobs/lifeatgoogle/benefits/.

An onsite fitness center is just one of the benefits that large companies have begun to offer employees. Such onsite benefits like fitness centers and child care are particularly important for employees who work long hours or who struggle to maintain a healthy work-life balance.

have forced a growing number of employers to trim this benefit. Even government workers, whose wages and benefits used to be virtually guaranteed safe, have seen reductions in health care and other benefits. Surveys have revealed that with the decrease in benefits comes a decrease in employee loyalty. Only 42 percent of employees say they feel a strong sense of loyalty to their employers. However, more than half of respondents indicated that employee benefits were important in decisions to stay with the company. Benefits are particularly important to younger generations of employees.[30] Starbucks recognizes the importance of how benefits can significantly affect an employee's health and well-being. As a result, it is one of only a few fast-food companies to offer its part-time employees health insurance.

A benefit increasingly offered is the employee assistance program (EAP). Each company's EAP is different, but most offer counseling for and assistance with those employees' personal problems that might hurt their job performance if not addressed. The most common counseling services offered include drug- and alcohol-abuse treatment programs, fitness programs, smoking cessation clinics, stress-management clinics, financial counseling, family counseling, and career counseling. Lowe's, for example, offers work/life seminars, smoking cessation clinics, and other assistance programs for its employees.[31] EAPs help reduce costs associated with poor productivity, absenteeism, and other workplace issues by helping employees deal with personal problems that contribute to these issues. For example, exercise and fitness programs reduce health insurance costs by helping employees stay healthy. Family counseling may help workers trying to cope with a divorce or other personal problems to focus better on their jobs.

Companies try to provide the benefits they believe their employees want, but diverse people may want different things. In recent years, some single workers have felt that co-workers with spouses and children seem to get special breaks and extra time off to deal with family issues. Some companies use flexible benefit programs to allow employees to choose the benefits they would like, up to a specified amount.

Fringe benefits include sick leave, vacation pay, pension plans, health plans, and any other extra compensation. Soft benefits include perks that help balance life and work. They include onsite child care, spas, food service, and even laundry services and hair salons. These soft benefits motivate employees and give them more time to focus on their job.

Cafeteria benefit plans provide a financial amount to employees so that they can select the specific benefits that fit their needs. The key is making benefits flexible, rather than giving employees identical benefits. As firms go global, the need for cafeteria or flexible benefit plans becomes even more important. For some employees, benefits are a greater motivator and differentiator in jobs than wages. For many Starbucks employees who receive health insurance when working part time, this benefit could be the most important compensation.

Over the past two decades, the list of fringe benefits has grown dramatically, and new benefits are being added every year.

labor unions
employee organizations formed to deal with employers for achieving better pay, hours, and working conditions

LO 10-6 Discuss some of the issues associated with unionized employees, including collective bargaining and dispute resolution.

FIGURE 10.5
Union Membership Rates by State

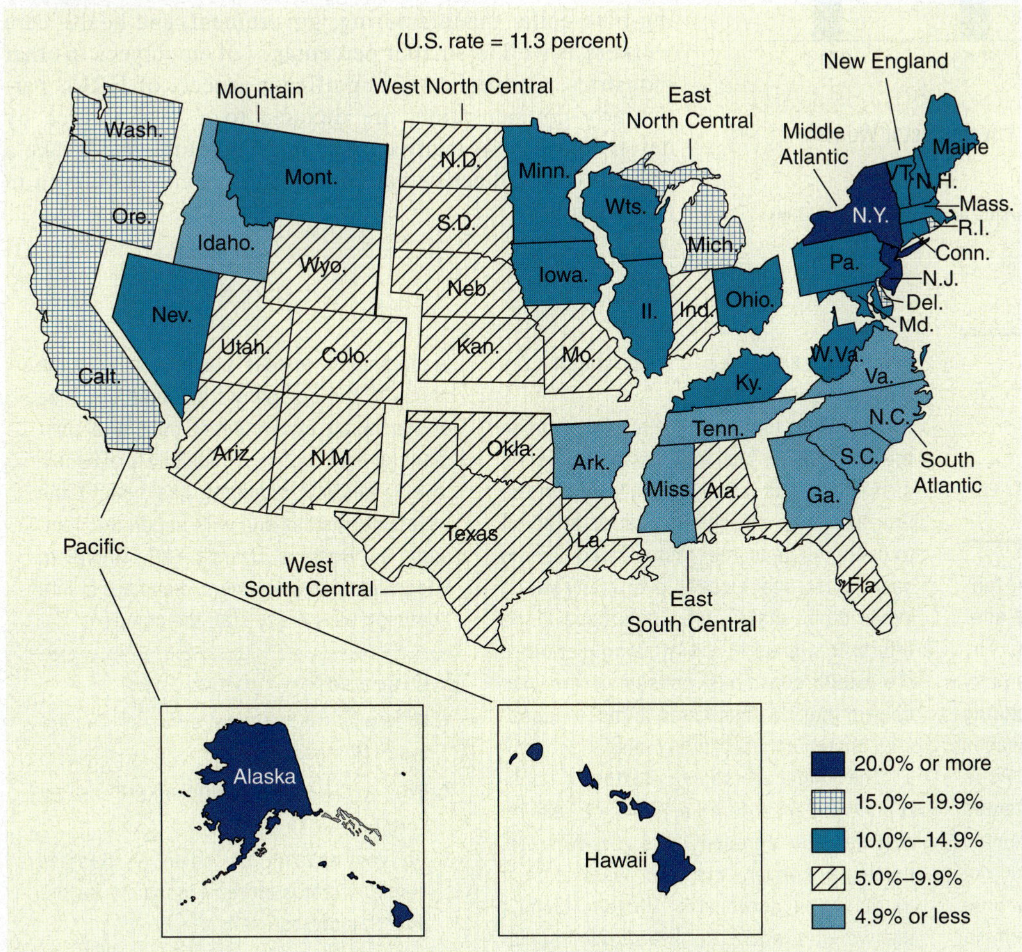

Source: Bureau of Labor Statistics U.S. Department of Labor, "Union Members—2012," www.bls.gov/news.release/pdf/union2.pdf.

MANAGING UNIONIZED EMPLOYEES

Employees who are dissatisfied with their working conditions or compensation have to negotiate with management to bring about change. Dealing with management on an individual basis is not always effective, however, so employees may organize themselves into **labor unions** to deal with employers and to achieve better pay, hours, and working conditions. Organized employees are backed by the power of a large group that can hire specialists to represent the entire union in its dealings with management. Union workers make significantly more than nonunion employees. The United States has a roughly 11.8 percent unionization rate. Figure 10.5 displays unionization rates by state. On average, the median usual weekly earnings of unionized full-time and salary workers are about $200 more than their nonunion counterparts.[32]

However, union growth has slowed in recent years, and

collective bargaining the negotiation process through which management and unions reach an agreement about compensation, working hours, and working conditions for the bargaining unit

labor contract the formal, written document that spells out the relationship between the union and management for a specified period of time—usually two or three years

picketing a public protest against management practices that involves union members marching and carrying antimanagement signs at the employer's plant or work site

strikes employee walkouts; one of the most effective weapons of labor unions

prospects for growth do not look good. One reason is that most blue-collar workers, the traditional members of unions, have already been organized. Factories have become more automated and need fewer blue-collar workers. The United States has shifted from a manufacturing to a service economy, further reducing the demand for blue-collar workers. Right-to-work laws in states such as Michigan limit the extent to which unions can require workers in certain industries to become members or pay dues. Figure 10.6 shows the decline in union membership among private-sector workers. Moreover, in response to foreign competition, U.S. companies are scrambling to find ways to become more productive and cost efficient. Job enrichment programs and participative management have blurred the line between management and workers. Because workers' say in the way plants are run is increasing, their need for union protection is decreasing.

FIGURE 10.6
Union Membership Rate for Private-Sector Workers

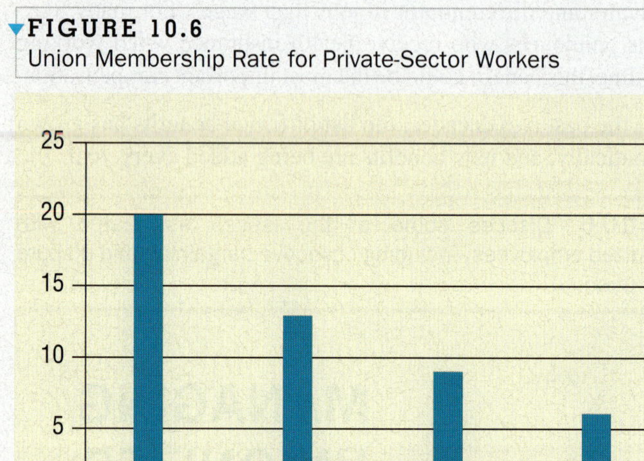

Source: Bloomberg BNA's 2012 Union Membership and Earnings Data Book.

Nonetheless, labor unions have been successful in organizing blue-collar manufacturing, government, and health care workers as well as smaller percentages of employees in other industries. Consequently, significant aspects of HRM, particularly compensation, are dictated to a large degree by union contracts at many companies. Therefore, we'll take a brief look at collective bargaining and dispute resolution in this section.

HOSTESS BRANDS SHUTTERS DOORS AFTER MEDIATION FAILS

After 82 years in existence, Hostess took action to liquidate the company after disagreements with worker unions. The company filed for bankruptcy in January 2012 and, as a measure for restructuring the company, reduced employees' wages and increased health care costs. As a result, employees became discontented with their work situation and commenced a strike. The company claimed it could not maintain production with so many workers on strike. When Hostess could not come to an agreement with one of the unions, the company announced it was shutting its doors for good.

Although the strike may have been the impetus for the immediate liquidation of Hostess, this is not the only reason the firm has been struggling. Failure to adapt to changing consumer tastes has dwindled sales of the snack cakes over many years. While other snack companies have made efforts to appeal to the growing market of the health-conscious consumer, analysts believe that Hostess failed to make necessary changes to its product mix.

The judge overseeing Hostess's bankruptcy request ordered a mediation session between the company and the workers' unions. However, the two were unable to reach an agreement. Hostess blames the workers' strike for the termination of the company, but the workers blame the leadership of Hostess, claiming that it is the cause of the company's downfall because of too much accumulated debt and poor management tactics. Thankfully for Twinkie lovers, another company has bought the assets of Hostess and will reopen the company as Hostess Brands LLC. However, according to management, plans are to hire nonunion workers to staff the company.[33]

Discussion Questions

1. Why was the workers' strike so damaging to Hostess?
2. Why was Hostess struggling prior to the workers' strike?
3. Do you believe the union or Hostess management is more responsible for the downfall of Hostess?

FIGURE 10.7
The Collective Bargaining Process

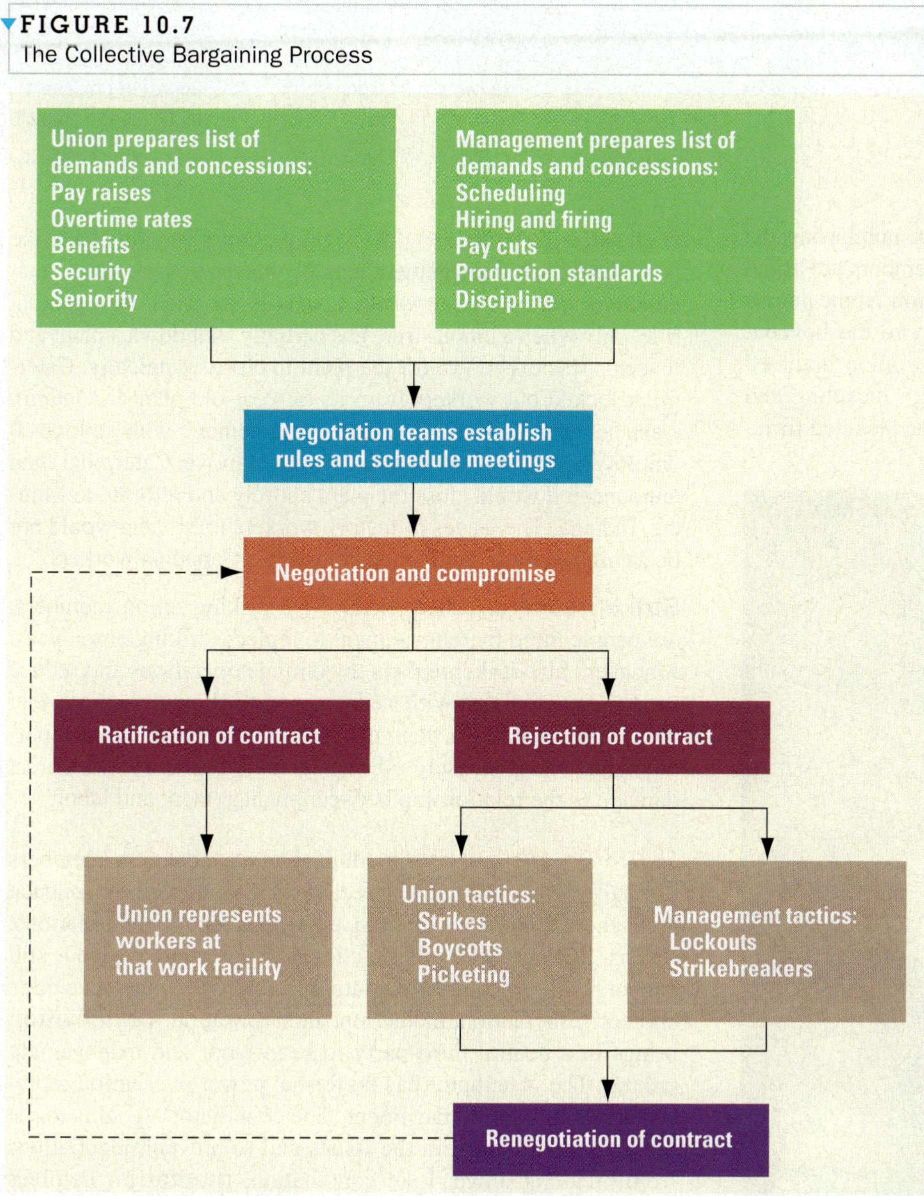

Collective Bargaining

Collective bargaining is the negotiation process through which management and unions reach an agreement about compensation, working hours, and working conditions for the bargaining unit (Figure 10.7). The objective of negotiations is to reach agreement about a **labor contract**, the formal, written document that spells out the relationship between the union and management for a specified period of time, usually two or three years.

In collective bargaining, each side tries to negotiate an agreement that meets its demands; compromise is frequently necessary. Management tries to negotiate a labor contract that permits the company to retain control over things like work schedules; the hiring and firing of workers; production standards; promotions, transfers, and separations; the span of management in each department; and discipline. Unions tend to focus on contract issues such as magnitude of wages; better pay rates for overtime, holidays, and undesirable shifts; scheduling of pay increases; and benefits. These issues will be spelled out in the labor contract, which union members will vote to either accept (and abide by) or reject.

Many labor contracts contain a *cost-of-living escalator* (or *adjustment*) *(COLA) clause,* which calls for automatic wage increases during periods of inflation to protect the "real" income of the employees. During tough economic times, unions may be forced to accept *givebacks*—wage and benefit concessions made to employers to allow them to remain competitive or, in some cases, to survive and continue to provide jobs for union workers.

Resolving Disputes

Sometimes, management and labor simply cannot agree on a contract. Most labor disputes are handled through collective bargaining or through grievance procedures. When these processes break down, however, either side may resort to more drastic measures to achieve its objectives.

Labor Tactics

Picketing is a public protest against management practices and involves union members marching (often waving antimanagement signs and placards) at the employer's plant or work site. Picketing workers hope that their signs will arouse sympathy for their demands from the public and from other unions. Picketing may occur as a protest or in conjunction with a strike.

Strikes (employee walkouts) are one of the most effective weapons labor has. By striking, a union makes carrying out the normal operations of a business difficult at best and impossible at worst. Strikes receive widespread publicity, but they remain a weapon of last resort. For example, the United Kingdom experienced significant disruption with closed schools, refusals to collect refuse, and the suspension of nonemergency hospital services after 2 million public-sector workers staged a strike. The workers were protesting against government announcements to change public-sector worker pension plans. Such disruption in daily operations is one reason both unions and companies try to avoid strikes.[34] The threat of a strike is often enough to get management to back down. In fact, the number of worker-days actually lost to strikes is lower than the number lost to the common cold.

boycott an attempt to keep people from purchasing the products of a company

lockout management's version of a strike, wherein a work site is closed so that employees cannot go to work

strikebreakers people hired by management to replace striking employees; called "scabs" by striking union members

conciliation a method of outside resolution of labor and management differences in which a third party is brought in to keep the two sides talking

mediation a method of outside resolution of labor and management differences in which the third party's role is to suggest or propose a solution to the problem

A **boycott** is an attempt to keep people from purchasing the products of a company. In a boycott, union members are asked not to do business with the boycotted organization. Some unions may even impose fines on members who ignore the boycott. To gain further support for their objectives, a union involved in a boycott may also ask the public—through picketing and advertising—not to purchase the products of the picketed firm.

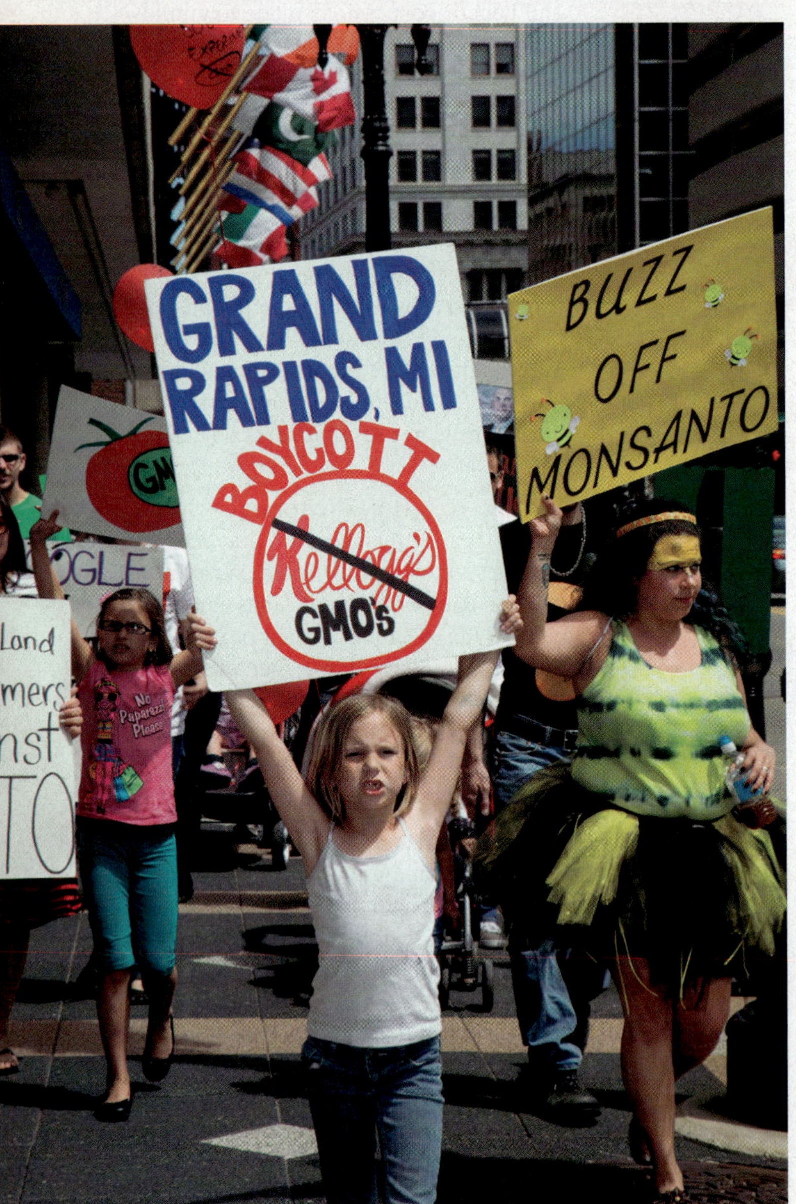

Protestors boycott Kellogg's and Monsanto for using or specializing in genetically modified food. The protestors hope their boycott will convince consumers to avoid genetically modified products.

Management Tactics

Management's version of a strike is the **lockout**; management actually closes a work site so that employees cannot go to work. Lockouts are used, as a general rule, only when a union strike has partially shut down a plant and it seems less expensive for the plant to close completely. Caterpillar locked out workers from its 62-year-old plant in Ontario, Canada, after failure to reach an agreement with unionized employees over wages. In a controversial move, Caterpillar then announced it would close the plant entirely and relocate to Muncie, Indiana. The wages of factory workers in Muncie would not be as high as those paid to the company's Canadian workers.[35]

Strikebreakers, called "scabs" by striking union members, are people hired by management to replace striking employees. Managers hire strikebreakers to continue operations and reduce the losses associated with strikes—and to show the unions that they will not bow to their demands. Strikebreaking is generally a last-resort measure for management because it does great damage to the relationship between management and labor.

Outside Resolution

Management and union members normally reach mutually agreeable decisions without outside assistance. Sometimes, though, even after lengthy negotiations, strikes, lockouts, and other tactics, management and labor still cannot resolve a contract dispute. In such cases, they have three choices: conciliation, mediation, and arbitration. **Conciliation** brings in a neutral third party to keep labor and management talking. The conciliator has no formal power over union representatives or over management. The conciliator's goal is to get both parties to focus on the issues and to prevent negotiations from breaking down. Like conciliation, **mediation** involves bringing in a neutral third party, but the mediator's role is to suggest or propose a solution to the problem. After employees from the American Licorice Co. went on strike, for instance, company officials met with union leaders at a federal mediator's office to work on the dispute.[36] Mediators have no formal power over either labor or management. With **arbitration**, a neutral third party is brought in to settle the dispute, but the arbitrator's solution is legally binding and enforceable. JP Morgan lost an arbitration case against American Century Investment Management and paid the firm $384 million in a settlement. The investment company maintained that JP Morgan had allegedly breached an agreement concerning the purchase of a retirement services business. JP Morgan continued to deny wrongdoing but complied with the arbitration decision.[37] Generally, arbitration takes place on a voluntary basis—management and labor must agree to it, and they usually split the cost (the arbitrator's fee and expenses) between them. Occasionally, management and labor submit to *compulsory* *arbitration,* in which an outside party (usually the federal government) requests arbitration as a means of eliminating a prolonged strike that threatens to disrupt the economy.

arbitration settlement of a labor/management dispute by a neutral third party whose solution is legally binding and enforceable

diversity the participation of different ages, genders, races, ethnicities, nationalities, and abilities in the workplace

THE IMPORTANCE OF WORKFORCE DIVERSITY

Customers, employees, suppliers—all the participants in the world of business—come in different ages, genders, races, ethnicities, nationalities, and abilities, a truth that business has come to label **diversity**. Understanding this diversity means recognizing and accepting differences as well as valuing the unique perspectives such differences can bring to the workplace.

LO 10-7 Describe the importance of diversity in the workforce.

The Characteristics of Diversity

When managers speak of diverse workforces, they typically mean differences in gender and race. Although gender and race are important characteristics of diversity, others are also important. We can divide these differences into primary and secondary characteristics of diversity. In the lower segment of Figure 10.8, age, gender, race, ethnicity, abilities, and sexual orientation represent *primary characteristics* of diversity that are inborn and cannot be changed. In the upper section of Figure 10.8 are eight *secondary characteristics* of diversity—work background, income, marital status, military experience, religious beliefs, geographic location, parental status, and education—which *can* be changed. We acquire, change, and discard them as we progress through our lives.

> "Once dominated by white men, today's workforce includes significantly more women, African Americans, Hispanics, and other minorities as well as disabled and older workers."

FIGURE 10.8
Characteristics of Diversity

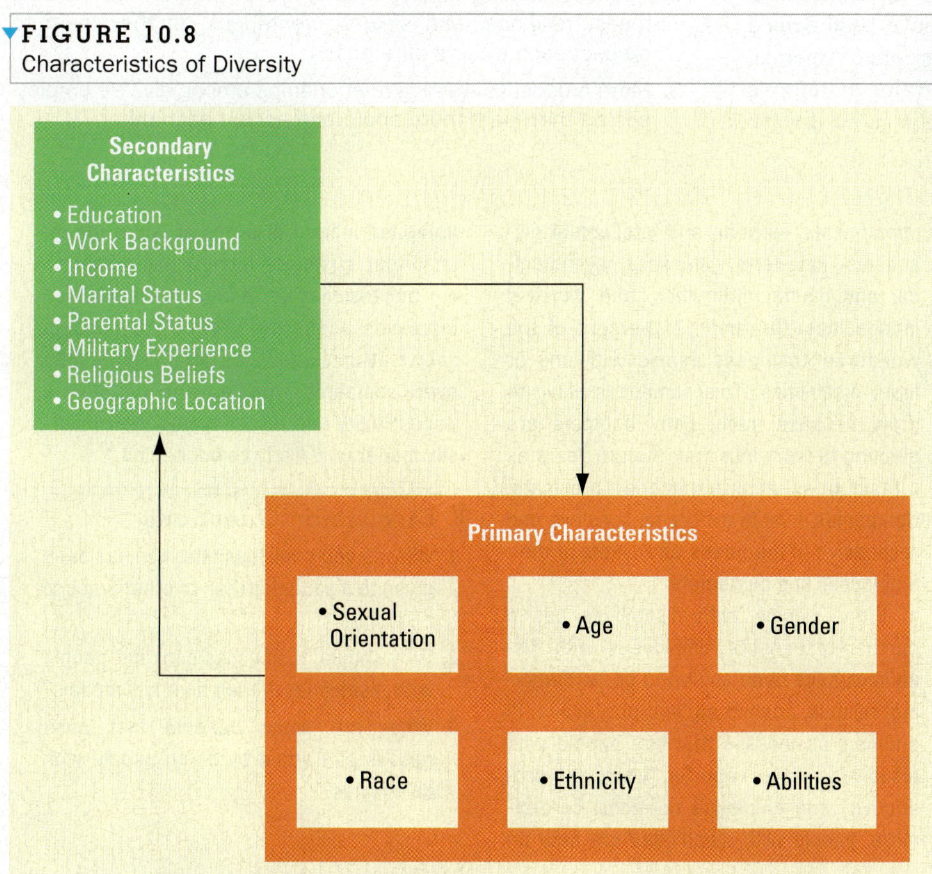

Source: Marilyn Loden and Judy B. Rosener, *Workforce America! Managing Employee Diversity as a Vital Resource,* © 1991, p. 20. Reprinted with permission of The McGraw-Hill Companies, Inc.

Defining characteristics of diversity as either primary or secondary enhances our understanding, but we must remember that each person is defined by the interrelation of all characteristics. In dealing with diversity in the workforce, managers must consider the complete person—not one or a few of a person's differences.

Why Is Diversity Important?

The U.S. workforce is becoming increasingly diverse. Once dominated by white men, today's workforce includes significantly more women, African Americans,

Some of the major benefits of diversity include a wider range of employee perspectives, greater innovation and creativity, and the ability to target a diverse customer base more effectively.

Hispanics, and other minorities as well as disabled and older workers. The Census Bureau has predicted that by 2042, minorities will make up more than 50 percent of the U.S. population.[38] These groups have traditionally faced discrimination and higher unemployment rates and have been denied opportunities to assume leadership roles in corporate America. Consequently, more and more companies are trying to improve HRM programs to recruit, develop, and retain more diverse employees to serve their diverse customers better. Some firms are providing special programs such as sponsored affinity groups, mentoring programs, and special career development opportunities. Kaiser Permanente has incorporated diversity into its goals and corporate strategies. Half of the company's board of directors consists of minorities, and more than one-third are women. Similar trends are seen with Kaiser Permanente's top management, with one-fourth consisting of women and more than one-third minorities. Diversity and equal rights are so important to Kaiser Permanente that it has established the Institute for Culturally Competent Care and the nine Centers of Excellence to pave the way for equal health care for all, including minorities, immigrants, and those with disabilities.[39] Table 10.9 shows the top 50 companies for minorities according to a study by DiversityInc. Effectively managing diversity in the workforce involves cultivating and valuing its benefits and minimizing its problems.

The Benefits of Workforce Diversity

There are a number of benefits to fostering and valuing workforce diversity, including the following:

1. More productive use of a company's human resources.
2. Reduced conflict among employees of different ethnicities, races, religions, and sexual orientations as they learn to respect each other's differences.
3. More productive working relationships among diverse employees as they learn more about and accept each other.

DISABILITIES CREATE DIVERSITY IN THE WORKPLACE

Diversity has been known to enhance productivity, increase responsiveness, widen the array of skill sets, and improve cultural understanding and sensitivity within the workplace. Although age, gender, ethnicity, and sexual orientation are often areas that managers target to increase office diversity, considerably less attention is given to workers with disabilities. Disability is most often thought of as a physical impairment or ailment, such as a person using a wheelchair. However, disability includes a much larger range of limitations, including hearing and vision impairments, learning and intellectual disabilities, long-term illnesses, psychological and mental difficulties, and physical incapacities. Currently, 21 percent of the workforce comprises people with one or more disabilities. This number is likely to grow because many baby boomers are electing to work into their mature years as a result of an uncertain economic climate. Companies must therefore be sensitive and responsive to the needs and wants of their employees and customers.

Hiring people with disabilities has a number of benefits. Employees with disabilities have been shown to be hardworking, reliable, committed, and productive. In addition, businesses that hire people with disabilities have reported improved productivity and employee relations. Furthermore, people with disabilities are both an untapped market in terms of labor and an important customer base. Finally, improving accessibility to those with disabilities increases accessibility for all, a concept known as universal access. Now more than ever, companies that do not incorporate accessibility and disability into their diversity models will likely be left behind.[40]

Discussion Questions

1. Why do you think less attention has been given to disabilities than to other types of diversity?
2. Why should businesses consider people with disabilities in their diversity models?
3. What are some benefits that businesses can attain by hiring people with disabilities?

affirmative action programs legally mandated plans that try to increase job opportunities for minority groups by analyzing the current pool of workers, identifying areas where women and minorities are underrepresented, and establishing specific hiring and promotion goals, with target dates, for addressing the discrepancy

4. Increased commitment to and sharing of organizational goals among diverse employees at all organizational levels.
5. Increased innovation and creativity as diverse employees bring new, unique perspectives to decision-making and problem-solving tasks.
6. Increased ability to serve the needs of an increasingly diverse customer base.[41]

Companies that do not value their diverse employees are likely to experience greater conflict as well as prejudice and discrimination. Among individual employees, for example, racial slurs and gestures, sexist comments, and other behaviors by co-workers harm the individuals at whom such behavior is directed. The victims of such behavior may feel hurt, depressed, or even threatened and suffer from lowered self-esteem, all of which harm their productivity and morale. In such cases, women and minority employees may simply leave the firm, wasting the time, money, and other resources spent on hiring and training them. When discrimination comes from a supervisor, employees may also fear for their jobs. A discriminatory atmosphere not only can harm productivity and increase turnover, but it may also subject a firm to costly lawsuits and negative publicity.

Astute businesses recognize that they need to modify their human resources management programs to target the needs of *all* their diverse employees as well as the needs of the firm itself. They realize that the benefits of diversity are long term in nature and come only to those organizations willing to make the commitment. Most important, as workforce diversity becomes a valued organizational asset, companies spend less time managing conflict and more time accomplishing tasks and satisfying customers, which is, after all, the purpose of business.

TABLE 10.9 The DiversityInc Top 50 Companies for Diversity

1. PricewaterhouseCoopers	26. Dell
2. Sodexo	27. Automatic Data Processing
3. Kaiser Permanente	28. General Mills
4. AT&T	29. Eli Lilly and Company
5. Procter & Gamble	30. Target
6. Ernst & Young	31. Bank of America
7. Kraft Foods	32. Starwood Hotels & Resorts Worldwide
8. Deloitte	33. Wells Fargo
9. Prudential Financial	34. WellPoint
10. Colgate-Palmolive	35. jcpenney
11. Johnson & Johnson	36. Booz Allen Hamilton
12. Accenture	37. Allstate Insurance Company
13. Novartis Pharmaceuticals Corporation	38. Medtronic
14. American Express	39. Verizon Communications
15. MasterCard Worldwide	40. Time Warner
16. Merck & Co.	41. Toyota Motor North America
17. IBM	42. Northrop Grumman
18. Cummins	43. Rockwell Collins
19. Health Care Service Corporation	44. Monsanto
20. Abbott	45. Chrysler Group
21. Marriott International	46. The Coca-Cola Company
22. KPMG	47. Capital One
23. CSX	48. Lockheed Martin
24. Aetna	49. Kellogg Company
25. Cox Communications	50. MetLife

Source: DiversityInc, "The DiversityInc Top 50 Companies for Diversity," *DiversityInc,* 2012, www.diversityinc.com/the-diversityinc-top-50-companies-for-diversity-2012/. © DiversityInc. Reproduced with permission.

Affirmative Action

Many companies strive to improve their working environment through **affirmative action programs**, legally mandated plans that try to increase job opportunities for minority groups by analyzing the current pool of workers, identifying areas where women and minorities are underrepresented, and establishing specific hiring and promotion goals along with target dates for meeting those goals to resolve the discrepancy. Affirmative action began in 1965 as Lyndon B. Johnson issued the first of a series of presidential directives. It was designed to make up for past hiring and promotion prejudices, to overcome workplace discrimination, and to provide equal employment opportunities for blacks and whites. Since then, minorities have made solid gains.

Legislation passed in 1991 reinforces affirmative action but prohibits organizations from setting hiring quotas that might result in reverse discrimination. Reverse discrimination occurs when a company's policies force it to consider only minorities or women instead of concentrating on hiring the person who is best qualified. More companies are arguing that affirmative action stifles their ability to hire the best employees, regardless of their minority status. Because of these problems, affirmative action became politically questionable.

TRENDS IN MANAGEMENT OF THE WORKFORCE

As unemployment reached 10 percent during the last recession, businesses laid off almost 9 million employees. Even after the recession and financial crisis, many firms reduced hiring and pushed workers to spend more time on the job for the same or less pay. Because of the economic uncertainty, this post-recession austerity has pervaded the workplace and inflated U.S. productivity. While companies are squeezing workers to cut costs, they are also drawing clear lines between workers and managers and are reducing privileges and benefits.

TEAM EXERCISE

Form groups. On monster.com, look up job descriptions for positions in business (account executive in advertising, marketing manager, human resources director, production supervisor, financial analyst, bank teller, and so on). What are the key requirements for the position that you have been assigned (education, work experience, language/computer skills, and so on)? Does the position announcement provide a thorough understanding of the job? Was any key information that you would have expected omitted? Report your findings to the class.

Many employees are developing grievances, claiming that they are being overworked. The number of lawsuits filed by employees against their employers rose 35 percent in a four-year period. Employee lawsuits involve, among other grievances, forcing employees to work off the clock and purposefully misclassifying jobs to eliminate overtime.[42]

The nature of the workplace is changing as well. The increasing use of smart phones and tablet computers is blurring the lines between leisure and work time, with some employers calling employees after hours.[43] Employees themselves are mixing work and personal time by using social media in the office. In fact, theft of time is the number-one ethical issue recorded by the Ethics Resource Center.[44]

SO YOU WANT TO WORK // in Human Resources /

Managing human resources is a challenging and creative facet of a business. It is the department that handles the recruiting, hiring, training, and firing of employees. Because of the diligence and detail required in hiring and the sensitivity required in firing, human resources managers have a broad skill set. Human resources, therefore, is vital to the overall functioning of the business because without the right staff, a firm will not be able to carry out its plans effectively. Like in basketball, a team is only as strong as its individual players, and those players must be able to work together and enhance strengths and downplay weaknesses. In addition, a good human resources manager can anticipate upcoming needs and changes in the business, hiring in line with the dynamics of the market and organization.

Once a good workforce is in place, human resources managers must ensure that employees are properly trained and oriented and that they clearly understand some elements of what the organization expects. Hiring new people is expensive, time consuming, and turbulent; thus, it is imperative for all employees to be carefully selected, trained, and motivated so that they will remain committed and loyal to the company. This is not an easy task, but it is one of the responsibilities of the human resources manager. Because even with references, a résumé, background checks, and an interview, it can be hard to tell how a person will fit in the organization—the HR manager needs to have skills to be able to anticipate how every individual will fit in. Human resources jobs include compensation, labor relations, benefits, training, ethics, and compliance managers. All of the tasks associated with the interface with hiring, developing, and maintaining employee motivation come into play in human resources management. Jobs are diverse and salaries will depend on responsibilities, education, and experience.

One of the major considerations for an HR manager is workforce diversity. A multicultural, multiethnic workforce consisting of men and women will help to bring a variety of viewpoints and improve the quality and creativity of organizational decision making. Diversity is an asset and can help a company from having blindspots or harmony in thought, background, and perspective, which stifles good team decisions. However, a diverse workforce can present some management challenges. Human resources management is often responsible for managing diversity training and compliance to make sure employees do not violate the ethical culture of the organization or break the law. Different people have different goals, motivations, and ways of thinking about issues that are informed by their culture, religion, and the people closest to them. No one way of thinking is more right or more wrong than others, and they are all valuable. A human resources manager's job can become very complicated, however, because of diversity. To be good at human resources, you should be aware of the value of differences, strive to be culturally sensitive, and ideally have a strong understanding and appreciation of different cultures and religions. Human resources managers' ability to manage diversity and those differences will affect their overall career success.

learn, practice, apply human resources management!

M: Business was developed just for you—students on the go who need information packaged in a concise yet interesting format with multiple learning options.

Check out the book's website to:

- Learn about the challenges of massive layoffs. (Solve the Dilemma)
- Consider ways to increase employee morale in difficult situations. (Solve the Dilemma)
- Understand the importance of diversity to an organization. (Build Your Skills)

While you are there, don't forget to enhance your skills. Practice and apply your knowledge, review the practice exercises, Student PPT® slides, and quizzes to review and apply chapter concepts. Additionally, *Connect® Business* is available for *M: Business*.

www.mhhe.com/ferrellm4e

This is requiring companies to come up with new policies that limit how employees can use social media in the workplace. Clearly, technology is changing the dynamics of the workplace in both positive and negative ways.

It is important for human resources managers to be aware of legal issues regarding worker rights. Strict criteria—such as having management responsibilities, having advanced degrees, or making more than $455 a week—determine whether an employee is exempt from overtime pay.[45] Interestingly, although it might currently be legal for employers to request an applicant's Facebook password, employees who rant about their employers on Facebook can receive some form of legal protection. Under the National Labor Relations Act of 1935, certain private-sector employees are allowed to complain about working conditions and pay—which seems to apply to social media sites as well. Threats, on the other hand, are not protected.[46] Hence, human resources managers should understand these issues to ensure that an employee is not wrongfully terminated.

Despite the grim outlook of the past few years, hiring trends appear to be on the rise. Companies are finding that as consumer demands rise, their current employees are hitting the limits of productivity, requiring firms to hire more workers.[47] This will require firms not only to know about relevant employee laws, but also to understand how benefits and employee morale can contribute to overall productivity. Many of the most successful firms have discovered ways to balance costs with the well-being of their employees. ■

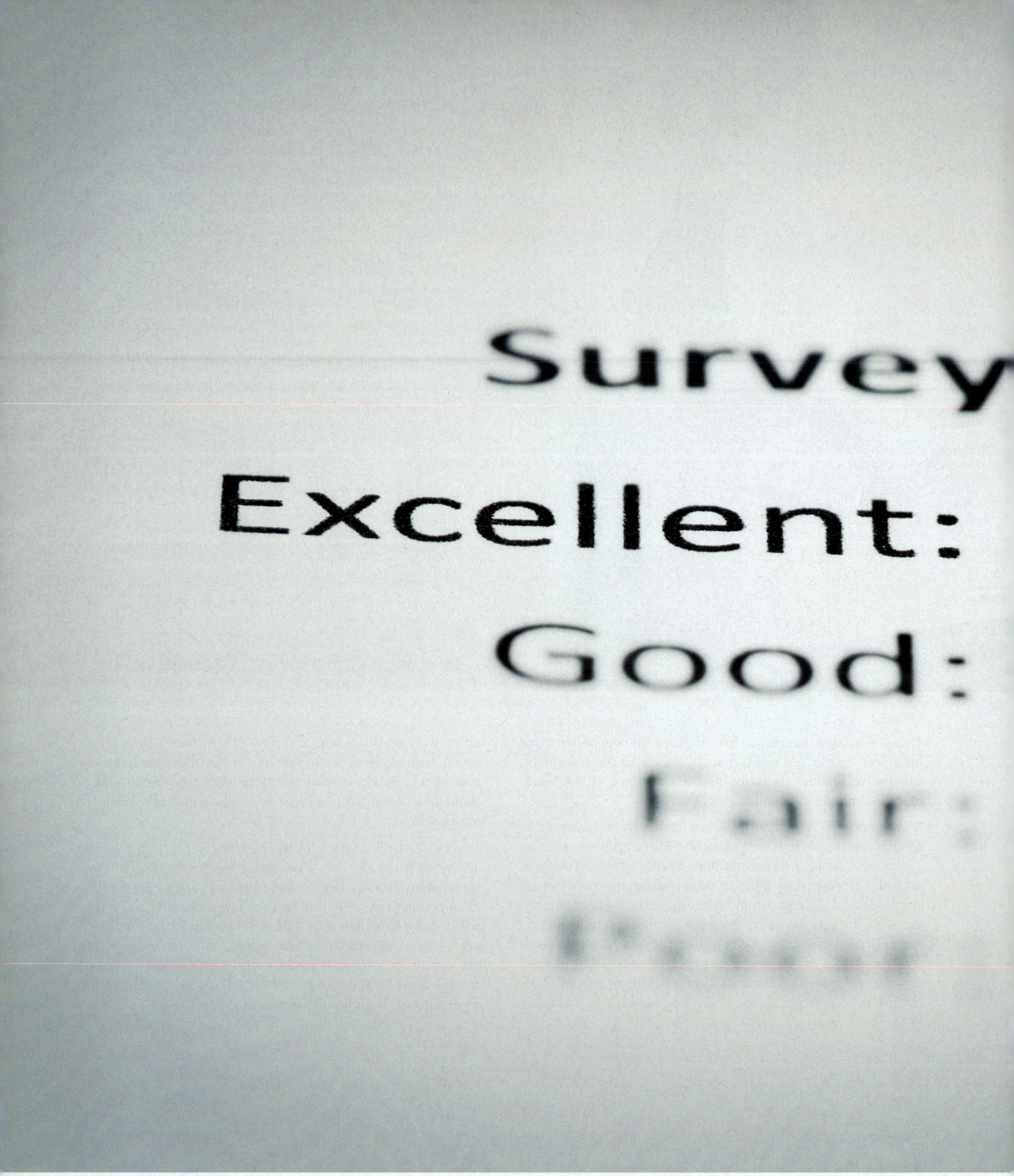
Survey
Excellent:
Good:
Fair:

chapter eleven

customer-driven marketing

Marketing involves planning and executing the development, pricing, promotion, and distribution of ideas, goods, and services to create exchanges that satisfy individual and organizational goals. These activities ensure that the products consumers want to buy are available at a price they are willing to pay and that consumers are provided with information about product features and availability. Organizations of all sizes and objectives engage in these activities.

In this chapter, we focus on the basic principles of marketing. First we define and examine the nature of marketing. Then we look at how marketers develop marketing strategies to satisfy the needs and wants of their customers. Next we discuss buying behavior and how marketers use research to determine what consumers want to buy and why. Finally, we explore the impact of the environment on marketing activities. ■

LEARNING OBJECTIVES

After reading this chapter, you will be able to:

- LO 11-1 Define marketing and describe the exchange process.
- LO 11-2 Specify the functions of marketing.
- LO 11-3 Explain the marketing concept and its implications for developing marketing strategies.
- LO 11-4 Examine the development of a marketing strategy, including market segmentation and marketing mix.
- LO 11-5 Investigate how marketers conduct marketing research and study buying behavior.
- LO 11-6 Summarize the environmental forces that influence marketing decisions.

LO 11-1 Define marketing and describe the exchange process.

NATURE OF MARKETING

A vital part of any business undertaking, **marketing** is a group of activities designed to expedite transactions by creating, distributing, pricing, and promoting goods, services, and ideas. These activities create value by allowing individuals and organizations to obtain what they need and want. A business cannot achieve its objectives unless it provides something that customers value. But just creating an innovative product that meets many users' needs isn't sufficient in today's volatile global marketplace. Products must be conveniently available, competitively priced, and uniquely promoted.

> "A business cannot achieve its objectives unless it provides something that customers value."

Marketing is an important part of a firm's overall strategy. It is the only business function that is directly responsible for creating sales and revenue. Other functional areas of the business—such as operations, finance, and all areas of management—must be coordinated with marketing decisions. Businesses try to respond to consumer wants and needs and to anticipate changes in the environment. Unfortunately, it is difficult to understand and predict what consumers want: Motives are often unclear; few principles can be applied consistently; and markets tend to fragment, each desiring customized products, new value, or better service.

It is important to note what marketing is not: It is not manipulating consumers to get them to buy products they do not want. It is not just selling and advertising; it is a systematic approach to satisfying consumers. Marketing focuses on the many activities—planning, pricing, promoting, and distributing products—that foster exchanges.

The Exchange Relationship

At the heart of all business is the **exchange**, the act of giving up one thing (money, credit, labor, goods) in return for

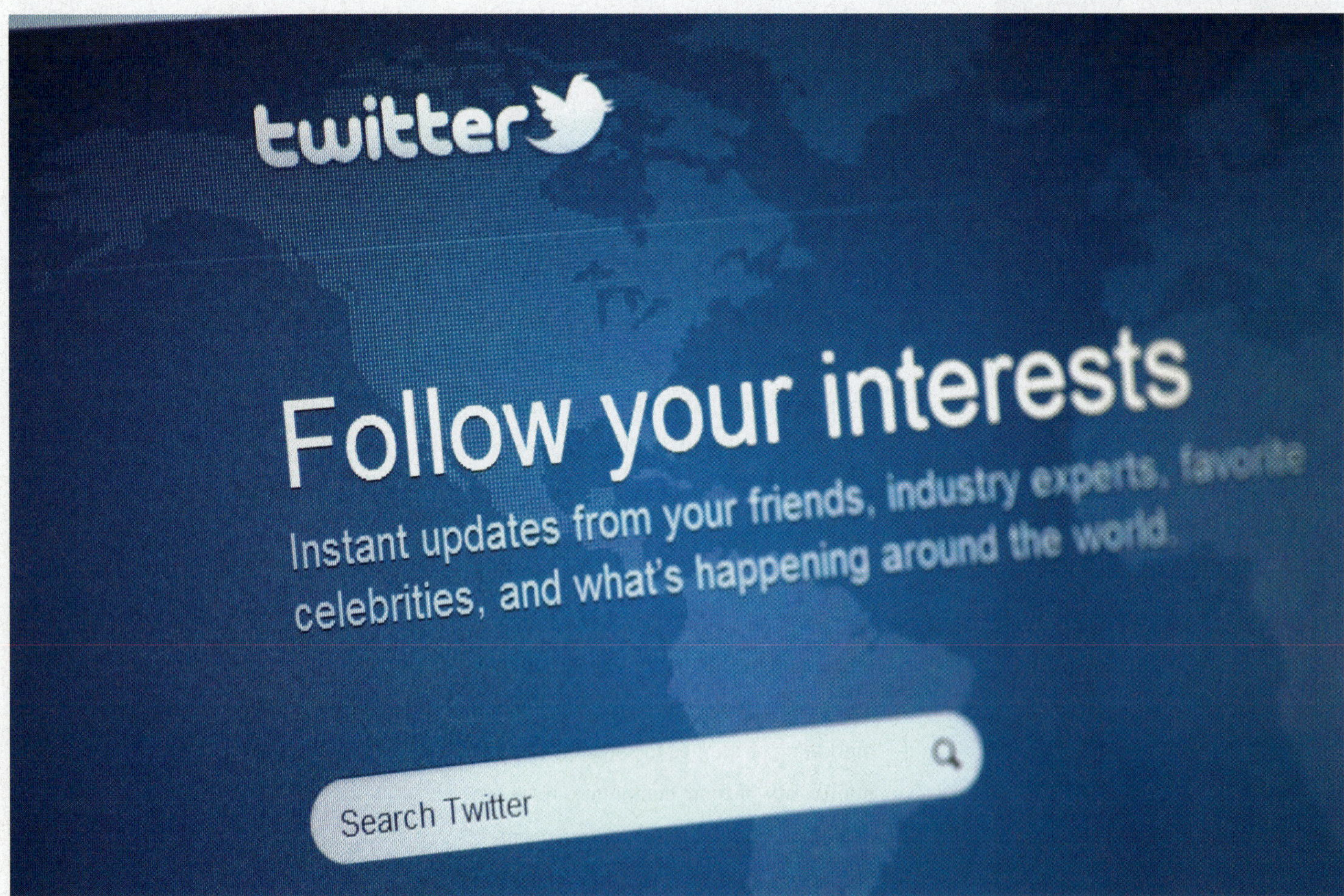

Companies find that communicating with customers through digital media sites can enhance customer relationships and create value for their brands.

marketing a group of activities designed to expedite transactions by creating, distributing, pricing, and promoting goods, services, and ideas

exchange the act of giving up one thing (money, credit, labor, goods) in return for something else (goods, services, or ideas)

FIGURE 11.1
The Exchange Relationship: Giving Up One Thing in Return for Another

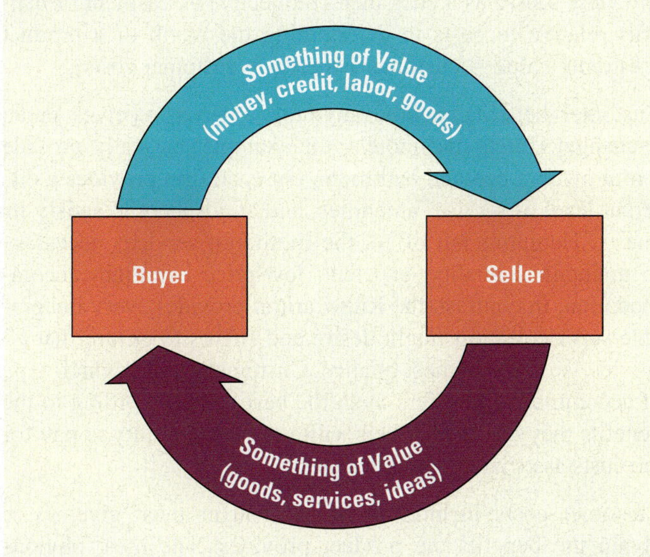

something else (goods, services, or ideas). Businesses exchange their goods, services, or ideas for money or credit supplied by customers in a voluntary *exchange relationship,* illustrated in Figure 11.1. The buyer must feel good about the purchase, or the exchange will not continue. If your cell phone service works everywhere, you will probably feel good about using its services. But if you have a lot of dropped calls, you will probably use another phone service next time.

For an exchange to occur, certain conditions are required. As indicated by the arrows in Figure 11.1, buyers and sellers must be able to communicate about the "something of value" available to each. An exchange does not necessarily take place just because buyers and sellers have something of value to exchange. Each participant must be willing to give up his or her respective "something of value" to receive the "something" held by the other. You are willing to exchange your "something of value"—your money or credit—for soft drinks, football tickets, or new shoes because you consider those products more valuable or more important than holding on to your cash or credit potential.

When you think of marketing products, you may think of tangible things—cars, MP3 players, or books, for example. What most consumers want, however, is a way to get a job done, solve a problem, or gain some enjoyment. You may purchase a Hoover vacuum cleaner not because you want a vacuum cleaner but because you want clean carpets. Starbucks serves coffee drinks at a premium price, providing convenience, quality, and an inviting environment. Therefore, the tangible product itself may not be as important as the image or the benefits associated with the product. This intangible "something of value" may be capability gained from using a product or the image evoked by it, or even the brand name. Good examples of brand names that are easy to remember include Avon's Skin So Soft, Tide detergent, and the Ford Mustang. The label or brand name may also offer the added bonus of being a conversation piece in a social environment, such as Dancing Bull or Smoking Loon wine.

LO 11-2 Specify the functions of marketing.

Functions of Marketing

Marketing focuses on a complex set of activities that must be performed to accomplish objectives and generate exchanges. These activities include buying, selling, transporting, storing, grading, financing, marketing research, and risk taking.

Buying Everyone who shops for products (consumers, stores, businesses, governments) decides whether and what to buy. A marketer must understand buyers' needs and desires to determine what products to make available.

Selling The exchange process is expedited through selling. Marketers usually view selling as a persuasive activity that is accomplished through promotion (advertising, personal selling, sales promotion, publicity, and packaging).

Transporting Transporting is the process of moving products from the seller to the buyer. Marketers focus on transportation costs and services.

Storing Like transporting, storing is part of the physical distribution of products and includes warehousing goods. Warehouses hold some products for lengthy periods to create time utility. Time utility has to do with being able to satisfy demand in a timely manner. This especially pertains to a seasonal good such as orange juice. Fresh oranges are available for only a few months annually, but consumers demand juice throughout the entire year. Sellers must arrange for cold storage of orange juice concentrate so that they can maintain a steady supply all of the time.

Grading Grading refers to standardizing products by dividing them into subgroups and displaying and labeling them so that consumers clearly understand their nature and quality. Many products, such as meat, steel, and fruit, are graded according to a set of standards that often are established by the state or federal government.

Financing For many products, especially large items such as automobiles, refrigerators, and new homes, the marketer arranges credit to expedite the purchase.

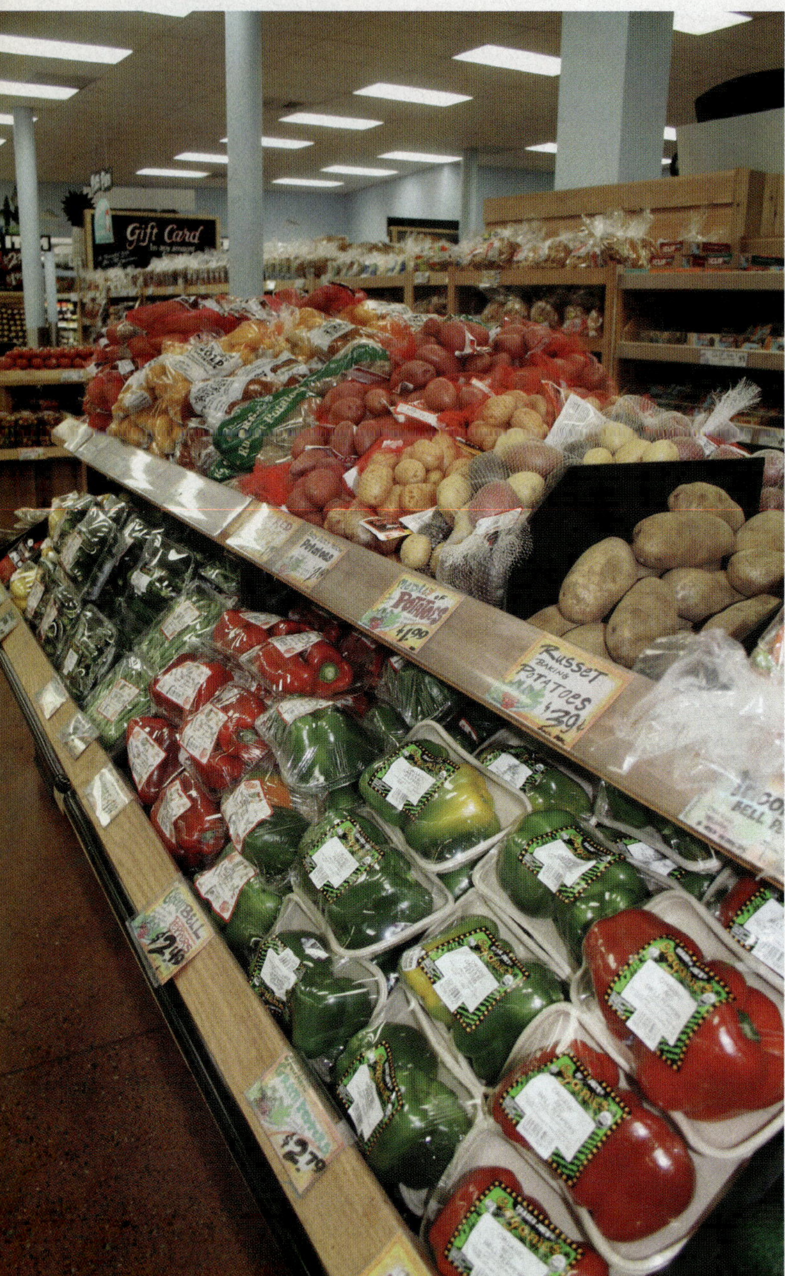

Trader Joe's, which sells many lines of organic and natural food products, is often thought to have better deals than some of its competitiors. The grocery chain attempts to meet consumer demands for high-quality food at reasonable prices.

Marketing Research Through research, marketers ascertain the need for new goods and services. By gathering information regularly, marketers can detect new trends and changes in consumer tastes.

Risk Taking Risk is the chance of loss associated with marketing decisions. Developing a new product creates a chance of loss if consumers do not like it enough to buy it. Spending money to hire a sales force or to conduct marketing research also involves risk. The implication of risk is that most marketing decisions result in either success or failure.

Creating Value with Marketing[1]

Value is an important element of managing long-term customer relationships and implementing the marketing concept. We view **value** as a customer's subjective assessment of benefits relative to costs in determining the worth of a product (customer value = customer benefits − customer costs).

Customer benefits include anything a buyer receives in an exchange. Hotels and motels, for example, basically provide a room with a bed and bathroom, but each firm provides a different level of service, amenities, and atmosphere to satisfy its guests. Hampton Inn offers the minimum services necessary to maintain a quality, efficient, low-price overnight accommodation. In contrast, the Ritz-Carlton provides every imaginable service a guest might desire and strives to ensure that all service is of the highest quality. Customers judge which type of accommodation offers them the best value according to the benefits they desire and their willingness and ability to pay for the costs associated with the benefits.

Customer costs include anything a buyer must give up to obtain the benefits the product provides. The most obvious cost is the monetary price of the product, but nonmonetary costs can be equally important in a customer's determination of value. Two nonmonetary costs are the time and effort customers expend to find and purchase desired products. To reduce time and effort, a company can increase product availability, thereby making it more convenient for buyers to purchase the firm's products. Another nonmonetary cost is risk, which can be reduced by offering good basic warranties for an additional charge. Another risk-reduction strategy is increasingly popular in today's catalog/telephone/Internet shopping environment. L.L. Bean, for example, uses a guarantee to reduce the risk involved in ordering merchandise from its catalogs.

In developing marketing activities, it is important to recognize that customers receive benefits based on their experiences. For example, many computer buyers consider services such as fast delivery, ease of installation, technical advice, and training assistance to be important elements of the product. Customers also derive benefits from the act of shopping and selecting products. These benefits can be affected by the atmosphere or environment of a store, such as Red Lobster's nautical/seafood theme.

LO 11-3 Explain the marketing concept and its implications for developing marketing strategies.

The Marketing Concept

A basic philosophy that guides all marketing activities is the **marketing concept**, the idea that an organization should try to satisfy customers' needs through coordinated activities that also allow it to achieve its own goals. According to the marketing concept, a business must find out what consumers desire and then develop the good, service, or idea that fulfills their needs or wants. The business must then get the product to the customer. In addition, the business must continually alter, adapt, and develop products to keep pace with changing consumer needs and wants. For instance, Domino's offers pizza with a gluten-free crust. With 6 to 8 percent of consumers on a gluten-free diet, many restaurants and fast-food companies are developing new food products to meet the needs of this growing segment.[2] To remain competitive, companies must be prepared to add to or adapt their product lines to satisfy customers' desires for new fads or changes in eating habits. Each business must determine how best to implement the marketing concept, given its own goals and resources.

Although customer satisfaction is the goal of the marketing concept, a business must also achieve its own objectives, such as boosting productivity, reducing costs, or achieving a percentage of a specific market. If it does not, it will not survive. For example, Dell could sell computers for $50 and give customers a lifetime guarantee, which would be great for customers but not so great for Dell. Obviously, the company must strike a balance between achieving organizational objectives and satisfying customers.

value a customer's subjective assessment of benefits relative to costs in determining the worth of a product

marketing concept the idea that an organization should try to satisfy customers' needs through coordinated activities that also allow it to achieve its own goals

> "To implement the marketing concept, a firm must have good information about what consumers want, adopt a consumer orientation, and coordinate its efforts throughout the entire organization."

Trying to determine customers' true needs is increasingly difficult because no one fully understands what motivates people to buy things. However, Estée Lauder, founder of her namesake cosmetics company, had a pretty good idea. When a prestigious store in Paris rejected her perfume in the 1960s, she "accidentally" dropped a bottle on the floor where nearby customers could get a whiff of it. So many asked about the scent that Galeries Lafayette was obliged to place an order. Lauder ultimately built an empire using then-unheard-of tactics such as free samples and gifts with purchases to market her "jars of hope."[3]

To implement the marketing concept, a firm must have good information about what consumers want, adopt a consumer orientation, and coordinate its efforts throughout the entire organization; otherwise, it may be awash with goods, services, and ideas that consumers do not want or need. Successfully implementing the marketing concept requires a business to view the

CHINESE BRANDS STRUGGLE TO LIFT QUALITY IMAGE

How do low cost and high quality come together to make a brand image? Not very well when your emphasis is on low cost. Chinese brands are in a perception predicament with U.S. consumers. Americans view products made in China as high quality if they are designed in the United States, but if they are both designed and manufactured in China, the perception of the product's quality is generally negative. Interestingly, Americans will respond positively to the quality of Chinese products when asked to assess them individually but not when asked about Chinese products. Furthermore, people will rate the quality of Chinese products highly if they don't realize that they were designed in China.

What can Chinese companies do to change this perception? Marketing and innovation are the key concepts. Chinese companies tend to take a follow-the-leader approach when it comes to creating products, focusing on a manufacturing or sales orientation rather than a market orientation. Instead of conveying to the American consumer something about the quality of their products and how it is something that could be of use to them, Chinese companies have tended to emphasize the fact that their items are low cost. When consumers see a low price without information about the quality of the product, they tend to perceive it as low quality. This is especially true when it comes to household appliances and electronics that are expected to have a long life. China also needs to work on letting the customer know that the quality of its products is guaranteed even after purchase. Implementing these aspects into its marketing mix could make Chinese brands top competitors in the international market.[4]

Discussion Questions

1. Why are Chinese brands struggling to break into the American market?
2. Why are consumer perceptions of brands so hard to change?
3. What might be some steps Chinese brands can take to improve perceptions of their brands' quality?

market orientation an approach requiring organizations to gather information about customer needs, share that information throughout the firm, and use that information to help build long-term relationships with customers

customer's perception of value as the ultimate measure of work performance and improving value, and the rate at which this is done, as the measure of success.[5] Everyone in the organization who interacts with customers—*all* customer-contact employees—must know what customers want. They are selling ideas, benefits, philosophies, and experiences—not just goods and services.

Someone once said that if you build a better mousetrap, the world will beat a path to your door. Suppose you do build a better mousetrap. What will happen? Actually, consumers are not likely to beat a path to your door because the market is so competitive. A coordinated effort by everyone involved with the mousetrap is needed to sell the product. Your company must reach out to customers and tell them about your mousetrap, especially how your mousetrap works better than those offered by competitors. If you do not make the benefits of your product widely known, in most cases, it will not be successful. One reason that Apple is so successful is its stores. Apple's 400 national and international retail stores market computers and electronics in a way unlike any other computer manufacturer or retail establishment. The upscale stores, located in high-rent shopping districts, show off Apple's products in modern, spacious settings to encourage consumers to try new things—like making a movie on a computer. The stores also incorporate its products into the selling process. Not only are consumers allowed to try out or "test drive" Apple's tech products, but the company has also begun to install iPad stations in its stores equipped with a customer service app to answer customer questions.[6] So for some companies, like Apple Inc., you need to create stores to sell your product to consumers. You could also find stores that are willing to sell your product to consumers for you. In either situation, you must implement the marketing concept by making a product with satisfying benefits and making it available and visible.

Orville Wright said that an airplane is "a group of separate parts flying in close formation." This is what most companies are trying to accomplish: They are striving for a team effort to deliver the right good or service to customers. A breakdown at any point in the organization—whether it be in production, purchasing, sales, distribution, or advertising—can result in lost sales, lost revenue, and dissatisfied customers.

Evolution of the Marketing Concept

The marketing concept may seem like the obvious approach to running a business and building relationships with customers. However, businesspeople are not always focused on customers when they create and operate businesses. Many companies fail to grasp the importance of customer relationships and fail to implement customer strategies. A firm's marketing department needs to share information about customers and their desires with the entire organization. Our society and economic system have changed over time, and marketing has become more important as markets have become more competitive.

The Production Orientation During the second half of the 19th century, the Industrial Revolution was well under way in the United States. New technologies, such as electricity, railroads, internal combustion engines, and mass-production techniques, made it possible to manufacture goods with ever increasing efficiency. Together with new management ideas and ways of using labor, products poured into the marketplace, where demand for manufactured goods was strong.

The Sales Orientation By the early part of the 20th century, supply caught up with and then exceeded demand, and businesspeople began to realize they would have to "sell" products to buyers. During the first half of the 20th century, businesspeople viewed sales as the primary means of increasing profits in what has become known as a sales orientation. Those who adopted the sales orientation perspective believed the most important marketing activities were personal selling and advertising. Today some people still inaccurately equate marketing with a sales orientation.

The Market Orientation By the 1950s, some businesspeople began to recognize that even efficient production and extensive promotion did not guarantee sales. These businesses, and many others since, found that they must first determine what customers want and then produce it, rather than making the products first and then trying to persuade customers that they need them. Managers at General Electric first suggested that the marketing concept was a companywide philosophy of

"Our society and economic system have changed over time, and marketing has become more important as markets have become more competitive."

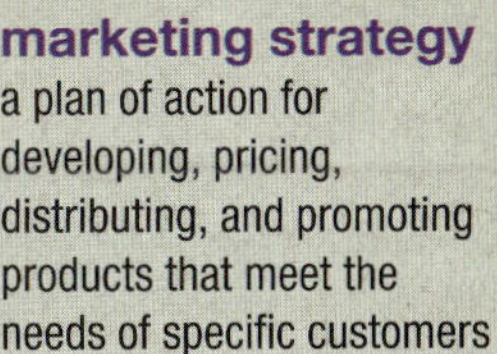
marketing strategy a plan of action for developing, pricing, distributing, and promoting products that meet the needs of specific customers

The Marquis Jet Card allows business travelers to have more flexible location-specific travel options at a much lower cost on NetJets-operated planes than that of operating a corporate jet or chartering a small plane.

doing business. As more organizations realized the importance of satisfying customers' needs, U.S. businesses entered the marketing era, one of market orientation.

A **market orientation** requires organizations to gather information about customer needs, share that information throughout the entire firm, and use it to help build long-term relationships with customers. Top executives, marketing managers, nonmarketing managers (those in production, finance, human resources, and so on), and customers all become mutually dependent and cooperate in developing and carrying out a market orientation. Nonmarketing managers must communicate with marketing managers to share information important to understanding the customer. Consider the 122-year history of Wrigley's gum. In 1891, the gum was given away to promote sales of baking powder (the company's original product). The gum was launched as its own product in 1893, and after four generations of Wrigley family CEOs, the company continues to reinvent itself and focus on consumers. Eventually, the family made the decision to sell the company to Mars. Wrigley now functions as a stand-alone subsidiary of Mars. The deal combined such popular brands as Wrigley's gums and Life Savers with Mars' M&M's, Snickers, and Skittles to form the world's largest confectionary company.

Trying to assess what customers want, which is difficult to begin with, is further complicated by the rate at which trends, fashions, and tastes can change. Businesses today want to satisfy customers and build meaningful long-term relationships with them. It is more efficient and less expensive for the company to retain existing customers and even increase the amount of business each customer provides the organization than to find new customers. Most companies' success depends on increasing the amount of repeat business; therefore, relationship building between company and customer is key. Many companies are turning to technologies associated with customer relationship management to help build relationships and boost business with existing customers.

Although it might be easy to dismiss customer relationship management as time-consuming and expensive, this mistake could destroy a company. Customer relationship management (CRM) is important in a market orientation because it can result in loyal and profitable customers. Without loyal customers, businesses would not survive; therefore, achieving the full profit potential of each customer relationship should be the goal of every marketing strategy. At the most basic level, profits can be obtained through relationships by acquiring new customers, enhancing the profitability of existing customers, and extending the duration of customer relationships. The profitability of loyal customers throughout their relationship with the company (their lifetime customer value) should not be underestimated. For instance, Pizza Hut has a lifetime customer value of approximately $8,000, whereas Cadillac's lifetime customer value is approximately $332,000.[7]

Communication remains a major element of any strategy to develop and manage long-term customer relationships. By providing multiple points of interactions with customers—that is, websites, telephone, fax, e-mail, and personal contact—companies can personalize customer relationships.[8] Like many online retailers, Amazon.com stores and analyzes purchase data in an attempt to understand each customer's interests. This information helps the online retailer improve its ability to satisfy individual customers and thereby increase sales of books, music, movies, and other products to each customer. The ability to identify individual customers allows marketers to shift their focus from targeting groups of similar customers to increasing their share of an individual customer's purchases. Regardless of the medium through which communication occurs, customers should ultimately be the drivers of marketing strategy because they understand what they want. Customer relationship management systems should ensure that marketers listen to customers to respond to their needs and concerns and build long-term relationships.

LO 11-4 Examine the development of a marketing strategy, including market segmentation and marketing mix.

DEVELOPING A MARKETING STRATEGY

To implement the marketing concept and customer relationship management, a business needs to develop and maintain a **marketing strategy**, a plan of action for developing, pricing,

market a group of people who have a need, purchasing power, and the desire and authority to spend money on goods, services, and ideas

target market a specific group of consumers on whose needs and wants a company focuses its marketing efforts

total-market approach an approach whereby a firm tries to appeal to everyone and assumes that all buyers have similar needs

market segmentation a strategy whereby a firm divides the total market into groups of people who have relatively similar product needs

market segment a collection of individuals, groups, or organizations who share one or more characteristics and thus have relatively similar product needs and desires

distributing, and promoting products that meet the needs of specific customers. This definition has two major components: selecting a target market and developing an appropriate marketing mix to satisfy that target market.

Selecting a Target Market

A **market** is a group of people who have a need, purchasing power, and the desire and authority to spend money on goods, services, and ideas. A **target market** is a more specific group of consumers on whose needs and wants a company focuses its marketing efforts. For instance, Lego focused on young boys as the target market for its products. This narrower strategic focus allowed the company to tailor products to attract this demographic with much success: Revenues have increased 105 percent since 2006. In the past few years, the company has performed market studies on girls to reposition its brand to attract both genders.[9]

Marketing managers may define a target market as a relatively small number of people within a larger market, or they may define it as the total market (Figure 11.2). Rolls Royce, for example, targets its products at a very exclusive, high-income market—people who want the ultimate in prestige in an automobile. On the other hand, Ford Motor Company manufactures a variety of vehicles including Lincolns, Mercurys, and Ford Trucks to appeal to varied tastes, needs, and desires.

Some firms use a **total-market approach**, in which they try to appeal to everyone and assume that all buyers have similar needs and wants. Sellers of salt, sugar, and many agricultural products use a total-market approach because everyone is a potential consumer of these products. Most firms, though, use **market segmentation** and divide the total market into groups of people. A **market segment** is a collection of individuals, groups, or organizations who share one or more characteristics and thus have relatively similar product needs and desires. Women are the largest market segment, with 51 percent of the U.S. population. At the household level, segmentation can identify each woman's social attributes, culture, and stages in life to determine preferences and needs.

Another market segment on which many marketers are focusing is the growing Hispanic population. MillerCoors sponsored a Mexican soccer league and placed more Spanish on its cartons and labels. Its rival Anheuser-Busch InBev developed Spanish advertisements and sponsored Cuban-American rapper Pitbull. The companies hope to create relationships with Hispanic consumers to gain their loyalty.[10] One of the challenges for marketers in the future will be to address an increasingly racially diverse United States effectively. The minority population of the United States is about 112 million (36 percent of the total population).[11] In future

FIGURE 11.2
Target Market Strategies

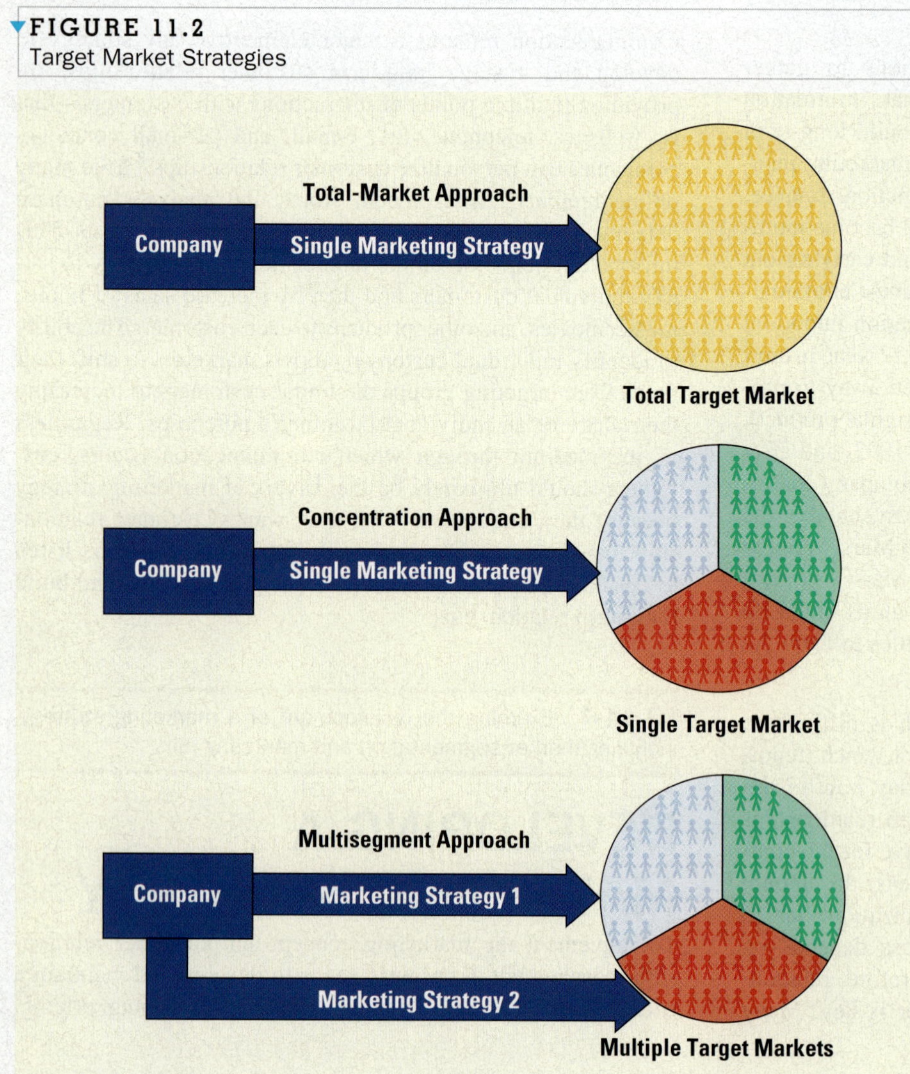

▼ TABLE 11.1 U.S. Buying Power Statistics by Race (billions)

	1990	2000	2010	2015
Total	$4,200	$7,300	$11,100	$14,100
White	3,800	6,350	9,400	11,800
Black	316	600	957	1,200
American Indian	19.6	40	67.7	90.4
Asian	117	274	544	775
Multiracial	N/A	58.4	115.5	164.6
Hispanic*	210	499	1,000	1,500

*Because Hispanic is an ethnic group, they may belong to any of the other races.

Sources: Jeffrey M. Humphreys, "The Multicultural Economy 2009," *GBEC* 69 (3rd Quarter, 2009), p. 3, www.terry.uga.edu/selig/docs/GBEC0903q.pdf; Jeffrey M. Humphreys, *The Multicultural Economy 2010*, www.diversityresources.com/att/pdfs/Multicultural%20Economy%202010.pdf.

> A firm can generate a large sales volume by penetrating a single market segment deeply.

decades, the purchasing power of minority market segments is set to grow by leaps and bounds. Table 11.1 shows the buying power and market share percentages of different market segments. Companies will have to learn how to reach these growing segments more effectively. Companies use market segmentation to focus their efforts and resources on specific target markets so that they can develop a productive marketing strategy. Two common approaches to segmenting markets are the concentration approach and the multisegment approach.

Zazzle

Market Segmentation Approaches In the **concentration approach**, a company develops one marketing strategy for a single market segment. The concentration approach allows a firm to specialize, focusing all its efforts on the one market segment. Porsche, for example, directs all its marketing efforts toward high-income individuals who want to own high-performance vehicles. A firm can generate a large sales volume by penetrating a single market segment deeply. The concentration approach may be especially effective when a firm can identify and develop products for a segment ignored by other companies in the industry.

In the **multisegment approach**, the marketer aims its marketing efforts at two or more segments, developing a marketing strategy for each. Many firms use a multisegment approach that includes different advertising messages for different segments. Companies also develop product variations to appeal to different market segments. The U.S. Postal Service, for example, offers personalized stamps, and Mars Inc. sells personalized M&M's through mymms.com. Many other firms also attempt to use a multisegment approach to market segmentation, such as the manufacturer of Raleigh bicycles, which has designed separate marketing strategies for racers, tourers, commuters, and children.

concentration approach a market segmentation approach whereby a company develops one marketing strategy for a single market segment

multisegment approach a market segmentation approach whereby the marketer aims its efforts at two or more segments, developing a marketing strategy for each

Niche marketing is a narrow market segment focus when efforts are on one small, well-defined group that has a unique, specific set of needs. Niche segments are usually very small compared to the total market for the products. Many airlines cater to first-class flyers, who comprise only 10 percent of international air travelers. To meet the needs of these elite customers, airlines include special perks along with the spacious seats. To take advantage of the growing market niche for gluten-free products, Anheuser-Busch launched Michelob Ultra Light Cider, a gluten-free beer.[12]

For a firm to use a concentration or multisegment approach to market segmentation successfully, several requirements must be met:

1. Consumers' needs for the product must be heterogeneous.
2. The segments must be identifiable and divisible.
3. The total market must be divided in a way that allows estimated sales potential, cost, and profits of the segments to be compared.
4. At least one segment must have enough profit potential to justify developing and maintaining a special marketing strategy.
5. The firm must be able to reach the chosen market segment with a particular market strategy.

marketing mix the four marketing activities—product, price, promotion, and distribution—that the firm can control to achieve specific goals within a dynamic marketing environment

price a value placed on an object exchanged between a buyer and a seller

distribution making products available to customers in the quantities desired

Bases for Segmenting Markets Companies segment markets on the basis of several variables:

1. *Demographic*—age, sex, race, ethnicity, income, education, occupation, family size, religion, social class. These characteristics are often closely related to customers' product needs and purchasing behavior, and they can be readily measured. For example, deodorants are often segmented by sex: Secret and Soft & Dri for women; Old Spice and Mennen for men.
2. *Geographic*—climate, terrain, natural resources, population density, subcultural values. These influence consumers' needs and product usage. Climate, for example, influences consumers' purchases of clothing, automobiles, heating and air conditioning equipment, and leisure activity equipment.
3. *Psychographic*—personality characteristics, motives, lifestyles. Soft-drink marketers provide their products in several types of packaging, including two-liter bottles and cases of cans, to satisfy different lifestyles and motives.
4. *Behavioristic*—some characteristic of the consumer's behavior toward the product. These characteristics commonly involve some aspect of product use.

?

DID YOU KNOW?

During its first year of operation, sales of Coca-Cola averaged just nine drinks per day for total first-year sales of $50. Today, Coca-Cola products are consumed at the rate of 1.8 billion drinks per day.[13]

Developing a Marketing Mix

The second step in developing a marketing strategy is to create and maintain a satisfying marketing mix. The **marketing mix** refers to four marketing activities—product, price, distribution, and promotion—that the firm can control to achieve specific goals within a dynamic marketing environment (Figure 11.3). The customer or the target market is the central focus of all marketing activities.

FIGURE 11.3
The Marketing Mix: Product, Price, Promotion, and Distribution

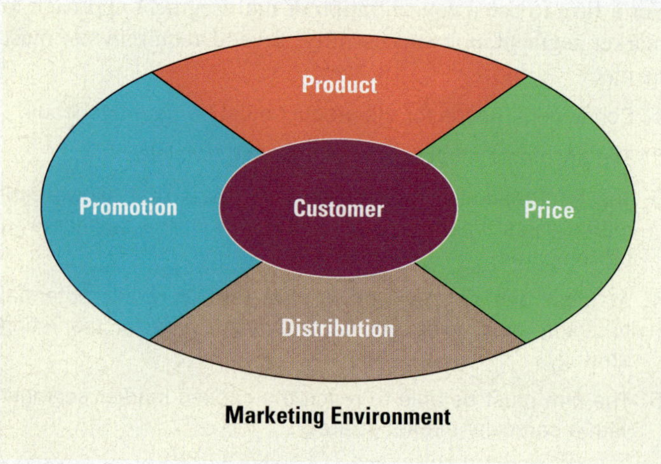

Product A product—whether a good, a service, an idea, or some combination—is a complex mix of tangible and intangible attributes that provide satisfaction and benefits. A *good* is a physical entity you can touch. A Porsche Cayenne, a Hewlett-Packard printer, and a kitten available for adoption at an animal shelter are examples of goods. A *service* is the application of human and mechanical efforts to people or objects to provide intangible benefits to customers. Air travel, dry cleaning, haircuts, banking, insurance, medical care, and day care are examples of services. *Ideas* include concepts, philosophies, images, and issues. For instance, an attorney, for a fee, may advise you about what rights you have in the event that the IRS decides to audit your tax return. Other marketers of ideas include political parties, churches, and schools.

A product has emotional and psychological, as well as physical, characteristics that include everything that the customer receives from an exchange. This definition includes supporting services such as installation, guarantees, product information, and promises of repair. Products usually have both favorable and unfavorable attributes; therefore, almost every purchase or exchange involves trade-offs as consumers try to maximize their benefits and satisfaction and minimize unfavorable attributes.

Products are among a firm's most visible contacts with consumers. If they do not meet consumer needs and expectations, sales will be difficult, and product life spans will be brief. The product is an important variable—often the central focus—of the marketing mix; the other variables (price, promotion, and distribution) must be coordinated with product decisions.

Price Almost anything can be assessed by a **price**, a value placed on an object exchanged between a buyer and a seller. Although the seller usually establishes the price, it may be negotiated between buyer and seller. The buyer usually exchanges purchasing power—income, credit, wealth—for the satisfaction or utility associated with a product. Because financial price is the measure of value commonly used in an exchange, it quantifies value and is the basis of most market exchanges.

Marketers view price as much more than a way of assessing value, however. It is a key element of the marketing mix because it relates directly to the generation of revenue and profits. Prices can also be changed quickly to stimulate demand

promotion a persuasive form of communication that attempts to expedite a marketing exchange by influencing individuals, groups, and organizations to accept goods, services, and ideas

marketing research a systematic, objective process of getting information about potential customers to guide marketing decisions

Netflix uses both traditional mail and streaming to distribute its products.

or respond to competitors' actions. The sudden increase in the cost of commodities such as oil can create price increases or a drop in consumer demand for a product. When gas prices rise, consumers purchase more-fuel-efficient cars; when prices fall, consumers return to larger vehicles.[14]

Promotion **Promotion** is a persuasive form of communication that attempts to expedite a marketing exchange by influencing individuals, groups, and organizations to accept goods, services, and ideas. Promotion includes advertising, personal selling, publicity, and sales promotion, all of which we will look at more closely in Chapter 12.

The aim of promotion is to communicate directly or indirectly with individuals, groups, and organizations to facilitate exchanges. When marketers use advertising and other forms of promotion, they must effectively manage their promotional resources and understand product and target-market characteristics to ensure that these promotional activities contribute to the firm's objectives.

Most major companies have set up websites on the Internet to promote themselves and their products. Although traditional advertising media such as television, radio, newspapers, and magazines remain important, digital advertising on websites and social media sites is growing. Not only can digital advertising be less expensive, but advertising offerings such as Google AdWords allow companies to pay only when users click the link or advertisement.[15] Additionally, social media sites offer advertising opportunities for both large and small companies. Firms can create a Facebook page and post corporate updates for free. To appeal to smaller businesses, Facebook has begun offering deals such as a certain amount in free advertising credits.[16] However, many companies—particularly big-name brands—continue to use Facebook's free features rather than pay much for advertising.[17]

["The aim of promotion is to communicate directly or indirectly with individuals, groups, and organizations to facilitate exchanges."]

Distribution **Distribution** (sometimes referred to as "place" because it helps to remember the marketing mix as the "4 Ps") is making products available to customers in the quantities desired. For example, consumers can rent DVDs and videogames from a physical store, a vending machine, or an online service. Intermediaries, usually wholesalers and retailers, perform many of the activities required to move products efficiently from producers to consumers or industrial buyers. These activities involve transporting, warehousing, materials handling, and inventory control as well as packaging and communication.

Critics who suggest that eliminating wholesalers and other middlemen would result in lower prices for consumers do not recognize that eliminating intermediaries would not do away with the need for their services. Other institutions would have to perform those services, and consumers would still have to pay for them. In addition, in the absence of wholesalers, all producers would have to deal directly with retailers or customers, keeping voluminous records and hiring extra people to deal with customers.

LO 11-5 Investigate how marketers conduct marketing research and study buying behavior.

MARKETING RESEARCH AND INFORMATION SYSTEMS

Before marketers can develop a marketing mix, they must collect in-depth, up-to-date information about customer needs. **Marketing research** is a systematic, objective process of

11.30.12

marketingnews

AMERICAN MARKETING ASSOCIATION MARKETINGPOWER.COM

TRUST MANAGEMENT

Continued economic uncertainty and Wall Street's bad rep are souring many consumers on investing, presenting a formidable challenge to financial services marketers. Here's how one company is working to counteract the negative perceptions and instill consumer confidence.

ALSO IN THIS ISSUE
The Marketing Power of Marketing Research

Marketing News is a good source for secondary marketing research. The publication contains up-to-date information on market trends and data.

getting information about potential customers to guide marketing decisions. Such information might include data about the age, income, ethnicity, gender, and educational level of people in the target market, their preferences for product features, their attitudes toward competitors' products, and the frequency with which they use the product. For instance, marketing research has revealed that consumers often make in-store purchase decisions in three seconds or less.[18] Marketing research is vital because the marketing concept cannot be implemented without information about customers.

A marketing information system is a framework for accessing information about customers from sources both inside and outside the organization. Inside the organization, there is a continuous flow of information about prices, sales, and expenses. Outside the organization, data are readily available through private or public reports and census statistics as well as from many other sources. Computer networking technology provides a framework for companies to connect to useful databases and customers with instantaneous information about product acceptance, sales performance, and buying behavior. This information is important to planning and marketing strategy development.

Two types of data are usually available to decision makers. **Primary data** are observed, recorded, or collected directly from respondents. If you've ever participated in a telephone survey about a product, recorded your TV viewing habits for A.C. Nielsen or Arbitron, or even responded to a political opinion poll, you provided the researcher with primary data. Primary data must be gathered by researchers who develop a method to observe phenomena or research respondents. Many companies use mystery shoppers to visit their retail establishments and report on whether the stores were adhering to the companies' standards of service. These undercover customers document their observations of store appearance, employee effectiveness, and customer treatment. Mystery shoppers provide valuable information that helps companies improve their organizations and refine their marketing strategies.[19] Companies also use surveys and focus groups to gauge customer opinion. Table 11.2 provides the results of a survey conducted by MSN Money-Zogby on organizations with the best customer service. A weakness of surveys is that respondents are sometimes untruthful to avoid seeming foolish or ignorant. Although focus groups can be more expensive than surveys, they allow marketers to understand how consumers express themselves as well as observe their behavior patterns.[20]

SPORT CLIPS: A NEW KIND OF SALON

In the early 1990s, Gordon Logan conducted market research in the hair care industry that revealed barber shops were a dying business. The only option was for men to go to salons, which are normally geared toward women. He decided to target a niche market with a salon specifically designed for men. Sport Clips was opened in 1993. Sport Clips is designed around the male demographic market segment. Its environment is customized to attract men with sports events aired on TVs and sports paraphernalia decorating the salon. The stylists are schooled in the area of men's haircuts and keep themselves apprised of the latest trends in men's hair styles. Just like a woman's salon, luxury is an element at Sport Clips, but speed is also a desirable factor. Men can go into the salon and get "The MVP Experience," which includes a quality haircut, steamed towel wrap, massaging shampoo, and a neck and shoulder massage—all in 20 minutes. Sport Clips is about to open its thousandth store and makes $250 million in sales.[21]

primary data marketing information that is observed, recorded, or collected directly from respondents

secondary data information that is compiled inside or outside an organization for some purpose other than changing the current situation

▼ **TABLE 11.2** Companies with the Best Customer Service

Rank	Companies	Excellence Ranking (%)
1	Amazon.com	53.5%
2	Google	43.8%
3	Apple	42.5%
4	UPS	42%
5	Sony (tie)	38.1%
5	Hilton Worldwide (tie)	38.1%
7	FedEx	37.5%
8	Marriott International	35.7%
9	American Express	34.3%
10	Southwest Airlines	33.9%

Source: Karen Aho, "The 2012 Customer Service Hall of Fame," *MSN Money*, http://money.msn.com/investing/2012-customer-service-hall-of-fame-1.

Some methods for marketing research use passive observation of consumer behavior and open-ended questioning techniques. Called ethnographic or observational research, the approach can help marketers determine what consumers really think about their products and how different ethnic or demographic groups react to them.

Secondary data are compiled inside or outside the organization for some purpose other than changing the current situation. Marketers typically use information compiled by the U.S. Census Bureau and other government agencies, databases created by marketing research firms, as well as sales and other internal reports to gain information about customers.

Online Marketing Research

The marketing of products and collecting of data about buying behavior—information on what people actually buy and how they buy it—represents marketing research of the future. New information technologies are changing the way businesses learn about their customers and market their products. Interactive multimedia research, or *virtual testing,* combines sight, sound, and animation to facilitate the testing of concepts as well as packaging and design features for consumer products. The evolving development of telecommunications and computer technologies is allowing marketing researchers quick and easy access to a growing number of online services and a vast database of potential respondents.

Marketing research can use digital media and social networking sites to gather useful information for marketing decisions. Sites such as Twitter and Facebook can be good substitutes for focus groups. Online surveys can serve as an alternative to mail, telephone, or personal interviews.

Social networks are a great way to obtain information from consumers who are willing to share their experiences about products and companies. In a way, this process identifies those consumers who develop an identity or passion for certain products as well as those consumers who have concerns about quality or performance. It is possible for firms to tap into existing online social networks and simply listen to what consumers have on their mind.

Starbucks attempts to influence consumers' buying behavior by offering free Wi-Fi and a comfortable retail environment.

buying behavior the decision processes and actions of people who purchase and use products

perception the process by which a person selects, organizes, and interprets information received from his or her senses

motivation inner drive that directs a person's behavior toward goals

learning changes in a person's behavior based on information and experience

attitude knowledge and positive or negative feelings about something

Firms can also encourage consumers to join a community or group so that they can share their opinions with the business.

A good outcome from using social networks is the opportunity to reach new voices and gain varied perspectives on the creative process of developing new products and promotions. For instance, Kickstarter gives aspiring entrepreneurs the ability to market their ideas online. Funders can then choose whether to fund those ideas in return for a finished product or a steep discount.[22] To some extent, social networking is democratizing design by welcoming consumers to join in the development process for new products.[23]

Online surveys are becoming an important part of marketing research. Traditionally, the process of conducting surveys online involved sending questionnaires to respondents either through email or through a website. However, digital communication has increased the ability of marketers to conduct polls on blogs and social networking sites. The amount that marketers spend on Internet surveys has increased 33 percent from 2005.[24] The benefits of online market research include lower costs and quicker feedback. For instance, when GNC launched its coconut-water beverage, it monitored online feedback to determine how customers viewed the product. The company found that feedback was negative, which convinced them to make product adjustments.[25] By monitoring consumers' feedback, companies can understand customer needs and adapt their products or services.

BUYING BEHAVIOR

Carrying out the marketing concept is impossible unless marketers know what, where, when, and how consumers buy; conducting marketing research into the factors that influence buying behavior helps marketers develop effective marketing strategies. **Buying behavior** refers to the decision processes and actions of people who purchase and use products. It includes the behavior of both consumers purchasing products for personal or household use and organizations buying products for business use. Marketers analyze buying behavior because a firm's marketing strategy should be guided by an understanding of buyers. People view pets as part of their families, and they want their pets to have the best of everything. Iams, which markets the Iams and Eukanuba pet food brands, recognized this trend and shifted

ARE YOUR CLOTHES GREEN? ASK THE HIGG INDEX

How do you determine whether you are purchasing green apparel? The Sustainable Apparel Coalition (SAC) is an initiative that was established by several apparel and footware retailers such as Nike, Target, and Adidas to address issues of sustainability. The apparel industry produces 21 billion pounds of waste every year, and the chemicals that are in the materials are damaging to the environment. Air pollution and water waste also occur in the process of making these materials.

One way SAC is trying to make green apparel more easily apparent is through the development of the Higg Index, which assigns scores to apparel and footware. These scores measure the levels of sustainability based on materials and the processes used to create the apparel. This is a significant development for sustainable products, especially in its quest to combat greenwashing. Greenwashing is a deceptive marketing tactic that makes sustainability claims for products that are not truly sustainable. This issue is compounded by the fact that many consumers and even businesses do not fully understand what constitutes a green product. The Higg Index will therefore act as an educational tool and help businesses see where they are deficient in sustainability throughout their supply chain.

Consumers today are more conscious of the environment and are willing to spend a little more money on products that they know are environmentally safe. This puts pressure on companies to offer green products, but analyzing green practices throughout the product development process is difficult. The Higg Index will help businesses understand how sustainable their products really are.[26]

Discussion Questions

1. What is the purpose of the Higg Index?
2. Why is it difficult to determine whether you are purchasing a green product?
3. Describe greenwashing and how it is becoming a growing problem in marketing communications.

personality the organization of an individual's distinguishing character traits, attitudes, or habits

social roles a set of expectations for individuals based on some position they occupy

reference groups groups with whom buyers identify and whose values or attitudes they adopt

social classes a ranking of people into higher or lower positions of respect

culture the integrated, accepted pattern of human behavior, including thought, speech, beliefs, actions, and artifacts

its focus. Today, it markets high-quality pet food, fancy pet treats, sauces, and other items. Both psychological and social variables are important to an understanding of buying behavior.

Psychological Variables of Buying Behavior

Psychological factors include the following:

- **Perception** is the process by which a person selects, organizes, and interprets information received from his or her senses, as when experiencing an advertisement or touching a product to understand it better.
- **Motivation**, as we said in Chapter 9, is an inner drive that directs a person's behavior toward goals. A customer's behavior is influenced by a set of motives rather than by a single motive. A buyer of a tablet computer, for example, may be motivated by ease of use, ability to communicate with the office, and price.
- **Learning** brings about changes in a person's behavior based on information and experience. For instance, a smart phone app that provides digital news or magazine content could eliminate the need for print copies. If a person's actions result in a reward, he or she is likely to behave the same way in similar situations. If a person's actions bring about a negative result, however—such as feeling ill after eating at a certain restaurant—he or she will probably not repeat that action.
- **Attitude** is knowledge and positive or negative feelings about something. For example, a person who feels strongly about protecting the environment may refuse to buy products that harm the earth and its inhabitants.
- **Personality** refers to the organization of an individual's distinguishing character traits, attitudes, or habits. Although market research on the relationship between personality and buying behavior has been inconclusive, some marketers believe that the type of car or clothing a person buys reflects his or her personality.

People's cultures have a big impact on what they buy. The food-seller Goya Foods sells more than three dozen types of beans to U.S. supermarkets because people with different cultural roots demand different types of beans. Which products are delivered to which stores depends on the heritage of those living in each area.

Social Variables of Buying Behavior

Social factors include **social roles**, which are a set of expectations for individuals based on some position they occupy. A person may have many roles: mother, wife, student, executive. Each of these roles can influence buying behavior. Consider a woman choosing an automobile. Her father advises her to buy a safe, gasoline-efficient car, such as a Volvo. Her teenaged daughter wants her to buy a cool car, such as a Ford Mustang; her young son wants her to buy a Ford Explorer to take on camping trips. Some of her colleagues at work say she should buy a hybrid Prius to help the environment. Thus, in choosing which car to buy, the woman's buying behavior may be affected by the opinions and experiences of her family and friends and by her roles as mother, daughter, and employee.

Other social factors include reference groups, social classes, and culture.

- **Reference groups** include families, professional groups, civic organizations, and other groups with whom buyers identify and whose values or attitudes they adopt. A person may use a reference group as a point of comparison or a source of information. A person new to a community may ask other group members to recommend a family doctor, for example.
- **Social classes** are determined by ranking people into higher or lower positions of respect. Criteria vary from one society to another. People within a particular social class may develop common patterns of behavior. People in the upper-middle class, for example, might buy a Lexus or a BMW as a symbol of their social class.
- **Culture** is the integrated, accepted pattern of human behavior, including thought, speech, beliefs, actions, and artifacts. Culture determines what people wear and

eat and where they live and travel. Many Hispanic Texans and New Mexicans, for example, buy *masa trigo*, the dough used to prepare flour tortillas, which are basic to Southwestern and Mexican cuisine.

Understanding Buying Behavior

Although marketers try to understand buying behavior, it is extremely difficult to explain exactly why a buyer purchases a particular product. The tools and techniques for analyzing consumers are not exact. Marketers may not be able to determine accurately what is highly satisfying to buyers, but they know that trying to understand consumer wants and needs is the best way to satisfy them. To combat declining gum sales, companies have begun to turn gum into a fashion statement. For instance, Kraft is engaging young artists to create designs for its gum packaging, and Rockstar Iced Mint Energy is touting its energy-boosting caffeine and taurine content. These overhauls are an attempt to reconnect with the teen market, which is the largest purchaser of gum products.[27]

LO 11-6 Summarize the environmental forces that influence marketing decisions.

THE MARKETING ENVIRONMENT

A number of external forces directly or indirectly influence the development of marketing strategies; the following political, legal, regulatory, social, competitive, economic, and technological forces comprise the marketing environment.

- *Political, legal, and regulatory forces*—laws and regulators' interpretation of laws, law enforcement and regulatory activities, regulatory bodies, legislators and legislation, and political actions of interest groups. Specific laws, for example, require advertisements to be truthful and all health claims to be documented.
- *Social forces*—the public's opinions and attitudes toward issues such as living standards, ethics, the environment, lifestyles, and quality of life. For example, social concerns have led marketers to design and market safer toys for children.
- *Competitive and economic forces*—competitive relationships such as those in the technology industry, unemployment, purchasing power, and general economic conditions (prosperity, recession, depression, recovery, product shortages, and inflation).
- *Technological forces*—computers and other technological advances that improve distribution, promotion, and new-product development.

TEAM EXERCISE

Form groups and assign the responsibility of finding examples of companies that excel in one dimension of the marketing mix (price, product, promotion, and distribution). Provide several company and product examples and defend why this would be an exemplary case. Present your research to the class.

Benetton appeals to environmentally responsible and fashion-conscious individuals.

Marketing requires creativity and consumer focus because environmental forces can change quickly and dramatically. Changes can arise from social concerns and economic forces such as price increases, product shortages, and altering levels of demand for commodities. Recently, climate change, global warming, and the impact of carbon emissions on our environment have become social concerns and are causing businesses to rethink marketing strategies. These environmental issues have persuaded governments to institute stricter limits on greenhouse gas emissions. For instance, in the United States the government has mandated that by 2025 vehicles must be able to reach 54.5 miles per gallon.[28] This is causing automobile companies such as General Motors to investigate ways to make their cars more fuel-efficient without significantly raising the price. At the same time, these laws are also introducing

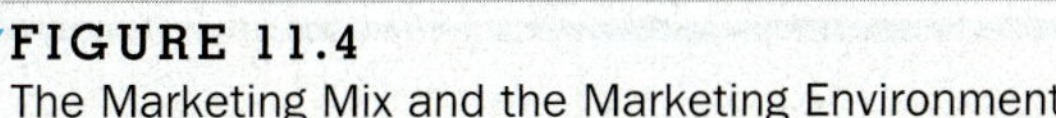

FIGURE 11.4
The Marketing Mix and the Marketing Environment

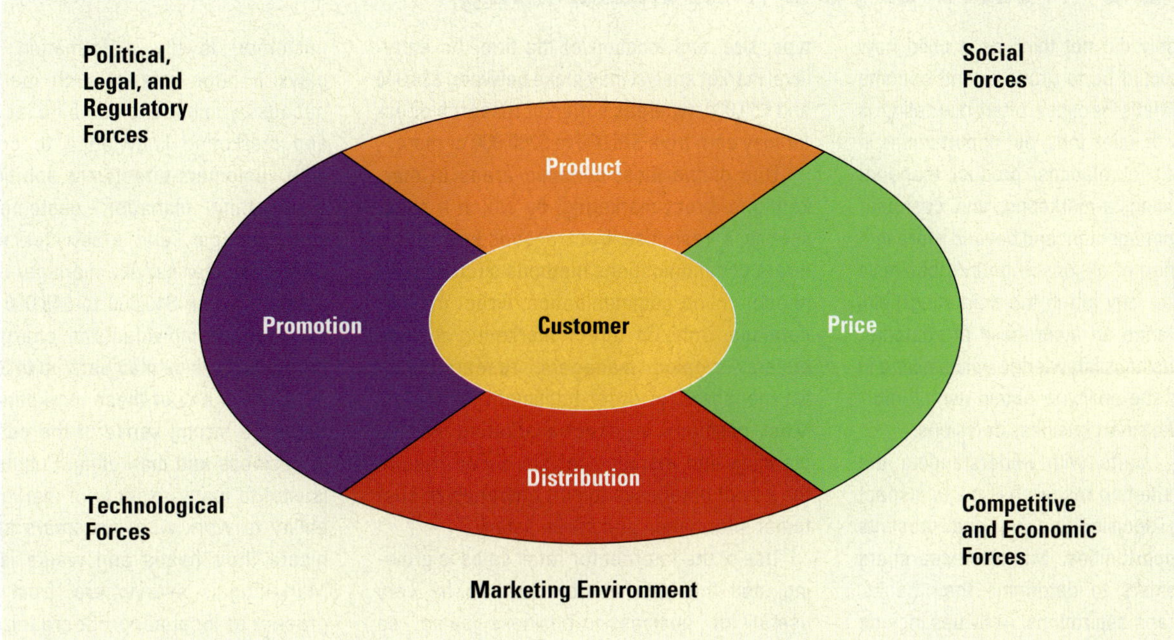

opportunities for new products. Concerns over the environment are encouraging automobile companies to begin releasing electric vehicles, such as the Chevrolet Volt and the Nissan Leaf.

Because such environmental forces are interconnected, changes in one may cause changes in others. Consider that because of evidence linking children's consumption of soft drinks and fast foods to health issues such as obesity, diabetes, and osteoporosis, marketers of such products have experienced negative publicity and calls for legislation regulating the sale of soft drinks in public schools.

Although the forces in the marketing environment are sometimes called uncontrollables, they are not totally so. A marketing manager can influence some environmental variables. For example, businesses can lobby legislators to dissuade them from passing unfavorable legislation. Figure 11.4 shows the variables in the marketing environment that affect the marketing mix and the buyer.

IMPORTANCE OF MARKETING TO BUSINESS AND SOCIETY

As this chapter has shown, marketing is a necessary function for reaching consumers, establishing relationships, and driving sales. Although some critics might view marketing as a way to change what consumers want, marketing is essential in communicating the value of goods and services. For consumers, marketing is necessary to ensure that they get the products they desire at the right places in the right quantities at a reasonable price. From the perspective of businesses, marketing is necessary to form valuable relationships with customers to increase profitability and customer support.

It is not just for-profit businesses that engage in marketing activities. Nonprofits, government institutions, and even people must market themselves to spread awareness and achieve desired outcomes. All organizations must reach their target markets, communicate their offerings, and establish high-quality services. For instance, nonprofit organization The Leukemia and Lymphoma Society uses print, radio, web, and other forms of media to market its Team in Training racing events to recruit participants and solicit support. Without marketing, it would be nearly impossible for organizations to connect with their target audiences. Marketing is therefore an important contributor to business and societal well-being. ■

SO YOU WANT A JOB // in Marketing /

You probably did not think as a child how great it would be to grow up and become a marketer. That's because often marketing is associated with sales jobs, but opportunities in marketing, public relations, product management, advertising, e-marketing, and customer relationship management and beyond represent almost one-third of all jobs in today's business world. To enter any job in the marketing field, you must balance an awareness of customer needs with business knowledge while mixing in creativity and the ability to obtain useful information to make smart business decisions.

Marketing starts with understanding the customer. Marketing research is a vital aspect in marketing decision making and presents many job opportunities. Market researchers survey customers to determine their habits, preferences, and aspirations. Activities include concept testing, product testing, package testing, test-market research, and new-product research. Salaries vary, depending on the nature and level of the position as well as the type, size, and location of the firm. An entry-level market analyst may make between $24,000 and $50,000, whereas a market research director may earn from $75,000 to $200,000 or more.

One of the most dynamic areas in marketing is direct marketing, by which a seller solicits a response from a consumer using direct communications methods such as telephone, online communication, direct mail, or catalogs. Jobs in direct marketing include buyers, catalog managers, research/mail-list managers, or order fulfillment managers. Most positions in direct marketing involve planning and market analysis. Some require the use of databases to sort and analyze customer information and sales history.

Use of the Internet for retail sales is growing, and the Internet continues to be very useful for business-to-business sales, so e-marketing offers many career opportunities, including customer relationship management (CRM). CRM helps companies market to customers through relationships, maintaining customer loyalty. Information technology plays a huge role in such marketing jobs because you need to combine technical skills and marketing knowledge to communicate with customers effectively. Job titles include e-marketing manager, customer relationship manager, and e-services manager. A CRM customer service manager may receive a salary in the $40,000 to $45,000 range, and experienced individuals in charge of online product offerings may earn up to $100,000.

A job in any of these marketing fields will require a strong sense of the current trends in business and marketing. Customer service is vital to many aspects of marketing, so the ability to work with customers and communicate their needs and wants is important. Marketing is everywhere, from the corner grocery or local nonprofit organization to the largest multinational corporations, making it a shrewd choice for an ambitious and creative person. We will provide additional job opportunities in marketing in Chapter 12.

learn, practice, apply how to market to customers!

M: Business was developed just for you—students on the go who need information packaged in a concise yet interesting format with multiple learning options.

Check out the book's website to:

- Evaluate the role of the marketing mix. (Solve the Dilemma)
- Analyze the marketing strategies of well-known companies. (Build Your Skills)
- Learn about the importance of market demand. (Solve the Dilemma)

While you are there, don't forget to enhance your skills. Practice and apply your knowledge, review the practice exercises, Student PPT® slides, and quizzes to review and apply chapter concepts. Additionally, *Connect® Business* is available for *M: Business*.

www.mhhe.com/ferrellm4e

TASTE
TO CALL OURSELVES
A ZERO
MAXIMUM
PEPSI TASTE
AUCTION HUNTERS
TOSHIBA
TOSHIBA
ERNST & YOUNG
SONY
NESPRESSO

chapter twelve

dimensions of marketing strategy

The key to developing a marketing strategy is selecting a target market and maintaining a marketing mix that creates long-term relationships with customers. Getting just the right mix of product, price, promotion, and distribution is critical if a business is to satisfy its target customers and achieve its own objectives (implement the marketing concept).

In Chapter 11, we introduced the marketing concept and the various activities important in developing a marketing strategy. In this chapter, we'll take a closer look at the four dimensions of the marketing mix—product, price, distribution, and promotion—used to develop the marketing strategy. The focus of these marketing mix elements is a marketing strategy that builds customer relationships and satisfaction. ■

LEARNING OBJECTIVES

After reading this chapter, you will be able to:

- **LO 12-1** Describe the role of product in the marketing mix, including how products are developed, classified, and identified.
- **LO 12-2** Define price and discuss its importance in the marketing mix, including various pricing strategies a firm might employ.
- **LO 12-3** Identify factors affecting distribution decisions, such as marketing channels and intensity of market coverage.
- **LO 12-4** Specify the activities involved in promotion as well as promotional strategies and promotional positioning.

THE MARKETING MIX

The marketing mix is the part of marketing strategy that involves decisions regarding controllable variables. After selecting a target market, marketers have to develop and manage the dimensions of the marketing mix to give their firm an advantage over competitors. Successful companies offer at least one dimension of value usually associated with a marketing mix element that surpasses all competitors in the marketplace in meeting customer expectations. However, this does not mean that a company can ignore the other dimensions of the marketing mix; it must maintain acceptable, and if possible distinguishable, differences in the other dimensions as well.

Walmart, for example, emphasizes price ("Save money, live better"). Procter & Gamble is well known for its promotion of top consumer brands such as Tide, Cheer, Crest, Ivory, and Head & Shoulders. Netflix has excelled at making movies available through regional warehouses and efficient distribution.

DID YOU KNOW?

Less than 10 percent of new products succeed in the marketplace, and 90 percent of successes come from a handful of companies.[1]

LO 12-1 Describe the role of product in the marketing mix, including how products are developed, classified, and identified.

PRODUCT STRATEGY

As mentioned previously, the term *product* refers to goods, services, and ideas. Because the product is often the most visible of the marketing mix dimensions, managing product decisions is crucial. In this section, we'll consider product development, classification, mix, life cycle, and identification.

Developing New Products

Each year, thousands of products are introduced, but few of them succeed. For example, Hewlett-Packard believed it could compete in the tablet computer industry with the TouchPad and its WebOS operating system. However, after six weeks of being on the market, HP dropped the TouchPad due to lackluster sales.

> "Each year, thousands of products are introduced, but few of them succeed."

While attending Yale in 1966, FedEx founder Fred Smith studied a mathematical discipline called topology, which inspired his vision for creating the company. Realizing the potential efficiencies of connecting all points on a network through a central hub, Smith used what he learned to get FedEx off the ground.

Many companies have similar stories of product failure.[2] Figure 12.1 shows the different steps in the product development process. Before introducing a new product, a business must follow a multistep process: idea development, the screening of new ideas, business analysis, product development, test marketing, and commercialization. A firm can take considerable time to get a product ready for the market: It took more than 20 years for the first photocopier, for example. Additionally, sometimes an idea or product prototype might be shelved only to be returned to later. Former Apple CEO Steve Jobs admitted that the iPad actually came before the iPhone in the product development process. Once it was realized that the scrolling mechanism he was thinking of using could be used to develop a phone, the iPad idea was placed on a shelf for the time being. Apple later returned to develop the product and released the iPad in 2010.[3]

Idea Generation New ideas can come from marketing research, engineers, and outside sources such as advertising agencies and management consultants. Microsoft has a separate division—Microsoft Research—where scientists devise technology of the future. The division has more than 800 researchers who work in a university-like research

FIGURE 12.1
Product Development Process

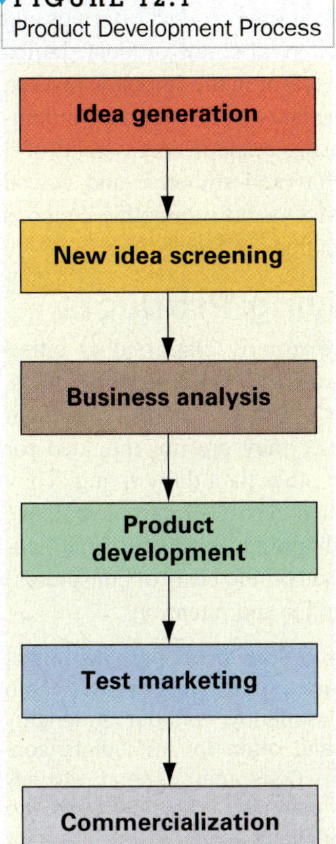

atmosphere. Research teams then present their ideas to Microsoft engineers who are developing specific products. As we said in Chapter 11, ideas sometimes come from customers, too. Other sources are brainstorming and intracompany incentives or rewards for good ideas. New ideas can even create a company. When Jeff Bezos came up with the idea to sell books over the Internet in 1992, he had no idea it would evolve into a firm with more than $61 billion in sales. After failing to convince his boss of the idea, Bezos left to start Amazon.com.[4]

New Idea Screening The next step in developing a new product is idea screening. In this phase, a marketing manager should look at the organization's resources and objectives and assess the firm's ability to produce and market the product. Important aspects to be considered at this stage are consumer desires, the competition, technological changes, social trends, and political, economic, and environmental considerations. Basically, there are two reasons new products succeed: They meet a need or solve a problem better than products already available, or they add variety to the product selection currently on the market. Bringing together a team of knowledgeable people including designers, engineers, marketers, and customers is a great way to screen ideas. Using the Internet to encourage collaboration represents a rich opportunity for marketers to screen ideas. Most new product ideas are rejected during screening because they seem inappropriate or impractical for the organization.

Business Analysis Business analysis is a basic assessment of a product's compatibility in the marketplace and its potential profitability. Both the size of the market and competing products are often studied at this point. The most important question relates to market demand: How will the product affect the firm's sales, costs, and profits?

Product Development If a product survives the first three steps, it is developed into a prototype that should reveal the intangible attributes it possesses as perceived by the consumer. Product development is often expensive, and few product ideas make it to this stage. New product research and development costs vary. Adding a new color to an existing item may cost $100,000 to $200,000, but launching a completely new product can cost millions of dollars. During product development, various elements of the marketing mix must be developed for testing. Copyrights, tentative advertising copy, packaging, labeling, and descriptions of a target market are integrated to develop an overall marketing strategy.

Test Marketing **Test marketing** is a trial minilaunch of a product in limited areas that represent the potential market. It allows a complete test of the marketing strategy in a natural environment, giving the organization an opportunity to discover weaknesses and eliminate them before the product is fully launched. Caterpillar Inc. often engages in test marketing before launching into full-scale production of its machinery and equipment. It introduced its Cat® CT660 Vocational Truck in limited markets to test the product as well as to ensure that it met quality standards. After successful test marketing, the Cat CT660 Vocational Truck was made ready for commercialization.[5] Because test marketing requires significant resources and expertise, market research companies such as ACNielsen can assist firms in test marketing their products. Figure 12.2 shows the permanent sites as well as custom locations for test marketing.

CROCS: A "SHOE IN" FOR SUCCESS

Crocs, Inc. was founded by Scott Seamans, Lyndon "Duke" Hanson, and George Boedecker Jr. in 2002. The company achieved success by creating a unique type of shoe made out of foam offered in a variety of colors. Although the shoe design was often perceived as ugly, it attracted customers because of its unique nature and comfortable qualities. The three men introduced the shoe at a boat show, selling out at 200 pairs.

Despite their early success, Crocs began experiencing dwindling sales because it offered only one type of shoe that could be purchased almost anywhere. In response, Crocs began to expand into other product lines to give the company more diversity. Today, the firm also sells fashionable flats, wedges, sneakers, and other products that offer the same comfort level. The firm launched an advertising campaign that touted the new styles while promising the same level of comfort as the original shoe. Thanks to these product lines and its widespread advertising campaign, the company is seeing $1 billion in sales and 30 percent in growth.[6]

FIGURE 12.2
ACNielsen Market Decisions

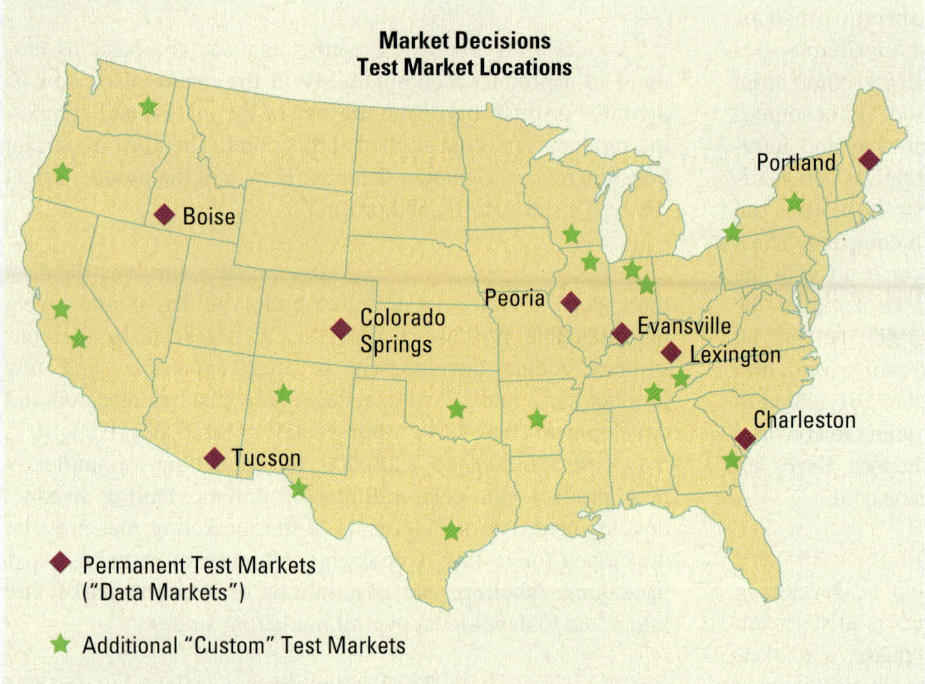

Source: "Test Marketing," ACNielsen (n.d.), www.acnielsen.com/services/testing/test1.htm. Reprinted with permission of ACNielsen Market Decisions.

Commercialization

Commercialization is the full introduction of a complete marketing strategy and the launch of the product for commercial success. During commercialization, the firm gears up for full-scale production, distribution, and promotion. After achieving success with its McCafé line, McDonald's expanded into the smoothie market. When the company entered the commercialization stage, it released coupons and free smoothie promotions to spread awareness about its newest product, Real Fruit Smoothies. During this stage, competitors often take the opportunity to emphasize their own product offerings and discredit their rival's new product. Jamba Juice, a competitor in the smoothie market, countered the launch of Real Fruit Smoothies by releasing a spoof commercial of a hamburger-flavored smoothie and vowed to redeem McDonald's smoothie coupons at Jamba locations in select cities.[7]

The DeLorean automobile from the 1980s is an example of a product that did not survive. However, it is still popular among car collectors. Because there are so few of these cars left, DeLoreans would be classified as specialty products requiring greater shopping effort.

Classifying Products

Products are usually classified as either consumer products or industrial products. **Consumer products** are for household or family use; they are not intended for any purpose other than daily living. They can be further classified as convenience products, shopping products, and specialty products on the basis of consumers' buying behavior and intentions.

- *Convenience products,* such as eggs, milk, bread, and newspapers, are bought frequently, without a lengthy search, and often for immediate consumption. Consumers spend virtually no time planning where to purchase these products and usually accept whatever brand is available.
- *Shopping products,* such as furniture, audio equipment, clothing, and sporting goods, are purchased after the consumer has compared competitive products and shopped around. Price, product features, quality, style, service, and image all influence the decision to buy.
- *Specialty products,* such as ethnic foods, designer clothing and shoes, art, and antiques, require even greater research and shopping effort. Consumers know what they want and go out of their way to find it; they are not willing to accept a substitute.

Business products are used directly or indirectly in the operation or manufacturing processes of businesses. They are usually purchased for the operation of an organization or the production of other products; thus, their purchase is tied to specific goals and objectives. They too can be further classified:

- *Raw materials* are natural products taken from the earth, oceans, and recycled solid waste. Iron ore, bauxite, lumber, cotton, and fruits and vegetables are examples.
- *Major equipment* covers large, expensive items used in production. Examples include earth-moving equipment, stamping machines, and robotic equipment used on auto assembly lines.
- *Accessory equipment* includes items used for production, office, or management purposes, which usually do not become part of the final product. Computers, fax machines, calculators, and hand tools are examples.

commercialization the full introduction of a complete marketing strategy and the launch of the product for commercial success

consumer products products intended for household or family use

business products products that are used directly or indirectly in the operation or manufacturing processes of businesses

product line a group of closely related products that are treated as a unit because of similar marketing strategy

product mix all the products offered by an organization

- *Component parts* are finished items, ready to be assembled into the company's final products. Tires, window glass, batteries, and spark plugs are component parts of automobiles.
- *Processed materials* are things used directly in production or management operations but are not readily identifiable as component parts. Varnish, for example, is a processed material for a furniture manufacturer.
- *Supplies* include materials that make production, management, and other operations possible, such as paper, pencils, paint, cleaning supplies, and so on.
- *Industrial services* include financial, legal, marketing research, security, janitorial, and exterminating services. Purchasers decide whether to provide these services internally or to acquire them from an outside supplier.

Product Line and Product Mix

Product relationships within an organization are of key importance. A **product line** is a group of closely related products that are treated as a unit because of a similar marketing strategy. At Colgate-Palmolive, for example, the oral-care product line includes Colgate toothpaste, toothbrushes, and dental floss. A **product mix** is all the products offered by an organization. Figure 12.3 displays a sampling of the product mix and product lines of the Colgate-Palmolive Company.

FIGURE 12.3
Colgate-Palmolive's Product Mix and Product Lines

← Product Mix →			
Oral Care	**Personal Care**	**Home Care**	**Pet Nutrition**
Toothpaste Colgate Total Advanced Colgate Optic White™	*Deodorant* Speed Stick Deodorant Irish Spring Deodorant Lady Speed Stick Deodorant	*Dishwashing* Palmolive AJAX Dermassage	Hill's Prescription Diet Hill's Science Diet Hill's Ideal Balance
Colgate Kids Colgate Dora the Explorer Colgate SpongeBob SquarePants Colgate 2in1	*Body Wash* Softsoap Body Wash Irish Spring Body Wash	*Fabric Conditioner* Suavitel	
Toothbrushes Colgate 360° Colgate Max White Colgate Total Professional	*Bar Soap* Softsoap Bar Soap Irish Spring Bar Soap	*Household cleaner* Murphy Oil Soap Fabuloso AJAX	

(Product Lines ↕)

Source: "Colgate World of Care," Colgate-Palmolive Company, www.colgate.com/app/Colgate/US/HomePage.cvsp.

Product Life Cycle

Like people, products are born, grow, mature, and eventually die. Some products have very long lives. Ivory Soap was introduced in 1879 and is still popular. In contrast, a new computer chip is usually outdated within a year because of technological breakthroughs and rapid changes in the computer industry. There are four stages in the life cycle of a product: introduction, growth, maturity, and decline (Figure 12.4). The stage a product is in helps determine marketing strategy. In the personal computer industry, desktop computers are in the decline stage, laptop computers have reached the maturity stage, and tablet computers are currently in the growth stage of the product life cycle. Manufacturers of these products are adopting different advertising and pricing strategies to maintain or increase demand for these types of computers.

In the *introduction stage,* consumer awareness and acceptance of the product are limited, sales are zero, and profits are negative. Profits are negative because the firm has spent money on research, development, and marketing to launch the product. During the introduction stage, marketers focus on making consumers aware of the product and its benefits. For instance, Google Glass is a gizmo consisting of glassless glasses with an embedded computer. Google Glass is currently in the introduction stage of the product life cycle.[8] Table 12.1 shows some familiar products at different stages of the product life cycle. Sales accelerate as the product enters the growth stage of the life cycle.

In the *growth stage,* sales increase rapidly and profits peak, then start to decline. One reason profits start to decline during the growth stage is that new companies enter the market, driving prices down and increasing marketing expenses. Android phones are currently in the growth stage. Launched in 2008, the Android operating system has been used in mobile devices sold by HTC, Motorola, Samsung, T-Mobile, and Sony. Android phones have attained between 47 and 52 percent market share, demonstrating incredible growth in their early years of existence.[9] Apple's iCloud service is also in the growth stage. The iCloud enables users to

branding the process of naming and identifying products

trademark a brand that is registered with the U.S. Patent and Trademark Office and is thus legally protected from use by any other firm

manufacturer brands initiated and owned by the manufacturer to identify products from the point of production to the point of purchase

private distributor brands brands, which may cost less than manufacturer brands, that are owned and controlled by a wholesaler or retailer

TABLE 12.1 Products at Different Stages of the Life Cycle

Introduction	Growth	Maturity	Decline
3D television	DVRs	Flat-screen televisions	AM/FM radios
Google Glass	Blu-ray Player	Laptop computers	VCRs
Electric cars	Tablet computers	Chevrolet Corvette	Desktop computers

store and coordinate information such as addresses, photos, and appointments across mobile devices. Adoption of the iCloud is growing, with 300 million current users.[10] During the growth stage, the firm tries to strengthen its position in the market by emphasizing the product's benefits and identifying market segments that want these benefits.

Sales continue to increase at the beginning of the *maturity stage,* but then the sales curve peaks and starts to decline while profits continue to decline. This stage is characterized by severe competition and heavy expenditures. In the United States, soft drinks have hit the maturity stage. Firms such as PepsiCo and Coca-Cola have taken many steps to revitalize sales, from introducing soda in smaller package sizes to adopting healthier product lines to expanding their reach internationally in places such as Africa.[11]

During the *decline stage,* sales continue to fall rapidly. Profits also decline and may even become losses as prices are cut and necessary marketing expenditures are made. As profits drop, firms may eliminate certain models or items. To reduce expenses and squeeze out any remaining profits, marketing expenditures may be cut back, even though such cutbacks accelerate the sales decline. Finally, plans must be made for phasing out the product and introducing new ones to take its place. General Motors discontinued the Chevrolet Cobalt in favor of the Chevrolet Cruze. The Cobalt was losing the company money, and critics claimed that the car was "mediocre" and behind technologically.[12] GM also phased out its Saturn, Hummer, and Pontiac brands.

At the same time, it should be noted that product stages do not always go one way. Some products that have moved to the maturity stage or to the decline stage can still rebound through redesign or new uses for the product. One prime example is baking soda. Originally, baking soda was used only for cooking, which meant it reached the maturity stage very quickly. However, once it was discovered that baking soda could be used as a deodorizer, sales shot up and bumped baking soda back into the growth stage.[13] Similarly, Mattel is trying to make a comeback with Barbie by releasing new lines of redesigned dolls. For instance, Mattel decided to use the online sensation Stardoll to create physical dolls to sell. The online Stardoll allows young girls to dress up virtual dolls digitally. By tapping into a brand that is already popular with young girls, Mattel plans to reinvigorate interest in its Barbie doll products.[14]

Identifying Products

Branding, packaging, and labeling can be used to identify or distinguish one product from others. As a result, they are key marketing activities that help position a product appropriately for its target market.

Branding

Branding is the process of naming and identifying products. A *brand* is a name, term, symbol, design, or combination that identifies a product and distinguishes it from other products. Consider that Google, iPod, and TiVo are brand names that are used to identify entire product categories, much like Xerox has become synonymous with photocopying and Kleenex with tissues. Protecting a brand name is important in maintaining a brand identity. The world's 10 most valuable brands are shown in Table 12.2. The brand name is the part of the brand that can be spoken and consists of letters, words, and numbers—such as WD-40 lubricant. A *brand mark* is the part of the brand that is a distinctive design, such as the silver star on the hood of a Mercedes or the McDonald's golden arches logo. A **trademark** is a brand that is registered with the U.S.

FIGURE 12.4
The Life Cycle of a Product

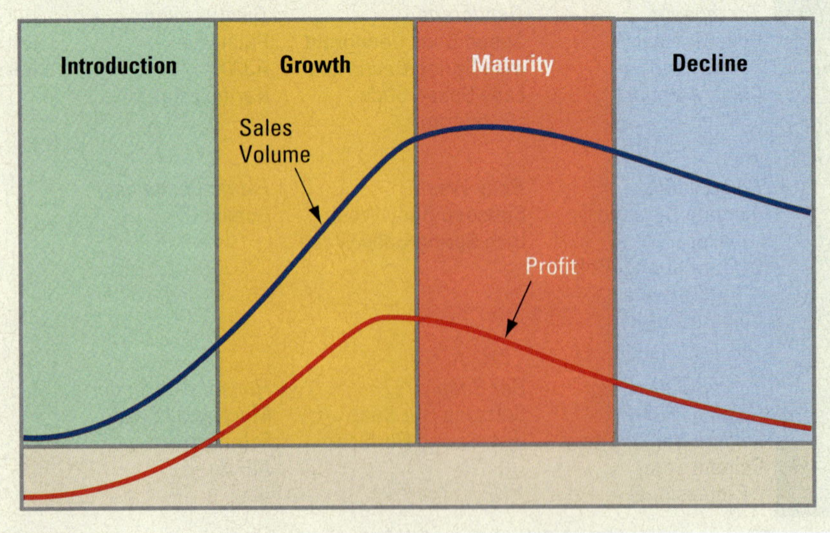

While VCRs are in the decline stage of the product life cycle, smart TVs and DVRs are in the growth stage.

▼ **TABLE 12.2** The 10 Most Valuable Brands in the World

Rank	Brand	Brand Value ($ Millions)
1	Apple	$182,951
2	IBM	115,985
3	Google	107,857
4	McDonald's	95,188
5	Microsoft	76,651
6	Coca-Cola	74,286
7	Marlboro	73,612
8	AT&T	68,870
9	Verizon	49,151
10	China Mobile	47,041

Source: Millward Brown, "BrandZ™ Top 100 Most Valuable Global Brands," www.millwardbrown.com/brandz/2012/Documents/2012_BrandZ_Top100_Chart.pdf. Reprinted with permission of Millward Brown.

Patent and Trademark Office and is thus legally protected from use by any other firm.

Two major categories of brands are manufacturer brands and private distributor brands. **Manufacturer brands** are brands initiated and owned by the manufacturer to identify products from the point of production to the point of purchase. Kellogg's, Sony, and Texaco are examples. **Private distributor brands**, which may be less expensive than manufacturer brands, are owned and controlled by a wholesaler or retailer, such as Kenmore appliances (Sears) and Sam's grocery products (Walmart and Sam's Wholesale Club). The names of private brands do not usually identify their manufacturer. Although private-label brands were once considered cheaper and of poor quality, such as Walmart's Ol'Roy dog food, many private-label brands are increasing in quality and image and are competing with national brands. For instance, a number of companies are hiring professional designers to design their private-label brands, replacing the traditional two-color

generic products products with no brand name that often come in simple packages and carry only their generic name

packaging the external container that holds and describes the product

labeling the presentation of important information on a package

quality the degree to which a good, service, or idea meets the demands and requirements of customers

packaging schemes often associated with private-label products. Target hired designer Jason Wu to design a limited-edition fashion collection, which sold out in a matter of hours.[15] The grocery retailer Tesco has several types of private-label brands, and its branding strategy has performed so effectively that consumers may end up paying more for Tesco's own products than for branded goods.[16] Manufacturer brands are fighting hard against private distributor brands to retain their market share.

Another type of brand that has developed is **generic products**—products with no brand name at all. They often come in plain, simple packages that carry only the generic name of the product—peanut butter, tomato juice, aspirin, dog food, and so on. They appeal to consumers who may be willing to sacrifice quality or product consistency to get a lower price. Although at one time generic brands represented as much as 10 percent of all retail grocery sales, today they account for less than half of 1 percent.

Companies use two basic approaches to branding multiple products. In one, a company gives each product within its complete product mix its own brand name. Warner-Lambert, for example, sells many well-known consumer products—Dentyne, Chiclets, Listerine, Halls, Rolaids, and Trident—each individually branded. This branding policy ensures that the name of one product does not affect the names of others, and different brands can be targeted at different segments of the same market, increasing the company's market share (its percentage of the sales for the total market for a product). Another approach to branding is to develop a family of brands with each of the firm's products carrying the same name or at least part of the name. Gillette, Sara Lee, and IBM use this approach. Finally, consumers may react differently to domestic versus foreign brands. Table 12.3 provides a snapshot of the most popular car brands.

TABLE 12.3 Best-Selling Vehicle Brands

Ranking	Vehicle Model	Country of Origin
1	Ford Focus	United States
2	Toyota Corolla	Japan
3	Volkswagen Jetta	Germany
4	Hyundai Elantra	South Korea
5	Ford Fiesta	United States
6	Volkswagen Golf	Germany
7	Toyota Camry	Japan
8	Volkswagen Polo	Germany
9	Chevrolet Cruze	United States
10	Honda Civic	Japan

Source: Joann Muller, "The World's Most Popular Cars: A New Champ," *Forbes*, December 19, 2012, www.forbes.com/sites/joannmuller/2012/12/19/the-worlds-most-popular-cars-a-new-champ/.

Packaging

The **packaging**, or external container that holds and describes the product, influences consumers' attitudes and their buying decisions. In a Harris Interactive Panel, three-fourths of respondents replied they would be willing to pay more money for certain packaging attributes. Some of the more important attributes cited included reusability, "staying fresh longer," and stating that the product is "made in the United States."[17] It is estimated that consumers' eyes linger only 2.5 seconds on each product on an average shopping trip; therefore, product packaging should be designed to attract and hold consumers' attention.

A package can perform several functions, including protection, economy, convenience, and promotion. Packaging can also be used to appeal to emotions. To appeal to consumers' fond memories of "the good ol' days," companies such as Mountain Dew and Frito-Lay have launched packages with designs reminiscent of the 1960s and the 1980s.[18] On the other hand, organizations must also exert caution before changing the designs of highly popular products.

Labeling

Labeling, the presentation of important information on the package, is closely associated with packaging. The content of labeling, often required by law, may include ingredients or content, nutrition facts (calories, fat, and so on), care instructions, suggestions for use (such as recipes), the manufacturer's address and toll-free number, website, and other useful information. This information can have a strong impact on sales. The labels of many products, particularly food and drugs, must carry warnings, instructions, certifications, or manufacturers' identifications.

Product Quality

Quality reflects the degree to which a good, service, or idea meets the demands and requirements of customers. Quality products are often referred to as reliable, durable, easily maintained, easily used, a good value, or a trusted brand name. The level of quality is the amount of quality that a product possesses, and the consistency of quality depends on the product maintaining the same level of quality over time.

Quality of service is difficult to gauge because it depends on customers' perceptions of how well the service meets or

Google built a high-quality search engine that soon dominated the industry and made it one of the most valuable brands worldwide. It also owns YouTube, the most popular video sharing site on the web. YouTube transformed an old phone booth into a YouTube Upload Booth at the Macworld Expo.

exceeds their expectations. In other words, service quality is judged by consumers, not the service providers. For this reason, it is quite common for perceptions of quality to fluctuate from year to year. For example, although Ford was considered to be the fifth highest in quality in 2010, it dropped to 27 in 2012 due to problems with its entertainment system. Ford responded by issuing upgrades to its entertainment system.[19] A bank may define service quality as employing friendly and knowledgeable employees, but the bank's customers may be more concerned with waiting time, ATM access, security, and statement accuracy. Similarly, an airline traveler considers on-time arrival, on-board Internet or TV connections, and satisfaction with the ticketing and boarding process. The American Customer Satisfaction Index produces customer satisfaction scores for 10 economic sectors, 47 industries, and more than 200 companies. The latest results show that overall customer satisfaction was 76.3 (out of a possible 100) with increases in some industries balancing out drops in others.[20]

> "Service quality is judged by consumers, not the service providers."

The quality of services provided by businesses on the Internet can be gauged by consumers on such sites as ConsumerReports.org and BBBOnline. The subscription service offered by ConsumerReports.org provides consumers with a view of digital marketing sites' business, security, and privacy policies; BBBOnline is dedicated to promoting responsibility online. As consumers join in by posting business and product reviews on the Internet on sites such as Yelp, the public can often get a much better idea of the quality of certain goods and services. Quality can also be associated with where the product is made. For example, "Made in U.S.A." labeling can be perceived as having a different value and quality. There are differences in the perception of quality and value between U.S. consumers and Europeans when comparing products made in the United States, Japan, Korea, and China.[21] Chinese brands are usually perceived as lower quality, whereas Japanese and Korean products are perceived as being of higher quality.

LO 12-2 Define price and discuss its importance in the marketing mix, including various pricing strategies a firm might employ.

PRICING STRATEGY

Previously, we defined price as the value placed on an object exchanged between a buyer and a seller. Buyers' interest in price stems from their expectations about the usefulness of a product or the satisfaction they may derive from it. Because buyers have limited resources, they must allocate those resources to obtain the products they most desire. They must decide whether the benefits gained in an exchange are worth the buying power sacrificed. Almost anything of value can be assessed by a price. Many factors may influence the evaluation of value, including time constraints, price levels, perceived quality, and motivations to use available information about prices.[22]

Indeed, consumers vary in their response to price: Some focus solely on the lowest price, whereas others consider quality or the prestige associated with a product and its price. Some types of consumers are increasingly trading up to more status-conscious products, such as automobiles, home appliances, restaurants, and even pet food, yet remain price-conscious for other products such as cleaning and grocery goods. In setting prices, marketers must consider not just a company's cost to produce a good or service, but the perceived value of that item in the marketplace. Products' perceived value has benefited marketers at Starbucks, Sub-Zero, BMW, and Petco—which can charge premium prices for high-quality, prestige products—as

price skimming charging the highest possible price that buyers who want the product will pay

penetration price a low price designed to help a product enter the market and gain market share rapidly

psychological pricing encouraging purchases based on emotional rather than rational responses to the price

reference pricing a type of psychological pricing in which a lower-priced item is compared to a more expensive brand in hopes that the consumer will use the higher price as a comparison price

discounts temporary price reductions, often employed to boost sales

marketing channel a group of organizations that moves products from their producer to customers; also called a channel of distribution

retailers intermediaries who buy products from manufacturers (or other intermediaries) and sell them to consumers for home and household use rather than for resale or for use in producing other products

well as Sam's Clubs and Costco—which offer basic household products at everyday low prices.

Price is a key element in the marketing mix because it relates directly to the generation of revenue and profits. In large part, the ability to set a price depends on the supply of and demand for a product. For most products, the quantity demanded goes up as the price goes down, and as the price goes up, the quantity demanded goes down, as illustrated in Chapter 1. Changes in buyers' needs, variations in the effectiveness of other marketing mix variables, the presence of substitutes, and dynamic environmental factors can influence demand. The demand and price for coal has decreased as the price for natural gas has decreased due to an increase in supply.

Price is probably the most flexible variable in the marketing mix. Although it may take years to develop a product, establish channels of distribution, and design and implement promotion, a product's price may be set and changed in a few minutes. Under certain circumstances, of course, the price may not be so flexible, especially if government regulations prevent dealers from controlling prices. Of course, price also depends on the cost to manufacture a good or provide a service or idea. A firm may temporarily sell products below cost to match competition, to generate cash flow, or even to increase market share, but in the long run, it cannot survive by selling its products below cost.

Morton's of Chicago uses a prestige pricing model to indicate the high quality of its food.

Pricing Objectives

Pricing objectives specify the role of price in an organization's marketing mix and strategy. They usually are influenced not only by marketing mix decisions but also by finance, accounting, and production factors. Maximizing profits and sales, boosting market share, maintaining the status quo, and survival are four common pricing objectives.

Specific Pricing Strategies

Pricing strategies provide guidelines for achieving the company's pricing objectives and overall marketing strategy. They specify how price will be used as a variable in the marketing mix. Significant pricing strategies relate to the pricing of new products, psychological pricing, and price discounting.

Pricing New Products Setting the price for a new product is critical: The right price leads to profitability; the wrong price may kill the product. In general, there are two basic strategies to setting the base price for a new product. **Price skimming** is charging the highest possible price that buyers who want the product will pay. Price skimming is used with luxury goods items. Gucci bags, for example, often run into the thousands of dollars. Price skimming is often used to allow the company to generate much-needed revenue to help offset the costs of research and development. Conversely, a **penetration price** is a low price designed to help a product enter the market and gain market share rapidly. When Netflix entered the market, it offered its rentals at prices much lower than the average rental stores and did not charge late fees. Netflix quickly gained market share and eventually drove many rental stores out of business. Penetration pricing is less flexible than price skimming; it is more difficult to raise a penetration price than to lower a skimming price. Netflix found this out the hard way when it faced consumer backlash for raising the fees on one of its most popular rental packages. Penetration pricing is used most often when marketers suspect that competitors will enter the market shortly after the product has been introduced.

Psychological Pricing **Psychological pricing** encourages purchases based on emotional rather than rational responses to the price. For example, the assumption behind *even/odd pricing* is that people will buy more of a product for $9.99 than $10 because it seems to be a bargain at the odd price. The assumption behind *symbolic/prestige pricing* is that high prices connote high quality. Thus the prices of certain fragrances and cosmetics are set artificially high to give the

DARDEN RESTAURANTS CHANGES TACTICS TO APPEAL TO CONSUMERS' CHANGING TASTES

Darden Restaurants, owner of chains such as Olive Garden and Red Lobster, is experiencing the consequences of marketing complacency. It is a well-known fact that large companies have difficulty changing the way they do business, especially if it has proved successful over long periods of time. Darden Restaurants' focus has traditionally been on quality dining. However, with changing market trends, this focus has led to a fall in sales. Consumers are now more concerned about cost, and Darden Restaurants is changing its marketing strategies to address these trends with smaller dishes, bigger appetizers (that could serve as meals), and a new marketing campaign that focuses on value. It is also introducing more nonseafood dishes on the Red Lobster menu to attract different types of customers. However, it must be careful of the effects of psychological pricing on its current customer base. Some customers may see the discount in price as a reflection of lower-quality foods.

The restaurant chains are also moving into vacant strip mall locations to expand and make themselves available to different types of customers. Retailers are welcoming their new neighbors because they can sell some of their parking spaces, and they hope the new restaurants will attract more business for their stores. This strategy will cut long-term costs for the restaurants because some of these existing spaces are large enough to place two restaurants near each other, which enables one truck delivery to service two locations at the same time.[23]

Discussion Questions

1. Why is it easy for companies to become complacent regarding changing market trends?
2. Do you think that Darden Restaurants' price discounts are a good move for the firm?
3. Name some of the advantages of locating restaurants in strip malls. Can you think of any disadvantages?

impression of superior quality. Some over-the-counter drugs are priced high because consumers associate a drug's price with potency.

Reference Pricing **Reference pricing** is a type of psychological pricing in which a lower-priced item is compared to a more expensive brand in hopes that the consumer will use the higher price as a comparison price. The main idea is to make the item appear less expensive compared to other alternatives. For example, Walmart might place its own Great Value brand next to a manufacturer's brand such as Bayer or Johnson & Johnson so that the Great Value brand will look like a better deal.

Price Discounting Temporary price reductions, or **discounts**, are often employed to boost sales. Although there are many types, quantity, seasonal, and promotional discounts are among the most widely used. Quantity discounts reflect the economies of purchasing in large volumes. Seasonal discounts to buyers who purchase goods or services out of season help even out production capacity. Promotional discounts attempt to improve sales by advertising price reductions on selected products to increase customer interest. Often promotional pricing is geared toward increased profits. Taco Bell, with its reputation for value, has been labeled the "best-positioned U.S. brand" to do well in a recession economy as consumers look for cheaper fast-food options. Taco Bell offers a Why Pay More? menu with selections priced at 89¢ and 99¢. KFC, Wendy's, and McDonald's all offer Value Menus as well, with items priced around $1.

LO 12-3 Identify factors affecting distribution decisions, such as marketing channels and intensity of market coverage.

DISTRIBUTION STRATEGY

The best products in the world will not be successful unless companies make them available where and when customers want to buy them. In this section, we will explore dimensions of distribution strategy, including the channels through which products are distributed, the intensity of market coverage, and the physical handling of products during distribution.

Marketing Channels

A **marketing channel**, or channel of distribution, is a group of organizations that moves products from their producer to customers. Marketing channels make products available to buyers when and where they desire to purchase them. Organizations that bridge the gap between a product's manufacturer and the ultimate consumer are called *middlemen,* or intermediaries. They create time, place, and ownership utility. Two intermediary organizations are retailers and wholesalers.

Retailers buy products from manufacturers (or other intermediaries) and sell them to consumers for home and household use rather than for resale or for use in producing other products. Toys 'Я' Us, for example, buys products from Mattel and other manufacturers and resells them to consumers. By bringing together an assortment of products from competing producers, retailers create utility. Retailers arrange for products to

wholesalers intermediaries who buy from producers or from other wholesalers and sell to retailers

be moved from producers to a convenient retail establishment (place utility). They maintain hours of operation for their retail stores to make merchandise available when consumers want it (time utility). They also assume the risk of ownership of inventories (ownership utility). Table 12.4 describes various types of general merchandise retailers.

Today, there are too many stores competing for too few customers, and, as a result, competition between similar retailers has never been more intense. Further, competition between different types of stores is changing the nature of retailing. Supermarkets compete with specialty food stores, wholesale clubs, and discount stores. Department stores compete with nearly every other type of store, including specialty stores, off-price chains, category killers, discount stores, and online retailers. For this reason, many businesses have turned to nonstore retailing to sell their products. Some nonstore retailing is performed by traditional retailers to complement their in-store offerings. For instance, Walmart and Macy's have created online shopping sites to retain customers and compete against other businesses. Other companies retail outside of physical stores entirely. The Internet, vending machines, mail-order catalogs, and entertainment such as going to a Chicago Bulls basketball game all provide opportunities for retailing outside of a store environment. For instance, although traditional vending machines are decreasing, some businesses are finding success by using vending machines in unusual ways. PA Live Bait Vending Machines use a refrigeration system and rotation process to sell minnows, mealworms, and nightcrawlers for fishing. PA Live Bait Vending now has 400 machines in operation.[24]

Wholesalers are intermediaries who buy from producers or from other wholesalers and sell to retailers. They usually do not sell in significant quantities to ultimate consumers. Wholesalers perform the functions listed in Table 12.5.

Wholesalers are extremely important because of the marketing activities they perform, particularly for consumer products. Although it is true that wholesalers can be eliminated, their functions must be passed on to some other entity, such as the producer, another intermediary, or even the customer. Wholesalers help consumers and retailers by buying in large quantities, then selling to retailers in smaller quantities. By stocking an assortment of products, wholesalers match products to demand. Sysco is a food wholesaler for the food services industry. The company provides food, preparation, and serving products to restaurants, hospitals, and other institutions that provide meals outside of the home.[25]

Supply Chain Management

In an effort to improve distribution channel relationships among manufacturers and other channel intermediaries, supply chain management creates alliances between channel members. In Chapter 8, we defined supply chain management as connecting and integrating all parties or members of the distribution system to satisfy customers. It involves long-term partnerships among marketing channel members working together to reduce costs, waste, and unnecessary movement in the entire marketing channel to satisfy customers. It goes beyond traditional channel members (producers, wholesalers, retailers, customers) to include *all* organizations involved in moving products from the producer to the ultimate customer. In a survey of business managers, a disruption in the supply chain

TABLE 12.4 General Merchandise Retailers

Type of Retailer	Description	Examples
Department store	Large organization offering wide product mix and organized into separate departments	Macy's, jcpenney, Sears
Discount store	Self-service, general merchandise store offering brand name and private brand products at low prices	Walmart, Target, Kmart
Convenience store	Small self-service store offering narrow product assortment in convenient locations	7-Eleven
Supermarket	Self-service store offering complete line of food products and some nonfood products	Kroger, Safeway, Publix
Superstore	Giant outlet offering all food and nonfood products found in supermarkets, as well as most routinely purchased products	Walmart Supercenters, SuperTarget
Hypermarket	Combination supermarket and discount store, larger than a superstore	Carrefour
Warehouse club	Large-scale, members-only establishments combining cash-and-carry wholesaling with discount retailing	Sam's Club, Costco
Warehouse showroom	Facility in a large, low-cost building with large on-premises inventories and minimum service	Ikea

Source: From William M. Pride and O.C. Ferrell, *Marketing Foundations*, 2013 Edition. © 2013 South-Western, a part of Cengage Learning, Inc. Reproduced by permission. www.cengage.com/permissions.

TABLE 12.5 Major Wholesaling Functions

Supply chain management	Creating long-term partnerships among channel members
Promotion	Providing a sales force, advertising, sales promotion, and publicity
Warehousing, shipping, and product handling	Receiving, storing, and stockkeeping Packaging Shipping outgoing orders Materials handling Arranging and making local and long-distance shipments
Inventory control and data processing	Processing orders Controlling physical inventory Recording transactions Tracking sales data for financial analysis
Risk taking	Assuming responsibility for theft, product obsolescence, and excess inventories
Financing and budgeting	Extending credit Making capital investments Forecasting cash flow
Marketing research and information systems	Providing information about market Conducting research studies Managing computer networks to facilitate exchanges and relationships

Source: From William M. Pride and O.C. Ferrell, *Marketing,* 2008 Edition. © 2008 South-Western, a part of Cengage Learning, Inc. Reproduced by permission. www.cengage.com/permissions.

was viewed as the number-one crisis that could decrease revenue.[26]

The focus shifts from one of selling to the next level in the channel to one of selling products *through* the channel to a satisfied ultimate customer. Information, once provided on a guarded, "as needed" basis, is now open, honest, and ongoing. Perhaps most importantly, the points of contact in the relationship expand from one-on-one at the salesperson–buyer level to multiple interfaces at all levels and in all functional areas of the various organizations.

Channels for Consumer Products Typical marketing channels for consumer products are shown in Figure 12.5. In Channel A, the product moves from the producer directly to the consumer. Farmers who sell their fruit and vegetables to consumers at roadside stands or farmer's markets use a direct-from-producer-to-consumer marketing channel.

In Channel B, the product goes from producer to retailer to consumer. This type of channel is used for products such as college textbooks, automobiles, and appliances. In Channel C, the product is handled by a wholesaler and a retailer before it reaches the consumer. Producer-to-wholesaler-to-retailer-to-consumer marketing channels distribute a wide range of products including refrigerators, televisions, soft

FIGURE 12.5
Marketing Channels for Consumer Products

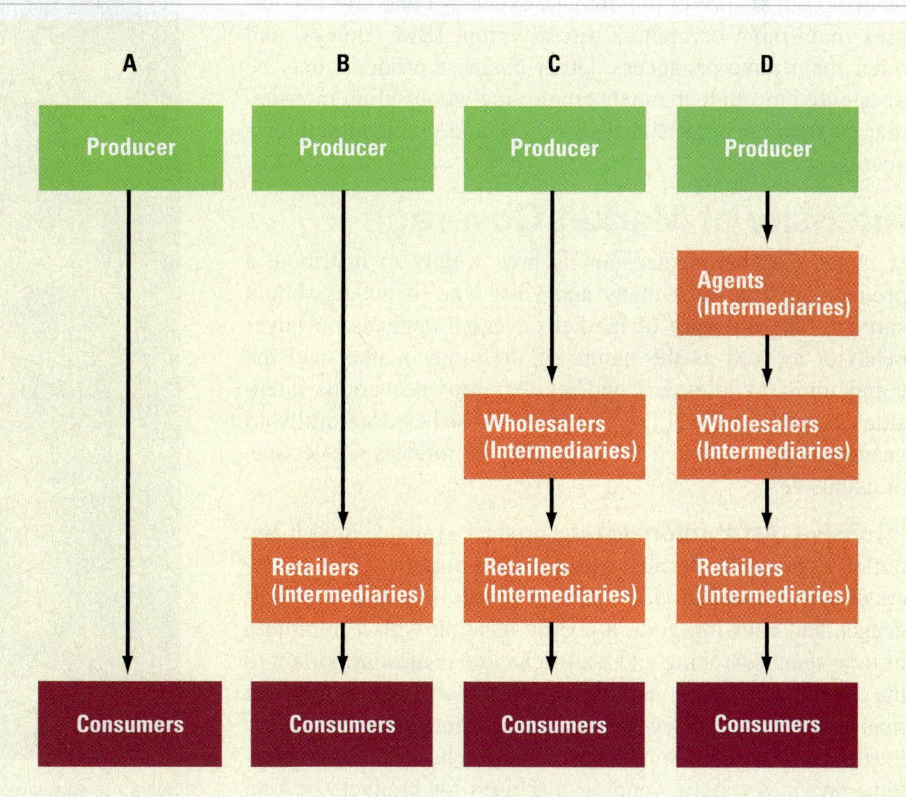

intensive distribution a form of market coverage whereby a product is made available in as many outlets as possible

selective distribution a form of market coverage whereby only a small number of all available outlets are used to expose products

exclusive distribution the awarding by a manufacturer to an intermediary of the sole right to sell a product in a defined geographic territory

physical distribution all the activities necessary to move products from producers to customers—inventory control, transportation, warehousing, and materials handling

transportation the shipment of products to buyers

warehousing the design and operation of facilities to receive, store, and ship products

drinks, cigarettes, clocks, watches, and office products. In Channel D, the product goes to an agent, a wholesaler, and a retailer before going to the consumer. This long channel of distribution is especially useful for convenience products. Candy and some produce are often sold by agents who bring buyers and sellers together.

Services are usually distributed through direct marketing channels because they are generally produced *and* consumed simultaneously. For example, you cannot take a haircut home for later use. Many services require the customer's presence and participation: The sick patient must visit the physician to receive treatment; the child must be at the day care center to receive care; the tourist must be present to sightsee and consume tourism services.

Channels for Business Products In contrast to consumer goods, more than half of all business products, especially expensive equipment or technically complex products, are sold through direct marketing channels. Business customers like to communicate directly with producers of such products to gain the technical assistance and personal assurances that only the producer can offer. For this reason, business buyers prefer to purchase expensive and highly complex mainframe computers directly from IBM, Unisys, and other mainframe producers. Other business products may be distributed through channels employing wholesaling intermediaries such as industrial distributors and/or manufacturer's agents.

Intensity of Market Coverage

A major distribution decision is how widely to distribute a product—that is, how many and what type of outlets should carry it. The intensity of market coverage depends on buyer behavior as well as the nature of the target market and the competition. Wholesalers and retailers provide various intensities of market coverage and must be selected carefully to ensure success. Market coverage may be intensive, selective, or exclusive.

Intensive distribution makes a product available in as many outlets as possible. Because availability is important to purchasers of convenience products such as bread, milk, gasoline, soft drinks, and chewing gum, a nearby location with a minimum of time spent searching and waiting in line is most important to the consumer. To saturate markets intensively, wholesalers and many varied retailers try to make the product available at every location a consumer might desire to purchase it. Zoom Systems provides robotic vending machines for products beyond candy and drinks. Zoom has more than a thousand machines in airports and hotels across the United States, some selling items such as Apple iPods, Neutrogena hair and skin products,

Sears has exclusive distribution of the Kardashian Kollection line of clothing.

and Sony products. The vending machines accept credit cards and allow sales to occur in places where storefronts would be impossible.[27] Through partnering with different companies, today's ZoomShops sell a variety of brands, including products from Sephora, Best Buy, Macy's, and Rosetta Stone.[28]

Selective distribution uses only a small number of all available outlets to expose products. It is used most often for products that consumers buy only after shopping and comparing price, quality, and style. Many products sold on a selective basis require salesperson assistance, technical advice, warranties, or repair service to maintain consumer satisfaction. Typical products include automobiles, major appliances, clothes, and furniture. Ralph Lauren is a brand that uses selective distribution.

Exclusive distribution exists when a manufacturer gives an intermediary the sole right to sell a product in a defined geographic territory. Such exclusivity provides an incentive for a dealer to handle a product that has a limited market. Exclusive distribution is the opposite of intensive distribution in that products are purchased and consumed over a long period of time, and service or information is required to develop a satisfactory sales relationship. Products distributed on an exclusive basis include high-quality musical instruments, yachts, airplanes, and high-fashion leather goods. Aircraft manufacturer Piper Aircraft uses exclusive distribution by choosing only a few dealers in each region. The company has only six dealers throughout the Americas.[29]

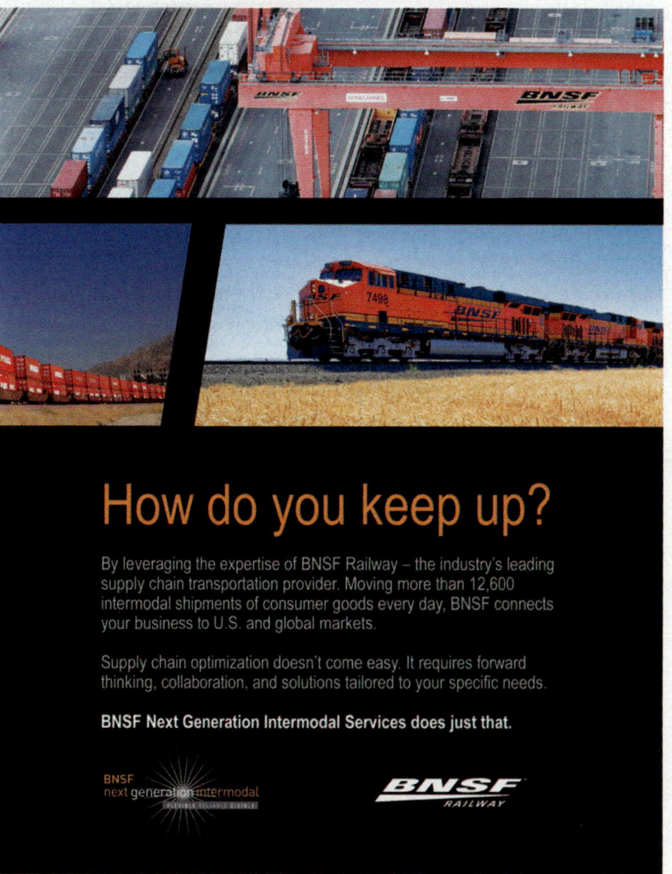

BNSF Railway is one of the largest freight railroads in North America. Although the popularity of passenger trains has dwindled in favor of other forms of transportation, railroads play a key role in keeping the U.S. supply chain competitive. (Reprinted with permission of BNSF Railway Company.)

Physical Distribution

Physical distribution includes all the activities necessary to move products from producers to customers—inventory control, transportation, warehousing, and materials handling. Physical distribution creates time and place utility by making products available when they are wanted, with adequate service and at minimum cost. Both goods and services require physical distribution. Many physical distribution activities are part of supply chain management, which we discussed in Chapter 8; we'll take a brief look at a few more now.

Transportation

Transportation, the shipment of products to buyers, creates time and place utility for products and thus is a key element in the flow of goods and services from producer to consumer. The five major modes of transportation used to move products between cities in the United States are railways, motor vehicles, inland waterways, pipelines, and airways.

Railroads are a cost-effective method of transportation for many products. Heavy commodities, foodstuffs, raw materials, and coal are examples of products carried by railroads. Trucks have greater flexibility than railroads because they can reach more locations. Trucks handle freight quickly and economically, offer door-to-door service, and are more flexible in their packaging requirements than are ships or airplanes. Air transport offers speed and a high degree of dependability but is the most expensive means of transportation; shipping is the slowest form. Pipelines are used to transport petroleum, natural gas, semiliquid coal, wood chips, and certain chemicals. Pipelines have the lowest costs for products that can be transported via this method. Many products can be moved most efficiently by using more than one mode of transportation.

Factors affecting the selection of a mode of transportation include cost, capability to handle the product, reliability, and availability, and, as suggested, selecting transportation modes requires trade-offs. Unique characteristics of the product and consumer desires often determine the mode selected.

Warehousing

Warehousing is the design and operation of facilities to receive, store, and ship products. A warehouse facility receives, identifies, sorts, and dispatches goods to storage; stores them; recalls, selects, or picks goods; assembles the shipment; and, finally, dispatches the shipment.

Companies often own and operate their own private warehouses that store, handle, and move their own products. Firms might want to own or lease a private warehouse when their goods require special handling and storage or when it has large warehousing needs in a specific geographic area. Private

materials handling the physical handling and movement of products in warehousing and transportation

integrated marketing communications coordinating the promotion mix elements and synchronizing promotion as a unified effort

advertising a paid form of nonpersonal communication transmitted through a mass medium, such as television commercials or magazine advertisements

advertising campaign designing a series of advertisements and placing them in various media to reach a particular target market

warehouses are beneficial because they provide customers with more control over their goods. However, fixed costs for maintaining these warehouses can be quite high.[30] They can also rent storage and related physical distribution services from public warehouses. Although public warehouses store goods for more than one company, providing firms with less control over distribution, they are often less expensive than private warehouses and are useful for seasonal production or low-volume storage.[31] Regardless of whether a private or a public warehouse is used, warehousing is important because it makes products available for shipment to match demand at different geographic locations.

Materials Handling **Materials handling** is the physical handling and movement of products in warehousing and transportation. Handling processes may vary significantly due to product characteristics. Efficient materials-handling procedures increase a warehouse's useful capacity and improve customer service. Well-coordinated loading and movement systems increase efficiency and reduce costs.

Importance of Distribution in a Marketing Strategy

Distribution decisions are among the least flexible marketing mix decisions. Products can be changed over time; prices can be changed quickly; and promotion is usually changed regularly. But distribution decisions often commit resources and establish contractual relationships that are difficult if not impossible to change. As a company attempts to expand into new markets, it may require a complete change in distribution. Moreover, if a firm does not manage its marketing channel in the most efficient manner and provide the best service, then a new competitor will evolve to create a more effective distribution system.

This ad for Hot Wheels conveys the fun and thrilling "ride" children can experience with this toy—so much so that it almost becomes a crime.

LO 12-4 Specify the activities involved in promotion as well as promotional strategies and promotional positioning.

PROMOTION STRATEGY

The role of promotion is to communicate with individuals, groups, and organizations to facilitate an exchange directly or indirectly. It encourages marketing exchanges by attempting to persuade individuals, groups, and organizations to accept goods, services, and ideas. Promotion is used not only to sell products but also to influence opinions and attitudes toward an organization, person, or cause. The state of Texas, for example, has successfully used promotion to educate people about the costs of highway litter and thereby reduce littering. Most people probably equate promotion with advertising, but it also includes personal selling, publicity, and sales promotion. The role that these elements play in a marketing strategy is extremely important.

The Promotion Mix

Advertising, personal selling, publicity, and sales promotion are collectively known as the promotion mix because a strong promotion program results from the careful selection and blending of these elements. The process of coordinating the promotion mix elements and synchronizing promotion as a unified effort is called **integrated marketing communications**. When planning promotional activities, an integrated marketing communications approach results in the desired message for customers. Different elements of the promotion mix are coordinated to play their appropriate roles in delivery of the message on a consistent basis.

Advertising Perhaps the best-known form of promotion, **advertising** is a paid form of nonpersonal communication transmitted through a mass medium, such as television commercials, magazine advertisements, or online ads. Even Google, one of the most powerful brands in the world, advertises. Google has turned to outdoor advertising on buses, trains, and ballparks in San Francisco and Chicago to promote its

DRIVING THE TIGER: DEMAND FOR SUVS GROWS IN CHINA

Sport utility vehicle (SUV) sales in the United States and Europe are declining, but the demand for these vehicles is growing rapidly in China. Despite China's overwhelming population, narrow roads, small parking lots, and high gas prices, Chinese moms are creating the demand for the SUV. However, it is not just any SUV they demand—they want a luxury SUV. Automakers are ready to meet the demand. After Toyota and Honda first introduced their SUVs to the Chinese market, interest grew for nicer models. Audi and BMW stepped in with luxury SUVs.

Another reason for this demand is that China's middle class is growing in both number and affluence, and it is choosing to express its status through the SUV. The cost of importing some of the SUV models into China is very high, which can make the cost of an SUV close to $100,000. This is not an issue for the Chinese consumer willing to pay the high price. Some automakers are establishing manufacturing factories in China to get the SUVs into the Chinese market more quickly. One concern, however, is about the effects that growing SUV use will have on the environment. Although American and European consumers are opting for cars with greater fuel efficiency, China's pollution problems might worsen if demand for these gas guzzlers continues to grow.[32]

Discussion Questions

1. Why is demand for SUVs growing in China?
2. How are automakers meeting this demand?
3. What are some potential issues with the growing demand for SUVs in China?

> "ADVERTISING MEDIA ARE THE VEHICLES OR FORMS OF COMMUNICATION USED TO REACH A DESIRED AUDIENCE."

Google Maps feature.[33] Commercials featuring celebrities, customers, or unique creations serve to grab viewers' attention and pique their interest in a product.

An **advertising campaign** involves designing a series of advertisements and placing them in various media to reach a particular target audience. The basic content and form of an advertising campaign are a function of several factors. A product's features, uses, and benefits affect the content of the campaign message and individual ads. Characteristics of the people in the target audience—gender, age, education, race, income, occupation, lifestyle, and other attributes—influence both content and form. When Procter & Gamble promotes Crest toothpaste to children, the company emphasizes daily brushing and cavity control, whereas it promotes tartar control and whiter teeth when marketing to adults. To communicate effectively, advertisers use words, symbols, and illustrations that are meaningful, familiar, and attractive to people in the target audience.

An advertising campaign's objectives and platform also affect the content and form of its messages. If a firm's advertising objectives involve large sales increases, the message may include hard-hitting, high-impact language and symbols. When campaign objectives aim at increasing brand awareness, the message may use much repetition of the brand name and words and illustrations associated with it. Thus, the advertising platform is the foundation on which campaign messages are built.

Advertising media are the vehicles or forms of communication used to reach a desired audience. Print media include newspapers, magazines, direct mail, and billboards, whereas electronic media include television, radio, and Internet advertising. Choice of media obviously influences the content and form of the message. Effective outdoor displays and short broadcast spot announcements require concise, simple messages. Magazine and newspaper advertisements can include considerable detail and long explanations. Because several kinds of media offer geographic selectivity, a precise message can be tailored to a particular geographic section of the target audience. For example, a company advertising in *Time* might decide to use one message in the New England region and another in the rest of the nation. A company may also choose to advertise in only one region. Such geographic selectivity lets a firm use the same message in different regions at different times. On the other hand, some companies are willing to pay extensive amounts of money to reach national audiences. Marketers spent approximately $545,000 for one 30-second ad spot in NBC Sunday Night Football.[34]

The use of online advertising is increasing. However, advertisers are demanding more for their ad dollars and proof that they are working, which is why Google AdWords charges companies only when users click the ad. Certain types of ads are more popular than pop-up ads and banner ads that consumers find annoying. One technique is to blur the lines between

personal selling direct, two-way communication with buyers and potential buyers

publicity nonpersonal communication transmitted through the mass media but not paid for directly by the firm

sales promotion direct inducements offering added value or some other incentive for buyers to enter into an exchange

television and online advertising. TV commercials may point viewers to a website for more information, where short "advertainment" films continue the marketing message. Marketers might also use the Internet to show advertisements or videos that were not accepted by mainstream television. When CBS rejected an ad from the National Football League Players Association involving the lockout of players during a collective bargaining dispute, the ad was played on the association's YouTube channel and other social media outlets.[35]

Infomercials—typically 30-minute blocks of radio or television air time featuring a celebrity or upbeat host talking about and demonstrating a product—have evolved as an advertising method. Toll-free numbers and website addresses are usually provided so consumers can conveniently purchase the product or obtain additional information. Although many consumers and companies have negative feelings about infomercials, apparently they get results.

Personal Selling

Personal selling is direct, two-way communication with buyers and potential buyers. For many products—especially large, expensive ones with specialized uses, such as cars, appliances, and houses—interaction between a salesperson and the customer is probably the most important promotional tool.

Personal selling is the most flexible of the promotional methods because it gives marketers the greatest opportunity to communicate specific information that might trigger a purchase. Only personal selling can zero in on a prospect and attempt to persuade that person to make a purchase. Although personal selling has a lot of advantages, it is one of the most costly forms of promotion. A sales call on an industrial customer can cost more than $400.

There are three distinct categories of salespersons: order takers (for example, retail sales clerks and route salespeople), creative salespersons (for example, automobile, furniture, and insurance salespeople), and support salespersons (for example, customer educators and goodwill builders who usually do not take orders). For most of these salespeople, personal selling is a six-step process:

1. *Prospecting:* Identifying potential buyers of the product.
2. *Approaching:* Using a referral or calling on a customer without prior notice to determine interest in the product.
3. *Presenting:* Getting the prospect's attention with a product demonstration.
4. *Handling objections:* Countering reasons for not buying the product.
5. *Closing:* Asking the prospect to buy the product.
6. *Following up:* Checking customer satisfaction with the purchased product.

Publicity

Publicity is nonpersonal communication transmitted through the mass media but not paid for directly by the firm. A firm does not pay the media cost for publicity and is not identified as the originator of the message; instead, the message is presented in news story form. Obviously, a company can benefit from publicity by releasing to news sources newsworthy messages about the firm and its involvement with the public. Many companies have *public relations* departments that try to gain favorable publicity and minimize negative publicity for the firm.

Although advertising and publicity are both carried by the mass media, they differ in several major ways. Advertising messages tend to be informative, persuasive, or both; publicity is mainly informative. Advertising is often designed to have an immediate impact or to provide specific information to persuade a person to act; publicity describes what a firm is doing, what products it is launching, or other newsworthy information, but seldom calls for action. When advertising is used, the organization must pay for media time and select the media that will best reach target audiences. The mass media willingly carry publicity because they believe it has general public interest. Advertising can be repeated a number of times; most publicity appears in the mass media once and is not repeated.

Advertising, personal selling, and sales promotion are especially useful for influencing an exchange directly. Publicity is extremely important when communication focuses on a company's activities and products and is directed at interest groups, current and potential investors, regulatory agencies, and society in general.

A variation of traditional advertising is buzz marketing, in which marketers attempt to create a trend or acceptance of a product. Companies seek out trendsetters in communities and get them to "talk up" a brand to their friends, family, co-workers, and others. Red Bull, often considered to be the king of buzz marketing, generated excitement when it sponsored daredevil Felix Baumgartner's jump from 23 miles above the Earth's surface. The jump broke sound barriers and caught the attention of much of the world. At one point, YouTube had 8 million viewers simultaneously watching the stunt.[36] Other marketers using the buzz technique include Hebrew National ("mom squads" grilled the company's hot dogs) and Chrysler (its retro PT Cruiser was planted in rental fleets). The idea behind buzz marketing is that an accepted member of a particular social group will be more credible than any form of paid communication.[37] The concept works best as part of an integrated marketing communication program that also includes traditional advertising, personal selling, sales promotion, and publicity.

A related concept is viral marketing, which describes the concept of getting Internet users to pass on ads and promotions to others. For example, the restaurant Kogi, which operates Korean taco trucks that traverse the Los Angeles area, was dubbed by *Newsweek* as "America's First Viral Restaurant" after it began using Twitter and the web to announce the whereabouts of its taco trucks.[38]

Jamba Juice increases demand for its fruit refreshers by offering coupons providing a discount.

Sales Promotion **Sales promotion** involves direct inducements offering added value or some other incentive for buyers to enter into an exchange. Sales promotions are generally easier to measure and less expensive than advertising. The major tools of sales promotion are store displays, premiums, samples and demonstrations, coupons, contests and sweepstakes, refunds, and trade shows. Coupon-clipping in particular has become more common during the recent recession. Although coupons in the past decade traditionally had a fairly low redemption rate, with about 2 percent being redeemed, the recent recession caused an upsurge in coupon usage. There has also been a major upsurge in the use of mobile coupons, or coupons sent to consumers over mobile devices. It is estimated that the redemption rates for mobile coupons will reach 8 percent of total coupon redemption rates by 2016.[39] Although coupons can be a valuable tool in sales promotion, they cannot be relied upon to stand by themselves but should be part of an overall promotion mix. Sales promotion stimulates customer purchasing and increases dealer effectiveness in selling products. It is used to enhance and supplement other forms of promotion. Sampling a product may also encourage consumers to buy. This is why many grocery stores provide free samples in the hopes of influencing consumers' purchasing decisions. In a given year, almost three-fourths of consumer product companies may use sampling.

Promotion Strategies: To Push or to Pull

In developing a promotion mix, organizations must decide whether to fashion a mix that pushes or pulls the product (Figure 12.6). A **push strategy** attempts to motivate intermediaries to push the product down to their customers. When a push strategy is used, the company attempts to motivate wholesalers and retailers to make the product available to their customers. Sales personnel may be used to persuade intermediaries to offer the product, distribute promotional materials, and offer special promotional incentives for those who agree to carry the product. For example, Kimberly-Clark is working with Red Dot Solutions to collaborate with retailers such as Walmart in developing virtual environments for customers to enhance their in-store shopping experience. In creating such favorable partnerships with retailers down the supply chain, Kimberly-Clark hopes to create favorable relationships with its intermediaries to push its products through the system.[40] A **pull strategy** uses promotion to create consumer demand for a product so that consumers exert pressure on marketing channel members

push strategy
an attempt to motivate intermediaries to push the product down to their customers

pull strategy
the use of promotion to create consumer demand for a product so that consumers exert pressure on marketing channel members to make it available

promotional positioning the use of promotion to create and maintain an image of a product in buyers' minds

to make it available. For a while, T-Mobile was the only major carrier that did not have the iPhone. The iPhone was not compatible with T-Mobile's 3G frequencies, so Apple largely sidestepped T-Mobile. However, the popularity of the iPhone and decreasing market share caused T-Mobile to revamp its spectrum to run on the iPhone better. This is an example of how consumer pull caused a company to change its practices.[41] In addition, offering free samples prior to a product rollout encourages consumers to request the product from their favorite retailer.

A company can use either strategy, or it can use a variation or combination of the two. The exclusive use of advertising indicates a pull strategy. Personal selling to marketing channel members indicates a push strategy. The allocation of promotional resources to various marketing mix elements probably determines which strategy a marketer uses.

Objectives of Promotion

The marketing mix a company uses depends on its objectives. It is important to recognize that promotion is only one element of the marketing strategy and must be tied carefully to the goals of the firm, its overall marketing objectives, and the other elements of the marketing strategy. Firms use promotion for many reasons, but typical objectives are to stimulate demand, to stabilize sales, and to inform, remind, and reinforce customers.

Increasing demand for a product is probably the most typical promotional objective. Stimulating demand, often through advertising and sales promotion, is particularly important when a firm is using a pull strategy.

Another goal of promotion is to stabilize sales by maintaining the status quo—that is, the current sales level of the product. During periods of slack or decreasing sales, contests, prizes, vacations, and other sales promotions are sometimes offered to customers to maintain sales goals. Advertising is often used to stabilize sales by making customers aware of slack use periods. For example, auto manufacturers often provide rebates, free options, or lower-than-market interest rates to stabilize sales and thereby keep production lines moving during temporary slowdowns. In addition, travel agents agree that Tuesdays and Wednesdays are generally the best time to purchase airline tickets. Airline sales are often launched on Monday night, and by Tuesday and Wednesday competing airlines tend to have lowered their fares to compete. The sales usually expire by Thursday and Friday, and ticket prices are highest on weekends due to peak demand. These different prices allow airlines to stabilize sales throughout the week.[42] A stable sales pattern allows the firm to run efficiently by maintaining a consistent level of production and storage and using all its functions so that it is ready when sales increase.

An important role of any promotional program is to inform potential buyers about the organization and its products. A major portion of advertising in the United States, particularly in daily newspapers, is informational. For example, if you pick up *USA Today,* you will find numerous advertisements on a variety of products at a variety of prices. Providing information

FIGURE 12.6
Push and Pull Strategies

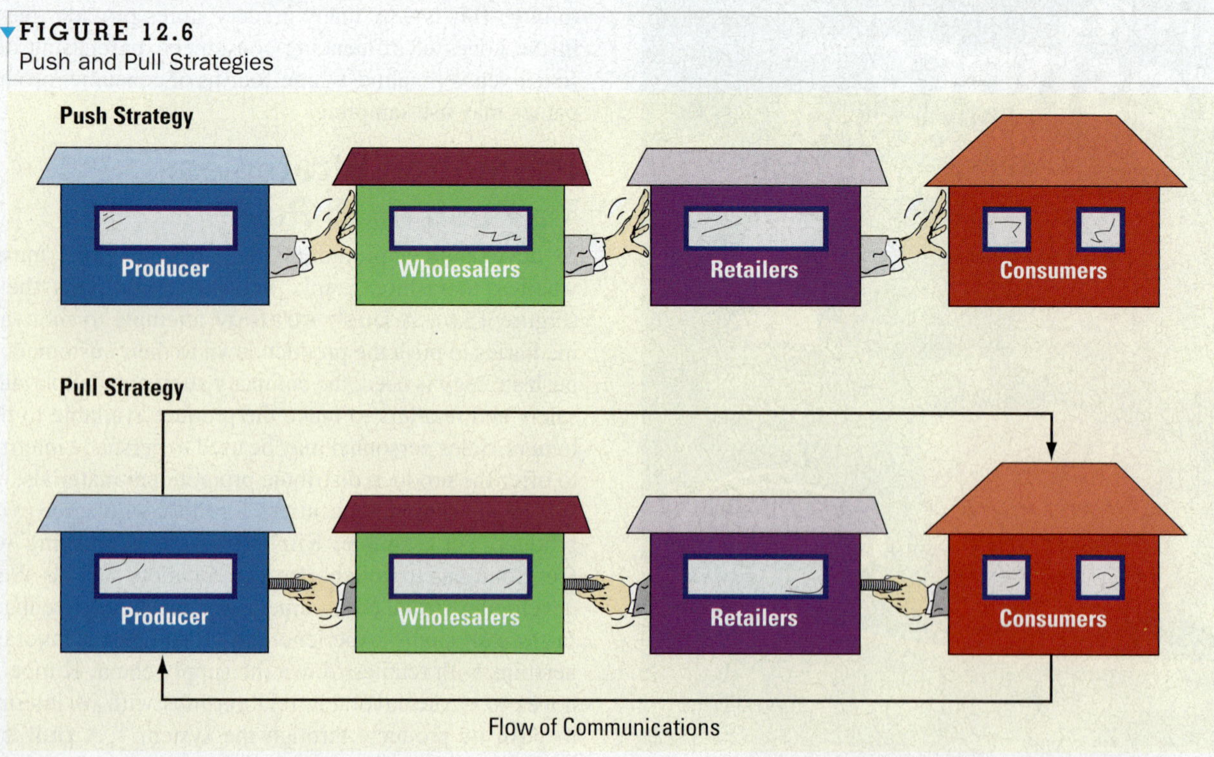

about the availability, price, technology, and features of a product is very important in encouraging a buyer to move toward a purchase decision. Nearly all forms of promotion involve an attempt to help consumers learn more about a product and a company.

Promotion is also used to remind consumers that an established organization is still around and sells certain products that have uses and benefits. Often advertising reminds customers that they may need to use a product more frequently or in certain situations. Pennzoil, for example, has run television commercials reminding car owners that they need to change their oil every 3,000 miles to ensure proper performance of their cars.

Reinforcement promotion attempts to assure current users of the product that they have made the right choice and tells them how to get the most satisfaction from the product. Also, a company could release publicity statements through the news media about a new use for a product. In addition, firms can have salespeople communicate with current and potential customers about the proper use and maintenance of a product—all in the hope of developing a repeat customer.

Promotional Positioning

Promotional positioning uses promotion to create and maintain an image of a product in buyers' minds. It is a natural result of market segmentation. In both promotional positioning and market segmentation, the firm targets a given product or brand at a portion of the total market. A promotional strategy helps differentiate the product and makes it appeal to a particular market segment. For example, to appeal to safety-conscious consumers, Volvo heavily promotes the safety and crashworthiness of Volvo automobiles in its advertising. Volkswagen has done the same thing with its edgy ads showing car crashes. Promotion can be used to change or reinforce an image. Effective promotion influences customers and persuades them to buy.

TEAM EXERCISE

Form groups and search for examples of convenience products, shopping products, specialty products, and business products. How are these products marketed? Provide examples of any ads that you can find to show examples of the promotional strategies for these products. Report your findings to the class.

IMPORTANCE OF MARKETING STRATEGY

Marketing creates value through selecting target markets and developing the marketing mix. For customers, value means receiving a product in which the benefit of the product outweighs the cost, or price paid for it. For marketers, value means that the benefits (usually monetary) received from selling the product outweigh the costs it takes to develop and sell it. This requires carefully integrating the marketing mix into an effective marketing strategy. One misstep could mean a loss in profits, whether from a failed product idea, shortages or oversupply of a product, a failure to promote the product effectively, or prices that are too high or too low. And although some of these marketing mix elements can be easily fixed, other marketing mix elements such as distribution can be harder to adapt.

On the other hand, firms that understand the consumer and develop an effective marketing mix to meet customer needs will gain competitive advantages. Often, these advantages occur when the firm excels at one or more elements of the marketing mix. Walmart has a reputation for its everyday low prices; Tiffany's is known for its high-quality jewelry. However, excelling at one element of the marketing mix does not mean that a company can neglect the others. The best product cannot succeed if consumers do not know about it or if they cannot find it in stores. Additionally, firms must constantly monitor the market environment to understand how demand is changing and whether adaptations in the marketing mix are needed. It is therefore essential for every element of the marketing mix to be carefully evaluated and synchronized with the marketing strategy. Only then will firms be able to achieve the marketing concept of providing products that satisfy customers' needs while allowing the organization to achieve its goals. Marketing in an organization is responsible for creating revenue. Without sales, a business will go out of existence. ■

SO YOU WANT TO BE // a Marketing Manager /

Many jobs in marketing are closely tied to the marketing mix functions: distribution, product, promotion, and price. Often, the job titles could be sales manager, distribution or supply chain manager, advertising account executive, or store manager.

A distribution manager arranges for transportation of goods within firms and through marketing channels. Transportation can be costly, and time is always an important factor, so minimizing their effects is vital to the success of a firm. Distribution managers must choose one or a combination of transportation modes from a vast array of options, taking into account local, federal, and international regulations for different freight classifications; the weight, size, and fragility of products to be shipped; time schedules; and loss and damage ratios. Manufacturing firms are the largest employers of distribution managers.

A product manager is responsible for the success or failure of a product line. This requires a general knowledge of advertising, transportation modes, inventory control, selling and sales management, promotion, marketing research, packaging, and pricing. Frequently, several years of selling and sales management experience are prerequisites for such a position, as well as college training in business administration. Being a product manager can be rewarding both financially and psychologically.

Some of the most creative roles in the business world are in the area of advertising. Advertising pervades our daily lives as businesses and other organizations try to grab our attention and tell us about what they have to offer. Copywriters, artists, and account executives in advertising must have creativity, imagination, artistic talent, and expertise in expression and persuasion. Advertising is an area of business in which a wide variety of educational backgrounds may be useful, from degrees in advertising itself to journalism or liberal arts degrees. Common entry-level positions in an advertising agency are found in the traffic department, account service (account coordinator), or the media department (media assistant). Advertising jobs are also available in many manufacturing or retail firms, nonprofit organizations, banks, professional associations, utility companies, and other arenas outside of an advertising agency.

Although a career in retailing may begin in sales, there is much more to retailing than simply selling. Many retail personnel occupy management positions, focusing on selecting and ordering merchandise, promotional activities, inventory control, customer credit operations, accounting, personnel, and store security. Many specific examples of retailing jobs can be found in large department stores. A section manager coordinates inventory and promotions and interacts with buyers, salespeople, and consumers. The buyer's job is fast-paced, often involving much travel and pressure. Buyers must be open-minded and foresighted in their hunt for new, potentially successful items. Regional managers coordinate the activities of several retail stores within a specific geographic area, usually monitoring and supporting sales, promotions, and general procedures. Retail management can be exciting and challenging. Growth in retailing is expected to accompany the growth in population and is likely to create substantial opportunities in the coming years.

Although a career in marketing can be very rewarding, marketers today agree that the job is getting tougher. Many advertising and marketing executives say the job has gotten much more demanding in the past 10 years, viewing their number-one challenge as balancing work and personal obligations. Other challenges include staying current on industry trends or technologies, keeping motivated and inspired on the job, and measuring success. If you are up to the challenge, you may find that a career in marketing is just right for you to use your business knowledge while exercising your creative side.

learn, practice, apply how to market to customers!

M: Business was developed just for you—students on the go who need information packaged in a concise yet interesting format with multiple learning options.

Check out the book's website to:

- Learn about designing a marketing strategy for a product line. (Solve the Dilemma)
- Evaluate the strengths and weaknesses of marketing strategies. (Solve the Dilemma)
- Learn about segmenting markets. (Build Your Skills)
- Practice developing a marketing mix (Build Your Skills)

While you are there, don't forget to enhance your skills. Practice and apply your knowledge, review the practice exercises, Student PPT® slides, and quizzes to review and apply chapter concepts. Additionally, *Connect® Business* is available for *M: Business.*

www.mhhe.com/ferrellm4e

chapter thirteen

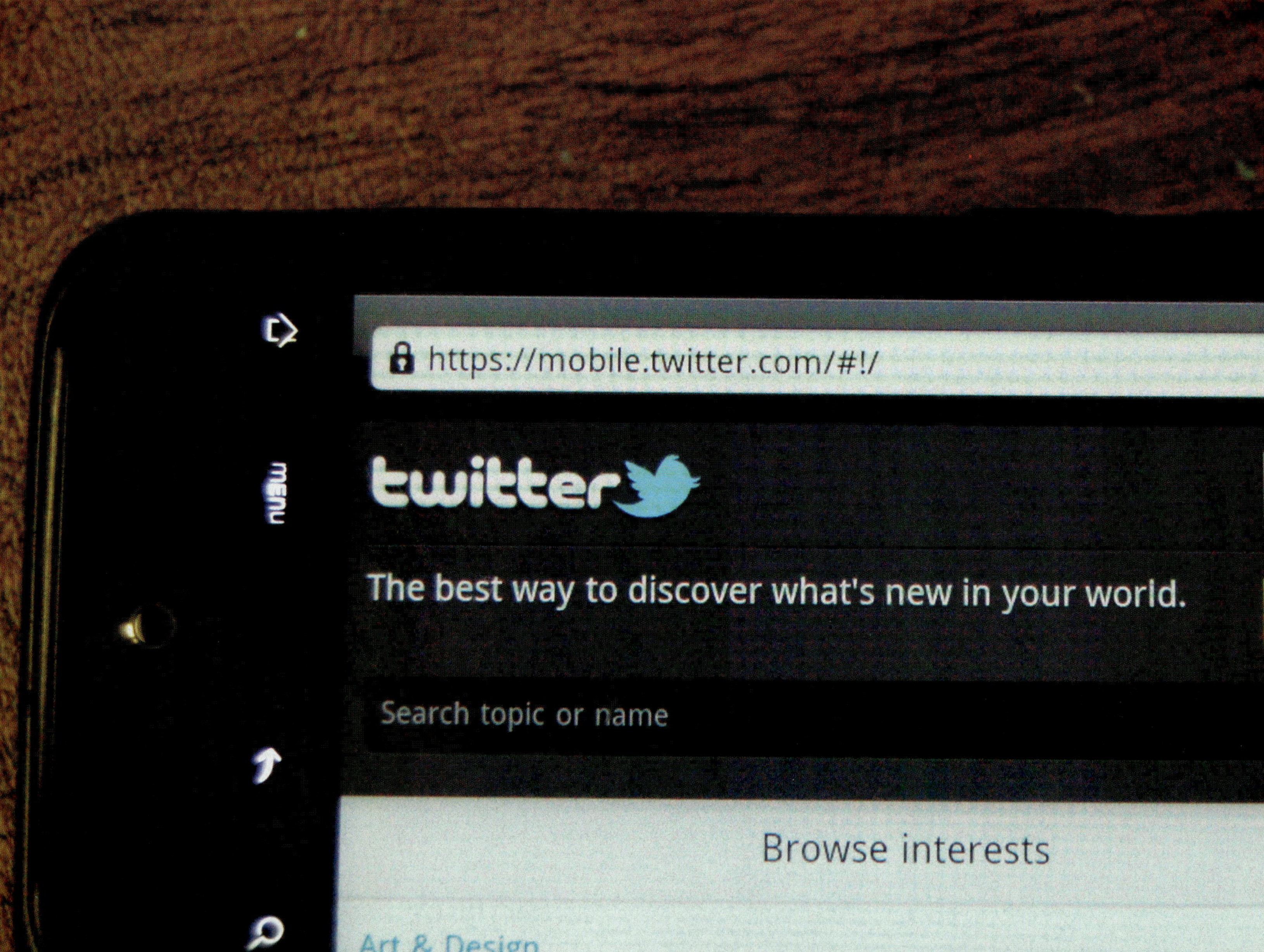

digital marketing + social networking

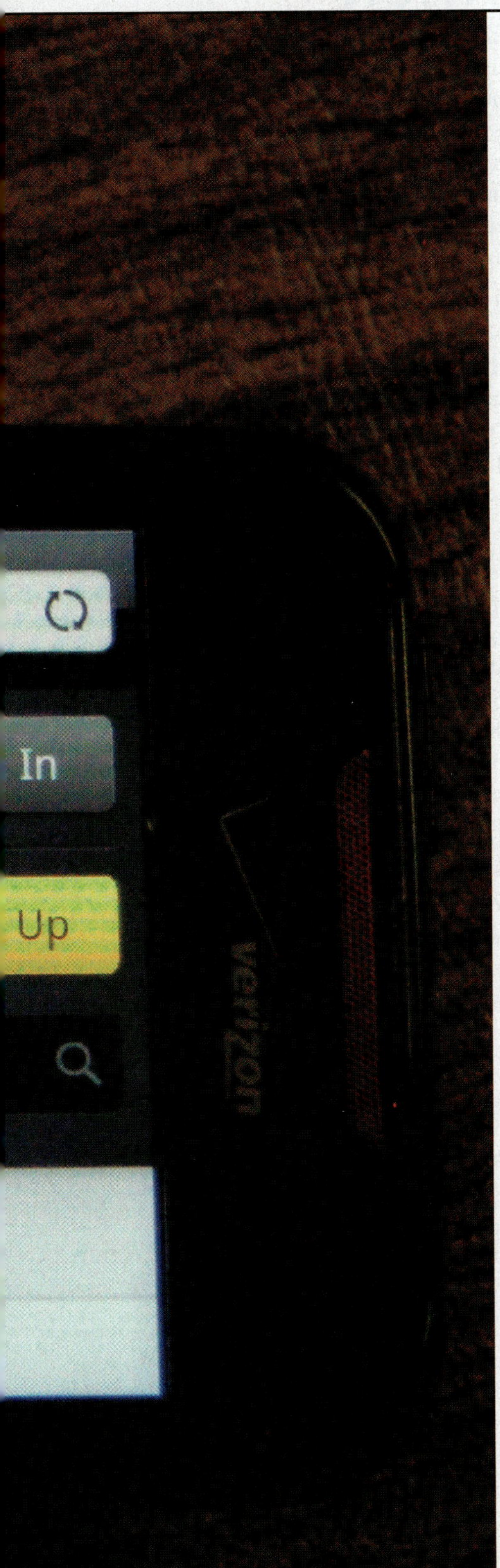

The Internet and information technology have dramatically changed the environment for business.[1] Marketers' new ability to convert all types of communications into digital media has created efficient, inexpensive ways of connecting businesses and consumers and has improved the flow and the usefulness of information. Businesses have the information they need to make more informed decisions, and consumers have access to a greater variety of products and more information about choices and quality.

The defining characteristic of information technology in the 21st century is accelerating change. New systems and applications advance so rapidly that it is almost impossible to keep up with the latest developments. Startup companies emerge that quickly overtake existing approaches to digital media. When Google first arrived on the scene, a number of search engines were fighting for dominance. With its fast, easy-to-use search engine, Google became number one and is now challenging many industries, including advertising, newspapers, mobile phones, and book publishing. Despite its victory, Google is constantly being challenged itself by competitors such as Yahoo! and Baidu. Baidu is gaining ground with 75 percent of the Chinese search engine market. Baidu has also announced it will create its own mobile technology to challenge Google's more than 40 percent market share in mobile operating systems in China.[2] Social networking continues to advance as the channel most observers believe will dominate digital communication in the near future. Today, people spend more time on social networking sites, such as Facebook, than they spend on e-mail.

continued on p. 266

LEARNING OBJECTIVES

After reading this chapter, you will be able to:

- **LO 13-1** Define digital media and digital marketing and recognize their increasing value in strategic planning.
- **LO 13-2** Demonstrate the role of digital marketing and social networking in today's business environment.
- **LO 13-3** Show how digital media affect the marketing mix.
- **LO 13-4** Define social networking and illustrate how businesses can use different types of social networking media.
- **LO 13-5** Identify legal and ethical considerations in digital media.

continued from p. 265

In this chapter, we first provide some key definitions related to digital marketing and social networking. Next, we discuss using digital media in business and digital marketing. We look at marketing mix considerations when using digital media and pay special attention to social networking. Then we focus on digital marketing strategies—particularly new communication channels such as social networks—and consider how consumers are changing their information searches and consumption behavior to fit emerging technologies and trends. Finally, we examine the legal and social issues associated with information technology, digital media, and e-business. ■

Amazon.com's mobile applications make it easier for users to shop and purchase items on the go.

LO 13-1 Define digital media and digital marketing and recognize their increasing value in strategic planning.

GROWTH AND BENEFITS OF DIGITAL COMMUNICATION

Let's start with a clear understanding of our focus in this chapter. First, we can distinguish **e-business** from traditional business by noting that conducting e-business means carrying out the goals of business through the use of the Internet. **Digital media** are electronic media that function using digital codes—when we refer to digital media, we mean media available via computers and other digital devices, including mobile and wireless ones such as smart phones.

Digital marketing uses all digital media, including the Internet and mobile and interactive channels, to develop communication and exchanges with customers. Digital marketing is a term we will use often because we are interested in all types of digital communications, regardless of the electronic channel that transmits the data. Digital marketing goes beyond the Internet and includes mobile phones, banner ads, digital outdoor advertisements, and social networks.

The Internet has created tremendous opportunities for businesses to forge relationships with consumers and business customers, target markets more precisely, and even reach previously inaccessible markets at home and around the world. The Internet also facilitates business transactions, allowing companies to network with manufacturers, wholesalers, retailers, suppliers, and outsource firms to serve customers more quickly and more efficiently. The telecommunication opportunities created by the Internet have set the stage for digital marketing's development and growth.

Digital communication offers a completely new dimension in connecting with others. Some of the characteristics that distinguish digital from traditional communication are addressability, interactivity, accessibility, connectivity, and control. These terms are discussed in Table 13.1.

LO 13-2 Demonstrate the role of digital marketing and social networking in today's business environment.

USING DIGITAL MEDIA IN BUSINESS

The phenomenal growth of digital media has provided new ways of conducting business. Given almost instant communication with precisely defined consumer groups, firms can use real-time exchanges to create and stimulate interactive

e-business carrying out the goals of business through use of the Internet

digital media electronic media that function using digital codes via computers, cellular phones, smart phones, and other digital devices that have been released in recent years

digital marketing the use of all digital media, including the Internet and mobile and interactive channels, to develop communication and exchanges with customers

communication, forge closer relationships, and learn more accurately about consumer and supplier needs. Consider Amazon.com, one of the most successful electronic businesses. It is a true digital marketer and was one of the early success stories in the industry, getting 50 percent of its revenue from international sales.[3] Many of you may not remember a world before Amazon because it has completely transformed how many people shop.

Because it is fast and inexpensive, digital communication is making it easier for businesses to conduct marketing research, provide and obtain price and product information, and advertise, as well as to fulfill their business goals by selling goods and services online. Even the U.S. government engages in digital marketing activities—marketing everything from Treasury bonds and other financial instruments to oil-drilling leases and wild horses. Procter & Gamble uses the Internet as a fast, cost-effective means for marketing research, judging consumer demand for potential new products by inviting online consumers to sample new-product prototypes and provide feedback. If a product gets rave reviews from the samplers, the company might decide to introduce it. By testing concepts online, companies can save significant time and money in getting new products to market.

New businesses and even industries are evolving that would not exist without digital media. Hulu is a video website that lets consumers watch a broad collection of premium videos from more than 410 content companies, any time and from anywhere. The company has partnered with several companies to advertise on their sites, including Johnson & Johnson and Best Buy. In fact, Hulu's growing popularity is allowing it to compete with YouTube.[4]

The reality, however, is that Internet markets are more similar to traditional markets than they are different. Thus, successful digital marketing strategies, like traditional business strategies, focus on creating products that customers need or want, not merely developing a brand name or reducing the costs associated with online transactions. Instead of changing all industries, digital technology has had much more impact in certain industries where the cost of business and customer transactions has been very high. For example, investment trading is less expensive online because customers can buy and sell investments, such as stocks and mutual funds, on their own. Firms such as Charles Schwab Corp., the biggest online brokerage firm, have been innovators in promoting online trading. Traditional brokers such as Merrill Lynch have had to follow with online trading for their customers.

Because the Internet lowers the cost of communication, it can contribute significantly to any industry or activity that depends on the flow of digital information such as entertainment, health care, government services, education, and computer services like software development. The publishing industry

"NEW BUSINESSES AND EVEN INDUSTRIES ARE EVOLVING THAT WOULD NOT EXIST WITHOUT DIGITAL MEDIA."

TABLE 13.1 Characteristics of Digital Marketing

Characteristic	Definition	Example
Addressability	The ability of the marketer to identify customers before they make a purchase	Amazon installs cookies on a user's computer that allows it to identify the owner when he or she returns to the website.
Interactivity	The ability of customers to express their needs and wants directly to the firm in response to its marketing communications	Texas Instruments interacts with its customers on its Facebook page by answering concerns and posting updates.
Accessibility	The ability for marketers to obtain digital information	Google can use web searches done through its search engine to learn about customer interests.
Connectivity	The ability for consumers to be connected with marketers along with other consumers	The Avon Voices website encouraged singers to upload their singing videos, which can then be voted on by other users for the chance to be discovered.
Control	Customers' ability to regulate the information they view as well as the rate and exposure to that information	Consumers use Kayak to discover the best travel deals.

Home Depot has an application that connects mobile users to its website to search and shop for products.

is transitioning away from print newspapers, magazines, and books as more consumers purchase e-readers, like the Kindle Fire or the new iPad, or read the news online. Even your textbook is available electronically. Because publishers save money on paper, ink, and shipping, many times electronic versions of books are cheaper than their paper counterparts.

Digital media can also improve communication within and between businesses. In the future, most significant gains will come from productivity improvements within businesses. Communication is a key business function, and improving the speed and clarity of communication can help businesses save time and improve employee problem-solving abilities. Digital media can be a communications backbone that helps to store knowledge, information, and records in management information systems so co-workers can access it when faced with a problem to solve. A well-designed management information system that uses digital technology can, therefore, help reduce confusion, improve organization and efficiency, and facilitate clear communications. Given the crucial role of communication and information in business, the long-term impact of digital media on economic growth is substantial, and it will inevitably grow over time.

Firms also need to control access to their digital communication systems to ensure worker productivity. This can be a challenge. For example, in companies across the United States, employees are surfing the Internet for as much as an hour during each workday. Many firms are trying to curb this practice by limiting employees' access to instant messaging services, streaming music, and websites with adult content.[5]

LO 13-3 Show how digital media affect the marketing mix.

DIGITAL MEDIA AND THE MARKETING MIX

Although digital marketing shares some similarities with conventional marketing techniques, a few valuable differences stand out. First, digital media make customer communications faster and interactive. Second, digital media help companies reach new target markets more easily, affordably, and quickly than ever before. Finally, digital media help marketers use new resources in seeking out and communicating with customers. One of the most important benefits of digital marketing is the ability of marketers and customers to share information easily. Through websites, social networks, and other digital media, consumers can learn about everything they consume and use in their lives, ask questions, voice complaints, indicate preferences, and otherwise communicate about their needs and desires. Many marketers use e-mail, mobile phones, social networking, wikis, media sharing, blogs, videoconferencing, and other technologies to coordinate activities and communicate with employees, customers, and suppliers. Twitter, considered both a social network and a micro-blog, illustrates how these digital technologies can combine to create new communication opportunities.

Nielsen Marketing Research revealed that consumers now spend more time on social networking sites than they do on e-mail, and social network use is still growing. As Figure 13.1 demonstrates, the United Kingdom and the United States are among the world's most avid social networkers. With digital media, even small businesses can reach new markets through these inexpensive communication channels. Brick-and-mortar companies such as Walmart use online catalogs and company websites and blogs to supplement their retail stores. Internet companies such as Amazon.com and Zappos.com that lack physical stores let customers post reviews of their purchases on their websites, creating company-sponsored communities.

FIGURE 13.1
Do You Use Social Networking Sites?

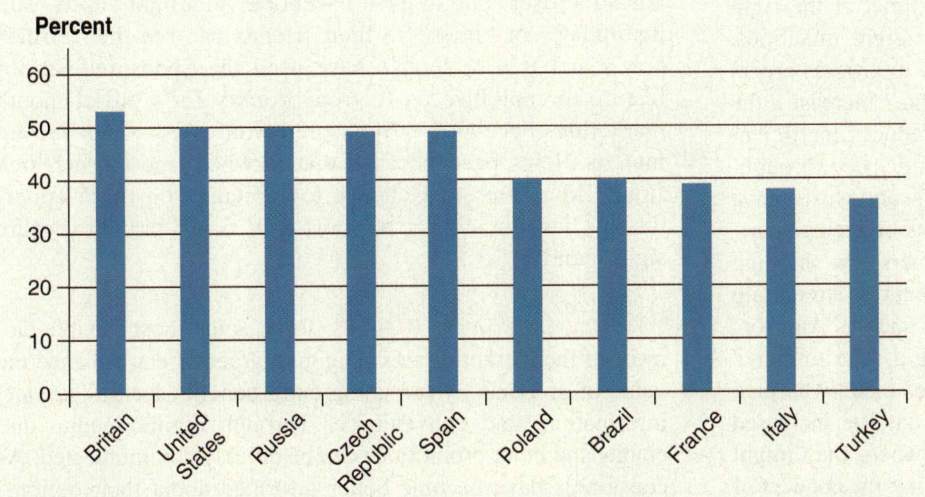

Source: Survey conducted across 21 nations by the Pew Research Center's Global Attitudes Project from March 17 to April 20, 2012.

One aspect of marketing that has not changed with digital media is the importance of achieving the right marketing mix. Product, distribution, promotion, and pricing are as important as ever for successful online marketing strategies. Nearly one-third of the world's population now uses the Internet.[6] That means it is essential for businesses large and small to use digital media effectively, not only to grab or maintain market share but also to streamline their organizations and offer customers entirely new benefits and convenience. Let's look at how businesses are using digital media to create effective marketing strategies on the web.

Product Considerations Like traditional marketers, digital marketers must anticipate consumer needs and preferences, tailor their goods and services to meet these needs, and continually upgrade them to remain competitive. The connectivity created by digital media provides the opportunity for adding services and can enhance product benefits. Some products, such as online games, applications, and virtual worlds, are available only via digital media. The more than 500,000 applications available on the iPad, for instance, provide examples of products that are available only in the digital world. Businesses can often offer more items online than they could in a retail store. In addition, Netflix offers a much wider array of movies and games than the average movie rental stores, along with a one-month free trial, quick delivery and easy returns, online video streaming of some movies, and no late fees. Netflix also prides itself on its recommendation engine, which recommends movies for users based on their previous rental history and how they rate movies they have seen. As Netflix demonstrates, the Internet can make it much easier to anticipate consumer needs. However, fierce competition makes quality product offerings more important than ever.[7]

FLIPPING THE PAGES IS A THING OF THE PAST: THE RISE OF E-TEXTBOOKS

With the onset of digital media, companies are finding ways to extend digital technology to the textbook industry. As a result, the popularity of electronic textbooks (e-textbooks) at universities is growing. Some universities are requiring students to purchase e-textbooks rather than print ones. Indiana University automatically charges the e-textbook to the student's account. In some cases, universities receive a percentage of the sales of the e-textbooks for promoting their use. Publishers are willing to offer the e-textbooks at lower prices because they do not have printing or shipping costs, and they get royalties on each copy that students use.

E-textbooks are more efficient for both the publisher and student because various intermediaries such as the bookstore can be eliminated, and publishers receive no revenue on used books. Therefore, each book contributes to covering overhead and development costs. Benefits of e-textbooks include less paper usage, lower prices for students, and less weight for students to carry around. However, some students prefer buying the printed version of the textbook because they like having an actual book to hold. Some say that it costs them more because they have to print the chapters of the electronic version. Another drawback is that some students find that reading e-textbooks takes more time, and their retention rate is lower.

Certain digital-media companies, such as Inkling, offer more options to attract students to their products. They provide textbooks with supplemental material such as quizzes and social networking features for students to share questions and thoughts with each other. They also offer the option for students to purchase chapters of the textbooks for $2.99 each if they choose not to purchase the entire textbook.[8]

Discussion Questions

1. What are the advantages of e-textbooks?
2. What are the disadvantages of e-textbooks?
3. What opportunities do e-textbooks offer to marketers?

social network a web-based meeting place for friends, family, co-workers, and peers that lets users create a profile and connect with other users for a wide range of purposes

Distribution Considerations

The Internet is a new distribution channel for making products available at the right time, at the right place, and in the right quantities. Marketers' ability to process orders electronically and increase the speed of communications via the Internet reduces inefficiencies, costs, and redundancies while increasing speed throughout the marketing channel. Shipping times and costs have become an important consideration in attracting customers, prompting many companies to offer consumers low shipping costs or next-day delivery. For example, Walmart is attempting to take market share away from e-marketers such as Amazon.com by reducing delivery time and creating a "site to store" system that eliminates shipping costs for consumers who pick up their deliveries in the store. This offer has the increased benefit of getting customers into the store, where they might make add-on purchases. Walmart is also testing the concept of delivering groceries to individual homes. Through even more sophisticated distribution systems, Walmart hopes to overtake online retailers to become the biggest online merchant.[9]

These changes in distribution are not limited to the Western world. In a revolutionary shift in China, where online shopping had not been widely adopted by consumers, businesses are now realizing the benefits of marketing online. One of the first adopters of Internet selling was the Chinese company Taobao, a consumer auction site that also features sections for Chinese brands and retailers. Taobao has been enormously successful; the majority of online sales in China take place there.[10] Consumer trends like these demonstrate that the shift of distributing through digital networks is well under way worldwide.

Promotion Considerations

Perhaps one of the best ways businesses can use digital media is for promotion purposes—whether they are increasing brand awareness, connecting with consumers, or taking advantage of social networks or virtual worlds (discussed later) to form relationships and generate positive publicity or buzz about their products. Thanks to online promotion, consumers can be more informed than ever, including reading customer-generated content before making purchasing decisions. Consumer consumption patterns are radically changing, and marketers must adapt their promotional efforts to meet them.

If marketers find it difficult to adapt their promotional strategies to online marketing, many social networks offer tools to help. For instance, Facebook's launch of Sponsored Stories lets advertisers pay to have Facebook "highlight" users' status updates or "likes" so their friends can see them. Burberry's and Ben & Jerry's have used the Sponsored Stories feature to capitalize on this opportunity for word-of-mouth marketing. Facebook's Sponsored Stories has been moved into its News Feed because that is where most users look first.[11] Marketers that choose to capitalize on these opportunities have the chance to boost their firms' brand exposure significantly.

Pricing Considerations

Price is the most flexible element of the marketing mix. Digital marketing can enhance the value of products by providing extra benefits such as service, information, and convenience. Through digital media, discounts and other promotions can be quickly communicated. As consumers have become better informed about their options, the demand for low-priced products has grown, leading to the creation of deal sites where consumers can directly compare prices. Expedia.com, for instance, provides consumers with a wealth of travel information about everything from flights to hotels that lets them compare benefits and prices. Many marketers offer buying incentives such as online coupons or free samples to generate consumer demand for their products. For the business that wants to compete on price, digital marketing provides unlimited opportunities.

LO 13-4 Define social networking and illustrate how businesses can use different types of social networking media.

Social Networking

A **social network** is "a web-based meeting place for friends, family, co-workers and peers that lets users create a profile and connect with other users for the purposes that range from getting acquainted, to keeping in touch, to building a work related network."[12] Social networks are a valued part of marketing because they are changing the way consumers communicate with each other and with firms. Sites such as Facebook and Twitter have emerged as opportunities for marketers to build communities, provide product information, and learn about consumer needs. By the time you read

> "Social networks are a valued part of marketing because they are changing the way consumers communicate with each other and with firms."

this, it is possible there will be new social networking sites that continue to advance digital communication and opportunities for marketers.

You might be surprised to know that social networks have existed in some form or other for 40 years. The precursors of today's social networks began in the 1970s as online bulletin boards that allowed users with common interests to interact with one another. The first modern social network was Six Degrees.com, launched in 1997. This system permitted users to create a profile and connect with friends—the core attributes of today's networks.[13] Although Six Degrees eventually shut down for lack of interest, the seed of networking had been planted.[14] Other social networks followed, with each new generation becoming increasingly sophisticated. Today's sites offer a multitude of consumer benefits, including the ability to download music, games, and applications; upload photos and videos; join groups; find and chat with friends; comment on friends' posts; and post and update status messages.

As the number of social network users increases, interactive marketers are finding opportunities to reach out to consumers in new target markets. CafeMom is a social networking site that offers mothers a forum in which to connect and write about parenting and other topics important to them. At 9 million unique monthly visitors, this particular site is an opportunity to reach out to mothers, a demographic that has a significant influence on family purchasing behavior. Walmart, Playskool, General Mills, and Johnson & Johnson have all advertised through this site.[15] We'll have more to say about how marketers use social networks later in this chapter.

An important question relates to how social media sites are adding value to the economy. Marketers at companies such as Ford and Zappos, for instance, are using social media to promote products and build consumer relationships. Most corporations are supporting Facebook pages and Yammer accounts for employees to communicate across departments and divisions. Professionals such as professors, doctors, and engineers also share ideas on a regular basis. Even staffing organizations use social media, bypassing traditional e-mail and telephone channels. Although billions of dollars in investments are being funneled into social media, it may be too early to assess the exact economic contribution of social media to the entire economy.[16]

TYPES OF CONSUMER-GENERATED MARKETING AND DIGITAL MEDIA

Although digital marketing has generated exciting opportunities for companies to interact with their customers, digital media are also more consumer-driven than traditional media. Internet users are creating and reading consumer-generated content as never before and are having a profound effect on marketing in the process.

Two factors have sparked the rise of consumer-generated information:

1. The increased tendency of consumers to publish their own thoughts, opinions, reviews, and product discussions through blogs or digital media.
2. Consumers' tendencies to trust other consumers over corporations. Consumers often rely on the recommendations of friends, family, and fellow consumers when making purchasing decisions.

Marketers who know where online users are likely to express their thoughts and opinions can use these forums to interact with them, address problems, and promote their companies. Types of digital media in which Internet users are likely to participate include social networks, blogs, wikis, video sharing sites, podcasts, virtual reality sites, and mobile applications. Let's look a little more closely at each.

Social Networks

The increase in social networking across the world is exponential. It is estimated that today's adults spend one of every five online minutes on social networking sites.[17] As social networks evolve, both marketers and the owners of social networking sites are realizing the opportunities such networks offer—an influx of advertising dollars for site owners and a large reach for the advertiser. As a result, marketers have begun investigating and experimenting with promotion on social networks. Two of the most prominent sites are Facebook and Twitter.

Facebook In April 2008, the social networking site Facebook surpassed Myspace in its number of members, becoming the most popular social networking site in the world.[18] Facebook users create profiles, which they can make public or

Threadless, an online community of artists, has developed a Facebook page to promote products and stay connected with consumers.

> **MANY MARKETERS ARE TURNING TO FACEBOOK TO MARKET PRODUCTS, INTERACT WITH CONSUMERS, AND GAIN FREE PUBLICITY.**

private, and then search the network for people with whom to connect. Many believe Facebook appeals to a broader demographic than does Myspace, attracting parents and grandparents as well as teens and college students.[19] In fact, the fastest-growing group on Facebook is consumers 55 and over.[20]

For this reason, many marketers are turning to Facebook to market products, interact with consumers, and gain free publicity. It is possible for a consumer to become a fan of a major company such as Starbucks by clicking the Like icon on the coffee retailer's Facebook page. Facebook partners with organizations to offer unique incentives to businesses. Facebook also offers businesses ways to engage in e-commerce. The organization launched a Gifts feature that enables users to purchase gifts—such as a Starbucks gift card—and send these gifts to their friends through the site.[21]

In addition, social networking sites are useful for relationship marketing, or the creation of relationships that mutually benefit the marketing business and the customer. Companies are using relationship marketing through Facebook to help consumers feel more connected to their products. For instance, New Belgium Brewing has more than 35 local Facebook pages and uses the website to target advertisements toward its fan base. After conducting a study on its Facebook fans, the company determined that its fans generate half of the company's annual sales.[22] Thanks to Facebook, companies like New Belgium are able to understand who their customers are and how they can meet their needs.

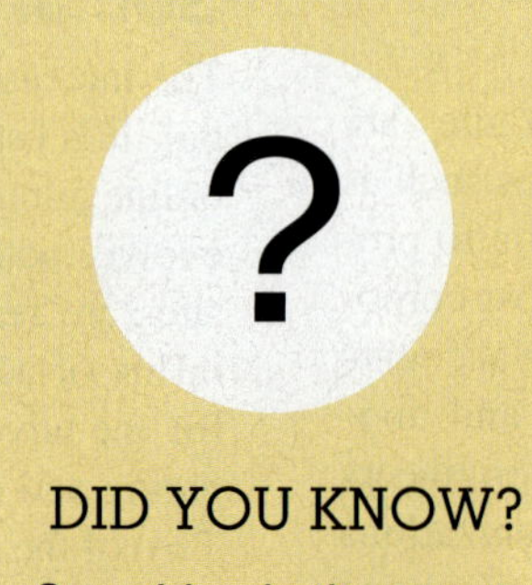

DID YOU KNOW?

Searching is the most popular online activity; social networking and blogging are fourth.[31]

Twitter Twitter is a hybrid of a social networking site and a micro-blogging site that asks users one simple question: "What's happening?" Members can post answers of up to 140 characters, which are then available for their registered followers to read. It sounds simple enough, but Twitter's effect on digital media has been immense. The site quickly progressed from a novelty to a social networking staple, attracting millions of viewers each month.[23]

Although 140 characters may not seem like enough for companies to send an effective message, some have become experts at using Twitter in their marketing strategies. Southwest Airlines has an entire team monitor its account during its business operations to answer questions on Twitter ranging from refunds to lost baggage.[24] These efforts are having an impact; approximately 88 percent of users report that they follow at least one brand on Twitter.[25]

Like other social networking tools, Twitter is also being used to build, or in some cases rebuild, customer relationships. For example, Zappos posts on Twitter to update followers on company activities and address customer complaints.[26] Other companies are using tweets to develop ideas for advertising campaigns. Samsung claims that its famous television ad mocking Apple's iPhone was inspired by comments posted on Twitter.[27]

Finally, companies are using Twitter to gain a competitive advantage. Marketers can pay Twitter to highlight advertisements or company brands to a wider range of users while they search for specific terms or topics.[28] The race is on among companies that want to use Twitter to gain a competitive edge.

Blogs and Wikis

Today's marketers must recognize that the impact of consumer-generated material like blogs and wikis and their significance to online consumers have increased a great deal. **Blogs** (short for web logs) are web-based journals in which writers can editorialize and interact with other Internet users. More than three-fourths of Internet users read blogs.[29] In fact, the blogging site Tumblr, which allows anyone to post text, hyperlinks, pictures, and other media for free, became one of the top ten online destinations. The site experiences approximately 18 billion page views per month.[30]

Blogs give consumers power, sometimes more than companies would like. Bloggers can post whatever they like about a company or its products, whether their opinions are positive or negative,

blog a web-based journal in which a writer can editorialize and interact with other Internet users

wiki a website where users can add to or edit the content of posted articles

true or false. For instance, although companies sometimes force bloggers to remove blogs, readers often create copies of the blog post and spread it across the Internet after the original's removal.[32] In other cases, a positive review of a product or service posted on a popular blog can result in large increases in sales. Thus, blogs can represent a potent threat or opportunity to marketers.

Rather than trying to eliminate blogs that cast their companies in a negative light, some firms are using their own blogs, or employee blogs, to answer consumer concerns or defend their corporate reputations. Boeing operates a corporate blog to highlight company news and to post correspondence from Boeing enthusiasts from all over the world.[33] As blogging changes the face of media, smart companies are using it to build enthusiasm for their products and create relationships with consumers.

Wikis are websites where users can add to or edit the content of posted articles. One of the best known is Wikipedia, an online encyclopedia with more than 22 million entries in more than 250 languages on nearly every subject imaginable. (Encyclopedia Britannica has only 120,000 entries.)[34] Wikipedia is one of the 10 most popular sites on the web, and because much of its content can be edited by anyone, it is easy for online consumers to add detail and supporting evidence and to correct inaccuracies in content. Wikipedia used to be completely open to editing, but to stop vandalism, the site had to make some topics off-limits that are now editable only by a small group of experts.

Like all digital media, wikis have advantages and disadvantages for companies. Wikis about controversial companies such as Walmart and Nike often contain negative publicity, such as about workers' rights violations. However, monitoring relevant wikis can provide companies with a better idea of how consumers feel about the company or brand. Some companies have also begun to use wikis as internal tools for teams working on projects that require a great deal of documentation.[35]

There is too much at stake financially for marketers to ignore wikis and blogs. Research has shown that approximately 46 percent of companies that use blogs have gained new customers from blog-generated leads.[36] Despite this fact, statistics show that only 28 percent of *Fortune* 500 companies have a corporate blog.[37] Marketers who want to form better customer relationships and promote their company's products must not underestimate the power of these two media outlets.

Media Sharing

Businesses can also share their corporate messages in more visual ways through media sharing sites. Media sharing sites allow marketers to share photos, videos, and podcasts. Media sharing sites are more limited in scope in how companies interact with consumers. They tend to be more promotional than reactive. This means that although firms can promote their products through videos or photos, they usually do not interact with consumers through personal messages or responses. At the same time, the popularity of these sites provides the potential to reach a global audience of consumers.

Video sharing sites allow virtually anybody to upload videos, from professional marketers at *Fortune* 500 corporations to the

MARKETERS FIND A NEW COMMUNICATION TOOL WITH PINTEREST

For marketers adept at recognizing new opportunities, the online bulletin board Pinterest can provide their companies with a competitive advantage. Pinterest is used to share photos and other images among Internet users. Users communicate mostly through images that they pin to their boards. Other users can repin these images to their boards, follow each other, like images, and make comments. Links to websites can be added to the images to move more traffic to company websites, turning Pinterest into an effective digital marketing tool.

Larger companies such as Dell and Whole Foods are more involved on Pinterest, but some smaller businesses are using it as well. The Pinterest community is dominated by the female demographic, so companies that target women have the opportunity to reach them in innovative ways. Companies are marketing their products by posting images that evoke an emotional response representing their brand. For example, Whole Foods has topic boards on Pinterest featuring recipes, farm scenes, and more. One image features a Nicaraguan who received a small loan to buy materials for her business to support herself. This reinforces Whole Foods' philanthropic program of providing small loans to entrepreneurs in developing countries.

Pinterest also serves as a customer relationship management tool because the images people pin to their boards reflect interests and aspirations, thus allowing marketers to interact with users on a more personal level. Marketers can inspire an emotional response among potential customers with the way they organize their boards. The effectiveness of this marketing can be monitored by how many repins, likes, and comments are posted. Marketers are reporting increased web traffic and sales because of Pinterest.[38]

Discussion Questions

1. Describe how marketers can use Pinterest to enhance their marketing communications.
2. Why might it be better to post an image that conveys an emotional response rather than a simple advertisement?
3. How does Pinterest act as a customer relationship management tool?

Flickr is a popular photo sharing sites. Marketers can use Flickr to post photos of products or company activities.

average Internet user. Some of the most popular video sharing sites include YouTube, Video.Yahoo.com, Metacafe.com, and Hulu. Video sharing sites give companies the opportunity to upload ads and informational videos about their products. A few videos become viral at any given time, and although many of these gain popularity because they embarrass the subject in some way, others reach viral status because people find them entertaining. **Viral marketing** is a marketing tool that uses the Internet, particularly social networking and video sharing sites, to spread a message and create brand awareness. Marketers are taking advantage of the viral nature of video sharing sites like YouTube, by either creating their own unique videos or advertising on videos that have already reached viral status. For instance, McDonald's partnered with YouTube to have advertisements posted during videos by YouTube's partners. Such exposure guarantees that McDonald's will reach a large audience.[39]

Businesses have also begun to use consumer-generated video content, saving money they would have spent on hiring advertising firms to develop professional advertising campaigns. GoPro was transformed from a small camera firm into a successful company due to the videos consumers took of themselves using GoPro cameras. The company is partnering with YouTube to create its own network for consumer-generated GoPro videos.[40] Marketers believe consumer videos appear more authentic and create enthusiasm for the product among consumer participants.

Photo sharing sites allow users to upload and share their photos and short videos with the world. Well-known photo sharing sites include Instagram and Flickr. Flickr is owned by Yahoo! and is one of the most popular photo sharing sites on the Internet. A Flickr user can upload images, edit them, classify the images, create photo albums, and share photos with friends without having to e-mail bulky image files or send photos through the mail. Although Flickr might be the most popular photo sharing site on the Internet, Instagram is the most popular mobile photo sharing application. Instagram allows users to make their photos look dreamy or retrospective with different tints. These photos can then be shared with other users. With more people using mobile apps or accessing the Internet through their smart phones, the use of photo sharing through mobile devices is likely to increase.[41]

Other sites are emerging that take photo sharing to a new level. Pinterest is a photo sharing bulletin board site that combines photo sharing with elements of bookmarking and social networking. Users can share photos and images among other Internet users, communicating mostly through images that they pin to their boards. Other users can repin these images to their boards, follow each other, like images, and make comments. Marketers have found that an effective way of marketing through Pinterest is to post images conveying emotions that represent their brand.[42]

Photo sharing represents an opportunity for companies to market themselves visually by displaying snapshots of company events, company staff, and/or company products. Keller Williams, for example, has used Flickr to show photographs of employees performing philanthropic services in their communities, a type of cause-related marketing.[43] Nike and MTV have

viral marketing a marketing tool that uses the Internet, particularly social networking and video sharing sites, to spread a message and create brand awareness

podcast an audio or video file that can be downloaded from the Internet with a subscription that automatically delivers new content to listening devices or personal computers

used Instagram for digital marketing campaigns.[44] Whole Foods has topic boards on Pinterest to reinforce its brand image.[45] Many businesses with pictures on Flickr have a link connecting their Flickr photostreams to their corporate websites.[46]

Podcasts are audio or video files that can be downloaded from the Internet via a subscription that automatically delivers new content to listening devices or personal computers. Podcasting offers the benefit of convenience, giving users the ability to listen to or view content when and where they choose.

It is estimated that by 2013, more than 37 million U.S. consumers will be downloading podcasts every month. Most current podcast users are between 18 and 29 years of age, making podcasts a good marketing tool for reaching this demographic.[47] For instance, the podcast *Mad Money,* hosted by Jim Cramer, gives investment advice and teaches listeners how to analyze stocks and other financial instruments. These are important topics for young adults who do not have much investment experience.[48]

> "Podcasting offers the benefit of convenience, giving users the ability to listen to or view content when and where they choose."

As podcasting continues to catch on, radio stations and television networks such as CBC Radio, NPR, MSNBC, and PBS are creating podcasts of their shows to profit from this growing trend. Many companies hope to use podcasts to create brand awareness, promote their products, and encourage customer loyalty.

Virtual Worlds

Games and programs allowing viewers to develop avatars that exist in an online virtual world have exploded in popularity in the 21st century. Virtual worlds include Second Life, Everquest, Sim City, and the role-playing game World of Warcraft. These sites can be described as social networks with a twist. Virtual realities are three-dimensional, user-created worlds that have their own currencies, lands, and residents that come in every shape and size. Internet users who participate in virtual realities such as Second Life choose a fictional persona, called an *avatar.* Residents of Second Life connect with other users, purchase goods with virtual Linden dollars (convertible to real dollars), and even own virtual businesses. For entertainment purposes, residents can shop, attend concerts, or travel to virtual environments—all while spending real money. Farmville provides a similar virtual world experience, except it is limited to life on a farm.

Although the businesses in Second Life are virtual ones, real-world marketers and organizations have been eager to capitalize on the site's popularity. For instance, in an effort to connect with consumers and build brand loyalty, Domino's Pizza created a shop in Second Life that allows users to order real pizza online.[49] Other businesses are looking toward virtual worlds to familiarize consumers with their products and services. For instance, McDonald's has partnered with the virtual gaming site Zynga to bring its virtual store and brand to Zynga's popular virtual gaming site CityVille.[50]

Firms are also using virtual technology for recruiting purposes. Major companies such as Boeing, Procter & Gamble, Citigroup, and Progressive Corp. have held virtual career fairs to recruit candidates from across the world. The companies promoted the fairs on Facebook and Twitter. By interacting with the public virtually, businesses hope to connect with younger generations of consumers.[51]

Mobile Marketing

As digital marketing becomes increasingly sophisticated, consumers are beginning to use mobile devices such as smart phones as a highly functional communication method. The

Second Life residents can purchase Linden dollars, the currency of Second Life, to purchase virtual products.

INSTAGRAM BECOMES AN INSTANT SUCCESS IN DIGITAL MARKETING

The story of Instagram began in a study abroad program at Stanford University. Founder Kevin Systrom had an instructor who replaced his digital camera with a Holga camera (an inexpensive plastic nondigital camera). The resulting retrospective photos had a nostalgic quality that charmed Systrom. He saw a market for a mobile photo sharing application because many people were taking low-quality photos with their mobile phones. Instagram's filters give users the ability to change the look and feel of photographs. With Instagram, photos can be made to look dreamy and romantic with a warm tint or austere with a cool tint. The application allows users to share their photos with friends, causing its popularity to soar. Its viral nature caught the attention of marketers such as Nike, Audi, and MTV, which have all used Instagram in digital marketing campaigns. On an interesting note, before he developed Instagram, Systrom was approached by Facebook's Mark Zuckerberg with a job offer. Systrom rejected the offer to finish his degree. In 2012, Systrom sold Instagram to Facebook for $1 billion, earning Systrom more money than if he had accepted Zuckerberg's original offer.[52]

iPhone and iPad have changed the way consumers communicate, and a growing number of travelers are using their smart phones to find online maps, travel guides, and taxis. In industries such as hotels, airlines, and car rental agencies, mobile phones have become a primary method for booking reservations and communicating about services. They can act as airline boarding passes, GPS devices, and even hotel room keys. FARELOGIX, a travel software company, is working with a number of airlines to introduce features that allow airlines to sell services such as priority boarding through mobile devices. Although airlines already make these services available on their websites, they also want to communicate with travelers who experience unexpected changes on their trips. Other marketing uses of mobile phones include sending shoppers timely messages related to discounts and shopping opportunities.[53] Figure 13.2 breaks down smart phone ownership by age. Mobile marketing is exploding—marketers spent $2.6 billion on mobile marketing in 2012.[54]

To avoid being left behind, brands must recognize the importance of mobile marketing. This makes it essential for companies to understand how to use mobile tools to create effective campaigns. Some of the more common mobile marketing tools include the following:

- *SMS messages:* SMS messages are text messages of 160 words or less. SMS messages have been an effective way to send coupons to prospective customers.[55]
- *Multimedia messages:* Multimedia messaging takes SMS messaging a step further by allowing companies to send video, audio, photos, and other types of media over mobile devices. Motorola's House of Blues multimedia campaign allowed users to receive access to discounts, tickets, music, and other digital content on their mobile phones.[56]
- *Mobile advertisements:* Mobile advertisements are visual advertisements that appear on mobile devices. Companies might choose to advertise through search engines, websites, or even games accessed on mobile devices. Comcast Corp. developed mobile advertising that allows users to click its ad and automatically send a call to the company.[57]
- *Mobile websites:* Mobile websites are websites designed for mobile devices. Mobile devices constitute 13 percent of web traffic.[58]

FIGURE 13.2
Smart Phone Ownership by Age

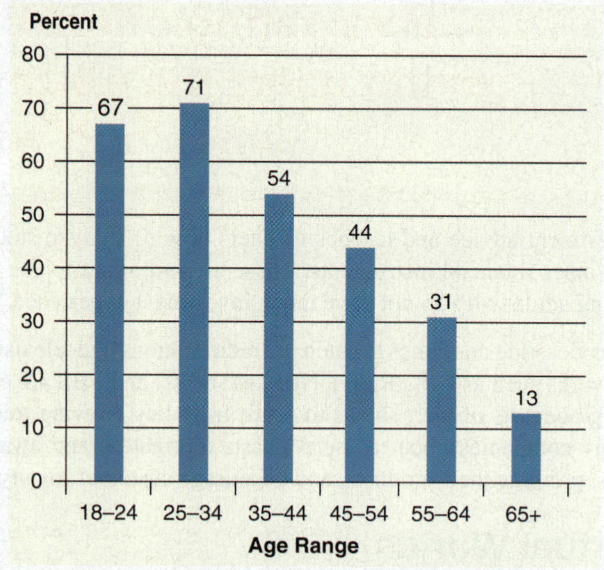

Source: Pew Research Center's Internet & American Life Project, April 26–May 22, 2011, and January 20–February 19, 2012, tracking surveys. For 2012 data, $n = 2{,}253$ adults and includes 901 cell phone interviews.

- *Location-based networks:* Location-based networks are built for mobile devices. One of the most popular location-based networks is Foursquare, which lets users check in and share their location with others. Businesses such as OpenTable have partnered with Foursquare to enable users to search for restaurants and make reservations with just a click of a button.[59]
- *Mobile applications:* Mobile applications (known as *apps*) are software programs that run on mobile devices and give users access to certain content.[60] Businesses release apps to help consumers access more information about their company or to provide incentives. Apps are discussed in further detail in the next section.

Applications and Widgets

Applications are adding an entirely new layer to the marketing environment; approximately half of all American adult cell phone users have applications on their mobile devices.[61] The most important feature of apps is the convenience and cost savings they offer to the consumer. Certain apps allow consumers to scan a product's barcode and then compare it with the prices of identical products in other stores. Mobile apps also enable customers to download in-store discounts.

To remain competitive, companies are beginning to use mobile marketing to offer additional incentives to consumers. International Hotel Group, for instance, has both a mobile website and a Priority Club Reward app. As a result of its mobile marketing strategy, the company experienced a 20 percent boost in mobile site jumps per month.[62] Another application that marketers are finding useful is the QR scanning app. QR codes are black-and-white squares that sometimes appear in magazines, posters, and storefront displays. Smart phone users who have downloaded the QR scanning application can open their smart phones and scan the code, which contains a hidden message accessible with the app. The QR scanning app recognizes the code and opens the link, video, or image on the phone's screen. Marketers are using QR codes to promote their companies and offer consumer discounts.[63]

Mobile payments are also gaining traction, and companies such as Google are working to capitalize on this opportunity.[64] Google Wallet is a mobile app that stores credit card information on the smart phone. When the shopper is ready to check out, he or she can tap the phone at the point of sale for the transaction to be registered.[65] The success of mobile payments in revolutionizing the shopping experience will largely depend on retailers to adopt this payment system, but companies such as Starbucks are already jumping at the opportunity. An estimated 70 percent of U.S. consumers will own smart phones by 2014, so businesses cannot afford to miss out on the chance to profit from these new trends.[66]

Widgets are small bits of software on a website, desktop, or mobile device that enables users "to interface with the application and operating system." Marketers might use widgets to display news headlines, clocks, or games on their web pages.[67] Widgets have been used by companies such as A&E Television Network as a form of viral marketing—users can download the widget and send it to their friends with a click of a button.[68] Widgets downloaded to a user's desktop can update the user on the latest company or product information, enhancing relationship marketing between companies and their fans. For instance, Krispy Kreme® Doughnuts developed a widget that will alert users when their Original Glazed® doughnuts are hot off the oven at their favorite Krispy Kreme shop.[69] Widgets are an innovative digital marketing tool to personalize web pages, alert users to the latest company information, and spread awareness of the company's products.

USING DIGITAL MEDIA TO REACH CONSUMERS

We've seen that customer-generated communications and digital media connect consumers as never before. These connections let consumers share information and experiences without company interference so they get more of the real story on a product or company feature. In many ways, these media take some of the professional marketer's power to control and dispense information and place it in the hands of the consumer.

However, this shift does not have to spell doom for marketers, who can choose to use the power of the consumer and Internet technology to their advantage. Although consumers use digital media to access more product information, marketers can use the same sites to get better and more targeted information about the consumer—often more than they could gather through traditional marketing venues. Marketers increasingly use consumer-generated content to aid their own marketing efforts, even going so far as to incorporate Internet bloggers in their publicity campaigns. Finally, marketers are also beginning to use the Internet to track the success of their online marketing campaigns, creating an entirely new way of gathering marketing research.

["The challenge for digital media marketers is to constantly adapt to new technologies and changing consumer patterns."]

The challenge for digital media marketers is to constantly adapt to new technologies and changing consumer patterns. Unfortunately, the attrition rate for digital media channels is very high, with some dying off each year as new ones emerge. As time passes, digital media are becoming more sophisticated so as to reach consumers in more effective ways. Those that are not able to adapt and change eventually fail.

Charlene Li and Josh Bernoff of Forrester Research, a technology and market research company, emphasize the need for marketers to understand these changing relationships in the online media world. By grouping consumers into different segments based on how they use digital media, marketers can gain a better understanding of the online market and how best to proceed.[70]

Table 13.2 shows seven ways that Forrester Research groups consumers based on their Internet activity (or lack thereof). The categories are not mutually exclusive; online consumers can participate in more than one at a time.

Creators are consumers who create their own media outlets, such as blogs, podcasts, consumer-generated videos, and wikis.[71] Consumer-generated media are increasingly important to online marketers as a conduit for addressing consumers directly. The second group of Internet users is *conversationalists.* Conversationalists regularly update their Twitter feeds or status updates on social networking sites. Although they are less involved than creators, conversationalists spend time at least once a week (and often more) on digital media sites posting updates.[72] The third category, *critics,* consists of people who comment on blogs or post ratings and reviews on review websites such as Yelp. Because many online shoppers read ratings and reviews to aid their purchasing decisions, critics should be a primary component in a company's digital marketing strategy. The next category is *collectors.* They collect information and organize content generated by critics and creators.[73] Because collectors are active members of the online community, a company story or site that catches the eye of a collector is likely to be posted, discussed on collector sites, and made available to other online users looking for information.

Joiners include all who become users of Twitter, Facebook, or other social networking sites. It is not unusual for consumers to be members of several social networking sites at once. Joiners use these sites to connect and network with other users, but as we've seen, marketers too can take significant advantage of these sites to connect with consumers and form customer relationships.[74] The last two segments are Spectators and Inactives.

TABLE 13.2 Social Technographics

Creators	Publish a blog Publish personal web pages Upload original video Upload original audio/music Write articles or stories and post them
Conversationalists	Update status on social networking sites Post updates on Twitter
Critics	Post ratings/reviews of products or services Comment on someone else's blog Contribute to online forums Contribute to/edit articles in a wiki
Collectors	Use RSS feeds Add tags to web pages or photos "Vote" for websites online
Joiners	Maintain profile on a social networking site Visit social networking sites
Spectators	Read blogs Watch video from other users Listen to podcasts Read online forums Read customer ratings/reviews
Inactives	None of the activities

Sources: Charlene Li and Josh Bernoff, *Groundswell* (Boston: Harvard Business Press, 2008), p. 43. "Forrester Unveils New Segment of Social Technographics–The Conversationalists," *360 Digital Connections,* January 21, 2010, http://blog.360i.com/social-media/forrester-new-segment-social-technographics-conversationalists.

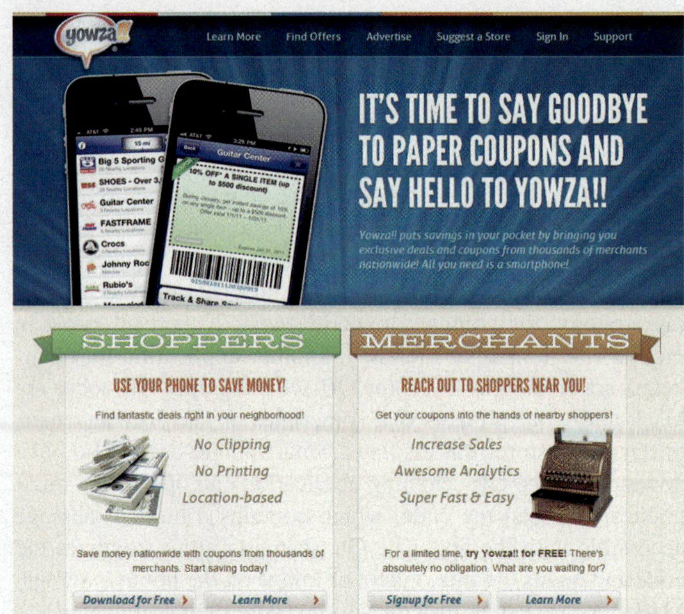

Yowza!!, a mobile phone app, uses the GPS devices in cell phones to locate consumers and send them coupons from retailers in that area.

Spectators, who read online information but do not join groups or post anywhere, are the largest group in most countries. *Inactives* are online users who do not participate in any digital online media, but their numbers are dwindling.

Marketers need to consider what proportion of online consumers are creating, conversing, rating, collecting, joining, or simply reading online materials. As in traditional marketing efforts, they need to know their target market. For instance, where spectators make up the majority of the online population, companies should post their own corporate messages through blogs and websites promoting their organizations.

USING DIGITAL MEDIA TO LEARN ABOUT CONSUMERS

Marketing research and information systems can use digital media and social networking sites to gather useful information about consumers and their preferences. Sites such as Twitter and Facebook can be good substitutes for focus groups. Online surveys can serve as an alternative to mail, telephone, or personal interviews.

Crowdsourcing describes how marketers use digital media to find out the opinions or needs of the crowd (or potential markets). Communities of interested consumers join sites such as threadless.com, which designs T-shirts, or crowdspring.com, which creates logos and print and web designs. These companies give interested consumers opportunities to contribute and give feedback on product ideas. Crowdsourcing lets companies gather and use consumers' ideas in an interactive way when creating new products.

Consumer feedback is an important part of the digital media equation. Ratings and reviews have become exceptionally popular; 25 percent of the U.S. online population reads this type of consumer-generated feedback.[75] Retailers such as Amazon, Netflix, and Priceline allow consumers to post comments on their sites about the books, movies, and travel arrangements they sell. Today, most online shoppers search the Internet for ratings and reviews before making major purchase decisions.

Although consumer-generated content about a firm can be either positive or negative, digital media forums do allow businesses to monitor closely what their customers are saying. In the case of negative feedback, businesses can communicate with consumers to address problems or complaints much more easily than through traditional communication channels. Yet despite the ease and obvious importance of online feedback, many companies do not yet take full advantage of the digital tools at their disposal.

LO 13-5 Identify legal and ethical considerations in digital media.

LEGAL AND SOCIAL ISSUES IN INTERNET MARKETING

The extraordinary growth of information technology, the Internet, and social networks has generated many legal and social issues for consumers and businesses. These issues include privacy concerns, the risk of identity theft and online fraud, and the need to protect intellectual property. The U.S. Federal Trade Commission (FTC) compiles an annual list of consumer complaints related to the Internet and digital media. We discuss these in this section, as well as steps that individuals, companies, and the government have taken to address them.

Privacy

Businesses have long tracked consumers' shopping habits with little controversy. However, observing the contents of a consumer's shopping cart or the process a consumer goes through when choosing a box of cereal generally does not result in the collection of specific, personally identifying data. Although using credit cards, shopping cards, and coupons forces consumers to give up a certain degree of anonymity in the traditional shopping process, they can still choose to remain anonymous by paying cash. Shopping on the Internet, however, allows businesses to track them on a far more personal level, from the contents of their online purchases to the websites they favor. Current technology has made it possible for marketers to amass vast quantities of personal information, often without consumers' knowledge, and to share and sell this information to interested third parties.

How is personal information collected on the web? Many sites follow users online by storing a cookie, or an identifying string of text, on users' computers. Cookies permit website operators to track how often a user visits the site, what he or she looks at while there, and in what sequence. They also allow website visitors to customize services, such as virtual shopping carts, as well as the particular content they see when they log onto a web page. Users have the option of turning off cookies on their machines; nevertheless, the potential for misuse has left many consumers uncomfortable with this technology.

About three-quarters of online shoppers read ratings and reviews before making a decision.

Facebook and other social networking sites have also come under fire for privacy issues. Facebook and Google both agreed to undergo independent privacy audits for 20 years due to alleged privacy transgressions. The Federal Trade Commission determined that Facebook's 2009 changes to its privacy policies were done without warning users. It charged Google with using the personal information from its Gmail users for its Google Buzz service, despite telling users otherwise. Such changes were deemed to have violated users' rights to know how their information was being used.[76] Another Internet privacy issue occurring more frequently is scraping, an activity by which companies offer to collect personal information from social networking sites and other forums.

Due to consumer concerns over privacy, the Federal Trade Commission (FTC) is considering developing regulations that would protect consumer privacy better by limiting the

identity theft occurs when criminals obtain personal information that allows them to impersonate someone else to use their credit to access financial accounts and make purchases

online fraud any attempt to conduct fraudulent activities online

amount of consumer information that businesses can gather online. Other countries are pursuing similar actions. The European Union passed a law requiring companies to get users' consent before using cookies to track their information. In the United States, one proposed solution for consumer Internet privacy is a "do not track" bill, similar to the "do not call" bill for telephones, to allow users to opt out of having their information tracked.[77] Although consumers may welcome such added protections, web advertisers, who use consumer information to target advertisements to online consumers, see it as a threat. In response to impending legislation, many web advertisers are attempting self-regulation to stay ahead of the game. For instance, the Interactive Advertising Board is encouraging its members to adopt a do-not-track icon that users can click to avoid having their online activity tracked. However, it is debatable whether members will choose to participate or honor users' do-not-track requests.[78]

Identity Theft

Identity theft occurs when criminals obtain personal information that allows them to impersonate someone else to use the person's credit to access financial accounts and make purchases. Many of these breaches occur at banks, universities, and other businesses that contain sensitive consumer information.[79] This requires organizations to implement increased security measures to prevent database theft. As you can see in Figure 13.3, the most common complaints relate to government documents/benefits fraud, followed by credit card fraud, utility fraud, bank fraud, and employment fraud.

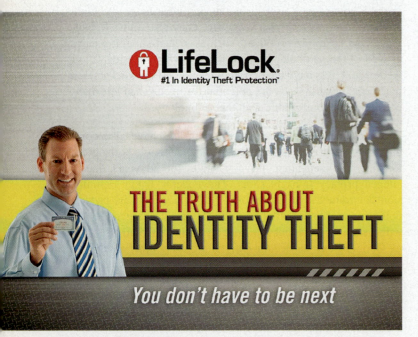

LifeLock protects consumers from identity theft by offering its identity theft protection system.

The Internet's relative anonymity and speed make possible both legal and illegal access to databases storing Social Security numbers, drivers' license numbers, dates of birth, mothers' maiden names, and other information that can be used to establish a credit card or bank account in another person's name to make fraudulent transactions. One growing scam used to initiate identity theft fraud is the practice of *phishing,* whereby con artists counterfeit a well-known website and send out e-mails directing victims to it. There visitors find instructions to reveal sensitive information such as their credit card numbers. Phishing scams have faked websites for PayPal, AOL, and the Federal Deposit Insurance Corporation.

Some identity theft problems are resolved quickly, whereas other cases take weeks and hundreds of dollars before a victim's bank balances and credit standings are restored. To deter identity theft, the National Fraud Center wants financial institutions to implement new technologies such as digital certificates, digital signatures, and biometrics—the use of fingerprinting or retina scanning.

Online Fraud

Online fraud includes any attempt to conduct fraudulent activities online, such as by deceiving consumers into releasing personal information. It is becoming a major source of frustration among users of social networking sites because cybercriminals are finding new ways to use sites such as Facebook and Twitter to commit fraudulent activities. For instance, they will create profiles under a company's name either to damage the company's reputation (particularly larger, more controversial companies) or to lure that company's customers into releasing personal information the perpetrators can use for monetary gain.

Mobile payments are another concern. It is estimated that with the growing use of mobile transactions, fraud will make up 1.5 percent of mobile transactions within the next few years.[80] Cybercriminals also create fake social network profiles to con people during times of natural disasters. Some criminals have posed as charitable institutions to solicit donations, whereas others have used fraudulent tactics to convince users to release their personal information. The best way for people to avoid being scammed through social media sites is to research charities before giving. After Hurricane Sandy, Apple and the Red Cross joined together to offer consumers a safe system for donating using their iTune accounts.[81]

Despite any number of safeguards, the best protection for consumers is to be careful when they divulge information online. The surest way to stay out of trouble is never to give out

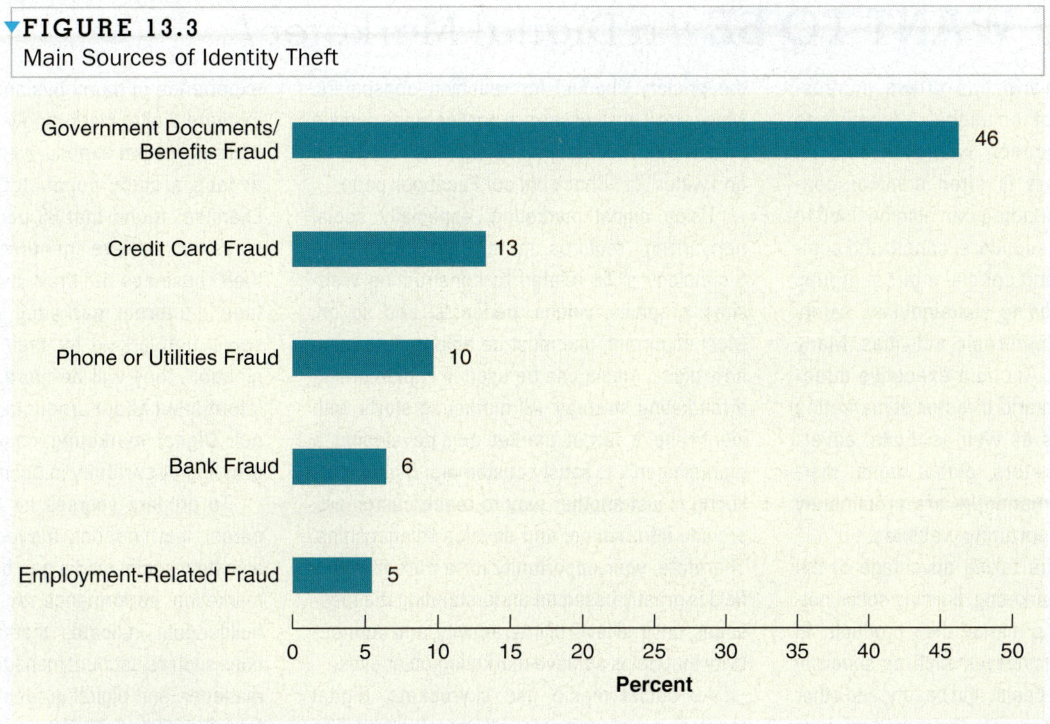

FIGURE 13.3
Main Sources of Identity Theft

Source: Federal Trade Commission, *Consumer Sentinel Network Data Book: January–December 2012,* February 2013, http://www.ftc.gov/sentinel/reports/sentinel-annual-reports/sentinel-cy2012.pdf.

personal information, like a Social Security or credit card number, unless it is a site you trust and that you know is legitimate.

Intellectual Property

In addition to protecting personal privacy, Internet users and others want to protect their rights to property they may create, including songs, movies, books, and software. Such intellectual property consists of the ideas and creative materials developed to solve problems, carry out applications, and educate and entertain others.

Although intellectual property is generally protected by patents and copyrights, each year losses from the illegal copying of computer programs, music, movies, compact discs, and books reach billions of dollars in the United States alone. This has become a particular problem with digital media sites. YouTube has often faced lawsuits on intellectual property infringement. With millions of users uploading content to YouTube, it can be hard for Google to monitor and remove all the videos that may contain copyrighted materials. The file hosting service Megaupload was shut down and owner Kim Dotcom arrested after prosecutors accused the site of being a front for massive Internet piracy. Legitimate users of the site were cut off from their files as well.[82]

Illegal sharing of content is another major intellectual property problem. Consumers rationalize the pirating of software, videogames, movies, and music for a number of reasons. First, many feel they just don't have the money to pay for what they want. Second, because their friends engage in piracy and swap digital content, some users feel influenced to engage in this activity. Others enjoy the thrill of getting away with something with a low risk of consequences. And finally, some people feel being tech-savvy allows them to take advantage of the opportunity to pirate content.[83]

The software industry loses more than $50 billion globally each year due to theft and illegal use of software products, according to the Business Software Alliance.[84] About 90 percent of illegal software copying is actually done by businesses. For example, a firm may obtain a license to install a specific application on 100 of its computers but actually installs it on 300. In some cases, software is illegally made available through the Internet by companies that have taken the software from the producer and set up their own distribution system.

TEAM EXERCISE

Develop a digital marketing promotion for a local sports team. Use Twitter, Facebook, and other social networking media to promote ticket sales for next season's schedule. In your plan, provide specific details and ideas for the content you would use on the sites. Also, describe how you would encourage fans and potential fans to go to your site. How would you use digital media to motivate sports fans to purchase tickets and merchandise and attend games?

SO YOU WANT TO BE // a Digital Marketer /

The business world has grown increasingly dependent on digital marketing to maintain communication with stakeholders. Reaching customers is often a major concern, but digital marketing can also be used to communicate with suppliers, concerned community members, and special interest groups about issues related to sustainability, safety practices, and philanthropic activities. Many types of jobs exist: Account executive directors of social media and director of marketing for digital products as well as digital advertisers, online marketers, global digital marketers, and brand managers are prominently listed on career opportunity websites.

Entrepreneurs are taking advantage of the low cost of digital marketing, building social networking sites to help market their products. In fact, some small businesses such as specialty publishing, personal health and beauty, and other specialty products can use digital marketing as the primary channel for reaching consumers. Many small businesses are posting signs outside their stores with statements such as "Follow us on Twitter" or "Check out our Facebook page."

Using digital marketing, especially social networking, requires more than information technology skills related to constructing websites, graphics, videos, podcasts, and so on. Most important, one must be able to determine how digital media can be used in implementing a marketing strategy. All marketing starts with identifying a target market and developing a marketing mix to satisfy customers. Digital marketing is just another way to reach customers, provide information, and develop relationships. Therefore, your opportunity for a career in this field is greatly based on understanding the messages, desired level of interactivity, and connectivity that helps achieve marketing objectives.

As social media use skyrockets, digital marketing professionals will be in demand. The experience of many businesses and research indicate digital marketing is a powerful way to increase brand exposure and generate traffic. In fact, a study conducted on Social Media Examiner found that 85 percent of marketers surveyed believe generating exposure for their business is their number-one advantage in Internet marketing. As consumers use social networking for their personal communication, they will be more open to obtaining information about products through this channel. Digital marketing could be the fastest-growing opportunity in business.

To prepare yourself for a digital marketing career, learn not only the technical aspects but also how social media can be used to maximize marketing performance. A glance at careerbuilder.com indicates that management positions such as account manager, digital marketing manager, and digital product manager can pay from $60,000 to $170,000 or more per year.

"DEVELOPING A STRATEGIC UNDERSTANDING OF HOW DIGITAL MARKETING CAN MAKE BUSINESS MORE EFFICIENT AND PRODUCTIVE IS INCREASINGLY NECESSARY."

DIGITAL MEDIA'S IMPACT ON MARKETING

To be successful in business, you need to know much more than how to use a social networking site to communicate with friends. Developing a strategic understanding of how digital marketing can make business more efficient and productive is increasingly necessary. If you are thinking of becoming an entrepreneur, then the digital world can open doors to new resources and customers. Smart phones, mobile broadband, and webcams are among the tools that can make the most of an online business world, creating greater efficiency at less cost. For example, rather than using traditional phone lines, Skype helps people make and receive calls via the Internet and provides free video calling and text messaging for about 10 percent of the cost of a land line.[85] It is up to businesses and entrepreneurs to develop strategies that achieve business success using existing and future technology, software, and networking opportunities.

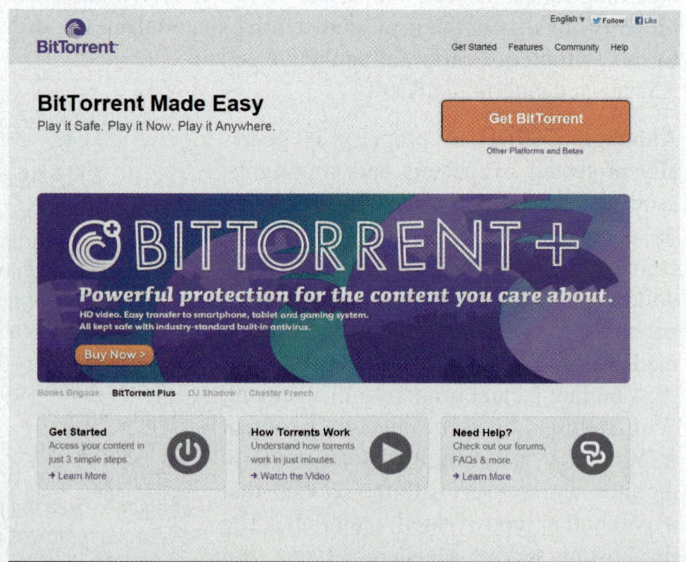

The file-sharing protocol BitTorrent allows users to share and download files. The U.S. Copyright Group recently obtained the IP addresses of users who downloaded specific movies using BitTorrent technology and are taking action against thousands of BitTorrent users for illegally downloading protected content.

Traditional businesses accustomed to using print media can find the transition to digital challenging. New media may require

learn, practice, apply digital marketing strategies!

M: Business **was developed just for you—students on the go who need information packaged in a concise yet interesting format with multiple learning options.**

Check out the book's website to:

- **Analyze ways to turn digital products into successful revenue-generators. (Solve the Dilemmas)**
- **Determine the types of digital media that would be helpful for promoting a product. (Build Your Skills)**
- **Practice planning digital marketing campaigns using digital media. (Build Your Skills)**

While you are there, don't forget to enhance your skills. Practice and apply your knowledge, review the practice exercises, Student PPT® slides, and quizzes to review and apply chapter concepts. Additionally, *Connect® Business* is available for *M: Business*.

www.mhhe.com/ferrellm4e

employees with new skills or additional training for current employees. There is often a gap between technical knowledge of how to develop sites and how to develop effective digital marketing strategies to enhance business success. Determining the correct blend of traditional and new media requires careful consideration; the mix will vary depending on the business, its size, and its target market. Future career opportunities will require skills in both traditional and digital media areas so that marketers properly understand and implement marketing strategies that help businesses achieve a competitive advantage. ■

accounting + financial statements

chapter fourteen

Accounting, the financial language that organizations use to record, measure, and interpret all of their financial transactions and records, is very important in business. All businesses—from a small family farm to a giant corporation—use the language of accounting to make sure they use their money wisely and to plan for the future. Nonbusiness organizations such as charities and governments also use accounting to demonstrate to donors and taxpayers how well they are using their funds and meeting their stated objectives.

This chapter explores the role of accounting in business and its importance in making business decisions. First, we discuss the uses of accounting information and the accounting process. Then, we briefly look at some simple financial statements and accounting tools that are useful in analyzing organizations worldwide. ■

LEARNING OBJECTIVES

After reading this chapter, you will be able to:

LO 14-1 Define accounting and describe the different uses of accounting information.

LO 14-2 Demonstrate the accounting process.

LO 14-3 Examine the various components of an income statement to evaluate a firm's bottom line.

LO 14-4 Interpret a company's balance sheet to determine its current financial position.

LO 14-5 Analyze the statement of cash flows to evaluate the increase and decrease in a company's cash balance.

accounting the recording, measurement, and interpretation of financial information

certified public accountant (CPA) an individual who has been state certified to provide accounting services ranging from the preparation of financial records and the filing of tax returns to complex audits of corporate financial records

private accountants accountants employed by large corporations, government agencies, and other organizations to prepare and analyze their financial statements

certified management accountants (CMAs) private accountants who, after rigorous examination, are certified by the National Association of Accountants and who have some managerial responsibility

LO 14-1 Define accounting and describe the different uses of accounting information.

THE NATURE OF ACCOUNTING

Simply stated, **accounting** is the recording, measurement, and interpretation of financial information. Large numbers of people and institutions, both within and outside businesses, use accounting tools to evaluate organizational operations. The Financial Accounting Standards Board has been setting the principles and standards of financial accounting and reporting in the private sector since 1973. Its mission is to establish and improve standards of financial accounting and reporting for the guidance and education of the public, including issuers, auditors, and users of financial information. However, the accounting scandals at the turn of the last century resulted when many accounting firms and businesses failed to abide by generally accepted accounting principles, or GAAP. Consequently, the federal government has taken a greater role in making rules, requirements, and policies for accounting firms and businesses through the Securities and Exchange Commission's (SEC) Public Company Accounting Oversight Board. For example, the Public Company Accounting Oversight Board charged the Chinese branch of Deloitte Touche Tohmatsu CPA Ltd. with not providing audit information related to a Chinese-based firm—a violation of U.S. securities law. The China-based audit firm was under investigation for possible accounting fraud. Chinese-based audit firms have been reluctant to allow U.S. authorities to investigate their activities.[1]

To understand the importance of accounting better, we must first understand who prepares accounting information and how it is used.

Accountants

Many of the functions of accounting are carried out by public or private accountants.

Public Accountants Individuals and businesses can hire a **certified public accountant (CPA)**, an individual who has been certified by the state in which he or she practices to provide accounting services ranging from the preparation of financial records and the filing of tax returns to complex audits of corporate financial records. Certification gives a public accountant the right to express, officially, an unbiased opinion regarding the accuracy of the client's financial statements. Most public accountants are either self-employed or members of large public accounting firms such as Ernst & Young, KPMG, Deloitte, and PricewaterhouseCoopers, together referred to as "the Big Four." In addition, many CPAs work for one of the second-tier accounting firms that are much smaller than the Big Four firms, as illustrated in Table 14.1.

Although there will always be companies and individual money managers who can successfully hide illegal or misleading accounting practices for a while, eventually they are exposed. After the accounting scandals of Enron and Worldcom in the early 2000s, Congress passed the Sarbanes-Oxley Act, which required firms to be more rigorous in their accounting and reporting practices. Sarbanes-Oxley made accounting firms separate their consulting and auditing businesses and punished corporate executives with potential jail sentences for inaccurate, misleading, or illegal accounting statements. This seemed to reduce the accounting errors among nonfinancial companies, but declining housing prices exposed some of the questionable practices by banks and mortgage companies. Only five years after the passage of the Sarbanes-Oxley Act, the world experienced a financial crisis starting in 2008—part of which was due to excessive risk taking and inappropriate accounting practices. Many banks failed to understand the true state of their financial health. Banks also developed questionable lending practices and investments based on subprime mortgages made to individuals who had poor credit. When housing prices declined and people suddenly found that they owed more on their mortgages than their homes were worth, they began to default. To prevent a depression, the government intervened and bailed out some of the United States' largest banks. Congress passed the Dodd-Frank Act in 2010 to strengthen the oversight of financial institutions. This act gave the Federal Reserve Board the task of implementing the legislation. It is expected that financial institutions will have at least one year to implement the requirements. This legislation will limit the types of assets commercial banks can buy; the amount of capital they must maintain; and the use of derivative instruments such as options, futures, and structured investment products.

?

DID YOU KNOW?

Corporate fraud costs are estimated at more than $3.5 trillion annually.[2]

KPMG is part of the "Big Four," or the four largest international accounting firms. The other three are PricewaterhouseCoopers, Ernst & Young, and Deloitte Touche Tohmatsu.

A growing area for public accountants is *forensic accounting,* which is accounting that is fit for legal review. It involves analyzing financial documents in search of fraudulent entries or financial misconduct. Functioning as much like detectives as accountants, forensic accountants have been used since the 1930s. In the wake of the accounting scandals of the early 2000s, many auditing firms are rapidly adding or expanding forensic or fraud-detection services. In addition, many forensic accountants root out evidence of cooked books for federal agencies such as the Federal Bureau of Investigation or the Internal Revenue Service. The Association of Certified Fraud Examiners, which certifies accounting professionals as *certified fraud examiners (CFEs),* has grown to more than 65,000 members.[3]

Private Accountants Large corporations, government agencies, and other organizations may employ their own **private accountants** to prepare and analyze their financial statements. With titles such as controller, tax accountant, or internal auditor, private accountants are deeply involved in many of the most important financial decisions of the organizations for which they work. Private accountants can be CPAs and may become **certified management accountants (CMAs)** by passing a rigorous examination by the Institute of Management Accountants.

TABLE 14.1 Prestige Ranking of Accounting Firms

Rank 2013	Rank 2012	Firm	Revenues (millions of $) 2011	Score	Location
1	22	Ernst & Young LLP	$22,000	7.941	New York, NY
2	1	Grant Thornton LLP	3,000	7.818	Chicago, IL
3	3	Deloitte LLP	28,000	7.615	New York, NY
4	2	PricewaterhouseCoopers LLP	29,200	7.612	New York, NY
5	23	KPMG LLP	22,700	7.452	New York, NY
6	27	Plante Moran	303	7.314	Southfield, MI
7	6	Moss Adams LLP	323	6.926	Seattle, WA
8	16	Baker Tilly Virchow Krause, LLP	242	6.833	Chicago, IL

* Rankings are based on issues that accounting professionals care most about.

Source: "Accounting Firms Rankings 2013: Vault Accounting 50," *Vault,* http://www.vault.com/wps/portal/usa/rankings/individual?rankingId1=252&rankingId2=−1&rankings=1®ionId=0&rankingYear=2013.

Accounting or Bookkeeping?

The terms *accounting* and *bookkeeping* are often mistakenly used interchangeably. Much narrower and far more mechanical than accounting, bookkeeping is typically limited to the routine, day-to-day recording of business transactions. Bookkeepers are responsible for obtaining and recording the information that accountants require to analyze a firm's financial position. They generally require less training than accountants. Accountants, on the other hand, usually complete course work beyond their basic four- or five-year college

managerial accounting the internal use of accounting statements by managers in planning and directing the organization's activities

cash flow the movement of money through an organization over a daily, weekly, monthly, or yearly basis

budget an internal financial plan that forecasts expenses and income over a set period of time

accounting degrees. This additional training allows accountants not only to record financial information but also to understand, interpret, and even develop the sophisticated accounting systems necessary to classify and analyze complex financial information.

The Uses of Accounting Information

Accountants summarize the information from a firm's business transactions in various financial statements (which we'll look at in a later section of this chapter) for a variety of stakeholders, including managers, investors, creditors, and government agencies. Many business failures may be directly linked to ignorance of the information "hidden" inside these financial statements. Likewise, most business successes can be traced to informed managers who understand the consequences of their decisions. Although maintaining and even increasing short-run profits is desirable, the failure to plan sufficiently for the future can easily lead an otherwise successful company to insolvency and bankruptcy court.

Basically, managers and owners use financial statements (1) to aid in internal planning and control and (2) for external purposes such as reporting to the Internal Revenue Service, stockholders, creditors, customers, employees, and other interested parties. Figure 14.1 shows some of the users of the accounting information generated by a typical corporation.

Internal Uses

Managerial accounting refers to the internal use of accounting statements by managers in planning and directing the organization's activities. Perhaps management's greatest single concern is **cash flow**, the movement of money through an organization over a daily, weekly, monthly, or yearly basis. Obviously, for any business to succeed, it needs to generate enough cash to pay its bills as they fall due. However, it is not at all unusual for highly successful and rapidly growing companies to struggle to make payments to employees, suppliers, and lenders because of an inadequate cash flow. One common reason for a so-called cash crunch, or shortfall, is poor managerial planning.

Managerial accountants also help prepare an organization's **budget**, an internal financial plan that forecasts expenses and income over a set period of time. It is not unusual for an organization to prepare separate daily, weekly, monthly, and yearly budgets. Think of a budget as a financial map, showing how the company expects to move from Point A to Point B over a specific period of time. Although most companies prepare *master budgets* for the entire firm, many also prepare budgets for smaller segments of the organization such as divisions, departments, product lines, or projects. Top-down master budgets begin at the upper management level and filter down to the individual department level, whereas bottom-up budgets start at the department or project level and are combined at the chief executive's office. Generally, the larger and more rapidly growing an organization, the greater will be the likelihood that it will build its master budget from the ground up.

Regardless of focus, the principal value of a budget lies in its breakdown of cash inflows and outflows. Expected operating expenses (cash outflows such as wages, materials costs, and taxes) and operating revenues (cash inflows in the form of payments from customers) over a set period of time are carefully forecast and subsequently compared with actual results. Deviations between the two serve as a trip wire or feedback loop to launch more detailed financial analyses in an effort to pinpoint trouble spots and opportunities.

External Uses

Managers also use accounting statements to report the business's financial performance to outsiders. Such statements are used for filing income taxes, obtaining credit from lenders, and reporting results to the firm's stockholders. They become the basis for the

FIGURE 14.1
The Users of Accounting Information

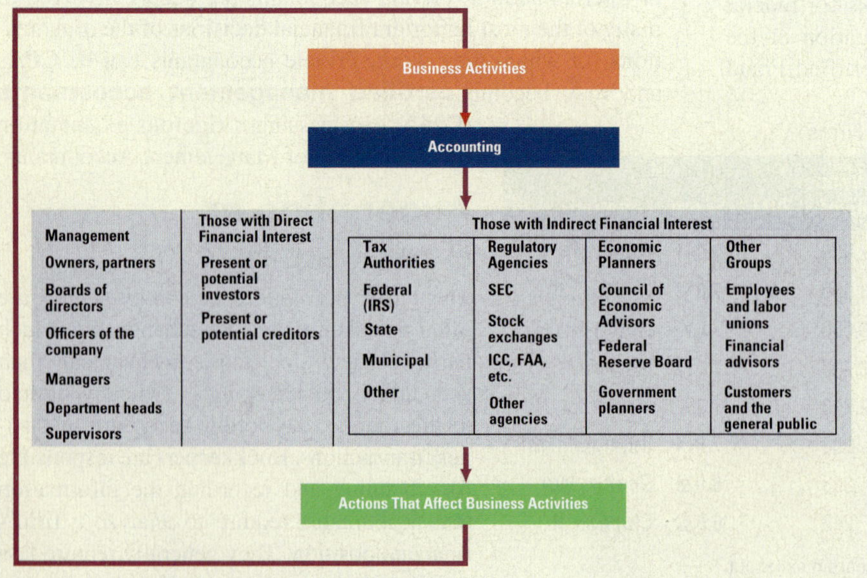

Source: From Needles/Powers/Crosson, *Principles of Accounting,* 12e. © 2014 South-Western, a part of Cengage Learning, Inc. Reproduced by permission.

annual report summary of a firm's financial information, products, and growth plans for owners and potential investors

information provided in the official corporate **annual report**, a summary of the firm's financial information, products, and growth plans for owners and potential investors. Although frequently presented between slick, glossy covers prepared by major advertising firms, the single most important component of an annual report is the signature of a certified public accountant attesting that the required financial statements are an accurate reflection of the underlying financial condition of the firm. Financial statements meeting these conditions are termed *audited.* The primary external users of audited accounting information are government agencies; stockholders and potential investors; and lenders, suppliers, and employees.

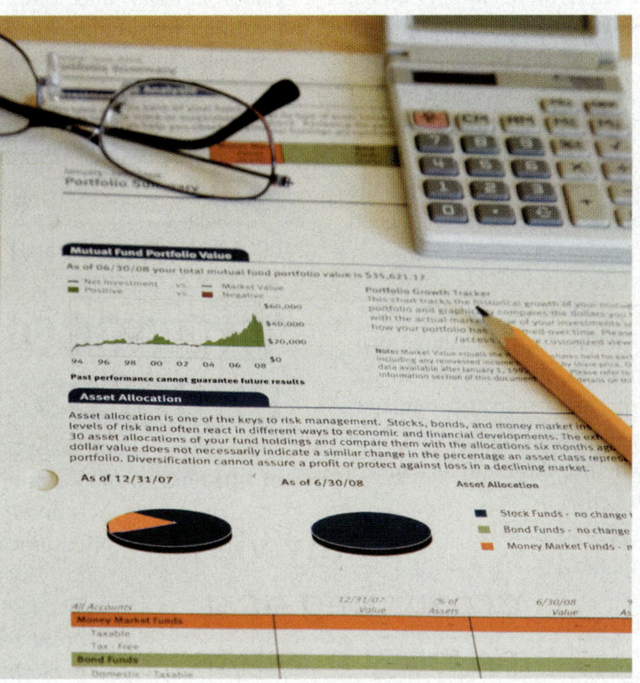

During the global financial crisis, it turns out that Greece had been engaging in deceptive accounting practices, with the help of U.S. investment banks. Greece was using financial techniques that hid massive amounts of debt from its public balance sheets. Eventually, the markets figured out the country might not be able to pay off its creditors. The European Union and the International Monetary Fund came up with a plan to give Greece some credit relief, but tied to this was the message to "get your financial house in order." By the middle of 2012, the European problem was often referred to as the PIGS. This referred to Portugal, Italy, Ireland, Greece, and Spain—all of which were having debt problems. The PIGS have caused cracks in the European Monetary Union. Whereas Germany demanded austerity, others, including Greece, wanted more growth-oriented strategies. Although the situation in the euro zone has calmed down, it is still simmering rather than boiling.

To top this off, *The New York Times* reported that many states, such as Illinois and California, seem to have the same problems as many EU countries—debt overload. These states have "budgets that will not balance,

GOODWILL CONTRIBUTES SIGNIFICANTLY TO FIRM VALUE

Suppose you purchase a company such as Starbucks. You might assume that you would pay for the net worth of Starbucks' assets, such as its cash, coffee inventory, property, and equipment. However, the majority of Starbucks' value is intangible. You would end up paying significantly more for Starbucks than just the value of its tangible assets. This additional cost is for the firm's goodwill, or the value of intangible assets such as reputation, relationships with customers, intellectual property, and brand value. Consider Apple Inc., for example. Its intellectual property, loyal customers, and strong reputation for quality make the company worth more than its hard, tangible assets. Companies must account for this goodwill on their balance sheet, which helps investors gain a better idea of the firm's financial situation as well as its return on investments.

However, sometimes a firm's goodwill exceeds its market value. This signals that the value of the firm's goodwill is too high, often because it made poor choices in deciding what companies to acquire. When this occurs, companies must mark down their goodwill value. Microsoft, Hewlett-Packard, and Boston Scientific Corp. all had to write off billions of dollars in goodwill after companies they acquired failed to live up to expectations. Hewlett-Packard announced that it would write off $8 billion of goodwill. What does this mean for investors? Not only does it reduce the firm's value, but it also indicates that the firms' leadership did not exercise good judgment when acquiring certain companies. Unfortunately, many companies on the S&P 500 index have goodwill ratios that are high compared to their market value.[4]

Discussion Questions

1. Why is goodwill important for a company?
2. What might be the problem if goodwill exceeds the market value of the firm?
3. What do goodwill write-offs indicate about leadership decisions?

assets a firm's economic resources, or items of value that it owns, such as cash, inventory, land, equipment, buildings, and other tangible and intangible things

liabilities debts that a firm owes to others

owners' equity all of the money that has ever been contributed to the company that never has to be paid back

accounting that masks debt, the use of derivatives to plug holes, and armies of retired public workers who are counting on pension benefits that are proving harder and harder to pay." Governor Brown of California has managed to work out some budget proposals with the state legislature to bring the state's revenue and spending back into balance over the next several years, but Illinois has been unable to reach a similar deal. Clearly, the economic downturn will have some lasting effects that need clear accounting solutions.[5]

Financial statements evaluate the return on stockholders' investment and the overall quality of the firm's management team. As a result, poor performance, as documented in the financial statements, often results in changes in top management. Potential investors study the financial statements in a firm's annual report to determine whether the company meets their investment requirements and whether the returns from a given firm are likely to compare favorably with similar companies.

Banks and other lenders look at financial statements to determine a company's ability to meet current and future debt obligations if a loan or credit is granted. To determine this ability, a short-term lender examines a firm's cash flow to assess its ability to repay a loan quickly with cash generated from sales. A long-term lender is more interested in the company's profitability and indebtedness to other lenders.

Labor unions and employees use financial statements to establish reasonable expectations for salary and other benefit requests. Just as firms experiencing record profits are likely to face added pressure to increase employee wages, so too are employees unlikely to grant employers wage and benefit concessions without considerable evidence of financial distress.

> "Many view accounting as a primary business language."

LO 14-2 Demonstrate the accounting process.

THE ACCOUNTING PROCESS

Many view accounting as a primary business language. It is of little use, however, unless you know how to speak it. Fortunately, the fundamentals—the accounting equation and the double-entry bookkeeping system—are not difficult to learn. These two concepts serve as the starting point for all currently accepted accounting principles.

The Accounting Equation

Accountants are concerned with reporting an organization's assets, liabilities, and owners' equity. To help illustrate these concepts, consider a hypothetical floral shop called Anna's Flowers, owned by Anna Rodriguez. A firm's economic resources, or items of value that it owns, represent its **assets**—cash, inventory, land, equipment, buildings, and other tangible and intangible things. The assets of Anna's Flowers include counters, refrigerated display cases, flowers, decorations, vases, cards, and other gifts as well as something known as goodwill, which in this case is Anna's reputation for preparing and delivering beautiful floral arrangements on a timely basis. **Liabilities**, on the other hand, are debts the firm owes to others. Among the liabilities of Anna's Flowers are a loan from the Small Business Administration and money owed to flower suppliers and other creditors for items purchased. The **owners' equity** category contains all of the money that has ever been contributed to the company that never has to be paid back. The funds can come from investors who have given money or assets to the company, or it can come from past profitable operations. In the case of Anna's Flowers, if Anna were to sell off, or liquidate, her business, any money left over after selling all the shop's assets and paying off its liabilities would comprise her owner's equity.

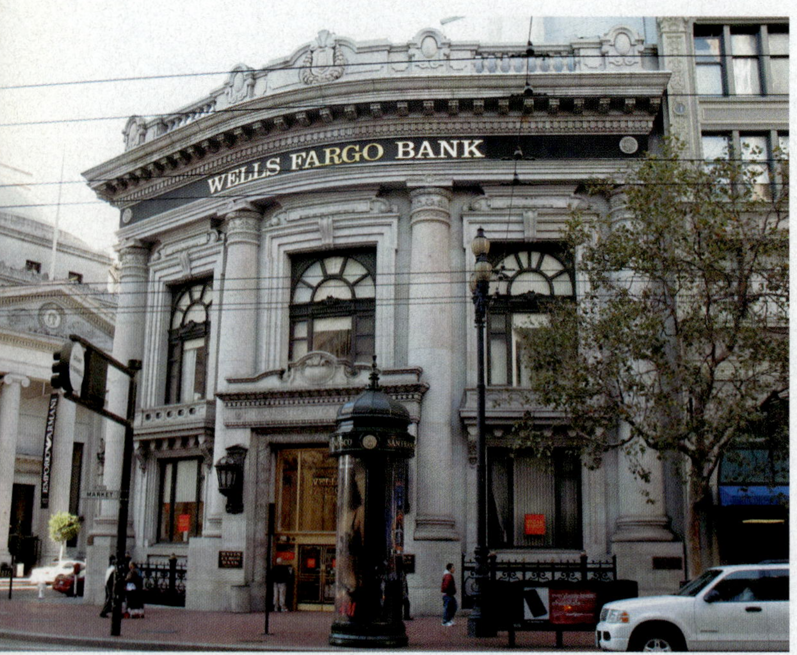

As one of the biggest banks in the United States, Wells Fargo specializes in banking, mortgage, and financial services. The data it provides can be used in financial statements.

accounting equation assets equal liabilities plus owners' equity

double-entry bookkeeping a system of recording and classifying business transactions in separate accounts to maintain the balance of the accounting equation

accounting cycle the four-step procedure of an accounting system: examining source documents, recording transactions in an accounting journal, posting recorded transactions, and preparing financial statements

journal a time-ordered list of account transactions

ledger a book or computer program with separate files for each account

The relationship among assets, liabilities, and owners' equity is a fundamental concept in accounting and is known as the **accounting equation**:

Assets = Liabilities + Owners' equity

Double-Entry Bookkeeping

Double-entry bookkeeping is a system of recording and classifying business transactions in separate accounts to maintain the balance of the accounting equation. Returning to Anna's Flowers, suppose Anna buys $325 worth of roses on credit from the Antique Rose Emporium to fill a wedding order. When she records this transaction, she will list the $325 as a liability or a debt to a supplier. At the same time, however, she will also record $325 worth of roses as an asset in an account known as inventory. Because the assets and liabilities are on different sides of the accounting equation, Anna's accounts increase in total size (by $325) but remain in balance:

Assets = Liabilities + Owners' equity

$325 = $325

Thus, to keep the accounting equation in balance, each business transaction must be recorded in two accounts.

In the final analysis, all business transactions are classified as assets, liabilities, or owners' equity. However, most organizations further break down these three accounts to provide more specific information about a transaction. For example, assets may be broken down into specific categories such as cash, inventory, and equipment; liabilities may include bank loans, supplier credit, and other debts.

Figure 14.2 shows how Anna used the double-entry bookkeeping system to account for all of the transactions that took place in her first month of business. These transactions include her initial investment of $2,500, the loan from the Small Business Administration, purchases of equipment and inventory, and the purchase of roses on credit. In her first month of business, Anna generated revenues of $2,000 by selling $1,500 worth of inventory. Thus, she deducts, or (in accounting notation that is appropriate for assets) *credits,* $1,500 from inventory and adds, or *debits,* $2,000 to the cash account. The difference between Anna's $2,000 cash inflow and her $1,500 outflow is represented by a credit to owners' equity, because it is money that belongs to her as the owner of the flower shop.

The Accounting Cycle

In any accounting system, financial data typically pass through a four-step procedure sometimes called the **accounting cycle**. The steps include examining source documents, recording transactions in an accounting journal, posting recorded transactions, and preparing financial statements. Figure 14.3 on page 293 shows how Anna works through them. Traditionally, all of these steps were performed using paper, pencils, and erasers (lots of erasers!), but today the process is often fully computerized.

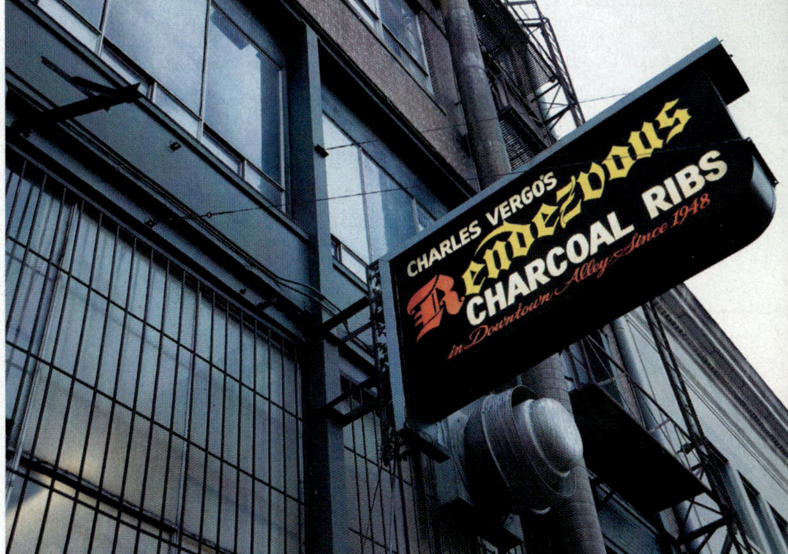

The owners' equity portion of a company's balance sheet, such as that of Rendezvous Barbecue in Memphis, Tennessee, includes the money the company's owners have put into the firm.

Step One: Examine Source Documents

Like all good managers, Anna Rodriguez begins the accounting cycle by gathering and examining source documents—checks, credit card receipts, sales slips, and other related evidence concerning specific transactions.

Step Two: Record Transactions

Next, Anna records each financial transaction in a **journal**, which is basically just a time-ordered list of account transactions. Although most businesses keep a general journal in which all transactions are recorded, some classify transactions into specialized journals for specific types of transaction accounts.

Step Three: Post Transactions

Anna next transfers the information from her journal into a **ledger**, a book or computer program with separate files for each account. This process is known as *posting.* At the end of the accounting period (usually yearly, but occasionally quarterly or monthly), Anna prepares a *trial balance,* a summary of the balances of all the accounts in the general ledger. If, upon totalling, the trial balance doesn't balance (that is, the accounting equation is not in

income statement
a financial report that shows an organization's profitability over a period of time—month, quarter, or year

balance), Anna or her accountant must look for mistakes (typically an error in one or more of the ledger entries) and correct them. If the trial balance is correct, the accountant can then begin to prepare the financial statements.

Step Four: Prepare Financial Statements The information from the trial balance is also used to prepare the company's financial statements. In the case of public corporations and certain other organizations, a CPA must *attest,* or certify, that the organization followed generally accepted accounting principles in preparing the financial statements. When these statements have been completed, the organization's books are "closed," and the accounting cycle begins anew for the next accounting period.

FINANCIAL STATEMENTS

The result of the accounting process is a series of financial statements. The income statement, the balance sheet, and the statement of cash flows are the best-known examples of financial statements. They are provided to stockholders and potential investors in a firm's annual report as well as to relevant outsiders such as creditors, government agencies, and the Internal Revenue Service.

It is important to recognize that not all financial statements follow precisely the same format. The fact that different organizations generate income in different ways suggests that when it comes to financial statements, one size definitely does not fit all. Manufacturing firms, service providers, and nonprofit organizations each use a different set of accounting principles or rules on which the public accounting profession has agreed. As we have already mentioned, these are sometimes referred to as *generally accepted accounting principles (GAAP).* Each country has a different set of rules that the businesses within that country are required to use for their accounting process and financial statements. However, a number of countries have adopted a standard set of accounting principles known as International Financial Reporting Standards. The United States has discussed adopting these standards to create a more standardized system of reporting for global investors. Moreover, as is the case in many other disciplines, certain concepts have more than one name. For example, *sales* and *revenues* are often interchanged, as are *profits, income,* and *earnings.* Table 14.2 lists a few common equivalent terms that should help you decipher their meaning in accounting statements.

LO 14-3 Examine the various components of an income statement to evaluate a firm's bottom line.

The Income Statement

The question "What's the bottom line?" derives from the income statement, where the bottom line shows the overall profit or loss of the company after taxes. Thus, the **income statement** is a financial report that shows an organization's profitability over a period of time, be that a month, quarter, or year. By its very design, the income statement offers one of the clearest possible pictures of the company's overall revenues and the costs incurred in generating those revenues. Other names for the income statement include profit and loss (P&L) statement or operating statement. A sample income statement

FIGURE 14.2
The Accounting Equation and Double-Entry Bookkeeping for Anna's Flowers

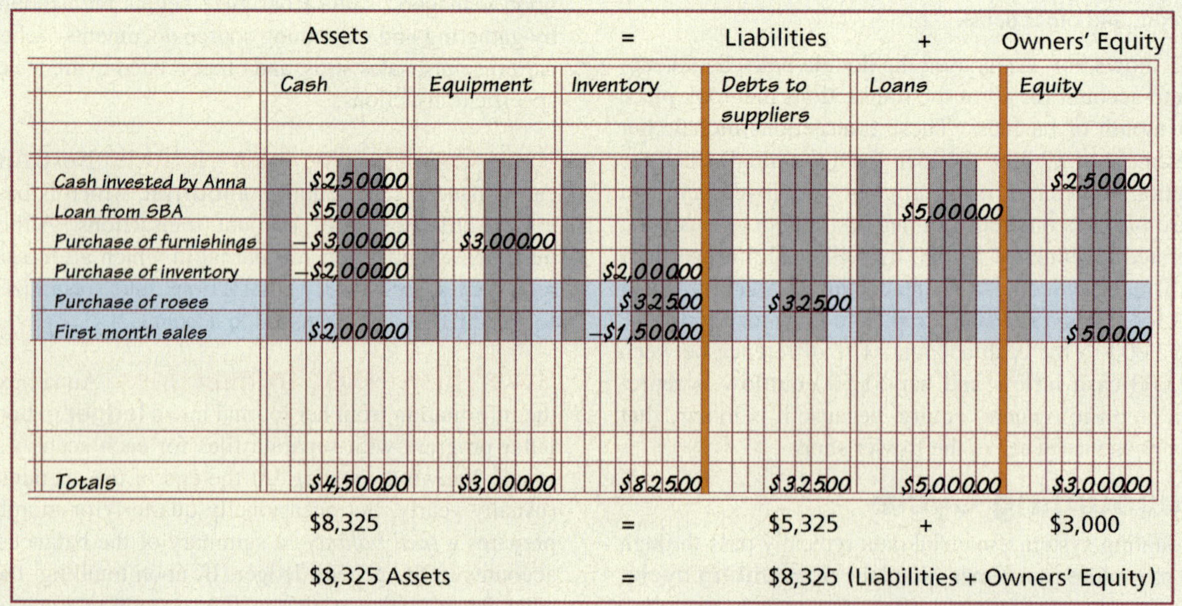

	Assets			= Liabilities		+ Owners' Equity
	Cash	*Equipment*	*Inventory*	*Debts to suppliers*	*Loans*	*Equity*
Cash invested by Anna	$2,500.00					$2,500.00
Loan from SBA	$5,000.00				$5,000.00	
Purchase of furnishings	–$3,000.00	$3,000.00				
Purchase of inventory	–$2,000.00		$2,000.00			
Purchase of roses			$325.00	$325.00		
First month sales	$2,000.00		–$1,500.00			$500.00
Totals	$4,500.00	$3,000.00	$825.00	$325.00	$5,000.00	$3,000.00

$8,325 = $5,325 + $3,000

$8,325 Assets = $8,325 (Liabilities + Owners' Equity)

FIGURE 14.3
The Accounting Process for Anna's Flowers

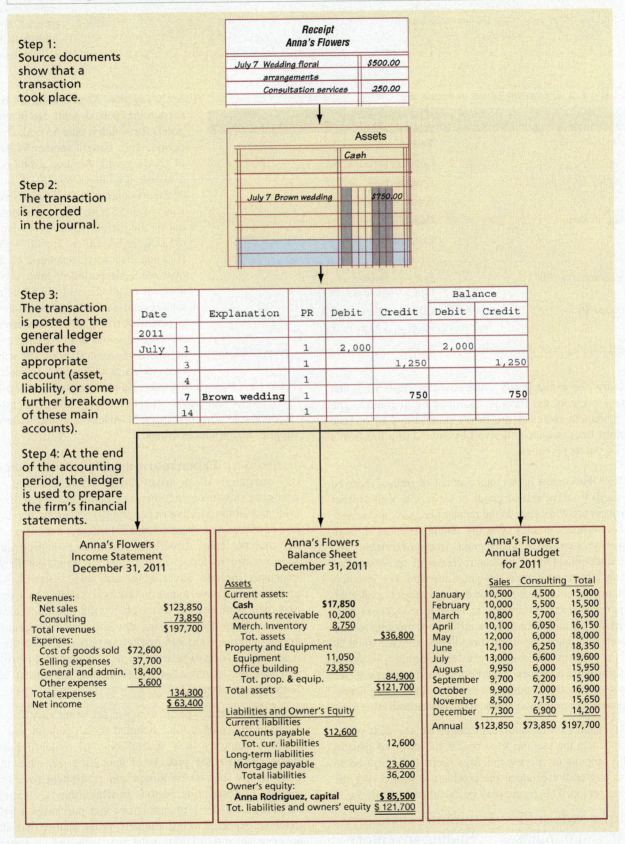

Step 1: Source documents show that a transaction took place.

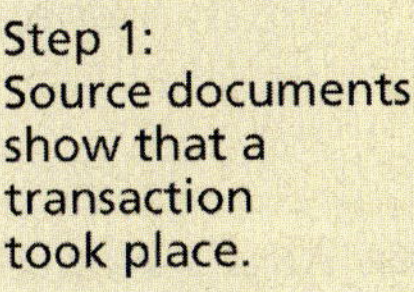

Receipt
Anna's Flowers

July 7 Wedding floral arrangements	$500.00
Consultation services	250.00

Step 2: The transaction is recorded in the journal.

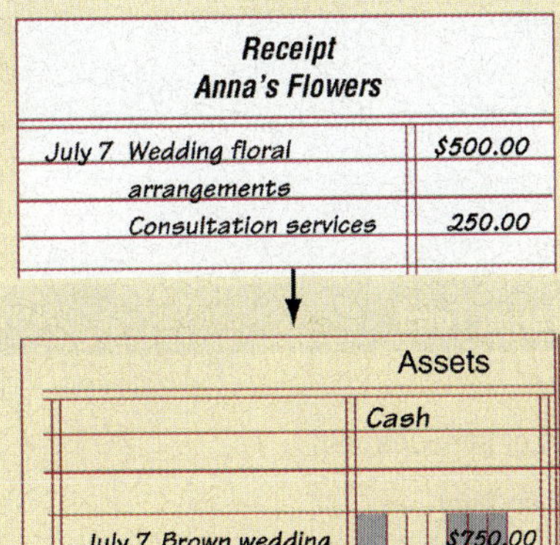

Step 3: The transaction is posted to the general ledger under the appropriate account (asset, liability, or some further breakdown of these main accounts).

Date		Explanation	PR	Debit	Credit	Balance Debit	Balance Credit
2011							
July	1		1	2,000		2,000	
	3		1		1,250		1,250
	4		1				
	7	Brown wedding	1		750		750
	14		1				

Step 4: At the end of the accounting period, the ledger is used to prepare the firm's financial statements.

Anna's Flowers
Income Statement
December 31, 2011

Revenues:		
Net sales		$123,850
Consulting		73,850
Total revenues		$197,700
Expenses:		
Cost of goods sold	$72,600	
Selling expenses	37,700	
General and admin.	18,400	
Other expenses	5,600	
Total expenses		134,300
Net income		$ 63,400

Anna's Flowers
Balance Sheet
December 31, 2011

Assets		
Current assets:		
Cash	**$17,850**	
Accounts receivable	10,200	
Merch. Inventory	8,750	
Tot. assets		$36,800
Property and Equipment		
Equipment	11,050	
Office building	73,850	
Tot. prop. & equip.		84,900
Total assets		$121,700
Liabilities and Owner's Equity		
Current liabilities		
Accounts payable	$12,600	
Tot. cur. liabilities		12,600
Long-term liabilities		
Mortgage payable		23,600
Total liabilities		36,200
Owner's equity:		
Anna Rodriguez, capital		**$ 85,500**
Tot. liabilities and owners' equity		$ 121,700

Anna's Flowers
Annual Budget
for 2011

	Sales	Consulting	Total
January	10,500	4,500	15,000
February	10,000	5,500	15,500
March	10,800	5,700	16,500
April	10,100	6,050	16,150
May	12,000	6,000	18,000
June	12,100	6,250	18,350
July	13,000	6,600	19,600
August	9,950	6,000	15,950
September	9,700	6,200	15,900
October	9,900	7,000	16,900
November	8,500	7,150	15,650
December	7,300	6,900	14,200
Annual	$123,850	$73,850	$197,700

revenue the total amount of money received (or promised) from the sale of goods or services as well as from related business activities

cost of goods sold the amount of money a firm spent (or promised to spend) to buy or produce the products it sold during the period to which the income statement applies

gross income (profit) revenues minus the cost of goods sold required to generate the revenues

expenses the costs incurred in the day-to-day operations of an organization

depreciation the process of spreading the costs of long-lived assets such as buildings and equipment over the total number of accounting periods in which they are expected to be used

TABLE 14.2 Equivalent Terms in Accounting

Term	Equivalent Term
Revenues	Sales
	Goods or services sold
Gross profit	Gross income
	Gross earnings
Operating income	Operating profit
	Earnings before interest and taxes (EBIT)
	Income before interest and taxes (IBIT)
Income before taxes (IBT)	Earnings before taxes (EBT) Profit before taxes (PBT)
Net income (NI)	Earnings after taxes (EAT)
	Profit after taxes (PAT)
Income available to common stockholders	Earnings available to common stockholders

with line-by-line explanations is presented in Table 14.3, and Table 14.4 presents the income statement of Starbucks. The income statement indicates the firm's profitability or income (the bottom line), which is derived by subtracting the firm's expenses from its revenues.

Revenue **Revenue** is the total amount of money received (or promised) from the sale of goods or services as well as from other business activities such as the rental of property and investments. Nonbusiness entities typically obtain revenues through donations from individuals and/or grants from governments and private foundations. One of the controversies in accounting has been when a business should recognize revenue. For instance, should an organization book revenue during a project or after the project is completed? Differences in revenue recognition have caused similar organizations to book different accounting results. A proposed rule states that firms should book revenue when "it satisfie[s] a performance obligation by transferring a promised good or service to a customer."[6] Starbucks' income statement (see Table 14.4) shows three sources of revenue: retail sales; licensing; and consumer processed goods, food service, and other.

For most manufacturing and retail concerns, the next major item included in the income statement is the **cost of goods sold**, the amount of money the firm spent (or promised to spend) to buy and/or produce the products it sold during the accounting period. This figure may be calculated as follows:

$$\text{Cost of goods sold} = \text{Beginning inventory} + \text{Interim purchases} - \text{Ending inventory}$$

Let's say that Anna's Flowers began an accounting period with an inventory of goods for which it paid $5,000. During the period, Anna bought another $4,000 worth of goods, giving the shop a total inventory available for sale of $9,000. If, at the end of the accounting period, Anna's inventory was worth $5,500, the cost of goods sold during the period would have been $3,500 ($5,000 + $4,000 − $5,500 = $3,500). If Anna had total revenues of $10,000 over the same period of time, subtracting the cost of goods sold ($3,500) from the total revenues of $10,000 yields the store's **gross income** or **profit** (revenues minus the cost of goods sold required to generate the revenues): $6,500. The same process occurs at Starbucks. As indicated in Table 14.4, the cost of goods sold was more than $4.9 million in 2011. Notice that Starbucks calls it cost of sales, rather than cost of goods sold. This is because Starbucks buys raw materials and supplies and produces drinks.

Expenses **Expenses** are the costs incurred in the day-to-day operations of an organization. Three common expense accounts shown on income statements are (1) selling, general, and administrative expenses; (2) research, development, and engineering expenses; and (3) interest expenses (remember that the costs directly attributable to selling goods or services are included in the cost of goods sold). Selling expenses include advertising and sales salaries. General and administrative expenses include salaries of executives and their staff and the costs of owning and maintaining the general office. Research and development costs include scientific, engineering, and marketing personnel and the equipment and information used to design and build prototypes and samples. Interest expenses include the direct costs of borrowing money.

The number and type of expense accounts vary from organization to organization. Included in the general and administrative category is a special type of expense known as **depreciation**, the process of spreading the costs of long-lived assets such as buildings and equipment over the total number of accounting periods in which they are expected to be used. Consider a manufacturer that purchases a $100,000 machine expected to last about 10 years. Rather than showing an expense of $100,000 in the first year and no expense for

net income the total profit (or loss) after all expenses, including taxes, have been deducted from revenue; also called net earnings

that equipment over the next nine years, the manufacturer is allowed to report depreciation expenses of $10,000 per year in each of the next 10 years because that better matches the cost of the machine to the years the machine is used. Each time this depreciation is written off as an expense, the book value of the machine is also reduced by $10,000. The fact that the equipment has a zero value on the firm's balance sheet when it is fully depreciated (in this case, after 10 years) does not necessarily mean that it can no longer be used or is economically worthless. Indeed, in some industries, machines used every day have been reported as having no book value whatsoever for more than 30 years.

Net Income **Net income** (or net earnings) is the total profit (or loss) after all expenses including taxes have been deducted from revenue. Generally, accountants divide profits into individual sections such as operating income and earnings before interest and taxes. Starbucks, for example, lists earnings before income taxes, net earnings, and earnings per share of outstanding stock (see Table 14.4). Like most companies, Starbucks presents not only the current year's results but also the previous two years' income statements to permit comparison of performance from one period to another.

Temporary Nature of the Income Statement Accounts Companies record their operational activities in the revenue and expense accounts during an accounting period. Gross profit, earnings before interest and taxes, and net income are the results of calculations made from the revenues and expenses accounts; they are not actual accounts. At the end of each accounting period, the dollar amounts in all

TABLE 14.3 Sample Income Statement

The following exhibit presents key components of an income statement with all the terms defined and explained.

Terms	Definitions
Revenues (sales)	Total dollar amount of products sold (includes income from other business services such as rental-lease income and interest income).
Less: Cost of goods sold	The cost of producing the goods and services, including the cost of labor and raw materials as well as other expenses associated with production.
Gross profit	The income available after paying all expenses of production.
Less: Selling and administrative expense	The cost of promoting, advertising, and selling products as well as the overhead costs of managing the company. This includes the cost of management and corporate staff. One noncash expense included in this category is depreciation, which approximates the decline in the value of plant and equipment assets due to use over time. In most accounting statements, depreciation is not separated from selling and administrative expenses. However, financial analysts usually create statements that include this expense.
Income before interest and taxes (operating income or EBIT)	This line represents all income left over after operating expenses have been deducted. This is sometimes referred to as operating income since it represents all income after the expenses of operations have been accounted for. Occasionally, this is referred to as EBIT, or earnings before interest and taxes.
Less: Interest expense	Interest expense arises as a cost of borrowing money. This is a financial expense rather than an operating expense and is listed separately. As the amount of debt and the cost of debt increase, so will the interest expense. This covers the cost of both short-term and long-term borrowing.
Income before taxes (earnings before taxes—EBT)	The firm will pay a tax on this amount. This is what is left of revenues after subtracting all operating costs, depreciation costs, and interest costs.
Less: Taxes	The tax rate is specified in the federal tax code.
Net income	This is the amount of income left after taxes. The firm may decide to retain all or a portion of the income for reinvestment in new assets. Whatever it decides not to keep it will usually pay out in dividends to its stockholders.
Less: Preferred dividends	If the company has preferred stockholders, they are first in line for dividends. That is one reason their stock is called "preferred."
Income to common stockholders	This is the income left for the common stockholders. If the company has a good year, there may be a lot of income available for dividends. If the company has a bad year, income could be negative. The common stockholders are the ultimate owners and risk takers. They have the potential for very high or very poor returns since they get whatever is left after all other expenses.
Earnings per share	Earnings per share is found by dividing the income available to the common stockholders by the number of shares of common stock outstanding. This is income generated by the company for each share of common stock.

balance sheet a snapshot of an organization's financial position at a given moment

current assets assets that are used or converted into cash within the course of a calendar year

accounts receivable money owed a company by its clients or customers who have promised to pay for the products at a later date

the revenue and expense accounts are moved into an account called "Retained Earnings," one of the owners' equity accounts. Revenues increase owners' equity; expenses decrease it. The resulting change in the owners' equity account is exactly equal to the net income. This shifting of dollar values from the revenue and expense accounts allows the firm to begin the next accounting period with zero balances in those accounts. Zeroing out the balances enables a company to count how much it has sold and how many expenses have been incurred during a period of time. The basic accounting equation (Assets = Liabilities + Owners' equity) will not balance until the revenue and expense account balances have been moved, or closed out, to the owners' equity account.

One final note about income statements: You may remember that corporations may choose to make cash payments called dividends to shareholders out of their net earnings. When a corporation elects to pay dividends, it decreases the cash account (in the assets category of the balance sheet) as well as a capital account (in the owners' equity category of the balance sheet). During any period of time, the owners' equity account may change because of the sale of stock (or contributions/withdrawals by owners), the net income or loss, or the dividends paid.

ExxonMobil has one of the highest incomes with almost $45 billion in 2012.

COMPANIES INVESTIGATE WAYS TO INTEGRATE FINANCIAL INFORMATION AND SUSTAINABILITY COSTS

Most people believe that financial statements such as income statements and balance sheets provide the entire picture of a firm's financial standing. In reality, however, this is not the case. It has been estimated that about 80 percent of a firm's value is not found on the balance sheet. One of the least understood areas involves sustainability. For instance, how much does violating an environmental law truly cost a firm, not only monetarily but also regarding its reputation? Some socially responsible businesses have adopted a triple bottom line approach in which the organization reports its financial results, its impact on society, and its impact on the planet. Yet even these companies find it difficult to add three dimensions up to provide an overall report.

A new pilot program consisting of 75 global companies wants to investigate ways to overcome these challenges. This program, monitored by the International Integrated Reporting Council, seeks to create an integrated reporting model that will give investors a holistic view of the company's operations and business strategies. Integrated reporting combines both financial and nonfinancial information. Companies testing this program include Microsoft, Unilever, Clorox, and Coca-Cola. Although most of these firms already develop sustainability or social responsibility reports, these reports are separate from the company's financial information. Such an endeavor requires the active participation of both company financial officers and accountants. Integrated reporting may soon become the new norm for investor reports—stock exchanges such as NASDAQ are beginning to require more information on a firm's corporate governance and environmental activities as well as its financial information.[7]

Discussion Questions

1. Why might it be important to include sustainability and other factors in a firm's financial reports?
2. What is the purpose of the Integrated Reporting Council?
3. Why do you think NASDAQ is beginning to require more information on a firm's corporate governance and environmental activities?

TABLE 14.4 Starbucks Corporation Consolidated Statements of Earnings (in millions, except per share data)

Fiscal Year Ended	Oct 2, 2011	Oct 3, 2010	Sep 27, 2009
Net revenues:			
Company-operated stores	$ 9,632.4	$ 8,963.5	$8,180.1
Licensed stores	1,007.5	875.2	795.0
CPG, foodservice and other	1,060.5	868.7	799.5
Total net revenues	11,700.4	10,707.4	9,774.6
Cost of sales including occupancy costs	4,949.3	4,458.6	4,324.9
Store operating expenses	3,665.1	3,551.4	3,425.1
Other operating expenses	402.0	293.2	264.4
Depreciation and amortization expenses	523.3	510.4	534.7
General and administrative expenses	636.1	569.5	453.0
Restructuring charges	0.0	53.0	332.4
Total operating expenses	10,175.8	9,436.1	9,334.5
Gain on sale of properties	30.2	0.0	0.0
Income from equity investees	173.7	148.1	121.9
Operating income	1,728.5	1,419.4	562.0
Interest income and other, net	115.9	50.3	37.0
Interest expense	(33.3)	(32.7)	(39.1)
Earnings before income taxes	1,811.1	1,437.0	559.9
Income taxes	563.1	488.7	168.4
Net earnings including noncontrolling interests	1,248.0	948.3	391.5
Net earnings (loss) attributable to noncontrolling interests	2.3	2.7	0.7
Net earnings attributable to Starbucks	$ 1,245.7	$ 945.6	$ 390.8
Earnings per share—basic	$ 1.66	$ 1.27	$ 0.53
Earnings per share—diluted	$ 1.62	$ 1.24	$ 0.52
Weighted average shares outstanding:			
Basic	748.3	744.4	738.7
Diluted	769.7	764.2	745.9
Cash dividends declared per share	$ 0.56	$ 0.36	$ 0.00

Source: Starbucks 2011 Annual Report, p. 43.

LO 14-4 Interpret a company's balance sheet to determine its current financial position.

The Balance Sheet

The second basic financial statement is the **balance sheet**, which presents a snapshot of an organization's financial position at a given moment. As such, the balance sheet indicates what the organization owns or controls and the various sources of the funds used to pay for these assets, such as bank debt or owners' equity.

The balance sheet takes its name from its reliance on the accounting equation: Assets *must* equal liabilities plus owners' equity. Table 14.5 provides a sample balance sheet with line-by-line explanations. Unlike the income statement, the balance sheet does not represent the result of transactions completed over a specified accounting period. Instead, the balance sheet is, by definition, an accumulation of all financial transactions conducted by an organization since its founding. Following long-established traditions, items on the balance sheet are listed on the basis of their original cost, less accumulated depreciation, rather than their present values.

Balance sheets are often presented in two formats. The traditional balance sheet format placed the organization's assets on the left side and its liabilities and owners' equity on the right. More recently, a vertical format, with assets on top followed by liabilities and owners' equity, has gained wide acceptance. Starbucks' balance sheet for 2010 and 2011 is presented in Table 14.6. In the sections that follow, we'll briefly describe the basic items found on the balance sheet; we'll take a closer look at a number of these in Chapter 16.

Assets All asset accounts are listed in descending order of *liquidity*—that is, how quickly each could be turned into cash. **Current assets**, also called short-term assets, are those that are used or converted into cash within the course of a calendar year. Cash is followed by temporary investments, accounts receivable, and inventory, in that order. **Accounts receivable** refers to money owed the company by its clients or customers who have promised to pay for the products at a later date. Accounts receivable usually includes an allowance for bad debts that management does not expect to collect. The bad-debts adjustment is normally based on historical collections experience and is deducted from the accounts receivable balance to present a more realistic view of the payments likely to be received in the future, called net

"The balance sheet takes its name from its reliance on the accounting equation: Assets *must* equal liabilities plus owners' equity."

TABLE 14.5 Sample Balance Sheet

The following exhibit presents key components of a balance sheet in word form with each item defined or explained.

Terms	Definitions
Assets	This is the major category for all physical, monetary, or intangible goods that have some dollar value.
Current assets	Assets that are either cash or are expected to be turned into cash within the next 12 months.
Cash	Cash or checking accounts.
Marketable securities	Short-term investments in securities that can be converted to cash quickly (liquid assets).
Accounts receivable	Cash due from customers in payment for goods received. These arise from sales made on credit.
Inventory	Finished goods ready for sale, goods in the process of being finished, or raw materials used in the production of goods.
Prepaid expense	A future expense item that has already been paid, such as insurance premiums or rent.
Total current assets	The sum of the preceding accounts.
Fixed assets	Assets that are long term in nature and have a minimum life expectancy that exceeds one year.
Investments	Assets held as investments rather than assets owned for the production process. Most often, the assets include small ownership interests in other companies.
Gross property, plant, and equipment	Land, buildings, and other fixed assets listed at original cost.
Less: Accumulated depreciation	The accumulated expense deductions applied to all plant and equipment over their life. Land may not be depreciated. The total amount represents in general the decline in value as equipment gets older and wears out. The maximum amount that can be deducted is set by the U.S. Federal Tax Code and varies by type of asset.
Net property, plant, and equipment	Gross property, plant, and equipment minus the accumulated depreciation. This amount reflects the book value of the fixed assets and not their value if sold.
Other assets	Any other asset that is long term and does not fit into the preceding categories. It could be patents or trademarks.
Total assets	The sum of all the asset values.
Liabilities and stockholders' equity	This is the major category. Liabilities refer to all indebtedness and loans of both a long-term and short-term nature. Stockholders' equity refers to all money that has been contributed to the company over the life of the firm by the owners.
Current liabilities	Short-term debt expected to be paid off within the next 12 months.
Accounts payable	Money owed to suppliers for goods ordered. Firms usually have between 30 and 90 days to pay this account, depending on industry norms.
Wages payable	Money owned to employees for hours worked or salary. If workers receive checks every two weeks, the amount owed should be no more than two weeks' pay.
Taxes payable	Firms are required to pay corporate taxes quarterly. This refers to taxes owed based on earnings estimates for the quarter.
Notes payable	Short-term loans from banks or other lenders.
Other current liabilities	The other short-term debts that do not fit into the preceding categories.
Total current liabilities	The sum of the preceding accounts.
Long-term liabilities	All long-term debt that will not be paid off in the next 12 months.
Long-term debt	Loans of more than one year from banks, pension funds, insurance companies, or other lenders. These loans often take the form of bonds, which are securities that may be bought and sold in bond markets.
Deferred income taxes	This is a liability owed to the government but not due within one year.
Other liabilities	Any other long-term debt that does not fit the preceding two categories.
Stockholders' equity	The following categories are the owners' investment in the company.
Common stock	The tangible evidence of ownership is a security called common stock. The par value is stated value and does not indicate the company's worth.

current liabilities a firm's financial obligations to short-term creditors, which must be repaid within one year

accounts payable the amount a company owes to suppliers for goods and services purchased with credit

accrued expenses an account representing all unpaid financial obligations incurred by the organization

▼ **TABLE 14.5** Sample Balance Sheet *(continued)*

Terms	Definitions
Capital in excess of par (a.k.a. contributed capital)	When shares of stock were sold to the owners, they were recorded at the price at the time of the original sale. If the price paid was $10 per share, the extra $9 per share would show up in this account at 100,000 shares times $9 per share, or $900,000.
Retained earnings	The total amount of earnings the company has made during its life and not paid out to its stockholders as dividends. This account represents the owners' reinvestment of earnings into company assets rather than payments of cash dividends. This account does not represent cash.
Total stockholders' equity	This is the sum of the preceding equity accounts representing the owners' total investment in the company.
Total liabilities and stockholders' equity	The total short-term and long-term debt of the company plus the owners' total investment. This combined amount *must* equal total assets.

receivables. Inventory may be held in the form of raw materials, work-in-progress, or finished goods ready for delivery.

Long-term, or fixed, assets represent a commitment of organizational funds of at least one year. Items classified as fixed include long-term investments, plant and equipment, and intangible assets, such as corporate goodwill, or reputation, as well as patents and trademarks.

Liabilities As seen in the accounting equation, total assets must be financed either through borrowing (liabilities) or through owner investments (owners' equity). **Current liabilities** include a firm's financial obligations to short-term creditors, which must be repaid within one year, whereas long-term liabilities have longer repayment terms. **Accounts payable** represents amounts owed to suppliers for goods and services purchased with credit. For example, if you buy gas with a BP credit card, the purchase represents an account payable for you (and an account receivable for BP). Other liabilities include wages earned by employees but not yet paid and taxes owed to the government. Occasionally, these accounts are consolidated into an **accrued expenses** account, representing all unpaid financial obligations incurred by the organization.

These machines from John Deere would be considered long-term assets on the balance sheet.

▼ **TABLE 14.6** Starbucks Corporation Consolidated Balance Sheets (in millions, except per share data)

ASSETS	Oct 2, 2011	Oct 3, 2010
Current assets:		
Cash and cash equivalents	$1,148.1	$1,164.0
Short-term investments—available-for-sale securities	855.0	236.5
Short-term investments—trading securities	47.6	49.2
Accounts receivable, net	386.5	302.7
Inventories	965.8	543.3
Prepaid expenses and other current assets	161.5	156.5
Deferred income taxes, net	230.4	304.2
Total current assets	3,794.9	2,756.4

(continued)

Owners' Equity Owners' equity includes the owners' contributions to the organization along with income earned by the organization and retained to finance continued growth and development. If the organization were to sell off all of its assets and pay off all of its liabilities, any remaining funds would belong to the owners. Not surprisingly, the accounts listed as owners' equity on a balance sheet may differ dramatically from company to company. Corporations sell stock to investors, who then become

statement of cash flows explains how the company's cash changed from the beginning of the accounting period to the end

the owners of the firm. Many corporations issue two, three, or even more classes of common and preferred stock, each with different dividend payments and/or voting rights. Because each type of stock issued represents a different claim on the organization, each must be represented by a separate owners' equity account, called contributed capital.

TABLE 14.6 Starbucks Corporation Consolidated Balance Sheets (in millions, except per share data) *(continued)*

	Oct 2, 2011	Oct 3, 2010
ASSETS		
Long-term investments—available-for-sale securities	107.0	191.8
Equity and cost investments	372.3	341.5
Property, plant and equipment, net	2,355.0	2,416.5
Other assets	297.7	346.5
Other intangible assets	111.9	70.8
Goodwill	321.6	262.4
TOTAL ASSETS	$7,360.4	$6,385.9
LIABILITIES AND EQUITY		
Current liabilities:		
Accounts payable	540.0	282.6
Accrued compensation and related costs	364.4	400.0
Accrued occupancy costs	148.3	173.2
Accrued taxes	109.2	100.2
Insurance reserves	145.6	146.2
Other accrued liabilities	319.0	262.8
Deferred revenue	449.3	414.1
Total current liabilities	2,075.8	1,779.1
Long-term debt	549.5	549.4
Other long-term liabilities	347.8	375.1
Total liabilities	2,973.1	2,703.6
Shareholders's equity:		
Common stock ($0.001 per value)—authorized, 1,200.0 shares; issued and outstanding, 744.8 and 742.6 shares, respectively (includes 3.4 common stock units in both periods)	0.7	0.7
Additional paid-in capital	1.1	106.2
Other additional paid-in capital	39.4	39.4
Retained earnings	4,297.4	3,471.2
Accumulated other comprehensive income	46.3	57.2
Total shareholders' equity	4,384.9	3,674.7
Noncontrolling interests	2.4	7.6
Total equity	4,387.3	3,682.3
TOTAL LIABILITIES AND EQUITY	$7,360.4	$6,385.9

Source: Starbucks 2011 Annual Report, p. 44.

LO 14-5 Analyze the statement of cash flows to evaluate the increase and decrease in a company's cash balance.

The Statement of Cash Flows

The third primary financial statement is called the **statement of cash flows**, which explains how the company's cash changed from the beginning of the accounting period to the end. Cash, of course, is an asset shown on the balance sheet, which provides a snapshot of the firm's financial position at one point in time. However, many investors and other users of financial statements want more information about the cash flowing into and out of the firm than is provided on the balance sheet to understand the company's financial health better. The statement of cash flows compares the cash balance from one year's balance sheet with the next while providing detail about how the firm used the cash. Table 14.7 presents Starbucks' statement of cash flows.

The change in cash is explained through details in three categories: cash from (used for) operating activities, cash from (used for) investing activities, and cash from (used for) financing activities. *Cash from operating activities* is calculated by combining the changes in the revenue accounts, expense accounts, current asset accounts, and current liability accounts. This category of cash flows includes all the accounts on the balance sheet that relate to computing revenues and expenses for the accounting period. If this amount is a positive number, as it is for Starbucks, then the business is making extra cash that it can use to invest in increased long-term capacity or to pay off debts such as loans or bonds. A negative number may indicate a business that is in a declining position regarding operations. Negative cash flow is not always a bad thing, however. It may indicate that a business is growing, with a very negative cash flow indicating rapid growth.

Cash from investing activities is calculated from changes in the long-term or fixed asset accounts. If this amount is negative, as is the case with Starbucks, the company is purchasing long-term assets for future growth. A positive figure indicates a business that is selling off existing long-term assets and reducing its capacity for the future.

ratio analysis calculations that measure an organization's financial health

▼ **TABLE 14.7** Starbucks Corporation Consolidated Statements of Cash Flows (in millions)

Fiscal Year Ended	Oct 2, 2011	Oct 3, 2010	Sep 27, 2009
OPERATING ACTIVITIES:			
Net earnings including noncontrolling interests	$1,248.0	$948.3	$ 391.5
Adjustments to reconcile net earnings to net cash provided by operating activities:			
Depreciation and amortization	550.0	540.8	563.3
Gain on sale of properties	(30.2)	0.0	0.0
Provision for impairments and asset disposals	36.2	67.7	224.4
Deferred income taxes, net	106.2	(42.0)	(69.6)
Equity in income of investees	(118.5)	(108.6)	(78.4)
Distributions of income from equity investees	85.6	91.4	53.0
Gain resulting from acquisition of joint ventures	(55.2)	(23.1)	0.0
Stock-based compensation	145.2	113.6	83.2
Excess tax benefit from exercise of stock options	(103.9)	(36.9)	(15.9)
Other	(2.9)	7.8	5.4
Cash provided/(used) by changes in operating assets and liabilities:			
Accounts receivable	(88.7)	(33.4)	59.1
Inventories	(422.3)	123.2	28.5
Accounts payable	227.5	(3.6)	(53.0)
Accrued taxes	104.0	0.6	59.2
Deferred revenue	35.8	24.2	16.3
Other operating assets	(22.5)	17.3	61.4
Other operating liabilities	(81.9)	17.6	60.6
Net cash provided by operating activities	1,612.4	1,704.9	1,389.0
INVESTING ACTIVITIES:			
Purchase of available-for-sale securities	(966.0)	(549.0)	(129.2)
Maturities and calls of available-for-sale securities	430.0	209.9	111.0
Sales of available-for-sale securities	0.0	1.1	5.0
Acquisitions, net of cash acquired	(55.8)	(12.0)	0.0
Net (purchases)/sales of equity, other investments, and other assets	(13.2)	1.2	(4.8)
Additions to property, plant, and equipment	(531.9)	(440.7)	(445.6)
Proceeds from sale of property, plant, and equipment	117.4	0.0	42.5
Net cash used by investing activities	(1,019.5)	(789.5)	(421.1)
FINANCING ACTIVITIES:			
Proceeds from issuance of commercial paper	0.0	0.0	20,965.4
Repayments of commercial paper	0.0	0.0	(21,378.5)
Proceeds from short-term borrowings	30.8	0.0	1,338.0
Repayments of short-term borrowings	0.0	0.0	(1,638.0)
Purchase of noncontrolling interest	(27.5)	(45.8)	0.0
Proceeds from issuance of common stock	235.4	127.9	57.3
Excess tax benefit from exercise of stock options	103.9	36.9	15.9

(continued)

Finally, *cash from financing activities* is calculated from changes in the long-term liability accounts and the contributed capital accounts in owners' equity. If this amount is negative, the company is likely paying off long-term debt or returning contributed capital to investors. As in the case of Starbucks, if this amount is positive, the company is either borrowing more money or raising money from investors by selling more shares of stock.

RATIO ANALYSIS: ANALYZING FINANCIAL STATEMENTS

The income statement shows a company's profit or loss, whereas the balance sheet itemizes the value of its assets, liabilities, and owners' equity. Together, the two statements provide the means to answer two critical questions: (1) How much did the firm make or lose? and (2) How much is the firm presently worth based on historical values found on the balance sheet? **Ratio analysis**, calculations that measure an organization's financial health, brings the complex information from the income statement and balance sheet into sharper focus so that managers, lenders, owners, and other interested parties can measure and compare the organization's productivity, profitability, and financing mix with other similar entities.

As you know, a ratio is simply one number divided by another, with the result showing the relationship between the two numbers. For example, we measure fuel efficiency with miles per gallon. This is how we know that 55 mpg in a Toyota Prius is much better than the average car. Financial ratios are used to weigh and evaluate a firm's performance. An absolute value such as earnings of $70,000 or accounts receivable of $200,000 almost never provides as much useful information as a well-constructed ratio. Whether

TABLE 14.7 Starbucks Corporation Consolidated Statements of Cash Flows (in millions) *(continued)*

Fiscal Year Ended	Oct 2, 2011	Oct 3, 2010	Sep 27, 2009
Principal payments on long-term debt	(4.3)	(6.6)	(0.7)
Cash dividends paid	(389.5)	(171.0)	0.0
Repurchase of common stock	(555.9)	(285.6)	0.0
Other	(0.9)	(1.8)	(1.6)
Net cash used by financing activities	(608.0)	(346.0)	(642.2)
Effect of exchange rate changes on cash and cash equivalents	(0.8)	(5.2)	4.3
Net increase/(decrease) in cash and cash equivalents	(15.9)	564.2	330.0
CASH AND CASH EQUIVALENTS:			
Beginning of period	1,164.0	599.8	269.8
End of period	$1,148.1	$1,164.0	$ 599.8
SUPPLEMENTAL DISCLOSURE OF CASH FLOW INFORMATION:			
Cash paid during the period for:			
Interest, net of capitalized interest	$ 34.4	$ 32.0	$ 39.8
Income taxes	$ 350.1	$ 527.0	$ 162.0

Source: Starbucks 2011 Annual Report, p. 45.

those numbers are good or bad depends on their relation to other numbers. If a company earned $70,000 on $700,000 in sales (a 10 percent return), such an earnings level might be quite satisfactory. The president of a company earning this same $70,000 on sales of $7 million (a 1 percent return), however, should probably start looking for another job!

Ratios by themselves are not very useful. It is the relationship of the calculated ratios to both prior organizational performance and the performance of the organization's peers, as well as its stated goals, that really matters. Remember, although the profitability, asset utilization, liquidity, debt ratios, and per share data we'll look at here can be very useful, you will never see the forest by looking only at the trees.

Profitability Ratios

Profitability ratios measure how much operating income or net income an organization is able to generate relative to its

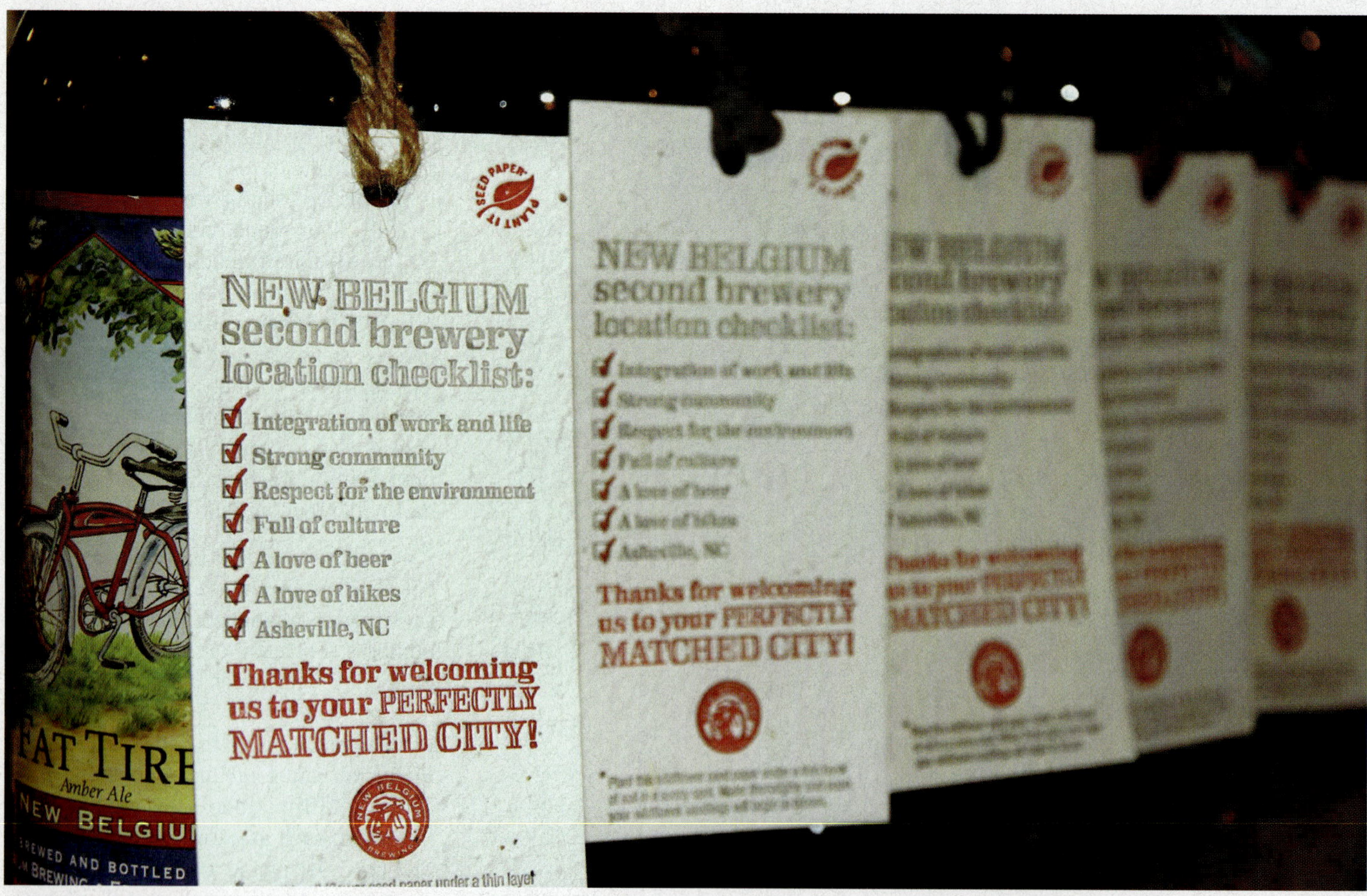

Increased profit margins allow companies such as New Belgium to invest in new production facilities in Asheville, North Carolina.

profitability ratios ratios that measure the amount of operating income or net income an organization is able to generate relative to its assets, owners' equity, and sales

profit margin net income divided by sales

return on assets net income divided by assets

return on equity net income divided by owners' equity; also called return on investment (ROI)

> ["The higher the profit margin, the better the cost controls within the company and the higher the return on every dollar of revenue."]

assets, owners' equity, and sales. The numerator (top number) used in these examples is always the net income after taxes. Common profitability ratios include profit margin, return on assets, and return on equity. The following examples are based on the 2011 income statement and balance sheet for Starbucks, as shown in Tables 14.4 and 14.6. Except where specified, all data are expressed in millions of dollars.

The **profit margin**, computed by dividing net income by sales, shows the overall percentage of profits earned by the company. It is based solely upon data obtained from the income statement. The higher the profit margin, the better the cost controls within the company and the higher the return on every dollar of revenue. Starbucks' profit margin is calculated as follows:

$$\text{Profit margin} = \frac{\text{Net income (Net earnings)}}{\text{Sales (Total net revenues)}}$$

$$= \frac{\$1{,}245.7}{\$11{,}700.4} = 10.65\%$$

Thus, for every $1 in sales, Starbucks generated profits after taxes of almost 11 cents.

Return on assets, net income divided by assets, shows how much income the firm produces for every dollar invested in assets. A company with a low return on assets is probably not using its assets very productively—a key managerial failing. For its construction, the return on assets calculation requires data from both the income statement and the balance sheet.

$$\text{Return on assets} = \frac{\text{Net income (Net earnings)}}{\text{Total assets}}$$

$$= \frac{\$1{,}245.7}{\$7{,}360.4} = 16.92\%$$

In the case of Starbucks, every $1 of assets generated a return of close to 17 percent, or profits of 16.92 cents per dollar.

Stockholders are always concerned with how much money they will make on their investment, and they frequently use the return on equity ratio as one of their key performance yardsticks. **Return on equity** (also called return on investment [ROI]), calculated by dividing net income by owners' equity, shows how much income is generated by each $1 the owners have invested in the firm. Obviously, a low return on equity means low stockholder returns and may indicate a need for immediate managerial attention. Because some assets may have been financed with debt not contributed by the owners, the value of the owners' equity is usually considerably lower

BUFFALO WILD WINGS: FROM ACCOUNTING MESS TO SUCCESS

Buffalo Wild Wings was founded in 1982 by James Disbrow and Scott Lowery after the two were unable to find a nearby restaurant that sold the buffalo wings they desired. After a few years in business, the founders got in trouble with the IRS for misusing the money they withheld from employee paychecks. With finances a mess, the company hired former KPMG tax specialist and current CEO Sally Smith to help sort out its financial records. With Smith's help, the company thrived. Same-store sales grew at a time when other restaurants were struggling. Today, the chain's 857 stores are well-known for their unique combination of beer, giant televisions featuring sports games, and buffalo wings with 16 sauces.

With $908 million in revenue, Buffalo Wild Wings is now eyeing the Middle East. The move might seem unusual: Alcohol is forbidden in many Middle Eastern countries, and the higher cost of chicken wings is affecting net profit margins. However, through local partnerships and menu changes, Buffalo Wild Wings is confident it can succeed with global expansion.[8]

asset utilization ratios ratios that measure how well a firm uses its assets to generate each $1 of sales

receivables turnover sales divided by accounts receivable

inventory turnover sales divided by total inventory

total asset turnover sales divided by total assets

liquidity ratios ratios that measure the speed with which a company can turn its assets into cash to meet short-term debt

current ratio current assets divided by current liabilities

quick ratio (acid test) a stringent measure of liquidity that eliminates inventory

debt utilization ratios ratios that measure how much debt an organization is using relative to other sources of capital, such as owners' equity

than the total value of the firm's assets. Starbucks' return on equity is calculated as follows:

$$\text{Return on equity} = \frac{\text{Net income}}{\text{Stockholders' equity}}$$

$$= \frac{\$1{,}245.7}{\$4{,}387.3} = 28.39\%$$

For every dollar invested by Starbucks stockholders, the company earned a 28.39 percent return, or 28.39 cents per dollar invested.

Asset Utilization Ratios

Asset utilization ratios measure how well a firm uses its assets to generate each $1 of sales. Obviously, companies using their assets more productively will have higher returns on assets than their less efficient competitors. Similarly, managers can use asset utilization ratios to pinpoint areas of inefficiency in their operations. These ratios (receivables turnover, inventory turnover, and total asset turnover) relate balance sheet assets to sales, which are found on the income statement.

The **receivables turnover**, sales divided by accounts receivable, indicates how many times a firm collects its accounts receivable in one year. It also demonstrates how quickly a firm is able to collect payments on its credit sales. Obviously, no payments means no profits. Starbucks collected its receivables a little more than 30 times per year. The reason the number is so high is that most of Starbucks' sales are for cash and not credit.

$$\text{Receivables turnover} = \frac{\text{Sales (Total net revenues)}}{\text{Receivables}}$$

$$= \frac{\$11{,}700.4}{\$386.5} = 30.27\times$$

Inventory turnover, sales divided by total inventory, indicates how many times a firm sells and replaces its inventory over the course of a year. A high inventory turnover ratio may indicate great efficiency but may also suggest the possibility of lost sales due to insufficient stock levels. Starbucks' inventory turnover indicates that it replaced its inventory 12.11 times last year, or slightly more than once a month.

$$\text{Inventory turnover} = \frac{\text{Sales (Total net revenues)}}{\text{Inventory}}$$

$$= \frac{\$11{,}700.4}{\$965.8} = 12.11\times$$

Total asset turnover, sales divided by total assets, measures how well an organization uses all of its assets in creating sales. It indicates whether a company is using its assets productively. Starbucks generated $1.59 in sales for every $1 in total corporate assets.

$$\text{Total asset turnover} = \frac{\text{Sales (Total net revenues)}}{\text{Total assets}}$$

$$= \frac{\$11{,}700.4}{\$7{,}360.4} = 1.59\times$$

Liquidity Ratios

Liquidity ratios compare current (short-term) assets to current liabilities to indicate the speed with which a company can turn its assets into cash to meet debts as they fall due. High liquidity ratios may satisfy a creditor's need for safety, but ratios that are too high may indicate that the organization is not using its current assets efficiently. Liquidity ratios are generally best examined in conjunction with asset utilization ratios because high turnover ratios imply that cash is flowing through an organization very quickly—a situation that dramatically reduces the need for the type of reserves measured by liquidity ratios.

The **current ratio** is calculated by dividing current assets by current liabilities. Starbucks' current ratio indicates that for every $1 of current liabilities, the firm had $1.83 of current assets on hand. This number improved from previous years and indicates that Starbucks has increased its liquidity as it restructures its business. Current assets increased faster than current liabilities between 2010 and 2011, making for a much improved current ratio. In addition, accounts receivable has increased over the same time period.

$$\text{Current ratio} = \frac{\text{Current assets}}{\text{Current liabilities}}$$

$$= \frac{\$3{,}794.9}{\$2{,}075.8} = 1.83\times$$

The **quick ratio** (also known as the **acid test**) is a far more stringent measure of liquidity because it eliminates inventory, the least-liquid current asset. It measures how well an organization can meet its current obligations without resorting to the sale of its inventory. In 2011, Starbucks had $1.36 invested in current assets (after subtracting inventory) for every $1 of current liabilities, an increase over previous years.

debt to total assets ratio a ratio indicating how much of the firm is financed by debt and how much by owners' equity

times interest earned ratio operating income divided by interest expense

per share data data used by investors to compare the performance of one company with another on an equal, per-share basis

earnings per share net income or profit divided by the number of stock shares outstanding

dividends per share paid by the corporation to the stockholders for each share owned

$$\text{Quick ratio} = \frac{\text{Current assets} - \text{Inventory}}{\text{Current liabilities}}$$

$$= \frac{\$2{,}829.1}{\$2{,}075.8} = 1.36 \times$$

Debt Utilization Ratios

Debt utilization ratios provide information about how much debt an organization is using relative to other sources of capital, such as owners' equity. Because the use of debt carries an interest charge that must be paid regularly regardless of profitability, debt financing is much riskier than equity. Unforeseen negative events such as recessions affect heavily indebted firms to a far greater extent than those financed exclusively with owners' equity. Because of this and other factors, the managers of most firms tend to keep debt-to-asset levels below 50 percent. However, firms in very stable and/or regulated industries, such as electric utilities, often are able to carry debt ratios well in excess of 50 percent with no ill effects.

The **debt to total assets ratio** indicates how much of the firm is financed by debt and how much by owners' equity. To find the value of Starbucks' total debt, you must add current liabilities to long-term debt and other liabilities.

$$\text{Debt to total assets} = \frac{\text{Debt (Total liabilities)}}{\text{Total assets}}$$

$$= \frac{\$2{,}973.1}{\$7{,}360.4} = 40\%$$

Thus, for every $1 of Starbucks' total assets, 40 percent is financed with debt. The remaining 60 percent is provided by owners' equity.

The **times interest earned ratio**, operating income divided by interest expense, is a measure of the safety margin a company has with respect to the interest payments it must make to its creditors. A low times interest earned ratio indicates that even a small decrease in earnings may lead the company into financial straits. Because Starbucks has more interest income than interest expense, it would appear that its times interest earned ratio cannot be calculated by using the income statement. However, in the statement of cash flows in Table 14.7 on the second line from the bottom, we can see that Starbucks paid $34.4 million in interest expense, an amount that was covered nearly 50.25 times by income before interest and taxes. A lender would not have to worry about receiving interest payments.

$$\text{Times interest earned} = \frac{\text{EBIT (Operating income)}}{\text{Interest}}$$

$$= \frac{\$1{,}728.5}{\$34.4} = 50.25 \times$$

Per Share Data

Investors may use **per share data** to compare the performance of one company with another on an equal, or per-share, basis. Generally, the more shares of stock a company issues, the less income is available for each share.

Earnings per share is calculated by dividing net income or profit by the number of shares of stock outstanding. This ratio is important because yearly changes in earnings per share, in combination with other economywide factors, determine a company's overall stock price. When earnings go up, so does a company's stock price—and so does the wealth of its stockholders.

$$\text{Diluted earnings per share} = \frac{\text{Net income}}{\text{Number of shares outstanding (diluted)}}$$

$$= \frac{\$1{,}245.7}{769.7} = \$1.62$$

We can see from the income statement that Starbucks' basic earnings per share more than tripled between 2009 and 2011 as Starbucks staged a dramatic turnaround. Notice that Starbucks lists diluted earnings per share, calculated here, of $0.52 per share in 2009 and $1.62 per share in 2011. You can see from the income statement that diluted earnings per share include more shares than the basic calculation; this is because diluted shares include potential shares that could be issued due to the exercise of stock options or the conversion of certain types of debt into common stock. Investors generally pay more attention to diluted earnings per share than basic earnings per share.

Dividends per share are paid by the corporation to the stockholders for each share owned. The payment is made from earnings after taxes by the corporation but is taxable income to the stockholder. Thus, dividends result in double taxation: The corporation pays tax once on its earnings, and the stockholder pays tax a second time on his or her dividend income. Starbucks began paying dividends in 2010 and increased them in 2011. The dividend declared on the income statement is 0 per share, but the actual dividends paid were $0.52. There is a difference between dividends paid and declared. Dividends are paid quarterly, and Starbucks declared a higher dividend in its fourth quarter, but it won't be paid until the next year.

$$\text{Dividends per share} = \frac{\text{Dividends paid}}{\text{Number of shares outstanding}}$$

$$= \frac{\$389.5}{748.3} = \$0.52$$

Industry Analysis

We have used McDonald's as a comparison to Starbucks because there are no real national and international coffee houses that compete with Starbucks on the same scale. Although McDonald's is almost two and one-half times larger than Starbucks in terms of sales, they both have a national and international presence and, to some extent, compete for the consumer's dollars. In recent years, McDonald's has moved into Starbucks' market by putting McCafé coffee shops in many of its locations. Table 14.8 indicates that McDonald's dominates Starbucks in two out of three profitability categories.

Since 2009, McDonald's has increased its after-tax profits by 21 percent, whereas Starbucks profits increased by more than 300 percent. Starbucks stumbled in 2007 and 2008 as it overexpanded and lost focus. Howard Schultz, the founder, returned as CEO and successfully restructured the company. Investors rewarded the company's turnaround by pushing the stock price from a low of $8.12 in early 2009 to a high of $62.00 in early 2012. Both companies have very little accounts receivables relative to the size of their sales, so the ratios are very high, indicating a lot of cash and credit card sales. McDonald's pushes off much of its inventory holding costs onto its suppliers, so it has much higher inventory turnover ratios. Both have current ratios that are reasonably solid given their level of profitability. The difference in the current ratios and the quick ratio is of little consequence to the financial analyst or lender because both companies have high times interest earned ratios. Starbucks has a much lower debt to asset ratio and therefore less financial risk than McDonald's, and this also is emphasized by Starbucks' much higher times interest earned ratio.

Although McDonald's net income has grown more slowly in the past three years, its earnings per share grew from $1.93 in 2007 to $5.27 in 2011. On the other hand, Starbucks' earnings per share in 2007 were $0.87. It dropped to $0.43 in 2008, recovered slightly to $0.52 in 2009, finally took off again in 2010, and reached $1.62 in 2011. Starbucks instituted its first dividend in 2010 and raised it from $0.10 per quarter to $0.13 per quarter to $0.17 per quarter for a projected annual rate of $0.68. Both companies are in good financial health, and Starbucks has regained its past glow. One thing is for sure: If Starbucks could earn the same profit margin as McDonald's, it would improve its other profitability ratios and its stock price.

TABLE 14.8 Industry Analysis, Year Ending 2011

	Starbucks	McDonald's
Profit margin	10.65%	20.38%
Return on assets	16.92%	16.68%
Return on equity	28.39%	38.24%
Receivables turnover	30.27×	20.23×
Inventory turnover	12.11×	231.22×
Total asset turnover	1.59×	0.82×
Current ratio	1.83×	1.25×
Quick ratio	1.36×	1.22×
Debt to total assets	40.00%	56%
Times interest earned	50.25×	17.43×
Diluted earnings per share	$1.62	$5.27
Dividends per share	$0.52	$2.53

Source: Data calculated from 2011 annual reports.

As another member of the "Big Four" accounting firms, Ernst & Young must maintain high standards of accounting ethics to secure its reputation for integrity.

IMPORTANCE OF INTEGRITY IN ACCOUNTING

The financial crisis and the recession that followed provided another example of a failure in accounting reporting. Many firms attempted to exploit loopholes and manipulate accounting processes and statements. Banks and other financial institutions often held assets off their books by manipulating their accounts. For instance, examiners for the Lehman Brothers' bankruptcy found that the most common example of removing assets or liabilities from the books was entering into what is called a repurchase agreement. In a repurchase agreement, assets are transferred to another entity with the contractual promise of buying them back at a set price. In the case of Lehman Brothers and other companies, repurchase agreements were used as a method of cooking the books that allowed them to manipulate accounting statements so that their ratios looked better than they actually were. If the accountants, the SEC, and the bank regulators had been more careful, these types of transactions would have been discovered and corrected.

On the other hand, strong compliance to accounting principles creates trust among stakeholders. The city of El Dorado, Kansas, makes transparency, accuracy, and disclosure of financial information top priorities. The city government wants to inform constituents about the amount of funds it receives as well as where that money is being spent. The government spends a significant amount of time in the audit process and creates an annual financial report that breaks down its financial information. Because of its diligence, the city has won the Certificate of Achievement for Financial Accounting from the Government Finance Officers Association every year since 1977.[9]

It is most important to remember that integrity in accounting processes requires ethical principles and compliance with both the spirit of the law and professional standards in the accounting profession. Most states require accountants preparing to take the CPA exam to take accounting ethics courses. Transparency and accuracy in reporting revenue, income, and assets develops trust from investors and other stakeholders. ■

TEAM EXERCISE

You can look at websites such as Yahoo! Finance (http://finance.yahoo.com/), under the company's Key Statistics link, to find many of its financial ratios, such as return on assets and return on equity. Have each member of your team look up a different company and explain why you think there are differences in the ratio analysis for these two ratios among the selected companies.

SO YOU WANT TO BE // an Accountant /

Do you like numbers and finances? Are you detail oriented, a perfectionist, and highly accountable for your decisions? If so, accounting may be a good field for you. If you are interested in accounting, there are always job opportunities available no matter the state of the economy. Accounting is one of the most secure job options in business. Of course, becoming an accountant is not easy. You will need at least a bachelor's degree in accounting to get a job, and many positions require additional training. Many states demand course work beyond the 120 to 150 credit hours collegiate programs require for an accounting degree. If you are really serious about getting into the accounting field, you will probably want to consider getting your master's in accounting and taking the CPA exam. The field of accounting can be complicated, and the extra training provided through a master's in accounting program will prove invaluable when you go out looking for a good job. Accounting is a volatile discipline affected by changes in legislative initiatives.

With corporate accounting policies changing constantly and becoming more complex, accountants are needed to help keep a business running smoothly and within the bounds of the law. In fact, the number of jobs in the accounting and auditing field is expected to increase 16 percent between 2010 and 2020, with more than 1.4 million jobs in the United States alone by 2020. Jobs in accounting tend to pay quite well, with the median salary standing at $61,690. If you go on to get your master's degree in accounting, expect to see an even higher starting wage. Of course, your earnings could be higher or lower than these averages, depending on where you work, your level of experience, the firm, and your particular position.

Accountants are needed in the public and the private sectors, in large and small firms, in for-profit and not-for-profit organizations. Accountants in firms are generally in charge of preparing and filing tax forms and financial reports. Public-sector accountants are responsible for checking the veracity of corporate and personal records to prepare tax filings. Basically, any organization that has to deal with money and/or taxes in some way or another will need an accountant, for either in-house service or occasional contract work. Requirements for audits under the Sarbanes-Oxley Act and rules from the Public Company Accounting Oversight Board are creating more jobs and increased responsibility to maintain internal controls and accounting ethics. The fact that accounting rules and tax filings tend to be complex virtually ensures that the demand for accountants will never decrease.[10]

learn, practice, apply accounting principles!

M: Business was developed just for you—students on the go who need information packaged in a concise yet interesting format with multiple learning options.

Check out the book's website to:

- Describe the information on the three basic accounting statements. (Solve the Dilemma)
- Understand the value of financial ratios. (Solve the Dilemma)
- Calculate profitability ratios and compare them to industry averages. (Build Your Skills)

While you are there, don't forget to enhance your skills. Practice and apply your knowledge, review the practice exercises, Student PPT® slides, and quizzes to review and apply chapter concepts. Additionally, *Connect® Business* is available for *M: Business.*

www.mhhe.com/ferrellm4e

chapter fifteen

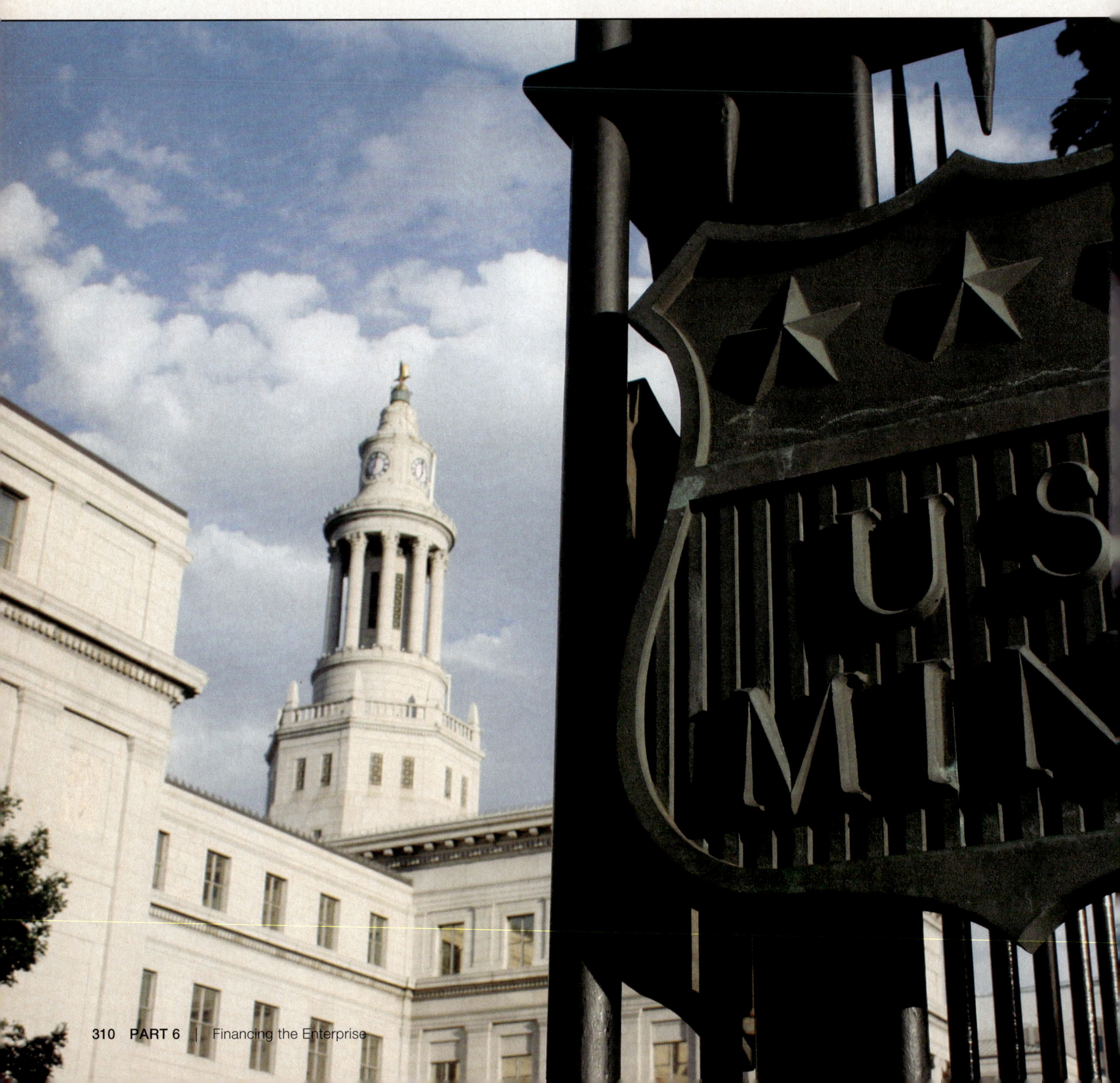

money + the financial system

From Wall Street to Main Street, both overseas and at home, money is the one tool used to measure personal and business income and wealth. **Finance** is the study of money: how it's made, how it's lost, and how it's managed. This chapter introduces you to the role of money and the financial system in the economy. Of course, if you have a checking account, automobile insurance, a college loan, or a credit card, you already have personal experience with some key players in the financial world.

We begin our discussion with a definition of money and then explore some of the many forms money may take. Next, we examine the roles of the Federal Reserve Board and other major institutions in the financial system. Finally, we explore the future of the finance industry and some of the changes likely to occur over the course of the next several years. ■

LEARNING OBJECTIVES

After reading this chapter, you will be able to:

LO 15-1 Define money, its functions, and its characteristics.

LO 15-2 Describe various types of money.

LO 15-3 Specify how the Federal Reserve Board manages the money supply and regulates the American banking system.

LO 15-4 Compare and contrast commercial banks, savings and loan associations, credit unions, and mutual savings banks.

LO 15-5 Distinguish among nonbanking institutions such as insurance companies, pension funds, mutual funds, and finance companies.

LO 15-6 Investigate the challenges ahead for the banking industry.

LO 15-1 Define money, its functions, and its characteristics.

MONEY IN THE FINANCIAL SYSTEM

Strictly defined, **money**, or *currency,* is anything generally accepted in exchange for goods and services. Materials as diverse as salt, cattle, fish, rocks, shells, cloth, as well as precious metals such as gold, silver, and copper, have long been used by various cultures as money. Most of these materials were limited-supply commodities that had their own value to society. (For example, salt can be used as a preservative and shells and metals as jewelry.) The supply of these commodities therefore determined the supply of "money" in that society. The next step was the development of IOUs, or slips of paper that could be exchanged for a specified supply of the underlying commodity. Gold notes, for instance, could be exchanged for gold, and the money supply was tied to the amount of gold available. Although paper money was first used in North America in 1685 (and even earlier in Europe), the concept of *fiat money*—a paper money not readily convertible to a precious metal such as gold—did not gain full acceptance until the Great Depression in the 1930s. The U.S. abandoned its gold-backed currency standard largely in response to the Great Depression and converted to a fiduciary, or fiat, monetary system. In the United States, paper money is really a government note, or promise, worth the value specified on the note.

> Money serves three important functions: as a medium of exchange, a measure of value, and a store of value.

For centuries, people on the Micronesian island of Yap have used giant round stones, like the ones shown here, for money. The stones aren't moved, but their ownership can change.

Functions of Money

Money serves three important functions: as a medium of exchange, a measure of value, and a store of value. For example, money allows a person or organization to pay expenses, to save and invest for future consumption, and to compare the price of competing goods and services.

Medium of Exchange Before fiat money, the trade of goods and services was accomplished through *bartering*—trading one good or service for another of similar value. As any school-age child knows, bartering can become quite inefficient—particularly in the case of complex, three-party transactions involving peanut butter sandwiches, baseball cards, and hair barrettes. There had to be a simpler way, and that was to decide on a single item—money—that can be freely converted to any other good upon agreement between parties.

Measure of Value As a measure of value, money serves as a common standard or yardstick of the value of goods and services. For example, $2 will buy a dozen large eggs and $25,000 will buy a nice car in the United States. In Japan, where the currency is known as the yen, these same transactions would cost about 198 yen and 2.47 million yen, respectively. Money, then, is a common denominator that allows people to compare the different goods and services that can be consumed on a particular income level. Although a star athlete and a burger-flipper are paid vastly different wages, each uses money as a measure of the value of their yearly earnings and purchases.

Store of Value As a store of value, money serves as a way to accumulate wealth (buying power) until it is needed. For example, a person making $1,000 per week who wants to buy a $500 computer could save $50 per week for each of the next 10 weeks. Unfortunately, the value of stored money is directly dependent on the health of the economy. If, due to rapid inflation, all prices double in one year, then the purchasing power value of the money "stuffed in the mattress" would fall by half. On the other hand, deflation occurs when prices of goods fall. Deflation might seem like a good thing for consumers, but in many ways it can be just as problematic as inflation. Periods of major deflation often lead to decreases in wages and

finance the study of money; how it's made, how it's lost, and how it's managed

money anything generally accepted in exchange for goods and services

increases in debt burdens.[1] Deflation also tends to be an indicator of problems in the economy. When Ireland experienced deflation in 2009—the first time it had experienced deflation in 49 years—the country blamed it on decreasing mortgage interest rate costs.[2] Ireland was undergoing a serious deficit and required a bailout from the European Commission, the International Monetary Fund, and the European Central Bank.[3]

Characteristics of Money

To be used as a medium of exchange, money must be acceptable, divisible, portable, stable in value, durable, and difficult to counterfeit.

Acceptability To be effective, money must be readily acceptable for the purchase of goods and services and for the settlement of debts. Acceptability is probably the most important characteristic of money: If people do not trust the value of money, businesses will not accept it as a payment for goods and services, and consumers will have to find some other means of paying for their purchases.

Divisibility Given the widespread use of quarters, dimes, nickels, and pennies in the United States, it is no surprise that the principle of divisibility is an important one. With barter, the lack of divisibility often makes otherwise preferable trades impossible, as would be an attempt to trade a steer for a loaf of bread. For money to serve effectively as a measure of value, all items must be valued in terms of comparable units—dimes for a piece of bubble gum, quarters for laundry machines, and dollars (or dollars and coins) for everything else.

Portability Clearly, for money to function as a medium of exchange, it must be easily moved from one location to the next. Large colored rocks could be used as money, but you couldn't carry them around in your wallet. Paper currency and metal coins, on the other hand, are capable of transferring vast purchasing power into small, easily carried (and hidden!) bundles. Few Americans realize it, but more U.S. currency is in circulation outside the United States than within. Currently, about $1.18 trillion of U.S. currency is in circulation, and the majority is held outside the United States.[4] Some countries, such as Panama, even use the U.S. dollar as their currency. Retailers in other countries often state prices in dollars and in their local currency.

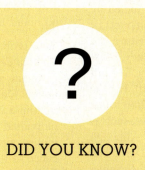

DID YOU KNOW?

Around 75 percent of counterfeit currency is found and destroyed before it ever reaches the public.[5]

Stability Money must be stable and maintain its declared face value. A $10 bill should purchase the same amount of goods or services from one day to the next. The principle of stability allows people who wish to postpone purchases and save their money to do so without fear that it will decline in value. As mentioned earlier, money declines in value during periods of inflation, when economic conditions cause prices to rise. Thus, the same amount of money buys fewer and fewer goods and services. In some countries, people spend their money as fast as they can to keep it from losing any more of its value. Instability destroys confidence in a nation's money and its ability to store value and serve as an effective medium of exchange. Ultimately, people faced with spiraling price increases avoid the increasingly worthless paper money at all costs, storing all of their savings in the form of real assets such as gold and land.

Durability Money must be durable. The crisp new dollar bills you trade at the music store for the hottest new CD will make their way all around town for about 20 months before being replaced (see Table 15.1). Were the value of an old, faded bill to fall in line with the deterioration of its appearance, the principles of stability and universal acceptability would fail (but, no doubt, fewer bills would pass through the washer!). Although metal coins, due to their much longer useful life, would appear to be an ideal form of money, paper currency is far more portable than metal because of its light weight. Today, coins are used primarily to provide divisibility.

Difficulty to Counterfeit Finally, to remain stable and enjoy universal acceptance, it almost goes without saying that money must be very difficult to counterfeit—that is, to duplicate illegally. Every country takes steps to make counterfeiting difficult. Most use multicolored money, and many use specially watermarked papers that are virtually impossible to duplicate. Counterfeit bills represent less than 0.03 percent of the currency

The U.S. government redesigns currency to stay ahead of counterfeiters and protect the public.

checking account money stored in an account at a bank or other financial institution that can be withdrawn without advance notice; also called a demand deposit

savings accounts accounts with funds that usually cannot be withdrawn without advance notice; also known as time deposits

money market accounts accounts that offer higher interest rates than standard bank rates but with greater restrictions

certificates of deposit (CDs) savings accounts that guarantee a depositor a set interest rate over a specified interval as long as the funds are not withdrawn before the end of the period—six months or one year, for example

credit cards means of access to preapproved lines of credit granted by a bank or finance company

TABLE 15.1 The Life Expectancy of Paper Currency

Denomination of Bill	Life Expectancy (Years)
$1	1.8
$5	1.3
$10	1.5
$20	2.0
$50	4.6
$100	7.4

Source: "How Currency Gets into Circulation," Federal Reserve Bank of Bank of New York, www.newyorkfed.org/aboutthefed/fedpoint/fed01.html.

in circulation in the United States,[6] but it is becoming increasingly easy for counterfeiters to print money with just a modest inkjet printer. This illegal printing of money is fueled by hundreds of people who often circulate only small amounts of counterfeit bills. To thwart the problem of counterfeiting, the U.S. Treasury Department redesigned the U.S. currency, starting with the $20 bill in 2003, the $50 bill in 2004, the $10 bill in 2006, the $5 bill in 2008, and the $100 bill in 2010. For the first time, U.S. money includes subtle colors in addition to the traditional green, as well as enhanced security features, such as a watermark, security thread, and color-shifting ink.[7] Although counterfeiting is not as much of an issue with coins, U.S. metal coins are usually worth more for the metal than their face value. It has begun to cost more to manufacture coins than what they are worth monetarily.

In 2006 the new Jefferson nickel was introduced, showing a profile of the nation's third president. Due to the increased price of metals, it costs a little over 10 cents to make the 5 cent piece.[8] As Table 15.2 indicates, it costs more than a penny to manufacture a penny, resulting in a call to discontinue it. Because it costs more to produce pennies and nickels than what they are worth, these coins have generated losses of $469 million in a seven-year period.[9]

TABLE 15.2 Costs to Produce Pennies and Nickels

Fiscal Year	Cent Unit Cost (¢)	Nickel Unit Cost (¢)	Revenue from Coins (millions)
2012	2.0	10.09	($109.20)
2011	2.41	11.18	($116.70)
2010	1.79	9.22	($42.60)
2009	1.62	6.03	($22.00)
2008	1.42	8.83	($47.00)
2007	1.67	9.53	($98.60)
2006	1.21	5.97	($32.90)
Total			($469.00)

Source: Michael Zielinksi, "Cost to Make Penny and Nickel Declines But Still Double Face Value," *Coin Update,* December 10, 2012, http://news.coinupdate.com/cost-to-make-penny-and-nickel-declines-but-still-double-face-value-1751/.

LO 15-2 Describe various types of money.

Types of Money

Although paper money and coins are the most visible types of money, the combined value of all of the printed bills and all of the minted coins is actually rather insignificant when compared with the value of money kept in checking accounts, savings accounts, and other monetary forms.

You probably have a **checking account** (also called a *demand deposit*), money stored in an account at a bank or other financial institution that can be withdrawn without advance notice. One way to withdraw funds from your account is by writing a *check,* a written order to a bank to pay the indicated individual or business the amount specified on the check from money already on deposit. Figure 15.1 explains the significance of the numbers found on a typical U.S. check. As legal instruments, checks serve as a substitute for currency and coins and are preferred for many transactions due to their lower risk of loss. If you lose a $100 bill, anyone who finds or steals it can spend it. If you lose a blank check, however, the risk of catastrophic loss is quite low. Not only does your bank have a sample of your signature on file to compare with a suspected forged signature, but you can render the check immediately worthless by means of a stop-payment order at your bank.

There are several types of checking accounts, with different features available for different monthly fee levels or specific minimum account balances. Some checking accounts earn interest (a small percentage of the amount deposited in the account that the bank pays to the depositor). One such interest-bearing checking account is the *NOW (Negotiable Order of Withdrawal) account* offered by most financial institutions. The interest rate paid on such accounts varies with the interest rates available in the economy but is typically quite low (more recently less than 1 percent but in the past between 2 and 5 percent).

Savings accounts (also known as *time deposits*) are accounts with funds that usually cannot be withdrawn without advance notice and/or have limits on the number of withdrawals

FIGURE 15.1
A Check

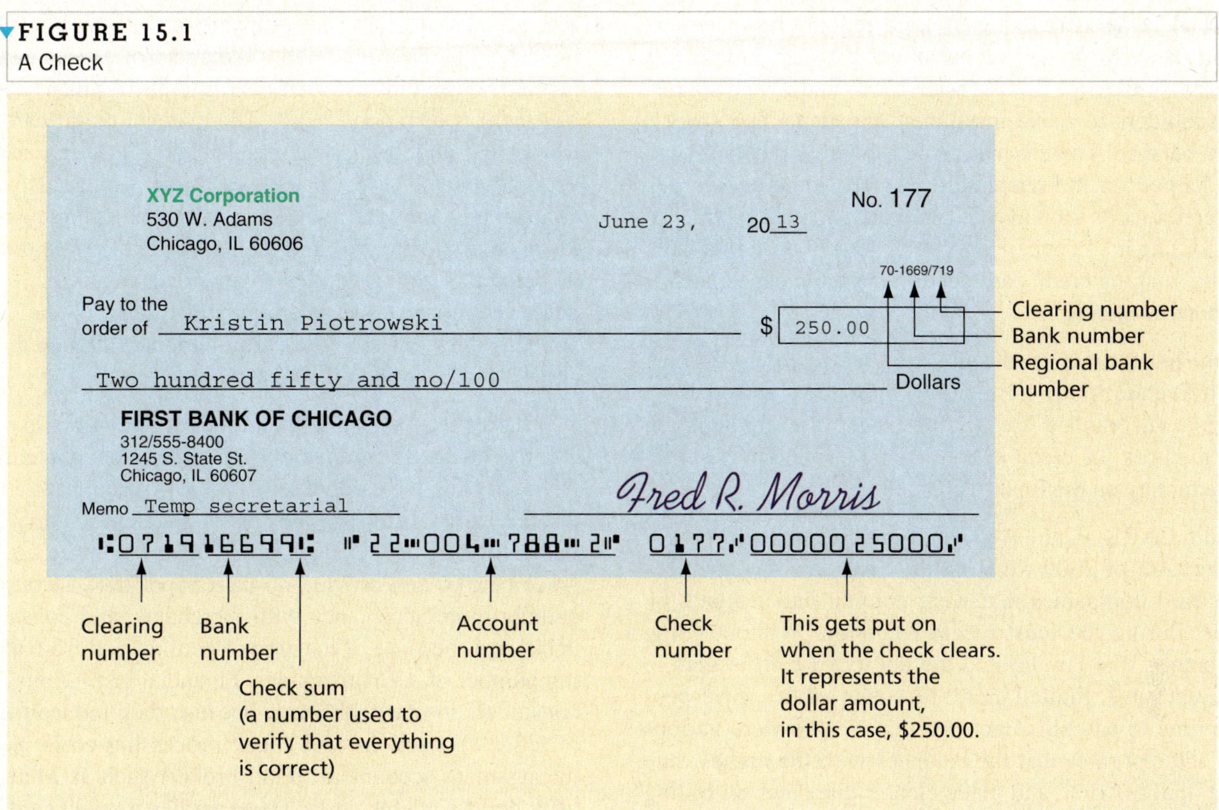

per period. Although seldom enforced, the fine print governing most savings accounts prohibits withdrawals without two or three days' notice. Savings accounts are not generally used for transactions or as a medium of exchange, but their funds can be moved to a checking account or turned into cash.

Money market accounts are similar to interest-bearing checking accounts, but with more restrictions. Generally, in exchange for slightly higher interest rates, the owner of a money market account can write only a limited number of checks each month, and there may be a restriction on the minimum amount of each check.

Certificates of deposit (CDs) are savings accounts that guarantee a depositor a set interest rate over a specified interval of time as long as the funds are not withdrawn before the end of the interval—six months, one year, or seven years, for example. Money may be withdrawn from these accounts prematurely only after paying a substantial penalty. In general, the longer the term of the CD, the higher is the interest rate it earns. As with all interest rates, the rate offered and fixed at the time the account is opened fluctuates according to economic conditions.

Credit cards allow you to promise to pay at a later date by using preapproved lines of credit granted by a bank or finance company. They are a popular substitute for cash payments because of their convenience, easy access to credit, and acceptance by merchants around the world. The institution that issues the credit card guarantees payment of a credit charge to merchants and assumes responsibility for collecting the money from the cardholders. Card issuers charge a transaction fee to the merchants for performing the credit check, guaranteeing the payment, and collecting the payment. The fee is typically between 2 and 5 percent, depending on the type of card. American Express fees are usually higher than Visa and MasterCard.

High interest rates on credit cards and the most recent recession have led the bulk of Americans to reduce credit card balances for the first time in years.

The original American Express cards require full payment at the end of each month, but American Express now offers credit cards similar to Visa, Master Card, and Discover that allow cardholders to make installment payments and carry a maximum balance. There is a minimum monthly payment with interest charged on the remaining balance. Some people pay off their credit cards monthly; others make monthly payments. Charges for unpaid balances can run 18 percent or higher at an annual rate, making credit card debt one of the most expensive ways to borrow money.

Besides the major credit card companies, many stores—Target, Saks Fifth Avenue, Macy's, Bloomingdales, Sears, and others—have their own branded credit cards. They use credit rating agencies to check the credit of the cardholders and they generally make money on the finance charges.

The Credit CARD (Card Accountability Responsibility and Disclosure) Act of 2009 was passed to regulate the practices of credit card companies that were coming under attack by consumers during the most recent recession. Without going into the details, the law limited the ability of card issuers to raise interest rates, limited credit to young adults, gave people more time to pay bills, required that if there were various levels of interest rates that the balances with the highest rate would be paid off first, and made clearer due dates on billing cycles, along with several other provisions. For college students, the most important part of the law is that young adults under the age of 21 will have to have an adult co-signer or show proof that they have enough income to handle the debt limit on the card.

This act is important to all companies and cardholders. Research indicates that approximately 40 percent of lower- and middle-income households use credit cards to pay for basic necessities. Yet there is also good news. The average credit card debt for lower- and middle-income households has decreased in recent years to about $7,145. On the other hand, studies also show that college students tend to lack the financial literacy needed to understand credit cards and their requirements. Approximately 90 percent of college students with credit cards have credit card debt. Therefore, vulnerable segments of the population such as college students should be careful about which credit cards to choose and how often they use them.[10]

A **debit card** looks like a credit card but works like a check. The use of a debit card results in a direct, immediate, electronic payment from the cardholder's checking account to a merchant or other party. Although they are convenient to carry and profitable for banks, they lack credit features, offer no purchase grace period, and provide no hard paper trail. Debit cards are gaining more acceptance with merchants, and consumers like debit cards because of the ease of getting cash from an increasing number of ATM machines. Financial institutions also want consumers to use debit cards because they reduce the number of teller transactions and check processing costs. Some cash management accounts at retail brokers such as Merrill Lynch offer deferred debit cards. These act like a credit card but debit to the cash management account once a month. During that time, the cash earns a money market return.

Traveler's checks, money orders, and cashier's checks are other common forms of near money. Although each is slightly

ARE PARTNERSHIPS BETWEEN UNIVERSITIES AND DEBIT CARD COMPANIES GOOD FOR STUDENTS?

Banks and universities have been partnering to offer student IDs that also function as debit cards. These practices raise ethical issues about marketing financial goods to students who may already have student loans and credit card debt. The universities claim that their agreements with the banks are written with regard for the students' best interests. However, universities have an interest of their own in these arrangements because they are receiving funding as a result of their partnerships. These additional funds are especially important because state funding for education has decreased. Universities stand to gain at least $1 million over a period of ten years, with the possibility of more money if more students open accounts.

Some concerns from critics include the fact that students may think the university is endorsing the financial institution because the card bears their school's logo. Other criticisms include the accusation that the partnerships enable banks to push debit cards onto young people. Critics are concerned that the partnerships will influence students' choices of other financial items such as credit cards or allow banks to market additional products. Incentives such as quicker access to the students' financial aid are offered if they open an account with the bank. Another worrisome aspect is fees. Some of these debit cards come with hefty fees that can drain the financial aid funds of the students (high overdraft fees, fees for using the debit card, and fees for using the card at other ATMs).[11]

Discussion Questions

1. What is the ethical issue of offering student ID cards that also function as debit cards?
2. How might this issue affect students in terms of debit card usage or other financial items?
3. Do you feel that it is ethical to offer students ID cards that function as debit cards?

different from the others, they all share a common characteristic: A financial institution, bank, credit company, or neighborhood currency exchange issues them in exchange for cash and guarantees that the purchased note will be honored and exchanged for cash when it is presented to the institution making the guarantee.

THE AMERICAN FINANCIAL SYSTEM

The U.S. financial system fuels our economy by storing money, fostering investment opportunities, and making loans for new businesses and business expansion as well as for homes, cars, and college educations. This amazingly complex system includes banking institutions, nonbanking financial institutions such as finance companies, and systems that provide for the electronic transfer of funds throughout the world. Over the past 20 years, the rate at which money turns over, or changes hands, has increased exponentially. Different cultures place unique values on saving, spending, borrowing, and investing. The combination of this increased turnover rate and increasing interactions with people and organizations from other countries has created a complex money system. First, we need to meet the guardian of this complex system.

LO 15-3 Specify how the Federal Reserve Board manages the money supply and regulates the American banking system.

The Federal Reserve System

The guardian of the American financial system is the **Federal Reserve Board**, or the Fed, as it is commonly called, an independent agency of the federal government established in 1913 to regulate the nation's banking and financial industry. The Federal Reserve System is organized into 12 regions, each with a Federal Reserve Bank that serves its defined area (Figure 15.2). All the Federal Reserve banks except those in Boston and

debit card a card that looks like a credit card but works like a check; using it results in a direct, immediate, electronic payment from the cardholder's checking account to a merchant or other party

Federal Reserve Board an independent agency of the federal government established in 1913 to regulate the nation's banking and financial industry

FIGURE 15.2
Federal Reserve System

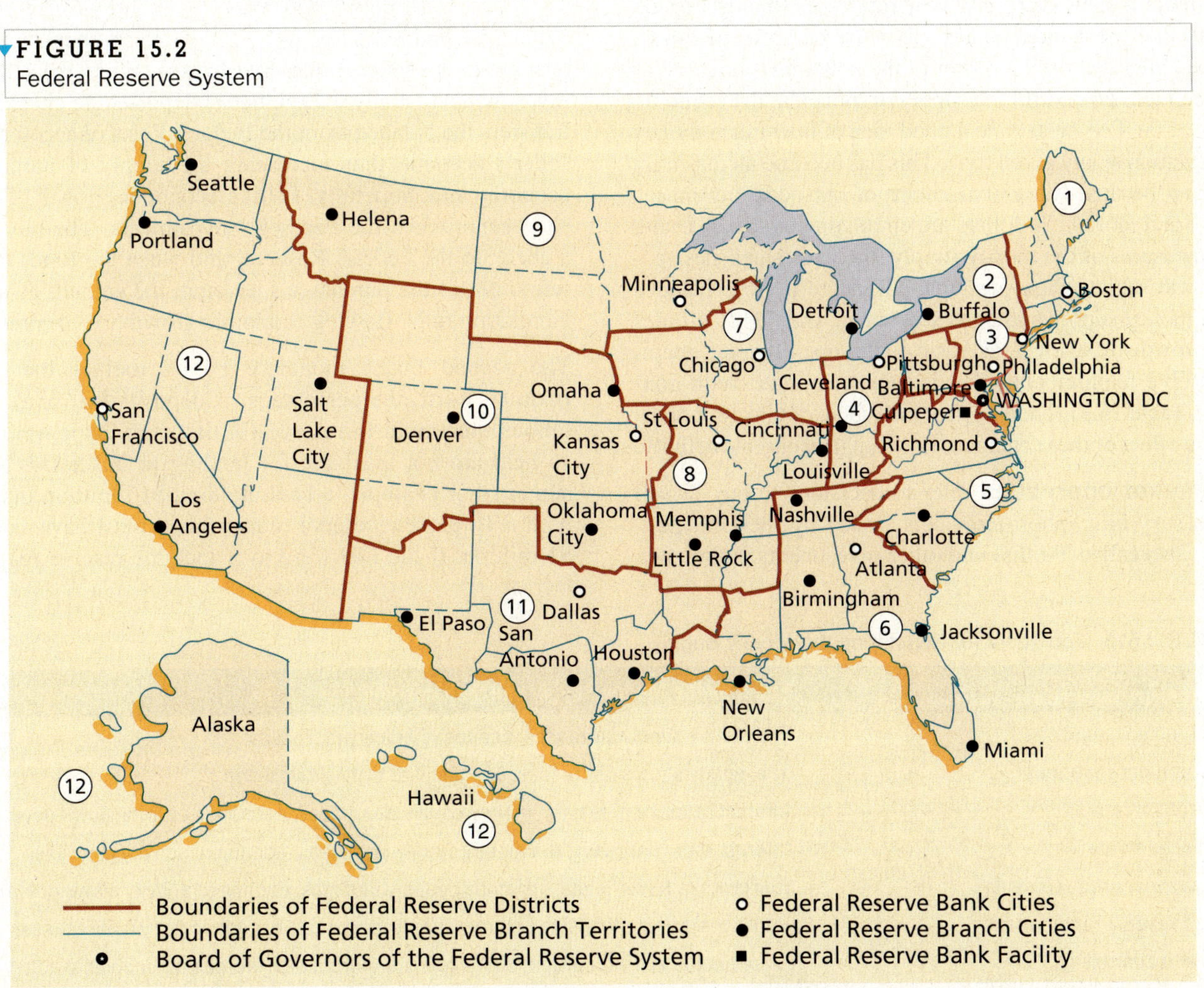

Philadelphia have regional branches. The Cleveland Federal Reserve Bank, for example, is responsible for branch offices in Pittsburgh and Cincinnati.

The Federal Reserve Board is the chief economic policy arm of the United States. Working with Congress and the president, the Fed tries to create a positive economic environment capable of sustaining low inflation, high levels of employment, a balance in international payments, and long-term economic growth. To this end, the Federal Reserve Board has four major responsibilities: (1) to control the supply of money, or monetary policy; (2) to regulate banks and other financial institutions; (3) to manage regional and national checking account procedures, or check clearing; and (4) to supervise the federal deposit insurance programs of banks belonging to the Federal Reserve System.

Monetary Policy The Fed controls the amount of money available in the economy through **monetary policy**. Without this intervention, the supply of and demand for money might not balance. This could result in either rapid price increases (inflation) because of too little money or economic recession and a slowdown of price increases (disinflation) because of too little growth in the money supply. In very rare cases (the depression of the 1930s) the United States has suffered from deflation, when the actual purchasing power of the dollar has increased as prices declined. To control the supply of money in the economy effectively, the Fed must have a good idea of how much money is in circulation at any given time. This has become increasingly challenging because the global nature of our economy means that more and more U.S. dollars are circulating overseas. Using several measures of the money supply, the Fed establishes specific growth targets that, presumably, ensure a close balance between money supply and money demand. The Fed fine-tunes money growth by using four basic tools: open market operations, reserve requirements, the discount rate, and credit controls (see Table 15.3). There is generally a lag of 6 to 18 months before the effect of these charges shows up in economic activity.

Open market operations refer to decisions to buy or sell U.S. Treasury bills (short-term debt issued by the U.S. government; also called T-bills) and other investments in the open market. The actual purchase or sale of the investments is performed by the New York Federal Reserve Bank. This monetary tool, the most commonly employed of all Fed operations, is performed almost daily in an effort to control the money supply.

One of the roles of the Federal Reserve is to use its policies to keep money flowing. Money is the lifeblood of the economy. If banks become too protective of their funds and stop lending money, the economy can grind to a halt.

When the Fed buys securities, it writes a check on its own account to the seller of the investments. When the seller of the investments (usually a large bank) deposits the check, the Fed transfers the balance from the Federal Reserve account into the seller's account, thus increasing the supply of money in the economy and, hopefully, fueling economic growth. The opposite occurs when the Fed sells investments. The buyer writes a check to the Federal Reserve, and when the funds are transferred out of the purchaser's account, the amount of money in circulation falls, slowing economic growth to a desired level.

The second major monetary policy tool is the **reserve requirement**, the percentage of deposits that banking institutions must hold in reserve (in the vault, as it were). Funds so held are not available for lending to businesses and consumers. For example, a bank holding $10 million in deposits, with a 10 percent reserve requirement, must have reserves of $1 million. If the Fed were to reduce the reserve requirement

TABLE 15.3 Fed Tools for Regulating the Money Supply

Activity	Effect on the Money Supply and the Economy
Buy government securities	The money supply increases; economic activity increases.
Sell government securities	The money supply decreases; economic activity slows down.
Raise discount rate	Interest rates increase; the money supply decreases; economic activity slows down.
Lower discount rate	Interest rates decrease; the money supply increases; economic activity increases.
Increase reserve requirements	Banks make fewer loans; the money supply declines; economic activity slows down.
Decrease reserve requirements	Banks make more loans; the money supply increases; economic activity increases.
Relax credit controls	More people are encouraged to make major purchases, increasing economic activity.
Restrict credit controls	People are discouraged from making major purchases, decreasing economic activity.

monetary policy means by which the Fed controls the amount of money available in the economy

open market operations decisions to buy or sell U.S. Treasury bills (short-term debt issued by the U.S. government) and other investments in the open market

reserve requirement the percentage of deposits that banking institutions must hold in reserve

discount rate the rate of interest the Fed charges to loan money to any banking institution to meet reserve requirements

credit controls the authority to establish and enforce credit rules for financial institutions and some private investors

to, say, 5 percent, the bank would need to keep only $500,000 in reserves. The bank could then lend to customers the $500,000 difference between the old reserve level and the new lower reserve level, thus increasing the supply of money. Because the reserve requirement has such a powerful effect on the money supply, the Fed does not change it very often, relying instead on open market operations most of the time.

The third monetary policy tool, the **discount rate**, is the rate of interest the Fed charges to loan money to any banking institution to meet reserve requirements. The Fed is the lender of last resort for these banks. When a bank borrows from the Fed, it is said to have borrowed at the discount window, and the interest rates charged there are often higher than those charged on loans of comparable risk elsewhere in the economy. This added interest expense, when it exists, serves to discourage banks from borrowing from the Fed.

When the Fed wants to expand the money supply, it lowers the discount rate to encourage borrowing. Conversely, when the Fed wants to decrease the money supply, it raises the discount rate. The increases in interest rates that occurred in the United States from 2003 through 2006 were the result of more than 16 quarter-point (0.25 percent) increases in the Fed discount rate. The purpose was to keep inflation under control and to raise rates to a more normal level as the economy recovered from the recession of 2001. During the most recent recession, which started in 2007, the Fed lowered interest rates from 5.25 percent to .125 percent at the beginning of 2009 and maintained this rate into 2013 to encourage borrowing. In an environment where credit markets were nearly frozen, the Fed used monetary policy to stimulate spending. Not surprisingly, economists watch changes in this sensitive interest rate as an indicator of the Fed's monetary policy.

> "The Fed establishes and enforces banking rules that affect monetary policy and the overall level of the competition between different banks."

The final tool in the Fed's arsenal of weapons is **credit controls**—the authority to establish and enforce credit rules for financial institutions and some private investors. For example, the Fed can determine how large a down payment individuals and businesses must make on credit purchases of expensive items such as automobiles, and how much time they have to finish paying for the purchases. By raising and lowering minimum down payment amounts and payment periods, the Fed can stimulate or discourage credit purchases of big-ticket items. The Fed also has the authority to set the minimum down payment investors must use for the credit purchases of stock. Buying stock with credit—buying on margin—is a popular investment strategy among individual speculators. By altering the margin requirement (currently set at 50 percent of the price of the purchased stocks), the Fed can effectively control the total amount of credit borrowing in the stock market.

Regulatory Functions The second major responsibility of the Fed is to regulate banking institutions that are members of the Federal Reserve System. Accordingly, the Fed establishes and enforces banking rules that affect monetary policy and the overall level of the competition between different banks. It determines which nonbanking activities, such as brokerage services, leasing, and insurance, are appropriate for banks and which should be prohibited. The Fed also has the authority to approve or disapprove mergers between banks and the formation of bank holding companies. In an effort to ensure that all rules are enforced and that correct accounting procedures are being followed at member banks, surprise bank examinations are conducted by bank examiners each year.

Check Clearing The Federal Reserve provides national check processing on a huge scale. Divisions of the Fed known as check clearinghouses handle almost all the checks written against a bank in one city and presented for deposit to a bank in a second city. Any banking institution can present the checks it has received from others around the country to its regional Federal Reserve Bank. The Fed passes the checks to the appropriate regional Federal Reserve Bank, which then sends the checks to the issuing bank for payment. With the advance of electronic payment systems and the passage of the Check Clearing for the 21st Century Act (Check 21 Act), checks can now be processed in a day. The Check 21 Act allows banks to clear checks electronically by presenting an electronic image of the check. This eliminates mail delays and time-consuming paper processing.

Depository Insurance The Fed is also responsible for supervising the federal insurance funds that protect the deposits of member institutions. These insurance funds will be discussed in greater detail in the following section.

LO 15-4 Compare and contrast commercial banks, savings and loan associations, credit unions, and mutual savings banks.

Banking Institutions

Banking institutions accept money deposits from and make loans to individual consumers and businesses. Some of the most important banking institutions include commercial banks, savings and loan associations, credit unions, and mutual savings banks. Historically, these have all been separate institutions. However, new hybrid forms of banking institutions that perform two or more of these functions have emerged over the past two decades. The following all have one thing in common: They are businesses whose objective is to earn money by managing, safeguarding, and lending money to others. Their sales revenues come from the fees and interest that they charge for providing these financial services.

Commercial Banks

The largest and oldest of all financial institutions are **commercial banks**, which perform a variety of financial services. They rely mainly on checking and savings accounts as their major source of funds and use only a portion of these deposits to make loans to businesses and individuals. Because it is unlikely that all the depositors of any one bank will want to withdraw all of their funds at the same time, a bank can safely loan out a large percentage of its deposits.

JPMorgan Chase is the second-largest commercial bank in the United States behind Bank of America.

Today, banks are quite diversified and offer a number of services. Commercial banks make loans for virtually any conceivable legal purpose, from vacations to cars, from homes to college educations. Banks in many states offer *home equity loans,* by which home owners can borrow against the appraised value of their already purchased homes. Banks also issue Visa and Master Card credit cards and offer CDs and trusts (legal entities set up to hold and manage assets for a beneficiary). Many banks rent safe deposit boxes in bank vaults to customers who want to store jewelry, legal documents, artwork, and other valuables. In 1999, Congress passed the Financial Services Modernization Act, also known as the Gramm-Leach-Bliley Bill. This act repealed the Glass-Steagall Act, which was enacted in 1929 after the stock market crash and prohibited commercial banks from being in the insurance and investment banking business. This puts U.S. commercial banks on the same competitive footing as European banks and provides a more level playing field for global banking competition. As commercial banks and investment banks have merged, the financial landscape has changed. Consolidation remains the norm in the U.S. banking industry. The financial crisis and the economic recession only accelerated the consolidation as large, healthy banks ended up buying weak banks that were in trouble. JP Morgan Chase bought Wachovia and the investment bank Bear Stearns; Wells Fargo bought Washington Mutual; PNC bought National City Bank; and Bank of America bought Countrywide Credit and Merrill Lynch. Most of these purchases were made with financial help from the U.S. Treasury and Federal Reserve. By 2012, the banks had paid back their loans, but the financial meltdown exposed some high-risk activities in the banking industry that Congress wanted to curtail. The result was the passage of the Dodd-Frank Act. This act added many new regulations, but the two most important changes raised the required capital banks had to hold on their balance sheet and limited certain types of high-risk trading activities. Despite these new regulations, in 2012 JP Morgan Chase lost billions of dollars in trading activities from taking excessive risks.[12]

> "Banks are quite diversified and offer a number of services."

Savings and Loan Associations

Savings and loan associations (S&Ls), often called thrifts, are financial institutions that primarily offer savings accounts and make long-term loans for residential mortgages. A mortgage is a loan made so that a business or individual can purchase real estate, typically a home; the real estate itself is pledged as a guarantee (called *collateral*) that the buyer will repay the loan. If the loan is not repaid, the savings and loan has the right to repossess the property. Prior to the 1970s, S&Ls focused almost exclusively

commercial banks the largest and oldest of all financial institutions, relying mainly on checking and savings accounts as sources of funds for loans to businesses and individuals

savings and loan associations (S&Ls) financial institutions that primarily offer savings accounts and make long-term loans for residential mortgages; also called "thrifts"

credit union a financial institution owned and controlled by its depositors, who usually have a common employer, profession, trade group, or religion

mutual savings banks financial institutions that are similar to savings and loan associations but, like credit unions, are owned by their depositors

Federal Deposit Insurance Corporation (FDIC) an insurance fund established in 1933 that insures individual bank accounts

BANKS INCREASE INVESTMENT IN SUSTAINABILITY

What does banking have to do with green technology? If companies such as Bank of America, Goldman Sachs, and Wells Fargo have their way, banks will be seen as major supporters of sustainability. Banks not only want to incorporate greener processes into their own operations, but they are also investing in green technology initiatives and grassroots organizations. For instance, in addition to reducing its paper and energy consumption, Bank of America is investing in projects that focus on areas such as water reduction and energy conservation. Goldman Sachs has pledged $40 billion toward solar, wind, energy storage, and transportation initiatives.

Wells Fargo has gained attention for setting lofty goals for the year 2020. Among its goals, the company announced that it was pledging $30 billion toward green technologies, increasing its own operational sustainability, and pledging $100 million in grants for grassroots environmental projects. In reducing its own environmental footprint, Wells Fargo plans to decrease its greenhouse gas emissions by 35 percent of 2008 levels and ensure that 35 percent of its buildings receive Leadership in Energy and Environmental Design (LEED) certification. Although these initiatives will cost Wells Fargo in the short-term, the company believes that sustainability is the future of business. In interacting with customers in an online forum, Wells Fargo found that 80 percent valued environmental commitment on the part of businesses. Wells Fargo also believes it can use its investments to help make consumers more aware of the importance of sustainability. By investing in greener initiatives, banks such as Wells Fargo and Bank of America could create competitive advantages through better customer relationships and a more positive reputation.[13]

Discussion Questions

1. Discuss some of the ways in which banks are investing in sustainability.
2. What are the advantages of investing in sustainability? The disadvantages?
3. Do you think Wells Fargo's sustainability goals represent a genuine commitment, or are they more window dressing to make the company look good?

on real estate lending and accepted only savings accounts. Today, following years of regulatory changes, S&Ls compete directly with commercial banks by offering many types of services.

Savings and loans have gone through a metamorphosis since the early 1990s, after having almost collapsed in the 1980s. Today, many of the largest savings and loans have merged with commercial banks. This segment of the financial services industry plays a diminished role in the mortgage lending market.

Credit Unions

A **credit union** is a financial institution owned and controlled by its depositors, who usually have a common employer, profession, trade group, or religion. The Aggieland Credit Union in College Station, Texas, for example, provides banking services for faculty, employees, and current and former students of Texas A&M University. A savings account at a credit union is commonly referred to as a share account, whereas a checking account is termed a share draft account. Because the credit union is tied to a common organization, the members (depositors) are allowed to vote for directors and share in the credit union's profits in the form of higher interest rates on accounts and/or lower loan rates. Although credit unions were originally created to provide depositors with a short-term source of funds for low-interest consumer loans for items such as cars, home appliances, vacations, and college, today they offer a wide range of financial services. Generally, the larger the credit union, the more sophisticated its financial service offerings will be.

Mutual Savings Banks

Mutual savings banks are similar to savings and loan associations, but, like credit unions, they are owned by their depositors. Among the oldest financial institutions in the United States, they were originally established to provide a safe place for savings of particular groups of people, such as fishermen. Found mostly in New England, they are becoming more popular in the rest of the country as some S&Ls have converted to mutual savings banks to escape the stigma created by the widespread S&L failures in the 1980s.

Insurance for Banking Institutions

The **Federal Deposit Insurance Corporation (FDIC)**, which insures individual bank accounts, was established in 1933 to help stop bank failures throughout the country during the Great Depression. As of this writing, the FDIC insures personal accounts up to a maximum of $250,000 at nearly 8,000 FDIC member

National Credit Union Administration (NCUA) an agency that regulates and charters credit unions and insures their deposits through its National Credit Union Insurance Fund

insurance companies businesses that protect their clients against financial losses from certain specified risks (death, accident, and theft, for example)

pension funds managed investment pools set aside by individuals, corporations, unions, and some nonprofit organizations to provide retirement income for members

mutual fund an investment company that pools individual investor dollars and invests them in large numbers of securities, thereby creating a diversified investment portfolio

brokerage firms firms that buy and sell stocks, bonds, and other securities for their customers and provide other financial services

institutions.[14] Although most major banks are insured by the FDIC, small institutions in some states may be insured by state insurance funds or private insurance companies. Should a member bank fail, its depositors can recover all of their funds, up to $250,000. Amounts over $250,000, although not legally covered by the insurance, are in fact usually covered because the Fed understands very well the enormous damage that would result to the financial system should these large depositors withdraw their money. When the financial crisis occurred, the FDIC was worried about people taking their money out of banks, so it increased the deposit insurance amount from $100,000 to $250,000. The amount is scheduled to revert to $100,000 on December 31, 2013. The *Federal Savings and Loan Insurance Corporation (FSLIC)* insured thrift deposits prior to its insolvency and failure during the S&L crisis of the 1980s. Now, the insurance functions once overseen by the FSLIC are handled directly by the FDIC through its Savings Association Insurance Fund. The **National Credit Union Administration (NCUA)** regulates and charters credit unions and insures their deposits through its National Credit Union Insurance Fund.

When they were originally established, Congress hoped that these insurance funds would make people feel secure about their savings so that they would not panic and withdraw their money when news of a bank failure was announced. The bank run scene in the perennial Christmas movie *It's a Wonderful Life,* when dozens of Bailey Building and Loan depositors attempted to withdraw their money (only to have the reassuring figure of Jimmy Stewart calm their fears), was not based on mere fiction. During the Great Depression, hundreds of banks failed and their depositors lost everything. The fact that large numbers of major financial institutions failed in the 1980s and 1990s—without a single major banking panic—underscores the effectiveness of the current insurance system.

Large bank failures occurred once again during the most recent recession. More than 380 banks failed between 2009 and 2011.[15] Although the future may yet bring unfortunate surprises, most depositors go to sleep every night without worrying about the safety of their savings.

LO 15-5 Distinguish among nonbanking institutions such as insurance companies, pension funds, mutual funds, and finance companies.

Nonbanking Institutions

Nonbank financial institutions offer some financial services, such as short-term loans or investment products, but do not accept deposits. These include insurance companies, pension funds, mutual funds, brokerage firms, nonfinancial firms, and finance companies. Table 15.4 lists some other diversified financial services firms.

Diversified Firms Recently, a growing number of traditionally nonfinancial firms have moved onto the financial field. These firms include manufacturing organizations, such as General Motors and General Electric, that traditionally confined their financial activities to financing their customers' purchases. GE was once so successful in the financial arena that its credit subsidiary accounted for more than 40 percent of the company's revenues and earnings. Unfortunately, GE Capital became a liability to GE during the financial crisis and is in the process of recovery as GE cuts the size of its finance unit and writes off billions of dollars in bad loans.

Insurance Companies **Insurance companies** are businesses that protect their clients against financial losses from certain specified risks (death, injury, disability, accident,

["A growing number of traditionally nonfinancial firms have moved onto the financial field."]

▼ **TABLE 15.4** Leading Diversified Financial Services Firms

Company	2012 Assets ($ Millions)	2012 Revenues ($ Millions)
JPMorgan Chase	$2,359,141	$106,198
MetLife	836,781	68,150
General Electric Capital*	539,223	46,039
SLM Corp.	181,260	6,110
American Express	153,140	33,808
Ameriprise Financial	134,729	10,259
Visa Inc.	40,013	10,421
Aon	30,486	11,514
Master Card	12,462	7,391

*GE Capital is a division of General Electric Corp.

Source: GE annual Report and Standard and Poor's Stock Reports.

fire, theft, and natural disasters, for example) in exchange for a fee, called a premium. Because insurance premiums flow into the companies regularly, but major insurance losses cannot be timed with great accuracy (though expected risks can be assessed with considerable precision), insurance companies generally have large amounts of excess funds. They typically invest these or make long-term loans, particularly to businesses in the form of commercial real estate loans.

Pension Funds **Pension funds** are managed investment pools set aside by individuals, corporations, unions, and some nonprofit organizations to provide retirement income for members. One type of pension fund is the *individual retirement account (IRA),* which is established by individuals to provide for their personal retirement needs. IRAs can be invested in a variety of financial assets, from risky commodities such as oil or cocoa to low-risk financial staples such as U.S. Treasury securities. The choice is up to each person and is dictated solely by individual objectives and tolerance for risk. The interest earned by all of these investments may be deferred tax-free until retirement.

In 1997, Congress revised the IRA laws and created a Roth IRA. Although similar to a traditional IRA in that investors may contribute $5,000 per year, the money in a Roth IRA is considered an after-tax contribution. When the money is withdrawn at retirement, no tax is paid on the distribution. The Roth IRA is beneficial to young people who can allow a long time for their money to compound and who may be able to have their parents or grandparents fund the Roth IRA with gift money.

Most major corporations provide some kind of pension plan for their employees. Many of these are established with bank trust departments or life insurance companies. Money is deposited in a separate account in the name of each individual employee, and when the employee retires, the total amount in the account can be either withdrawn in one lump sum or taken as monthly cash payments over some defined time period (usually for the remaining life of the retiree).

Social Security, the largest pension fund, is publicly financed. The federal government collects Social Security funds from payroll taxes paid by both employers and employees. The Social Security Administration then uses these monies to make payments to those eligible to receive Social Security benefits—the retired, the disabled, and the young children of deceased parents.

Mutual Funds A **mutual fund** pools individual investor dollars and invests them in large numbers of securities, thereby creating a diversified investment portfolio. Individual investors buy shares in a mutual fund in the hope of earning a high rate of return and in much the same way as people buy shares of stock. Because of the large numbers of people investing in any one mutual fund, the funds can invest in hundreds of securities at any one time, minimizing the risks of any single security that does not do well. Mutual funds provide professional financial management for people who lack the time and/or expertise to invest in particular securities, such as government bonds. Although there are no hard-and-fast rules, investments in one or more mutual funds are one way for people to plan for financial independence at the time of retirement.

A special type of mutual fund called a *money market fund* invests specifically in short-term debt securities issued by governments and large corporations. Although they offer services such as check-writing privileges and reinvestment of interest income, money market funds differ from the money market accounts offered by banks primarily in that the former represent a pool of funds, whereas the latter are basically specialized, individual checking accounts. Money market funds usually offer slightly higher rates of interest than bank money market accounts.

Brokerage Firms and Investment Banks **Brokerage firms** buy and sell stocks, bonds, and other securities for their customers and provide other financial services. Larger

State Farm Insurance allows users to input their information on its website to receive an auto insurance quote quickly and conveniently.

investment banker underwrites new issues of securities for corporations, states, and municipalities

finance companies businesses that offer short-term loans at substantially higher rates of interest than banks

electronic funds transfer (EFT) any movement of funds by means of an electronic terminal, telephone, computer, or magnetic tape

automated teller machine (ATM) the most familiar form of electronic banking, which dispenses cash, accepts deposits, and allows balance inquiries and cash transfers from one account to another

automated clearinghouses (ACHs) a system that permits payments such as deposits or withdrawals to be made to and from a bank account by magnetic computer tape

brokerage firms such as Merrill Lynch, Charles Schwab, and Edward Jones offer financial services unavailable at their smaller competitors. Merrill Lynch, for example, offers the Merrill Lynch Cash Management Account (CMA), which pays interest on deposits and allows clients to write checks, borrow money, and withdraw cash much like a commercial bank. The largest of the brokerage firms (including Merrill Lynch) have developed so many specialized services that they may be considered financial networks—organizations capable of offering virtually all of the services traditionally associated with commercial banks. The rise of online brokerage firms has helped investors who want to do it themselves at low costs. Firms such as E-Trade, TDAmeritrade, and Scottrade offer investors the ability to buy and sell securities for $7 to $10 per trade, whereas the same trade at Morgan Stanley might cost $125. E-Trade offers banking services, debit cards, wire transfers, and many of the same services that the traditional brokerage firms offer.

Most brokerage firms are really part financial conglomerates that provide many kinds of services besides buying and selling securities for clients. For example, Merrill Lynch also is an investment banker, as are Morgan Stanley, Smith Barney, and Goldman Sachs. The **investment banker** underwrites new issues of securities for corporations, states, and municipalities needed to raise money in the capital markets. The new issue market is called a *primary market* because the sale of the securities is for the first time. After the first sale, the securities trade in the *secondary markets* by brokers. The investment banker advises on the price of the new securities and generally guarantees the sale while overseeing the distribution of the securities through the selling brokerage houses. Investment bankers also act as dealers who make markets in securities. They do this by offering to sell the securities at an asked price (which is a higher rate) and buy the securities at a bid price (which is a lower rate)—the difference in the two prices represents the profit for the dealer.

Finance Companies

Finance companies are businesses that offer short-term loans at substantially higher rates of interest than banks. Commercial finance companies make loans to businesses, requiring their borrowers to pledge assets such as equipment, inventories, or unpaid accounts as collateral for the loans. Consumer finance companies make loans to individuals. Like commercial finance companies, these firms require some sort of personal collateral as security against the borrowers' possible inability to repay their loans. Because of the high interest rates they charge and other factors, finance companies typically are the lender of last resort for individuals and businesses whose credit limits have been exhausted and/or those with poor credit ratings.

Electronic Banking

Since the advent of the computer age, a wide range of technological innovations has made it possible to move money all across the world electronically. Such paperless transactions have allowed financial institutions to reduce costs in what has been, and continues to be, a virtual competitive battlefield. **Electronic funds transfer (EFT)** is any movement of funds by means of an electronic terminal, telephone, computer, or magnetic tape. Such transactions order a particular financial institution to subtract money from one account and add it to another. The most commonly used forms of EFT are automated teller machines, automated clearinghouses, and online banking systems.

Automated Teller Machines

Probably the most familiar form of electronic banking is the **automated teller machine (ATM)**, which dispenses cash, accepts deposits, and allows balance inquiries and cash transfers from one account to another. ATMs provide 24-hour banking services—both at home (through a local bank) and far away (via worldwide ATM networks such as Cirrus and Plus). Rapid growth, driven by both strong consumer acceptance and lower transaction costs for banks (about half the cost of teller transactions), has led to the installation of hundreds of thousands of ATMs worldwide. Table 15.5 presents some interesting statistics about ATMs.

Automated Clearinghouses

Automated clearinghouses (ACHs) permit payments such as deposits or withdrawals to be made to and from a bank account by magnetic

TABLE 15.5 Facts about ATM Use

There are 2.2 million ATM machines currently in use.
The average cash withdrawal from ATMs is $60.
The typical ATM consumer will visit an ATM 7.4 times per month.
The total ratio of people per ATM machine is 3,000:1.
ATM users spend approximately 23 percent more than non-ATM users.
The top ATM owners are Cardtronics, Payment Alliance, Bank of America, JPMorgan Chase, and Wells Fargo.

Source: Lenpenzo, Trends Today, "ATM Machines Statistics," March 2, 2012, www.statisticbrain.com/atm-machine-statistics/.

computer tape. Most large U.S. employers, and many others worldwide, use ACHs to deposit their employees' paychecks directly to the employees' bank accounts. Although direct deposit is used by only 50 percent of U.S. workers, nearly 100 percent of Japanese workers and more than 90 percent of European workers use it. The largest user of automated clearinghouses in the United States is the federal government, with 99 percent of federal government employees and 65 percent of the private workforce receiving their pay via direct deposit. More than 82 percent of all Social Security payments are made through an ACH system. The Social Security Administration is trying to reduce costs and reduce theft and fraud, so if you apply for Social Security benefits on or after May 1, 2011, you must receive your payments electronically.

The advantages of direct deposits to consumers include convenience, safety, and potential interest earnings. It is estimated that more than 4 million paychecks are lost or stolen annually, and FBI studies show that 2,000 fraudulent checks are cashed every day in the United States. Checks can never be lost or stolen with direct deposit. The benefits to businesses include decreased check-processing expenses and increased employee productivity. Research shows that businesses that use direct deposit can save more than $1.25 on each payroll check processed. Productivity could increase by $3 to $5 billion annually if all employees were to use direct deposit rather than taking time away from work to deposit their payroll checks.

Some companies also use ACHs for dividend and interest payments. Consumers can also use ACHs to make periodic (usually monthly) fixed payments to specific creditors without ever having to write a check or buy stamps. The estimated number of bills paid annually by consumers is 20 billion, and the total number paid through ACHs is estimated at only 8.5 billion. The average consumer who writes 10 to 15 checks each month would save $41 to $62 annually in postage alone.[16]

Online Banking Many banking activities are now conducted on a computer at home or at work or through wireless devices such as cell phones and PDAs anywhere there is a wireless hot point. Consumers and small businesses can now make a bewildering array of financial transactions at home or on the go 24 hours a day. Functioning much like a vast network of personal ATMs, companies such as Google and Apple provide online banking services through mobile phones, allowing subscribers to make sophisticated banking transactions, buy and sell stocks and bonds, and purchase products and airline tickets without ever leaving home or speaking to another human being. Many banks allow customers to log directly into their accounts to check balances, transfer money between accounts, view their account statements, and pay bills via home computer or other Internet-enabled devices. Computer and advanced telecommunications technology have revolutionized world commerce; 62 percent of adults list Internet banking as their preferred banking method, making it the most popular banking method in the United States.[17]

Computers and handheld devices have made online banking extremely convenient. However, hackers have stolen millions from banking customers by tricking them into visiting websites and downloading malicious software that gives the hackers access to their passwords.

LO 15-6 Investigate the challenges ahead for the banking industry.

Future of Banking after the Financial Crisis

Rapid advances and innovations in technology are challenging the banking industry and requiring it to change. As we said earlier, more and more banks, both large and small, are offering electronic access to their financial services. ATM technology is rapidly changing, with machines now dispensing more than just cash. Online financial services, ATM technology, and bill presentation are just a few of the areas where rapidly changing technology is causing the banking industry to change as well. The newest innovation is banking on your smart phone. The problem is that smart phones are more easily hacked than computers.

The premise that banks will get bigger over the next 10 years is uncertain. During 2007–2008, the financial markets collapsed under the weight of declining housing prices, subprime mortgages (mortgages with low-qualifying borrowers), and risky securities backed by these subprime mortgages. Because the value of bank assets declined dramatically, most large banks such as CitiBank and Bank of America had a shrinking capital base. That is, the amount of debt in relation to their equity was so high that they were below the minimum required capital requirements. In this financial environment, banks did not trust the counterparties to their loans and asset-backed securities, and the markets ceased to function in an orderly fashion. To keep the banking system from total collapse, the U.S. Treasury and the Federal Reserve created the TARP program, an acronym for Troubled Asset Relief Program. This program allowed the Treasury to purchase up to $250 billion of senior preferred shares of bank securities.[18]

Most of the big banks either needed to take the cash infusion from the U.S. Treasury or were forced to sell preferred stock to the Treasury. The rationale from the government's point of view was that it didn't want to signal to the financial community which banks were strong and which ones were weak for fear that depositors would move massive amounts of money from weak banks to strong banks. This phenomenon actually occurred several times and forced banks such as Wachovia to be merged with Wells Fargo.

The total amount of preferred stock bought amounted to $204 billion. In the case of Citibank (Citigroup), its Tier 1 capital ratio fell under the minimum because it had to write off billions of dollars in bad loans, which reduced its asset base. This forced Citibank to give the Treasury common stock in exchange for the preferred stock, and so, as of spring 2010, the U.S. government was the largest stockholder in Citigroup. By December of that year, the U.S. government sold its remaining shares of Citigroup. Not only did the government get the return of its original investment, but it reaped a profit of $12 billion. By spring 2012, all the banks had repaid their loans.[19]

During this period, the Federal Reserve took unprecedented actions that included buying up troubled assets from the banks and lending money at the discount window to nonbanks such as investment banks and brokers. The Fed also entered into the financial markets by making markets in commercial paper and other securities where the markets had ceased to function in an orderly fashion. In addition, the Fed began to pay interest on reserves banks kept at the Fed and finally, it kept interest rates low to stimulate the economy and help the banks regain their health. Because banks make money by the spread between their borrowing and lending rates, the Fed managed the spread between long- and short-term rates to generate a fairly large spread for the banks.

Last, the future of the structure of the banking system is in the hands of the U.S. Congress. In reaction to the financial meltdown and severe recession, Congress passed the Dodd-Frank Wall Street Reform and Consumer Protection Act. The full name implies that the intent of the act is to eliminate the ability of banks to create this type of problem in the future. The regulations for achieving its goals are still being created and implemented over time by the Federal Reserve. We do know that there will be a consolidation of regulatory agencies, increased transparency of derivative products, a new consumer protection agency, and improved international standards for banks. ■

TEAM EXERCISE

Mutual funds pool individual investor dollars and invest them in a number of securities. Go to **http://finance.yahoo.com/** and select some top-performing funds, using criteria such as sector, style, or strategy. Assume that your group has $100,000 to invest in mutual funds. Select five funds in which to invest, representing a balanced (varied industries, risk, and so on) portfolio, and defend your selections.

TIME TO SQUARE UP WITHOUT CASH OR CREDIT CARDS

Square, a startup founded by Twitter co-founder Jack Dorsey, enables businesses that do not have traditional credit card readers to accept credit card payments by plugging a plastic dongle into their mobile devices. These dongles are small credit card swipers attached to a smart phone. As a result, Square allows businesses to bypass fees associated with owning a traditional credit card reader. Businesses can choose to pay Square a monthly fee of $275 for their services or 2.75 percent of every transaction.

A major success for Square occurred after it signed an agreement with Starbucks. This agreement allows Starbucks customers to pay for their purchases without physically swiping a credit card or using a dongle. Starbucks customers can pay for their purchases before they even enter the store with the information in their Square accounts. This partnership has increased Square's visibility among other businesses interested in its services. Because of options like these, money and credit cards are quickly becoming a thing of the past as companies like Square redefine the future of payments.[20]

SO YOU'RE INTERESTED // in Financial Systems or Banking /

You think you might be interested in going into finance or banking, but it is so hard to tell when you are a full-time student. Classes that seem interesting when you take them might not translate to an interesting work experience after you graduate. A great way to see whether you would excel at a career in finance is to get some experience in the industry. Internships, whether they are paid or unpaid, not only help you figure out what you might really want to do after you graduate but they are also a great way to build up your résumé, put your learning to use, and start generating connections within the field.

For example, Pennsylvania's Delaware County District Attorney's Office has been accepting business students from Villanova University for a six-month internship. The student works in the economic-crime division, analyzing documents of people under investigation for financial crimes ranging from fraud to money laundering. The students get actual experience in forensic accounting and have the chance to see whether this is the right career path. On top of that, the program has saved the county an average of $20,000 annually on consulting and accounting fees, not to mention that detectives now have more time to take on larger caseloads. One student who completed the program spent his six months investigating a case in which the owner of a sewage treatment company had embezzled a total of $1 million over the course of nine years. The student noted that the experience helped him gain an understanding about how different companies handle their financial statements as well as how accounting can be applied in forensics and law enforcement.

Internship opportunities are plentiful all over the country, although you may need to do some research to find them. To start, talk to your program advisor and your professors about opportunities. Also, you can check company websites where you think you might like to work to see whether they have any opportunities available. City, state, or federal government offices often provide student internships as well. No matter where you end up interning, the real-life skills you pick up, as well as the résumé boost you get, will be helpful in finding a job after you graduate. When you graduate, commercial banks and other financial institutions offer major employment opportunities. In 2008–2009, a major downturn in the financial industry resulted in mergers, acquisitions, and financial restructuring for many companies. Although the immediate result was a decrease in job opportunities, as the industry recovers, many challenging job opportunities are becoming available.[21]

learn, practice, apply knowledge of the financial system!

M: Business **was developed just for you—students on the go who need information packaged in a concise yet interesting format with multiple learning options.**

Check out the book's website to:

- **Understand the functions of various financial institutions. (Solve the Dilemma)**
- **Determine which financial services are helpful for a type of business. (Solve the Dilemma)**
- **Learn about how to select financial service institutions that are right for your situation. (Build Your Skills)**

While you are there, don't forget to enhance your skills. Practice and apply your knowledge, review the practice exercises, Student PPT® slides, and quizzes to review and apply chapter concepts. Additionally, *Connect® Business* is available for *M: Business*.

www.mhhe.com/ferrellm4e

Highlights
MONEY RATES
EMERGING COMPANIES
CURRENCIES
INVEST
MONEY
STOCK EXCHANGE
Diary
Most active
Gainers
Losers
Volume: 17,224,000

chapter **sixteen**

financial management + securities markets

Although it's certainly true that money makes the world go around, financial management is the discipline that makes the world turn more smoothly. Indeed, without effective management of assets, liabilities, and owners' equity, all business organizations are doomed to fail—regardless of the quality and innovativeness of their products. Financial management is the field that addresses the issues of obtaining and managing the funds and resources necessary to run a business successfully. It is not limited to business organizations: All organizations, from the corner store to the local nonprofit art museum, from giant corporations to county governments, must manage their resources effectively and efficiently if they are to achieve their objectives.

In this chapter, we look at both short- and long-term financial management. First, we discuss the management of short-term assets, which companies use to generate sales and conduct ordinary day-to-day business operations. Next we turn our attention to the management of short-term liabilities, the sources of short-term funds used to finance the business. Then, we discuss the management of long-term assets such as plants, equipment, and the use of common stock (equity) and bonds (long-term liability) to finance these long-term corporate assets. Finally, we look at the securities markets, where stocks and bonds are traded. ■

LEARNING OBJECTIVES

After reading this chapter, you will be able to:

- **LO 16-1** Describe some common methods of managing current assets.
- **LO 16-2** Identify some sources of short-term financing (current liabilities).
- **LO 16-3** Summarize the importance of long-term assets and capital budgeting.
- **LO 16-4** Specify how companies finance their operations and manage fixed assets with long-term liabilities, particularly bonds.
- **LO 16-5** Discuss how corporations can use equity financing by issuing stock through an investment banker.
- **LO 16-6** Describe the various securities markets in the United States.

working capital management the managing of short-term assets and liabilities

transaction balances cash kept on hand by a firm to pay normal daily expenses such as employee wages and bills for supplies and utilities

LO 16-1 Describe some common methods of managing current assets.

MANAGING CURRENT ASSETS AND LIABILITIES

Managing short-term assets and liabilities involves managing the current assets and liabilities on the balance sheet (discussed in Chapter 14). Current assets are short-term resources such as cash, investments, accounts receivable, and inventory. Current liabilities are short-term debts such as accounts payable, accrued salaries, accrued taxes, and short-term bank loans. We use the terms *current* and *short term* interchangeably because short-term assets and liabilities are usually replaced by new assets and liabilities within three or four months, and always within a year. Managing short-term assets and liabilities is sometimes called **working capital management** because short-term assets and liabilities continually flow through an organization and are thus said to be working.

Managing Current Assets

The chief goal of financial managers who focus on current assets and liabilities is to maximize the return to the business on cash, temporary investments of idle cash, accounts receivable, and inventory.

Managing Cash A crucial element facing any financial manager is effectively managing the firm's cash flow. Remember that cash flow is the movement of money through an organization on a daily, weekly, monthly, or yearly basis. Ensuring that sufficient (but not excessive) funds are on hand to meet the company's obligations is one of the single most important facets of financial management.

Idle cash does not make money, and corporate checking accounts typically do not earn interest. As a result, astute money managers try to keep just enough cash on hand, called **transaction balances**, to pay bills—such as employee wages, supplies, and utilities—as they fall due. To manage the firm's cash and ensure that enough cash flows through the organization quickly and efficiently, companies try to speed up cash collections from customers.

To facilitate collection, some companies have customers send their payments to a **lockbox**, which is simply an address for receiving payments, instead of directly to the company's main address. The manager of the lockbox, usually a commercial bank, collects payments directly from the lockbox several times a day and deposits them into the company's bank account. The

FINANCE EXECUTIVES RECOGNIZE THE BENEFITS OF METHOD'S GREEN EFFICIENCIES

Method is a green company in more ways than one. Not only does it sell eco-friendly household supplies, but it also generates more than $100 million in annual revenues. Thanks to companies such as Method, finance executives are beginning to realize the financial benefits of going green. At a time when the prices of commodities are rapidly fluctuating, finance executives are looking for ways to cut costs. Eco-friendly options such as decreasing energy use, using recycled materials, and reducing packaging are becoming viable methods for saving money and improving efficiency. A recent poll found that 40 percent of finance executives are increasing their facilities' efficiency through better energy management, and one-third are undertaking initiatives to increase the efficiency of their shipping, including the adoption of more fuel-efficient vehicles. Method, for instance, has significantly increased its use of biodiesel trucks, which get 13 percent more miles per gallon than traditional trucks.

Method aligns its environmental objectives with its cost-saving goals. The operations and finance departments routinely work together to look at what ingredients and processes would save money while reducing Method's environmental impact. Sometimes this requires the company to adopt additional costs in the short run to save money in the long term. Method's long-term perspective, efficient operations, and popularity with customers are catching on with competitors. It is estimated that eco-friendly household supplies will grow from 3 percent of the household cleaning market in 2008 to 30 percent by 2013. Method has a head start on this increasing trend toward the use of green products and operational processes.[1]

Discussion Questions

1. If greener operations cut company costs, how will this affect Method's current assets and liabilities?
2. Why might Method decide to pursue greener business activities that are costly in the short run?
3. Do you think other household supply companies are beginning to realize how green products can improve their financial conditions?

lockbox an address, usually a commercial bank, at which a company receives payments to speed collections from customers

marketable securities temporary investment of "extra" cash by organizations for up to one year in U.S. Treasury bills, certificates of deposit, commercial paper, or eurodollar deposits

Treasury bills (T-bills) short-term debt obligations the U.S. government sells to raise money

commercial certificates of deposit (CDs) certificates of deposit issued by commercial banks and brokerage companies, available in minimum amounts of $100,000, which may be traded prior to maturity

bank can then start clearing the checks and get the money into the company's checking account much more quickly than if the payments had been submitted directly to the company. However, there is no free lunch: The costs associated with lockbox systems make them worthwhile only for those companies that receive thousands of checks from customers each business day.

More and more companies are now using electronic funds transfer systems to pay and collect bills online. Companies generally want to collect cash quickly but pay out cash slowly. When companies use electronic funds transfers between buyers and suppliers, the speed of collections and disbursements increases to one day. Only with the use of checks can companies delay the payment of cash by three or four days until the check is presented to their bank and the cash leaves their account.

Investing Idle Cash As companies sell products, they generate cash on a daily basis, and sometimes cash comes in faster than it is needed to pay bills. Organizations often invest this "extra" cash, for periods as short as one day (overnight) or for as long as one year, until it is needed. Such temporary investments of cash are known as **marketable securities**. Examples include U.S. Treasury bills, certificates of deposit, commercial paper, and eurodollar deposits. Table 16.1 summarizes a number of marketable securities used by businesses and some sample interest rates on these investments as of June 23, 2006, and April 22, 2013. The safety rankings are relative. Although all of the listed securities are very low risk, the U.S. government securities are the safest. You can see from the table that interest rates have declined during the two periods presented and are currently some of the lowest rates in the history of the United States.

You may never see interest rates this low again in your lifetime. The Fed used monetary policy to lower interest rates to stimulate borrowing and investment during the severe recession of 2007–2009 and continued to maintain low rates into 2012 to stimulate employment and economic growth. The Fed has stated that it expects to continue with low interest rates into 2014, which would be unprecedented.

Many large companies invest idle cash in U.S. **Treasury bills (T-bills)**, which are short-term debt obligations the U.S. government sells to raise money. Issued weekly by the U.S. Treasury, T-bills carry maturities of between one week and one year. U.S. T-bills are generally considered to be the safest of all investments and are called risk free because the U.S. government will not default on its debt.

Individuals and companies can invest their idle cash in marketable securities such as U.S. Treasury bills, commercial paper, and eurodollar deposits.

Commercial certificates of deposit (CDs) are issued by commercial banks and brokerage companies. They are available in minimum amounts of $100,000 but are typically in

commercial paper a written promise from one company to another to pay a specific amount of money

eurodollar market a market centered in London for trading U.S. dollars in foreign countries

▼ **TABLE 16.1** Short-Term Investment Possibilities for Idle Cash

Type of Security	Maturity	Seller of Security	Interest Rate 6/23/2006	Interest Rate 4/22/2013	Safety Level
U.S. Treasury bills	90 days	U.S. government	4.80%	0.06%	Excellent
U.S. Treasury bills	180 days	U.S. government	5.05	0.09	Excellent
Commercial paper	30 days	Major corporations	5.14	0.07	Very good
Certificates of deposit	90 days	U.S. commercial banks	5.40	0.20	Very good
Certificates of deposit	180 days	U.S. commercial banks	5.43	0.27	Very good
Eurodollars	90 days	European commercial banks	5.48	0.28	Very good

Source: "Selected Interest Rates," *Federal Reserve Statistical Release*, www.federalreserve.gov/releases/h15/current/.

units of $1 million for large corporations investing excess cash. Unlike consumer CDs (discussed in Chapter 15), which must be held until maturity, commercial CDs may be traded prior to maturity. Should a cash shortage occur, the organization can simply sell the CD on the open market and obtain needed funds.

One of the most popular short-term investments for the largest business organizations is **commercial paper**—a written promise from one company to another to pay a specific amount of money. Because commercial paper is backed only by the name and reputation of the issuing company, sales of commercial paper are restricted to only the largest and most financially stable companies. Because commercial paper is frequently bought and sold for durations of as short as one business day, many players in the market find themselves buying commercial paper with excess cash on one day and selling it to gain extra money the following day.

During 2007 and 2008, the commercial paper market simply stopped functioning. Investors no longer trusted the IOUs of even the best companies. Companies that had relied on commercial paper to fund short-term cash needs had to turn to the banks for borrowing. Those companies who had existing lines of credit at their bank were able to draw on their line of credit. Others were in a tight spot. Eventually, the Federal Reserve entered the market to buy and sell commercial paper for its own portfolio. This is something the Fed was not in the habit of doing. But it rescued the market, and the market functioned well during 2011 and 2012.

Some companies invest idle cash in international markets such as the **eurodollar market**, a market centered in London for trading U.S. dollars in foreign countries. Because the eurodollar market was originally developed by London banks, any dollar-denominated deposit in a non-U.S. bank is called a eurodollar deposit, regardless of whether the issuing bank is actually located in Europe, South America, or anyplace else. For example, if you travel overseas and deposit $1,000 in a German bank, you will have created a eurodollar deposit in the amount of $1,000. Because the U.S. dollar is accepted by most countries for international trade, these dollar deposits can be used by international companies to settle their accounts. The market created for trading such investments offers firms with extra dollars a chance to earn a slightly higher rate of return with just a little more risk than they would face by investing in U.S. Treasury bills.

Maximizing Accounts Receivable After cash and marketable securities, the balance sheet lists accounts receivable and inventory. Remember that accounts receivable is money owed to a business by credit customers. For example, if you charge your Shell gasoline purchases, until you actually pay for them with cash or a check, they represent an account receivable to Shell. Many businesses make the vast majority of their sales on credit, so managing accounts receivable is an important task.

Each credit sale represents an account receivable for the company, the terms of which typically require customers to pay the full amount due within 30, 60, or even 90 days from the date of the sale. To encourage quick payment, some businesses offer some of their customers discounts of between 1 and 2 percent if they pay off their balance within a specified period of time (usually between 10 and 30 days). On the other hand, late payment charges of between 1 and 1.5 percent serve to discourage slow payers from sitting on their bills forever. The larger the early payment discount offered, the faster customers will tend to pay their accounts. Unfortunately, although discounts increase cash flow, they also reduce profitability. Finding the right balance between the added advantages of early cash receipt and the disadvantages of reduced profits is no simple matter. Similarly, determining the optimal balance between the higher sales likely to result from extending credit to customers with less than sterling credit ratings and the higher bad-debt losses likely to result from a more lenient credit policy is also challenging. Information on company credit ratings is provided by local credit bureaus, national credit-rating agencies such as Dun and Bradstreet, and industry trade groups.

Optimizing Inventory Although the inventory that a firm holds is controlled by both production needs and marketing considerations, the financial manager has to coordinate inventory purchases to manage cash flows. The object is to minimize the firm's investment in inventory without experiencing production cutbacks as a result of critical materials shortfalls or lost sales due to insufficient finished goods inventories. Every dollar invested in inventory is a dollar unavailable for investment in some other area of the organization. Optimal inventory levels are determined in large part by the method of production.

Loans are important for most consumers purchasing a home. Interest rates have been at historic lows over the past few years but are expected to increase in the long-run.

If a firm attempts to produce its goods just in time to meet sales demand, the level of inventory will be relatively low. If, on the other hand, the firm produces materials in a constant, level pattern, inventory increases when sales decrease and decreases when sales increase. One way that companies are optimizing inventory is through the use of radio frequency identification (RFID) technology. Companies such as Walmart manage their inventories better by using RFID tags. An RFID tag, which contains a silicon chip and an antenna, allows a company to use radio waves to track and identify the products to which the tags are attached. These tags are primarily used to track inventory shipments from the manufacturer to the buyer's warehouses and then to the individual stores and cut down on trucking theft because the delivery truck and its contents can be tracked.

The automobile industry is an excellent example of an industry driven almost solely by inventory levels. Because it is inefficient to lay off workers continually in slow times and call them back in better times, Ford, General Motors, and Chrysler try to set and stick to quarterly production quotas. Automakers typically try to keep a 60-day supply of unsold cars. During particularly slow periods, however, it is not unusual for inventories to exceed 100 days of sales.

Although less publicized, inventory shortages can be as much of a drag on potential profits as too much inventory. Not having an item on hand may send the customer to a competitor—forever. Complex computer inventory models are frequently employed to determine the optimum level of inventory a firm should hold to support a given level of sales. Such models can indicate how and when parts inventories should be ordered so that they are available exactly when required—and not a day before. Developing and maintaining such an intricate production and inventory system is difficult, but it can often prove to be the difference between experiencing average profits and spectacular ones.

trade credit credit extended by suppliers for the purchase of their goods and services

line of credit an arrangement by which a bank agrees to lend a specified amount of money to an organization upon request

secured loans loans backed by collateral that the bank can claim if the borrowers do not repay them

unsecured loans loans backed only by the borrowers' good reputation and previous credit rating

prime rate the interest rate that commercial banks charge their best customers (usually large corporations) for short-term loans

LO 16-2 Identify some sources of short-term financing (current liabilities).

Managing Current Liabilities

Although having extra cash on hand is a delightful surprise, the opposite situation—a temporary cash shortfall—can be a crisis. The good news is that there are several potential sources of short-term funds. Suppliers often serve as an important source through credit sales practices. Also, banks, finance companies, and other organizations offer short-term funds through loans and other business operations.

Accounts Payable Remember from Chapter 14 that accounts payable is money an organization owes to suppliers for goods and services. Just as accounts receivable must be actively managed to ensure proper cash collections, so too must accounts payable be managed to make the best use of this important liability.

The most widely used source of short-term financing, and therefore the most important account payable, is **trade credit**—credit extended by suppliers for the purchase of their goods and services. Although varying in formality, depending on both the organizations involved and the value of the items purchased, most trade credit agreements offer discounts to organizations that pay their bills early. A supplier, for example, may offer trade terms of "1/10 net 30," meaning that the purchasing organization may take a 1 percent discount from the invoice amount if it makes payment by the 10th day after receiving the bill. Otherwise, the entire amount is due within 30 days. For example, pretend that you are the financial manager in charge of payables. You owe Ajax Company $10,000, and it offers trade terms of 2/10 net 30. By paying the amount due within 10 days, you can save 2 percent of $10,000, or $200. Assume you place orders with Ajax once per month and have 12 bills of $10,000 each per year. By taking the discount every time, you will save 12 times $200, or $2,400, per year. Now assume you are the financial manager of Gigantic Corp., and it has monthly payables of $100 million per month. Two percent of $100 million is $2 million per month. Failure to take advantage of such trade discounts can add up to large opportunity losses over the span of a year.

Bank Loans Virtually all organizations—large and small—obtain short-term funds for operations from banks. In most instances, the credit services granted these firms take the form of a line of credit or fixed dollar loan. A **line of credit** is an arrangement by which a bank agrees to lend a specified amount of money to the organization upon request—provided that the bank has the required funds to make the loan. In general, a business line of credit is very similar to a consumer credit card, with the exception that the preset credit limit can amount to millions of dollars.

In addition to credit lines, banks also make **secured loans**—loans backed by collateral that the bank can claim if the borrowers do not repay the loans—and **unsecured loans**—loans backed only by the borrowers' good reputation and previous credit rating. Both individuals and businesses build their credit rating from their history of borrowing and repaying borrowed funds on time and in full. The three national credit-rating services are Equifax, TransUnion, and Experian. A lack of credit history or a poor credit history can make it difficult to get loans from financial institutions. The *principal* is the amount of money borrowed; *interest* is a percentage of the principal that the bank charges for use of its money. As we mentioned in Chapter 15, banks also pay depositors interest on savings accounts and some checking accounts. Thus, banks charge borrowers interest for loans and pay interest to depositors for the use of their money. In addition, these loans may include origination fees.

One of the complaints from borrowers during the financial meltdown and recession was that banks weren't willing to lend. There were several causes. Banks were trying to rebuild their capital, and they didn't want to take the extra risk that lending offers in an economic recession. They were drowning in bad debts and were not sure how future loan losses would affect their capital. The banks' lack of lending caused problems for small businesses. Smaller regional banks did a better job of maintaining small business loans than the major money center banks who suffered most in the recession.

The **prime rate** is the interest rate commercial banks charge their best customers (usually large corporations) for short-term loans. Although for many years, loans at the prime rate represented funds at the lowest possible cost, the rapid development of the market for commercial paper has dramatically reduced the importance of commercial banks as a source of short-term loans. Today, most "prime" borrowers are actually small- and medium-sized businesses.

The interest rates on commercial loans may be either fixed or variable. A variable, or floating-rate, loan offers an advantage when interest rates are falling but represents a distinct disadvantage when interest rates are rising. Between 1999 and 2004, interest rates plummeted, and borrowers refinanced their loans with low-cost fixed-rate loans. Nowhere was this more visible than in the U.S. mortgage markets, where homeowners lined up to refinance their high-percentage home mortgages with lower-cost loans, in some cases as low as 5 percent on a 30-year loan. These mortgage interest rates had returned to 6.5 percent by mid-2006, but by 2012 they had declined to less than 4.0 percent. Individuals and corporations have the same motivation: to minimize their borrowing costs.

factor a finance company to which businesses sell their accounts receivable—usually for a percentage of the total face value

long-term (fixed) assets production facilities (plants), offices, and equipment—all of which are expected to last for many years

capital budgeting the process of analyzing the needs of the business and selecting the assets that will maximize its value

Nonbank Liabilities Banks are not the only source of short-term funds for businesses. Indeed, virtually all financial institutions, from insurance companies to pension funds, from money market funds to finance companies, make short-term loans to many organizations. The largest U.S. companies also actively engage in borrowing money from the eurodollar and commercial paper markets. As noted earlier, both of these funds' sources are typically slightly less expensive than bank loans.

In some instances, businesses actually sell their accounts receivable to a finance company known as a **factor**, which gives the selling organizations cash and assumes responsibility for collecting the accounts. For example, a factor might pay $60,000 for receivables with a total face value of $100,000 (60 percent of the total). The factor profits if it can collect more than what it paid for the accounts. Because the selling organization's customers send their payments to a lockbox, they may have no idea that a factor has bought their receivables.

Additional nonbank liabilities that must be efficiently managed to ensure maximum profitability are taxes owed to the government and wages owed to employees. Clearly, businesses are responsible for many types of taxes, including federal, state, and local income taxes, property taxes, mineral rights taxes, unemployment taxes, Social Security taxes, workers' compensation taxes, excise taxes, and more. Although the public tends to think that the only relevant taxes are on income and sales, many industries must pay other taxes that far exceed those levied against their income. Taxes and employees' wages represent debt obligations of the firm, which the financial manager must plan to meet as they fall due.

LO 16-3 Summarize the importance of long-term assets and capital budgeting.

MANAGING FIXED ASSETS

Up to this point, we have focused on the short-term aspects of financial management. Although most business failures are the result of poor short-term planning, successful ventures must also consider the long-term financial consequences of their actions. Managing the long-term assets and liabilities and the owners' equity portion of the balance sheet is important for the long-term health of the business.

Long-term (fixed) assets are expected to last for many years—production facilities (plants), offices, equipment, heavy machinery, furniture, automobiles, and so on. In today's fast-paced world, companies need the most technologically advanced, modern facilities and equipment they can afford. Automobile, oil refining, and transportation companies depend on fixed assets.

Modern and high-tech equipment carry high price tags, and the financial arrangements required to support these investments are by no means trivial. Leasing is just one approach to financing. Obtaining major long-term financing can be challenging for even the most profitable organizations. For less successful firms, such challenges can prove nearly impossible. One approach is leasing assets such as equipment, machines, and buildings. Leasing involves paying a fee for usage rather than owning the asset. There are two kinds of leases: capital leases and operating leases. A capital lease is a long-term contract and shows up on the balance sheet as an asset and liability. The operating lease is a short-term cancelable lease and does not show up on the balance sheet. We'll take a closer look at long-term financing in a moment, but first let's address some issues associated with fixed assets, including capital budgeting, risk assessment, and the costs of financing fixed assets.

Capital Budgeting and Project Selection

One of the most important jobs performed by the financial manager is to decide what fixed assets, projects, and investments will earn profits for the firm beyond the costs necessary to fund them. The process of analyzing the needs of the business and selecting the assets that will maximize its value is called **capital budgeting**, and the capital budget is the amount of money budgeted for investment in such long-term assets. But capital budgeting does not end with the selection and purchase of a particular piece of land, equipment, or major investment. All assets and projects must be continually reevaluated to ensure their compatibility with the organization's needs. Financial executives believe most budgeting activities are occasionally or frequently unrealistic or irrelevant. If a particular asset does not live up to expectations, then management must determine why and take necessary corrective action. Budgeting is not an exact process, and managers must be flexible when new information is available.

> "All assets and projects must be continually reevaluated to ensure their compatibility with the organization's needs."

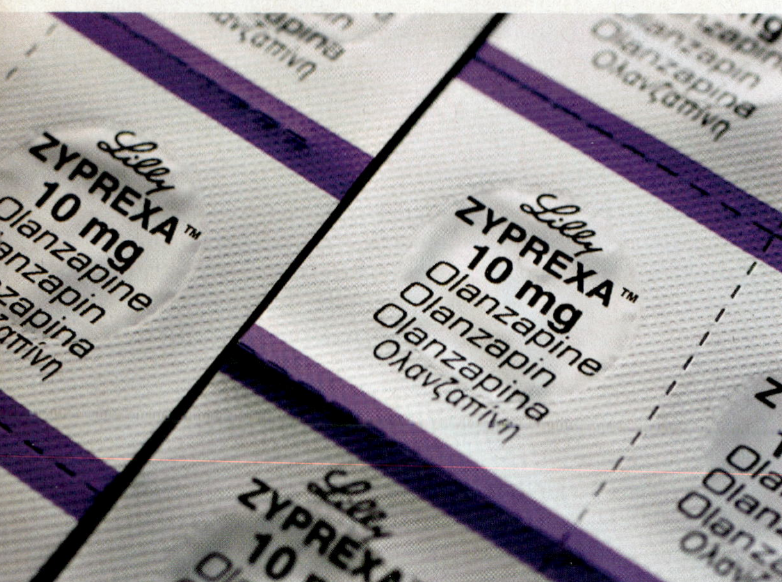

Pharmaceutical companies spend millions of dollars developing drugs such as Zyprexa without knowing if the drug will pass FDA approval and have a significant margin.

Assessing Risk

Every investment carries some risk. Figure 16.1 ranks potential investment projects according to estimated risk. When considering investments overseas, risk assessments must include the political climate and economic stability of a region. The decision to introduce a product or build a manufacturing facility in England would be much less risky than a decision to build one in the Middle East, for example.

The longer a project or asset is expected to last, the greater its potential risk because it is hard to predict whether a piece of equipment will wear out or become obsolete in 5 or 10 years. Predicting cash flows one year down the road is difficult, but projecting them over the span of a 10-year project is a gamble.

The level of a project's risk is also affected by the stability and competitive nature of the marketplace and the world economy as a whole. IBM's latest high-technology computer product is far more likely to become obsolete overnight than is a similar $10 million investment in a manufacturing plant. Dramatic changes in the marketplace are not uncommon. Indeed, uncertainty created by the rapid devaluation of Asian currencies in the late 1990s wrecked a host of assumptions in literally hundreds of projects worldwide. Financial managers must constantly consider such issues when making long-term decisions about the purchase of fixed assets.

Pricing Long-Term Money

The ultimate profitability of any project depends not only on accurate assumptions of how much cash it will generate but also on its financing costs. Because a business must pay interest on money it borrows, the returns from any project must cover not only the costs of operating the project but also the interest expenses for the debt used to finance its construction. Unless an organization can effectively cover all of its costs—both financial and operating—it will eventually fail.

FIGURE 16.1
Qualitative Assessment of Capital Budgeting Risk

Clearly, only a limited supply of funds is available for investment in any given enterprise. The most efficient and profitable companies can attract the lowest-cost funds because they typically offer reasonable financial returns at very low relative risks. Newer and less prosperous firms must pay higher costs to attract capital because these companies tend to be quite risky. One of the strongest motivations for companies to manage their financial resources wisely is that they will, over time, be able to reduce the costs of their funds and in so doing increase their overall profitability.

In our free-enterprise economy, new firms tend to enter industries that offer the greatest potential rewards for success. However, as more and more companies enter an industry, competition intensifies, eventually driving profits down to average levels. The digital music player market of the early 2000s provides an excellent example of the changes in profitability that typically accompany increasing competition. The sign of a successful capital budgeting program is that the new products create higher than normal profits and drive sales and the stock price up. This has certainly been true for Apple when it made the decision to enter the electronics industry. In 2001, Apple

long-term liabilities debts that will be repaid over a number of years, such as long-term loans and bond issues

Apple went from $6.30 a share in 2003 to over $700 in 2012 and down to less than $400 in 2013 before rebounding. Its move into the electronics industry has led to such hits as the Apple iPod, iPhone, and iPad.

introduced the first iPod. Since then, the iPod has undergone many enhancements in size, style, and different versions such as the small Nano. These modifications have been largely successful; in 2012, the iPod sold 35.4 million units, accounting for sales of $5.6 billion. But the offshoot of this successful product was the iTunes Store, which added another $7.5 billion in sales. The iPhone, introduced in 2007, has now gone through many annual updates with the latest being the iPhone 5. During 2012, the iPhone sold 125 million units accounting for $80.5 billion in sales. Finally, the iPad tablet was introduced in 2010 and is now in its third version. In 2012, Apple sold 58.3 million iPad units, generating $32.4 billion in revenue. Interestingly, Apple did not appear to be negatively affected by the recession. In fact, its sales grew from $42.9 billion in 2009 to $156.5 billion in 2012. It is on track to keep up its growth as it expands into China, India, and other emerging markets. An interesting development was that the ease of synchronization with all Apple computers caused an increase in the sale of iMacs and MacBooks.

Even with a well-planned capital budgeting program, it may be difficult for Apple to stay ahead of the competition because the Google Android platform is being used by Apple's competitors. This intense competition may make it difficult to continue market dominance for any extended period. Apple was valued at $373 billion in April 2013. The company's common stock has gone from a low price of $6.36 per share in 2003 to $702 per share in September 2012. However, it fell to $392 per share in April 2013 as investors worried about future growth prospects. If you had invested $1,000 at the low price and still held the shares at the high price, your holdings would have been worth $110,377, but seven months later they would have been worth only $61,635, which is still not a bad return. The problem is having the patience to continue to hold such a winner without taking some profits along the way.[2]

Maintaining market dominance is also difficult in the personal computer industry, particularly because tablet computers are taking away market share. With increasing competition, prices have fallen dramatically since the 1990s. Even Dell, with its low-cost products, has moved into other markets such as servers to maintain growth in a maturing market. Weaker companies have failed, leaving the most efficient producers/marketers scrambling for market share. The expanded market for personal computers dramatically reduced the financial returns generated by each dollar invested in productive assets. The glory days of the personal computer industry—the time in which fortunes could be won and lost in the space of an average-sized garage—have long since passed into history. Personal computers have essentially become commodity items, and profit margins for companies in this industry have shrunk as the market matures.

LO 16-4 Specify how companies finance their operations and manage fixed assets with long-term liabilities, particularly bonds.

FINANCING WITH LONG-TERM LIABILITIES

As we said earlier, long-term assets do not come cheaply, and few companies have the cash on hand to open a new store across town, build a new manufacturing facility, research and develop a new life-saving drug, or launch a new product worldwide. To develop such fixed assets, companies need to raise low-cost long-term funds to finance them. Two common choices for raising these funds are attracting new owners *(equity financing)*, which we'll look at in a moment, and taking on long-term liabilities *(debt financing)*, which we'll look at now.

Long-term liabilities are debts that will be repaid over a number of years, such as long-term bank loans and bond issues. These take many forms, but in the end, the key word is *debt*. Companies may raise money by borrowing it from commercial banks or other financial institutions in the form of lines of credit, short-term loans, or long-term loans. Many corporations acquire debt by borrowing money from pension funds, mutual funds, or life-insurance funds.

bonds debt instruments that larger companies sell to raise long-term funds

unsecured bonds debentures, or bonds that are not backed by specific collateral

secured bonds bonds that are backed by specific collateral that must be forfeited in the event that the issuing firm defaults

serial bonds a sequence of small bond issues of progressively longer maturity

floating-rate bonds bonds with interest rates that change with current interest rates otherwise available in the economy

Companies that rely too heavily on debt can get into serious trouble should the economy falter; during these times, they may not earn enough operating income to make the required interest payments (remember the times-interest-earned ratio in Chapter 14). In severe cases when the problem persists too long, creditors will not restructure loans but will instead sue for the interest and principal owed and force the company into bankruptcy.

Bonds: Corporate IOUs

Much long-term debt takes the form of **bonds**, which are debt instruments that larger companies sell to raise long-term funds. In essence, the buyers of bonds (bondholders) loan the issuer of the bonds cash in exchange for regular interest payments until the loan is repaid on or before the specified maturity date. The bond itself is a certificate, much like an IOU, that represents the company's debt to the bondholder. Bonds are issued by a wide variety of entities, including corporations; national, state, and local governments; public utilities; and nonprofit corporations. Most bondholders need not hold their bonds until maturity; rather, the existence of active secondary markets of brokers and dealers allows for the quick and efficient transfer of bonds from owner to owner.

The bond contract, or *indenture,* specifies all of the terms of the agreement between the bondholders and the issuing organization. The indenture, which can run more than 100 pages, specifies the basic terms of the bond, such as its face value, maturity date, and the annual interest rate. Table 16.2 briefly explains how to determine these and more things about a bond from a bond quote as it might appear in *The Financial Times.* The face value of the bond, its initial sales price, is typically $1,000. After this, however, the price of the bond on the open market will fluctuate along with changes in the economy (particularly, changes in interest rates) and in the creditworthiness of the issuer. Bondholders receive the face value of the bond along with the final interest payment on the maturity date. The annual interest rate (often called the *coupon rate*) is the guaranteed percentage of face value that the company will pay to the bond owner every year. For example, a $1,000 bond with a coupon rate of 7 percent would pay $70 per year in interest. In most cases, bond indentures specify that interest payments be made every six months. In the preceding example, the $70 annual payment would be divided into two semiannual payments of $35.

In addition to the terms of interest payments and maturity date, the bond indenture typically covers other important topics, such as repayment methods, interest payment dates, procedures to be followed in case the organization fails to make the interest payments, conditions for the early repayment of the bonds, and any conditions requiring the pledging of assets as collateral.

TABLE 16.2 Bonds—Global Investment Grade Quoted in US $

	Red Date[a]	Coupon[b]	S[c]	M[c]	F[c]	Bid Price[d]	Bid Yield[e]	Spread vs. Govts.[f]
GE Capital	01/16	5.00	AA+	Aa3	AA−	103.7	4.01	1.56
AT&T Wireless	03/31	8.75	A	A2	A	128.2	6.3	1.53
Goldman Sachs	02/33	6.13	A	A1	A+	98.29	6.27	1.49

[a]Red Date—the month and year that the bond matures and must pay back the borrowed amount.

[b]Coupon—the percentage in interest payment that the bond pays based on a $1,000 bond. For example, the GE Capital bond pays 5 percent on $1,000 or $50 per year, whereas the AT&T bond pays $87.50.

[c]S-M-F—the ratings provided by the three major rating agencies: S (Standard and Poor's), M (Moody's), and F (Fitch). Using Standard and Poor's as an example, a rating of AAA would be the highest quality and lowest risk bond. Any bond in the A category is investment grade and considered high quality.

[d]Bid Price—the price as a percentage of par value ($1,000) that investors are willing to pay for a bond. For example, the GE Capital bond has a bid price of $103.69, which would translate into 103% of $1,000 or a price of $1,036.90.

[e]Bid Yield—the annual rate of return the investor would receive if he or she held the bond to maturity. For example, with the GE bond you would get $50 per year until the bond matured in January 2016, and you would receive $1,000 par value at maturity. Because you paid $1,036.90, you would lose $36.90 on your investment. The 4.01 percent bid yield reflects both the income from the interest payment and the loss on the investment.

[f]Spread vs. Govts.—represents the premium yield the corporate bond pays over a U.S. government bond of equal maturity. Because corporate bonds are riskier than government bonds, an investor would expect the corporation to pay more than a risk-free government bond. In the case of GE Capital, the premium the company pays is an extra 1.56 percent.

Source: *The Financial Times,* March 31, 2010, p. 23.

Types of Bonds

Not surprisingly, there are a great many types of bonds. Most are **unsecured bonds**, meaning that they are not backed by collateral; such bonds are termed *debentures*. **Secured bonds**, on the other hand, are backed by specific collateral that must be forfeited in the event that the issuing firm defaults. Whether secured or unsecured, bonds may be repaid in one lump sum or with many payments spread out over a period of time. **Serial bonds**, which are different from secured bonds, are actually a sequence of small bond issues of progressively longer maturity. The firm pays off each of the serial bonds as it matures. **Floating-rate bonds** do not have fixed interest payments; instead, the interest rate changes with current interest rates otherwise available in the economy.

In recent years, a special type of high-interest-rate bond has attracted considerable attention (usually negative) in the financial press. High-interest bonds, or **junk bonds** as they are popularly known, offer relatively high rates of interest because they have higher inherent risks. Historically, junk bonds have been associated with companies in poor financial health and/or startup firms with limited track records. In the mid-1980s, however, junk bonds became a very attractive method of financing corporate mergers; they remain popular today with many investors as a result of their very high relative interest rates. But higher risks are associated with those higher returns (upward of 12 percent per year in some cases) and the average investor would be well-advised to heed those famous words: Look before you leap!

LO 16-5 Discuss how corporations can use equity financing by issuing stock through an investment banker.

FINANCING WITH OWNERS' EQUITY

A second means of long-term financing is through equity. Remember from Chapter 14 that owners' equity refers to the owners' investment in an organization. Sole proprietors and partners own all or part of their businesses outright, and their equity includes the money and assets they have brought into their ventures. Corporate owners, on the other hand, own stock or shares of their companies, which they hope will provide them with a return on their investment. Stockholders' equity includes common stock, preferred stock, and retained earnings.

> A second means of long-term financing is through equity.

Common stock (introduced in Chapter 4) is the single most important source of capital for most new companies. On the balance sheet, the common stock account is separated into two basic parts—common stock at par and capital in excess of par. The *par value* of a stock is simply the dollar amount printed on the stock certificate and has no relation to actual *market value*—the price at which the common stock is currently trading. The difference between a stock's par value and its offering price is called *capital in excess of par*. Except in the case of some very low-priced stocks, the capital in excess of par account is significantly larger than the par value account. Table 16.3 briefly explains how to gather

TABLE 16.3 A Basic Stock Quote

1		2	3	4	5	6	7	8
Stock Price 52 week								
High	Low	Stock	Symbol	Dividend	Dividend Yield (%)	Volume	Close	Net Change
114.81	76.98	Nike	NKE	1.44	1.30%	2,408,500	110.92	+2.13
19.00	11.21	Sketchers USA	SKX	0.0	0.0	905,754	17.78	+0.33
44.13	30.77	Wolverine Worldwide	WWW	0.48	1.13	861,544	44.64	+0.72

1. The **52-week high and low**—the highest and lowest prices, respectively, paid for the stock in the last year; for Nike stock, the highest was $114.81 and the lowest price, $76.98.
2. **Stock**—the name of the issuing company. When followed by the letters "pf," the stock is a preferred stock.
3. **Symbol**—the ticker tape symbol for the stock; NKE.
4. **Dividend**—the annual cash dividend paid to stockholders; Nike paid a dividend of $1.44 per share of stock outstanding.
5. **Dividend yield**—the dividend return on one share of common stock; Nike, 1.30 percent.
6. **Volume**—the number of shares traded on this day; Nike, 2,408,500.
7. **Close**—Nike's last sale of the day was for $110.92.
8. **Net change**—the difference between the previous day's close and the close on the day being reported; Nike was up $2.13.

Source: Yahoo! Finance, May 29, 2012, http://finance.yahoo.com/q?s.

junk bonds a special type of high-interest-rate bond that carries higher inherent risks

retained earnings earnings after expenses and taxes that are reinvested in the assets of the firm and belong to the owners in the form of equity

dividend yield the dividend per share divided by the stock price

primary market the market where firms raise financial capital

secondary markets stock exchanges and over-the-counter markets where investors can trade their securities with other investors

investment banking the sale of stocks and bonds for corporations

securities markets the mechanism for buying and selling securities

VENTURE FIRM FOCUSES ON SMALLER CLEAN-TECH INVESTMENTS

Robert Fenwick-Smith leaves the large-scale investments in alternative energy to large corporations. He prefers smaller clean-tech companies that are capital efficient, can reach profitability more quickly, and yield smaller but still profitable returns. His venture capital firm Aravaipa Ventures, founded in 2008 in Colorado, does just that. Rather than investing large amounts of money in a few companies, Aravaipa invests in several smaller firms. It also limits its investments to four key areas: transportation efficiency, building efficiency, water efficiency, and location efficiency. This enables Aravaipa to spread out the risks so the failure of one company will not lead to enormous losses. In addition, Aravaipa invests only in firms that need no more than $5 million in funding and have the ability to generate revenue within the next year and a half. Although this might seem to create limitations for Aravaipa, the company has been able to invest in innovative smaller companies that might be ignored by larger corporations. Due to Fenwick-Smith's leadership skills in green investing, he won the Governor's Award for Excellence in Clean-tech Leadership 2012.[3]

important information from a stock quote, as it might appear in *The Wall Street Journal* or on the NASDAQ website.

Preferred stock was defined in Chapter 14 as corporate ownership that gives the stockholder preference in the distribution of the company's profits but not the voting and control rights accorded to common stockholders. Thus, the primary advantage of owning preferred stock is that it is a safer investment than common stock.

All businesses exist to earn profits for their owners. Without the possibility of profit, there can be no incentive to risk investors' capital and succeed. When a corporation has profits left over after paying all of its expenses and taxes, it has the choice of retaining all or a portion of its earnings and/or paying them out to its shareholders in the form of dividends. **Retained earnings** are reinvested in the assets of the firm and belong to the owners in the form of equity. Retained earnings are an important source of funds and are, in fact, the only long-term funds that the company can generate internally.

When the board of directors distributes some of a corporation's profits to the owners, it issues them as cash dividend payments. But not all firms pay dividends. Many fast-growing firms retain all of their earnings because they can earn high rates of return on the earnings they reinvest. Companies with fewer growth opportunities typically pay out large proportions of their earnings in the form of dividends, thereby allowing their stockholders to reinvest their dividend payments in higher-growth companies. Table 16.4 presents a sample of companies and the dividend each paid on a single share of stock. As shown in the table, when the dividend is divided by the price, the result is the **dividend yield**. The dividend yield is the cash return as a percentage of the price but does not reflect the total return an investor earns on the individual stock. If the dividend yield is 3.59 percent on Campbell Soup and the stock price increases by 10 percent from $32.60 to $35.86, then the total return would be 13.59 percent. It is not clear that stocks with high dividend yields will be preferred by investors to those with little or no dividends. Most large companies pay their stockholders dividends on a quarterly basis.

DID YOU KNOW?

A single share of Coca-Cola stock purchased during its original 1919 IPO would be worth more than $5 million today.[4]

INVESTMENT BANKING

A company that needs more money to expand or take advantage of opportunities may be able to obtain financing by issuing stock. The first-time sale of stocks and bonds directly to the public is called a *new issue*. Companies that already have stocks or bonds outstanding may offer a new issue of stock to raise additional funds for specific projects. When a company offers its stock to the public for the very first time, it is said to be going public, and the sale is called an *initial public offering*.

New issues of stocks and bonds are sold directly to the public and to institutions in what is known as the **primary market**—the market where firms raise financial capital. The primary market differs from **secondary markets**, which are stock exchanges and over-the-counter markets where investors can trade their securities with other investors rather than the company that

TABLE 16.4 Estimated Common Stock Price/Earnings Ratios and Dividends for Selected Companies

Ticker Symbol	Company Name	Price Per Share	Dividend Per Share	Dividend Yield	Earnings Per Share (*)	Price/Earnings Ratio$^{P/E}$
AEO	American Eagle	$20.02	$0.44	2.20%	$0.83	24.12
AXP	American Express	56.62	0.8	1.41%	4.22	13.42
AAPL	Apple	570.58	10.6	1.86%	41.04	13.90
CPB	Campbell Soup	32.6	1.16	3.56%	2.31	14.11
DIS	Disney	45.09	0.6	1.33%	2.79	16.16
F	Ford	10.8	0.2	1.85%	4.71	2.29
HOG	Harley Davidson	48.02	0.62	1.29%	2.78	17.27
HD	Home Depot	49.45	1.16	2.35%	2.65	18.66
MCD	McDonald's	91.27	2.8	3.07%	5.35	17.06
PG	Procter & Gamble	62.83	2.25	3.58%	3.26	19.27
LUV	Southwest Airlines	8.89	0.04	0.45%	0.35	25.40
SBUX	Starbucks	55.18	0.68	1.23%	1.73	31.90

* Earnings per share are for a 12-month period and do not necessarily match year-end numbers.

** Apple declared a dividend of $2.65 per quarter to begin in mid-2012 for an annual rate of $10.60.

Source: *Yahoo! Finance,* May 29, 2012, http://finance.yahoo.com/.

issued the stock or bonds. Primary market transactions actually raise cash for the issuing corporations, whereas secondary market transactions do not.

Investment banking, the sale of stocks and bonds for corporations, helps such companies raise funds by matching people and institutions who have money to invest with corporations in need of resources to exploit new opportunities. Corporations usually employ an investment banking firm to help sell their securities in the primary market. An investment banker helps firms establish appropriate offering prices for their securities. In addition, the investment banker takes care of the myriad details and securities regulations involved in any sale of securities to the public.

Just as large corporations such as IBM and Microsoft have a client relationship with a law firm and an accounting firm, they also have a client relationship with an investment banking firm. An investment banking firm such as Merrill Lynch, Goldman Sachs, or Morgan Stanley Smith Barney can provide advice about financing plans, dividend policy, or stock repurchases as well as advice on mergers and acquisitions. Many now offer additional banking services, making them one-stop shopping banking centers. When Pixar merged with Disney, both companies used investment bankers to help them value the transaction. Each firm wanted an outside opinion about what it was worth to the other. Sometimes mergers fall apart because the companies cannot agree on the price each company is worth or the structure of management after the merger. The advising investment banker, working with management, often irons out these details. Of course, investment bankers do not provide these services for free. They usually charge a fee of between 1 and 1.5 percent of the transaction. A $20 billion merger can generate between $200 and $300 million in investment banking fees. The merger mania of the late 1990s allowed top investment bankers to earn huge sums. Unfortunately, this type of fee income is dependent on healthy stock markets, which seem to stimulate the merger fever among corporate executives.

LO 16-6 Describe the various securities markets in the United States.

THE SECURITIES MARKETS

Securities markets provide a mechanism for buying and selling securities. They make it possible for owners to sell their stocks and bonds to other investors. Thus, in the broadest sense, stocks and bonds markets may be thought of as providers of liquidity—the ability to turn security holdings into cash quickly and at minimal expense and effort. Without liquid securities markets, many potential investors would sit on the sidelines rather than invest their hard-earned savings in securities. Indeed, the ability to sell securities at well-established market prices is one of the very pillars of the capitalistic society that has developed over the years in the United States.

Unlike the primary market, in which corporations sell stocks directly to the public, secondary markets permit the trading of previously issued securities. There are many secondary markets for both stocks and bonds. If you want to purchase 100 shares of Google common stock, for example, you must purchase this stock from another investor or institution. It is the active buying and selling by many thousands of investors that establishes the prices of all financial securities. Secondary market trades may take place on organized exchanges or in what is

over-the-counter (OTC) market a network of dealers all over the country linked by computers, telephones, and Teletype machines

known as the over-the-counter market. Many brokerage houses exist to help investors with financial decisions, and many offer their services through the Internet. One such broker is Charles Schwab. Its site offers a wealth of information and provides educational material to individual investors.

Stock Markets

Stock markets exist around the world in New York, Tokyo, London, Frankfurt, Paris, and other world locations. The two biggest stock markets in the United States are the New York Stock Exchange (NYSE) and the NASDAQ market. The American Stock Exchange is now part of the New York Stock Exchange, and NASDAQ bought both the Boston and Philadelphia regional exchanges. The Chicago Stock Exchange still exists as a regional exchange, but it has a difficult time justifying its existence as a stand-alone exchange.

Exchanges used to be divided into organized exchanges and over-the-counter markets, but during the past several years, dramatic changes have occurred in the markets. Both the NYSE and NASDAQ became publicly traded companies. They were previously not-for-profit organizations but are now for-profit companies. In addition, both exchanges bought or merged with electronic exchanges, the NYSE with Archipelago and the NASDAQ with Instinet. Electronic trading is faster and less expensive than floor trading (where brokers meet to transact business) and now accounts for most of the stock trading done worldwide.

In an attempt to expand its markets, NASDAQ acquired the OMX, a Nordic stock exchange headquartered in Sweden, and the New York Stock Exchange merged with Euronext, a large European electronic exchange that trades options and futures contracts as well as common stock. Both the NYSE and NASDAQ have expanded their reach, their product line, and their ability to trade around the world. What we are witnessing is the globalization of the world's financial markets.

Traditionally, the NASDAQ market has been an electronic market, and many of the large technology companies such as Microsoft, Oracle, and Apple Inc. trade on the NASDAQ market. The NASDAQ operates through dealers who buy and

The New York Stock Exchange is the world's biggest stock exchange in terms of market capitalization.

SOCIAL MEDIA COMPANIES FACE OBSTACLES GOING PUBLIC

When large companies wish to expand, one way to raise funds is by becoming a public company and financing with owner's equity through the issuance of stock. In determining the initial stock price, growth projections are important because investors do not want to risk their capital without strong growth prospects. A failure to foresee obstacles or rely too much on past success can cause a company's stock to be overvalued. This has been the case for many social media companies.

For example, with an initial offering of $38 a share, Facebook made a major debut as a public company. Within four months its stock had slid 45 percent, leading to a number of investor lawsuits claiming that they had been misled about Facebook's future growth prospects. The social gaming company Zynga saw its stock drop 70 percent in less than a year.

While Facebook's share value dropped significantly after its IPO, later in 2013 the value of the stock had recovered to over $40 a share. It is possible that the valuation of social media companies is very difficult to estimate, and it can be hard to determine how profitable they might be in the future. Those investors who thought they had been misled can now see a gain in their initial investments.[5]

Discussion Questions

1. Why might a company's stock be overvalued?
2. In hindsight, were lawsuits claiming that investors were misled about Facebook's value merited?
3. Why is it so hard to determine the value of a social media company?

"Many investors follow the activity of the Dow Jones Industrial Average to see whether the stock market has gone up or down."

sell common stock (inventory) for their own accounts. The NYSE has traditionally been a floor-traded market, where brokers meet at trading posts on the floor of the New York Stock Exchange to buy and sell common stock. The brokers act as agents for their clients and do not own their own inventory. This traditional division between the two markets is becoming less significant as the exchanges become electronic.

The Over-the-Counter Market

Unlike the organized exchanges, the **over-the-counter (OTC) market** is a network of dealers all over the country linked by computers, telephones, and Teletype machines. It has no central location. Today, the OTC market consists of small stocks, illiquid bank stocks, penny stocks, and companies whose stocks trade on the "pink sheets." Once NASDAQ was classified as an exchange by the SEC, it was no longer part of the OTC market. Further, because most corporate bonds and all U.S. securities are traded over the counter, the OTC market regularly accounts for the largest total dollar value of all of the secondary markets.

Measuring Market Performance

Investors, especially professional money managers, want to know how well their investments are performing relative to the market as a whole. Financial managers also need to know how their companies' securities are performing when compared with their competitors'. Thus, performance measures—averages and indexes—are very important to many people. They not only indicate the performance of a particular securities market but also provide a measure of the overall health of the economy.

Indexes and averages are used to measure stock prices. An *index* compares current stock prices with those in a specified base period, such as 1944, 1967, or 1977. An *average* is the average of certain stock prices. The averages used are usually not simple calculations, however. Some stock market averages (such as the Standard & Poor's Composite Index) are weighted averages, where the weights employed are the total market values of each stock in the index (in this case 500). The Dow Jones Industrial Average is a price-weighted average. Regardless of how they are constructed, all market averages of stocks move together closely over time. See Figure 16.2, which graphs the Dow Jones Industrial Average. The recession of 2007–2009 caused more than a 50 percent decline in the market, but by May 2013, the DJIA hit new highs. Young investors should focus on the long-term trends and not the monthly or yearly fluctuations. It is very difficult to outsmart the market.

Many investors follow the activity of the Dow Jones Industrial Average to see whether the stock market has gone up or down. Table 16.5 lists the 30 companies that currently make up the Dow. Although these companies are only a small fraction of the total number of companies listed on the New York Stock Exchange, because of their size they account for about 25 percent of the total value of the NYSE.

The numbers listed in an index or average that tracks the performance of a stock market are expressed not as dollars but as a number on a fixed scale. If you know, for example, that the Dow Jones Industrial Average climbed from 860 in August 1982 to a high of 11,497 at the beginning of 2000, you can see clearly that the value of the Dow Jones Average increased more than 10 times in this 19-year period, making it one of the highest rate of return periods in the history of the stock market.

Unfortunately, prosperity did not last long once the Internet bubble burst. Technology

FIGURE 16.2
Recent Performance of Stock Market and Dow Jones Industrial Average (^DJI)

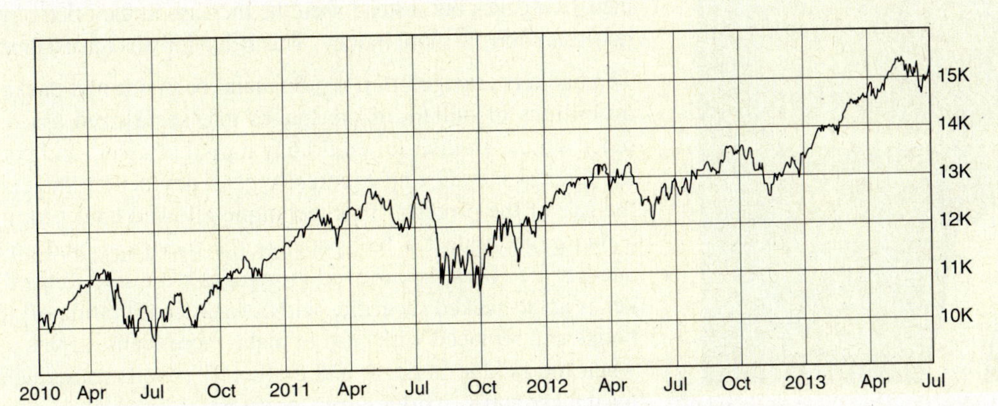

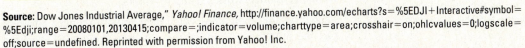

Source: Dow Jones Industrial Average," *Yahoo! Finance,* http://finance.yahoo.com/echarts?s=%5EDJI+Interactive#symbol=%5Edji;range=20080101,20130415;compare=;indicator=volume;charttype=area;crosshair=on;ohlcvalues=0;logscale=off;source=undefined. Reprinted with permission from Yahoo! Inc.

TABLE 16.5 The 30 Stocks in the Dow Jones Industrial Average

3M Co	General Electric	Nike
American Express Co	Goldman Sachs	Pfizer
AT&T Inc.	Home Depot	Procter & Gamble
Boeing	Intel	Travelers Companies
Caterpiller	IBM	United Technologies
Chevron	Johnson & Johnson	UnitedHealth Group
Cisco Systems	JPMorgan Chase	Verizon
Coca-Cola	McDonald's	Visa
Du Pont	Merck	Walmart
ExxonMobil	Microsoft	Walt Disney

Source: "Dow Jones Industrial Average," *Yahoo! Finance,* http://finance.yahoo.com/q/cp?s=%5EDJI.

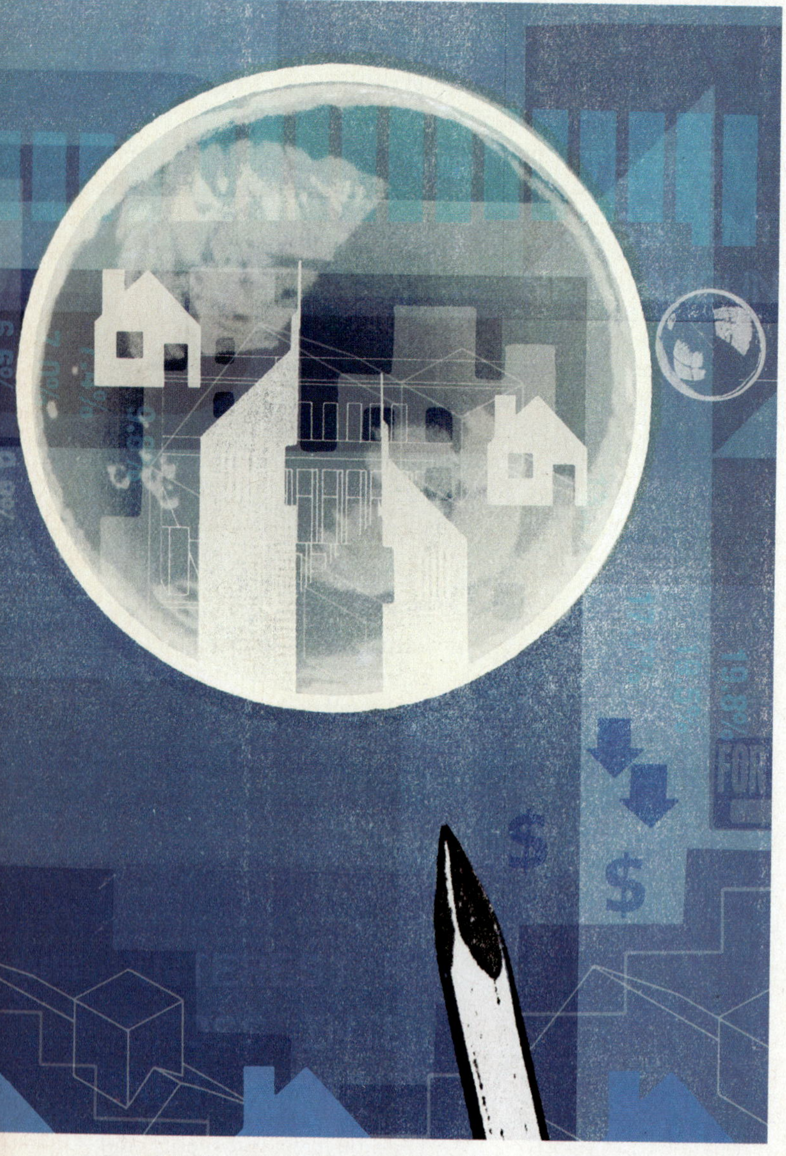

During the housing bubble, banks provided loans to riskier subprime borrowers. Although these loans were highly profitable, it was only a matter of time before the bubble burst.

stocks and new Internet companies were responsible for the huge increase in stock prices. Even companies with few sales and no earnings were selling at prices that were totally unreasonable. It is always easier to realize that a bubble existed after it has popped. By September 2002, the Dow Jones Industrial Average hit 7,461. The markets stabilized and the economy kept growing; investors were euphoric when the Dow Jones Industrial Average hit an all-time high of 14,198 in October 2007. However, once the housing bubble burst, the economy and the stock market went into a free fall. The Dow Jones Industrial Average bottomed out at 6,470 in March 2009. The market entered a period of wild fluctuations, and by April 2010, it hit a new high for the year of 10,975. By the end of May 2012, it was at 12,454, and by May 2013, it had set an all-time high of 15,521, more than double its 2009 low. In addition to any capital gains (change in prices), an investor would have collected dividends, which are not reflected in the index. Perhaps this roller-coaster ride indicates why some people are afraid to enter the market and buy common stocks. If you look at the long-term trend and long-term returns in common stocks, they far outdistance bonds and government securities. When you are young, you should be playing the long-term trends, and as you get older your investments should become more conservative.

Recognizing financial bubbles can be difficult. It is too easy to get caught up in the enthusiasm that accompanies rising markets. Knowing what something is worth in economic terms is the test of true value. During the housing bubble, banks made loans to subprime borrowers to buy houses. (Remember that the prime rate is the rate for the highest-quality borrowers, and subprime loans are generally made to those who do not qualify for regular ones.) As more money poured into the housing market, the obvious supply and demand relationship from economics would indicate that housing prices would rise. As prices rose, speculators entered the real estate market trying to make a fast buck. States such as Florida, Arizona, Nevada, and California were the favorite speculative spots and the states with the largest decline in house prices. To make matters worse, banks had created the home equity loan years ago so that borrowers could take out a second mortgage against their house and deduct the interest payment for tax purposes. Many homeowners no longer thought about paying off their mortgages but instead used the increase in the price of their houses to borrow more money. This behavior was unsustainable.

The bankers engaged in risky financial behavior and packaged up billions of dollars of mortgages into securitized assets. In other words, an investor could buy a pool of assets and collect the interest income and eventually get a payment at the end of the life of the product. This technique allowed banks to make a mortgage, collect a fee, package the mortgage, and collect another fee. These securitized mortgages were sold to the market as asset-backed securities with a AAA credit rating off their books and replaced with cash to make more loans. In this case, when the bubble burst, it had extremely severe consequences for the economy, workers, and investors.

People defaulted on loans when they could no longer afford to pay the mortgage. Many of these people shouldn't have been able to borrow in the first place. The defaults caused housing prices to fall, and some people who had home equity loans no longer had any equity left in their house. Some homeowners owed the bank more than the house was worth, and they started walking away from their mortgage. At the same time, investors realized that the mortgage-backed securities they owned were probably not worth what they thought they were worth, and prices of these assets plummeted. Banks and other financial service firms that had these assets on their books suffered a double whammy. They had loan losses and losses on mortgage-backed securities that another division of the bank had bought for investment purposes. Soon, many banks were close to violating their capital requirement, and the U.S. Treasury and Federal Reserve stepped in—with the help of funding from Congress—to make banks loans, buy securities that were illiquid, and invest in the capital of the banks by buying preferred stocks.

The consensus of most economists is that through the actions of the U.S. Treasury and the Federal Reserve, the U.S. economy escaped what might have been another depression equal to or worse than the depression of the 1930s. The recession of 2007–2009 lasted 18 months and was the longest recession since the 1930s. Hundreds of banks went bankrupt during 2008–2009, and the Federal Deposit Insurance Corporation closed these banks and reopened them as part of another healthy bank with no losses for the depositors. Given that the stock market is a leading indicator, it has been rising since the bottom in March 2009, and everyone—from investors to people relying on pensions tied to the market—hopes the rising market is a sign of an improving economy. Now you know why investing in the stock market takes discipline, knowledge, and the willingness to weather economic storms.

TEAM EXERCISE

Compare and contrast financing with long-term liabilities, such as bonds versus financing with owners' equity, typically retained earnings, common stock, and preferred stock. Form groups and suggest a good mix of long-term liabilities and owner's equity for a new firm that makes wind turbines for generating alternate energy and would like to grow quickly.

For investors to make sound financial decisions, it is important for them to stay in touch with business news, markets, and indexes. Of course, business and investment magazines, such as *Bloomberg Businessweek, Fortune,* and *Money,* offer this type of information. Many Internet sites, including CNN/*Money, Business Wire, USA Today,* other online newspapers, and *PR Newswire,* offer this information as well. Many sites offer searchable databases of information by topic, company, or keyword. However investors choose to receive and review business news, doing so is a necessity in today's market. ■

SO YOU WANT TO WORK // in Financial Management or Securities /

Taking classes in financial and securities management can provide many career options, from managing a small firm's accounts receivables to handling charitable giving for a multinational to investment banking to stock brokerage. We have entered into a less certain period for finance and securities jobs, however. In the world of investment banking, the past few years have been especially challenging. Tens of thousands of employees from Wall Street firms have lost their jobs. This phenomenon is not confined to New York City either, leaving the industry with a lot fewer jobs around the country. This type of phenomenon is not isolated to the finance sector. In the early 2000s, the tech sector experienced a similar downturn, from which it has subsequently largely recovered. Undoubtedly, markets will bounce back and job creation in finance and securities will increase again—but until that happens, the atmosphere across finance and securities will be more competitive than it has been in the past. However, this does not mean that there are no jobs. All firms need financial analysts to determine whether a project should be implemented, when to issue stocks or bonds, or when to initiate loans. These and other forward-looking questions such as how to invest excess cash must be addressed by financial managers. Economic uncertainty in the financial and securities market has made for more difficulty in finding the most desirable jobs.

Why this sudden downturn in financial industry prospects? A lot of these job cuts came in response to the subprime lending fallout and subsequent bank failures such as Bear Stearns, which alone lost around 7,000 employees. All of these people had to look for new jobs in new organizations, increasing the competitive level in a lot of employment areas. For young jobseekers with relatively little experience, this may result in a great deal of frustration. On the other hand, by the time you graduate, the job market for finance majors could be in recovery and rebuilding with new employees. Uncertainty results in hiring freezes and layoffs but leaves firms lean and ready to grow when the cycle turns around, resulting in hiring from the bottom up.

Many industries require people with finance skills. So do not despair if you have a difficult time finding a job in exactly the right firm. Most students switch companies a number of times over the course of their careers. Many organizations require individuals trained in forecasting, statistics, economics, and finance. Even unlikely places like museums, aquariums, and zoos need people who are good at numbers. It may require some creativity, but if you are committed to a career in finance, look to less obvious sources—not just the large financial firms.[6]

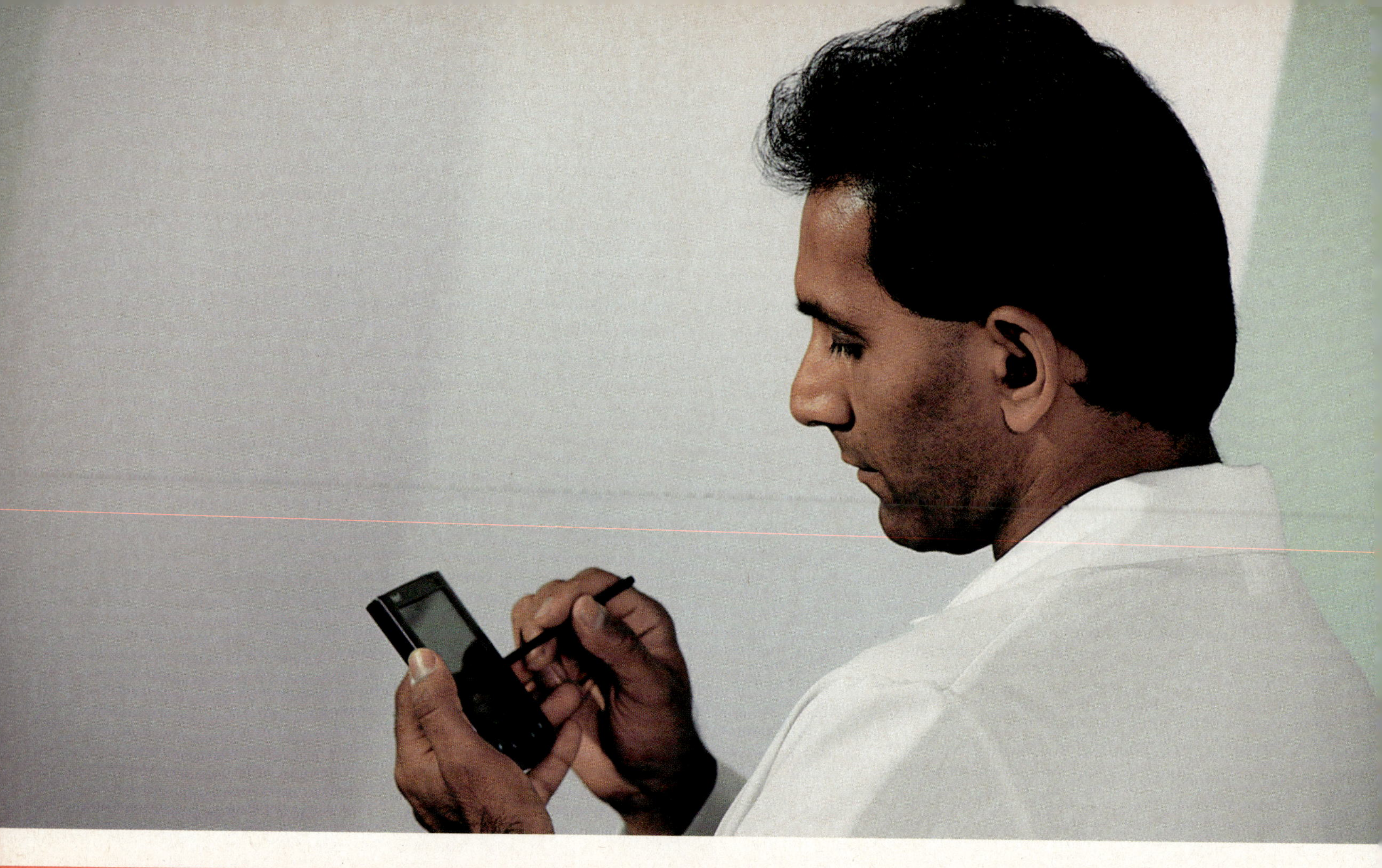

learn, practice, apply financial management!

M: Business was developed just for you—students on the go who need information packaged in a concise yet interesting format with multiple learning options.

Check out the book's website to:

- Learn about the importance of a firm's working capital to its financial health. (Solve the Dilemma)
- Determine how to improve working capital with current liabilities techniques. (Solve the Dilemma)
- Categorize projects based on their risks, and determine which project would be most beneficial. (Build Your Skills)

While you are there, don't forget to enhance your skills. Practice and apply your knowledge, review the practice exercises, Student PPT® slides, and quizzes to review and apply chapter concepts. Additionally, *Connect® Business* is available for *M: Business.*

www.mhhe.com/ferrellm4e

notes

CHAPTER 1

1. Lindsay Blakely, "Erasing the Line between Marketing and Philanthropy," *CBS News*, April 21, 2011, **www.cbsnews.com/8301-505143_162-40244368/erasing-the-line-between-marketingand-philanthropy/**; "The Best of 2011," Charlotte Street Computers, **http://charlottestreetcomputers.com/the-best-of-2011/**.
2. The Graduate Management Admissions Council website, **www.gmac.com/**; "Diversity Advisory Group, **www.gmac.com/reach-and-recruit-students/recruit-students-for-your-program/diversify-your-candidate-pool/diversity-advisory-group.aspx**.
3. David A. Kaplan, "Chipotle's Growth Machine," *CNNMoney*, September 12, 2011, **http://features.blogs.fortune.cnn.com/2011/09/12/chipotles-growth-machine/**.
4. Craig Torres and Anthony Field, "Campbell's Quest for Productivity," *Bloomberg Businessweek*, November 2–December 5, 2010, pp. 15–16.
5. Tahman Bradley, "Michelle Obama and Walmart Join Forces Promoting Healthy Food," *ABC News*, January 20, 2011, **http://abcnews.go.com/Politics/WorldNews/michelle-obama-walmartjoin-forces-promote-healthy-eating/story?id=12723177**.
6. Martinne Geller, "PepsiCo Lineup to Look Healthier in 10 Years: CEO," *Reuters*, October 17, 2011, **www.reuters.com/article/2011/10/17/us-pepsico-ceo-idUSTRE79G4Z020111017**.
7. "The Breakfast Project," **www.whymilk.com/celeb.php**.
8. "About Bill Daniels," **www.danielsfund.org/About-Us/About-Bill-Daniels.asp**.
9. "Reforms Please Cubans, But Is It Communism?" *Associated Press*, April 2, 2008, **www.msnbc.msn.com/id/23925259**.
10. "Special Report: The Visible Hand," *The Economist*, January 21, 2012, pp. 3–5.
11. James T. Areddy and Craig Karmin, "China Stocks Once Frothy, Fall by Half in Six Months," *The Wall Street Journal*, April 16, 2008, pp. 1, 7.
12. "Special Report: The Visible Hand."
13. "Special Report: The World in Their Hands," *The Economist*, January 21, 2012, pp. 15–17.
14. Felicity Barringer, "U.S. Declines to Protect the Overfished Bluefin Tuna," *The New York Times*, May 27, 2011, **www.nytimes.com/2011/05/28/science/earth/28tuna.html**; David Helvarg, "Oil, Terror, Tuna and You," *The Huffington Post*, May 9, 2011, **www.huffingtonpost.com/david-helvarg/oil-terror-tuna-and-you_b_859106.html**; "Endangered Species Listing for Atlantic Bluefin Tuna Not Warranted," NOAA, May 27, 2011, **www.noaanews.noaa.gov/stories2011/20110527_bluefintuna.html**; David Jolly, "Many Mediterranean Fish Species Threatened with Extinction, Report Says," *The New York Times*, April 19, 2011, **http://green.blogs.nytimes.com/2011/04/19/mediterranean-fish-species-threatened-with-extinction/**; "Giant Bluefin Tuna Sells for Record Breaking Price: Big Pic," *Discovery News*, January 5, 2011, **http://news.discovery.com/animals/bluefin-tuna-record-auction-110105.html**; "The King of Sushi," CBS—*60 Minutes*, **www.youtube.com/watch?v=dsbx6dQuRhQ**; Associated Press, "Bluefin Tuna Goes for Record $736,000 at Tokyo's Tsukiji Fish Market," *Huffington Post*, March 6, 2012, **www.huffingtonpost.com/2012/01/05/bluefin-tuna-record_n_1185770.html**.
15. *Shark Tank*, ABC, **http://abc.go.com/shows/shark-tank/bios**.
16. John D. Sutter and Doug Gross, "Apple Unveils the 'Magical' iPad," *CNN Tech*, January 28, 2010, **www.cnn.com/2010/TECH/01/27/apple.tablet/index.html?section=cnn_latest**.
17. "China Patent Filings Could Overtake US, Japan in 2011," *Solid State Technology*, October 11, 2010, **www.electroiq.com/articles/sst/2010/10/china-patent_filings.html**.
18. John Kell, "Foot Locker Sales Get Olympics Lift," *The Wall Street Journal*, August 18–19, 2012, p. B3; Hannah Elliott, "Running Man," *Forbes*, August 20, 2012, pp. 32–34; Amanda D'Amico, "When the Shoe Fits for a Corporate Turnaround," *Wharton Magazine*, February 27, 2012, **http://whartonmagazine.com/blogs/when-the-shoe-fits-for-a-corporate-turnaround/**.
19. "Zimbabwe," *CIA—The World Factbook*, **www.cia.gov/library/publications/the-world-factbook/geos/zi.html**.
20. Greg Wilson, "US Debt Tops $16 Trillion: So Who Do We Owe Most of the Money To?" *Fox News*, September 4, 2012, **www.foxnews.com/politics/2012/09/04/who-do-owe-most-that-16-trillion-to-hint-it-isnt-china/**.
21. Mayorga Coffee website, **www.mayorgacoffee.com**; Darren Dahl, "Senor Coffee Helping to Grow a Better Bean," *Inc.*, **www.inc.com/magazine/201206/darren-dahl/senor-coffee-inc-5000-update.html**.
22. "Facts about Working Women," *Women Employed*, **www.womenemployed.org/index.php?id=20**.
23. Haya El Nasser, Gregory Korte, and Paul Overberg, "308.7 Million," *USA Today*, December 22, 2010, p. 1A.
24. Liz Welch, "Wolfgang Puck: From Potato Peeler to Gourmet-Pizza Tycoon," *Inc.*, October 2009, pp. 87–88; "Restaurants," Wolfgang Puck, **www.wolfgangpuck.com/restaurants**.
25. "About the Hershey Company," The Hershey Company, **www.thehersheycompany.com/**.
26. Fortune, "Largest U.S. Corporations," *Fortune 167*(7), May 20, 2013, pp. F1–F26.; Anthony Bianco and Wendy Zellner, "Is Wal-Mart Too Powerful?" *BusinessWeek*, October 6, 2003, pp. 100–110; "Wal Mart Stores, Inc. Business Information, Profile, and History," **http://companies.jrank.org/pages/4725/Wal-Mart-Stores-Inc.html**; "Investors," Wal-Mart Corporate, **http://investors.walmartstores.com/phoenix.zhtml?c=112761&p=irol-irhome**; Mike Duke, "CEO Letter," *2012 Annual Report*, **www.walmartstores.com/sites/annual-report/2012/CEOletter.aspx**.
27. "Samuel Robson Walton," *Bloomberg*, **http://topics.bloomberg.com/samuel-robson-walton/**.
28. "Stopping SOPA," *The Economist*, January 21, 2012, p. 33.
29. "The 2011 World's Most Ethical Companies," *Ethisphere*, 2011, Q1, pp. 37–43.
30. Isabelle Maignon, Tracy L. Gonzalez-Padron, G. Tomas, M. Hult, and O.C. Ferrell, "Stakeholder Orientation: Development and

Testing of a Framework for Socially Responsible Marketing," *Journal of Strategic Marketing* 19, no. 4 (July 2011), pp. 313–338.

31. Joel Holland, "Save the World, Make a Million," *Entrepreneur*, April 2010, **www.entrepreneur.com/magazine/entrepreneur/2010/april/205556.html**.

CHAPTER 2

1. Kimberly Blanton, "Creating a Culture of Compliance," *CFO*, July/August 2011, pp. 19–21.
2. Zynga.org website, **http://zynga.org/**; Eric Chang Ding, "Executive Profile: Laura Pincus Hartman, Chairwoman of the Board of Directors for the School of Choice Education Organization," *Chicago Tribune*, July 30, 2012, **http://articles.chicagotribune.com/2012-07-30/business/ct-biz-0730-executive-profile-hartman-20120730_1_zynga-virtual-goods-board-chairwoman**; Ellen McGirt, "Meet the League of Extraordinary Women: 60 Influencers Who Are Changing the World," *Fast Company*, June 18, 2012, **www.fastcompany.com/1839862/meet-league-extraordinary-women-60-influencers-who-are-changing-world**.
3. "Medicare Fraud Strike Force Charges 107 Individuals for Approximately $452 Million in False Billing," *The United States Department of Justice*, May 2, 2012, **www.justice.gov/opa/pr/2012/May/12-ag-568.html**.
4. Ronald Alsop, "Corporate Scandals Hit Home," *The Wall Street Journal*, February 19, 2004, **http://online.wsj.com/article/SB107715182807433462.html**.
5. Ruth Simon and Victoria McGrane, "Wells Penalty: $85 Million," *The Wall Street Journal*, July 21, 2011, p. C3.
6. O.C. Ferrell, John Fraedrich, and Linda Ferrell, *Business Ethics: Ethical Decision Making and Cases*, 8th ed. (Mason, OH: South-Western Cengage Learning, 2011), p. 7.
7. Christian Berthelsen, "Dimon's Pay Cut by 50%," *The Wall Street Journal*, January 16, 2013, **http://online.wsj.com/article/SB1000142412788732396830457824538173450958O.html**.
8. Cameron McWhirter, "Ex-New Orleans Mayor Indicted for Corruption," *The Wall Street Journal*, January 19–20, 2013, p. A6.
9. Reed Albergotti and Vanessa O'Connell, "Cyclist Swerves to Fix Image," *The Wall Street Journal*, January 15, 2013, pp. A1, A14.
10. Ferrell, Fraedrich, and Ferrell, *Business Ethics*.
11. Kimberly Blanton, "Creating a Culture of Compliance," *CFO*, July/August 2011, pp. 19–21.
12. Ethics Resource Center, *2011 National Business Ethics Survey® : Ethics in Transition* (Arlington, VA: Ethics Resource Center, 2012).
13. Bobby White, "The New Workplace Rules: No Video Watching," *The New York Times*, March 3, 2008, p. B1.
14. Laura Petrecca, "Bullying in Workplace Is Common, Hard to Fix," *USA Today*, December 28, 2010, pp. 1B–2B.
15. Peter Lattman, "Boeing's Top Lawyer Spotlights Company's Ethical Lapses," *The Wall Street Journal*, Law Blog, January 30, 2006, **http://blogs.wsj.com/law/2006/01/31/boeings-top-lawyer-rips-into-his-company/**.
16. Stephen J. Dunn, "Lawyer Charged with Tax Evasion for Paying Personal Expenses from Firm," *Forbes*, July 28, 2011, **www.forbes.com/sites/stephendunn/2011/07/28/lawyer-charged-with-tax-evasion-for-paying-personal-expenses-from-firm/**.
17. "Proper Use of Company, Customer, and Supplier Resources," Boeing, November 19, 2009, **www.boeing.com/companyoffices/aboutus/ethics/pro10.pdf**.
18. Barbara Kiviat, "A Bolder Approach to Credit-Agency Rating Reform," *Time*, September 18, 2009, **http://business.time.com/2009/09/18/a-bolder-approach-to-credit-rating-agency-reform/** (accessed January 28, 2010).
19. Reuters, "Rajat Gupta's Lawyer: Government 'Wildly Expanding' Case against Ex-Goldman Director," *Huffington Post*, February 7, 2010, **www.huffingtonpost.com/2012/02/07/rajat-gupta_n_1261313.html**.
20. "Corruption Perceptions Index 2009," Transparency International, **www.transparency.org/policy_research/surveys_indices/cpi/2009/cpi_2009_table**.
21. "Employee Theft: The Largest Source of Shrink in North America," *PI Newswire*, October 18, 2011, **www.pinewswire.net/article/employeetheftthe-largest-source-of-shrink-innorth-america/**.
22. Nathalie Tadena, "Pool Agrees to Settle FTC Charges of Anticompetitive Tactics," *The Wall Street Journal*, November 21, 2011, **http://online.wsj.com/article/BT-CO-20111121-709935.html**.
23. Ibid.
24. David Voreacos, Alex Nussbaum, and Greg Farrell, "Johnson & Johnson's Quality Catastrophe," *Bloomberg Businessweek*, March 31, 2011, **www.businessweek.com/magazine/content/11_15/b4223064555570.htm**.
25. "Campaign Warns about Drugs from Canada," *CNN*, February 5, 2004, **www.cnn.com**; Gardiner Harris and Monica Davey, "FDA Begins Push to End Drug Imports," *The New York Times*, January 23, 2004, p. C1.
26. Lara Salahi, "FDA Appeals Block on Cigarette Warning Label," *ABC News*, November 30, 2011, **http://abcnews.go.com/Health/Wellness/fda-appealsblock-cigarette-warning-labels/story?id=15059707**.
27. Ethics Resource Center, *2005 National Business Ethics Survey* (Washington, DC: Ethics Resource Center, 2005), p. 43.
28. Thomas M. Jones, "Ethical Decision Making by Individuals in Organizations: An Issue-Contingent Model," *Academy of Management Review* 2 (April 1991), pp. 371–73.
29. Sir Adrian Cadbury, "Ethical Managers Make Their Own Rules," *Harvard Business Review* 65 (September–October 1987), p. 72.
30. Associated Press, "NFL Alleges Saints Issued Bounties on Foes," *The Wall Street Journal*, March 2, 2012, **http://online.wsj.com/article/SB1000142405297020375370457725773288314 8466.html**; Mike Freeman, "Saints Took Common Practice of Bounties to New, Dangerous Level," *CBS Sports*, March 5, 2012, **www.cbssports.com/nfl/story/17595418/saints-took-common-practice-of-a-bounty-system-to-new-dangerous-level**; "NFL Bans Saints' Payton a Year for 'Bounties'; Williams Out, Too," *NFL*, March 21, 2012, **www.nfl.com/news/story/09000d5d827c0dd9/article/nfl-suspends-saints-coach-payton-for-one-year-without-pay?module=HP11_breaking_news**; Adam Schefter and the Associated Press, "Joe Vitt to Coach New Orleans Saints," *ESPN NFL*, April 13, 2012, **http://espn.go.com/nfl/story/_/id/7806938/joe-vitt-tabbed-coach-new-orleans-saints-sean-payton-absence**; Kevin Clark, "Appeals Panel Lifts Saints Suspensions," *The Wall Street Journal*, September 7, 2012, **http://online.wsj.com/article/SB10000872396390443819404577637852187484014.html**.

31. Ferrell, Fraedrich, and Ferrell, *Business Ethics,* pp. 174–75.

32. Ethics Resource Center, *2009 National Business Ethics Survey* (Washington, DC: Ethics Resource Center, 2009), p. 41.

33. "The 2010 World's Most Ethical Companies—Company Profile: Granite Construction," *Ethisphere,* Q1, p. 33.

34. Ethics Resource Center, *2011 National Business Ethics Survey®,* p. 23.

35. Skadden, Arps, Slate, Meagher & Flom LLP & Affiliates, *The Dodd Frank Act: Commentary and Insights,* July 12, 2010, **www.skadden.com/sites/default/files/ckeditor/files/Skadden_Insights_Special_Edition_Dodd-Frank_Act1.pdf**; Ethics Resource Center, *2011 National Business Ethics Survey®,* p. 43.

36. Ferrell, Fraedrich, and Ferrell, *Business Ethics,* p. 13.

37. "Trust in the Workplace: 2010 Ethics & Workplace Survey," Deloitte LLP, **www.deloitte.com/assets/Dcom-UnitedStates/Local%20Assets/Documents/us_2010_Ethics_and_Workplace_Survey_report_071910.pdf.**

38. Archie B. Carroll, "The Pyramid of Corporate Social Responsibility: Toward the Moral Management of Organizational Stakeholders," *Business Horizons* 34 (July/August 1991), p. 42.

39. Bryan Walsh, "Why Green Is the New Red, White and Blue," *Time,* April 28, 2008, p. 46.

40. Adam Shriver, "Not Grass-Fed, But at Least Pain-Free," *The New York Times,* February 18, 2010, **www.nytimes.com/2010/02/19/opinion/19shriver.html?scp=4&sq=animal%20rights&st=cse.**

41. Alan Beattie, "Countries Rush to Restrict Trade in Basic Foods," *Financial Times,* April 2, 2008, p. 1.

42. Bill Roth, "Marketing Opportunity: Consumers Want Green and Health Explanations from Companies on Their Brand Claims," *Earth 2017,* April 1, 2011, **www.earth2017.com/best-practices/marketing-opportunity-consumers-want-green-and-health-explanations-from-companies-on-their-brand-claims/.**

43. "2010 World's Most Ethical Companies," *Ethisphere,* **http://ethisphere.com/wme2010/.**

44. Indra Nooyi, "The Responsible Company," *The Economist, The World in 2008 Special Edition,* March 2008, p. 132.

45. Ferrell, Fraedrich, and Ferrell, *Business Ethics,* pp. 13–19.

46. Ann Zimmerman, "U.S. Charges Bass Pro Shops with Racial Bias," *The Wall Street Journal,* September 22, 2011, **http://online.wsj.com/article/SB10001424053111904563904576585090889465336.html.**

47. Amy Schatz, "Phone-Bill 'Cramming' Takes a Toll, Study Finds," *The Wall Street Journal,* July 14, 2011, **http://online.wsj.com/article/SB10001424052702304911104576443863004059774.html.**

48. Todd Littman, "Win-Win Emissions Reductions Strategies," Victoria Transport Policy Institute, **www.vtpi.org/wwclimate.pdf.**

49. Lauren Etter, "Earth Day: 36 Years on, Plenty of Concerns Remain," *The Wall Street Journal,* April 22–23, 2006, p. A7.

50. Cornelia Dean, "Drugs Are in the Water, Does It Matter?" *The New York Times,* April 3, 2007, HEALTH, **www.nytimes.com/2007/04/03/science/earth/03water.html?_r=1&scp=55&sq=%22cornelia+dean%22&st=nyt&oref=slogin.**

51. Kitt Doucette, "The Plastic Bag Wars," *Rolling Stone,* July 25, 2011, **www.rollingstone.com/politics/news/the-plastic-bag-wars-20110725.**

52. Whole Foods, "Whole Foods to Sack Disposable Plastic Grocery Bags," January 22, 2008, **http://media.wholefoodsmarket.com/news/whole-foods-market-to-sack-disposable-plastic-grocery-bags-by-earth-day/.**

53. Josh Glasser, "T. Boone Pickens on Natural Gas: You Can't Beat it," *Fortune,* July 14, 2009, **http://money.cnn.com/2009/07/14/news/economy/pickens_natural_gas.fortune/**; Brian Merchant, "The US Imports $1.5 Billion Barrels of Oil a Year from 'Dangerous or Unstable' Nations," Treehugger.com, January 14, 2010, **www.treehugger.com/files/2010/01/us-imports-1-5-billionbarrels-oil-year-dangerous-unstablenations.php**; "US Spent Over $30 Billion for Foreign Oil in April," *BusinessWire,* May 17, 2010, **www.businesswire.com/news/home/20100517006122/en/U.S.-Spent-30-Billion-Foreign-Oil-April.**

54. Paul Sonne, "Unilever Takes Palm Oil in Hand," *The Wall Street Journal,* April 24, 2012, **http://online.wsj.com/article/SB10001424052702303978104577362160223536388.html**; "How it works," *Green Palm Sustainability,* **www.greenpalm.org/en/what-is-greenpalm/how-it-works**; "Unilever's Europe-wide palm oil covered sustainably," Unilever, July 4, 2010, **www.unilever.com/mediacentre/pressreleases/2010/UnileversEuropewidepalmoilcoveredsustainably.asp.**

55. Nathan Myhrvold, "Energy Subsidies Stymie Wind, Solar Innovation," *Bloomberg Businessweek,* November 27, 2011, **www.bloomberg.com/news/2011-11-27/energy-subsidies-stymie-wind-solar-innovation-nathan-myhrvold.html**; Michael Scherer, "The Solyndra Syndrome," *Time,* October 10, 2011, pp. 42–45.

56. "Wal-Mart's Motive Is No Secret: Going Green Saves It Money," *Los Angeles Times,* June 4, 2011, **http://articles.latimes.com/2011/jun/04/business/la-fi-walmart-green-20110604.**

57. Jim Rogers, "Point of View: A New Model for Energy Efficiency," *The News & Observer,* February 19, 2008, **www.newsobserver.com/print/tuesday/opinion/story/951188.html.**

58. "GreenChoice: The #1 Green Power Program in America," Austin Energy, **www.austinenergy.com/Energy%20Efficiency/Programs/Green%20Choice/index.htm.**

59. "Certification," Home Depot, **https://corporate.homedepot.com/CorporateResponsibility/Environment/WoodPurchasing/Pages/Certification.aspx.**

60. Mark Calvey, "Profile: Safeway's Grants Reflect Its People," *San Francisco Business Times,* July 14, 2003, **http://sanfrancisco.bizjournals.com/sanfrancisco/stories/2003/07/14/focus9.html.**

61. Jim Puzzanghera, "Fed Brightens Projections for Unemployment Rate in 2013," *Los Angeles Times,* December 12, 2012, **http://articles.latimes.com/2012/dec/12/business/la-fi-mo-federal-reserve-economic-projection-bernanke-20121212.**

62. "Occupy Wall Street," Case written for the Daniels Fund Ethics Initiative, **http://danielsethics.mgt.unm.edu/pdf/Occupy%20Wall%20Street%20DI.pdf.**

63. James R. Hagerty, "Caterpillar Closes Plant in Canada after Lockout," *The Wall Street Journal,* February 4–5, 2012, p. B1.

64. Peter Cappelli, "Why Companies Aren't Getting the Employees They Need," *The Wall Street Journal,* October 24, 2011, pp. R1, R6.

65. Christie Garton, "Corporations Add Their Know-How to Charitable Efforts," *USA Today,* July 25, 2011, **http://usatoday30.usatoday.com/money/companies/management/2011-07-22-corporate-giving-chronicle-of-philanthropy_n.htm**; REDcard, **https://redcard.target.com/redcard/rc_main.jsp.**

66. "100 Best Companies to Work For," *CNNMoney,* **http://money.cnn.com/magazines/fortune/bestcompanies/2011/snapshots/2.html.**

67. "Who Really Pays for CSR Initiatives," *Environmental Leader,* February 15, 2008, **www.environmentalleader.com/2008/02/**

15/who-really-pays-for-csr-initiatives/; "Global Fund," www.joinred.com/globalfund; Reena Jana, "The Business of Going Green," *Businessweek Online,* June 22, 2007, www.businessweek.com/innovate/content/jun2007/id20070622_491833.htm?chan=search.

68. M.P. McQueen, "Agency Misses Chance to Curb Lead in Jewelry," *The Wall Street Journal,* February 12, 2008, p. D1.
69. "2ND UPDATE: AT&T Hit by iPhone Costs, T-Mobile Breakup Fee," *The Wall Street Journal,* January 26, 2012, http://online.wsj.com/article/BT-CO-20120126-713581.html.
70. Maureen Dorney, "Congress Passes Federal Anti-Spam Law: Preempts Most State Anti-Spam Laws," *DLA Piper,* December 3, 2003, http://franchiseagreements.com/global/publications/detail.aspx?pub=622.
71. Elizabeth Alterman, "As Kids Go Online, Identity Theft Claims More Victims," *CNBC,* October 10, 2011, www.cnbc.com/id/44583556/As_Kids_Go_Online_Identity_Theft_Claims_More_Victims.
72. Abby Ellin, "F.T.C. Updates Online Privacy Regulations For Kids," *ABC News*, August 3, 2012, http://abcnews.go.com/Business/ftc-update-online-privacy-regulations-kids/story?id=16916132#.UKaX62c8eVA; Anton Troianovski, "New Rules on Kids' Web Ads," *The Wall Street Journal,* August 1, 2012, http://online.wsj.com/article/SB10000872396390444130304577561411341883468.html; Somini Sengupta, "Update Urged on Children's Online Privacy," *The New York Times,* September 15, 2011, www.nytimes.com/2011/09/16/technology/ftc-proposes-updates-to-law-on-childrens-online-privacy.html?_r=0; Natasha Singer, "A Trail of Clicks, Culminating in Conflict," *The New York Times,* November 5, 2012, www.nytimes.com/2012/11/06/technology/silicon-valley-objects-to-online-privacy-rule-proposals-for-children.html?pagewanted=all&_r=0.
73. Joelle Tessler, "Disney's Playdom to Pay $3M to Settle Kids Privacy Case," *The Wall Street Journal,* May 13, 2011, p. 3B.
74. Jean Eaglesham and Ashby Jones, "Whistle-blower Bounties Pose Challenges," *The Wall Street Journal,* December 13, 2010, pp. C1, C3.
75. "Office of Financial Research," U.S. Department of Treasury, www.treasury.gov/initiatives/ofr/Pages/default.aspx; "Initiatives: Financial Stability Oversight Council," U.S. Department of Treasury, www.treasury.gov/initiatives/Pages/FSOC-index.aspx.

CHAPTER 3

1. Tim Kelly, "Squash the Caterpillar," *Forbes,* April 21, 2008, p. 136.
2. Julie Jargon, "Subway Runs Past McDonald's Chain," *The Wall Street Journal,* March 9, 2011, p. B4; Subway, http://world.subway.com/Countries/frmMainPage.aspx?CC=CAN.
3. "Starbucks Coffee International," Starbucks, www.starbucks.com/bsusiness/international-stores.
4. Elisabeth Sullivan, "Choose Your Words Wisely," *Marketing News,* February 15, 2008, p. 22.
5. Matthew Boyle, "Unilever: Taking on the World, One Stall at a Time," *Bloomberg Businessweek,* January 7–January 13, 2013, pp. 18–20.
6. Sullivan, "Choose Your Words Wisely."
7. Michelle Yun and Kathy Chu, "Philippines May Answer Call," *USA Today,* January 10, 2011, pp. 1B–2B.
8. "U.S. International Transactions: Fourth Quarter and Year 2012," U.S. Department of Commerce Bureau of Labor Economic Analysis, www.bea.gov/newsreleases/international/transactions/transnewsrelease.htm.
9. D. Roberts and D. Rocks, "China: Let a Thousand Brands Bloom," *Bloomberg Businessweek,* October 16, 2005, www.businessweek.com/stories/2005-10-16/china-let-a-thousand-brands-bloom.
10. Joseph O'Reilly, "Global Logistics: In China, Bigger Bull's-eye Better," *Inbound Logistics,* April 2008, p. 26.
11. "U.S. International Transactions: Fourth Quarter and Year 2012," U.S. Department of Commerce Bureau of Labor Economic Analysis, www.bea.gov/newsreleases/international/transactions/transnewsrelease.htm.
12. Ibid.
13. Keith Bradsher, "GM Plans to Develop Electric Cars with China," *The New York Times,* September 20, 2011, www.nytimes.com/2011/09/21/business/global/gm-plans-to-develop-electric-cars-with-chinese-automaker.html.
14. Brett Forrest, "The Skype Killers of Belarus," *Bloomberg Businessweek,* August 27–September 2, 2012, pp. 62–65; Brian Blum, "Top 10 iPhone apps from Israel," Israel 21c, http://techcrunch.com/2010/12/02/viber-iphone/; Viber website, www.viber.com/; Jordan Crook, "With 70 Million Registered Users, Viber Brings Beta Data Apps to Blackberry, Windows Phone," *TechCrunch,* May 8, 2012, http://techcrunch.com/2012/05/08/with-70-million-registered-users-viber-brings-beta-apps-to-blackberry-windows-phone/.
15. Amol Sharma and Prasanta Sahu, *The Wall Street Journal,* January 11, 2012, http://online.wsj.com/article/SB10001424052970204257504577152342214405180.html; Indranil Bose, Shilpi Banerjee, and Edo de Vries Robbe, "Wal-Mart and Bharti: Transforming Retail in India," *Harvard Business Review,* August 27, 2009, http://hbr.org/product/wal-mart-and-bhartitransforming-retail-in-india/an/HKU845-PDF-ENG.
16. O'Reilly, "Global Logistics: New Tax Treaty Raises U.S. Stakes in Belgium's Lowlands," p. 24.
17. Amol Sharma, "India to Western Tech Firms: To Sell It Here, Build It Here," *The Wall Street Journal,* January 8, 2013, p. B1; Amol Sharma, Megha Bahree, and Paul Beckett, "Rising Risk: Foreign Firms Sense Hostility in India," *The Wall Street Journal,* March 30, 2012, p. B1.
18. Business Software Alliance, *Eighth Annual BSA Global Software 2010 Piracy Study,* http://global.bsa.org/globalpiracy2008/index.html.
19. "USA: President Obama Should Take the Lead on Lifting Embargo against Cuba," Amnesty International, September 2, 2009, www.amnesty.org/en/for-media/press-releases/usa-president-obama-should-take-lead-lifting-embargo-against-cuba-200909; Kitty Bean Yancey, "Back to Cuba: 'People-to-People Trips' Get the Green Light," *USA Today,* August 4, 2011, p. 4A.
20. Kitty Bean Yancey and Laura Bly, "Door May Be Inching Open for Tourism," *USA Today,* February 20, 2008, p. A5; Sue Kirchhoff and Chris Woodyard, "Cuba Trade Gets 'New Opportunity'," *USA Today,* February 20, 2008, p. B1.
21. Ryan Tracy, "Washington to Hit Beijing with Solar-Panel Tariffs," *The Wall Street Journal,* November 7, 2012, http://online.wsj.com/article/SB10001424127887323894704578105123838714546.html.
22. Malavika Sharma, "India's Plague of Knockoffs," *Bloomberg Businessweek,* May 7, 2012–May 13, 2012, pp. 28–29; "Counterfeit, Fake and Smuggled Goods Impacting 'Brand India' (Comment)," *Daily News,* July 8 2012, http://india.nydailynews.com/business/d4b61258b418e1ad19d2d91f0978b8f2/counterfeit-fake-and-smuggled-goods-impacting-brand-india-comment; Shilpa Cannan, "Counterfeit Drugs Targeted by

Technology in India," *BBC News*, October 11, 2011, **www.bbc.co.uk/news/business-15208595.**

23. Julie Bennett, "Product Pitfalls Proliferate in Global Cultural Maze," *The Wall Street Journal*, May 14, 2001, p. B11.
24. Ann Blackman/Moscow, "Moscow's Big Mac Attack," *Time*, February 5, 1990, **www.time.com/time/magazine/article/0,9171,969321,00.html.**
25. "Slogans Gone Bad," Joe-ks, **www.joe-ks.com/archives_apr2004/slogans_gone_bad.htm.**
26. David Ricks, *Blunders in International Business*, 4th ed. (Malden, MA: Blackwell Publishing, 2006), p. 70.
27. J. Bonasia, "For Web, Global Reach Is Beauty—and Challenge," *Investor's Business Daily*, June 13, 2001, p. A6.
28. Chris Nutall, "Lenovo knocks HP Off Computer Top Spot," *Financial Times*, October 11, 2012, **www.ft.com/cms/s/0/29767c00-1324-11e2-bca6-00144feabdc0.html#axzz2JbNSvRkX.**
29. World Trade Organization, "What Is the WTO?" **www.wto.org/english/thewto_e/whatis_e/whatis_e.htm.**
30. Joe McDonald, "China Files Trade Case against U.S.," *USA Today*, September 18, 2012, **http://usatoday30.usatoday.com/USCP/PNI/Business/2012-09-18-ChinaUSTrade-917_ST_U.htm.**
31. The CIA, *The World Factbook*, **https://www.cia.gov/library/publications/the-world-factbook/rankorder/rankorderguide.html.**
32. "Trade in Goods (Imports, Exports and Trade Balance) with Canada," U.S. Bureau of the Census, **www.census.gov/foreign-trade/balance/c1220.html;** "North America: Canada," *CIA—WorldFactbook*, **https://www.cia.gov/library/publications/the-world-factbook/geos/ca.html.**
33. "America's Biggest Partners," *CNBC*, **www.cnbc.com/id/31064179?slide=11.**
34. The CIA, *The World Factbook*, **https://www.cia.gov/library/publications/the-world-factbook/rankorder/rankorderguide.html.**
35. "Trade in Goods with Mexico," U.S. Bureau of the Census: Foreign Trade, **www.census.gov/foreign-trade/balance/c2010.html.**
36. "Special Report: Mexico," *The Economist*, November 24, 2012, pp. 3–16.
37. "A Tale of Two Mexicos: North and South," *The Economist*, April 26, 2008, pp. 53–54.
38. Josh Mitchell, "U.S. Jump-Starts Bid to End Truck Dispute with Mexico," *The Wall Street Journal*, January 7, 2011, **http://online.wsj.com/article/SB1000142405274870441510457606 5924125822128.html;** Elizabeth Williamson, "U.S., Mexico Agree to Settle Truck Feud," *The Wall Street Journal*, March 4, 2011, **http://online.wsj.com/article/SB10001424052748703300904576178511087875924.html.**
39. Geri Smith and Cristina Lindblad, "Mexico: Was NAFTA Worth It?" *BusinessWeek*, December 23, 2003, **www.businessweek.com/magazine/content/03_51/b3863008.htm.**
40. "Europein12Lessons," **http://europa.eu/abc/12lessons/lesson_2/index_en.htm;** "EU Backs Croatia to Join in July as 28th Member State," *BBC*, March 26, 2013, **www.bbc.co.uk/news/world-europe-21937076.**
41. "Country Comparison: GDP (Purchasing Power Parity)," *The World Factbook*, **https://www.cia.gov/library/publications/the-world-factbook/rankorder/2001rank.html.**
42. Stanley Reed, with Ariane Sains, David Fairlamb, and Carol Matlack, "The Euro: How Damaging a Hit?" *BusinessWeek*, September 29, 2003, p. 63; "The Single Currency," *CNN*, **www.cnn.com/SPECIALS/2000/eurounion/story/currency/.**
43. Stephen Fidler and Jacob Bunge, "NYSE Deal Nears Collapse," *The Wall Street Journal*, January 11, 2012, pp. A1, A9.
44. Abigail Moses, "Greek Contagion Concern Spurs European Sovereign Default Risk to Record," *Bloomberg*, April 26, 2010, **www.bloomberg.com/news/2010-04-26/greek-contagion-concern-spurs-european-sovereign-default-risk-to-record.html.**
45. James G. Neuger and Joe Brennan, "Ireland Weighs Aid as EU Spars over Debt-Crisis Remedy," *Bloomberg*, **www.bloomberg.com/news/2010-11-16/ireland-discusses-financial-bailout-as-eu-struggles-to-defuse-debt-crisis.html.**
46. "EU Raises Flags over French, Italian, Spanish Economies," *Reuters Canada*, April 10, 2013, **http://ca.reuters.com/article/businessNews/idCABRE9390HI20130410?pageNumber=1&virtualBrandChannel=0.**
47. "Powerhouse Deutschland," *Bloomberg Businessweek*, January 3, 2011, 93; Alan S. Blinder, "The Euro Zone's German Crisis," *The Wall Street Journal*, **http://online.wsj.com/article/SB10001424052970203430404577094313707190708.html.**
48. "About APEC," Asia-Pacific Economic Cooperation, **www.apec.org/about-us/about-apec.aspx.**
49. Jack Perkowski, "Managing the Dragon's 2013 China Predictions," *Forbes*, January 7, 2013, **www.forbes.com/sites/jackperkowski/2013/01/07/managing-the-dragons-2013-china-predictions/.**
50. James T. Areddy, James Hookway, John Lyons, and Marcus Walker, "U.S. Slump Takes Toll across Globe," *The Wall Street Journal*, April 3, 2008, p. A1; Pam Woodall, "The New Champions," *The Economist*, November 15, 2008, p. 55; Matt Jenkins, "A Really Inconvenient Truth," *Miller-McCune*, April/May 2008, p. 42.
51. Dexter Roberts, "Corporate China's Black Hole of Debt," *Bloomberg Businessweek*, November 19–November 22, 2012, pp. 15–16.
52. Elizabeth Holmes, "U.S. Apparel Retailers Turn Their Gaze beyond China," *The Wall Street Journal*, June 16, 2010, p. B1.
53. "Overview," Association of Southeast Asian Nations, **www.aseansec.org/64.htm.**
54. Wang Yan, "ASEAN Works to 'Act as Unison' on Global Stage," *China Daily*, November 19, 2011, **www.chinadaily.com.cn/cndy/2011-11/19/content_14122972.htm.**
55. ASEAN website, **www.aseansec.org/.**
56. "Common Effective Preferential Tariff (CEPT)," The Malaysia Government's Official Portal, **www.malaysia.gov.my/EN/Relevant%20Topics/IndustryInMalaysia/Business/BusinessAndEBusiness/BusinessAndAgreement/CEPT/Pages/CEPT.aspx.**
57. R.C., "No Brussels Sprouts in Bali," *The Economist*, November 18, 2011, **www.economist.com/blogs/banyan/2011/11/asean-summits.**
58. Eric Bellman, "Asia Seeks Integration Despite EU's Woes," *The Wall Street Journal*, July 22, 2011, p. A9.
59. David J. Lynch, "The IMF Is . . . Tired Fund Struggles to Reinvent Itself," *USA Today*, April 19, 2006, p. B1.
60. Jeff Chu, "Bridging the Gap," *Fast Company*, July/August 2012, pp. 88–95; Barbara Thau, "Can Uniqlo's Clever Clothes Refashion the U.S. Retail Market?" *The Daily Finance*, October 29, 2011, **www.dailyfinance.com/2011/10/29/can-uniqlos-clever-clothes-refashion-the-u-s-retail-market/;** Stephanie Clifford, "A U.S. Retailer's Retreat, a Japanese Chain Sees an Opening," *New York Times*, May 22, 2012, **www.nytimes.com/2012/05/23/business/uniqlo-sees-room-for-growth-in-the-us.html?_r=1&pagewanted=all.**

61. Walter B. Wriston, "Ever Heard of Insourcing?" Commentary, *The Wall Street Journal,* March 24, 2004, p. A20.

62. "Here, There and Everywhere," A Special Report, *The Economist,* January 19, 2013, pp. 1–20.

63. Barclays Wealth, **www.census.gov/hhes/w/cpstables/032009/hhinc/new01_009.htm**; Nick Heath, "Banks: Offshoring, Not Outsourcing," *BusinessWeek,* March 10, 2009, **www.businessweek.com/globalbiz/content/mar2009/gb20090310_619247.htm**.

64. Kejal Vyas, "Venezuela's PdVSA Forms Joint Venture with Brazil's Odebrecht," *The Wall Street Journal,* September 29, 2011, **http://online.wsj.com/article/BT-CO-20110929-710025.html**.

65. Matt O'Sullivan, "Virgin Blue Mines Fly-In, Fly-Out Boom," *The Sydney Morning Herald,* January 10, 2011, **www.smh.com.au/business/virgin-blue-minesflyin-flyout-boom-20110110-19kb3.html**; Matt O'Sullivan, "Virgin Blue Hooks Up with Regional Skywest," *The Sydney Morning Herald,* January 11, 2011, **www.smh.com.au/business/virgin-blue-hooks-up-withregional-skywest-20110110-19l7d.html**.

66. Sharon Silk Carty, "Ford Plans to Park Jaguar, Land Rover with Tata Motors," *USA Today,* March 26, 2008, p. B1.

67. Guo Changdong and Ren Ruqin, "Nestlé CEO Visits Tianjin," *China Daily,* August 12, 2010, **www.chinadaily.com.cn/m/tianjin/e/2010-08/12/content_11146560.htm**; "Employee Profiles," Nestlé, **www.nestle-ea.com/en/jobssite/beingatnestleear/Pages/EmployessProfiles.aspx**.

68. O.C. Ferrell, John Fraedrich, and Linda Ferrell, *Business Ethics,* 6th ed. (Boston: Houghton Mifflin, 2005), pp. 227–30.

69. Export.gov, **www.export.gov/about/index.asp**; CIBER Web, **http://CIBERWEB.msu.edu**.

CHAPTER 4

1. Maggie Overfelt, "Start-Me-Up: How the Garage Became a Legendary Place to Rev Up Ideas," *Fortune Small Business,* September 1, 2003, **http://money.cnn.com/magazines/fsb/fsb_archive/2003/09/01/350784/index.htm**.

2. Mark Henricks, B2B Service, Special Franchise Advertising Section, *Inc.,* February 2012; Stratus Building Solutions website, **www.stratusbuildingsolutions.com/**.

3. Judith Ohikuare, "Let's Get Physical," *Inc.,* September 2012, **www.inc.com/magazine/201209/judith-ohikuare/dana-salazar-of-vital-farms-free-range-chicken-farm.html**; "Vital Farms," *The Cornucopia Institute,* **www.cornucopia.org/organic-egg-scorecard/egg_profiles/FarmID_21.html**; Vital Farms website, **http://vitalfarms.com/**; "Vital Farms Sets the National Standard for Humane, Environmentally Responsible Egg Farming," *PR Newswire,* **www.prnewswire.com/news-releases/vital-farms-sets-the-national-standard-for-humane-environmentally-responsible-egg-farming-134862058.html**.

4. Christian Sylt, "Cirque du Soleil May Leap for New Partner," *The Telegraph,* January 30, 2011, **www.telegraph.co.uk/finance/newsbysector/banksandfinance/privateequity/8290380/Cirque-du-Soleil-may-leap-for-new-partner.html#**.

5. "The 2011 Global 100: Most Profits Per Partner," *The American Lawyer,* March 12, 2010, **www.law.com/jsp/tal/PubArticleTAL.jsp?id=1202514395169**.

6. Laura Petrecca, "A Partner Can Give Your Business Shelter or a Storm," *USA Today,* October 9, 2009, **www.usatoday.com/money/smallbusiness/startup/week4-partnerships.htm**.

7. Thomson Reuters, "2012 Top 100 Firms," *Accounting Today,* 2012, p. 15; Clarissa French, "Diversification Accounts for BKD Revenue Results," *sbj.net,* March 5, 2010, **http://sbj.net/main.asp?SectionID=48&SubSectionID=108&ArticleID=86481**; "About BKD," BKD website, **www.bkd.com/about/AtaGlance.htm**.

8. Alexandra Berzon and Kate O'Keefe, "A Partners' Fight Erupts at Wynn," *The Wall Street Journal,* January 13, 2012, **http://online.wsj.com/article/SB10001424052970204542404577156491314541590.html**.

9. *Warren Buffett's Berkshire Hathaway Letter to Shareholders,* **www.berkshirehathaway.com/letters/2010ltr.pdf**.

10. Vita Coco website, **http://vitacoco.com**; Michael Kirban and Reshma Yaqub, "The Way I Work," *Inc.,* July/August 2012, pp. 102–104; Mike Esterl, "The Beverage Wars Move to Coconuts," *The Wall Street Journal,* February 11, 2012, **http://online.wsj.com/article/SB10001424052970203315804577207313086829188.html**.

11. Andrea Murphy, "America's Largest Private Companies 2012," *Forbes,* November 28, 2012, **www.forbes.com/sites/andreamurphy/2012/11/28/americas-largest-private-companies-2012/**.

12. Ibid.

13. Deborah Orr, "The Secret World of Mars," *Forbes,* April 28, 2008, **www.forbes.com/2008/04/28/billionaires-mars-wrigley-biz-billies-cz_do_0428marsfamily.html**.

14. Jay Hart, "Not His Father's CEO," *Yahoo! Sports,* January 22, 2010, **http://sports.yahoo.com/nascar/news?slug=jh-france012209**.

15. Scott DeCarlo, "The World's Leading Companies," *Forbes,* April 18, 2012, **www.forbes.com/sites/scottdecarlo/2012/04/18/the-worlds-biggest-companies/**.

16. Henry Blodget, "Facebook Bankers Secretly Cut Facebook's Revenue Estimates in Middle of IPO Roadshow," *Yahoo! Finance,* **http://finance.yahoo.com/blogs/daily-ticker/facebook-bankers-secretly-cut-facebook-revenue-estimates-middle-133648905.html**; Olivia Oran and Alistair Barr, "Facebook prices at top of range in landmark IPO," *Reuters,* May 17, 2012, **www.reuters.com/article/2012/05/17/us-facebook-idUSBRE84G14Q20120517**; Jenny Strasburg and Jean Eaglesham, "NASDAQ Faces Facebook Fine," *The Wall Street Journal*, February 5, 2013, **http://online.wsj.com/article/SB10001424127887324761004578286200951471148.html**.

17. Niraj Sheth and Jeff McCracken, "RCN Is Sold to Firm in $535 Million Deal," March 5, 2010, **http://online.wsj.com/article/SB10001424052748703915204575103362665861820.html?KEYWORDS=private+equity+buy+out**.

18. O.C. Ferrell, John Fraedrich, and Linda Ferrell, *Business Ethics: Ethical Decision Making and Cases,* 8th ed. (Mason, OH: South-Western Cengage Learning, 2011), p. 109.

19. Floyd Norris, "For Boards, S.E.C. Keeps the Bar Low," *The New York Times,* March 3, 2011, **www.nytimes.com/2011/03/04/business/04norris.html?pagewanted=1&_r=1&src=busln**.

20. Gary Strauss, "Company Directors See Pay Skyrocket," *USA Today,* October 26, 2011, **www.usatoday.com/money/companies/management/story/2011-10-25/director-compensation-rising/50918332/1**; Gary Strauss, "$228,000 for a Part-Time Job? Apparently, That's Not Enough," *USA Today,* March 4–6, 2011, p. 1A.

21. Caleb Melby, "New Cola War? SodaStream Refuses to Comply with Coca-Cola Cease-and-Desist Letter," *Forbes,* June 18, 2012, **www.forbes.com/sites/calebmelby/2012/06/18/new-cola-war-sodastream-refuses-to-comply-with-coca-cola-cease-and-desist-letter/**; "Company Overview," SodaStream, 2011, **http://sodastream.investorroom.com/sodastreamoverview**; Caleb_Melby, "Bubble Man," *Forbes,* August 2012, pp. 60–62.

22. "PROCTER & GAMBLE CO/THE (PG:New York)," *Bloomberg Businessweek*, **http://investing.businessweek.com/research/stocks/people/board.asp?ticker=PG:US.**

23. Joseph Nathan Kane, *Famous First Facts*, 4th ed. (New York: The H.W. Wilson Company, 1981), p. 202.

24. CHS Inc., "CHS and Cargill Expand TEMCO Grain Export Operations," *Sacramento Bee*, February 1, 2011, **www.sacbee.com/2012/02/01/4231825/chs-andcargill-expand-temco-grain.html**; "TEMCO LLC," *Bloomberg Businessweek*, **http://investing.businessweek.com/research/stocks/private/snapshot.asp?privcapId=31014255.**

25. Robert D. Hisrich and Michael P. Peters, *Entrepreneurship*, 5th ed. (Boston: McGraw-Hill, 2002), pp. 315–16.

26. Russell Gold, "Biomass Power Generates Traction," *The Wall Street Journal*, June 1, 2009, p. A4.

27. Brent Kendall and Valerie Bauerlein, "U.S. Sues to Block Big Beer Merger," *The Wall Street Journal*, February 1, 2013, pp. A1–A2.

28. Dow Jones Newswires, "Openwave Adopts Poison Pill with 4.99% Trigger to Protect Tax Assets," *The Wall Street Journal*, January 30, 2012, **http://online.wsj.com/article/BT-CO-20120130-706082.html.**

CHAPTER 5

1. "FAQs," U.S. Small Business Administration, **http://web.sba.gov/faqs/faqIndexAll.cfm?areaid=24.**

2. "Let a Million Flowers Bloom," *The Economist*, March 12–18, 2011, pp. 79–81.

3. "FAQs," U.S. Small Business Administration, **http://web.sba.gov/faqs/faqIndexAll.cfm?areaid=24.**

4. "Nation's Women-Owned Firms Contribute Nearly $3 Trillion to U.S. Economy According to Groundbreaking Research," Center for Women's Business Research, October 2, 2009, **www.career-women.org/dateien/dateien/cfwbreconomicimpactrelease100209.pdf.**

5. "FAQs," U.S. Small Business Administration, **http://web.sba.gov/faqs/faqIndexAll.cfm?areaid=24.**

6. "Statistics of U.S. Businesses (SUSB)," *Statistics of U.S. Businesses*, **www.census.gov/econ/susb/index.html.**

7. "Bittersweet Synergy: Domestic Outsourcing in India," *The Economist*, October 22, 2009, p. 74.

8. Joseph Schumpeter, "Brand Royalty," *The Economist*, November 26, 2009, p. 78.

9. "Small Biz Stats & Trends," *SCORE*, **www.score.org/node/148155.**

10. Lindsay Blakely, "One-Man Brands," *Money.CNN.com*, July 6, 2007, **http://money.cnn.com/galleries/2007/biz2/0706/gallery.building_brands.biz2/2.html.**

11. Darren Dahl, "The Cost of Starting Up a Retail Shop," *Inc.*, August 8, 2011, **www.inc.com/articles/201108/business-start-up-costs-retail-store.html.**

12. Leigh Buchanan, "We Will Be the Best-Run Business in America," *Inc.*, February 2012, pp. 72–78.

13. "News Room," *Facebook*, **http://newsroom.fb.com/**; FacebookPublic Policy Europe, "Measuring Facebook's Economic Impact in Europe," *Facebook*, January 24, 2012, **www.facebook.com/notes/facebook-brussels/measuring-facebooks-economic-impact-in-europe/309416962438169.**

14. "Statistics of U.S. Businesses (SUSB)," U.S. Bureau of the Census, updated December 21, 2010, **www.census.gov/econ/susb/.**

15. Steven Kurutz, "On Kickstarter, Designers' Dream Materializes," *The New York Times*, September 21, 2011, **www.nytimes.com/2011/09/22/garden/on-kickstarter-designers-dreams-materialize.html?pagewanted=all**; Jenna Wortham, "A Few Dollars at a Time, Patrons Support Artists on the Web," *The New York Times*, August 24, 2009, **www.nytimes.com/2009/08/25/technology/start-ups/25kick.html?_r=1&em**; Brittany Shammas, "Funding Sites Match Entrepreneurs, Contributors," *Indy.com*, August 6, 2011, **www.indy.com/posts/funding-sites-match-entrepreneurs-contributors-2**; "What Is Kickstarter?" Kickstarter, **www.kickstarter.com/**; Roger Yu, "Need Cash? Ask a Crowd," *USA Today*, May 31, 2012, pp. 2A–2B.

16. Geoff Williams, "Rico Elmore, Fatheadz: When Regular Glasses Just Won't Fit," *Huffington Post*, July 29, 2011, **www.huffingtonpost.com/2011/07/29/rico-elmore-fatheadz-when-regular-glasses-wont-fit_n_917425.html.**

17. "FAQs," U.S. Small Business Administration, **http://web.sba.gov/faqs/faqIndexAll.cfm?areaid=24.**

18. Damon Tabor, "Clean Green," *Bloomberg Businessweek*, September 17–September 23, 2012, p. 101; Scott Stiffler, "An Eco-Friendly Spin on the Dirty Business of Laundry," *Chelsea Now*, August 8, 2012, **http://chelseanow.com/articles/2012/08/08/news/doc5022a40c20a38868348003.txt**; Eco Laundry website, **http://ecolaundrycompany.com/**; "Probably the Most Famous Laundry Company in the World," Relevansi Blog, March 31, 2011, **http://relevansi.com/blog/probably-the-most-famous-laundry-company-in-the-world/.**

19. Nadine Heintz, "Close-up: Matt Chatham," *Inc.*, September 2011, p. 32; "SkyCrepers," *Facebook*, **www.facebook.com/#!/pages/SkyCrepers-LLC/210480242315950**; "Former Patriots Player Matt Chatham Is Opening SkyCrepers in North Attleboro," *Boston Restaurant Talk*, **http://bostonrestaurants.blogspot.com/2011/07/former-patriots-player-matt-chatham-is.html**; Michael Chmura, "2011 MBA Business Plan Competition Winner SkyCrepers, LLC Announces Grand Opening at Emerald Square Mall," *Babson*, August 1, 2011, **www.babson.edu/News-Events/babson-news/Pages/SkyCrepersOpening8-11.aspx.**

20. Anthony Ha, "Food-Guide Site Foodspotting Gets Backing from Super Angels," *Venture Beat*, August 25, 2010, **http://venturebeat.com/2010/08/25/foodspotting-backed-by-super-angels/**; Anthony Ha, "Foodspotting Bites into $3M of New Funding," *Venture Beat*, January 10, 2011, **http://venturebeat.com/2011/01/10/foodspotting-funding/**; Shatterbox Staff, "Change Generation: How Alexa Andrzejewski Started Foodie-Photo Site Foodspotting," *Fast Company*, December 21, 2010, **www.fastcompany.com/1711463/change-generation-how-alexa-andrzejewski-started-foodie-photo-site-foodspotting.**

21. Thomas W. Zimmerer and Norman M. Scarborough, *Essentials of Entrepreneurship and Small Business Management*, 6th ed. (Upper Saddle River, NJ: Pearson Prentice Hall, 2005), pp. 118–124.

22. Ibid.

23. "The SCORE Association Media Fact Sheet," *SCORE*, **www.score.org/system/files/u209922/SCORE_media_fact_sheet_2011_0.pdf.**

24. Interview between Jerry Murrell and Liz Welch, "How I Did It: Jerry Murrell, Five Guys Burgers and Fries," *Inc.*, April 2010, 77–80); "History," Five Guys Burgers and Fries, **www.fiveguys.com/history.aspx**; Karen Weise, "Behind Five Guys' Beloved Burgers," *Bloomberg Businessweek*, August 11, 2011, 70–73; Lottie Joiner, "Five Guys Family Keeps It Simple," special for *USA Today*, July 30, 2012, p. 3B; Monte Burke, "All in the Family," *Forbes*, August 6, 2012, pp. 93–97.

25. Adapted from "Tomorrow's Entrepreneur," *Inc. State of Small Business* 23, no. 7 (2001), pp. 80–104.

26. U.S. Bureau of the Census, *Statistical Abstract of the United States, 2011* (Washington, DC: Government Printing Office, 2009), p. 12.

27. Molly Smith, "Managing Generation Y as They Change the Workforce," *Reuters,* January 8, 2008, **www.reuters.com/article/2008/01/08/idUS129795+08-Jan-2008+BW20080108.**

28. Jeffrey Passal and D'Vera Cohn, "Immigration to Play Lead Role in Future U.S. Growth," Pew Research, February 11, 2008, **http://pewresearch.org/pubs/729/united-states-population-projections;** U.S. Bureau of the Census, *Statistical Abstract of the United States, 2011.*

29. Daniel McGinn, "How I Did It: Arianna Huffington," *Inc.,* February 10, 2010, p. 65, **www.inc.com/magazine/20100201/how-i-did-it-arianna-huffington.html;** "AOL Agrees to Acquire *The Huffington Post,*" *The Huffington Post,* February 7, 2011, **www.huffingtonpost.com/2011/02/07/aol-huffington-post_n_819375.html.**

30. Gifford Pinchott III, *Intrapreneuring* (New York: Harper & Row, 1985), p. 34.

31. Paul Brown, "How to Cope with Hard Times," *The New York Times,* June 10, 2008, **www.nytimes.com/2008/06/10/business/smallbusiness/10toolkit.html?pagewanted=print.**

CHAPTER 6

1. "Ford Fiesta," *Automobile,* April 2010, p. 14.

2. "Letter to Stakeholders," General Electric Ecomagination, **http://ge.ecomagination.com/annual-reports/letter-to-stakeholders.html.**

3. Clarkston Consulting, "Taking Lessons from Our Clients, Clarkston Consulting Goes Green," May 7, 2012, **www.clarkstonconsulting.com/our-story/news-events/press-releases/taking-lessons-from-our-clients-clarkston-consulting-goes-green.**

4. "The Most Influential Women in Direct Selling, Shelli Gardner Co-Founder and CEO, Stampin' Up!" *Direct Selling News* 8, no. 10 (October 2012), pp. 28–30; Judi Kauffman, "Shelli Gardner, CEO and Cofounder, Stampin' Up!" **www.scrapbooking.com,** October 18, 2012, **http://scrapbooking.com/article/77527;** Linda Fantin, "Great Impressions," **www.sltrib.com,** March 20, 2005, **www.sltrib.com/search/ci_2614579;** "The $100M Club," *Direct Selling News,* June 1, 2012, **http://directsellingnews.com/index.php/view/dsn_global_100_the_top_direct_selling_companies_in_the_world/P8#.UJg2y_Umx8E.**

5. Mary Schlangenstein, "FedEx Relies on Express Revamp to Meet $1.7 Billion Goal," *Bloomberg,* October 10, 2012, **www.bloomberg.com/news/2012-10-10/fedex-sets-1-7-billion-savings-and-profit-goal-over-three-years.html.**

6. Don Bain, "Will Jennifer Lopez's Popularity Drive Sales for Fiat?" *Torque News,* November 22, 2011, **www.torquenews.com/397/fiat-jennifer-lopez-popularity-drive-sales-fiat-500;** Anita Lienert, "Chrysler Offers Lease Deal to Move 2012 Fiat 500," *Edmunds Inside Line,* **www.insideline.com/fiat/500/2012/chrysleroffers-lease-deal-to-move-2012-fiat-500.html.**

7. G. Tomas, M. Hult, David W. Cravens, and Jagdish Sheth, "Competitive Advantage in the Global Marketplace: A Focus on Marketing Strategy," *Journal of Business Research* 51 (January 2001), p. 1.

8. Henry Dewing, "Cisco Strategy Evolves and Tactics Mature," *Forrester Blogs,* July 15, 2011, **http://blogs.forrester.com/henry_dewing/11-07-15-cisco_strategy_evolves_and_tactics_mature;** Rosabeth Moss Kanter, "Cisco and a Cautionary Tale about Teams," *Harvard Business Review,* May 9, 2011, **http://blogs.hbr.org/kanter/2011/05/cisco-and-a-cautionary-tale-ab.html;** Tom Foremski, "Is It Time for Cisco to Ditch Its Councils?" *ZD Net,* April 14, 2011, **www.zdnet.com/blog/foremski/is-it-time-for-ciscoto-ditch-its-councils/1755.**

9. "Study: 87 Percent of Small to Mid-Sized Businesses Have Inadequate or Out of Date Disaster Recovery Plans," Contingency Planning and Management Conference and Expo, February 1, 2012, **http://contingencyplanning.com/articles/2012/02/01/small-to-midsized-businesses-have-inadequate-or-out-of-date-disaster-recovery-plans.aspx.**

10. Tamara Lytle, "Rising for the Bubble," *Society for Human Resource Management,* 56, no. 9 (September 1, 2011), **www.shrm.org/Publications/hrmagazine/EditorialContent/2011/0911/Pages/0911lytle.aspx.**

11. Mariko Yasu, "Panasonic Plans to Eliminate 17,000 Jobs in Reorganization," *Bloomberg Businessweek,* April 28, 2011, **www.bloomberg.com/news/2011-04-28/panasonic-plans-to-reduce-its-workforce-by-17-000-to-350-000-by-march-2013.html.**

12. John Barfield, "Staffing Up for Growth," *Fortune,* May 5, 2008, p. S10.

13. "Labor Force Statistics from the Current Population Survey," Bureau of Labor Statistics, **www.bls.gov/data/.**

14. C. O. Trevor and A. J. Nyberg. "Keeping Your Headcount When All about You Are Losing Theirs: Downsizing, Voluntary Turnover Rates, and the Moderating Role of HR Practices," *Academy of Management Journal* 51 (2008), pp. 259–76.

15. "Women CEOs in the Fortune 500," *CNN Money,* May 9, 2013, **http://management.fortune.cnn.com/2013/05/09/women-ceos-fortune-500/.**

16. Adam Lashinsky, "How Tim Cook Is Changing Apple," *Fortune,* June 11, 2012; Rocco Pendola, "Amazon vs. Apple: Jeff Bezos Just Squashed Tim Cook," September 7, 2012, **www.forbes.com/sites/thestreet/2012/09/07/amazon-vs-apple-jeff-bezos-just-squashed-tim-cook/;** Kit Eaton, "Steve Jobs vs. Tim Cook: Words of Wisdom," August 26, 2011, **www.fastcompany.com/1776013/steve-jobs-vs-tim-cook-words-wisdom;** "Inside the Minds of America's Most Hard-Charging CEOs," *Inc.,* September 2012, pp. 142–46.

17. Del Jones, "Autocratic Leadership Works—Until It Fails," *USA Today,* June 5, 2003, **www.usatoday.com/news/nation/2003-06-05-raines-usat_x.htm.**

18. George Manning and Kent Curtis, *The Art of Leadership* (New York: McGraw-Hill, 2003), p. 125.

19. "Hewlett-Packard Replaces Leo Apotheker with Meg Whitman," *BBC News,* September 23, 2011, **www.bbc.co.uk/news/business-15028509;** James B. Stewart, "For Seamless Transitions, Don't Look to Hewlett," *The New York Times,* August 26, 2011, **www.nytimes.com/2011/08/27/business/for-seamless-transitions-at-the-top-dont-consult-hewlett-packard.html?pagewanted=all.**

20. Bill George, Peter Sims, Andrew M. McLean, and Diana Mayer, "Discovering Your Authentic Leadership," *Harvard Business Review,* February 2007, **http://hbr.org/2007/02/discovering-your-authentic-leadership/ar/1.**

21. John P. Kotter, "What Leaders Really Do," *Harvard Business Review,* December 2001, **http://fs.ncaa.org/Docs/DIII/What%20Leaders%20Really%20Do.pdf.**

22. Rich Karlgaard, "Innovation Rules," *Forbes.com,* November 2, 2011, **www.forbes.com/forbes/2009/1102/opinions-rich-karlgaard-digital-rules.html;** Johnny Rich, "Example of Democratic Leadership Style–Persuasion Element 2," **http://howcanisucceedinlife.com/example-of-democratic-leadership-style-persuasion-element-2/;** "Understanding Your Leadership Style," **www.marsdd.com/articles/understanding-your-leadership-style/;** Michael Maccoby, "Narcissistic Leaders: The Incredible Pros, the Inevitable Cons," *The Harvard Business Review,* January–February 2000, **www.maccoby.com/Articles/NarLeaders.**

shtml; Rich Karlgaard, "Leadership Lessons from Google," *Forbes.com*, November 23, 2009, **www.forbes.com/2009/11/23/ken-auletta-leadership-intelligent-technology-google.html**; Nicholas Carlson, "Google CEO Eric Schmidt: 'We Don't Really Have a Five Year Plan,'" May 20, 2009, **http://articles.businessinsider.com/2009-05-20/tech/30099731_1_google-ceo-eric-schmidt-googlers-google-people**; Leigh Buchanan, "13 Ways of Looking at a Leader," *Inc. Magazine*, June 2012, pp. 74–76; "Inside the Minds of America's Most Hard-Charging CEOs," *Inc. Magazine*.

23. Lisa Baertlein, "McDonald's CEO Jim Skinner to retire," *Reuters*, March 22, 2012, **www.reuters.com/article/2012/03/22/us-mcdonalds-idUSTRE8170YW20120322**.
24. C. L. Pearce and C. C. Manz, "The New Silver Bullets of Leadership: The Importance of Self- and Shared Leadership in Knowledge Work," *Organizational Dynamics* 34 no. 2, (2005), pp. 130–40.
25. Deborah Harrington-Mackin, *The Team Building Tool Kit* (New York: New Directions Management, Inc., 1994); Joseph P. Folger, Marshall Scott Poole, and Randall K. Stutman, *Working through Conflict: Strategies for Relationships, Groups, and Organizations*, 6th ed. (Upper Saddle River, NJ: Pearson Education Inc., 2009).
26. Kerrie Unsworth, "Unpacking Creativity," *Academy of Management Review* 26 (April 2001), pp. 289–297.
27. Pallavi Gogoi, "A Bittersweet Deal for Wrigley," *BusinessWeek*, May 12, 2008, p. 034; Wrigley, "About Us," **www.wrigley.com/global/about-us.aspx**.
28. James P. Kotter, "What Effective General Managers Really Do," *Harvard Business Review* 60 (November–December 1982), p. 160.
29. Dan Schawbel, "5 Reasons Why Your Online Presence Will Replace Your Resume in 10 Years," *Forbes*, February 21, 2012, **www.forbes.com/sites/danschawbel/2011/02/21/5-reasons-why-your-online-presence-will-replace-your-resume-in-10-years/**.
30. "Salary after Taxes," *Employment Spot*, **www.employmentspot.com/employment-articles/salary-after-taxes**.
31. Bureau of Labor Statistics, "May 2012 National Industry-Specific Occupational Employment and Wage Estimates," **www.bls.gov/oes/current/naics4_551100.htm**.

CHAPTER 7

1. Mina Kimes, "What Admired Firms Don't Have in Common," *CNNMoney*, March 6, 2009, **http://money.cnn.com/2009/03/06/news/companies/hay.survey.fortune/index.htm**.
2. "The Container Store: An Employee-Centric Retailer," Daniels Fund Ethics Initiative website, **http://danielsethics.mgt.unm.edu/pdf/Container%20Store%20Case.pdf**.
3. Alex Harris, "A New Future for Toms Shoes, Tweed Shire and Room to Read," Reputation Report, August 7, 2009, **www.reputationreport.com.au/2009/08/a-new-future-by-toms-shoes-tweed-shire-and-room-to-read/**; "Our Movement," TOMS Shoes, **www.toms.com/our-movement**.
4. "Best Companies to Work For: Happy Campers," *CNNMoney*, **http://money.cnn.com/galleries/2011/news/companies/1104/gallery.best_companies_happy_campers.fortune/2.html**; Christopher Palmeri, "Zappos Retails Its Culture," *Bloomberg Businessweek*, December 30, 2009, **www.businessweek.com/magazine/content/10_02/b4162057120453.htm**.
5. Joe Light, "Finance and Tech Signal Attitudes on Ethics," *The Wall Street Journal*, March 7, 2011, **http://online.wsj.com/article/SB10001424052748704728004576176711042012064.html**.
6. Rachel Emma Silverman and Leslie Kwoh, "Peer Performance Reviews Take Off," *The Wall Street Journal*, August 1, 2012, p. B6; Eric Mosley, "Crowdsource Your Performance Reviews," *Harvard Business Review*, June 15, 2012, **http://blogs.hbr.org/cs/2012/06/crowdsource_your_performance_r.html**; Catherine Lovering, "The Advantages of the Peer Review Appraisal System," *Small Business Chronicle*, 2012, **http://smallbusiness.chron.com/advantages-peer-review-appraisal-method-34573.html**.
7. FSB 100, *CNNMoney.com*, **http://money.cnn.com/magazines/fsb/fsb100/2009/snapshots/72.html**; "Nathan's Famous, Inc. Reports Year-End and Fourth Quarter Results," *Seeking Alpha*, June 4, 2012, **http://seekingalpha.com/news-article/3050201-nathan-s-famous-inc-reports-year-end-and-fourth-quarter-results**; "A Treasured Tradition," **http://nathansfamous.com/index.php/nathan-today**.
8. Adam Smith, *The Wealth of Nations* (New York: Modern Library, 1937; originally published in 1776).
9. Malcolm Moore, "What Has Triggered the Suicide Cluster at Foxconn?" *The Telegraph*, May 16, 2010, **http://blogs.telegraph.co.uk/news/malcolmmoore/100039883/what-has-triggered-the-suicide-clusterat-foxconn/**.
10. "2011 Update of the Corporate Social Responsibility Report," Campbell's, **www.campbellsoupcompany.com/csr/success_profile.asp**.
11. Rachel Emma Silverman, "Who's the Boss? There Isn't One," *The Wall Street Journal*, June 20, 2012, pp. B1 and B8; Jason Fried, "Why I Run a Flat Company," *Inc. Magazine*, April 2011, **www.inc.com/magazine/20110401/jason-fried-why-i-run-a-flat-company.html**; Dana Griffin, "Benefits in a Flat Organizational Structure," *Chron.com*, **http://smallbusiness.chron.com/benefits-flat-organizational-structure-281.html**.
12. McDonald's India, **www.mcdonaldsindia.com/**.
13. "Why Work Here?" **www.wholefoodsmarket.com/careers/workhere.php**.
14. PespiCo, "PepsiCo Unveils New Organizational Structure, Names CEOs of Three Principal Operating Units," Boston.com, November 5, 2007, **http://finance.boston.com/boston/news/read/3696031/pepsico_unveils_new_organizational_structure**; "The PepsiCo Family," PepsiCo, **www.pepsico.com/Company/The-Pepsico-Family/PepsiCo-Americas-Beverages.html**.
15. Jon R. Katzenbach and Douglas K. Smith, "The Discipline of Teams," *Harvard Business Review* 71 (March–April 1993), p. 19.
16. Ibid.
17. "The Secret to Team Collaboration: Individuality," *Inc.*, January 18, 2012, **www.inc.com/john-baldoni/the-secret-to-team-collaboration-is-individuality.html**.
18. Anne Fisher, "How to Build a (Strong) Virtual Team," *CNNMoney*, November 20, 2009, **http://money.cnn.com/2009/11/19/news/companies/ibm_virtual_manager.fortune/index.htm**.
19. Esther Shein, "Making the Virtual Team Real," *The Network*, April 2, 2008, **http://newsroom.cisco.com/dlls/2008/ts_040208.html**.
20. Patrick Kiger, "Task Force Training Develops New Leaders, Solves Real Business Issues and Helps Cut Costs," *Workforce*, September 7, 2011, **www.workforce.com/article/20070521/NEWS02/305219996/task-force-training-develops-new-**

leaders-solves-real-business-issues-and-helps-cut-costs; Duane D. Stanford, "Coca-Cola Woman Board Nominee Bucks Slowing Diversity Trend," *Bloomberg,* February 22, 2013, www.bloomberg.com/news/2013-02-22/coca-cola-s-woman-director-nominee-bucks-slowing-diversity-trend.html.

21. Jerry Useem, "What's That Spell? TEAMWORK," *Fortune,* June 12, 2006, p. 66.
22. Jia Lynnyang, "The Power of Number 4.6," *Fortune,* June 12, 2006, p. 122.
23. AMVAC Chemical Corporation, "Business and Product Development Team," www.amvac-chemical.com/AboutUs/BusinessandProductDevelopmentTeam/tabid/69/Default.aspx; "Company Overview of AMVAC Chemical Corporation," *Bloomberg Businessweek,* http://investing.businessweek.com/research/stocks/private/snapshot.asp?privcapId=763493.
24. "The Most Influential Women in Direct Selling: Bonnie Kelly and Teresa Walsh, Co-Founders, Silpada," *Direct Selling News* 8, no. 10 (October 2012), pp. 39–40; Barbara Seale, "Sterling Strategy: Avon Acquires Silpada," *Direct Selling News,* September 1, 2010, http://directsellingnews.com/index.php/view/sterling_strategy_avon_acquires_silpada#.UIBfRfUmx8E; Hearst Communication, Inc., "Make Your Work Work for You," *Redbook,* www.redbookmag.com/money-career/tips-advice/make-work-work.
25. Richard S. Wellins, William C. Byham, and Jeanne M. Wilson, *Empowered Teams: Creating Self-Directed Work Groups That Improve Quality, Productivity, and Participation* (San Francisco: Jossey-Bass Publishers, 1991), p. 5.
26. Matt Krumrie, "Are Meetings a Waste of Time? Survey Says Yes," *Minneapolis Workplace Examiner,* May 12, 2009, www.examiner.com/article/are-meetings-a-waste-of-time-survey-says-yes.
27. Peter Mell and Timothy Grance, "The NIST Definition of Cloud Computing," National Institute of Standards and Technology, Special Publication 800-145, September 2011, http://csrc.nist.gov/publications/nistpubs/800-145/SP800-145.pdf.
28. Michael Christian, "Top 10 Ideas: Making the Most of Your Corporate Intranet," *Claromentis,* April 2, 2009, www.claromentis.com/blog/top-10-ideas-making-the-most-of-your-corporate-intranet/#.UWxdQvUmx8E.
29. "Corporate America vs. Workers: Companies Do More with Fewer Employees," *NY Daily News,* November 5, 2009, www.nydailynews.com/money/2009/11/05/2009-11-05_corporate_america_vs_workers_companies_do_more_with_fewer_employees.html.
30. Kim Komando, "Why You Need a Company Policy on Internet Use," Microsoft Corporation, www.microsoft.com/business/en-us/resources/management/employee-relations/why-you-need-a-company-policy-on-internet-use.aspx?fbid=YtCe0AAlh2X.
31. *PBSNewsHour,* "Apple Supplier Foxconn Pledges Better Working Conditions, but Will It Deliver?" *You Tube,* www.youtube.com/watch?v=ZduorbCkSBQ.

CHAPTER 8

1. Tom Van Ripper, "Stadium Stuffer," *Forbes,* August 6, 2012, pp. 64–65; The Aspire Group website, www.theaspiregroupinc.com.
2. Rina Rapuano, "Check Please!" *The Washingtonian Blog,* February 18, 2010, www.washingtonian.com/blogarticles/restaurants/bestbites/15008.html.
3. Leonard L. Berry, *Discovering the Soul of Service* (New York: The Free Press, 1999), pp. 86–96.
4. Valerie A. Zeithaml and Mary Jo Bitner, *Services Marketing,* 3rd ed. (Boston: McGraw-Hill Irwin, 2003), pp. 3, 22.
5. Bernard Wysocki Jr., "To Fix Health Care, Hospitals Take Tips from the Factory Floor," *The Wall Street Journal,* April 9, 2004, http://online.wsj.com/article/0,,SB108146068260878363,00.html.
6. Chris Woodyard and James Healey, "Ford Looking to Aluminum for Pickups?" *USA Today,* July 26, 2012, www.usatoday.com/money/autos/story/2012-07-26/-ford-f-150/56515524/1; Danny Hakim, "Study Says Lighter Cars Would Cost More Lives," *The New York Times,* October 15, 2003, www.nytimes.com/2003/10/15/business/study-says-lighter-cars-would-cost-more-lives.html; Sonari Glinton, "A Push to Make Gasoline Engines More Efficient," *NPR,* November 23, 2011, www.npr.org/2011/11/23/142662849/a-push-to-make-gasoline-engines-more-efficient.
7. "20 Awesome Facebook Pages," *Inc.,* www.inc.com/20-awesome-facebook-fan-pages-2011/.
8. Faith Keenan, "Opening the Spigot," *BusinessWeek* e.biz, June 4, 2001, www.businessweek.com/magazine/content/01_23/b3735616.htm.
9. "Dell Laptop Parts," Parts people, www.parts-people.com/.
10. Ryan Underwood, "Dear Customer . . . Managing E-mail Campaigns," *Inc.,* March 2008, p. 59.
11. Amy Brantley, "Fun Facts about Hershey's Chocolate," *Yahoo! Voices,* July 30, 2007, http://voices.yahoo.com/fun-facts-hersheys-chocolate-469131.html.
12. "Green Factories/Green Building," Honda, November 30, 2012, www.honda.com/newsandviews/article.aspx?id=4056-en; "ISO 14000 Essentials," ISO, www.iso.org/iso/iso_14000_essentials.
13. "Top 10 Solar Friendly States," *Cooler Planet,* http://solar.coolerplanet.com/Articles/top-10-solar-friendly-states.aspx.
14. Robotic Industries Association, "North American Robotics Market Sets New Records in 2012," February 5, 2013, www.robotics.org/content-detail.cfm/Industrial-Robotics-News/North-American-Robotics-Market-Sets-New-Records-in-2012/content_id/3906.
15. Hugh Aston, "The Quest for Hidden Treasures," *Businessweek Special Advertisement Section,* 2012, www.businessweek.com/adsections/2012/pdf/120319_Panasonic3.pdf; Alison Moodle, "Why Companies' Top Struggles Lie in Sustainable Supply Chains," *GreenBiz,* October 26, 2012, www.greenbiz.com/news/2012/10/26/why-companies-top-struggle-sustainable-supply-chains; Manish Bapna, "3 Lessons for a Greener and More Profitable Supply Chain," *Forbes,* October 10, 2012, www.forbes.com/sites/manishbapna/2012/10/10/3-lessons-for-better-supply-chain-management/; Marc Gunther, "What Sustainable Consumption Looks Like," *GreenBiz,* October 10, 2012, www.greenbiz.com/blog/2012/10/10/what-sustainable-consumption-looks-like?page=0%2C2.
16. Johnson Controls, *2011 Business and Sustainability Report: Growth in Every Dimension* (Milwaukee, WI: Johnson Controls, Inc., 2011).
17. Bryan Walsh, "Why Green Is the New Red, White and Blue," *Time,* April 28, 2008, p. 53.
18. "2012 Chevrolet Volt," Chevrolet, www.chevrolet.com/volt-electric-car/.
19. Megan Kamerick, "How to Go Green," *New Mexico Business Weekly,* May 23–29, 2008, p. 3.
20. O.C. Ferrell and Michael D. Hartline, *Marketing Strategy* (Mason, OH: South-Western, 2011), p. 215.

21. John Edwards, "Orange Seeks Agent," *Inbound Logistics*, January 2006, pp. 239–242.

22. Ferrell and Hartline, *Marketing Strategy*, p. 215.

23. "Broken Links," *The Economist*, March 31, 2011, **www.economist.com/node/18486015**.

24. Ari Lavaux, "Chocolate's Dark Side," *The Weekly Alibi*, February 9–15, 2012, p. 22.

25. Susan Carey, "Airlines Play Up Improvements in On-Time Performance," *The Wall Street Journal*, February 10, 2010, p. B6.

26. "Four U.S. Organizations Honored with the 2012 Baldrige National Quality Award," Baldrige Performance Excellence Program, November 14, 2012, **www.nist.gov/baldrige/baldrige_recipients2012.cfm**.

27. Roger Yu, "Kia Looks to Buff Image with Value, New Designs," *USA Today*, June 29, 2011, **www.usatoday.com/money/autos/2011-06-27-kia-rising_n.htm**.

28. Philip B. Crosby, *Quality Is Free: The Art of Making Quality Certain* (New York: McGraw-Hill, 1979), pp. 9–10.

29. Nigel F. Piercy, *Market-Led Strategic Change* (Newton, MA: Butterworth-Heinemann, 1992), pp. 374–85.

30. "Compuware Gomez Introduces Free Web Performance Benchmarking Tool," *Bloomberg*, **www.bloomberg.com/apps/news?pid=newsarchive&sid=a3bTx6JLIx7I**.

31. "ISO 9001 Certification," GE Power & Water, **www.geinstruments.com/company/iso-9001-certification.html**.

32. "Mouthing Off By the Numbers," *Ethisphere*, 2011, Q3, p. 9.

33. Charles Duhigg and David Barboza, "Apple's iPad and the Human Costs for Workers in China," The New York Times, January 25, 2012, **www.nytimes.com/2012/01/26/business/ieconomy-apples-ipad-and-the-human-costs-for-workers-in-china.html?pagewanted=all**.

34. "Monitoring and Auditing Global Supply Chains Is a Must," *Ethisphere*, 2011, Q3, pp. 38–45.

35. "Employment Opportunities," Careers in Supply Chain Management, **www.careersinsupplychain.org/career-outlook/empopp.asp**.

CHAPTER 9

1. Dan Heath and Chip Heath, "Business Advice from Van Halen," *Fast Company*, March 1, 2010, **www.fastcompany.com/1550881/business-advice-van-halen**.

2. "100 Best Companies to Work for 2010," *Fortune*, **http://money.cnn.com/magazines/fortune/bestcompanies/2010/snapshots/4.html**; "Benefits," Google Jobs, **www.google.com/about/jobs/lifeatgoogle/benefits/**.

3. Scott Martin, "Perksville, USA," *USA Today*, July 5, 2012, pp. 1A–2A.

4. Ira S. Wolfe, "How Much Does Absenteeism Cost Your Business?" The Perfect Labor Storm 2.0, December 10, 2008, **http://hrblog.typepad.com/perfect_labor_storm/2008/12/how-much-does-absenteeism-cost-your-business.html#axzz2QZOxYx2w**.

5. "America's Highest Paid Chief Executives," *Forbes*, **www.forbes.com/lists/2012/12/ceo-compensation-12_rank.html**.

6. Sony Pictures, "A Greener World," **www.sonypictures.com/green/act/employee-involvement/employees-go-green.php**; Lockheed Martin, "A Foundation of Credibility," **www.lockheedmartin.com/us/who-we-are/sustainability/credibility.html**; Tiffany Hsu, "Google Creates $280 Million Solar Power Fund," *Los Angeles Times*, June 14, 2011, **http://articles.latimes.com/2011/jun/14/business/la-fi-google-solar-20110614**; Alison van Diggelen, "Working @ Google: Green Carrots & Pogo Sticks," *Fresh Dialogues*, **www.freshdialogues.com/2011/08/23/working-google-green-carrots-pogo-sticks/**; Google, "We Commute Sustainably," *Google Green*, **www.google.com/green/efficiency/oncampus/#commuting**.

7. "25 Well-Paying Jobs That Most People Overlook (and Why)," *Business Pundit*, **www.businesspundit.com/25-well-paying-jobs-that-most-peopleoverlook-and-why/**.

8. "For Third Year Running, L.L. Bean Ranks Number One In Customer Service," National Retail Federation, **www.nrf.com/modules.php?name=news&op=viewlive&sp_id=876**; Jena McGregor, "Customer Service Champs 2010," *Bloomberg Businessweek*, **http://images.businessweek.com/ss/10/02/0218_customer_service_champs/2.htm**.

9. Douglas McGregor, *The Human Side of Enterprise* (New York: McGraw-Hill, 1960), pp. 33–34.

10. Leslie Kwoh, "Firms Bow to Generation Y's Demands," *The Wall Street Journal*, August 22, 2012, p. B6; Susanne Gargiulo, "'Generation Y' Set to Transform Office Life," *CNN*, August 21, 2012, **http://edition.cnn.com/2012/08/20/business/generation-y-global-office-culture/index.html**; Emily Jane Fox, "Best Companies for Generation Y," *CNN Money*, August 21, 2012, **http://money.cnn.com/2012/08/21/pf/jobs/gen-y-jobs/index.html**; Julie Labrie, "Generation Clash: Is Having Four Generations in the Workplace a Liability or an Asset?" *Workopolis*, December 21, 2011, **www.workopolis.com/solutions/en/article/1688-generation-clash-is-having-four-generations-in-the-workplace-a-liability-or-an-asset**; Maud Purcell, "Generation Y Can Be an Asset to Employers," September 14, 2012, *Times Union*, **www.timesunion.com/living/article/Generation-Y-can-be-an-asset-to-employers-3866333.php**.

11. McGregor, *The Human Side of Enterprise.*

12. Bharat Mediratta, "The Google Way: Give Engineers Room," *The New York Times*, October 21, 2007, **www.nytimes.com/2007/10/21/jobs/21pre.html**.

13. Jon L. Pierce, Tatiana Kostova, and Kurt T. Kirks, "Toward a Theory of Psychological Ownership in Organizations, *Academy of Management Review* 26, no. 2 (2001), p. 298.

14. Liz Rappaport, "Goldman Cuts Blankfein's Bonus," *The Wall Street Journal*, February 4, 2012, **http://online.wsj.com/article/SB10001424052970204662204577201483347787346.html**.

15. Ethics Resource Center, *2011 National Business Ethics Survey®: Ethics in Transition* (Arlington, VA: Ethics Resource Center, 2012), p. 16.

16. Archie Carroll, "Carroll: Do We Live in a Cheating Culture?" *Athens Banner-Herald*, February 21, 2004, **www.onlineathens.com/stories/022204/bus_20040222028.shtml**.

17. Geoff Colvin, "How Top Companies Breed Stars," September 20, 2007, **http://money.cnn.com/magazines/fortune/fortune_archive/2007/10/01/100351829/index.htm**.

18. My Guides USA.com, "Which Jobs Offer Flexible Work Schedules?" **http://jobs.myguidesusa.com/answers-to-my-questions/which-jobs-offer-flexible-work-schedules?/**.

19. Robert Preidt, "Workplace Flexibility Can Boost Healthy Behaviors," *The Washington Post*, December 14, 2007, **www.washingtonpost.com/wp-dyn/content/article/2007/12/14/AR2007121401583.html**.

20. My Guides USA.com, "Which Jobs Offer Flexible Work Schedules?"

21. "GEN XYZ Companies," *Coloradobiz Magazine,* October 2012, p. 31; FullContact website, **www.fullcontact.com**; Craig Kanalley, "FullContact Pays Its Employees $7,500 to Go on Vacation," *The Huffington Post,* July 13, 2012, **www.huffingtonpost.com/2012/07/12/fullcontact-employees-vacation_n_1669668.html**.
22. "The Latest Telecommuting Statistics," Telework Research Network, **www.teleworkresearchnetwork.com/telecommuting-statistics**.
23. Dori Meinert, "Make Telecommuting Pay Off," *Society for Human Resource Management,* June 1, 2011, **www.shrm.org/Publications/hrmagazine/EditorialContent/2011/0611/Pages/0611meinert.aspx**.
24. Ibid.
25. "Best Places For Business and Careers," *Forbes,* March 25, 2009, **www.forbes.com/lists/2009/1/bizplaces09_Best-Places-For-Business-And-Careers_Rank.html**.
26. Kurt Badenhausen, "The Best Places for Business and Careers," *Forbes,* June 29, 2011, **www.forbes.com/sites/kurtbadenhausen/2011/06/29/the-best-places-for-business-and-careers/**.

CHAPTER 10

1. "About O*NET," O*NET Resource Center, **www.onetcenter.org/overview.html**.
2. Procter & Gamble, "Hiring Process," **www.pg.com/en_US/careers/hiring_process.shtml**.
3. U.S. Department of Health and Human Services, "Results from the 2010 National Survey on Drug Use and Health: Summary of National Findings," September 2011, **www.samhsa.gov/data/NSDUH/2k10NSDUH/2k10Results.htm#3.1.7**.
4. "Substance Abuse Costs Employers Billions," *The National Registry of Workers' Compensation Specialists,* **www.nrwcs.com/substance-abuse-costs-billions**.
5. Manuel Valdes and Shannon McFarland, "Job Seekers' Facebook Password Asked for During U.S. Interviews," *Huffington Post,* March 20, 2012, **www.huffingtonpost.com/2012/03/20/facebook-passwordsjob-seekers_n_1366577.html**.
6. Abram Brown, "Yahoo CEO Quits Amid Furor over Bogus Resume," *Forbes,* May 13, 2012, **www.forbes.com/sites/abrambrown/2012/05/13/yahoo-ceo-plans-to-quit-as-company-tries-to-appease-hedge-fund-manager/**.
7. Christopher T. Marquet and Lisa J.B. Peterson, "Résumé Fraud: The Top Ten Lies," Marquet International, Ltd., **www.marquetinternational.com/pdf/Resume%20Fraud-Top%20Ten%20Lies.pdf**.
8. U.S. Equal Employment Opportunity Commission, "EEOC Reports Nearly 100,000 Job Bias Charges in Fiscal Year 2012," January 28, 2013, **www.eeoc.gov/eeoc/newsroom/release/1-28-13.cfm**.
9. "Fortune 500 Black, Latino, Asian CEOs," DiversityInc, February 19, 2012, **http://diversityinc.com/leadership/fortune-500-black-latino-asian-ceos/**; Alliance for Board Diversity, "Missing Pieces: Women and Minorities on *Fortune* 500 Boards," *2010 Alliance for Board Diversity Census, 2011,* **http://theabd.org/Missing_Pieces_Women_and_Minorities_on_Fortune_500_Boards.pdf**.
10. "Compulsory Retirement Age at 65 Fully Abolished," *BBC News,* October 1, 2011, **www.bbc.co.uk/news/business-15127835**; "Can You Legally Force Someone to Retire or Is It Age Discrimination?" *LawInfo blog,* **http://blog.lawinfo.com/2011/04/10/can-you-legally-force-someone-to-retire-or-is-it-age-discrimination/**.
11. Stephen Bastien, "12 Benefits of Hiring Older Workers," *Entrepreneur.com,* September 20, 2006, **www.entrepreneur.com/humanresources/hiring/article167500.html**.
12. Catherine Rampell, "The Gender Wage Gap, Around the World," March 9, 2010, **http://economix.blogs.nytimes.com/2010/03/09/the-gender-wage-gap-around-the-world/**.
13. "Our Curriculum," Hamburger University, **www.aboutmcdonalds.com/mcd/careers/hamburger_university/our_curriculum.html**.
14. "100 Best Companies to Work for, 2011," *Fortune,* February 7, 2011, **http://money.cnn.com/magazines/fortune/best-companies/2011/snapshots/21.html**.
15. Doug Stewart, "Employee-Appraisal Software," *Inc.,* **www.inc.com/magazine/19940615/3288_pagen_2.html**.
16. Maury A. Peiperl, "Getting 360-Degree Feedback Right," *Harvard Business Review,* January 2001, pp. 142–48.
17. Chris Musselwhite, "Self Awareness and the Effective Leader," Inc.com, www.inc.com/resources/leadership/articles/20071001/musselwhite.html.
18. Rebecca Vesely, "Companies Aim to Improve Wellness of Telecommuting, Traveling Employees, Too," *Workforce,* October 30, 2012, **www.workforce.com/article/20121030/NEWS02/121039996/companies-aim-to-improve-wellness-of-telecommuting-traveling-employees-too**.
19. Marcia Zidle, "Employee Turnover: Seven Reasons Why People Quit Their Jobs," **http://ezinearticles.com/?Employee-Turnover:-Seven-Reasons-Why-People-Quit-Their-Jobs&id=42531**.
20. Andrea Chang, "Gap to Close about 200 Stores in N. America as It Expands Overseas," *The Los Angeles Times,* October 14, 2011, **http://articles.latimes.com/2011/oct/14/business/la-fi-gap-downsize-20111014**.
21. "Wage and Hour Division (WHD)," U.S. Department of Labor, **www.dol.gov/whd/flsa/index.htm**.
22. "Fair Labor Standards Act Advisor," U.S. Department of Labor, **www.dol.gov/elaws/faq/esa/flsa/002.htm**.
23. Associated Press, "Santa Fe Not Likely to Raise Minimum Wage," kvia.com, December 22, 2009, **www.kvia.com/global/story.asp?s11716158**.
24. Zelie Pollon, "Santa Fe, N.M., to Have Nation's Highest Minimum Wage," *Reuters,* January 27, 2012, **www.reuters.com/article/2012/01/27/us-minimum-wage-santa-fe-idUSTRE80Q24K20120127**.
25. Rachel Emma Silverman, "My Colleague, My Paymaster," *The Wall Street Journal,* April 3, 2012, **http://online.wsj.com/article/SB1000142405270230475040457732203112852050 6.html**; Dan Beucke, "The Web's Next Big Thing: Cheap Labor," *Bloomberg Businessweek,* November 7, 2011, **www.businessweek.com/finance/occupy-wall-street/archives/2011/11/a_web-site_that_buys_and_sells_work.html**; Quentin Hardy, "Bit by Bit, Work Exchange Site Aims to Get Jobs Done," *The New York Times,* November 6, 2011, **www.nytimes.com/2011/11/07/technology/coffee-and-power-site-aims-to-get-jobs-done-bit-by-bit.html?_r=0**.
26. "Kele & Co: First Innovative Jewelry Company in Direct Sales," PRLog, April 29, 2008, **www.prlog.org/10067694-kele-co-the-first-innovative-jewelry-company-in-direct-sales.html**; Kele & Co, "About Kele & Co," 2012, **www.keleonline.com/pages/about.html**.

27. Frederick E. Allen, "Boss Gives $3 Million of His Bonus to His Employees," *Forbes,* July 20, 2012, **www.forbes.com/sites/frederickallen/2012/07/20/boss-gives-3-million-of-his-bonus-to-employees/**.

28. The National Center for Employee Ownership, ESOP (Employee Stock Ownership Plan) Facts, 2013, **www.esop.org/**.

29. Bureau of Labor Statistics, U.S. Department of Labor, "Employer Costs for Employee Compensation—December 2012," **www.bls.gov/news.release/pdf/ecec.pdf**.

30. Stephen Miller, "Employee Loyalty Hits 7-Year Low; Benefits Promote Retention," *Society for Human Resource Management,* March 22, 2012, **www.shrm.org/hrdisciplines/benefits/Articles/Pages/LoyaltyLow.aspx**.

31. "Work/Life," Lowe's, **https://careers.lowes.com/benefits_work.aspx**.

32. "Union Members—2011," *Bureau of Labor Statistics,* January 27, 2012, **www.bls.gov/news.release/pdf/union2.pdf**.

33. Bruce Horovitz, "Twinkie Reigns as Pop Culture Rock Star, but Can It Survive?" *USA Today,* November 19, 2012, p. 3B; Rachel Feintzeig and Mike Spector, "Hostess Union Clings to Hope," *The Wall Street Journal,* November 19, 2012, p. B1; Mark Schneider, "Hostess Twinkies: The Last Bite?" *www.examiner.com,* November 18, 2012, **www.examiner.com/article/hostess-twinkies-the-last-bite**; David Benoit, "Twinkies Never Die? Hostess CEO Says He's Hopeful Brands Will Be Sold," *The Wall Street Journal,* November 16, 2012, **http://blogs.wsj.com/deals/2012/11/16/twinkies-never-die-hostess-ceo-says-hes-hopeful-brands-will-be-sold/?KEYWORDS=hostess**; Tom Gara, "The Demise of the Twinkie: Hostess Files Motion to Liquidate," *The Wall Street Journal,* November 16, 2012, **http://blogs.wsj.com/corporate-intelligence/2012/11/16/the-end-of-the-twinkie-hostess-files-motion-to-liquidate/?KEYWORDS=hostess**; Julie Jargon and Annie Gasparro, "Rush to Grab Last Twinkies, Ho-Hos," *The Wall Street Journal,* November 16, 2012, **http://online.wsj.com/article/SB10001424127887324595904578123300611324768.html?user=welcome&mg=id-wsj**; Julie Jargon and Mike Spector, "More Suitors Signal Interest in Hostess," *The Wall Street Journal,* November 19, 2012, **http://blogs.wsj.com/deals/2012/11/19/more-suitors-signal-interest-in-hostess/?KEYWORDS=hostess**; Charles Passy, "Why We Love Twinkies–But Haven't Eaten Them in Years," *The Wall Street Journal,* November 19, 2012, **http://blogs.wsj.com/speakeasy/2012/11/19/why-we-love-twinkies-but-havent-eaten-them-in-years/?KEYWORDS=hostess**; Jacqueline Palank and Rachel Feintzeig, "Hostess, Bakers Union Agree to Mediation," *The Wall Street Journal,* November 19, 2012, **http://online.wsj.com/article/SB10001424127887324307204578129282170898870.html?user=welcome&mg=id-wsj**; Hank Cardello, "Mediation Could Never Have Saved Hostess: Its Problems Ran Much Deeper," *Forbes,* November 21, 2012, **www.forbes.com/sites/forbesleadershipforum/2012/11/21/mediation-could-never-have-saved-hostess-its-problems-ran-much-deeper/**; Chris Isidore and James O'Tool, "Hostess Closing Ok'd by Judge," *CNN,* November 21, 2012, **http://money.cnn.com/2012/11/21/news/companies/hostess-closing/index.html**; George F. Will, "Digesting Hostess Twinkies Lessons," *Boston Herald,* November 25, 2012, **www.bostonherald.com/news/opinion/op_ed/view/20221125digesting_hostess_twinkies_lessons_markets_may_let_boomers_eat_cake/**; ABC News, "Hostess Reopening Plants, Without Union Workers," *ABC News,* April 26, 2013, **http://abcnews.go.com/Business/twinkies-return-hostess-unions/story?id=19043854#.UYAizvUmx8E**.

34. Severin Carrell, Dan Milmo, Alan Travis, and Nick Hopkins, "Day of Strikes as Millions Heed Unions' Call to Fight Pension Cuts," *The Guardian,* November 29, 2011, **www.guardian.co.uk/society/2011/nov/30/public-sector-workers-strike-uk**.

35. James R. Hagerty, "Caterpillar Closes Plant in Canada after Lockout," *The Wall Street Journal,* February 3, 2012, **http://online.wsj.com/article/SB10001424052970203889904577200953014575964.html**.

36. "Union City Licorice Company Heads to Mediation," *CBS San Francisco,* January 9, 2012, **http://sanfrancisco.cbslocal.com/2012/01/09/union-city-licorice-company-strike-heads-to-mediation/**.

37. Reuters, "JP Morgan Discloses It Lost in an Arbitration Last Year," *The New York Times,* March 22, 2012, **www.nytimes.com/2012/03/23/business/jpmorgan-discloses-it-lost-in-arbitration-to-american-century.html**.

38. "US Will Have Minority Whites Sooner, Says Demographer," *NPR,* June 27, 2011, **www.npr.org/2011/06/27/137448906/us-will-have-minoritywhites-sooner-says-demographer**.

39. DiversityInc, "The DiversityInc Top 50 Companies for Diversity," *DiversityInc,* 2012, **www.diversityinc.com/the-diversityinc-top-50-companies-for-diversity-2012/**.

40. Judy Owen, "The Benefits of Disability in the Workplace," *Forbes,* May 12, 2012, **www.forbes.com/sites/judyowen/2012/05/12/a-cost-benefit-analysis-of-disability-in-the-workplace/**; Office of Disability Employment Policy, "Disability Policy. Employment Practice. Full Inclusion," *Department of Labor,* September 2012, **www.dol.gov/odep/**; *Huffington Post,* "Hiring Disabled Workers Can Make Workers More Efficient," *Huffington Post,* July 12, 2012, **www.huffingtonpost.com/2012/07/26/workers-with-disabilities_n_1707421.html**; Peggy Klaus, "A Chance to See Disabilities as Assets," *The New York Times,* February 4, 2012, **www.nytimes.com/2012/02/05/jobs/disabilities-can-be-workplace-assets.html**; disAbility Resource Center, "Accessible Design/Universal Design Resources," May 28, 2012, **www.makoa.org/accessible-design.htm**; NC State University, "Center for Universal Design," **www.ncsu.edu/project/design-projects/udi/**; "DLLR's Division of Workforce Development and Adult Learning," *Maryland's Department of Labor, Licensing and Regulation,* May 17, 2010, **www.dllr.state.md.us/employment/businessservices1.shtml**; Hill Country Disabled Group, "What Is a Disability?" **http://hcdg.org/definition.htm**.

41. Taylor H. Cox Jr., "The Multicultural Organization," *Academy of Management Executives* 5 (May 1991), pp. 34–47; Marilyn Loden and Judy B. Rosener, *Workforce America! Managing Employee Diversity as a Vital Resource* (Homewood, IL: Business One Irwin, 1991).

42. Paul Davidson, "Overworked and Underpaid?" *USA Today,* April 16, 2012, pp. 1A–2A.

43. Ibid.

44. Ethics Resource Center, *2011 National Business Ethics Survey® : Ethics in Transition* (Arlington, VA: Ethics Resource Center, 2012), pp. 39–40.

45. Davidson, "Overworked and Underpaid?"

46. Melanie Trottman, "For Angry Employees, Legal Cover for Rants," *The Wall Street Journal,* December 2, 2011, **http://online.wsj.com/article/SB10001424052970203710704577049822809710332.html**.

47. Martin Crutsinger, "Hiring Grows as Companies Hit Limits with Workers," *MPR News,* March 7, 2012, **http://minnesota.publicradio.org/display/web/2012/03/07/hiring-grows-as-companies-hit-limit/**.

CHAPTER 11

1. Adapted from William Pride and O.C. Ferrell, "Value-Driven Marketing," *Foundations of Marketing,* 4th ed. (Mason, OH: South-Western Cengage Learning), pp. 13–14.
2. Bruce Horovitz, "Domino's Offers Gluten-Free Pizza Crust," *USA Today,* May 7, 2012, p. B1.
3. "Beauty Queen," *People,* May 10, 2004, p. 187.
4. Bruce Einhorn, "China Is Really Big. Its Brands, Not So Much," *Bloomberg Businessweek,* July 30–August 5, 2012, pp. 19–20; Thomas Isaac, "Made in China, the Fear Factor," *Asian Conversations,* January 2012, **www.asianconversations.com/ChinaBrands.php**.
5. Michael Treacy and Fred Wiersema, *The Discipline of Market Leaders* (Reading, MA: Addison Wesley, 1995), p. 176.
6. Jefferson Graham, "At Apple Stores, iPads at Your Service," *USA Today,* May 23, 2011, p. 1B; "Apple Stores," AAPLInvestors, **www.apple.com/retail/storelist/**.
7. Customer Insight Group Inc., "Program Design: Loyalty and Retention," **www.customerinsightgroup.com/loyalty_retention.php**.
8. Venky Shankar, "Multiple TouchPoint Marketing," American Marketing Association, Faculty Consortium on Electronic Commerce, Texas A&M University, July 14–17, 2001.
9. Brad Wieners, "Lego Is for Girls," *Bloomberg Businessweek,* December 19–25, 2011, pp. 68–73.
10. David Kesmodel, "Brewers Go Courting Hispanics," *The Wall Street Journal,* July 12, 2011, p. B8.
11. "Minority Report," *The Economist,* March 31, 2011, **www.economist.com/node/18488452**.
12. Horovitz, "Domino's Offers Gluten-Free Pizza Crust," p. B1.
13. "The Coca-Cola Company Fact Sheet," **http://assets.coca-colacompany.com/90/11/5f21b88444bab46d430b4c578e80/Company_Fact_Sheet.pdf**; "Growth, Leadership, and Sustainability," The Coca-Cola Company, **www.thecocacolacompany.com/ourcompany**.
14. Hannah Elliott, "Most Fuel-Efficient Cars for the Buck," *Forbes,* March 30, 2009, **www.forbes.com/2009/03/30/fuel-efficient-cars-lifestyle-vehicles-efficient-cars.html**.
15. "AdWords," Google, **https://adwords.google.com/um/gaiaauth?apt%3DNone%26ltmpl%3Djfk%26ltmpl%3Djfk&error=newact&sacu=1&sarp=1**.
16. Sarah E. Needleman, "Facebook 'Likes' Small Business," *The Wall Street Journal,* September 26, 2011, p. B11.
17. Emily Steel and Geoffrey A. Fowler, "Big Brands Like Facebook, But They Don't Like to Pay," *The Wall Street Journal,* November 2, 2011, **http://online.wsj.com/article/SB10001424052970204294504576613232804554362.html?mg5comwsj**.
18. Christine Birkner, "10 Minutes with . . . Raul Murguia Villegas," *Marketing News,* July 30, 2011, pp. 26–27.
19. "MSPA North America," Mystery Shopping Providers Association, **http://mysteryshop.org/**.
20. Piet Levy, "10 Minutes with . . . Robert J. Morais," *Marketing News,* May 30, 2011, pp. 22–23.
21. Emily Maltby, "Not a Barber Shop: A Salon for Men," *The Wall Street Journal,* August 16, 2012, B7; Sports Clip website, **www.sportclips.com**.
22. Steven Kurutz, "On Kickstarter, Designers' Dream Materialize," *The New York Times,* September 21, 2011, **www.nytimes.com/2011/09/22/garden/on-kickstarter-designers-dreams-materialize.html?pagewanted=all**.
23. Mya Frazier, "CrowdSourcing," *Delta Sky Mag,* February 2010, p. 73.
24. Sue Shellenbarger, "A Few Bucks for Your Thoughts?" *The Wall Street Journal,* May 18, 2011, **http://online.wsj.com/article/SB10001424052748703509104576329110724411724.html**.
25. David Rosenbaum, "Who's Out There?" *CFO,* January/February 2012, pp. 44–49.
26. Sustainable Coalition website, **www.apparelcoalition.org/**; Eliana Dockerman, "Eco Chic: How U.S Clothing Brands Are Getting Greener," *Time,* August 20, 2012, p. 13; "Target, Walmart and Kohl's Launch Higg Index," August 2, 2012, *Green Retail Decisions,* **www.greenretaildecisions.com/news/2012/08/02/target-walmart-and-kohls-launch-higg-index**.
27. Bruce Horovitz, "Gum Goes from Humdrum to Teen Fashion Statement," *USA Today,* May 8, 2012, p. B1.
28. Jon Gertner, "How Do You Solve a Problem Like GM, Mary?" *Fast Company,* October 2011, pp. 104–108, 148; Sharon Terlep, "The Secrets of the GM Diet," *The Wall Street Journal,* August 5, 2011, pp. B1, B4.

CHAPTER 12

1. Narendra Rao, "The Keys to New Product Success (Part 1): Collecting Unarticulated & Invisible Customer Needs," *Product Management & Strategy,* June 19, 2007, **http://productstrategy.wordpress.com/2007/06/19/the-keys-to-new-product-succeess-part-1-collecting-unarticulated-invisible-customer-needs/**.
2. Nicholas Kolakowski, "HP's Touch Pad Proves a Bestseller in Its Dying Moments," eWeek.com, August 22, 2011, **www.eweek.com/c/a/Mobile-and-Wireless/HPs-TouchPad-Proves-a-Bestseller-In-its-Dying-Moments-373816/**.
3. Associated Press, "Jobs Says iPad Idea Came before iPhone," *Fox News,* June 2, 2010, **www.foxnews.com/tech/2010/06/02/jobs-says-ipad-idea-came-iphone/**.
4. "Amazon.com Inc.," *Yahoo! Finance,* **http://finance.yahoo.com/q/is?s=AMZN+Income+Statement&annual**; John A. Byrne, "Greatest Entrepreneurs of Our Time," *Fortune,* April 9, 2012, pp. 68–86.
5. "Cat® CT660 Vocational Trucks Ready for Work," Caterpillar Press Release, September 2011.
6. Lisa Ryckman, "25th Anniversary Top Company, Crocs Inc.," *Coloradobiz Magazine,* November 2012; Andrew Adam Newman, "Crocs Campaign Nods to its Clog," *The New York Times,* January 11, 2012, **www.nytimes.com/2012/01/12/business/media/crocs-expands-line-but-honors-its-clog-advertising.html?n=Top%2fNews%2fBusiness%2fCompanies%2fCrocs%20Inc.&_r=0**; Elizabeth Wellington, "Fashion Attack," *Philadelphia Inquirer,* July 5, 2007, **http://articles.philly.com/2007-07-05/news/24994606_1_crocs-soft-shoe-socks**.
7. Julia Scott, "Jamba Juice Honoring McDonald's Smoothie Coupons," *Daily Finance,* August 10, 2010, **www.dailyfinance.com/2010/08/10/jamba-juice-honoring-mcdonalds-smoothie-coupons/**.
8. Diana Falzone, "Google Glass: Half Empty, or Half Full?" *Fox,* May 6, 2013, **www.foxnews.com/entertainment/2013/05/06/google-glass-half-empty-or-half-full/**.
9. Kent German, "A Brief History of Android Phones," *CNET,* August 2, 2011, **http://reviews.cnet.com/8301-19736_7-20016542-251/a-brief-history-of-android-phones/**; Mike Luttrell, "Android Suffers First-Ever Market Share Decline," *TG Daily,* January 27, 2012, **www.tgdaily.com/mobility-brief/61070-android-suffers-first-ever-market-sharedecline**.

10. Sean Ludwig, "Apple Now Has More Than 300M iCloud Users," *Venture Beat,* April 23, 2013, **http://venturebeat.com/2013/04/23/apple-now-has-300m-icloud-users/**.
11. Duane Stanford, "Africa: Coke's Last Frontier," *Bloomberg Businessweek,* October 28, 2010, **www.businessweek.com/magazine/content/10_45/b4202054144294.htm**; Kim Peterson, "Coke Debuts Smaller Bottles," *MSN Money,* September 19, 2011, **http://money.msn.com/top-stocks/post.aspx?post=2e4eaa5c-2162-4135-81c6-6d41a02d91b9**; Meghra Bahree and Mike Esterl, "PepsiCo's Health Push," *The Wall Street Journal,* July 7, 2011, p. B8.
12. MSN Autos, "Good Riddance! Worst Discontinued Cars for 2011: Chevrolet Cobalt," **http://autos.ca.msn.com/specials/buyers-guide/gallery.aspx?cp-documentid=26951603&page=7**.
13. "Product Life Cycle," Answers.com, **www.answers.com/topic/product-lifecycle**.
14. Bruce Horovitz, "Barbie Ventures into Online World with Stardolls," *The Wall Street Journal,* November 14, 2011, p. 1B.
15. ABC News, "Jason Wu for Target Apparel Sells Out in Hours," February 6, 2011, **http://abcnewsradioonline.com/business-news/jason-wu-for-target-apparel-sells-out-in-hours.html**.
16. "Private Label Gets Personal," *Shopper Culture,* October 1, 2009, **www.shopperculture.com/shopper_culture/2009/10/private-label-gets-personal.html**.
17. Mona Doyle, "What Packaging Will Consumers Pay More For?" *Food & Beverage Packaging,* August 1, 2008, **www.foodandbeveragepackaging.com/Articles/Article_Rotation/BNP_GUID_9-5-2006_A_10000000000000401665**.
18. Bruce Horovitz, "Marketers Capitalize on Fond Thoughts of the Good Ol' Days," *USA Today,* March 11–13, 2011, p. 1A.
19. Mike Ramsey, "Ford Drops in Quality Survey," *The Wall Street Journal,* June 24, 2011, **http://online.wsj.com/article/SB10001424052702304569504576403824202399548.html**; Nick Bunkley, "After Ratings Drop, Ford Reworks Touch Screen," *The New York Times,* March 5, 2012, **www.nytimes.com/2012/03/06/business/after-ratings-drop-ford-reworks-touch-screens.html?_r=0**; Associated Press, "Lexus Tops Quality Survey, Ford Stumbles Again," *Fox News,* June 20, 2012, **www.foxnews.com/leisure/2012/06/20/lexus-tops-quality-survey-ford-stumbles-again/**.
20. American Customer Satisfaction Index, "Map of ACSI Structure," **www.theacsi.org/about-acsi/acsi-benchmarks-national-sector-industry**.
21. "American Demographics 2006 Consumer Perception Survey," *Advertising Age,* January 2, 2006, p. 9. Data by Synovate.
22. Rajneesh Suri and Kent B. Monroe, "The Effects of Time Constraints on Consumers' Judgments of Prices and Products," *Journal of Consumer Research 30*(June 2003), p. 92.
23. Annie Gasparro, "Darden to Update Its Restaurants," *The Wall Street Journal,* September 24, 2012, p. B9; Candice Choi and Michelle Chapman, "Darden's Profit Rises ahead of Revamps for Olive Garden, Red Lobster," September 21, 2012, **www.startribune.com/business/170673236.html?refer=y**; Julie Jargon and Kris Hudson, "Growing Restaurant Chains Flock to Malls," *The Wall Street Journal,* September 18, 2012, **http://online.wsj.com/article/SB1000087239639044477280457762395147857756 4.html?KEYWORDS=growing+restaurant+chains+flock+to+malls**.
24. Emily Maltby, "Restocking the Old Vending Machine with Live Bait and Prescription," *The Wall Street Journal,* March 22, 2012, p. B1.
25. Sysco, "The Sysco Story," **www.sysco.com/about-sysco.html#**.
26. "Top Threats to Revenue," *USA Today,* February 1, 2006, p. A1.
27. Brad Howarth, "Hear This, iPods from a Vending Machine," *The Sydney Morning Herald,* November 14, 2006, **www.smh.com.au/news/biztech/hearthis-ipods-from-a-vending-machine/2006/11/13/1163266481869.html**.
28. "Welcome to the Future of Shopping," Zoom Systems, **www.zoomsystems.com/zoomshops/zs_index.html**.
29. Piper Aircraft, "International Dealers and Sales Locations," **www.piper.com/docs/DealerMap_Intl.pdf**.
30. William Pride and O.C. Ferrell, *Marketing Foundations,* 5th ed. (Mason, OH: Cengage South-Western Learning, 2013), pp. 415–416.
31. Ibid.
32. Bloomberg News, "China's Soccer Moms Want SUVs, Too" *Bloomberg Businessweek,* May 3, 2012, **www.businessweek.com/articles/2012-05-03/chinas-soccer-moms-want-suvs-too**; Yingling Liu, "China's SUV Culture: Flaunting Fat Wallets While Choking on Dirty Air," *Worldwatch Institute,* October 8, 2012, **www.worldwatch.org/node/5657**; David Pierson, "SUVs Are Big in China," *Los Angeles Times,* April 24, 2012, **http://articles.latimes.com/2012/apr/24/business/la-fi-china-suv-20120425**.
33. Abbey Klaassen, "Even Google Has to Advertise," *Advertising Age,* June 2, 2008, p. 4.
34. Brian Steinberg, "TV Ad Prices: 'Idol' No Match for Football," *Advertising Age,* October 21, 2012, **http://adage.com/article/media/tv-ad-prices-idol-match-football/237874/**.
35. Rich Thomaselli, "National Football League Players: CBS Rejected Let Us Play Ad," *Advertising Age,* January 31, 2011, **http://adage.com/article/news/nationalfootball-league-players-cbs-rejectedplay-ad/148580/**.
36. Dan Bigman, "Big Risk, Big Reward: Felix Baumgartner and Red Bull Deserve All the Marketing Buzz They Get," *Forbes,* October 14, 2012, **www.forbes.com/sites/danbigman/2012/10/14/big-risk-big-reward-felix-baumgartner-and-red-bull-deserve-all-the-marketing-buzz-they-can-get/**.
37. Gerry Khermouch and Jeff Green, "Buzz Marketing," *BusinessWeek,* July 30, 2001, pp. 50–56.
38. Andrew Romano, "Now 4 Restaurant 2.0," *Newsweek,* February 28, 2009, **www.newsweek.com/id/187008**.
39. Lauren Johnson, "Mobile Coupon Redemption Expected to Reach 8pc by 2016: Study," *Mobile Commerce Daily,* January 6, 2012, **www.mobilecommercedaily.com/mobile-coupon-redemption-expected-to-reach-8pc-by-2016-study**.
40. Ken Harris, *Forbes,* April 27, 2010, **www.forbes.com/2010/04/27/retail-manufacturing-cooperation-safeway-wal-mart-target-unilever-cmo-network-ken-harris.html**.
41. Evan Niu, "At Long Last, T-Mobile Is Getting the iPhone," *Daily Finance,* December 7, 2012, **www.dailyfinance.com/2012/12/07/at-long-last-t-mobile-is-getting-the-iphone/**.
42. Scott McCartney, "Whatever You Do, Don't Buy an Airline Ticket . . . ," *The Wall Street Journal,* January 27, 2011, **http://online.wsj.com/article/SB1000142405274870406260457610 5953506930800.html**.

CHAPTER 13

1. The material in this chapter is reserved for use in the authors' other textbooks and teaching materials.
2. Brad Stone and Bruce Einhorn, "Baidu China," *Bloomberg Businessweek,* November 15–21, 2010, pp. 60–67; Trefis Team, "Baidu Girds for Google Battle in China," *Forbes,*

www.forbes.com/sites/greatspeculations/2011/12/07/baidu-girds-for-google-battle-in-china/.

3. "Fortune 500: Amazon.com," *Fortune,* 2009, **http://money.cnn.com/magazines/fortune/fortune500/2009/snapshots/10810.html**; Josh Quittner, "How Jeff Bezos Rules the Retail Space," *Fortune,* May 5, 2008, pp. 127–132.
4. Hulu website, **www.hulu.com/about**.
5. Bobby White, "The New Workplace Rules: No Video-Watching," *The Wall Street Journal,* March 4, 2008, p. B1.
6. "Internet Usage Statistics," Internet World Stats, **www.Internetworldstats.com/stats.htm**.
7. Michael V. Copeland, "Tapping Tech's Beautiful Mind," *Fortune,* October 12, 2009, pp. 35–36.
8. Yasmeen Abutaleb, "Universities Push E-Textbook Sales," *USA Today,* August 14, 2012, p. 1B; Richard Nieva, "Banking on Better Books," *Fortune Magazine,* July 2, 2012, p. 32; Stephanie Brookes, "Should Universities Force E-Books on Students?" **TeleRead.com**, September 7, 2012, **www.teleread.com/university/should-universities-force-e-textbooks-on-students/**.
9. Matthew Boyle and Douglas MacMillan, "Wal-Mart's Rocky Path from Bricks to Clicks," *Bloomberg Businessweek,* July 25–31, 2011, pp. 31–33; "Free Shipping with Site to Store®," Walmart, **www.walmart.com/cp/Siteto-Store/538452**.
10. Aaron Back, "China's Big Brands Tackle Web Sales," *The Wall Street Journal,* December 1, 2009, p. B2; "The Taobao Affair from China Largest Auction Website," *PR Log,* February 7, 2010, **www.prlog.org/10552554-thetaobao-affair-from-china-largestauction-website.html**.
11. Shayndi Raice, "The Man behind Facebook's Marketing," *The Wall Street Journal,* February 3, 2012, p. B7; "Interacting with Ads," Facebook, **www.facebook.com/help/?page=154500071282557**.
12. "2009 Digital Handbook," *Marketing News,* April 30, 2009, p. 13.
13. Cameron Chapman, "The History and Evolution of Social Media," *WebDesigner Depot,* October 7, 2009, **www.webdesignerdepot.com/2009/10/the-history-and-evolution-of-social-media/**.
14. "The History of Social Media in a Blink," *Nightshift,* November 22, 2007, **http://marcbresseel.wordpress.com/2007/11/22/the-history-of-social-media-in-a-blink/**.
15. "CafeMom," Highland Capital Partners, **www.hcp.com/cafemom**; "Top 15 Most Popular Social Networking Sites," *eBiz,* February 2012, **www.ebizmba.com/articles/social-networking-websites**; "Advertise with Us," CafeMom website, **www.cafemom.com/about/advertise.php**.
16. Zachary Karabell, "To Tweet or Not to Tweet," April 12, 2011, *Time,* p. 24.
17. "It's a Social World: Social Networking Leads as Top Online Activity Globally, Accounting for 1 in Every 5 Online Minutes," *comScore,* December 21, 2011, **www.comscore.com/Press_Events/Press_Releases/2011/12/Social_Networking_Leads_as_Top_Online_Activity_Globally**.
18. "Facebook: Largest, Fastest Growing Social Network," *Tech Tree,* August 13, 2008, **www.techtree.com/India/News/Facebook_Largest_Fastest_Growing_Social_Network/551-92134-643.html**.
19. Nick Summers, "Heated Rivalries: #9 Facebook vs. MySpace," *Newsweek,* **www.2010.newsweek.com/top-10/heated-rivalries/facebook-vs-myspace.html**.
20. Courtney Rubin, "Internet Users over Age 50 Flocking to Social Media," *Inc.,* August 30, 2010, **www.inc.com/news/articles/2010/08/users-over-50-are-fastest-growing-social-media-demographic.html**.
21. Trefis Team, "Facebook's Gifts and Collections Could Spur E-Commerce Growth," *Forbes,* October 10, 2012, **www.forbes.com/sites/greatspeculations/2012/10/10/facebooks-gifts-and-collections-could-spur-e-commerce-growth/**.
22. Cotton Delo, "New Belgium Toasts to Its Facebook Fans," *Advertising Age,* February 13, 2012, **http://adage.com/article/news/belgium-toasts-facebookfans/232681/**.
23. Jefferson Graham, "Cake Decorator Finds Twitter a Tweet Recipe for Success," *USA Today,* April 1, 2009, p. 5B.
24. Bruce Horovitz, "Marketers Step Up Their Rewards for Twitter Buzz," *USA Today,* November 17, 2010, p. 2B.
25. Anthony Ha, "Twitter Says More Than Half Its Users Follow Six or More Brands," October 2, 2012, **http://techcrunch.com/2012/10/02/twitter-follow-brands/**.
26. Zachary Karabell, "To Tweet or Not to Tweet," *Time,* April 11, 2011, p. 24.
27. Suzanne Vranica, "Tweets Spawn Ad Campaigns," *The Wall Street Journal,* October 22, 2012, p. B5.
28. "As Twitter Grows and Evolves, More Manpower Is Needed," *Marketing News,* March 15, 2011, p. 13.
29. "2012 Social Media Summit," Harrisburg University, May 23, 2012, **www.harrisburgu.edu/news/event-details.php?id=348&cid=5**.
30. Jeff Bercovici, "Tumblr: David Karp's $800 Million Art Project," *Forbes,* January 2, 2013, **www.forbes.com/sites/jeffbercovici/2013/01/02/tumblr-david-karps-800-million-art-project/**.
31. A.C. Nielsen, "Global Faces and Networked Places: A Nielsen Report on Social Networking's New Global Footprint," March 2009, **www.nielsen.com/content/dam/corporate/us/en/newswire/uploads/2009/03/nielsen_globalfaces_mar09.pdf**.
32. Hyejin Kim, "Couldn't Stop the Spread of the Conversation in Reactions from Other Bloggers," May 4, 2007, blog post, "Korea: Bloggers and Donuts" on the Global Voices blog, **http://globalvoicesonline.org/2007/05/04/korea-bloggers-and-donuts/**.
33. Randy Tinseth, "Randy's Journal," Boeing, **http://boeingblogs.com/randy/**.
34. Drake Bennett, "Ten Years of Inaccuracy and Remarkable Detail: Wikipedia," *Bloomberg Businessweek,* January 10, 2011, pp. 57–61; "Wikipedia: About," *Wikipedia,* **http://en.wikipedia.org/wiki/Wikipedia:About**.
35. Charlene Li and Josh Bernoff, *Groundswell* (Boston: Harvard Business Press, 2008), pp. 25–26.
36. Paula Berg, "Why Every Brand-Conscious Business Should Blog," *Colorado Business,* October 2012, p. 12.
37. MarketingCharts staff, "Adoption of Blogs Rises among Fortune 500 Cos.," *Marketing Charts,* September 4, 2012, **www.marketingcharts.com/interactive/blogging-up-among-fortune-500-cos-23135/**,
38. Laura Schlereth, "Marketers' Interest in Pinterest," *Marketing News,* April 30, 2012, pp. 8–9; The Creative Group, "PINTEREST INTEREST: Survey: 17 Percent of Marketers Currently Using or Planning to Join Pinterest," August 22, 2012, **www.sacbee.com/2012/08/22/4747399/pinterest-interest-survey-17-percent.html**; Jason Falls, "How Pinterest Is Becoming the Next Big Thing in Social Media for Business," *Entrepreneur,* February 7, 2012, **www.entrepreneur.com/article/222740**; Pinterest website, **http://pinterest.com/**; "Whole Foods Foundation," Pinterest, **http://pinterest.com/wholefoods/whole-planet-foundation/**.

39. Emily Glazer, "Who Is Ray WJ? YouTube's Top Star," *The Wall Street Journal*, February 2, 2012, p. B1.

40. Tom Foster, "The GoPro Army," *Inc.*, February 2012, pp. 52–59.

41. Steven Bertoni, "How Stanford Made Instagram an Instant Success," *Forbes*, August 20, 2012, pp. 56–63; Jefferson Graham, "Instagram Is a Start-up Magnet," *USA Today*, August 9, 2012, **www.usatoday.com/tech/news/story/2012-08-07/instagram-economy/56883474/1**; Karen Rosenberg, "Everyone's Lives, in Pictures," *The New York Times*, April 12, 2012, **www.nytimes.com/2012/04/22/sunday-review/everyones-lives-in-pictures-from-instagram.html**; Kelly Clay, "3 Things You Can Learn about Your Business with Instagram," *Forbes*, August 9, 2012, **www.forbes.com/sites/kellyclay/2012/08/09/3-things-you-can-learn-about-your-business-with-instagram/**; Ian Crouch, "Instagram's Instant Nostalgia," *The New Yorker*, April 10, 2012, **www.newyorker.com/online/blogs/culture/2012/04/instagrams-instant-nostalgia.html#slide_ss_0=1**.

42. Laura Schlereth, "Marketers' Interest in Pinterest," *Marketing News*, April 30, 2012, pp. 8–9; The Creative Group, "PINTEREST INTEREST: Survey: 17 Percent of Marketers Currently Using or Planning to Join Pinterest," August 22, 2012, **www.sacbee.com/2012/08/22/4747399/pinterest-interest-survey-17-percent.html**; Jason Falls, "How Pinterest Is Becoming the Next Big Thing in Social Media for Business," *Entrepreneur*, February 7, 2012, **www.entrepreneur.com/article/222740**; Pinterest website, **http://pinterest.com/wholefoods/whole-planet-foundation/**.

43. "Keller Williams Reality Photo Stream," **www.flickr.com/photos/kellerwilliamsrealty/**.

44. Kelly Clay, "3 Things You Can Learn about Your Business with Instagram," *Forbes*, August 9, 2012, **www.forbes.com/sites/kellyclay/2012/08/09/3-things-you-can-learn-about-your-business-with-instagram/**.

45. Pinterest, "Whole Planet Foundation," **http://pinterest.com/wholefoods/whole-planet-foundation/**.

46. Matt McGee, "How to Market on Flickr," Small Business Search Marketing, June 15, 2006, **www.smallbusinesssem.com/how-to-market-on-flickr/6031/**.

47. "2009 Digital Handbook," p. 14.

48. "About Made Money," *CNBC*, **www.cnbc.com/id/17283246/**.

49. "Dominos Pizza, Second Places," **www.secondplaces.net/opencms/opencms/portfolio/caseStudies/caseStudy_dominospizza.html**.

50. Brandy Shaul, "CityVille Celebrates the Golden Arches with Branded McDonald's Restaurant," *Games.com*, October 19, 2011, **http://blog.games.com/2011/10/19/cityville-mcdonalds-restaurant/**.

51. Emily Glazer, "Virtual Fairs Offer Real Jobs," *The Wall Street Journal*, October 31, 2011, p. B9.

52. Steven Bertoni, "How Stanford Made Instagram an Instant Success," *Forbes*, August 20, 2012, pp. 56–63; Jefferson Graham, "Instagram Is a Start-up Magnet," *USA Today*, August 9, 2012, **www.usatoday.com/tech/news/story/2012-08-07/instagram-economy/56883474/1**; Karen Rosenberg, "Everyone's Lives, in Pictures," *The New York Times*, April 12, 2012, **www.nytimes.com/2012/04/22/sunday-review/everyones-lives-in-pictures-from-instagram.html**; Kelly Clay, "3 Things You Can Learn about Your Business with Instagram," *Forbes*, August 9, 2012, **www.forbes.com/sites/kellyclay/2012/08/09/3-things-you-can-learn-about-your-business-with-instagram/**; Ian Crouch, "Instagram's Instant Nostalgia," *The New Yorker*, April 10, 2012, **www.newyorker.com/online/blogs/culture/2012/04/instagrams-instant-nostalgia.html#slide_ss_0=1**.

53. Roger Yu, "Smartphones Help Make Bon Voyages," *USA Today*, March 5, 2010, p. B1.

54. Kate Freeman, "Majority of Marketers Plan to Increase Mobile Budgets in 2013," July 6, 2012, **http://mashable.com/2012/07/06/marketers-increase-budgets-for-mobile/**.

55. Mark Milian, "Why Text Messages Are Limited to 160 Characters," *Los Angeles Times*, May 3, 2009, **http://latimesblogs.latimes.com/technology/2009/05/invented-text-messaging.html**; "Eight Reasons Why Your Business Should Use SMS Marketing," *Mobile Marketing Ratings*, **www.mobilemarketingratings.com/eight-reasons-sms-marketing.html**.

56. Lauren Folino and Michelle V. Rafter, "How to Use Multimedia for Business Marketing," *Inc.*, January 25, 2010, **www.inc.com/guides/multimedia-for-business-marketing.html**; "Motorola Powers House of Blues(R)," *PR Newswire*, **www.prnewswire.com/news-releases/motorola-powers-house-of-bluesr-54990822.html**.

57. Shira Ovide, "Mobile-Ad Tactics That Work," *The Wall Street Journal*, September 28, 2012, p. B1.

58. Steven Musil, "Mobile Internet Traffic Gaining Fast on Desktop Internet Traffic," *cnet*, December 3, 2012, **http://news.cnet.com/8301-1023_3-57556943-93/mobile-internet-traffic-gaining-fast-on-desktop-internet-traffic/**.

59. "Foursquare and OpenTable Just Made It Even Easier to Plan Your Perfect Night Out," September 28, 2012. **http://blog.foursquare.com/2012/09/28/foursquare-and-opentable-just-made-it-even-easier-to-plan-your-perfect-night-out/**.

60. Anita Campbell, "What the Heck Is an App?" *Small Business Trends*, March 7, 2011, **http://smallbiztrends.com/2011/03/what-is-an-app.html**.

61. "Half of Adult Cell Phone Users Have Apps on Their Phones," Pew Internet and American Life Project, November 2, 2011, **http://pewinternet.org/~/media/Files/Reports/2011/PIP_Apps-Update-2011.pdf**.

62. Todd Wasserman, "5 Innovative Mobile Marketing Campaigns," *Mashable*, March 8, 2011, **http://mashable.com/2011/03/08/mobile-marketing-campaigns/**.

63. Umika Pidaparthy, "Marketers Embracing QR Codes, for Better or Worse," *CNN Tech*, March 28, 2011, **http://articles.cnn.com/2011-03-28/tech/qr.codes.marketing_1_qr-smartphone-users-symbian?_s=PM:TECH**.

64. Brad Stone and Olga Kharif, "Pay As You Go," *Bloomberg Businessweek*, July 18–24, 2011, pp. 66–71.

65. "Google Wallet," **www.google.com/wallet/what-is-google-wallet.html**.

66. Miriam Gottfried, "Mobile Banking Gets Riskier," *The Wall Street Journal*, July 10, 2011, p. B7.

67. Vangie Beal, "All About Widgets," *Webopedia*™, August 31, 2010, **www.webopedia.com/DidYouKnow/Internet/2007/widgets.asp**.

68. Rachael King, "Building a Brand with Widgets," *Bloomberg Businessweek*, March 3, 2008, **www.businessweek.com/technology/content/feb2008/tc20080303_000743.htm**.

69. "Barkley Develops Krispy Kreme® 'Hot Light' App and Widget," *PR Newswire*, December 23, 2011, **www.prnewswire.com/news-releases/barkley-develops-krispy-kreme-hot-light-app-and-widget-136140073.html**.

70. Li and Bernoff, *Groundswell*, p. 41.

71. Li and Bernoff, *Groundswell*, pp. 41–42.

72. "Forrester Unveils New Segment of Social Technographics—The Conversationalists," *360 Digital Connections*, January 21, 2010, **http://blog.360i.com/social-marketing/forrester-new-segment-social-technographics-conversationalists**.

73. Li and Bernoff, *Groundswell,* p. 44.
74. Li and Bernoff, *Groundswell,* pp. 44–45.
75. Li and Bernoff, *Groundswell,* pp. 26–27.
76. Julia Angwin, Shayndi Raice, and Spencer E. Ante, "Facebook Retreats on Privacy, *The Wall Street Journal,* November 11, 2011, **http://online.wsj.com/article/SB10001424052970204224604577030383745515166.html**.
77. Jon Swartz, "Facebook Changes Its Status in Washington," *USA Today,* January 13, 2011, pp. 1B–2B; John W. Miller, "Yahoo Cookie Plan in Place," *The Wall Street Journal,* March 19, 2011, **http://online.wsj.com/article/SB10001424052748703512404576208700813815570.html**.
78. Byron Acohido, "Net Do-Not-Track Option Kicks Off to Criticism," *USA Today,* August 30, 2011, p. 2B.
79. Larry Barrett, "Data Breach Costs Surge in 2009: Study," *eSecurityPlanet,* January 26, 2010, **www.esecurityplanet.com/features/article.php/3860811/Data-Breach-Costs-Surge-in-2009-Study.htm**.
80. Olga Kharif, "A New Frontier for Criminals," *Bloomberg Businessweek,* October 8–October 14, 2012, p. 62.
81. Christine Dugas, "Now, It's a Severe Scam Warning," *USA Today,* November 2, 2012, p. 1B.
82. Brett Molina, "Legit Megaupload Users Cut Off from Their Files," *The Wall Street Journal,* February 1, 2012, p. 3B.
83. Kevin Shanahan and Mike Hyman, "Motivators and Enablers of SCOURing," *Journal of Business Research* 63 (September–October 2010), pp. 1095–1102.
84. "Seventh Annual BSA and IDC Global Software Piracy Study," BSA, **http://globalstudy.bsa.org/2009/**.
85. Max Chafkin, "The Case, and the Plan, for the Virtual Company," *Inc.,* April 2010, p. 68.

CHAPTER 14

1. "SEC Charges Deloitte & Touche in Shanghai with Violating U.S. Securities Laws in Refusal to Produce Documents," U.S. Securities & Exchange Commission, May 9, 2012, **www.sec.gov/news/press/2012/2012-87.htm**.
2. Association of Certified Fraud Examiners, *Report to the Nation on Occupational Fraud and Abuse* (Austin, TX: Association of Certified Fraud Examiners, 2012).
3. "About the ACFE," ACFE website, **www.acfe.com/about-the-acfe.aspx**.
4. Scott Thurm, "Buyers Beware: The Goodwill Games," *The Wall Street Journal,* August 14, 2012, p. B1; Amanda McMullen, "Examples of Goodwill in Accounting," *Chron.com,* **http://smallbusiness.chron.com/examples-goodwill-accounting-38665.html**; Rick Wayman, "Impairment Charges: The Good, the Bad, and the Ugly," *Investopedia,* July 29, 2012, **www.investopedia.com/articles/analyst/110502.asp#axzz24yPuObAe**.
5. Mary Williams Walsh, "State Woes Grow Too Big to Camouflage," *The New York Times,* March 29, 2010, **www.nytimes.com/2010/03/30/business/economy/30states.html**.
6. Sarah Johnson, "Averting Revenue-Recognition Angst," *CFO,* April 2012, p. 21.
7. "Integrated Reporting," **www.theiirc.org/**; Kathleen Hoffelder, "What Does Sustainability *Really* Cost?" *CFO,* August 28, 2012, **www3.cfo.com/article/2012/8/cash-flow_integrated-reporting-edelman-sustainability-vancity-cash-flow-iirc?currpage=0**; "Triple Bottom Line," *The Economist,* November 17, 2009, **www.economist.com/node/14301663**.
8. Buffalo Wild Wings website, **www.buffalowildwings.com/wings/**; "About Buffalo Wild Wings," *Entrepreneur,* **www.entrepreneur.com/franchises/buffalowildwings/282167-0.html**; Claire Cain Miller, "Girl's Night Out," *Forbes,* October 29, 2007, **www.forbes.com/forbes/2007/1029/098.html**; Meghan Casserly, "Taking Flight," *Forbes,* November 5, 2012, p. 104.
9. Julie Clements, "City of El Dorado Receives Accounting Award," *El Dorado Times,* April 3, 2012, **www.eldoradotimes.com/article/20120403/NEWS/304039932**.
10. "Accountants and Auditors: Occupational Outlook Handbook," *Bureau of Labor Statistics,* August 31, 2012, **www.bls.gov/ooh/Business-and-Financial/Accountants-and-auditors.htm**.

CHAPTER 15

1. Paul Krugman, "Why Is Deflation Bad?" *The New York Times,* August 2, 2010, **http://krugman.blogs.nytimes.com/2010/08/02/why-is-deflation-bad**.
2. "First Annual Negative Inflation in 49 Years," *RTE News,* February 12, 2009, **www.rte.ie/news/2009/0212/inflation.html**.
3. Phillip Inman, "Ireland Back in Recession as Global Slowdown Hits Exports," *guardian.co.uk,* March 22, 2012, **www.guardian.co.uk/business/2012/mar/22/ireland-recession-global-slowdown-exports**.
4. "Currency in Circulation (WCURCIR)," *Economic Research,* May 1, 2013. **http://research.stlouisfed.org/fred2/series/WCURCIR**.
5. "Weird and Wonderful Money Facts and Trivia," *Happy Worker,* **www.happyworker.com/magazine/facts/weird-and-wonderful-money-facts**.
6. Ibid.
7. "About the Redesigned Currency," The Department of the Treasury Bureau of Engraving and Printing, **www.newmoney.gov/newmoney/currency/aboutnotes.htm**.
8. Michael Zielinski, "Cost to Make Penny and Nickel Declines but Still Double Face Value," *Coin Update,* December 10, 2012, **http://news.coinupdate.com/cost-to-make-penny-and-nickel-declines-but-still-double-face-value-1751/**.
9. Ibid.
10. Jessica Dickler, "Americans Still Relying on Credit Cards to Get By," *CNN Money,* May 23, 2012, **http://money.cnn.com/2012/05/22/pf/credit-card/index.htm**; Martin Merzer, "Survey: Students Fail the Credit Card Test," *Fox Business,* April 16, 2012, **www.foxbusiness.com/personal-finance/2012/04/09/survey-students-fail-credit-card-test/**.
11. Anne Ryman, "ASU to Cash In on Student-ID, Debit-Card Deal with Bank," *The Arizona Republic,* June 21, 2012, **www.azcentral.com/community/tempe/articles/2012/06/23/20120623asu-cash-student-id-debit-card-deal-bank.html**; Andrew Martin, "On Campus, New Deals with Banks," *The New York Times,* May 30, 2012, **www.nytimes.com/2012/05/31/business/on-campus-new-deals-with-banks.html**; Christina Couch, "Fees on Debit Cards Cut into College Aid," Bankrate.com, **www.bankrate.com/finance/banking/fees-debit-cards-cut-college-aid.aspx**.
12. Roben Farzad, Mary Childs, and Shannon D. Harrington, "How JP Morgan Lost $2 Billion without Really Trying," *Bloomberg Businessweek,* May 24–27, 2012, pp. 44–46.
13. Joel Makower, "Why Wells Fargo Is Banking on Sustainability," *GreenBiz.com,* April 23, 2012, **www.greenbiz.com/**

blog/2012/04/23/why-wells-fargo-banking-sustainability; Wells Fargo, "Wells Fargo: $30+ Billion in Environmental Investments by 2020," April 23, 2012, **https://www.wellsfargo.com/press/2012/20120423_WellsFargo30Billion**; Nelson D. Schwartz, "Banks Look to Burnish Their Images by Backing Green Technology Firms," *The New York Times*, June 10, 2012, **www.nytimes.com/2012/06/11/business/banks-look-to-burnish-their-images-by-backing-green-technology-firms.html?_r=0**.

14. "Deposit Insurance Simplification Fact Sheet," FDIC website, **www.fdic.gov/deposit/deposits/DIfactsheet.html**.
15. "Bank Failures in Brief," Federal Deposit Insurance Corporation, **www.fdic.gov/bank/historical/bank/**.
16. "NACHA Reports More Than 18 Billion ACH Payments in 2007," NACHA: The Electronic Payments Association, May 10, 2008, **http://nacha.org/News/news/pressreleases/2008/Volume_Final.pdf**.
17. "From the Vault . . ." Ohio Commerce Bank, winter 2012, **www.ohiocommercebank.com/PDF/OCB%20Newsletter%20Winter%202012.pdf**.
18. Federal Deposit Insurance Corporation website, **www.fdic.gov**.
19. Shira Ovide, "Government Exits Citigroup: Is a Dividend Next?" *The Wall Street Journal*, December 7, 2010, **http://blogs.wsj.com/deals/2010/12/07/government-exits-citigroup-is-a-dividend-next/**.
20. Jon Swartz, "Starbucks Gets a Square Deal," *USA Today*, October 5, 2012, pp. 1B, 2B; Eric Savitz, "Jack Dorsey: Leadership Secrets of Twitter and Square," *Forbes Magazine*, November 5, 2012, pp. 64–70, **www.forbes.com/sites/ericsavitz/2012/10/17/jack-dorsey-the-leadership-secrets-of-twitter-and-square/**; Robin Shreeves, "How Does the Pay with Square App Work?" *Mother Nature Network*, August 8, 2012, **www.mnn.com/money/personal-finance/blogs/how-does-the-pay-with-square-app-work**; Aaron Smith and Laurie Segall, "Starbucks in Mobile Payment Deal with Square," *CNNMoney.com*, August 8, 2012, **http://money.cnn.com/2012/08/08/technology/starbucks-square-mobile/?iid=SF_BN_Lead**.
21. "CSI Pennsylvania," *CFO Magazine*, March 2008, p. 92.

CHAPTER 16

1. Kate O'Sullivan, "Going for the Other Green," *CFO*, September 2011, pp. 52–57; Carlye Adler, "Thinking Big," *Time*, May 3, 2011, **http://bx.businessweek.com/carbon-markets/view?url=http%3A%2F%2Fc.moreover.com%2Fclick%2Fhere.pl%3Fr4627673218%26f%3D9791**.
2. Calculated by Geoff Hirt from Apple's annual reports and website on May 27, 2012.
3. David Lewis, "Cleantech 2.0: Pragmatic and Capital-Efficient," *Coloradobiz Magazine*, November 2012, pp. 42–43; "Investment Focus & Criteria," Aravaipa Ventures, **www.aravaipaventures.com/Page_2.html**; "Colorado Cleantech Industry Association Selects the 2012 Finalists Honoring Leadership in Advancing Colorado's Cleantech Economy," PR Web, October 10, 2012, **www.prweb.com/releases/2012/10/prweb9992932.htm**.
4. Joshua Kennon, "Should You Invest in an IPO?" About.com, **http://beginnersinvest.about.com/od/investmentbanking/a/aa073106a.htm**.
5. Matt Krantz, "4 Reasons Investors Don't Like Facebook," *The Wall Street Journal*, August 2, 2012, p. 1B; Aaron Lucchetti, "Facebook's Next Fight: Suits, and More Suits," *The Wall Street Journal*, September 26, 2012; Shayndi Raice and Shira Ovide, "Groupon Investors Give Up," *The Wall Street Journal*, August 20, 2012, **http://online.wsj.com/article/SB10000872396390443989204577599273177326912.html**.
6. Vincent Ryan, "From Wall Street to Main Street," *CFO Magazine*, June 2008, pp. 85–86.

photo credits

FRONT MATTER

Page v: Jorg Greuel/Getty Images RF; p. vi (top): Doug Armand/Getty Images RF; p. vi (bottom): Comstock Images/Alamy RF; p. vii: Purestock/Superstock RF; p. viii (top): Ingram Publishing RF; p. viii (bottom): pictafolio/Getty Images RF; p. ix: © Stockbyte/PunchStock RF.

CHAPTER 1

Opener: Chris Hondros/Staff/Getty Images; p. 4: © 2013 Seventh Generation, Inc.; p. 6: GEICO/Google+; p. 7: Courtesy of Young Americans Center for Financial Education; p. 9: PAUL J. RICHARDS/AFP/Getty Images; p. 10: Purestock/Superstock RF; p. 14: Courtesy of the U.S. Department of the Treasury Bureau of the Public Debt.; p. 17 (top): Chris Ratcliffe/Bloomberg via Getty Images; p. 17 (bottom): Jin Lee/Bloomberg via Getty Images; p. 18: Courtesy of The Home Depot; p. 21: Fuse/Getty Images RF.

CHAPTER 2

Opener: Photodisc/Getty Images RF; p. 24: Courtesy of Sustainable Harvest; p. 26: SC Johnson via AP Images; p. 27 (top): NC1 WENN Photos/Newscom; p. 27 (bottom): ©Studio Lambert All Rights Reserved.; p. 30: RODRIGO BUENDIA/AFP/Getty Images; p. 31: Courtesy of Plagiarism.org; p. 34: Courtesy of Harpo Studios, Inc., George Burns/AP Images; p. 38: These materials have been reproduced with the permission of eBay Inc. © 2013 EBAY INC. ALL RIGHTS RESERVED; p. 40: Idealink Photography/Alamy RF; p. 41: MANDEL NGAN/AFP/Getty Images; p. 44: Bill Pugliano/Getty Images; p. 51: © The McGraw-Hill Companies, Inc./Mark Dierker, photographer; p. 55: Frederick Bass/Getty Images RF.

CHAPTER 3

Opener: Robert Churchill/Getty Images RF; p. 59: AFP/Getty Images; p. 60: Anat Givon/AP Images; p. 61: © Bob Henry/Alamy; p. 63: The McGraw-Hill Companies, Inc./Christopher Kerrigan, photographer; p. 64: © Henri Conodul/Iconotec.com; p. 65 (left): © Ryan McVay/Getty Images RF; p. 65 (right): © Stockbyte RF; p. 67: Joseph Van Os/The Image Bank/Getty Images; p. 69: PhotoLink/Getty Images RF; p. 70: Jennifer Thermes/Getty Images RF; p. 71: The APEC Logo reproduced with permission from the APEC Secretariat, www.apec.org; p. 73: Tulsa World, James Gibbard/AP Images; p. 75: © Walter Bibikow/Corbis; p. 76: Mark Ralston/AFP/Getty Images; p. 79: © Paul Bradbury/age fotostock RF.

CHAPTER 4

Opener: © 2013 Federal Express Corporation. All Rights Reserved; p. 83: © Ariel Skelley/Blend Images LLC RF; p. 85: Justin Sullivan/Getty Images; p. 86: Ben Margot/AP Images; p. 90: UNCLE BEN'S®, M&M'S®, SNICKERS®, MILKY WAY®, PEDIGREE®, and WHISKAS® are registered trademarks of Mars, Incorporated and its affiliates. WINTERFRESH®, BIG RED®, and ORBIT® are registered trademarks of Wrigley Co. These trademarks and product images are used with permission. Mars, Incorporated, Wrigley and its affiliates are not associated with McGraw-Hill Higher Education; p. 92: © Gregg Segal; p. 93: Stockbyte/Getty Images RF; p. 94: BEN STANSALL/AFP/Getty Images; p. 96: M.O. Stevens/Wikimedia Commons 3.0; p. 97: Donna McWilliam/Getty Images; p. 99: Ilene MacDonald/Alamy RF.

CHAPTER 5

Opener: Siri Stafford/Getty Images RF; p. 104: © Georgella/Alamy; p. 105: Ross Patten/Photoshot/Newscom; p. 106: © Little Man Ice Cream; p. 107: © John Foxx/Imagestate Media RF; p. 110 (top): Jonathan Wiggs/The Boston Globe via Getty Images; p. 110 (bottom): Ariel Skelley/Getty Images; p. 113: Maria Teijeiro/Getty Images RF; p. 114: Jack Dorsey/© jack; p. 117: Stockbyte/Getty Images RF.

CHAPTER 6

Opener: Bloomberg via Getty Images; p. 120: © Giuseppe Aresu/Bloomberg via Getty Images; p. 122: The Republic, Joe Harpring/AP Images; p. 123: Courtesy of Nokia; p. 124: © 2013 Monster; p. 126: © Yuriko Nakao/AFP/Getty Images; p. 129: Courtesy of Southwest Airlines; p. 132: Sakchai Lalit/AP Images; p. 134: © The McGraw-Hill Companies, Inc./Mark Dierker, photographer; p. 135: Screenshot © 2013 LinkedIn; p. 137: © Max Power/Corbis RF.

CHAPTER 7

Opener: U.S. Navy photo by Mass Communication Specialist 1st Class Roger S. Duncan; p. 141: The El Dorado News-Times, Michael Orrell/AP Images; p. 143: U. Baumgarten via Getty Images; p. 144: © Bloomberg via Getty Images; p. 153: Google and the Google logo are registered trademarks of Google Inc., used with permission; p. 154: Klapaucjusz/Public Domain; p. 157: Jacobs Stock Photography/Getty Images RF.

CHAPTER 8

Opener: Compassionate Eye Foundation/Getty Images RF; p. 162: © Elan Fleisher/Getty Images; p. 163: © Doctor's Associates Inc.; p. 166: Mark Lennihan/AP Images; p. 169: © ZUMA Press, Inc./Alamy; p. 170: Bloomberg via Getty Images; p. 171: Courtesy of DHL; p. 172: JOHN ANGELILLO/UPI/Newscom; p. 176: © Kent Knudson/PhotoLink/Getty Images RF; p. 179: Inti St. Clair/Getty Images RF.

CHAPTER 9

Opener: © Photodisc/Getty Images RF; p. 182: Ann Heisenfelt/AP Images; p. 183: © Jason Smith/iStockphoto; p. 185: Jens Kalaene/dpa/picture-alliance/Newscom; p. 187: Bloomberg via Getty Images; p. 190: © Jack Hollingsworth/Corbis RF; p. 192: Jupiterimages/Getty Images RF; p. 193: © Erik Snyder/Getty Images RF; p. 283: © Laura Doss/Corbis RF; p. 195: Hill Street Studios/Getty Images RF.

CHAPTER 10

Opener: © Digital Vision RF; p. 198: © Yuri Arcurs/Cutcaster RF; p. 199: Courtesy of The-Ladders; p. 201: © Kirby Hamilton/iStockphoto; p. 202: Good Hire, LLC; p. 203: U.S. Equal Employment Opportunity Commission; p. 204: Used with permission of McDonald's Corporation; p. 206: © Nika Dreamscape; p. 207: © Royalty-Free/Corbis; p. 210: © Mark Bowden/iStockphoto; p. 214: © Jim West/Alamy; p. 216: © Jupiterimages/Getty Images RF; p. 219: Digital Vision/Getty Images RF.

CHAPTER 11

Opener: Ravi Tahilramani/Getty Images RF; p. 222: © Zoonar GmbH/Alamy; p. 224: Francinegirvan/Public Domain; p. 227: © LUDOVIC/REA/Redux; p. 229: © Zazzle Inc.; p. 231: Wilfredo Lee/AP Images; p. 232: American Marketing Association; p. 233: The McGraw-Hill Companies, Inc./John Flournoy, photographer; p. 235: Photo provided courtesy of Goya © Foods, Inc.; p. 236: Photo, Gustavo Millon/Illustration, Philip Bone/FABRICA/Benetton Group; p. 238: Pixtal/age fotostock RF.

CHAPTER 12

Opener: Jumper/Getty Images RF; p. 242: © Joe Raedle/Getty Images; p. 244: © www.delorean.com; p. 247: Sean Gallup/Getty Images; p. 248: GREEN WORKS® is a registered trademark of The Clorox Company. Used with permission. © 2013 The Clorox Company. Reprinted with permission; p. 249: © Kim White/Bloomberg via Getty Images; p. 250: © Richard Levine/Alamy; p. 254 (left): © Paul Fenton/ZUMAPRESS.Com/Alamy; p. 254 (right): Reprinted with permission of BNSF Railway Company; p. 256: Photo provided by Spectrum Photofile. © Mattel, Inc. All Rights Reserved; p. 258: Bloomberg via Getty Images; p. 259: Jamba Juice Company © Copyright 2013. All Rights Reserved; p. 263: © Jack Hollingsworth/Blend Images/Corbis RF.

CHAPTER 13

Opener: Denise McCullough RF; p. 266: LearningStockImages/Alamy; p. 268: Courtesy of The Home Depot; p. 271: The NBA and individual member team identifications reproduced herein are used with permission from NBA Properties, Inc. © 2013 NBA Properties, Inc. All rights reserved. Screen-capture taken on Twitter, Inc.; p. 272: Screenshot © Facebook.com/Threadless; p. 274: Courtesy of Aaron Coyle/Flickr; p. 275: Nico Time/Flickr/CC2.0; p. 278: © Yowza!! All rights reserved; p. 279: © JGI/Jamie Grill/Blend Images LLC RF; p. 280: LifeLock, Inc.; p. 282: Screenshot © Bittorrent.com; p. 283: © Laura Doss/Corbis RF.

CHAPTER 14

Opener: © Tetra Images/Corbis RF; p. 287: VIEW Pictures Ltd/Alamy; p. 289: © KingWu/iStockphoto; p. 290: © 2006 Kjetil Ree/CC3.0; p. 291: Courtesy of Rendezvous BBQ; p. 296: Benjamin Lowy/Getty Images; p. 299: © Andrey Rudakov/Bloomberg via Getty Images; p. 302: Courtesy of New Belgium Brewing; p. 306: Stephen Yang/Bloomberg via Getty Images; p. 308: Ingram Publishing RF.

CHAPTER 15

Opener: © Colin Smith/Alamy RF; p. 312: Photo © FSM Visitors Board; p. 313: Courtesy of the U.S. Department of the Treasury, Bureau of Engraving and Printing; p. 315: © Daniel Acker/Bloomberg via Getty Images; p. 318: © Erik Dreyer/Getty Images; p. 320: © Chris McGrath/Getty Images; p. 322: National Credit Union Administration; p. 323: State Farm/Flickr/CC2.0; p. 323: Royalty-Free/Corbis; p. 327: © Graham Bell/Corbis RF.

CHAPTER 16

Opener: Photodisc/Getty Images RF; p. 331: Tetra Images/Getty Images RF; p. 333: Phillip Spears/Getty Images RF; p. 336: © Ehrbahn Jacob/POLFOTO; p. 337: Kevork Djansezian/Getty Images; p. 338: The McGraw-Hill Companies, Inc.; p. 342: © Brand X Pictures/PunchStock RF; p. 344: Alex Williamson/Getty Images; p. 346: © Comstock/PunchStock RF.

index

A

B

C

D

G

H

I

M

N

O

P

Q

R

S

Z

chapter one

active review card
The Dynamics of Business and Economics

in a nutshell

Goals, activities, and participants make up the fundamentals of business. Understanding the basics of economics and applying them to the United States economy will further your understanding of how business works and provide a framework for learning about business.

The following statements will test your take-away knowledge from this chapter. Do your best to explain each one in the space provided.

LO 1-1 Define basic concepts such as business, product, and profit.

LO 1-2 Identify the main participants and activities of business and explain why studying business is important.

LO 1-3 Define economics and compare the four types of economic systems.

LO 1-4 Describe the role of supply, demand, and competition in a free-enterprise system.

LO 1-5 Specify why and how the health of the economy is measured.

LO 1-6 Trace the evolution of the American economy and discuss the role of the entrepreneur in the economy.

 ISBN 0078023157 | Ferrell M 4e

Did your answers include the following important points?

LO 1-1. Define basic concepts such as business, product, and profit.

- A business is individuals or organizations who try to earn a profit by providing products that satisfy people's needs.
- A product is a good, service, or idea that has both tangible and intangible characteristics that provide satisfaction and benefits.
- Profit, the basic goal of business, is the difference between what it costs to make and sell a product and what a customer pays for it.

LO 1-2. Identify the main participants and activities of business and explain why studying business is important.

- The three main participants in business are owners, employees, and customers, but others—government regulators, suppliers, social groups, and so on—are also important.
- Management involves planning, organizing, and controlling the tasks required to carry out the work of the company.
- Marketing refers to those activities—research, product development, promotion, pricing, and distribution—designed to provide goods and services that satisfy customers.
- Finance refers to activities concerned with funding a business and using its funds effectively, and studying business can help you prepare for a career and become a better consumer.

LO 1-3. Define economics and compare the four types of economic systems.

- Economics is the study of how resources are distributed for the production of goods and services within a social system, and an economic system describes how a particular society distributes its resources.
- Communism is an economic system in which the people, without regard to class, own all the nation's resources, whereas in a socialist system, the government owns and operates basic industries, but individuals own most businesses.
- Under capitalism, individuals own and operate the majority of businesses that provide goods and services.
- Mixed economies have elements from more than one economic system; most countries have mixed economies.

LO 1-4. Describe the role of supply, demand, and competition in a free-enterprise system.

- Supply is the number of goods or services that businesses are willing to sell at different prices at a specific time.
- Demand is the number of goods and services that consumers are willing to buy at different prices at a specific time.
- Competition is the rivalry among businesses to persuade consumers to buy goods or services.

LO 1-5. Specify why and how the health of the economy is measured.

- A country measures the state of its economy to determine whether it is expanding or contracting and whether the country needs to take steps to minimize fluctuations.
- One commonly used measure is gross domestic product (GDP), the sum of all goods and services produced in a country during a year.
- A budget deficit occurs when a nation spends more than it takes in from taxes.

LO 1-6. Trace the evolution of the American economy and discuss the role of the entrepreneur in the economy.

- The American economy has evolved through the early economy, the Industrial Revolution, the manufacturing economy, the marketing economy, and the service- and Internet-based economy of today.
- Entrepreneurs play an important role because they risk their time, wealth, and efforts to develop new goods, services, and ideas that fuel the growth of the American economy.

Practical Application

LO 1-1.

- When purchasing a product, the consumer is actually buying its anticipated benefits and ______________.
- If a business is to be successful in the long run, it must treat its customers, employees, and community with social ______________.
- The goal of business is to earn ______________.

LO 1-2.

- ______________ involves activities designed to provide goods and services that fulfill needs and desires of consumers.
- When a business fails or does not make a profit, ______________ have the most to lose.
- Advertising, personal selling, coupons, and sweepstakes are forms of ______________ .

LO 1-3.

- Private property, profits, independent business decisions, and choice are rights associated with ______________.
- In ______________, consumers have a limited choice of goods and services, and prices are usually high.
- Most countries operate as ______________, which have elements from more than one economic system.

LO 1-4.

- In ______________, there are many small businesses selling one standardized product.
- The market structure that exists when there are very few businesses selling a product is called a(n) ______________.
- The quantity of products that businesses are willing to sell at different prices at specific times is called ______________.

LO 1-5.

- During ______________ there is a decline in production, employment, and income.
- ______________ is the sum of all goods and services produced in a country during a year.
- A(n) ______________ occurs when a nation spends more than it takes in from taxes.

LO 1-6.

- The Industrial Revolution changed the United States from an agricultural economy to a(n) ______________ one.
- ______________ industries account for almost 80 percent of the American economy today.
- A person who risks his or her wealth and time to develop an innovative product or idea for profit is called a(n) ______________.

ANSWERS LO 1-1 •satisfaction •responsibility •a profit LO 1-2 •Marketing •owners •promotion LO 1-3 •free enterprise •communist economies •mixed economies LO 1-4 •pure competition •oligopoly •supply LO 1-5 •recession •Gross domestic product •budget deficit LO 1-6 •manufacturing •Service •entrepreneur

chapter two

active review card

Business Ethics and Social Responsibility

in a nutshell

You must understand the role of ethics and social responsibility in making good business decisions. Learning to recognize business ethics issues, how businesses can improve their ethical behavior, and the impact of how companies respond to these issues is the basis of social responsibility.

The following statements will test your take-away knowledge from this chapter. Do your best to explain each one in the space provided.

LO 2-1 Define business ethics and social responsibility and examine their importance.

LO 2-2 Detect some of the ethical issues that may arise in business.

LO 2-3 Specify how businesses can promote ethical behavior.

LO 2-4 Explain the four dimensions of social responsibility.

LO 2-5 Debate an organization's social responsibilities to owners, employees, consumers, the environment, and the community.

 ISBN 0078023157 | Ferrell M 4e

Did your answers include the following important points?

LO 2-1. Define business ethics and social responsibility and examine their importance.

- The principles and standards that determine acceptable conduct in business organizations are defined as business ethics.
- A business's obligation to maximize its positive impact and minimize its negative impact on society illustrates the concept of social responsibility.
- Business ethics relates to an individual's or a work group's decisions that society evaluates as right or wrong, whereas social responsibility is a broader concept that concerns the impact of the entire business's activities on society.
- Socially responsible businesses win the trust and respect of their employees, customers, and society and increase profits.
- Ethics is important in business because it builds trust and confidence in business relationships.

LO 2-2. Detect some of the ethical issues that may arise in business.

- An ethical issue is an identifiable problem, situation, or opportunity requiring a person or organization to choose from among several actions that must be evaluated as right or wrong.
- Ethical issues can be categorized in the context of their relation with conflicts of interest, fairness and honesty, communications, and business associations.

LO 2-3. Specify how businesses can promote ethical behavior.

- Businesses can promote ethical behavior among employees by limiting their opportunity to engage in misconduct.
- Formal codes of ethics, ethical policies, and ethics training programs reduce incidences of unethical behavior by informing employees what is expected of them and providing punishments for those who fail to comply.

LO 2-4. Explain the four dimensions of social responsibility.

- The four dimensions of social responsibility are economic (being profitable), legal (obeying the law), ethical (doing what is right, just, and fair), and voluntary (being a good corporate citizen).

LO 2-5. Debate an organization's social responsibilities to owners, employees, consumers, the environment, and the community.

- Businesses must maintain proper accounting procedures, provide all relevant information about the performance of the firm to investors, and protect the owners' rights and investments.
- In relations with employees, businesses are expected to provide a safe workplace, pay employees adequately for their work, and treat them fairly.
- Consumerism refers to the activities undertaken by independent individuals, groups, and organizations to protect their rights as consumers.
- Increasingly, society expects businesses to take greater responsibility for the environment, especially with regard to animal rights as well as water, air, land, and noise pollution.
- Many businesses engage in activities to make the communities in which they operate better places for everyone to live and work.

Practical Application

LO 2-1.

- If a very successful professional football team has been ignoring the players' use of illegal muscle-building steroids, the owners should begin focusing on improving the organization's ______________.
- A company's obligation to increase its positive impact and decrease its negative impact is its ______________.
- The ______________ criminalized securities fraud and stiffened penalties for corporate fraud.

LO 2-2.

- A(n) ___________ exists when a person must choose whether to advance his or her own personal interests or those of others.
- Any payment, gift, or special favor intended to influence the outcome of a decision can be considered a(n) ______________.
- If a person takes someone's work and presents it as his or her own without mentioning the source, it would be considered an act of ______________.

LO 2-3.

- ______________ occurs when an employee exposes an employer's wrongdoing to outsiders.
- A set of formalized rules and standards that describe what a company expects of its employees is called a(n) ______________ .
- According to the text, ethical decisions in an organization are influenced by (1) individual moral standards, (2) the influence of managers and co-workers, and (3) ______________.

LO 2-4.

- Being profitable relates to ______________ social responsibility.
- Consumers vote against firms they view as socially irresponsible by not ______________.
- Philanthropic contributions made by a business to a charitable organization represent ______________ social responsibility.

LO 2-5.

- Businesses must first be responsible to their ______________.
- Many of the laws regulating safety in the workplace are enforced by ______________.
- ______________ ensures the fair treatment of consumers who voice complaints about a purchased product.

ANSWERS LO 2-1 •ethics •social responsibility •Sarbanes-Oxley Act LO 2-2 •conflict of interest •bribe •plagiarism LO 2-3 •Whistleblowing •code of ethics •the opportunity to engage in misconduct LO 2-4 •economic •buying their products •voluntary LO 2-5 •owners or shareholders •OSHA •The right to be heard

chapter three

active review card
Business in a Borderless World

in a nutshell

To learn about business in a global marketplace, you need to understand the nature of international business, including barriers to and promoters of trade across international boundaries. You must also consider the levels of organizational involvement in international business and the strategies used for trading across national borders.

The following statements will test your take-away knowledge from this chapter. Do your best to explain each one in the space provided.

LO 3-1 Explore some of the factors within the international trade environment that influence business.

LO 3-2 Investigate some of the economic, legal-political, social, cultural, and technological barriers to international business.

LO 3-3 Specify some of the agreements, alliances, and organizations that may encourage trade across international boundaries.

LO 3-4 Summarize the different levels of organizational involvement in international trade.

LO 3-5 Contrast two basic strategies used in international business.

 ISBN 0078023157 | Ferrell M 4e

Did your answers include the following important points?

LO 3-1. Explore some of the factors within the international trade environment that influence business.

- International business is the buying, selling, and trading of goods and services across national boundaries.
- Importing is the purchase of products and raw materials from another nation; exporting is the sale of domestic goods and materials to another nation.
- A nation's balance of trade is the difference in value between its exports and its imports: a negative balance of trade is a trade deficit.
- An absolute or comparative advantage in trade may determine what products a company from a particular nation will export.

LO 3-2. Investigate some of the economic, legal-political, social, cultural, and technological barriers to international business.

- Companies engaged in international trade must consider the effects of economic, legal, political, social, and cultural differences between nations.
- Wide-ranging legal and political barriers include differing laws (and enforcement), tariffs, exchange controls, quotas, embargoes, political instability, and war.
- Ambiguous cultural and social barriers involve differences in spoken and body language, time, holidays, and other observances and customs.

LO 3-3. Specify some of the agreements, alliances, and organizations that may encourage trade across international boundaries.

- Among the most important promoters of international business are the General Agreement on Tariffs and Trade, the World Trade Organization, the North American Free Trade Agreement, the European Union, the Asia-Pacific Economic Cooperation, the Association of Southeast Asian Nations, the World Bank, and the International Monetary Fund.

LO 3-4. Summarize the different levels of organizational involvement in international trade.

- Countertrade agreements occur at the import/export level and involve bartering products for other products, and a trading company links buyers and sellers in different countries to foster trade.
- Licensing and franchising occurs when one company allows a foreign company to use its name, products, patents, brands, trademarks, raw materials, and production process in exchange for a flat fee or royalty.
- Contract manufacturing occurs when a company hires a foreign company to produce a specified volume of the firm's product and allows the final product to carry the domestic firm's name. In a joint venture, companies work as a partnership and share the costs and operation of the business. A strategic alliance is a partnership formed to create competitive advantage on a worldwide basis.
- Direct investment involves purchasing overseas production and marketing facilities, whereas outsourcing involves transferring manufacturing to countries where labor and supplies are cheap. A multinational corporation is one that operates on a worldwide scale, without ties to any one nation or region. Offshoring is the relocation of a business process by a company, or a subsidiary, to another country.

LO 3-5. Contrast two basic strategies used in international business.

- A multinational strategy customizes products, promotion, and distribution according to cultural, technological, regional, and national differences, whereas a global strategy (globalization) standardizes products for the whole world as if it were a single entity.

Practical Application

LO 3-1.

- South Africa holds a(n) ______________ in diamond deposits in the world.
- The difference between the flow of money into and out of a country is called its ______________.
- The transfer of manufacturing and other tasks to places where labor and other supplies are less expensive is called ______________.

LO 3-2.

- The United States' prohibition of imported Cuban cigars is an example of a(n) ______________.
- A group of nations or companies that band together to act as a monopoly is known as a(n) ______________.
- A country/business that wants to gain a quick entry into a new market sometimes engages in ______________ its products.

LO 3-3.

- The ______________ makes short-term loans to member countries with trade deficits and provides foreign currencies to member nations.
- The ______________ is the largest source of advice and assistance with loans for developing countries.
- Until 1993, each nation of the ______________ functioned as a separate market.

LO 3-4.

- When a company hires a foreign company to produce a specified volume of the firm's product to specification, it is engaging in ______________.
- PepsiCo allows a Canadian firm to use its name, formula, and brands in return for a royalty. This arrangement is known as ______________.
- In some industries, ______________ allow companies to create competitive advantage on a worldwide basis.

LO 3-5.

- Standardizing products for the whole world as if it were a single entity is a characteristic of ______________ strategy.
- Most companies doing international business have used the ______________ strategy; that is, they have customized their products and distribution to cultural and regional differences.
- The ______________ is the global business solutions unit of the U.S. Department of Commerce that offers U.S. firms practical knowledge of international markets and industries, along with a global network.

ANSWERS LO 3-1 •absolute advantage •balance of payments •outsourcing LO 3-2 •embargo •cartel •dumping LO 3-3 •International Monetary Fund •World Bank •European Union LO 3-4 •contract manufacturing •licensing •strategic alliances LO 3-5 •global •multinational •Commercial Service

active review card
Options for Organizing Business

in a nutshell

Sole proprietorship, partnership, and corporation are three primary forms of business that are used in traditional business, online-only business, or a combination of both. Other forms of business include S corporations, limited liability companies, and cooperatives. In organizing a business, it is helpful to understand the advantages and disadvantages of these forms of business as well as business trends.

The following statements will test your take-away knowledge from this chapter. Do your best to explain each one in the space provided.

LO 4-1 Define and examine the advantages and disadvantages of the sole proprietorship form of organization.

LO 4-2 Identify two types of partnership and evaluate the advantages and disadvantages of the partnership form of organization.

LO 4-3 Describe the corporate form of organization and cite the advantages and disadvantages of corporations.

LO 4-4 Define and debate the advantages and disadvantages of mergers, acquisitions, and leveraged buyouts.

 ISBN 0078023157 | Ferrell M 4e

Did your answers include the following important points?

LO 4-1. Define and examine the advantages and disadvantages of the sole proprietorship form of organization.

- The most common form of business is the sole proprietorship. The advantages of this form of business include the fact that it is easy and inexpensive to form, it allows for a high level of secrecy, all profits belong to the owner, the owner has complete control over the business, government regulation is minimal, taxes are paid only once, and the business can be closed easily.
- Disadvantages include the fact that the owner may have to use personal assets to borrow money, sources of external funds are difficult to find, the owner must have many diverse skills, the survival of the business is tied to the life of the owner and his or her ability to work, qualified employees are hard to find, and wealthy sole proprietors pay a higher tax rate than they would under the corporate form of business.

LO 4-2. Identify two types of partnership and evaluate the advantages and disadvantages of the partnership form of organization.

- Partnerships may be general or limited and offer the following advantages: They are easy to organize, they may have higher credit ratings because partners may have more combined wealth, partners can specialize, partnerships can make decisions faster than larger businesses, and government regulations are few.
- Disadvantages include the fact that general partners have unlimited liability for the debts of the partnership, partners are responsible for each other's decisions, the death or termination of one partner requires a new partnership agreement, it is difficult to sell a partnership interest at a fair price, the distribution of profits may not correctly reflect the amount of work done by each partner, and partnerships cannot find external sources of funds as easily as large corporations.

LO 4-3. Describe the corporate form of organization and cite the advantages and disadvantages of corporations.

- A corporation, which is owned by stockholders, is a legal entity created by the state, whose assets and liabilities are separate from those of its owners. They are chartered by a state through articles of incorporation and have a board of directors made up of corporate officers or people from outside the company.
- Advantages include the fact that owners have limited liability, ownership (stock) can be easily transferred, corporations are long-lasting, raising money is easier, and expansion into new businesses is simpler.
- Disadvantages include the fact that the company is taxed on its income and owners pay a second tax on any profits received as dividends, forming a corporation can be expensive, keeping trade secrets is difficult because so much information must be made available to the public and to government agencies, and owners and managers are not always the same and can have different goals.

LO 4-4. Define and debate the advantages and disadvantages of mergers, acquisitions, and leveraged buyouts.

- A merger occurs when two companies (usually corporations) combine to form a new company. An acquisition occurs when one company buys most of another company's stock, whereas in a leveraged buyout, a group of investors borrows money to acquire a company, using the assets of the purchased company to guarantee the loan.
- Advantages include the fact that they can help merging firms gain a larger market share in their industries, acquire valuable assets, and realize lower costs. They can also benefit stockholders by improving companies' market value and stock prices.
- Disadvantages include the fact that they can hurt companies if they force managers to focus on avoiding takeovers at the expense of productivity and profits, they may lead a company to take on too much debt, and they can harm employee morale and productivity.

Practical Application

LO 4-1.

- One of the most popular and easiest to establish forms of business in the United States is the ______________.
- An individual who is the sole owner of a business faces ____________ liability in case of debt.

LO 4-2.

- ______________ are the least used form of business organization in the United States.
- The decision-making process in a partnership tends to be faster when the partnership is ______________.
- In a partnership, owners must share ______________, even though a bad decision may have been taken by one of them.

LO 4-3.

- Another often-used name for stockholder is ______________.
- A(n) ______________ is one whose stocks anyone may buy, sell, or trade.
- The organizational form that many consider to be a blend of the best characteristics of corporations, partnerships, and sole proprietorships is the ______________.

LO 4-4.

- When two companies combine to form a new company, it is called a(n) ______________.
- When companies operating at different, but related, levels of an industry merge, it is known as a(n) ______________.
- XYZ, Inc. is attempting to avoid a hostile takeover by a corporate raider by allowing stockholders to buy more shares of stock at prices lower than current market value; the ______________ method is being used here to avoid the takeover.

ANSWERS LO 4-1 •sole proprietorship •unlimited LO 4-2 •Partnerships •small •business responsibility LO 4-3 •shareholder •public corporation •limited liability company
LO 4-4 •merger •vertical merger •poison pill

active review card

Small Business, Entrepreneurship, and Franchising

A successful entrepreneur or small-business owner understands the advantages and disadvantages of owning a small business, challenges facing small businesses today, and why small businesses succeed or fail.

The following statements will test your take-away knowledge from this chapter. Do your best to explain each one in the space provided.

LO 5-1 Define entrepreneurship and small business.

LO 5-2 Investigate the importance of small business in the U.S. economy and why certain fields attract small business.

LO 5-3 Specify the advantages of small-business ownership.

LO 5-4 Summarize the disadvantages of small-business ownership and analyze why many small businesses fail.

LO 5-5 Describe how you go about starting a small business and what resources are needed.

LO 5-6 Evaluate the demographic, technological, and economic trends that are affecting the future of small business.

LO 5-7 Explain why many large businesses are trying to "think small."

 ISBN 0078023157 | Ferrell M 4e

Did your answers include the following important points?

LO 5-1. Define entrepreneurship and small business.

- An entrepreneur is a person who creates a business or product and manages his or her resources and takes risks to gain a profit; entrepreneurship is the process of creating and managing a business to achieve desired objectives.
- A small business is one that is not dominant in its competitive area and does not employ more than 500 people.

LO 5-2. Investigate the importance of small business in the U.S. economy and why certain fields attract small business.

- Small businesses are vital to the American economy because they provide products, jobs, innovation, and opportunities.
- Retailing, wholesaling, services, manufacturing, and high technology attract small businesses because these industries are relatively easy to enter, require relatively low initial financing, and may experience less heavy competition.

LO 5-3. Specify the advantages of small-business ownership.

- Small-business ownership offers some personal advantages, including independence, freedom of choice, and the option of working at home.
- Business advantages include flexibility, the ability to focus on a few key customers, and the chance to develop a reputation for quality and service.

LO 5-4. Summarize the disadvantages of small-business ownership and analyze why many small businesses fail.

- Small businesses have many disadvantages for their owners, such as expense, physical and psychological stress, and a high failure rate.
- Small businesses fail for many reasons: undercapitalization, management inexperience or incompetence, neglect, disproportionate burdens imposed by government regulation, and vulnerability to competition from larger companies.

LO 5-5. Describe how you go about starting a small business and what resources are needed.

- Have an idea for developing a small business and devise a business plan to guide the development of the business. Then you must decide what form of business ownership to use and provide funds, either your own or funds provided by friends, families, banks, investors, or other organizations.
- You must also decide whether to start a new business from scratch, buy an existing one, or buy a franchise operation.

LO 5-6. Evaluate the demographic, technological, and economic trends that are affecting the future of small business.

- Changing demographic trends include more elderly people as baby boomers age; a large gain in the 11- to 28-year-old age range known as echo boomers, millennials, or Generation Y; and an increasing number of immigrants to the United States.
- Technological advances and an increase in service exports have created new opportunities for small companies to expand their operations abroad, whereas trade agreements and alliances have created an environment in which small business has fewer regulatory and legal barriers.
- Economic turbulence presents both opportunities for and threats to the survival of small businesses.

LO 5-7. Explain why many large businesses are trying to "think small."

- Large companies are copying small businesses in an effort to make their firms more flexible, resourceful, and innovative, and improve the bottom line.
- This involves downsizing and intrapreneurship, by which an employee takes responsibility for developing innovations within the larger organization.

Practical Application

LO 5-1.

- Small businesses provide opportunities for _______________ and _______________ to succeed in business.
- The Small Business Administration was established to provide _______________ assistance to small businesses.
- Small business refers to an owner-managed business that employs not more than _______________ people.

LO 5-2.

- Small businesses generated _______________ of all new jobs created in the United States in recent years.
- _______________ attracts entrepreneurs because gaining experience and exposure is relatively easy.
- The fastest growing sector of the U.S. economy is represented by _____.

LO 5-3.

- When market conditions change rapidly, a small business usually has fewer layers of management to work through in making decisions; this advantage of a small business is called _______________.
- _______________ is one of the leading reasons that entrepreneurs choose to go into business for themselves.
- Unlike many large corporations, small businesses can focus on developing products for a defined _______________, that is, specific customers.

LO 5-4.

- Many people turn a hobby into a business without identifying a(n) _______________ for that product; this leads to failure.
- _______________ is one of the leading reasons for business failure because most businesses suffer from seasonal variations in sales.
- Initially, the factor that probably affects a company's reputation more than anything else is poorly managed _______________.

LO 5-5.

- Since Rachel Hollings decided to purchase the rights to own and operate a McDonald's fast-food restaurant rather than start her own operation, she is probably a(n) _______________.
- A mortgage is an example of _______________.
- ________ are persons or organizations that agree to provide some funds for a new business in exchange for an ownership interest or stock.

LO 5-6.

- The _______________ segment of the population is probably the wealthiest in the United States.
- The _______________ population, the nation's largest minority group, is a vast untapped market for small businesses.
- Deregulation of the _______________ market and an interest in fuel conservation has spawned many small businesses.

LO 5-7.

- Reducing management layers, corporate staff, and work tasks to make a firm more flexible, resourceful, and innovative is known as _______.
- Individuals who take responsibility for the development of innovations of any kind within larger organizations are called _______________.

ANSWERS LO 5-1 • minorities, women • managerial and financial • 500 LO 5-2 • two-thirds • Retailing • service providers LO 5-3 • flexibility • Independence • market niche LO 5-4 • need • Undercapitalization • growth LO 5-5 • franchisee • debt financing • Venture capitalists LO 5-6 • baby boomer • Latino • energy LO 5-7 • downsizing • intrapreneurs

chapter six

active review card
The Nature of Management

in a nutshell

A successful manager needs to possess certain skills and follow steps for effective decision making. In doing so, managers accomplish various functions and participate in differing levels and areas of management.

The following statements will test your take-away knowledge from this chapter. Do your best to explain each one in the space provided.

LO 6-1 Define management and explain its role in the achievement of organizational objectives.

LO 6-2 Describe the major functions of management.

LO 6-3 Distinguish among three levels of management and the concerns of managers at each level.

LO 6-4 Specify the skills managers must have to be successful.

LO 6-5 Describe the different types of leaders and how leadership can be used to empower employees.

LO 6-6 Summarize the systematic approach to decision making used by many business managers.

 ISBN 0078023157 | Ferrell M 4e

Did your answers include the following important points?

LO 6-1. Define management and explain its role in the achievement of organizational objectives.

- Management is a process designed to achieve an organization's objectives by using its resources effectively and efficiently in a changing environment.
- Managers make decisions about the use of the organization's resources and are concerned with planning, organizing, staffing, directing, and controlling the organization's activities to reach its objectives.

LO 6-2. Describe the major functions of management.

- Planning is the process of determining the organization's objectives and deciding how to accomplish them. Organizing is the structuring of resources and activities to accomplish those objectives efficiently and effectively.
- Staffing is the hiring of people with the necessary skills to carry out the work of the company.
- Directing is motivating and leading employees to achieve organizational objectives and controlling the process of evaluating and correcting activities to keep the organization on course.

LO 6-3. Distinguish among three levels of management and the concerns of managers at each level.

- Top management is responsible for the whole organization and focuses primarily on strategic planning. Middle management develops plans for specific operating areas and carries out the general guidelines set by top management.
- First-line, or supervisory, management supervises the workers and day-to-day operations.
- Managers can also be categorized according to their area of responsibility: finance, production and operations, human resources, marketing, or administration.

LO 6-4. Specify the skills managers must have to be successful.

- Managers need leadership skills, technical expertise, conceptual skills, analytical skills, and human relations skills.

LO 6-5. Describe the different types of leaders and how leadership can be used to empower employees.

- Leadership is the ability to influence employees to work toward organizational goals.
- Managers can be classified into three types based on their leadership style. *Autocratic leaders* make all the decisions and then tell employees what must be done and how to do it. *Democratic leaders* involve their employees in decisions. *Free-rein leaders* let their employees work without much interference.
- Another type of leadership gaining in popularity is authentic leadership. Authentic leaders are passionate about the goals and mission of the company, display corporate values in the workplace, and form long-term stakeholder relationships.
- Employee empowerment occurs when employees are provided with the ability to take on responsibilities and make decisions about their jobs. To empower employees, leaders should adopt systems that support their ability to provide input and feedback on company decisions, encourage them to participate in decision making, and train them in leadership skills.

LO 6-6. Summarize the systematic approach to decision making used by many business managers.

- A systematic approach to decision making follows these steps: recognizing and defining the situation, developing options, analyzing options, selecting the best option, implementing the decision, and monitoring the consequences.

Practical Application

LO 6-1.

- If a manager is concerned about doing work with the least cost and waste, her primary managerial concern is ________.
- ________ make decisions about the use of an organization's resources and are concerned with planning, organizing, leading, and controlling the organization's activities.
- Managers need to make efficient use of the company's ________ to reach organizational objectives.

LO 6-2.

- The type of planning conducted on a long-range basis by top managers is usually called ________.
- Dividing work into small units and assigning it to individuals are tasks related to ________.
- Hiring people to carry out the work of the organization is known as ________.

LO 6-3.

- ________ are responsible for tactical planning that will implement the general guidelines established by the top management.
- Decisions regarding adding new products, acquiring companies, and moving into foreign markets would most typically be made by the ________.
- Most people get their first managerial experience as ________ supervising workers and daily operations.

LO 6-4.

- Joe met with department heads to listen to their opinions about buying a new machine. Although they all thought it was a good idea, Joe did not buy the machine. Joe's leadership style is ________.
- To train employees, answer questions, and provide guidance in doing a task, managers need ________.
- Those managers who can communicate well, understand the needs of others, and deal effectively with people inside and outside the organization are said to have good ________ skills.

LO 6-5.

- ________ leaders let their employees work without much interference.
- Authentic leaders are passionate about the goals and mission of the company, display ________ in the workplace, and form long-term ________.
- ________ occurs when employees are provided with the ability to take on responsibilities and make decisions about their jobs.

LO 6-6.

- When analyzing options in the decision-making process, managers must consider the appropriateness and ________ of each option.
- Effective implementation of a major decision requires ________.
- Managers need to spend a lot of time in ________ with those who can help in the realization of organizational objectives.

ANSWERS LO 6-1 •efficiency •Managers •resources LO 6-2 •strategic •organizing •staffing LO 6-3 •Middle managers •top management •first-line managers LO 6-4 •democratic •technical expertise •human resource LO 6-5 •Free-rein •corporate values; stakeholder relationships •Employee empowerment LO 6-6 •practicality •planning •networking

chapter seven

active review card
Organization, Teamwork, and Communication

in a nutshell

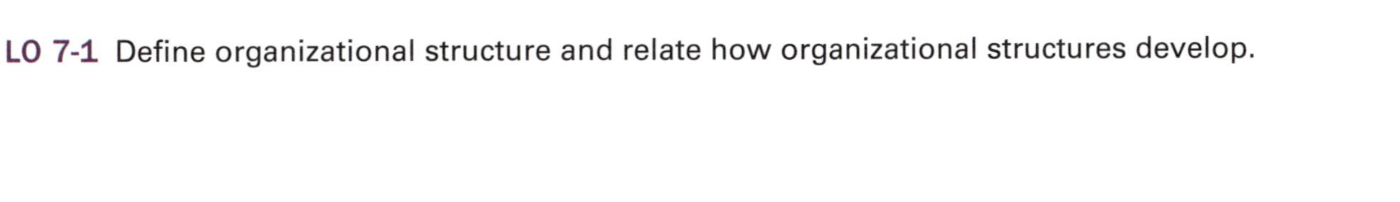

An organization's culture affects its operations. It is important in organizing a business to understand the development of structure, including how tasks and responsibilities are organized through specialization and departmentalization, as well as the different forms organizational structure may take.

The following statements will test your take-away knowledge from this chapter. Do your best to explain each one in the space provided.

LO 7-1 Define organizational structure and relate how organizational structures develop.

LO 7-2 Describe how specialization and departmentalization help an organization achieve its goals.

LO 7-3 Determine how organizations assign responsibility for tasks and delegate authority.

LO 7-4 Compare and contrast some common forms of organizational structure.

LO 7-5 Distinguish between groups and teams and identify the types of groups that exist in organizations.

LO 7-6 Describe how communication occurs in organizations.

 ISBN 0078023157 | Ferrell M 4e

Did your answers include the following important points?

LO 7-1. Define organizational structure and relate how organizational structures develop.

- Structure is the arrangement or relationship of positions within an organization; it develops when managers assign work activities to work groups and specific individuals and coordinate the diverse activities required to attain organizational objectives.
- Organizational structure evolves to accommodate growth, which requires people with specialized skills.

LO 7-2. Describe how specialization and departmentalization help an organization achieve its goals.

- Structuring an organization requires that management assign work tasks to specific individuals and groups. Under specialization, managers break labor into small, specialized tasks and assign employees to do a single task, fostering efficiency.
- Departmentalization is the grouping of jobs into working units.
- Businesses may departmentalize by function, product, geographic region, or customer, or they may combine two or more of these.

LO 7-3. Determine how organizations assign responsibility for tasks and delegate authority.

- Delegation of authority means assigning tasks to employees and giving them the power to make commitments, use resources, and take whatever actions are necessary to accomplish the tasks.
- The extent to which authority is delegated throughout an organization determines its degree of centralization.

LO 7-4. Compare and contrast some common forms of organizational structure.

- Line structures have direct lines of authority that extend from the top manager to employees at the lowest level of the organization.
- A multidivisional structure gathers departments into larger groups called divisions. A matrix or project-management structure sets up teams from different departments, thereby creating two or more intersecting lines of authority.

LO 7-5. Distinguish between groups and teams and identify the types of groups that exist in organizations.

- A group is two or more persons who communicate, have a common identity, and have a common goal, whereas a team is a small group whose members have complementary skills, a common purpose, goals, and approach, and who hold themselves mutually accountable.
- The major distinction is that individual performance is most important in groups, while collective work group performance counts most in teams.
- Special kinds of groups include task forces, committees, project teams, product-development teams, quality-assurance teams, and self-directed work teams.

LO 7-6. Describe how communication occurs in organizations.

- Communication occurs both formally and informally in organizations. Formal communication may be downward, upward, horizontal, and even diagonal.
- Informal communication takes place through friendships and the grapevine.

Practical Application

LO 7-1.

- The arrangement or relationship of positions within an organization is called ______________.
- Work philosophies, values, dress codes, work habits, extracurricular activities, and stories make up ______________.

LO 7-2.

- ______________ departmentalization arranges jobs around the needs of various types of customers.
- General Motors is organized into these groups: GMC Trucks, Chevrolet, Buick, and Cadillac. This is called ______________ departmentalization.
- Adam Smith illustrated improvements in efficiency through the application of ______________.

LO 7-3.

- An organization with many layers of managers is considered to be ______________.
- An organization operating in a complex and unpredictable environment is likely to be ______________.
- When the decisions of a company are very risky and low-level managers lack decision-making skills, the company will tend to ______________.

LO 7-4.

- The ______________ of organization allows managers to specialize in their area of expertise.
- The ______________ organizational form is likely to be complex and expensive.
- ______________ permit delegation of decision-making authority, and ensure that better decisions are made faster.

LO 7-5.

- A temporary group of employees responsible for bringing about a particular change is a(n) ______________.
- A special type of project team formed to devise, design, and implement a new product is a(n) ______________.
- A(n) ______________ is a group of employees responsible for an entire work process or segment that delivers a product to an internal or external customer.

LO 7-6.

- When managers recognize that a(n) ______________ exists, they should use it to their advantage.
- Progress reports and complaints are part of ______________ communication.
- When individuals from different organizational units and levels communicate with each other, it is called ______________ communication.

ANSWERS LO 7-1 •organizational structure •organizational culture LO 7-2 •Customer •product •specialization LO 7-3 •tall •decentralized •centralize LO 7-4 •line-and-staff structure •matrix structure •Multidivisional structures LO 7-5 •task force •product-development team •self-directed work team LO 7-6 •grapevine •upward •diagonal

chapter eight

active review card
Managing Service and Manufacturing Operations

in a nutshell

Production and operations management involves planning and designing the processes that will transform resources into finished products, managing the movement of resources through the transformation process, and ensuring that the products are of the quality expected by customers.

The following statements will test your take-away knowledge from this chapter. Do your best to explain each one in the space provided.

LO 8-1 Define operations management and differentiate between operations and manufacturing.

LO 8-2 Explain how operations management differs in manufacturing and service firms.

LO 8-3 Describe the elements involved in planning and designing an operations system.

LO 8-4 Specify some techniques managers may use to manage the logistics of transforming inputs into finished products.

LO 8-5 Assess the importance of quality in operations management.

 ISBN 0078023157 | Ferrell M 4e

Did your answers include the following important points?

LO 8-1. Define operations management and differentiate between operations and manufacturing.

- Operations management (OM) is the development and administration of the activities involved in transforming resources into goods and services.
- The terms *manufacturing* and *production* are used interchangeably to describe the activities and processes used in making tangible products, whereas *operations* is a broader term used to describe the process of making both tangible and intangible products.

LO 8-2. Explain how operations management differs in manufacturing and service firms.

- Manufacturers and service firms both transform inputs and outputs, but service providers differ from manufacturers in several ways: They have greater customer contact because the service occurs at the point of consumption; their inputs and outputs are more variable than those of manufacturers; because of the human element, service providers are generally more labor intensive, and their productivity measurement is more complex.

LO 8-3. Describe the elements involved in planning and designing an operations system.

- Operations planning relates to decisions about what products to make and for whom and what processes and facilities are needed to produce them.
- Common facility layouts include fixed-position layouts, process layouts, and product layouts.
- Where to locate operations facilities is a crucial decision that depends on proximity to market, availability of raw materials, availability of transportation, availability of power, climatic influences, availability of labor, and community characteristics.
- Technology is also vital to operations, particularly computer-assisted design, computer-assisted manufacturing, flexible manufacturing, robotics, and computer-integrated manufacturing.

LO 8-4. Specify some techniques managers may use to manage the logistics of transforming inputs into finished products.

- Logistics, or supply chain management, includes all the activities involved in obtaining and managing raw materials and component parts, managing finished products, packaging them, and getting them to customers.
- Common approaches to inventory control include the economic order quantity (EOQ) model, the just-in-time (JIT) inventory concept, and material-requirements planning (MRP).
- Logistics also includes routing and scheduling processes and activities to complete products.

LO 8-5. Assess the importance of quality in operations management.

- Quality is a critical element of operations management because low-quality products can hurt people and harm business.
- Quality control refers to the processes an organization uses to maintain its established quality standards.
- To control quality, a company must establish what standard of quality is desired and determine whether its products meet that standard through inspection.

Practical Application

LO 8-1.

- Viewed from the perspective of operations, the money used to purchase a carpenter's tools and the electricity used to run his power saw are _______________.
- If an employee is involved with transforming resources into goods and services, then she is in _______________.
- From an operations perspective, food sold at a restaurant and services provided by a plumbing company are _______________.

LO 8-2.

- Due to the high degree of automation, products in the manufacturing industry are more _______________ than those in the service industry.
- Most goods are manufactured _______________ purchase, whereas most services are performed _______________ purchase.
- The service industry is _______________ intensive, whereas the manufacturing industry is _______________ intensive.

LO 8-3.

- Television sets, ballpoint pens, and tortilla chips are _______________ products because they are produced on an assembly line.
- If ABC Computer Company is trying to determine the demand for its future products and how much consumers are willing to pay, the company will probably rely on _______________.
- When a customer goes to a print shop to order business cards, the manufacturing process used would most likely be _______________.

LO 8-4.

- A company that requires all its resources to be brought to a central location is using a(n) _________________.
- Materials that have been purchased to be used as inputs in making other products are included in _______________.
- _______________ helps engineers design components, products, and processes on the computer instead of on paper.

LO 8-5.

- Determining how many items are to be inspected is called _______________.
- The degree to which a good or service meets the demands and requirements of customers is called _______________.
- _______________ is a philosophy that a uniform commitment to quality in all areas of an organization will promote a culture that meets customers' perceptions of quality.

ANSWERS LO 8-1 •inputs •operations •outputs LO 8-2 •uniform •before; after •labor-; capital- LO 8-3 •standardized •market research •customization LO 8-4 •fixed-position layout •raw materials inventory •Computer-assisted design (CAD) LO 8-5 •sampling •quality •Total quality management

chapter nine

active review card
Motivating the Workforce

in a nutshell

Managers who understand the needs and motivations of workers and strategies for motivating them can help workers reach higher levels of productivity, subsequently contributing to the achievement of organizational goals.

The following statements will test your take-away knowledge from this chapter. Do your best to explain each one in the space provided.

LO 9-1 Define human relations and determine why its study is important.

LO 9-2 Summarize early studies that laid the groundwork for understanding employee motivation.

LO 9-3 Compare and contrast the human-relations theories of Abraham Maslow and Frederick Herzberg.

LO 9-4 Investigate various theories of motivation, including Theories X, Y, and Z; equity theory; and expectancy theory.

LO 9-5 Describe some of the strategies that managers use to motivate employees.

 ISBN 0078023157 | Ferrell M 4e

Did your answers include the following important points?

LO 9-1. Define human relations and determine why its study is important.

- Human relations is the study of the behavior of individuals and groups in organizational settings. Its focus is what motivates employees to perform on the job.
- Human relations is important because businesses need to understand how to motivate their employees to be more effective, boost workplace morale, and maximize employees' productivity and creativity.

LO 9-2. Summarize early studies that laid the groundwork for understanding employee motivation.

- Time and motion studies by Frederick Taylor and others helped them analyze how employees perform specific work tasks in an effort to improve their productivity.
- Taylor and the early practitioners of the classical theory of motivation felt that money and job security were the primary motivations of employees; however, the Hawthorne studies revealed that human factors also influence workers' behavior.

LO 9-3. Compare and contrast the human-relations theories of Abraham Maslow and Frederick Herzberg.

- Abraham Maslow defined five basic needs of all people and arranged them in the order in which they must be satisfied: physiological, security, social, esteem, and self-actualization.
- Frederick Herzberg divided the characteristics of jobs into hygiene factors and motivational factors.
- Herzberg's hygiene factors can be compared to Maslow's physiological and security needs; motivational factors may include Maslow's social, esteem, and self-actualization needs.

LO 9-4. Investigate various theories of motivation, including Theories X, Y, and Z; equity theory; and expectancy theory.

- Douglas McGregor contrasted two views of management: Theory X suggests workers dislike work, whereas Theory Y suggests that workers not only like work but seek out responsibility to satisfy their higher-order needs.
- Theory Z stresses employee participation in all aspects of company decision making, whereas the equity theory indicates that how much people are willing to contribute to an organization depends on their assessment of the fairness, or equity, of the rewards they will receive in exchange.
- The expectancy theory states that motivation depends not only on how much a person wants something but also on the person's perception of how likely he or she is to get it.

LO 9-5. Describe some of the strategies that managers use to motivate employees.

- Strategies for motivating workers include behavior modification and job design. Among the job design strategies businesses use are job rotations, job enlargement, job enrichment, and flexible scheduling strategies.

Practical Application

LO 9-1.

- An inner drive that directs behavior toward objectives is called ________.
- Good morale in an employee is likely to result in ________.
- A(n) ________ is the personal satisfaction that we feel from achieving a goal.

LO 9-2.

- Prior to the Hawthorne studies, management theorists believed that the primary motivators of employees were job security and ________.
- The birth of the study of human relations can be traced to ________ and ________ studies.

LO 9-3.

- According to Maslow, living life to the fullest is most closely associated with fulfilling one's ________ need.
- According to Frederick Herzberg, the aspects that relate to the work setting form the ________ factors.

LO 9-4.

- Jim has learned that his company is offering a Hawaiian vacation to its best salesperson. He almost won last year and really wants the trip. He is working very hard because he thinks he has a good chance to win. This exemplifies the ________ theory.
- Jack believes that he can get some extra work completed before the deadline by withholding his workers' vacation schedules until the job is completed. Jack is a manager who follows ________.
- The approach that suggests that imagination, ingenuity, and creativity can help solve organizational problems is ________.

LO 9-5.

- A work system that allows employees to choose their starting and ending times as long as they are at work during a specified core period is called ________.
- ________ adds tasks to a job instead of treating each task as a separate job.
- When Kelly reprimands Sarah each time Sarah is late for work, Kelly is applying ________.

ANSWERS LO 9-1 • motivation • loyalty • intrinsic reward LO 9-2 • money • time; motion LO 9-3 • self-actualization • hygiene LO 9-4 • expectancy • Theory X • Theory Y LO 9-5 • flex-time • job enlargement • behavior modification

chapter ten

active review card
Managing Human Resources

in a nutshell

Human resources managers need to plan for, recruit, and select qualified employees. Yet another aspect of the human resources manager's job is to train, appraise, compensate, and retain valued employees, which can present an added challenge among unionized and diverse employees.

The following statements will test your take-away knowledge from this chapter. Do your best to explain each one in the space provided.

LO 10-1 Define human resources management and explain its significance.

LO 10-2 Summarize the processes of recruiting and selecting human resources for a company.

LO 10-3 Discuss how workers are trained and their performance appraised.

LO 10-4 Identify the types of turnover companies may experience and explain why turnover is an important issue.

LO 10-5 Specify the various ways a worker may be compensated.

LO 10-6 Discuss some of the issues associated with unionized employees, including collective bargaining and dispute resolution.

LO 10-7 Describe the importance of diversity in the workforce.

 ISBN 0078023157 | Ferrell M 4e

Did your answers include the following important points?

LO 10-1. Define human resources management and explain its significance.

- Human resources management refers to all the activities involved in determining an organization's human resources needs and acquiring, training, and compensating people to fill those needs.
- It is concerned with maximizing the satisfaction of employees and improving their efficiency to meet organizational objectives.

LO 10-2. Summarize the processes of recruiting and selecting human resources for a company.

- Human resources managers must determine the firm's human resources needs, develop a strategy to meet those needs, and recruit qualified applicants from whom management will select the employees.
- Selection is the process of collecting information about applicants, using that information to decide which to hire, and putting potential hires through the process of application, interview, testing, and reference checking.

LO 10-3. Discuss how workers are trained and their performance appraised.

- Training teaches employees how to do their job tasks, whereas development is training that augments the skills and knowledge of managers and professionals as well as current employees.
- Appraising performance involves identifying an employee's strengths and weaknesses on the job. Performance appraisals may be subjective or objective.

LO 10-4. Identify the types of turnover companies may experience and explain why turnover is an important issue.

- A promotion is an advancement to a higher-level job with increased authority, responsibility, and pay. A transfer is a move to another job within the company, typically at the same level and wage.
- Separations occur when employees resign, retire, are terminated, or are laid off. Turnovers due to separation are expensive because of the time, money, and effort required to select, train, and manage new employees.

LO 10-5. Specify the various ways a worker may be compensated.

- Wages are financial compensation based on the number of hours worked or the number of units produced, whereas commissions are a fixed amount or percentage of a sale paid as compensation.
- Salaries are compensation calculated on a weekly, monthly, or annual basis, regardless of the number of hours worked or the number of items produced.
- Bonuses and profit sharing are types of financial incentives; benefits are nonfinancial forms of compensation such as vacation, insurance, and sick leave.

LO 10-6. Discuss some of the issues associated with unionized employees, including collective bargaining and dispute resolution.

- Collective bargaining is the negotiation process through which management and unions reach an agreement on a labor contract.
- If labor and management cannot agree on a contract, labor union members may picket, strike, or boycott the firm; management may lock out striking employees, hire strikebreakers, or form employers' associations.
- In a deadlock, labor disputes may be resolved by a third party.

LO 10-7. Describe the importance of diversity in the workforce.

- Companies with diverse workforces experience more productive use of human resources, reduced conflict, better work relationships among workers, increased commitment to and sharing of organizational goals, increased innovation and creativity, and enhanced ability to serve diverse customers.

Practical Application

LO 10-1.

- In some companies, the department that handles the human resources management function is still called _______________.
- The observation and study of information about a job is called ________.
- The qualifications required for a job are spelled out in a job ________.

LO 10-2.

- _______________ tests are restricted to specific government jobs and those involving security or access to drugs.
- Professionals who specialize in luring qualified people away from other companies are known as _______________.
- Recruiting for entry-level managerial and professional positions is often carried out on _______________.

LO 10-3.

- The _______________ includes a panel consisting of the employee's peers, superiors, and subordinates.
- If Greta received training by watching videotapes and discussing case studies, she received _______________ training.
- Joseph has worked at his position for years. He is currently participating in management seminars at company expense. This is an example of _______________.

LO 10-4.

- Sandy Smith moved to a new job that involved more responsibility and an increase in compensation. She received a(n) _____________.
- Susan was terminated from her job by her employer because she was repeatedly late to work. She was _______________.
- A(n) _______________ rate signifies problems with the selection and training program.

LO 10-5.

- To motivate employees such as car salespersons to sell as much as they can, they are paid _______________.
- June works at McDonald's part-time as a grill operator. She will probably be paid with the _______________ compensation method.
- An employee stock ownership plan is an example of _______________.

LO 10-6.

- Workers seeking to improve pay and working conditions may join together to form a(n) _______________.
- _______________ make carrying out normal business operations difficult, if not impossible.
- A(n) ___________ might be brought in as a neutral third party to keep union and management representatives talking.

LO 10-7.

- Age, gender, and race are __________ characteristics of diversity.
- Secondary characteristics of diversity _______________.
- Having a diverse workforce has many benefits. One benefit is the _______________ use of a company's human resources.

ANSWERS LO 10-1 •personnel •job analysis •specification LO 10-2 •Polygraph •headhunters •college and university campuses LO 10-3 •360-degree feedback system •classroom •development LO 10-4 •promotion •fired •high turnover LO 10-5 •commissions •time-wage •profit sharing LO 10-6 •labor union •Strikes •conciliator LO 10-7 •primary •can be changed •more productive

chapter eleven

active review card
Customer-Driven Marketing

in a nutshell

Marketers develop marketing strategies to satisfy the needs and wants of their customers; they also need to consider buying behavior and use research to determine what consumers want to buy and why. Marketers also need to consider the impact of the environment on marketing activities.

The following statements will test your take-away knowledge from this chapter. Do your best to explain each one in the space provided.

LO 11-1 Define marketing and describe the exchange process.

LO 11-2 Specify the functions of marketing.

LO 11-3 Explain the marketing concept and its implications for developing marketing strategies.

LO 11-4 Examine the development of a marketing strategy, including market segmentation and marketing mix.

LO 11-5 Investigate how marketers conduct marketing research and study buying behavior.

LO 11-6 Summarize the environmental forces that influence marketing decisions.

 ISBN 0078023157 | Ferrell M 4e

Did your answers include the following important points?

LO 11-1. Define marketing and describe the exchange process.

- Marketing is a group of activities designed to expedite transactions by creating, distributing, pricing, and promoting goods, services, and ideas.
- Marketing facilitates exchange, the act of giving up one thing in return for something else. The central focus is to satisfy needs.

LO 11-2. Specify the functions of marketing.

- Marketing includes many varied and interrelated activities: buying, selling, transporting, storing, grading, financing, marketing research, and risk taking.

LO 11-3. Explain the marketing concept and its implications for developing marketing strategies.

- The marketing concept is the idea that an organization should try to satisfy customers' needs through coordinated activities that also allow it to achieve its goals.
- If a company does not implement the marketing concept by providing products that consumers need and want while achieving its own objectives, it will not survive.

LO 11-4. Examine the development of a marketing strategy, including market segmentation and marketing mix.

- A marketing strategy is a plan of action for creating a marketing mix for a specific target market. Some firms use a total-market approach, designating everyone as the target market.
- Most firms divide the total market into segments of people who have relatively similar product needs.
- A company using a concentration approach develops one marketing strategy for a single market segment, whereas a multisegment approach aims marketing efforts at two or more segments, developing a different marketing strategy for each segment.

LO 11-5. Investigate how marketers conduct marketing research and study buying behavior.

- Carrying out the marketing concept is impossible unless marketers know what, where, when, and how consumers buy; marketing research into the factors that influence buying behavior helps marketers develop effective marketing strategies.
- Marketing research is a systematic, objective process of getting information about potential customers to guide marketing decisions.
- Buying behavior is the decision processes and actions of people who purchase and use products.

LO 11-6. Summarize the environmental forces that influence marketing decisions.

- Several forces influence marketing activities: political, legal, regulatory, social, competitive, economic, and technological.

Practical Application

LO 11-1.

- James Johnson has developed a new product, found a store willing to sell it, and agreed to help promote the product's sale. He is engaging in ______________.
- When a customer hands the cashier $1 and receives a loaf of bread, a(n) ______________ has occurred.

LO 11-2.

- When a storeowner spends a lot of money for new products that have yet to be proved sales items, the owner is engaging in the marketing function of ______________.
- Richard has acquired a supply of canned fruits and vegetables. He does not yet have a buyer for them, but he's using promotion and other activities to find a buyer. He is performing the marketing function of ______________.

LO 11-3.

- The goal of the marketing concept is ______________.
- ______________ remains a major element of any strategy to develop and manage long-term customer relationships.
- During the Industrial Revolution, new technologies fueled strong ______________.

LO 11-4.

- A plan of action for developing, pricing, distributing, and promoting products that meets the needs of a specific customer is a(n) ______________.
- People visiting a ski resort would be viewed by a ski equipment storeowner as the business's ______________.
- The aim of ______________ is to communicate directly or indirectly with individuals, groups, and organizations to facilitate exchanges.

LO 11-5.

- ______________ is a systematic and objective process of getting information on potential customers.
- ______________ is a psychological variable of buyer behavior.
- ______________ are the least expensive data to collect.

LO 11-6.

- Purchasing power, recession, and inflation are associated with ______________ forces.
- The public's opinions and attitudes toward living standards, ethics, and the environment are considered ______________ forces.

ANSWERS LO 11-1 •marketing •exchange LO 11-2 •risk taking •selling LO 11-3 •customer satisfaction •Communication •demand LO 11-4 •marketing strategy •market •promotion LO 11-5 •Market research •Personality •Secondary data LO 11-6 •economic •social

chapter twelve

active review card

Dimensions of Marketing Strategy

in a nutshell

There are four dimensions of marketing—product, price, distribution, and promotion. These elements are used to develop a marketing strategy that builds customer relationships and satisfaction.

The following statements will test your take-away knowledge from this chapter. Do your best to explain each one in the space provided.

LO 12-1 Describe the role of product in the marketing mix, including how products are developed, classified, and identified.

LO 12-2 Define price and discuss its importance in the marketing mix, including various pricing strategies a firm might employ.

LO 12-3 Identify factors affecting distribution decisions, such as marketing channels and intensity of market coverage.

LO 12-4 Specify the activities involved in promotion as well as promotional strategies and promotional positioning.

Did your answers include the following important points?

LO 12-1. Describe the role of product in the marketing mix, including how products are developed, classified, and identified.

- Products are among a firm's most visible contacts with consumers and must meet consumers' needs to be successful. New-product development is a multistep process including idea development, the screening of new ideas, business analysis, product development, test marketing, and commercialization.
- Products are classified as either consumer or business products. Consumer products can be further classified as convenience, shopping, or specialty products.
- The business product classifications are raw materials, major equipment, component parts, processed materials, supplies, and industrial services.
- Products can also be classified by the stage of the product life cycle. Identifying products includes branding, packaging, and labeling.

LO 12-2. Define price and discuss its importance in the marketing mix, including various pricing strategies a firm might employ.

- Price is the value placed on an object exchanged between a buyer and a seller. Pricing objectives include survival, maximization of profits and sales volume, and maintenance of the status quo.
- A firm may use price skimming or penetration pricing when introducing a new product. Psychological pricing, reference pricing, and price discounting are other strategies.

LO 12-3. Identify factors affecting distribution decisions, such as marketing channels and intensity of market coverage.

- Making products available to customers is facilitated by middlemen or intermediaries, who bridge the gap between the producer of the product and its ultimate user.
- A marketing channel is a group of marketing organizations that directs the flow of products from producers to consumers.
- Market coverage relates to the number and variety of outlets that make products available to customers; it may be intensive, selective, or exclusive.

LO 12-4. Specify the activities involved in promotion as well as promotional strategies and promotional positioning.

- Promotion encourages marketing exchanges by persuading individuals, groups, and organizations to accept goods, services, and ideas. The promotion mix includes advertising, personal selling, publicity, and sales promotion.
- A push strategy attempts to motivate intermediaries to push the product down to the customers, whereas a pull strategy tries to create consumer demand for a product so that the consumers exert pressure on marketing channel members to make the product available.
- Typical promotion objectives are to stimulate demand; stabilize sales; and inform, remind, and reinforce customers. Promotional positioning is the use of promotion to create and maintain an image of the product in the mind of the buyer.

Practical Application

LO 12-1.

- ______________ allows a company to discover the strengths and weaknesses of a product before it is fully launched in the market.
- ______________ are less expensive than manufacturer brands and are owned and controlled by a wholesaler or retailer.
- ______________ generally appeal to those consumers who are willing to sacrifice quality and product consistency for the sake of lower prices.

LO 12-2.

- The pricing policy that allows a company to cover the product's development cost most quickly is ______________.
- ______________ enables a product to enter the market and rapidly gain market share.
- A cosmetics company believes that it makes more sense to sell its eye shadow at $11.99 rather than $12.00; it is using ______________.

LO 12-3.

- ______________ buy products from manufacturers and sell them to consumers for home and household use.
- When a product is to be made available in as many outlets as possible, wholesalers and retailers engage in ______________.

LO 12-4.

- When Ford pays a television network to air its commercial, it is using ______________.
- When Chiquita uses newspaper ads to introduce its new fruit drink to consumers before introducing it to supermarkets, it is using the ______________.
- The mass media willingly carry ______________ for a company or product, believing it has general public interest.

ANSWERS LO 12-1 •Test marketing •Private distributor brands •Generic products LO 12-2 •price skimming •Penetration price •psychological pricing LO 12-3 •Retailers •intensive distribution LO 12-4 •advertising •pull strategy •publicity

chapter thirteen

active review card

Digital Marketing and Social Networking

in a nutshell

You must understand the concepts of digital media and digital marketing and how they have become extremely important in strategic planning. The Internet and social networking are becoming increasingly important in people's lives, so you need to understand their impact on business today.

The following statements will test your take-away knowledge from this chapter. Do your best to explain each one in the space provided.

LO 13-1 Define digital media and digital marketing and recognize their increasing value in strategic planning.

LO 13-2 Demonstrate the role of digital marketing and social networking in today's business environment.

LO 13-3 Show how digital media affect the marketing mix.

LO 13-4 Define social networking and illustrate how businesses can use different types of social networking media.

LO 13-5 Identify legal and ethical considerations in digital media.

 ISBN 0078023157 | Ferrell M 4e

Did your answers include the following important points?

LO 13-1. Define digital media and digital marketing and recognize their increasing value in strategic planning.

- Digital media are electronic media that function using digital codes—available via computers and other digital services such as cell phones and smart phones.
- Digital marketing uses digital media to create communications and exchanges with customers.

LO 13-2. Demonstrate the role of digital marketing and social networking in today's business environment.

- Firms can use real-time exchanges to stimulate interactive communication, forge closer relationships, and learn more accurately about consumer and supplier needs.
- Digital communication is making it easier for businesses to conduct marketing research, provide price and product information, and advertise.

LO 13-3. Show how digital media affect the marketing mix.

- The Internet is a new distribution channel making products available at the right time, at the right place, and in the right quantities.
- Online promotions are creating well-informed consumers.
- Digital media enhance the value of products by providing extra benefits such as service, information, and convenience.
- The Internet gives consumers access to more information about costs and prices.

LO 13-4. Define social networking and illustrate how businesses can use different types of social networking media.

- A social network is a web-based meeting place for friends, family, co-workers, and peers that lets users create a profile and connect with other users for different purposes.
- Internet users participate in blogs, wikis, social networks, media sharing sites, virtual reality sites, mobile marketing, and applications and widgets.
- Marketers have begun investigating and experimenting with promotion on social networks.
- Blogs answer consumer concerns and obtain free publicity, whereas wikis give marketers a better understanding of how consumers feel about their companies.
- Photo-sharing sites enable companies to share images of their businesses or products with consumers and often have links that connect users to company-sponsored blogs. Video sharing is allowing many businesses to engage in viral marketing. Podcasts are audio or video files that can be downloaded from the Internet with a subscription that automatically delivers new content to listening devices or personal computers.
- Companies are using the virtual world to gather information about consumer tastes and preferences as well as feedback on products.
- Mobile phones are also being used for communicating with consumers and conducting business, especially in the service industry.
- Apps can help consumers perform services and make purchases more easily; widgets can be used to inform consumers about company updates and can easily go viral.

LO 13-5. Identify legal and ethical considerations in digital media.

- The Internet and e-business have raised concerns such as privacy concerns, the risk of identity theft, online fraud, and intellectual property rights.

Practical Application

LO 13-1.

- ________ are electronic media that function using digital codes and are available via computers, cell phones, smart phones, and other digital devices.
- ________ uses digital media to develop communication and exchanges with customers.
- ________ means carrying out the goals of business through the use of the Internet.

LO 13-2.

- The Internet ________ the cost of communication and is therefore significant in industries such as entertainment, health care, and education.
- Digital media can be a(n) ________ backbone that helps store knowledge, information, and records in management information systems for the employees of a company.

LO 13-3.

- The Internet has become a new ________ to make products available for people.
- A recent market research study reveals that people today spend more time on ________ than they do on ________.
- The aspect of marketing that still remains unchanged by the digital media is the importance of achieving the ________.

LO 13-4.

- Some companies have started using ________ as internal tools for projects that require a lot of documentation.
- Marketers generally engage in ________ of their products on social networking sites.
- ________ only read online information and are the largest group in most countries.

LO 13-5.

- The BBBOnline program is managed by the ________, which follows guidelines on self-regulation and monitoring established by the U.S. Department of Commerce.
- ________ is a method of initiating identity theft fraud that is growing rapidly.
- ________ of content is a major intellectual property problem especially in the areas of software, music, movies, and videogames.

ANSWERS LO 13-1 •Digital media •Digital marketing •E-business LO 13-2 •lowers •communications LO 13-3 •distribution channel •social networking sites; e-mail •right marketing mix LO 13-4 •wikis •promotion •Spectators LO 13-5 •Council of Better Business Bureaus •Phishing •Illegal sharing

chapter fourteen

active review card

Accounting and Financial Statements

in a nutshell

The use of accounting information and the accounting process is important in making business decisions. Understanding simple financial statements and accounting tools is useful in analyzing organizations worldwide.

The following statements will test your take-away knowledge from this chapter. Do your best to explain each one in the space provided.

LO 14-1 Define accounting and describe the different uses of accounting information.

LO 14-2 Demonstrate the accounting process.

LO 14-3 Examine the various components of an income statement to evaluate a firm's bottom line.

LO 14-4 Interpret a company's balance sheet to determine its current financial position.

LO 14-5 Analyze the statement of cash flows to evaluate the increase and decrease in a company's cash balance.

 ISBN 0078023157 | Ferrell M 4e

Did your answers include the following important points?

LO 14-1. Define accounting and describe the different uses of accounting information.

- Accounting is the language businesses and other organizations use to record, measure, and interpret financial transactions.
- Financial statements are used internally to judge and control an organization's performance and to plan and direct its future activities and measure goal attainment.
- External organizations such as lenders, governments, customers, suppliers, and the Internal Revenue Service are major consumers of the information generated by the accounting process.

LO 14-2. Demonstrate the accounting process.

- Assets are an organization's economic resources; liabilities are debts the organization owes to others; owners' equity is the difference between the value of an organization's assets and liabilities.
- This principle can be expressed as the accounting equation: Assets = Liabilities + Owners' equity.
- The double-entry bookkeeping system is a system of recording and classifying business transactions in accounts that maintain the balance of the accounting equation.
- The accounting cycle involves recording transactions in a journal, posting transactions, and preparing financial statements on a continuous basis throughout the life of the organization.

LO 14-3. Examine the various components of an income statement to evaluate a firm's bottom line.

- The income statement indicates a company's profitability over a specific period of time. It shows the bottom line, the total profit (or loss) after all expenses have been deducted from revenue.
- Major components of the income statement include revenue, expenses, and net income.

LO 14-4. Interpret a company's balance sheet to determine its current financial position.

- The balance sheet, which summarizes the firm's assets, liabilities, and owners' equity since its inception, portrays its financial position as of a particular point in time.
- Major classifications included in the balance sheet are current assets, fixed assets, current liabilities, long-term liabilities, and owners' equity.

LO 14-5. Analyze the statement of cash flows to evaluate the increase and decrease in a company's cash balance.

- The statement of cash flows explains how the company's cash changed from the beginning of the accounting period to the end.
- The change in cash is explained through details in three categories: cash from (used for) operating activities, cash from (used for) investing activities, and cash from (used for) financing activities.

Practical Application

LO 14-1.

- A(n) _______________ is an individual who has been state-certified to provide accounting services ranging from the preparation of financial records and the filing of tax returns to complex audits of corporate financial records.
- An internal financial plan that forecasts expenses and income over a set period of time is known as an organization's _______________.
- A(n) _______________ is a summary of the firm's financial information, products, and growth plans for owners and potential investors.

LO 14-2.

- Trendy, an organization that specializes in hand-stitched clothes, owes money to its suppliers and to the Small Business Administration. The money owed is an example of Trendy's ____________.
- The system of recording and classifying business transactions in separate accounts to maintain the balance of the accounting equation is called _______________.
- A(n) _______________ is a book or computer program with separate files for each account.

LO 14-3.

- The _______________ is the amount of money the firm spent to buy and/or produce the products it sold during the accounting period.
- _______________ is the process of spreading the costs of long-lived assets such as buildings and equipment over the total number of accounting periods in which they are expected to be used.
- The _______________ shows the profit or loss once all taxes and expenses have been deducted from the revenue.

LO 14-4.

- Short-term assets that are used or converted into cash within the course of a calendar year are also known as _______________.
- _______________ represents amounts owed to suppliers for goods and services purchased with credit.
- All unpaid financial obligations of a company are kept in the _______________ account.

LO 14-5.

- The _______________ explains how the company's cash changed from the beginning of the accounting period to the end.
- Cash from _______________ is calculated by combining the changes in the revenue accounts, expense accounts, current asset accounts, and current liability accounts.
- Cash from _______________ is calculated from changes in the long-term liability accounts and the contributed capital accounts in owners' equity.

ANSWERS LO 14-1 •certified public accountant •budget •annual report LO 14-2 •liabilities •double-entry bookkeeping •ledger LO 14-3 •cost of goods sold •Depreciation •net income LO 14-4 •current assets •Accounts payable •accrued expenses LO 14-5 •statement of cash flows •operating activities •financing activities

chapter fifteen active review card
Money and the Financial System

in a nutshell

The Federal Reserve Board and other major financial institutions play significant roles in the financial system. In understanding finance, you need to consider the definition of money and the forms money may take. You also need to consider the future of the finance industry and the changes likely to occur over the course of the next several years.

The following statements will test your take-away knowledge from this chapter. Do your best to explain each one in the space provided.

LO 15-1 Define money, its functions, and its characteristics.

LO 15-2 Describe various types of money.

LO 15-3 Specify how the Federal Reserve Board manages the money supply and regulates the American banking system.

LO 15-4 Compare and contrast commercial banks, savings and loan associations, credit unions, and mutual savings banks.

LO 15-5 Distinguish among nonbanking institutions such as insurance companies, pension funds, mutual funds, and finance companies.

LO 15-6 Investigate the challenges ahead for the banking industry.

 ISBN 0078023157 | Ferrell M 4e

Did your answers include the following important points?

LO 15-1. Define money, its functions, and its characteristics.

- Money is anything generally accepted as a means of payment for goods and services. Money serves as a medium of exchange, a measure of value, and a store of wealth.
- To serve effectively in these functions, money must be acceptable, divisible, portable, durable, stable in value, and difficult to counterfeit.

LO 15-2. Describe various types of money.

- Money may take the form of currency, checking accounts, or other accounts.
- Checking accounts are funds left in an account in a financial institution that can be withdrawn without advance notice.
- Other types of accounts include savings accounts, money market accounts, certificates of deposit, credit cards, and debit cards as well as traveler's checks, money orders, and cashier's checks.

LO 15-3. Specify how the Federal Reserve Board manages the money supply and regulates the American banking system.

- The Federal Reserve Board regulates the U.S. financial system. The Fed manages the money supply by buying and selling government securities, raising or lowering the discount rate, raising or lowering bank reserve requirements, and adjusting down payment and repayment terms for credit purchases.
- It also regulates banking practices, processes checks, and oversees federal depository insurance for institutions.

LO 15-4. Compare and contrast commercial banks, savings and loan associations, credit unions, and mutual savings banks.

- Commercial banks are financial institutions that take and hold deposits in accounts for and make loans to individuals and businesses.
- Savings and loan associations are financial institutions that primarily specialize in offering savings accounts and mortgage loans. Mutual savings banks are similar to S&Ls, except that they are owned by their depositors.
- Credit unions are financial institutions owned and controlled by their depositors.

LO 15-5. Distinguish among nonbanking institutions such as insurance companies, pension funds, mutual funds, and finance companies.

- Insurance companies are businesses that protect their clients against financial losses due to certain circumstances, in exchange for a fee.
- Pension funds are investments set aside by organizations or individuals to meet retirement needs.
- Mutual funds pool investors' money and invest in large numbers of different types of securities, brokerage firms buy and sell stocks and bonds for investors, and finance companies make short-term loans at higher interest rates than banks.

LO 15-6. Investigate the challenges ahead for the banking industry.

- Future changes in financial regulations are likely to result in fewer but larger banks and other financial institutions.

Practical Application

LO 15-1.

- Trading one good or service for another of similar value is known as ______________.
- When a dollar bill is handled hundreds of times and is still being used, it has ______________.
- When inflation is very high, people no longer believe that money is ______________.

LO 15-2.

- Another name for a savings account is a(n) ______________.
- In general, the longer the term of a certificate of deposit, the higher its ______________.
- The acronym NOW, when used in financial circles, stands for ______________.

LO 15-3.

- To carry out its functions of controlling the supply of money, the Federal Reserve Board uses its ______________.
- When the Federal Reserve buys securities, it ______________.

LO 15-4.

- If employees of a local school district conduct their financial business through the same financial institution that they own and only they are allowed to join, the institution is probably a(n) ______________.
- ______________ are the oldest and largest of all financial institutions.
- The ______________ was established in 1933 to help stop bank failures throughout the country during the Great Depression and has nearly 8,000 member institutions at present.

LO 15-5.

- Insurance companies invest premiums from insured individuals and businesses or make short-term loans, particularly to businesses in the form of ______________.
- ______________ permits home computer users to conduct banking activities through their personal computers.

LO 15-6.

- The Federal Reserve and the U.S Treasury created the ______________ to save the banking system from total collapse.
- The future of the structure of the American banking system is largely in the hands of the ______________.

ANSWERS LO 15-1 • bartering • durability • stable LO 15-2 • time deposit • interest rate • negotiable order of withdrawal LO 15-3 • monetary policy • increases the money supply LO 15-4 • credit union • Commercial banks • Federal Deposit Insurance Corporation (FDIC) LO 15-5 • commercial real estate loans • Online banking LO 15-6 • Troubled Asset Relief Program (TARP) • U.S. Congress

chapter sixteen

active review card

Financial Management and Securities Markets

in a nutshell

Companies use short-term assets to generate sales and conduct ordinary day-to-day business operations and short-term liabilities to finance business. They also use long-term assets such as plant and equipment and long-term liabilities such as stocks and bonds to finance corporate assets. Financial management depends on the management of these assets and liabilities as well as the trade of stocks and bonds.

The following statements will test your take-away knowledge from this chapter. Do your best to explain each one in the space provided.

LO 16-1 Describe some common methods of managing current assets.

LO 16-2 Identify some sources of short-term financing (current liabilities).

LO 16-3 Summarize the importance of long-term assets and capital budgeting.

LO 16-4 Specify how companies finance their operations and manage fixed assets with long-term liabilities, particularly bonds.

LO 16-5 Discuss how corporations can use equity financing by issuing stock through an investment banker.

LO 16-6 Describe the various securities markets in the United States.

 ISBN 0078023157 | Ferrell M 4e

Did your answers include the following important points?

LO 16-1. Describe some common methods of managing current assets.

- Current assets are short-term resources such as cash, investments, accounts receivable, and inventory.
- Financial managers focus on minimizing the amount of cash kept on hand and increasing the speed of collections through lockboxes and electronic funds transfer and by investing in marketable securities.
- Marketable securities include U.S. Treasury bills, certificates of deposit, commercial paper, and money market funds.
- Managing accounts receivable requires judging customer creditworthiness and creating credit terms that encourage prompt payment.
- Inventory management focuses on determining optimum inventory levels that minimize the cost of storing the ordering inventory without sacrificing too many lost sales due to stockout.

LO 16-2. Identify some sources of short-term financing (current liabilities).

- Current liabilities are short-term debt obligations that must be repaid within one year, such as accounts payable, taxes payable, and notes payable.
- Trade credit is extended by suppliers for the purchase of their goods and services, whereas a line of credit is an arrangement by which a bank agrees to lend a specified amount of money to a business whenever the business needs it.
- Secured loans are backed by collateral; unsecured loans are backed only by the borrower's good reputation.

LO 16-3. Summarize the importance of long-term assets and capital budgeting.

- Long-term or fixed assets are expected to last for many years, such as production facilities, offices, and equipment. Businesses need up-to-date equipment to succeed in today's competitive environment.
- Capital budgeting is the process of analyzing company needs and selecting the assets that will maximize its value; a capital budget is the amount of money budgeted for the purchase of fixed assets.

LO 16-4. Specify how companies finance their operations and manage fixed assets with long-term liabilities, particularly bonds.

- Two common choices for financing are equity financing and debt financing. Long-term liabilities are debts that will be repaid over a number of years, such as long-term bank loans and bond issues.
- A bond is a long-term debt security that an organization sells to raise money. The bond indenture specifies the provisions of the bond contract—maturity date, coupon rate, repayment methods, and others.

LO 16-5. Discuss how corporations can use equity financing by issuing stock through an investment banker.

- Owners' equity represents what owners have contributed to the company and includes common stock, preferred stock, and retained earnings.
- To finance operations, companies can issue new common and preferred stock through an investment banker that sells stocks and bonds to corporations.

LO 16-6. Describe the various securities markets in the United States.

- Securities markets provide the mechanism for buying and selling stocks and bonds. Primary markets allow companies to raise capital by selling new stock directly to investors through investment bankers.
- Secondary markets allow the buyers of previously issued shares of stock to sell them to other owners. Major secondary markets are the New York Stock Exchange, the American Stock Exchange, and the over-the-counter market.
- Investors measure stock market performance by watching stock market averages and indexes.

Practical Application

LO 16-1.

- A(n) _______________ is an address for receiving payments from customers.
- _______________ are short-term debt obligations that the U.S. government sells to raise money.
- Good financial managers minimize the amount of cash available to pay bills in _______________.

LO 16-2.

- A finance company to which businesses sell their accounts receivable, usually for a percentage of the total face value, is a(n) _______________.
- The most widely used source of short-term financing is _______________.

LO 16-3.

- Plants, offices, and equipment are considered _______________ assets.
- The process of analyzing the needs of the business and selecting the assets that will maximize its value is called _______________.
- In general, the longer the expected life of a project or asset, the _______________ the potential risk.

LO 16-4.

- _______________ are a sequence of small bond issues of progressively longer maturity.
- Items such as a bond's value, date, and rate are specified in the _______________.
- A method of long-term financing that requires repaying funds with interest is _______________ .

LO 16-5.

- The first-time sale of stocks and bonds to the public directly is called _______________.
- If a company retains all of its earnings, it will not pay _______________.
- Corporations usually employ an investment banking firm to help sell their securities in the _______________.

LO 16-6.

- A(n) _______________ is a network of dealers rather than an organized exchange.
- A(n) _______________ compares current stock prices with those in a specified base period.

ANSWERS LO 16-1 •lockbox • Treasury bills (T-bills) •transaction balances LO 16-2 •factor •trade credit LO 16-3 •long-term •capital budgeting •greater LO 16-4 •Serial bonds •indenture •issuing bonds LO 16-5 •new issue •dividends •primary market LO 16-6 •over-the-counter (OTC) market •index